ISBN 978-0-260-45348-8
PIBN 10949225

This book is a reproduction of an important historical work. Forgotten Books uses
state-of-the-art technology to digitally reconstruct the work, preserving the original format
whilst repairing imperfections present in the aged copy. In rare cases, an imperfection in
the original, such as a blemish or missing page, may be replicated in our edition. We do,
however, repair the vast majority of imperfections successfully; any imperfections that
remain are intentionally left to preserve the state of such historical works.

JOURNAL OF PROCEEDINGS

OF THE

ELEVENTH

ÆNNUÆL COUNCIL

OF THE

PROTESTÆNT EPISCOPAL CHURCH

IN THE

DIOCESE OF ARKANSAS,

HELD IN ST. JOHN'S CHURCH, CAMDEN, ARKANSAS, ON THE
6TH, 7TH AND 8TH DAYS OF APRIL, A. D. 1883.

LITTLE ROCK, ARK.:
PRINTED BY THE KELLOGG PRINTING COMPANY,
1883.

OFFICERS OF THE DIOCESE OF ARKANSAS:

President:
THE RT.-REV. HENRY NILES PIERCE, D.D., LL.D.

Secretary:
THE REV. TULLIUS C. TUPPER, Little Rock.

Assistant Secretary:
MR. WILLIAM COPPEÉ STEVENS, Little Rock.

Treasurer:
MR. LOGAN H. ROOTS, Little Rock.

Registrar:
REV. W. C. STOUT, Morrilton.

Chancellor:
MR. WILLIAM G. WHIPPLE, Little Rock.

Trustee of the Episcopate Fund:
MR. P. K. ROOTS, Little Rock.

Trustees of the University of the South:
REV. INNES O. ADAMS.
MESSRS. M. L. BELL AND LOGAN H. ROOTS.

Trustee of the General Theological Seminary:
REV. W. B. BURROWS, Helena.

Standing Committee:
REV. T. C. TUPPER, President.
THE REV. MESSRS. W. C. STOUT AND INNES O. ADAMS,
MESSRS. M. L. BELL AND P. K. ROOTS, Secretary.

Deputies to the General Convention:

Rev. T. C. TUPPER.   Mr. R. V. McCRACKEN.

Rev. J. J. VAULX.   Mr. WILLIAM C. STEVENS.

Rev. W. C. STOUT.   Mr. J. J. HORNER.

Rev. INNES O. ADAMS.   Mr. A. WASSELL.

Alternates:

Rev. W. B. BURROWS.   Mr. C. H. STONE.

Rev. D. L. TRIMBLE.   Mr. M. L. BELL.

Rev. D. McMANUS.   Mr. C. A. MAGILL.

Rev. J. A. MATTHEWS.   Mr. L. MINOR.

Board of Missions:

The Rt.-Rev. the Bishop of the Diocese, and the Clerical Members of the Standing Committee.

CLERGY OF THE DIOCESE:

The Rt.-Rev. Henry N. Pierce, D.D., LL.D.. Little Rock.

The Rev. Innes O. Adams............Trinity, Pine Bluff.

The Rev. Edwin C. Alcorn.........St. Paul's, Newport.

*The Rev. Joseph L. Berne........St. John's, Fort Smith.

The Rev. William B. Burrows........St. John's, Helena.

†The Rev. C. A. Bruce..........................Helena.

*†The Rev. H. C. E. Costelle..........Grace, Washington.

†The Rev. Geo. S. Gibbs.........St. Luke's, Hot Springs.

The Rev. D. McManus...........Grace, Phillips County.

†The Rev. D. F. McDonald, D. D............Dardanelle.

†The Rev. James A. Matthews........Trinity, Van Buren.

†The Rev. A. W. Pierce, *Deacon*..............Mississippi.

The Rev. W. C. Stout.....................Lewisburg.

The Rev. David L. Trimble................Pine Pluff.

The Rev. T. C. Tupper........Christ Church, Little Rock.

The Rev. J. J. Vaulx.............St. Paul's, Fayetteville.

*Not Canonically connected.
†Absent from Council.

LIST OF PARISHES AND LAY DEPUTIES:

W. G. WHIPPLE, ESQ., Chancellor.

Arkadelphia, St. Mark's.

Augusta, St. Paul's.

Batesville, St. Paul's.

Camden, St. John's.—C. A. Magill, H. A. Millen, C. H. Stone. Alternates: H. Higinbotham and J. A. Reeves.

Dardanelle, St. Paul's.

Fayetteville, St. Paul's.

Fort Smith, St. John's.

Helena, St. John's.—J. J. Horner, Greenfield Quarles.

Hot Springs, St. Luke's.—J. P. Mellard, I. W. Carhart.

Jacksonport, Grace Church.—P. Lynch Lee.

Lake Village, Emmanuel.

Little Rock, Christ Church.—L. H. Roots, W. C. Stevens, Albert Wassell. Alternates: G. H. VanEtten, H. H. Bein, J. C. Alexander.

Newport, St. Paul's.—Launcelot Minor, Frank Orff.

Phillips County, Grace Church.

Pine Bluff, Trinity.—M. L. Bell, R. V. McCracken.

Prescott, St. James.

Van Buren, Trinity.

Washington, Grace Church.

LIST OF MISSIONS:

Columbus.	Conway.	Forrest City.	Hope.
Marianna.	Morrilton.	Osceola.	Richmond.
Rocky Comfort.		Searcy.	

List of Lay Delegates who attended the Council:

W. G. Whipple, Chancellor....................Little Rock.
Logan H. Roots...............Christ Church, Little Rock.
Wm. C. Stevens...............   "   "   "   "
M. L. Bell.....................Trinity Church, Pine Bluff.
R. V. McCracken ....   "   "   "   "
P. Lynch Lee.................Grace Church, Jacksonport.
C. H. Stone...................St. John's Church, Camden.
H. Higinbotham..............   "   "   "
Chas. A. Magill...............

.

PROCEEDINGS

OF THE

⊲ELEVENTH ANNUAL COUNCIL⊳

FIRST DAY.

St. John's Church, Camden, Ark., }
Friday, April 6, 1883. }

The Eleventh Annual Council of the Diocese of Arkansas met in St. John's Church, Camden, Friday morning, the 6th of April, 1883.

After morning prayer, and the ante-communion service was said, the Rt.-Rev., the Bishop of the Diocese, read his Annual Address:

THE BISHOP'S ADDRESS

To the Eleventh Annual Council of the Diocese of Arkansas.

My last Annual Address closed on April 20, 1882, the day before the opening of the Annual Council.

April 21—In St. Luke's Church, Hot Springs, Ark., I celebrated the Holy Eucharist at the opening services of the Annual Council of the Diocese of Arkansas, and presided during its sessions.

April 22—Read my Annual Address.

April 23—The second after Easter. I assisted at the services, morning and afternoon, in St. Luke's, Hot Springs.

April 24—At 5:30 a.m., in St. Luke's Church, Hot Springs,

assisted by the Rector, Rev. George S. Gibbs, I celebrated the Holy Eucharist. At 6 a.m. the Council was called to order, and at 8:30 a.m. adjourned *sine die.* Returned to Little Rock, and at night, assisted by Rev. Messrs. McManus, Vaulx and Ramsey, I examined the Rev. W. B. Burrows, Deacon, on the third examination for Priests' Orders.

APRIL 30—Sunday, the third after Easter. In Trinity Church, Pine Bluff, I said the morning and evening services, and preached twice. The offertory, amounting to $4.85, I donated to Diocesan Missions.

MAY 7—Sunday, the fourth after Easter. In St. Luke's Church, Hot Springs, I assisted in saying service twice, morning and night, and preached twice.

MAY 8—Attended morning service at St. Luke's Church. At night began a very heavy rain, which flooded the valley and interrupted travel on the Hot Springs and Malvern, and on the Iron Mountain Railroads, for about ten days. For nearly a week we had not even telegraphic communication with the world without.

MAY 14—Sunday, the fifth after Easter. In St. Luke's Church, Hot Springs, I assisted in saying morning service and preached. At night I preached again; confirmed five persons, and addressed the newly confirmed.

MAY 15—I attended morning prayers at St. Luke's.

MAY 16—I said morning prayer in St. Luke's Church, Hot Springs. At 8 p.m. I preached in said Church, and confirmed three persons and addressed the class.

MAY 18—Ascension Day. Much to my regret, I felt it necessary to avail myself of the first opportunity to leave the valley after my long detention. I started for Little Rock by the morning train.

MAY 21—Sunday after Ascension. In Christ Church, Little Rock, I assisted at morning service and preached.

MAY 28—Whitsun·Day. In Trinity Church, Pine Bluff, I said morning service, preached and celebrated the Holy Eucharist. At night I said evening prayer and preached again.

MAY 29—I baptized a child at Pine Bluff.

JUNE 2—Attended morning prayer in St. Mary's Cathedral, Memphis, Tenn.

JUNE 4—Trinity Sunday. In St. Peter's Church, Columbia, Tenn., I assisted at morning service and celebrated the Holy Eucharist. At night I preached in St. Peter's.

JUNE 6—I delivered the Commencement Address at the Institute, Columbia, Tennessee, and the same day I was elected a member of the Board of Trustees of the Institute. The more I see of this noble Church School, the more I am pleased with it, and I again recommend it to churchmen, and to the citizens of Arkansas in general, as the best place to educate their daughters. I am happy to say that it is in a very flourishing condition.

JUNE 11—First Sunday after Trinity. In St. Peter's Church, Columbia, Tennessee, I assisted in saying morning service and preached. At night I said evening prayer and preached again.

JUNE 18—The second Sunday after Trinity. In St. John's Church, Camden, Ark., I assisted in saying morning service, preached and celebrated the Holy Eucharist, assisted by the Rector, the Rev. I. O. Adams. The offertory, amounting to $5, I donated to Diocesan Missions. At night I preached again, confirmed seven persons and addressed the class.

JUNE 21—In St. John's, Camden, Ark., I preached and confirmed one person, and made an address.

JUNE 25—The third Sunday after Trinity. In St. James' Church, Texarkana, Texas, I assisted in saying the morning service and preached. In the afternoon I visited the Sunday-School and addressed it. At night I preached again and confirmed eleven persons, and addressed the class. These services were at the request of the Rt.-Rev., the Missionary Bishop of Northern Texas, then lying very ill at his home in Dallas.

JULY 1—In Grace Church, Washington, Arkansas, I said evening prayer and preached.

JULY 2—The fourth Sunday after Trinity. In Grace Church, Washington, Arkansas, I said morning service, baptized a child, preached and celebrated the Holy Eucharist. At night I said evening prayer and preached again.

JULY 3—At 8 p. m. I said evening prayer in the Methodist Church, Hope, Ark., and preached. The Church at this point was blown down several months ago, but the Parish, with an energy worthy of all praise, began at once to rebuild. They deserve help.

JULY 5—I paid $8 to reinsure the Church at Prescott, Ark.

JULY 7—In Little Rock I confirmed three persons—a sick man, his wife and daughter—in private. The candidates were presented by the Rev. T. C. Tupper, Rector of Christ Church. I, at the same time, administered the Holy Communion to them.

JULY 9—The fifth Sunday after Trinity. In Christ Church, Little Rock, I assisted at morning service and preached. At night I assisted in saying evening prayer, confirmed five persons and addressed the class.

JULY 16—The sixth Sunday after Trinity. In Christ Church, Little Rock, I assisted in saying morning service and preached.

JULY 23—The seventh Sunday after Trinity. In Christ Church, Little Rock, I assisted at morning service and preached.

JULY 27—At Sewanee, Tenn., attended morning prayers in St. Augustine's Chapel. After service, a meeting of the Bishops at Bishop Green's residence.

JULY 28—Meeting of the Bishops again.

JULY 29—At the University of the South, Sewanee, Tenn., I took part in the opening services at the meeting of the Board of Trustees.

JULY 30—The eighth Sunday after Trinity. Attended morning service at St. Augustine's Chapel. At night attended evening service at St. Paul's Church in the village.

JULY 31—Attending the meetings of the Board.

AUGUST 1—Meeting of the Board.

AUGUST 2—As yesterday.

AUGUST 3—Thursday, Commencement Day. Attended the exercises.

AUGUST 4—Attending the meeting of the Board and on Committee.

AUGUST 5—Meeting of the Board, which adjourned *sine die* at 5 p.m.

AUGUST 6—The ninth Sunday after Trinity. In the morning attended divine service in St. Augustine's Chapel. At night I preached in St. Paul's Church, Sewanee, Tenn.

AUGUST 13—The tenth Sunday after Trinity. In Christ Church, Little Rock, Ark., I assisted at morning service and preached.

AUGUST 18—In St. James' Church, Prescott, Ark., I said evening prayer and preached.

AUGUST 20—The eleventh Sunday after Trinity. In St. James' Church, Prescott, I said morning and evening service, preached twice and baptized a child.

AUGUST 27—The twelfth Sunday after Trinity. In St. John's Church, Fort Smith, I assisted in saying morning service, preached, confirmed two persons and addressed the newly confirmed, and, assisted by the Rev. J. L. Berne, celebrated the Holy Eucharist. At night I preached again and confirmed seventeen persons, and addressed the class.

AUGUST 28—In Trinity Church, Van Buren, after evening prayer said by the Rector, Rev. J. A. Matthews, I preached.

SEPTEMBER 3—The thirteenth Sunday after Trinity. In Christ Church, Little Rock, I assisted at morning service and celebrated the Holy Eucharist.

SEPTEMBER 10—The fourteenth Sunday after Trinity. In Christ Church, Little Rock, I assisted at morning service and preached.

SEPTEMBER 17—The fifteenth Sunday after Trinity. In Calvary Church, Memphis, Tennessee. I assisted in saying morning and evening services and preached twice.

SEPTEMBER 22—I purchased three lots in the City of Little Rock as a site for the Cathedral Church.

SEPTEMBER 24—The sixteenth Sunday after Trinity. I said morning and evening services in Christ Church, Little Rock, and preached twice.

OCTOBER 1—The seventeenth Sunday after Trinity. In Trinity Church, Pine Bluff, I assisted at morning service, preached, and celebrated the Holy Eucharist, assisted by the Rev. Mr. Burrows, of Helena, Arkansas. At night, I assisted in saying the service, and the Rev. Mr. Burrows preached.

OCTOBER 2—I administered the Holy Communion to the sick at Pine Bluff.

OCTOBER 8—The eighteenth Sunday after Trinity, I assisted in saying morning service in Christ Church, Little Rock.

OCTOBER 10—In Christ Church, Little Rock, Arkansas, at 11 a. m., the Rev. D. L. Trimble began morning prayer. The Rev. T. C. Tupper said the prayers. I preached. The Rev. Mr. Trimble read the Epistle. The Rev. T. C. Tupper presented and I ordered Priest, the Rev. William Bamford Burrows, Deacon. I celebrated the Holy Eucharist, and administered the elements unassisted, as the rubric seems to require.

OCTOBER 12—At 11 a. m., in Christ Church, Little Rock, Arkansas, I joined in Holy Matrimony, Mr. William Coppee Stevens, son of the Rt. Rev. the Bishop of Pennsylvania, and Miss Susan Shepperd Pierce, my second daughter.

OCTOBER 15—The nineteenth Sunday after Trinity. In Christ Church, Little Rock, I assisted at morning service and preached.

OCTOBER 17—I officiated in the religious services at the opening session of the Cotton Planters' Association, at Little Rock, Arkansas.

OCTOBER 22—The twentieth Sunday after Trinity. This day, when I should have been at Fort Sill, Indian Territory, was spent at Fort Worth, Texas. Owing to delays in the trains, I was unable to make the expected connections.

OCTOBER 27—Visited the Arapahoe School of Darlington, Indian Territory, and made a little talk to the pupils.

OCTOBER 29—The twenty-first Sunday after Trinity. In the morning, the Rev. J. B. Wicks and myself visited the Sunday-School at the Cheyenne Indian school-house, three miles or so from Darlington, where we both made short addresses to the children, and to the adult Indians. The Rev. David Pendleton Oakerhater, the Cheyenne Deacon, acted as my interpreter on this occasion. At 3 p. m., at the residence of the Rev. J. B.

Wicks, Darlington, the Rev. Mr. Wicks said evening prayer, and I addressed the congregation on the subject of Confirmation. This service is held by the missionary specially for the Indians, who are more or less acquainted with English. It was very pleasant to hear them joining in the service and responding heartily. At night, at the Arapahoe school-house, Rev. Mr. Wicks said evening prayer, and I preached, to a congregation mostly of whites.

OCTOBER 31—In the morning visited the Cheyenne school, and observed the modes of teaching in the different rooms. In the evening, I met in conference, at Wolfrobe's lodge, several of the Cheyenne chiefs. We spent two hours or more together, and I addressed them, the Rev. David P. Oakerhater acting as my interpreter. The occasion was one of great interest to me, and I was specially gratified to see how thoroughly the Rev. Mr. Wicks has now the confidence of the Indians.

NOVEMBER 1—At night, at the Cheyenne school-house, I made a short address, and the Rev. Mr. Wicks baptized three young men, all Cheyennes. It was one of the most solemn services I ever joined in, and there were many moist eyes in the room.

NOVEMBER 5—The twenty-second Sunday after Trinity. At 10:30 a. m., at the Cheyenne school-house, the Rev. Mr. Wicks said the litany and the ante-communion service. I made an address and confirmed fifteen persons (seven males and eight females), all Cheyennes. In the afternoon, at 3 o'clock, I attended the service at Mr. Wick's residence. At night, Rev. Mr. Wicks said evening prayer, and I preached in the Chapel at Fort Reno. The Chapel is just completed, and this was, I believe, the first religious services ever held in it.

NOVEMBER 7—At Anadarko, Indian Territory, I visited the evening assembly at the Comanche and Kiowa school, and made a brief talk to the pupils.

NOVEMBER 9—Visited the same school, and made an address.

NOVEMBER 12—The twenty-third Sunday after Trinity. At the Kiowa and Comanche school-house, Anadarko, the Rev J.

B. Wicks said the litany and the ante-communion service, and baptized six young men, Indians. At 3 p. m., Mr. Wicks said evening prayer, and I preached and confirmed twelve persons (ten males, two females), eight Kiowas, two Comanches, one Apache, one Seminole, and addressed the class.

NOVEMBER 19—The twenty-fourth Sunday after Trinity. At Fort Sill, Indian Territory, the Rev. Mr. Wicks said morning service. I preached, and confirmed one person, Mrs. Julia Faulkner Henry, the wife of Col. Guy V. Henry, the commandant, and, assisted by the Rev. Mr. Wicks, celebrated the Holy Eucharist. In the afternoon I baptized a child. At night, Rev. Mr. Wicks said evening prayer. I preached, confirmed one person, and made an address on Confirmation, etc.

NOVEMBER 26—The twenty-fifth Sunday after Trinity. In Christ Church, Little Rock, Arkansas, I assisted in saying morning service, and baptized a child.

NOVEMBER 30—St. Andrews' Day and National Thanksgiving. I attended morning service in Christ Church, Little Rock.

DECEMBER 3—The first Sunday in Advent. In Trinity Church, Pine Bluff, Arkansas, I said the service morning and evening, and preached twice.

DECEMBER 10—The second Sunday in Advent. In Grace Church, Newport, Arkansas, the Rev. Edwin C. Alcorn, of the Diocese of Fond du Lac, said morning prayer and litany, and read the Epistle. I said the ante-communion, preached, and, assisted by the Rev. Mr. Alcorn, celebrated the Holy Eucharist. At 3:30 p. m., I preached again.

DECEMBER 13—Mr. George W. Hunt, of Anadarka, Indian Territory, was this day admitted a candidate for Holy Orders, and he was duly notified of the fact by letter.

DECEMBER 17—The third Sunday in Advent. In Christ Church, Little Rock, I assisted at morning service and preached.

DECEMBER 24—The fourth Sunday in Advent. In Christ Church, Little Rock, I assisted at morning service and preached. At night I assisted in saying the service.

DECEMBER 25—Christmas Day. In Christ Church, Little

Rock, I assisted at morning service, and celebrated the Holy Eucharist.

DECEMBER 29—In St. Paul's Church, Fayetteville, Arkansas. After evening prayer, said by Rev. J. J. Vaulx, I preached.

DECEMBER 30—Preached at night service in St. Paul's, Fayetteville.

DECEMBER 31—Sunday after Christmas. In St. Paul's Church, Fayetteville, I assisted in saying morning service, preached, and, assisted by the Rector, celebrated the Holy Eucharist. At night I preached again.

JANUARY 1, 1883—The Circumcision of Our Lord. I attended service at 10 o'clock, and received the Holy Sacrament. Rev. Mr. Vaulx celebrated.

JANUARY 4—I preached in St. Paul's Church.

JANUARY 6—The Epiphany. In St. Paul's Church, Fayetteville, Arkansas, I assisted at morning service, preached, and celebrated the Holy Eucharist. At night I preached again.

JANUARY 7—The first Sunday after Epiphany. In St. St. Paul's, Fayetteville, I assisted at morning service, preached, and celebrated the Holy Eucharist. The offertory, for Diocesan Missions, amounted to $3.90. In the afternoon, after a special service, said by the Rev. J. J. Vaulx, I preached, and confirmed ten persons and addressed the class.

JANUARY 9—At Fayetteville, I confirmed one person, the candidate being presented by the Rev. Mr. Vaulx.

JANUARY 14—The second Sunday after the Epiphany. In St. John's Church, Fort Smith. After morning service, said by Rev. J. A. Matthews, of Van Buren, and Rev. J. L. Berne, I preached, and celebrated the Holy Eucharist. In the afternoon, at the request of Rev. J. L. Berne, I baptized a child. The offertory at morning service, amounting to $7.55, of which I took charge, was devoted to Sewanee. At night I preached in the same church, and confirmed one person.

JANUARY 21—Septuagesima Sunday. In Christ Church, Little Rock, I assisted in saying morning service and preached.

JANUARY 22—Gave my canonical consent to the consecration of Rev. Hugh Miller Thompson. D. D., Assistant Bishop-

Elect of the Diocese of Mississippi. Gave notice of my acceptance of letters dismissary from the Diocese of Fond du Lac, presented by Rev. Edwin C. Alcorn, Deacon.

JANUARY 28—Sexuagesima Sunday. In Christ Church, Little Rock, I said morning and evening services, and preached twice. In the afternoon of the same day I officiated at a funeral.

JANUARY 31—I officiated at a funeral, at Little Rock, Arkansas.

FEBRUARY 4—Quinquagesima Sunday. At Grace Church, Phillip's County, Arkansas. No congregation assembled, being prevented by the severest storm of the winter.

FEBRUARY 7—Ash Wednesday. In St. John's Church, Helena, Arkansas, I assisted at morning service and preached. The offertory was devoted to Sewanee, and amounted to $2.00 only, the weather being very bad and the congregation small. This collection the Rector, Rev. W. B. Burrows, took in charge, promising to add to it and forward the whole.

FEBRUARY 11—The first Sunday in Lent. In St. John's Church, Helena, Arkansas, I assisted in saying morning service, preached, and, assisted by the Rector, celebrated the Holy Eucharist. The offertory, for Diocesan Missions, amounted to $4.35, of which I took charge. At night I preached again, confirmed two persons, and addressed the newly confirmed.

FEBRUARY 14—In St. John's Church, Helena, I assisted in saying morning service and preached.

FEBRUARY 16—Attended morning service in St. John's.

FEBRUARY 18—The second Sunday in Lent. At Marianna, Arkansas, the Rev. C. A. Bruce said morning prayer, and baptized an adult and a child. I said the ante-communion, preached, and, assisted by the Rev. Mr. Bruce, celebrated the Holy Eucharist. The offertory, which amounted to $2.65, I devoted to Sewanee. At night I preached again, confirmed two persons, and addressed the newly confirmed.

FEBRUARY 24—In St. Paul's Church, Dardanelle, after evening service, said by the Rev. D. F. McDonald, D. D., I preached.

FEBRUARY 25—The third Sunday in Lent. In St. Paul's Church, Dardanelle, I assisted in saying morning service and preached. The offertory, for Diocesan Missions, amounted to $5.65, of which I took charge. At 4 p. m. I preached again, and confirmed one person.

FEBRUARY 28—In St. John's Church, Fort Smith, Arkansas, I attended Lenten service in the morning. Rev. J. L. Berne officiated.

MARCH 2—In the evening I attended Lenten service in St. John's Church.

MARCH 4—The fourth Sunday in Lent. In St. John's Church, Fort Smith, Arkansas, I assisted in saying morning service, preached, and, assisted by the Rev. J. L. Berne, celebrated the Holy Eucharist. The offertory, for Diocesan Missions, amounted to $9.75, of which I took charge. At night I preached in the same Church, confirmed five persons, and addressed the class. This makes the whole number of confirmations in this Parish for the year twenty-five.

MARCH 7—Attended Lenten service in Trinity Church, Van Buren, Arkansas.

MARCH 8—Attended Lenten service in Trinity Church.

MARCH 9—Attended Lenten service in Trinity Church. Met and conferred with the members of the vestry, and gave my counsel as to the completion of the beautiful new Church now in process of erection.

MARCH 11—The fifth Sunday in Lent. In Trinity Church, Van Buren, Arkansas, I assisted in saying morning service, preached, and, assisted by the Rev. J. A. Matthews, Rector, celebrated the Holy Eucharist. The offertory, which I devoted to Sewanee, amounted to $2.75. At night I preached again, confirmed three persons, and addressed the newly confirmed.

MARCH 14—Attended Lenten service in Christ Church, Little Rock.

MARCH 15—Accepted letters dismissary from the Diocese of Indiana, presented by the Rev. D. L. Trimble.

MARCH 16—Attended Lenten service in Christ Church, Little Rock.

MARCH 18—The sixth Sunday in Lent. In St. Luke's Church, Hot Springs, Arkansas, I assisted in saying morning service and preached. The offertory, which I took charge of and devoted to Sewanee, amounted to $13.64. At night I preached again.

MARCH 19—Monday in Holy Week. In St. Luke's Church, Hot Springs, after evening prayer, said by the Rector, Rev. George S. Gibbs, I preached. During the day I visited the Parish School, taught by Miss Coleman, a daughter of the late Rev. Dr. Coleman, and made an address to the pupils. I was glad to see this Parish School in so flourishing a condition. Were there accommodations for that number, it is said, the pupils, now thirty or forty, might be increased to one hundred or more.

MARCH 20—Tuesday in Holy Week. I preached at evening service in St. Luke's, Hot Springs.

MARCH 22—Thursday in Holy Week. I attended morning service in Christ Church, Little Rock.

MARCH 23—Good Friday. In Christ Church, Little Rock, I assisted in saying morning service and preached. I assisted in saying evening prayer in the same Church.

MARCH 25—Easter Sunday. In Christ Church, Little Rock, Arkansas, I assisted in saying the morning service, preached, and, assisted by the Rector, the Rev. T. C. Tupper, celebrated the Holy Eucharist. The Rector also celebrated at an early service. In the afternoon, I preached again and confirmed eighteen persons, and addressed the class.

MARCH 26—Easter Monday. In Christ Church, Little Rock, I confirmed two persons, making the whole number confirmed in this Parish during the past year twenty-eight.

APRIL 1—The first Sunday after Easter. This Sunday I had an appointment to officiate in St. John's Church, Camden. But, mistaking the indistinct call of the brakesman, I got off the cars at Curtis, instead of at Gurdon, where I should have alighted, and thus lost the opportunity of reaching my destination in time. I would have officiated at Curtis, but no occasion presented itself, and I spent part of the day in attending to the wants of a young German whom I found lying ill at my stopping place.

APRIL 4—At night I attended at the parsonage a donation party given to the Rector of St. John's, Camden. Though the weather was unpropitious, the evening was, socially, a very pleasant one. On this occasion I was presented by the Rector, the Rev. I. O. Adams, in behalf of St. John's Guild and St. John's Sisterhood, with a beautiful set of Eucharistic vestments. This Guild and this Sisterhood have shown great efficiency in Parish work. To their efforts is mainly due the nice little parsonage, which has been such a comfort to the Rector. They, continuing their good work, have on hand several hundred dollars towards the erection of a new Church. To this abstract of my journal, as brief as I could well make it, I add the following tabular statement of my official acts:

TABULAR STATEMENT:

Eucharists celebrated.............................. 22
Sermons preached.... 84
Addresses made.... 28
Confirmed.... 88
Baptized, infants............................ 6
Ordinations, to the Priesthoood.... 1
Marriages......... 1
Funerals.............. 2
Number of miles traveled...........................6201

Besides the confirmations in the Diocese of Arkansas, I have confirmed beyond our borders as follows:

In the Diocese of Northern Texas 11
In the Indian Territory............................. 29

Of the six infants baptized by me, five will probably be reported by the Parishes where the baptisms took place, and so also with the funerals and the marriages.

I have taken no time since the last Council for recreation,

and all the days passed out of Arkansas have been spent in works pertaining to my office.

I have received into the Diocese the Rev. D. L. Trimble, Priest, on letters dismissary from the Diocese of Indiana, and the Rev. Edwin·C. Alcorn, Deacon, on letters dismissary from the Diocese of Fond du Lac.

The Rev. Mr. Alcorn is officiating at Batesville and Newport. The Rev. D. L. Trimble has but recently been transferred, and has not yet entered upon regular work. The Rev. I. O. Adams has been called to the Rectorship of Trinity Church, Pine Bluff, and will, God willing, take charge of that important point before many weeks elapse. I have given letters dismissary to the Rev. D. B. Ramsey to the Diocese of Mississippi. The Rev. A. W. Pierce, Deacon, is at present officiating in the Diocese of Mississippi, but canonically resident in Arkansas. The Rev. P. A. Johnson and the Rev. C. H. Newman are not within the bounds of Arkansas, and I have no late reports from them. The Rev. P. G. Jenkins, so long with us, has been transferred to the Diocese of South Carolina. The Rev. J. L. Berne, who is working with such marked success at Fort Smith, is not yet canonically connected with the Diocese of Arkansas, but I hope soon will be.

The Church of Hope, which was blown down by a hurricane about a year ago, as I have already mentioned, is partly rebuilt. The Churchmen of Hope have shown an energy worthy of all praise, and I beg that you, brethren, will aid those who so well merit assistance, in completing what they have so nobly begun. I am ashamed to say that the appeal I made for them, in my last report to the Board of Missions, has brought in only the pitiful sum of $10.25. When I see appeals in our Church papers, for fonts and altars, altar-cloths and bells, I think of the pressing necessities of the little band of HOPE.

At Fort Smith a lot has been paid for, on which, before long, I hope to see a nice Rectory standing. At Van Buren the new Church is in a state of forwardness, and one vigorous effort will give Trinity Church a beautiful house of worship.

At Dardanelle, the Rev. Dr. McDonald has put up at his own expense a small residence, which, I trust, will become a commodious Rectory by proper enlargement.

The Church in Arkansas is steadily advancing, but the Churchmen of this Diocese must rouse themselves to greater efforts. Most of our Clergy are living on totally inadequate salaries, and their Parishioners should realize that no Clergyman worth the having will consent to remain long where he cannot possibly live honestly, and without incurring debts, which he is unable to meet.

I reported to the last Council that the collections for Diocesan Missions, made during my visitation of the Diocese, amounted in all to $79.75. Of this sum, the collection at Pine Bluff, $12.05, was left in the hands of the Priest, to be forwarded to the Treasurer; this was afterwards paid over to me. The collection at Grace Church, Phillips County, $1.55, was given to the Rev. D. McManus. This last sum being deducted, there was a balance in my hands of seventy-eight dollars and twenty cents ($78.20), to which add the following collections since made:

Trinity Church, Pine Bluff	$ 4	85
St. John's, Camden	5	00
St. Paul's, Fayetteville	3	90
St. John's, Helena	4	35
St. Paul's, Dardanelle	5	65
St. John's, Fort Smith	9	75
Christ Church, Little Rock	17	50
Total	$51	00
Grand total	$129	20

Of this amount, I have paid to the Rev. Dr. Mc-

Donald.................................. 105 65

And I have now in hand a balance of.............$ 23 55

What moneys have been received from the two annual collections ordered by the last Council to be made in every Parish for Diocesan Missions, I do not at present know, as nothing from these regular collections has passed into my hands.

This year I have appropriated some of the collections made on my visitations to meet the quota due from Arkansas to sustain the Theological Department at Sewanee, Tennessee, our University. I have collected and now hold in hand the following sums:

St. John's, Fort Smith....	$ 7 55
Marianna Mission...........	2 65
Trinity, Van Buren.......	2 75
St. Luke's, Hot Springs.	13 64
St. Paul's, Fayetteville...	12 00
St. John's, Camden....	8 00
Total........	$46 59

The whole amount collected for this purpose will be made known in the report of the Commissioner for the University of the South, the Rev. I. O. Adams. If the whole equals an *average* of $12.00 to each Clergyman actually resident in Arkansas, our quota will be duly made up. If it is found to fall short of this amount, I hope this Council will immediately take steps to make it up. The Theological Department at Sewanee is our Theological School. It depends on the offerings of the Church in the Dioceses interested in it, for the support of the professors. To not meet our fair proportion of its necessary expenses, would be a disgrace to us, which I should feel most deeply.

As to events and movements in the Church at large in this land, I shall follow my former custom and say nothing. You are informed through the Church periodicals, or at least you *should* be so informed on all such topics, and what I could add, in the brief space which I could devote to these subjects, would add but little to your own knowledge.

I therefore close, and leave you to proceed with your regular business, and may the source of all wisdom give you grace to perceive what you ought to do, and strength to perform the same—through Christ our Lord.   H. N. PIERCE.

The Holy Communion was then celebrated by the Bishop, assisted by the Rector of the Parish, the Rev. Innes O. Adams.

The Council was called to order immediately after the services. The roll of the Clergy was called by the Secretary, and the following answered to their names: Rt.-Rev. Henry Niles Pierce, D. D., LL.D., the Rev. Messrs. I. O. Adams, D. McManus, W. C. Stout, D. L. Trimble, T. C. Tupper and J. J. Vaulx; also the Rev. J. L. Berne, not canonically connected.

The list of Parishes was then called, and the following found to be represented in the Council: St. John's Church, Camden; Christ Church, Little Rock; Trinity Church, Pine Bluff.

A quorum of Lay Representatives not being present, the Council adjourned until Saturday morning, the 7th inst., at 9:30 a. m.

SECOND DAY.

Saturday Morning, April 7, 1883.

Council met pursuant to adjournment.

The roll was called, and, in addition to those present yesterday, the following answered to their names: The Rev. Messrs. W. B. Burrows and J. L. Alcorn; also, Mr. W. G. Whipple, Chancellor of the Diocese.

On calling the roll of Parishes, a quorum of Lay Delegates not being present, the Council took a recess until 9:30 p. m.

Saturday, 9:30 p. m.

Council met pursuant to adjournment.

The Secretary called the list of Clergy; those present this morning answered to their names.

On calling the list of Parishes, four were found to be represented in the Council.

The Rt.-Rev. President appointed the Rev. Messrs. Adams and Burrows a Committee on Credentials, who reported the following Parishes were duly represented in the Council, viz.:

St. John's Church, Camden; Christ Church, Little Rock; Grace Church, Newport, and Trinity Church, Pine Bluff.

The roll of Lay Delegates being called, the following answered to their names: Mr. Wm. G. Whipple, Chancellor; Messrs. C. A. Magill, C. H. Stone, H. Higinbotham, St. John's Church, Camden; Mr. Wm. C. Stevens, Christ Church, Little Rock; Mr. P. Lynch Lee, Grace Church, Newport; Mr. R. V. McCracken, Trinity Church, Pine Bluff.

A quorum of Lay Delegates being present, the Council proceeded to the next business, the election of a Secretary. On motion, the Rev. Tullius C. Tupper was unanimously re-elected, and the Council was declared to be organized.

The Secretary appointed as Assistant Secretary, Mr. Wm. C. Stevens.

The Rt.-Rev. President announced the following Standing Committees:

On Constitution and Canons—Rev. W. C. Stout, Rev. D. L. Trimble, Chancellor Whipple, Mr. C. A. Magill.

On State of the Church—Revs. D. McManus, E. C. Alcorn, W. B. Burrows, and Messrs. Wm. C. Stevens and R. V. McCracken.

On Auditing and Finance—Messrs. R. V. McCracken, C. H. Stone, Wm. C. Stevens and P. Lynch Lee.

On New Parishes—Rev. Mr. Adams and the Chancellor.

On Unfinished Business—The Rev. Secretary.

The Standing Committee of the Diocese submitted the following report:

"The Standing Committee met in St. Luke's Church, Hot Springs, Saturday, the 22d of April, 1882, and organized by electing Rev. T. C. Tupper, President, and P. K. Roots, Secretary.

"Met in Little Rock, December 13, 1882. Testimonials were signed recommending Mr. G. W. Hunt, postulant, to be admitted a candidate for Holy Orders. At the same time and place, unanimous consent was given to the consecration of the Rev. Hugh Miller Thompson, D. D., Assistant Bishop-Elect of

Mississippi, and his testimonials accordingly signed. At the same time and place, the Rev. Innes O. Adams was elected a clerical member of the Standing Committee, to fill the place made vacant by the removal of the Rev. D. B. Ramsey to the Diocese of Mississippi.

" The Committee met in Camden the 6th of April, 1883, and signed the testimonials of the Rev. E. C. Alcorn, Deacon, recommending his admission to the Sacred Order of Priests.

" Respectfully submitted,

"T. C. TUPPER, *President*."

The following reports of the Treasurer of the Diocese and the Trustees of the different funds were submitted, which were referred to the Finance and Auditing Committee :

REPORT OF LOGAN H. ROOTS, TREASURER DIOCESAN FUND.

RECEIPTS.

1882. DR.

April 29, Balance per last report	$ 202 30
May 6, St. John's, Helena	15 00
June 19, Trinity Parish, Van Buren	5 00
1883.	
March 10, Christ Church, Little Rock	75 00
March 24, St. John's, Helena	20 00
April 7, Grace Church, Phillips County	4 50
" " St. John's, Camden	17 50
" " St. John's, Fort Smith	56 00
" " Trinity, Pine Bluff	20 00
" " St. Paul's, Batesville	17 00
" " St. Paul's, Newport	3 50
" " St. Luke's, Hot Springs	12 00
Total to be accounted for	$ 447 80

DISBURSEMENTS.

1882 CR.

June 5, T. C. Tupper, Secretary	$ 68 20
July 20, P. K. Roots, Trustee Episcopal Fund	104 10
1883.	
February 26, T. C Tupper, Secretary	5 50
April 7, Balance on hand	270 00
	$ 447 80
April 9, 1883, Balance on hand	270 00

Respectfully submitted,   LOGAN H. ROOTS, *Treasurer.*

AMOUNTS REPORTED AS RECEIVED BY LOGAN H. ROOTS AS TREASURER OF THE FUND FOR DIOCESAN MISSIONS.

1882.

July 9, St. John's Parish, Camden	$ 3 40
December 26, Christ Church, Little Rock	10 00

1883.

March 22, St John's, Helena 6 15

       Total.......... .. .. $ 19 55

    Respectfully submitted,   LOGAN H. ROOTS, *Treasurer.*

REPORT OF P. K. ROOTS, TRUSTEE OF THE EPISCOPATE FUND.

RECEIVED, ETC.

1882.

Balance per last report   .   ... $ 125 58

May 6, St. John's, Helena 10 55

June 30,   "   " 4 50

July 20, From Treasurer Diocesan Fund 104 10

November 6, From Treasurer Diocesan Fund 493 50

December 21, Grace Church, Phillips County 4 70

1883.

January 10, St. John's, Camden 3 95

February 23,   "   " 1 70

    "   26, Christ Church, Little Rock, Sunday School 11 60

    "   "   "   "   "   "   .... :.. .....   4 50

March 5,   "   "   "   " 4 50

March 22, St John's, Helena 11 00

                                                                      ————
                                                                    $ 780 18

       Balance on hand 270 70

EXPENDITURES, ETC.

1882

September 23, Building Association $200 75

October 14,   "   " 20 00

November 16,   "   " 20 00

December 16,   "   " 20 00

1883.

January 2,   "   " 130 50

    "   16,   "   " 30 00

February 16.   "   " 30 00

March 16,   "   " 30 00

                                                                      ——————— $481 25

April 7, City Tax on Lots 10, 11 and 12, Block 200   . .   .   .   8 40

    "   " State and County Tax on Lots 10, 11 and 12, Block 200, $20.65, at 96 cents. ..   19 83

Balance on hand 270 70

                                                                      ——————
                                                                    $ 780 18

ASSETS.

$3,000 stock in Building Association, worth   .   .   .. $ 481 25

Lots 10, 11 and 12, Block 200 . .. .   700 00

Cash on hand 270 70

                                                                    $1,451 95

REPORT OF LOGAN H. ROOTS, AS TREASURER OF THE FUND FOR DISABLED
CLERGYMEN, ETC.

1881.

April, Balance per last report   . . . . $ 19 35

1882.

August 31, Grace Church, Phillips County........................ ... .   3 00

       Balance now on hand .   ...$ 22 35

The Committee on Finance and Auditing reported that they found the said reports correct as submitted.

The Rev. Mr. Adams submitted the following report of his duties as Diocesan Agent for the Theological Department of the University of the South:

CAMDEN, April 7, 1883.

To the Rt.-Rev. the President and the Members of the Eleventh Annual Council of the Diocese of Arkansas:

As Diocesan Agent for the Theological Department of the University of the South, I submit the following report as to the amounts that have been forwarded to the Treasurer since the last Council, so far as known to me:

St. John's, Fort Smith	.$ 12 00
St. John's, Camden	5 00
Grace Church, Phillips County	7 60
Amount collected at last Council	4 00
Christ Church, Little Rock	30 00
Total..........	.$ 58 60—$ 58 60

Now in the hands of the Bishop to be forwarded by him—

Additional from St. John's, Fort Smith	.$ 7 55
Marianna	2 65
Trinity, Van Buren	2 75
St Luke's, Hot Springs	13 64
St. Paul's, Fayetteville	12 00
St. John's, Camden ...	8 00
[Total ..	$ 46 59— 46 59
Grand total	$105 19

Respectfully submitted,

INNES O ADAMS,

Diocesan Agent for Theological Department University of the South

The Council went into the election of the Standing Committee, which resulted as follows: Revs. Tullius C. Tupper, W. C. Stout, Innes O. Adams, Messrs. M. L. Bell and P. K. Roots.

The following were elected Deputies and Alternates to the General Convention, the vote being by orders:

Of the Clergy—Deputies: Rev. Messrs. T. C. Tupper, J. J. Vaulx, W. C. Stout, Innes O. Adams. Alternates: Rev. Messrs. W. B. Burrows, D. L. Trimble, D. McManus, J. A. Matthews.

Of the Laity—Deputies: Messrs. R. V. McCracken, William C. Stevens, J. J. Horner, A. Wassell. Alternates: Messrs. C. H. Stone, M. L. Bell, C. A. Magill, L. —. Minor.

The Rev. Mr. Stout was on motion unanimously re-elected Registrar of the Diocese.

The Rev. W. B. Burrows was unanimously elected Trustee of the General Theological Seminary.

The Special Committee on Constitution and Canons, appointed at the Tenth Council, submitted the following report, which was on motion referred to the Standing Committee on Constitution and Canons, and the Special Committee discharged:

Report of Special Committee on Constitution and Canons:

" Your Committee appointed by the Tenth Annual Council, and instructed 'to report to the next Council a Digest of the Constitution and Canons,' have given due attention to their instruction, and beg to report that they find so few amendments that a republication at this time is not of sufficient importance to justify the expense.

" It is deemed highly creditable to the members of former Councils of this Diocese that in ten years so few changes have been made.

" The only change in the Constitution is in regard to the time of the Annual Council, changed from 'second Tuesday in May,' to 'such time as the Council may determine.' *Vide* Journal of Third Council, page 16.

" The first five Councils made no alterations or amendments in or to the Canons.

" The Sixth Annual Council adopted a new Canon, to be known as Title I, Canon XII, of the Chancellor. *Vide* page 12, 1878. This Council also amended Section 2, Canon 1, Title I ; but that amendment was repealed by the⹁Seventh Council. *Vide* page 18, Journal, 1879. Said Sixth Council also adopted a second section to Canon IX, Title I, providing for an election of a Trustee for the Episcopal Fund ; also, amended the Order of Business in conformity therewith. *Vide* pages 15 and 16, Journal, 1878.

" The Seventh Council having repealed the amendment to Section 2, Canon 1, Title I, passed at the Sixth Council, en-acted another amendment to the same Section 2, Canon I, Title I. *Vide* pages 18 and 19, Journal, 1879. This amend-ment pertains to the financial question.

" The Eighth Council made no change in the Canons.

" The Ninth Annual Council added a clause to Section 5, Title III, Canon I—*vide* page 13—and enacted a Canon, enti-tled Canon III, of Title III, providing 'a form of organization for a Missionary Station.' *Vide* pages 15, 16 and 17, Journal, 1881.

" The Tenth Annual Council made a verbal change in Section 2, Title I, Canon I, and repealed Section 3, Canon VIII, Title II. *Vide* Journal, 1882.

" The above are all the changes that have been made, and may be easily noted and referred to.

"Respectfully submitted,

" W. C. STOUT,

" T. C. TUPPER,

"Approved: " WM. G. WHIPPLE.

" H. N. PIERCE, Bishop."

At 12:30 a. m., on motion, the Council adjourned until 4 p. m., Sunday, April 8th.

THIRD DAY.

ST. JOHN'S CHURCH, CAMDEN, ARK., }
April 8, 1883, 4 p. m. }

The Council was called to order by the Rt.-Rev. President, the Bishop of the Diocese. Present: same as yesterday. On motion, the calling of the roll and reading of minutes of last session were dispensed with.

The Rev. Mr. Trimble offered the following, which was on motion referred to the Committee on Constitution and Canons:

Resolved, That at the end of Canon I, Title II, the following be added: "And it shall be the duty of such vacant Parishes, thus supplied, to defray all the expenses incident to such occasional services."

The Standing Committee on Constitution and Canons, to whom was referred the report of the Special Committee on Constitution and Canons, reported as follows, which was adopted:

Report of Committee on Constitution and Canons:

"Your Committee on Constitution and Canons, to whom were referred the recommendations of the Special Committee appointed at the last Council, have considered the same, and report the following resolutions:

"*Resolved*, That every repeal, amendment or enactment of a Canon, hereafter, shall be voted as a distinct proposition, after the same has been plainly read, and the question shall be put by the Chairman in this form: Shall this Canon, or amendment, pass? And on such question the roll shall be called, and the yeas and nays taken, and so entered on the journal.

"*Resolved*, That Canon V, Title I, be amended to read: 'A quorum for ordinary business at the Annual Council shall consist of such Clergy and Delegates from the Parishes as may be present, the Bishop also being present; but, if the Bishop be not present, such quorum shall only have power to receive the reports of Committees and Parishes, and refer the same; to elect the ordinary Officers and Committees, and to fix the time and place for the next Council. In the election of a Bishop, two-thirds of the Clergy and a majority of all the Parishes shall be present before the Council proceed to elect. At any *called* Council, other than as provided for in Section 1, Canon I, Title I, a quorum shall consist of a majority of all the Clergy entitled to seats, and Lay Delegates from four or more Parishes.'

"W. C. STOUT,
"D. L. TRIMBLE,
"W. G. WHIPPLE,
"C. A. MAGILL.

"*Approved:*
"H. N. PIERCE, Bishop."

The Committee on New Parishes respectfully reported,
" That it finds no business requiring its attention.

" I. O. ADAMS,

" WM. G. WHIPPLE,

" *Committee.*"

On motion, it was

Resolved, That, when this Council adjourns, it does so to
meet in St. Paul's Church, Fayetteville, on the second Friday
after Easter, A. D. 1884.

On motion, the following was adopted :

Resolved, That a Committee be appointed, to consist of the
Rev. J. J. Vaulx, to prepare a memorial to the General Convention, urging that body to pass a General Canon for the trial
of Ministers, and to establish a Court of Appeals from the Diocesan Courts.

The following was offered, but failed to pass :

Resolved, That the Deputies to the General Convention be,
and are hereby, instructed to vote for and use their best en-
deavors to have that body pass a General Canon for the trial of
Ministers, and to establish a Court of Appeals from the Diocesan Courts.

On motion, the following were adopted :

Resolved, That the Secretary be authorized to have printed
500 copies of the Journal of this Council, and the Treasurer be,
and is hereby, instructed to pay from the Diocesan funds the
expense incurred in carrying out this order.

Resolved, That, after paying the assessment against the
Diocese by the General Convention, and retaining $50 for con-
tingent expenses, the Treasurer pay over the balance to the
Trustee of the Episcopal Fund.

On motion, the following was unanimously adopted :

Resolved, That the members of the Council express hereby
their grateful appreciation of the kindness and hospitality extended to them by the Rector, vestry and congregation of St.
John's Church, Camden.

The following amendment, which was recommended by the Committee on Constitution and Canons, was adopted:

Resolved, That at the end of Section 1, Canon I, Title IV, the following words be added: "And at such election of a vestry, no vote by proxy shall be received."

The following was offered, but failed to receive the votes necessary to pass it:

Resolved, That the necessary expenses incurred by members of the Standing Committee in attending meetings of the Committee be defrayed by this Council out of Diocesan funds.

The Committee on the State of the Church reported as follows:

The Committee on the State of the Church respectfully report that the number of Clergy at present in this Diocese is the same as last year. This must be a source of much pleasure to all who feel an interest in the work of the Church, in view of the inadequate means available for their support, but it is still more gratifying to find that the results of their efforts in building up God's Kingdom are larger than in any year since our first Arkansas Council was organized. In truth, the increase seems to be concurrent with the increase of our population. The Church does not stand still. It would be sad, indeed, if the mightiest factor in civilization could become inert while other elements are in a high state of activity. The age in which we live is progressive. The land is being filled with living souls in its remotest corners. Countless broad acres are being opened up. Commerce, as it were, takes wings, and material interests do, we fear, to a large extent predominate, but will never, we believe, reach to universal dominion so long as the Church of God can have a clear stage and a fair fight with the powers of evil that are in the world, and we are the more led to believe this from our experience of the public sentiment at many points in our noble State. The influence of the Church is not confined to the Parish or the town where it is organized and established. Like the atmosphere, it is expansive, and is felt and seen in unnumbered places, where men congregate for social purposes. Hence, we find that not only in the Church proper, but among our whole people, there are no agnostics, no blatant infidels, no coteries who pretend not to know whether they are living souls or brute beasts. This is not said merely for the sake of making a statement with a view of filling out a report. Did the time permit, or the occasion call for it, we could cite many instances which would fully confirm what we say; but we will, for the present, confine ourselves to the immediate object for which your Committee was appointed, and will only add the subjoined statistics, which have been carefully made out, and are now submitted, with all due respect, to the Bishop and brethern in Council assembled.

> " D. McManus, *Chairman,*
> " W. B. Burrows,
> " E. C. Alcorn,
> " R. V. McCracken,
> " Wm. C. Stevens."

SUMMARY.

Baptisms—Adults, 36; Infants, 94—Totals 130

Confirmations 95

Marriages 42

Burials 78

Sunday-School Teachers 75

    "   "   Scholars 649

Communicants last report 1,010

   Dropped 14

   Died 12

   Removed . . . . 30—56

Leaving 954

   Add—Confirmations 95

   Otherwise . . . . 89—184

Present number 1,138

   Gain since last Council 128

Contribution $7,504 20

Increase for 1882-3 . . . . 2,553 37

PARISHES	BAPTISMS			MARRIAGES	BURIALS	SUNDAY-SCHOOLS		COMMUNICANTS									CONTRIBUTIONS	RECTOR OR MISSIONARY
	ADULT	INFANT	TOTAL			TEACHERS	SCHOLARS	LAST REPORT	CONFIRMED	ADD ANEW	REMOVED INTO PARISH	TOTAL	REMOVED FROM PARISH	DROPPED	DIED	TOTAL		
St. John's .... Camden	3	6	8	1	1	7	60	12	9		10	51		1	3	48	$ 759 08	I. O. Adams.
St. Paul's .... Newport	3	7	10	1		5	40	27				27				37	131 70	E. C. Alcorn.
St. Paul's .... Batesville		1	1			7	27	66			1	61	5		5	56	198 37	E. C. Alcorn.
Christ Church .. Little Rock	21	36	61	22	38	20	230	292	28		30	329	1	2	1	312	3,157 48	T. C. Tupper.
Trinity Church .. Pine Bluff		3	3	3	3	8	80	56	43			70			1	69	14 85	
St. John's Church . Fort Smith	7	30	37	4	11	10	102	68	25	20	1	123	9		2	112	1,291 62	J. L. Berne.
Grace Church .. Phillips County	2		2					17	2		14	17	3		1	13	22 95	D. McManus.
St. John's Church .. Helena	1		1						11	6	3	8	2			8	8 60	W. B. Burrows.
St. Paul's .... Fayetteville		10	11	6	15	10	60	63			4	86			1	99	218 60	J. Vaulx.
Trinity .... Hot Springs		6	6	3	4	5	80	6	6			99	9			30	118 00	J. S. Gibbs.
St. Luke's .... Van Buren		1	1	3	6	3	30	25	2			40				46	1,591 58	J. A. Matthews.
St. Andrew's .... Marianna								46				46				29		C. A. Bruce.
St. Paul's .... Hope								16				20				24		
.... Dardanelle								24				24				17		
.... Bentonville								17				17				8		
.... Eureka Springs								8				8				8		
.... Huntsville								8				8				6		
.... Prescott								4				6				4		
.... Washington								6				4				34		
St. Mark's .... Arkadelphia								34				34				4		
.... Lake Village								4				16				16		
.... Augusta								66				16				6		
St. Paul's .... Morrilton								6				4				4		
.... Forrest City								16				16				16		
.... Southwest Arkansas								46				46				46		
.... Russellville								4				4				4		
.... Alma								4				4				4		
.... Wallaceburg								4				4				4		
.... Mineral Springs								4				6				6		
.... Stony Point								6				5				5		
.... Lonoke								3										
.... Clarendon								11				11						W. C. Stout.
At large													11	11				
Total	36	94	130	42	78	75	689	1,010	124	26	63	1,189	30	14	12	1,138	$ 7,504 20	

*No report—figures estimated.

On motion, the following was adopted :

Resolved, That the Deputies to the General Convention shall report to the President of the Standing Committee, for the information of the Bishop, one month before the meeting of that body, as to their ability to attend its meeting, that should any be unable to attend, the Bishop may appoint an Alternate Deputy.

On motion, the following was adopted :

Resolved, That the Council adjourn until after service to-night.

Sunday Evening, 9 p. m.

Present : same as the afternoon.

No business being before the Council, the Rt.-Rev. President declared the Eleventh Annual Council of the Diocese of Arkansas adjourned *sine die*.

Attest :

T. C. TUPPER,
Secretary.

W. C. STEVENS,
Assistant Secretary.

PAROCHIAL REPORTS.

ST. PAUL'S, BATESVILLE.

Baptisms—
 Infants ....

Communicants—
 Last reported...... 58
 Added anew................................. 2
 Removed into the Parish..... 1
 Removed from the Parish 5
 Present number.............................56

Sunday-School—.
 Teachers..................................... 7
 Pupils 27

OFFERINGS.

Weekly offertory...................... ...$ 31 32
All other sources........................ 167 05
              ————
 Total................................$198 37

APPROPRIATIONS.

Convention assessment...................$ 17 00
Diocesan Missions 8 22
Parochial purposes..................... 168 15
Other expenses....................... 5 00
              ————
 Total................................$198 37

 H. S. COLEMAN, *Treasurer.*

Remarks: In addition to the above amount, the "Ladies' Aid Society" of the Parish have raised by sewing and otherwise $193 towards building a Rectory.

E. C. ALCORN, Rector.

In addition to the number of Communicants above reported, there are ten persons in the Parish who have been Confirmed, but have never Communed.

___

ST. JOHN'S, CAMDEN.

Baptisms—
- Adults......................... 2
- Infants c

Total......................... 8
Confirmations 9

Communicants—
- Last reported......................... 42
- Added anew 9
- Removed from the Parish.. 1
- Dropped......................... 1
- Died 1
- Present number.... 48
- Marriages......................... 1
- Burials 1

Sunday-School—
- Teachers... 7
- Pupils 60

OFFERINGS.

Communion alms......................... $ 21 30
Weekly offertory......................... 30. 90
All other sources......................... 706 85

Total......................... $759 05

APPROPRIATIONS.

Convention assessment......................... $ 17 50
Endowment of the Episcopate......................... 3 95
Diocesan Missions 10 25
University of the South......................... 5 00
Parochial purposes......................... 719 50

Other expenses........................... 2 85

Total.............................$759 05

P. LYNCH LEE, *Treasurer.*

INNES O. ADAMS, *Rector.*

ST. PAUL'S, FAYETTEVILLE.

Baptisms—
Infants 6
Confirmations 11
Communicants—
Last reported........... 65
Present number............................. 90
Marriages.. 2
Burials 4
Sunday-School—
Teachers........... 5
Pupils 80

OFFERINGS.

Communion alms $30 00
Weekly offertory........................... 56 00

Total............... ....$86 00

APPROPRIATIONS.

University of the South.................$ 12 00
Domestic Missions...................... 17 50
Mission to Jews........................ 2 50
Parochial purposes..................... 86 00

Total.............................$118 00

J. L. CRAVENS, *Treasurer.*

JAMES J. VAULX, *Rector.*

ST. JOHN'S, FORT SMITH.

Baptisms—
Adults...................................... /

Infants 30

Total 37
Communicants—
Last reported 68
Confirmations 25
Removed into Parish 6
Returned to Communion .24
Removed from Parish 9
Died 2
Present number 112
Number of celebrations of the Holy Communion . .45
Marriages 4
Burials 11
Sunday-School—
Teachers 10
Pupils 102

OFFERINGS.

Weekly offertory . . . .$ 291 00
All other sources 1,000 62

Total $1,291 62

APPROPRIATIONS.

Convention assessment . . . .$ 34 00
Endowment of the Episcopate 9 75
Diocesan Missions 9 00
University of the South 19 70
Sunday-School expenses 141 10
Christmas expenses 46 00
Prof. Botefuhr, Organist 60 00
Salary of Rector 800 00
Incidentals 172 07

Total $1,291 62

C. M. BARNES, *Secretary of Vestry.*

JAMES L. BERNE, *Rector.*

ST. JOHN'S, HELENA.

Baptisms—
Adults	1
Infants	10
Total	11
Confirmations	2

Communicants—
Last reported	63
Added anew	20
Removed into Parish	3
Died	1
Removed from Parish	2
Present number	83
Marriages	5
Burials	15

Sunday-School—
Teachers	10
Pupils	60

OFFERINGS.

Weekly offertory	$162 65
Communion alms	55 95
Total	$218 60

APPROPRIATIONS.

Convention assessment	$ 20 00
Endowment of the Episcopate	11 00
Diocesan Missions	15 00
University of the South	2 00
Jewish Missions	3 20
Parochial purposes	168 40
Total	$218 60

JOHN J. HORNER, *Treasurer.*

W. B. BURROWS, *Rector.*

ST. LUKE'S, HOT SPRINGS.

Baptisms—

Infants .,... 1

Confirmations 6

Communicants—

Last reported..... 25

Added anew...................... 6

Removed into the Parish..................... 3

Removed from the Parish 9

Died ...; 1

Present number.............................24

Marriages............................. 3

Burials 6

Sunday-School—

Teachers...... 3

Pupils 20

OFFERINGS.

Communion alms.............. ....$ 144 00

Weekly offertory.... .... 246 00

All other sources....................... .... 1,201 58

Total $1,591 58

APPROPRIATIONS.

Convention assessment .... $ 12 00

Diocesan Missions, Bishop's visitation 13 67

Parochial purposes........ .... 1,527 41

Other expenses, insurance on Church 38 50

Total $1,591 58

J. A. POLHAMIUS, *Treasurer.*

Remarks: It will appear from this report that no collections have been made in behalf of either the Diocesan or general institutions of the Church during the past year. This is because of the constant demand made largely on my people for means with which to minister to the dying and dead. They come here from all parts of the country, utterly destitute. It is not a charitable work, but one that is forced upon us.

GEO. S. GIBBS, *Rector.*

CHRIST CHURCH, LITTLE ROCK.

Baptisms—
    Adults..21
    Infants 30

        Total.... 51
    Confirmations 28
Communicants—
    Last reported..............................292
    Removed from the Parish.................... 1
    Dropped. 2
    Died 5
    Present number........ 312
    Marriages....... 22
    Burials 38
Sunday-School—
    Teachers.... 20
    Pupils 220

OFFERINGS.

Communion alms and private offerings for
    poor ....$ 227 55
Weekly offertory. 444 13
All other sources, including pew rents..... 2,485 80

    Total $3,157 48

APPROPRIATIONS.

Convention assessment..... ....$ 75 00
Endowment of the Episcopate........... 21 00
Diocesan Missions.................... 27 50
University of the South 30 00
General Missions of the Church by in-
    dividuals 105 05
Society for promoting Christianity among
    the Jews.......................... 9 75
Parochial purposes 2,644 13
" Pious and charitable uses"..... .... 227 55
Nashotah 7 50

Bible and P. B. Society 10 00

Total $3,157 48

R. H. PARHAM, JR., *Treasurer.*

TULLIUS C. TUPPER, *Rector.*

ST. PAUL'S, NEWPORT.

Baptisms—

Adults 3

Infants 7

Total......... 10

Communicants—

Present number...... 27

Marriages.................................. 1

Sunday-School—

Teachers.. 5

Pupils 40

OFFERINGS.

Communion alms ....$ 6 60

Weekly offertory...................... 18 15

All other sources 103 50

Sunday-School 3 45

Total...... . ...$131 70

APPROPRIATIONS.

Convention assessment ... .$ 3 50

Diocesan Missions 6 40

Parochial purposes 111 75

Other expenses 6 60

Total....... ....$128 25

Remarks: In addition to the above sums, $25 has been raised by the Ladies' Guild, and $150 more has been promised, towards the building of a Rectory.

E. C. ALCORN, *Deacon in Charge.*

GRACE CHURCH, PHILLIPS COUNTY.

Baptisms—
    Adults............................. 2
Communicants—
    Last reported........................... ..17
    Removed from the Parish.'.... 3
    Died 1
    Present number............................13

OFFERINGS.

Communion alms $17 45
All other sources........ .... 5 50
                                              ———
    Total..............................$22 95

APPROPRIATIONS.

Convention assessment ....$ 4 50
Endowment of the Episcopate 4 70
University of the South........... .... 4 00
Domestic Missions..... .... 5 00
Parochial purposes....................... 4 75
                                              ———
    Total............................ ....$22 95

J. B. PILLOW, *Treasurer.*

Remarks: The Parishioners live at such distances from the
Church that it seems almost impossible to have the children
assembled early enough on Sunday mornings, but it is gratifying to know that they are being faithfully instructed by their
parents.   D. McMANUS, *Rector.*

TRINITY CHURCH, PINE BLUFF.

Baptisms—Infants 3
    Confirmations 14
Communicants—
    Died 1
    Present number....... .... .20
    Marriages...... 3
    Burials 3

Sunday-School—
 Teachers.. 8
 Pupils 80

APPROPRIATIONS.

Convention assessment $10 00
Diocesan Missions 4 85
                    ————
 Total.... ....:...........$14 85

R. V. McCRACKEN, Secretary of the Vestry.

TRINITY CHURCH, VAN BUREN.

Confirmations 3
Communicants—
 Nominally .... .38
 Added 4
 Removed from the Parish..................... 2
 Died 1
 Marriages................................. 1
 Burials 1

J. A. MATTHEWS, Rector.

☞ Collections required to be made:

For Diocesan Missions—On the first Sunday in Lent, and on Trinity Sunday.

For the Episcopate Fund—On the first Sunday in Advent.

In addition to these the Clergy of the Diocese are requested to devote an offertory to the Theological Department of the University of the South, and also to make collections for the General Missions of the Church.

JOURNAL OF PROCEEDINGS

OF THE

TWELFTH ANNUAL COUNCIL

OF THE

PROTESTANT EPISCOPA. CHURCH,

IN THE

Diocese of Arkansas.

Held in St. Paul's Church, Fayetteville, Arkansas, on the 25th, 26th and 28th days of April, A. D 1884.

LITTLE ROCK:
THE O'NEALE AND STEVENS COMPANY,
STATIONERS.
1884.

OFFICERS OF THE DIOCESE OF ARKANSAS.

President:
THE RT. REV. HENRY NILES PIERCE, D. D., LL.D.,
Little Rock.

Secretary:
THE REV. TULLIUS C. TUPPER, D. D., Little Rock.

Assistant Secretary:
MR. WILLIAM COPPEÉ STEVENS, Little Rock.

Treasurer:
MR. LOGAN H. ROOTS, Little Rock.

Registrar:
REV. WILLIAM C. STOUT, Morrillton.

Chancellor:
MR. M. L. BELL, Pine Bluff.

Trustee of the Episcopate Fund:
MR. P. K. ROOTS, Little Rock.

Trustees of the University of the South:
REV. JOSEPH L. BERNE,
MESSRS. W. G. WHIPPLE AND ALBERT WASSELL.

Trustee of the General Theological Seminary:
REV. W. B. BURROWS, Helena.

Standing Committee:

REV. T. C. TUPPER, D. D. President,

THE REV. MESSRS. J. L. BERNE AND INNES O. ADAMS,

MESSRS. M. L. BELL AND P. K. ROOTS, Secretary.

Deputies to the General Convention:

REV. J. J. VAULX,   MR. J. L. CRAVENS,

REV. T. C. TUPPER, D. D.,   MR. G. H. VAN ETTEN,

REV. INNES O. ADAMS,   MR. M. L. BELL,

REV. W. B. BURROWS,   MR. A. WASSELL.

Board of Missions:

The Rt. Rev. the Bishop of the Diocese, and the Clerical Members of the Standing Committee.

CLERGY OF THE DIOCESE.

The Rt. Rev. HENRY N. PIERCE, D.D., LL.D., Little Rock.
The Rev. INNES O. ADAMS...............Trinity, Pine Bluff.
The Rev. JOSEPH L. BERNE........St. John's, Fort Smith.
The Rev. WILLIAM B. BURROWS.........St. John's, Helena.
†The Rev. C. A. BRUCE.....................................Helena.
†The Rev. H. C. E. COSTELLE............Grace, Washington.
The Rev. D. McMANUS..............................Fort Smith.
†The Rev. D. F. McDONALD, D. D.................Dardanelle.
The Rev. W. J. MILLER............St. Luke's, Hot Springs.
†The Rev. A. W. PIERCE, *Deacon*................Little Rock.
†The Rev. W. C. STOUT..............................Lewisburg.
†The Rev. DAVID L. TRIMBLE......................Pine Bluff.
The Rev. T. C. TUPPER, D. D., Christ Church, Little Rock.
The Rev. J. J. VAULX...............St. Paul's, Fayetteville.

†Absent from Council.

W. G. Whipple, Esq., *Chancellor.*

Arkadelphia, St. Mark's.

Augusta, St. Paul's.

Batesville, St. Paul's.

Camden, St. John's.

Dardanelle, St. Paul's.

Fayetteville, St. Paul's—J. L. Cravens, C. H. Leaverett.

Fort Smith, St. John's.

Helena, St. John's—H. S. Hornor, P. O. Thweatt.

Hot Springs, St. Luke's—I. W. Carhart, G. G. Latta.

Jacksonport, Grace Church.

Lake Village, Emmanuel.

Little Rock, Christ Church—W. G. Whipple, Albert L. O'Neale and Albert Wassell.

Newport, St. Paul's.

Phillips County, Grace Church.

Pine Bluff, Trinity—M. L. Bell, R. V. McCracken, Geo. E. Valliant and F. Heakes.

Prescott, St. James.

Van Buren, Trinity.

Washington, Grace Church.

PROCEEDINGS

OF THE

TWELFTH ANNUAL COUNCIL.

ST. PAUL'S CHURCH, FAYETTEVILLE, ARK.,
April 25, 1884.

The Twelfth Annual Council of the Protestant Episcopal Church in the Diocese of Arkansas, met in St. Paul's Church, Fayetteville, Friday morning, the twenty-fifth of April, 1884.

After morning prayer, and the ante-communion service was said, the Rev. D. McManus preached, and the Rt. Rev. the Bishop of the Diocese, celebrated the holy communion.

The Council then took a recess until 4 p. m.

4:30 O'CLOCK P. M.

The Council reassembled according to notice, and on call of the roll, the following Clergymen answered to their names: The Rt. Rev. H. N. Pierce, D.D., LL.D., Bishop; the Rev. Innes O. Adams, Rector of Trinity Church, Pine Bluff; the Rev. Joseph L. Berne, Rector of St. John's Church, Fort Smith; the Rev. D. McManus; the Rev. T. C. Tupper, D. D., Rector of Christ Church, Little Rock;

and the Rev. J. J. Vaulx, B. D., Rector of St. Paul's Church, Fayetteville.

On calling the roll of parishes, the following were found to be represented: Christ Church, Little Rock, and Trinity Church, Pine Pluff.

The Rt. Rev. President appointed Rev. Messrs. D. McManus and J. J. Vaulx, a Committee on Credentials, who reported that they find on examination that the following Lay Delegates have been duly elected to this Council, viz.: From St. Paul's Church, Fayetteville, Messrs. J. L. Cravens and C. II. Leaverett ; from St. John's Church, Helena, Alternates II. S. Hornor and P. O. Thweatt; from St. Luke's Church, Hot Springs, Messrs. Geo. G. Latta and I. W. Carhart; from Christ Church, Little Rock, Messrs. W. G. Whipple, Albert L. O'Neale and Albert Wassell ; from Trinity Church, Pine Bluff, Messrs. M. L. Bell, Geo. E. Valliant, F. Heakes and R. V. McCracken.

The roll of Lay Representatives being called, the following answered to their names ; Fayetteville, J. L. Cravens; Christ Church, Little Rock, A. L. O'Neale and Albert Wassell ; Trinity Church, Pine Bluff, M. L. Bell.

On motion, St. Paul's Church, Fayetteville, was excused from payment of the Diocesan assessment for the present year.

On motion, the Rev. Dr. Tupper was unanimously re-elected Secretary of the Council, and the Chairman then declared the Council duly organized and ready for business.

The Secretary gave notice that he had appointed Mr. Wm. C. Stevens, of Little Rock, Assistant Secretary.

The Bishop then appointed the following Standing Committees :

On the State of the Church—Rev. T. C. Tupper, Rev. J. L. Berne, Mr. A. L. O'Neale, Mr. C. H. Leaverett.

On Constitutions and Canons—Rev. J. J. Vaulx, Rev. I.

O. Adams, Rev. D. McManus, Mr. M. L. Bell, Mr. Albert Wassell.

On Unfinished Business—Rev. D. McManus, Mr. A. L. O'Neale.

Finance and Auditing Committee—Messrs. J. L. Cravens, M. L. Bell, A. Wassell.

The following report of the Standing Committee was then submitted:

To THE RT. REV. H. N. PIERCE, D. D., LL. D., AND THE TWELFTH AN-
NUAL COUNCIL OF THE DIOCESE OF ARKANSAS:

April 7, 1883, Committee met at Camden, and approved the testimonials of Rev. E. C. Alcorn, applying for Priest's orders.

January 30, 1884, the Committee met at Little Rock, and approved
unanimously the consecration of the Rev. Alfred Augustin Watson, D. D.,
Bishop Elect of the Diocese of East Carolina, to the Episcopate. The application of the Rev. A. W. Pierce, Deacon, for Priest's orders, was presented, and his testimonials recommending him for ordination to the second order of Priests, signed.

Also, the application of Isaiah Daniels (colored), as a candidate for Holy
Orders, was approved.

Respectfully submitted.   T. C. TUPPER, *President.*

The following report of the Treasurer of the Diocese was submitted:

TREASURER'S REPORT.

To THE TWELFTH ANNUAL COUNCIL OF THE DIOCESE OF ARKANSAS:

In my report, as published in the Proceedings of the Eleventh Annual
Council, page 27, I accounted for all funds received previous to and during
the session of the Council of last year. The following statement is now
submitted:

RECEIPTS.

1883.   DR.

April 16, balance on hand last report............................$270 00

1884.

April 19, Hope and Washington.................... .... 10 00

April 22, St. Paul's Parish, Newport....,....... .... 2 50

April 25, St. Luke's Parish, Hot Springs............. .... 15 00

May 1, St. John's Parish, Fort Smith......................... 54 50

May 3, Christ Church, Little Rock........... .... 75 00

———— Trinity Church, Pine Bluff............................. 18 00

May 13, St. John's Parish, Camden.......................... 18 00

May 17, St. John's Parish, Helena............................. 25 00

        Total receipts...... ....$488 00

DISBURSEMENTS.

1883.   CR.
April 20, printing Reports.............................. $4 50
June 9, printing and mailing Reports.................. 76 00
August 21, stamps to Rev. T. C. Tupper, Secretary...... 2 25
October 19, dues to General Convention.... .... 45 00
Jan. 25, P. K. Roots, Trustee Episcopate Fund..... ....135 00
Feb. 5, express charges on Proceedings (G. C.).......... 2 40
April 15, postage, printing and stationery.............. 4 00—$269 15

Leaving balance on hand.............................$218 85

All of which is respectfully submitted,

LOGAN H. ROOTS,
Trustee of Diocesan Fund.

REPORT OF TRUSTEE OF EPISCOPATE FUND.

TO THE RT. REV. THE PRESIDENT AND MEMBERS OF THE TWELFTH AN-
NUAL COUNCIL OF THE DIOCESE OF ARKANSAS:

As Trustee of the Episcopate Fund, I submit the following statement:

RECEIPTS, ETC.

1883.
April 7, balance on hand......................................$270 70
Dec. 4, from Rev. E. C. Alcorn, Batesville..................... 5 00
1884.
Jan. 25, from Diocesan Fund................................. 135 00
Feb. 21, from St. John's, Fort Smith....................... ... 7 25
March 20, from Advent collection, Helena..................... 12 65
April 19, from Christ Church Sunday-School, Little Rock........ 13 30
April 19, from Trinity Church, Pine Bluff..................... 4 65
May —, from $500 Building Association stock sold at par........ 145 00

Total receipts...$593 55

DISBURSEMENTS, ETC.

1883.
April, paid Building Association dues $30 00
May,   "   "   "   ." 30 00
June,   "   " 30 00
July,   "   " 30 00
August, "   " 30 00
Sept., "   " 30 00
Oct.,   "   " 30 00
Nov.,   "   " 30 00
Dec.,   "   " 30 00

```
    1884.
Jan.,    "       "         ..      ..    ........ 30 00
Feb.,    "       "         ..      ..    ........ 30 00
March,   "       "         ..      ..    ........ 30 00
April,   "       "         ..      ..    ........ 30 00
May,     "       "         "       "     ........ 25 00—$415 00
Feb. 11, Taxes on Lots 10, 11 and 12, Block 200........  33 61 — $448 61

May 20, leaving cash balance on hand..........................$144 94
```

ASSETS.

```
$2500 stock in Building Association, worth.. ....................$751 25
Lots 10, 11 and 12, Block 200..................................  700 00
Cash on hand...............................................  144 94

         Total fund at this date..............................$1596 19
```
All of which is respectfully submitted,

P. K. ROOTS,
Trustee of Episcopate Fund.

REPORT OF THE TREASURER OF THE FUND FOR DIOCE-SAN MISSIONS.

To THE RT. REV. THE PRESIDENT AND MEMBERS OF THE ANNUAL COUN-
CIL OF THE DIOCESE OF ARKANSAS :

As Treasurer of the Fund for Diocesan Missions, I would respectfully report :

RECEIPTS.

```
    1883.
April 9, balance on hand.......................................$19 55
Dec. 13, received from Christ Church, Little Rock...............  10 05
    1884.
March 30, St. Johns, Helena, Trinity collection.................   3 25
          "        "    Lenten collection.................   3 50
——— Trinity, Pine Bluff...................................   6 85
                                                              ———————
                                                              $43 20
```

EXPENDITURES, ETC.

```
    1884.
April 17, gave Rt. Rev. Bishop for the Mission at Dardanelle......  35 00

      Leaving balance on hand.............................   $8 20
```

As Treasurer of the Fund for Disabled Clergymen, etc., I would respectfully report that I had a balance on hand at the close of last Council of $22.35; since which time I have not received nor disbursed anything on said account, so that there is still in my possession the said amount of $22.35.

All of which is respectfully submitted,

LOGAN H. ROOTS,
Treasurer of respective Funds.

The above reports were referred to the Auditing Committee, who reported as follows:

To THE TWELFTH ANNUAL COUNCIL:

Your Committee to whom was referred the report of the Treasurer of the Diocese, beg leave to report that they have examined the same and find it correct, and that the Treasurer has on hand as per statement rendered, a balance of $218.85.

Your Committee also beg leave to report that they find the statement of the Trustee of the Episcopate Fund correct, and that the assets of that fund amount to $1596.19.

Your Committee also beg leave to report that they have examined the report of the Treasurer of the fund for Diocesan Missions and Disabled Clergymen, etc., and find the same correct. We find the balance of the Fund for Diocesan Missions on hand, $8.20, and that for Disabled Clergymen, $22.35.

Respectfully submitted,   M. L. BELL, *Chairman.*

The election of the Standing Committee for the ensuing year being next in order, an election was had as provided by canon, which resulted as follows: Rev. T. C. Tupper, Rev. I. O. Adams, Rev. J. L. Berne, Mr. M. L. Bell, Mr. P. K. Roots.

The following gentlemen were elected Deputies to the General Convention: Rev. J. J. Vaulx, Rev. T. C. Tupper, D. D., Rev. I. O. Adams, Rev. W. B. Burrows, Mr. J. L. Cravens, Mr. G. H. Van Etten, Mr. M. L. Bell, Mr. A. Wassell.

Rev. William C. Stout, of Morrillton, was re-elected Registrar of the Diocese by acclamation.

On motion of Rev. I. O. Adams, Mr. M. L. Bell was elected Chancellor of the Diocese, to serve for the ensuing three years, as required by canon.

On motion, the Rev. Joseph L. Berne, Mr. Wm. G. Whipple and Mr. Albert Wassell were elected Trustees of the University of the South at Sewanee, Tennessee, to serve for three years.

The following amendment to Section 3, Canon X, Title I, of the Diocese, was presented to the consideration of the Council by the Rev. T. C. Tupper:

   *   *   * or shall be filled by appointment of the Bishop from the Clergy Canonically connected with the Diocese, and from the Lay Communicants residing in any Parish admitted into union with the Council.

Which was, on his motion, referred to the Committee on Constitution and Canons.

On motion, the Council adjourned to meet in St. Paul's Church to-morrow morning, the 26th inst., at 9:30 o'clock.

  *   *   *   *   *   *   *   *   *   *

Evening prayer was said at 8 o'clock of the evening of the 25th inst., by Rev. Messrs. J. J. Vaulx and D. McManus, after which the Rev. Innes O. Adams, Rector of Trinity Church, Pine Bluff, preached the Convention Sermon from the text, Second Corinthians, iv, 7.

SECOND DAY.

St. Paul's Church, April 26, 1884.

Council met pursuant to adjournment.

Morning prayer was said by the Rev. J. L. Berne and T. C. Tupper, D. D., after which the Rt.-Rev. the Bishop of the Diocese, read before the Council his Annual Address, as follows:

BISHOP'S ADDRESS.

BRETHREN OF THE CLERGY AND LAITY: We meet once more in Annual Council. The thin attendance of the Clergy is not due to decrease in the Clerical force of the Diocese. The Clerical list has undergone some changes in the past year, but the number of laborers is about the same. Though the period since we last assembled has been one filled with cares and toils, yet it has not been unmarked by decided progress, nor without encouragement.

We have, as usual, vacant Parishes, from which evil we have so often and so severely suffered, but, thank God, I see in a future that I trust may be near, a remedy for the ills arising from this source. I believe that the Cathedral and the Cathedral system, of which I have long dreamed, and for which I have long planned and worked, will soon be a reality, and a living, acting power in Arkansas. Every year has more and more convinced me that, for vigorous Church growth in this Diocese, the Cathedral is a necessity. No Layman or Clergyman can so well appreciate this fact as the Bishop, upon whom mainly rests the responsibility of keeping alive the Church where it is feeble, and of planting it in fields yet unoccupied. But of this and other matters, more hereafter.

My first duty is to lay before you an abstract of my Journal for the past Counciliar year. My last report of official work, as shown in an abstract of my Journal, was closed on April 5, 1883.

APRIL 6—The Annual Council of the Diocese of Arkansas met in St. John's Church, Camden. After morning prayer and litany said by the Rev. Messrs. D. L. Trimble, T. C. Tupper and J. J. Vaulx, I said the Ante-Communion, the Rev. I. O. Adams reading the Epistle, and the Rev. D. McManus, the Gospel. I then read my Annual Address, and, assisted by the Rector, the Rev. I. O. Adams, I celebrated the Holy Eucharist. On calling the Council to order, no quorum was found to be present, and nearly two whole days were passed waiting for a quorum, the deficiency being in the Lay representation. The attendance of the Clergy was unusually full. I am glad to say that one of the first things done, when the requisite quorum was obtained, was to repeal the Canon that has caused us such trouble, and occasioned such loss of time in years past. Hereafter, those who do meet on the day and at the place appointed, will constitute a Canonical quorum for the transaction of all business. Of course, when Brethren are known to be on the way and detained by untoward circumstances, Christian courtesy will lead us to await their arrival before proceeding to the more important matters before the Council. But in no case will a Council hereafter waste day after day waiting for absentees. If the Parishes will not take the pains to be represented in the Diocesan Council, let them not find fault with the proceedings of those who are sufficiently interested to obey the Church's summons; for the work will be done hereafter, however negligent Clergy or Lay Delegates may be in their attendance. As long as this Canon remains unchanged we cannot be tied up to inaction; and I believe this change in regard to a quorum will soon result in a larger attendance of the Laity than we have generally been favored with. If it have this effect, I shall be doubly thankful for the change.

APRIL 7—Attended morning prayer in St. John's Church. At night, after service, and a sermon by the Rev. J. L. Berne, I confirmed one person.

A quorum having been secured, the Council proceeded to business, and I presided till its final adjournment, as the Journal shows.

APRIL 8—The second Sunday after Easter. At 11 a. m., at St. John's Church, Camden, morning prayer having been said at an earlier hour, the Rev. T. C. Tupper preached; the Rev. I. O. Adams presented and I ordered Priest the Rev. Edwin Cheney Alcorn, Deacon. The Rev. J. J. Vaulx read the Epistle, and the Rev. W. C. Stout, the Gospel. All the Priests present united in imposition of hands. I celebrated the Holy Eucharist unassisted. The offertory, amounting to $8, was devoted to the Theological Department of the University of the South, at Sewanee, Tennessee. At night, the Rev. D. L. Trimble preached, and, after giving a short address, I declared the Council adjourned *sine die*.

APRIL 9—In St. John's Church, Camden, after evening prayer said, I delivered an address on "Woman's place in creation, and mission to the world," being the Commencement Address at the Institute, Columbia, Tennessee, the previous June.

APRIL 15—The third Sunday after Easter. Assisted in saying morning service in Christ Church, Little Rock. At night I preached in the same Church.

APRIL 22—The fourth Sunday after Easter. In Christ Church, Little Rock, I assisted in saying morning service, and preached. Also assisted in saying evening service.

APRIL 29—The fifth Sunday after Easter. In Christ Church, Little Rock, I assisted in saying morning service. Also assisted in saying evening service, and preached.

MAY 3—Ascension Day. In Christ Church, Little Rock, assisted in saying morning service, and preached. The Rector celebrated the Holy Eucharist.

MAY 6 - The Sunday after Ascension. In Christ Church, Little Rock, I assisted in saying morning service, and preached, and celebrated the Holy Eucharist. I assisted in saying evening service in the same Church.

MAY 7—I gave notice to the Rt. Rev. Dr. Brown, Bishop of Fond du Lac, that the Letters Dimissory presented by the Rev. H. C. E. Costelle, had been presented and accepted.

MAY 13—Whitsunday. In Christ Church, Little Rock, I assisted in saying morning service, and preached.

MAY 14—This day I executed and had recorded a Declaration of Trust concerning the Cathedral lots, showing that I held the same three lots as Trustee, for the benefit of Trinity Cathedral, Little Rock.

MAY 29—Trinity Sunday. In St. Paul's Church, Fayetteville, Ark., I celebrated the Holy Eucharist, and preached morning and night.

MAY 31—At 4:30 p. m., I preached in same Church, and after service held a meeting of the vestry, and gave them my counsel on certain matters pertaining to the well-being of the Parish. At 8 p. m., after evening prayer, I preached again.

MAY 22—In St. Paul's, Fayetteville, I preached at 4:30 p. m. At 8 p. m. I preached again, and confirmed three persons, and addressed the class. The Rector, Rev. J. J. Vaulx, said the service on all these occasions.

MAY 23—In Trinity Church, Van Buren, Arkansas, after evening prayer said by the Rev. James A. Matthews, I preached, confirmed two persons, and addressed the class.

MAY 27—The first Sunday after Trinity. At 10:30 a. m., in Trinity Church, Pine Bluff, Arkansas, the Rev. D. L. Trimble and the Rev. D. B. Ramsey said morning prayer. Rev. Mr. Ramsey preached, and I instituted Rector of Trinity Church, Pine Bluff, Arkansas, the Rev. I. O. Adams. At 8 p. m. I preached, and confirmed seven persons, and addressed the class.

MAY 28—At Pine Bluff, Arkansas. I confirmed, in private, one person. The Rector of Trinity Church presented the candidate.

JUNE 1—I gave Letters Dismissary to the Rev. P. A. Johnson, transferring him to the Diocese of Minnesota.

JUNE 3—The second Sunday after Trinity. In Christ Church, Little Rock, I assisted in saying morning service, preached, and celebrated the Holy Eucharist.

JUNE 8—I gave Letters Dimissory to the Rev. George S. Gibbs, transferring him to the Diocese of Colorado.

JUNE 10—The third Sunday after Trinity. In Christ Church, Little Rock, I assisted in saying morning service.

JUNE 16—Attended at morning and evening prayers in St. Luke's Church, Jackson, Tennessee.

JUNE 17—The fourth Sunday after Trinity. In St. Luke's Church, Jackson, Tennessee, at 7 a. m., I attended the celebration of the Holy Eucharist, and received. At 10:30 service, in same Church, I preached, and made an appeal for my Cathedral. The offertory was appropriated to that object. [As a full report will be made in due time of all moneys collected for Cathedral, I shall not take the space to enter on this abstract the sums collected from time to time.] At 8 p. m. I preached again in the same Church.

JUNE 18—Attended daily prayers in St. Luke's, Jackson, morning and evening, and at the evening service I preached, and confirmed one person. This confirmation was held under peculiar circumstances, and I rightly judged that the Rt. Rev. the Bishop of Tennessee, would heartily approve of my seeming intrusion into his jurisdiction.

JUNE 19—Attended morning and evening prayers in St. Luke's Church.

JUNE 24—The fifth Sunday after Trinity, and St. John Baptist's Day. Attended early celebration and received in St. Peter's Church, Columbia, Tennessee; the Rector, Dr. Beckett, was the celebrant. At 11 a. m., I assisted in saying the service, and preached, and made an appeal for the Cathedral. The offertory was appropriated to that object. At night 1 preached again.

JULY 1—The sixth Sunday after Trinity. In St. Peter's Church, Columbia, Tennessee, I assisted in saying morning service, and preached, and celebrated the Holy Eucharist.

JULY 8—The seventh Sunday after Trinity. In Christ Church, Louisville, Ky., the Rector, Rev. Mr. Craik, said morning prayer and litany. I said the ante-communion, preached, and made appeal for the Cathedral, and with good success. The offertory was kindly appropriated to that object. At 6 p. m., in Calvary Church, Louisville, after evening prayer by the Rev. Mr. Minegerode, the Rector, I made an appeal for the Cathedral, and obtained the offertory. At 8 p. m., after evening prayer by the Rev. Dr. Tschiffely, Rector of Grace Church, I preached in St. Peter's Church, Portland, Louisville. The Tuesday, Wednesday, Thursday and Friday following were spent in soliciting funds for my Cathedral, and with encouraging success, which result I owe very largely to the kindness and influence of the Rev. Dr. Tschiffely.

JULY 12—I received the Holy Communion at the Chapel of the Church Orphanage, in Louisville; Dr. Tschiffely was the celebrant.

JULY 15—The eighth Sunday after Trinity. In Trinity Church, Covington, Kentucky, I said morning service, preached, made an appeal for Cathedral, and took up an offertory for the same.

JULY 22—The ninth Sunday after Trinity. In Grace Church, Cleveland, Ohio, after morning prayer said by the Rector, the Rev. Mr. Trimble, and by Rev. Dr. James A. Bolles, Rector Emeritus of Trinity Church, Cleveland, I said the ante-communion, preached, made an appeal for the Cathedral, and celebrated the Holy Eucharist, assisted by the Rector. The offertory was devoted to Arkansas, and it was a large one for the Parish. At 7:30 p. m., I assisted at evening prayer in the same Church, and preached again. The week I spent in Cleveland was occupied in soliciting funds for the Cathedral, with a success as marked as it was unexpected. I am most deeply indebted to the Rev. Dr. Bolles for his kindly hospitality, as well as for his most generous espousal of my cause.

JULY 29—The tenth Sunday after Trinity, was spent with friends in the country in the State of New Jersey. 1 was unable to attend Church in the neighboring town, but said the service and read a sermon in the family circle.

AUGUST 3—I baptized, in private, a gentleman, an old friend, in New Jersey.

AUGUST 5—The eleventh Sunday after Trinity. In St. Paul's Church, Rahway, New Jersey, I assisted the Rector, the Rev. Dr. Norton, in saying morning service, preached, and made an appeal for my Cathedral, and took up an offertory for the same. At 4 p. m., in the Church of the Holy Com-

forter, after evening prayer said by the Rector, the Rev. Mr. Bartow, I
preached, and made an appeal for Cathedral, and received the offertory for
the same. At night I preached again in St. Paul's Church.

AUGUST 12—The twelfth Sunday after Trinity. At 10:30 a. m., in
Grace Church, Newark, New Jersey, I assisted in saying morning service,
'preached, made an appeal for Cathedral, and, assisted by the Rev. Mr.
Meade, celebrated the Holy Eucharist. At 8 p. m., after evening prayer
said by the Rev. A. L. Wood, I preached in the House of Prayer, Newark,
and made an appeal for Cathedral. Neither of the offertories taken were
devoted to my work, but the appeals were not fruitless; for they resulted
in a small contribution from Grace Church, and a very generous one from
the House of Prayer, as will appear more clearly on some future occasion.

AUGUST 19—The thirteenth Sunday after Trinity. I assisted in saying
morning service in St. Paul's Church, New York City, and preached, also
assisted at evening prayer in the same Church.

AUGUST 26—The fourteenth Sunday after Trinity. In Trinity Church,
Newport, Rhode Island, I assisted the Rector, the Rev. Dr. Magill, in saying morning service, and preached, and made an appeal for Cathedral;
which appeal was warmly seconded by Dr. Magill. No offertory was
taken for Arkansas; but the response was a liberal one, as will be shown in
due time. I assisted also at evening prayer in the same Church.

SEPTEMBER 2—The fifteenth Sunday after Trinity. In Trinity Church,
Pawtucket, Rhode Island, I assisted in saying morning service, and
preached, and made an appeal for Cathedral. The Rector, the Rev. Mr.
Tucker, promised to take an offertory after a while, which promise was
duly fulfilled. A gentleman of the congregation handed me $5 for the
object, after the service. At 7 p. m. I preached in St. Paul's Church, Pawtucket, and made my appeal. Rev. Mr. Porter promised a collection in
the future, which promise was duly fulfilled. Here, as in the morning, $5
were handed me for the object after the service. All of which will be
duly and more minutely reported at a subsequent time.

SEPTEMBER 9—The sixteenth Sunday after Trinity. In Christ Church,
Norwich, Connecticut, I assisted the Rector, the Rev. Dr. Giess, in the
morning service, preached, and made an appeal for Cathedral. The offertory was forwarded to the Board of Missions as a *special* for Arkansas. At
7:30 I preached in Trinity Church, Norwich, and made my appeal. The
Rector, the Rev. Dr. Jewett, kindly promised me a collection in the future,
which promise has been made good.

SEPTEMBER 16—The seventeenth Sunday after Trinity. In St. Peter's
Church, Westchester, New York, I assisted the Rector, the Rev. Mr. Johnson, in saying morning service, preached, and made an appeal for Arkansas, in which I was kindly seconded by the Rector. At night I preached
again. Offertories were taken at both services for my Cathedral and Mission work, and they were most liberal. In this Church I confirmed, at the

request of the Rt. Rev. Horatio Potter, D. D., Bishop of New York, quite a large class.

SEPTEMBER 23—The eighteenth Sunday after Trinity. In St. Matthew's Church, Jersey City, I assisted in saying morning service, preached, and made an appeal for Cathedral and Clergy House. The Rev. Dr. Abercrombie, the Rector, kindly promised me an offertory for my work later in the season, which promise was duly fulfilled. At night I preached in the Church of the Holy Spirit, Madison Avenue, New York City. The Rector, Rev. Dr. Guilbert, kindly contributed to my Cathedral fund, and gave me hopes of further assistance at some future time.

SEPTEMBER 30—The nineteenth Sunday after Trinity. In St. Paul's Church, New York City, I preached, and made an appeal for my Cathedral and Missionary Cause. The Rev. Dr. Mulchahey strongly endorsed my undertaking, and asked the people to send in to him their contributions. The sum subsequently received was a very liberal one, and will, in due time, be reported to the Church.

OCTOBER 3—Attended the opening services of the General Convention, in Christ Church, Philadelphia. From this time till the twenty-sixth of October, I was in attendance on the sessions of the House of Bishops, and on the sessions of the General Convention sitting as the Board of Missions. This General Convention was second in importance to none preceding it. The amount of work accomplished was very great. As to the chief fruit of our labors, the revision of the Prayer-Book, I shall speak further on.

OCTOBER 5—In answer to the call of the Domestic Committee, I addressed the Board of Missions in regard to the work in Arkansas and the Indian Territory. The brief time allowed each speaker prevented as full a statement of the subject as was desirable. At times, twenty minutes would give ample opportunity of setting forth the facts which should be known; at other times an hour would hardly suffice. At the close of my speech the Rev. Dr. Saul kindly promised to help me in my work, which promise was subsequently made more than good by a contribution which doubled the amount pledged to me. The Rev. E. Spruille Buford also kindly pledged me his aid. He subsequently fixed on Easter, 1884, as the time when his contribution would be forwarded to me, and it is probably now awaiting me on my return home.

OCTOBER 7—The twentieth Sunday after Trinity. In the Church of the Ascension, Philadelpnia, I assisted in saying morning service, and preached a Missionary Sermon, and, assisted by the Rector, Rev. Mr. Hodge, celebrated the Holy Eucharist. Here I received a small contribution for my work in Arkansas. At night, in St. Clement's Church, Philadelphia, I took part in a Missionary Meeting, and made a brief statement of the work to be done in Arkansas, and how I proposed, by God's help, to do it. The Rev. Father Maturin added a few eloquent words in my behalf, and announced that the offertory would be appropriated to Arkansas. It was the largest collection nace for ny Cathedral and Clergy-House in any Church where I nace ny appeal. It was sent to the Board of Missions as a *special* for Arkansas.

OCTOBER 10—I presiced at a neeting of the Clergy and Laity held in Philadelphia, to take steps for the preservation of the docunentary history of the Church in the Confederate States. It was the unanimous desire of the meeting that the Rev. John Fulton. D. D., of St. Louis, should gather, edit and publish these documents. At another meeting, attenced by all the Southern Bishops, and other Bishops specially interested in the Southern Dioceses, the Rev. Dr. Fulton was requested and appointed to take charge of this natter. I would suggest that a connittee of two or nore Clergy and Laity who have been long conversant with the Church in Arkansas, be appointed by this Council to aid the Rev. Dr. Fulton in his important work. Perhaps one Clergyman and one Layman would form the nost efficient Connittee, and I believe that the Council will agree in ny opinion that the Rev. Willian C. Stout is the Clergyman best qualified for this labor; no one of us is so well inforned as to the history of the Church in Arkansas during those troublous cays.

OCTOBER 14—The twenty-first Suncay after Trinity. In Trinity Church, Pittsburgh, Pennsylvania, I assisted the Rev. Mr. Maxwell, the Rector, in saying norning service, preached, mace an appeal for my Cathedral and Clergy-House, etc., and, assistec by the Rector, celebrated the Holy Eucharist. At night I preached again, and made a further explanation of ny plans and statenents showing the need of a Missionary centre in Arkansas. The offertories taken morning and evening were very generous, and were forwarced to the Board of Missions as a *special* for Arkansas.

OCTOBER 20—I attended the consecration of the Rev. Dr. H. C. Potter, as Assistant Bishop of the Diocese of New York. Dr. Potter's advancenent to the Episcopate has been hailed with great satisfaction by the whole Church. The approbation of the choice of the Diocese of New York has been universal. The consecration took place in Grace Church, New York City.

OCTOBER 21—The twenty-second Suncay after Trinity. I attended service in the Church of the Atonenent, Philadelphia.

OCTOBER 26—I joinec in the closing services of the General Convention in Holy Trinity Church, Philadelphia.

OCTOBER 28—The twenty-third Suncay after Trinity. In the Church of the Nativity, Philacelphia, I assistec the Rector, the Rev. Mr. Jeffers, in saying morning service, preachec, and nade an appeal for Cathedral, Clergy-House and Missions in Arkansas. The offertory, a large one, was sent to the Board of Missions as a *special* for Arkansas. At 4 p. m. I preached in St. Clenent's Church, Philadelphia. At night I preached in the Church of the Annunciation, Philadelphia.

NOVEMBER 4—The twenty-fourth Sunday after Trinity. In Grace Church, Plainfield, New Jersey, I assisted the Very Rev. Dr. Rodman, Rector, in saying morning service, preached, and made an appeal for ny work in Arkansas, after which, assisted by the Rector, I celebrated the Holy Eucharist. The offertory, a liberal one, was sent to the Board of Missions as a *special* for Arkansas. In the afternoon I addressed the children of the Parish on Missionary work anong the Indians.

NOVEMBER 11—The twenty-fifth Sunday after Trinity. In Grace Church, Memphis, Tennessee, I attended the early celebration and received the Holy Communion; the Rector, Rev. Edgar Organ, was the celebrant. At 11 a. m. I assisted in saying norning service, and preached. At night I preached again, and made an appeal for Cathedral, etc., and, acting for and at the request of the Rt. Rev. the Bishop of Tennessee, confirmed one person. The offertory at the evening service was devoted to Arkansas.

NOVEMBER 18—The twenty-sixth Sunday after Trinity. In Christ Church, Little Rock, I assisted in saying morning service.

NOVEMBER 25 - The twenty-seventh Sunday after Trinity. In Christ Church, Little Rock, I assisted in saying morning service, and preached.

NOVEMBER 29 – Thanksgiving Day. In Christ Church, Little Rock, I assisted in saying morning service.

NOVEMBER 30—St. Andrew's Day. I assisted the Rector of Christ Church in saying morning service.

DECEMBER 2 – The first Sunday in Advent. I assisted in saying norning service, and preached in Christ Church, Little Rock, and, assisted by the Rev. T. C. Tupper, Rector, celebrated the Holy Eucharist.

DECEMBER 9 -- The second Suncay in Acvent. In Christ Church, Little Rock, I assisted in saying norning service. At night I preached, and confirned six persons, and acdressed the class.

DECEMBER 16—The third Sunday in Advent. In Christ Church, Little Rock, I assisted in saying morning service, and preached.

DECEMBER 23—The fourth Sunday in Advent. I assisted in saying morning service in Christ Church, Little Rock.

DECEMBER 25—Christmas Day. In Christ Church, Little Rock, I assisted in saying norning service, preached, and celebrated the Holy Eucharist, assisted by the Rector.

DECEMBER 30—The Sunday after Christmas. Assisted in saying norning service in Christ Church, Little Rock.

JANUARY 6, 1884 -- The Epiphany. In Christ Church, Little Rock, I assisted in saying norning service, preached, and celebrated the Holy Eucharist, assisted by the Rector.

JANUARY 13—The first Sunday after Epiphany. In Christ Church, Little Rock, assisted in saying morning service, and preached.

JANUARY 20—The second Sunday after Trinity. In Trinity Church, Pine Bluff, I assisted in saying norning service, preached, and, assisted by the Rector, the Rev. 1. O. Adams, celebrated the Holy Eucharist. In the afternoon, assisted by the Rev. D. L. Trimble and the Rev. I. O. Adams, I held a special service in the Northern Methodist (Colored) Church, and addressed the congregation on the Church, and explained our plans. The Rev. Messrs. Trimble and Adams followed with appropriate remarks. The Rev. Mr. Trimble has nobly determined to begin a work among the colored people. I believe the time is now opportune, and if I can get a special appropriation from the Board of Missions for two years, I think the work will prove a great success. Mr. Trimble donates a fine lot for the Church, and will aid in erecting it also. The opening is a promising one, and I trust the Church will listen to my appeal. The undertaking will be connected directly with my Cathedral work. At night I preached again in Trinity Church. I was much rejoiced to see the Rectory of Trinity Church approaching its completion. This is the second Rectory the Rev. Mr. Adams has been instrumental in erecting in Arkansas. I hope the time is not distant when every Parish in the Diocese will have a comfortable home of its own for the Rector.

JANUARY 27- -The third Sunday after Epiphany.—In Christ Church, Little Rock, I assisted in saying morning service, and preached.

FEBRUARY 3—The fourth Sunday after Epiphany. In St. John's Church, Fort Smith, I assisted in saying morning service, preached, and, assisted by the Rector, the Rev. J. L. Berne, celebrated the Holy Eucharist. At night I preached again, confirmed two persons, and addressed the class. The offertory, amounting to $10.10, which was augmented by a kind friend to $20.10, I devoted to the Cathedral.

FEBRUARY 7 In Trinity Church, Van Buren, after evening prayer said by the Rev. D. McManus, I preached.

FEBRUARY 10—Septuagesima Sunday. In St. Paul's Church, Fayetteville, I assisted in saying morning service, and preached, and, assisted by the Rev. J. J. Vaulx, Rector, celebrated the Holy Eucharist. In the afternoon I preached again, and confirmed one person.

FEBRUARY 17—Sexagesima. In St. Paul's Church, Fayetteville, I said morning service, preached, and celebrated the Holy Eucharist. The heavy rains had caused an interruption of travel, and I was forced to remain north of the mountains a week longer than I had proposed to myself.

FEBRUARY 20- I spent several hours in carefully inspecting the new Church at Van Buren. I was greatly relieved to find that the exaggerated stories of its unsafety were wholly groundless. Some mistakes have been made in its erection, but none which can not be easily rectified. There is no good reason why it should not be completed as fast as the people are ple are able to obtain the funds.

FEBRUARY 22 Gave my Canonical consent to the consecration of the Rev. Dr. Watson, Bishop-elect of the new Diocese of East Carolina.

FEBRUARY 24—Quinquagesima. In Christ Church, Little Rock, I assisted in saying morning service, and preached.

FEBRUARY 27—Ash Wednesday. I assisted in saying morning service in Christ Church, Little Rock.

MARCH 2—The first Sunday in Lent. In Christ Church, Little Rock, I assisted in saying morning service, and preached.

MARCH 5—I preached at morning service in Christ Church, Little Rock.

MARCH 9—The second Sunday in Lent. In Christ Church, Little Rock, I assisted in saying morning service, and preached.

MARCH 10—Attended evening prayer in Christ Church.

MARCH 11—At Little Rock, I confirmed, in private, two persons, the candidates being presented by the Rector of Christ Church. Attended evening prayer at the Church.

MARCH 12—I preached at morning service in Christ Church, Little Rock.

MARCH 13—Attended evening prayer in Christ Church.

MARCH 14—Attended evening prayer in Christ Church.

MARCH 16—The third Sunday in Lent. In St. Mark's Church, Hope, I assisted in saying morning service, preached, confirmed two persons, and addressed the class. After which, assisted by the Rector, the Rev. H. C. E. Costelle, I celebrated the Holy Eucharist. The offertory, amounting to $3.20, was donated to the Cathedral. At night, in Grace Church, Washington, I preached, confirmed four persons, and addressed the class.

MARCH 19—After evening prayer said by the Rev. Mr. Costelle, I preached in Grace Church, Washington. I am rejoiced to say that the Parish at Washington has purchased a lot with a house upon it, which, when properly repaired and fitted up, will make a very comfortable Rectory. There is much evidence of new life in this Parish, and the Rev. Mr. Costelle is doing excellent work here.

MARCH 23—The fourth Sunday in Lent. In St. John's Church, Camden, at 10 o'clock a. m., I said morning prayer, baptized an adult, and made an address on baptism. At 11 a. m. I said the litany and ante-communion, preached, and celebrated the Holy Eucharist. The offertory, amounting to $5.10. I donated to the Cathedral. At night I said evening prayer, preached, confirmed three persons, and made an address.

MARCH 25—Attended evening prayer in Christ Church, Little Rock.

MARCH 26—Preached in Christ Church, Little Rock, at morning service.

MARCH 30—The fifth Sunday in Lent. In Trinity Church, Pine Bluff, I assisted in saying morning service, and preached. In the afternoon I confirmed a person in private. At night I preached again, and confirmed two persons.

APRIL 1—Attended evening prayer in Christ Church, Little Rock.

APRIL 2—Preached at morning service in Christ Church, Little Rock.

APRIL 3—Attended evening prayer in Christ Church, Little Rock.

APRIL 6—The sixth Sunday in Lent. In St. Luke's Church. Hot Springs. I assisted the Rector. the Rev. William J. Miller. in saying morning service. preached. and confirmed five persons. and made a brief address to the newly confirmed: after which. assisted by the Rector. I celebrated the Holy Eucharist and. at 4:30 p. m. I preached again. The offertory. amounting to $32.45. I devoted to the Cathedral.

APRIL 8—Tuesday in Holy Week. I attended morning service in Christ Church, Little Rock.

APRIL 9—Wednesday in Holy Week. I attended morning service in Christ Church.

APRIL 10—Maundy Thursday. Attended morning service in Christ Church.

APRIL 11—Good Friday. I assisted in saying morning service in Christ Church. and preached.

APRIL 13—I assisted in saying morning service in Christ Church. Little Rock, preached, and. assisted by the Rector. Rev. T. C. Tupper, celebrated the Holy Eucharist. At night I assisted in the evening service, and confirmed eight persons and addressed the class. The offertory at night was devoted to the Cathedral. It was $18.26.

APRIL 14—Easter Monday. Attended morning service in Christ Church.

APRIL 17—In St. Paul's Church, Dardanelle. After evening prayer said by the Rev. Dr. MacDonald, Rector, I preached.

APRIL 20—Low Sunday. In Trinity Church, Van Buren. the Rev. D. McManus said morning prayer and litany, and read the epistle. I said the ante-communion, made an address encouraging the people to complete their new Church, and preached. At night. after evening prayer by the Rev. J. L. Berne, Rector, I preached in St. John's Church, Fort Smith, and confirmed eight persons, and addressed the class.

You will see from this condensed statement of my work during the interval between this Annual Council and the Council of 1883, that a portion of the Diocese remains to be yet visited. God willing, I shall visit the Eastern border, and other points, shortly. The erection of the west end of the Cathedral required my presence and attention for months after my return to the State, after an absence of five months. I believed that work to be so important that every other interest should, for the time, be placed in abeyance. Besides this reason, I postponed by visit to the Eastern portion of the Diocese because the whole Mississippi front and the Valley of White River, have suffered so much from high water and overflows that a visitation there would have been almost fruitless.

Before proceeding further I will here add a summary of the work done, as shown by the above abstract.

SUMMARY.

Sermons.. 90

Addresses 43

Eucharists 23

Confirmed 58

Ordinations.. 1

Institutions... 1

Miles traveled..7193

I have received on Letters Dimissory from the Diocese of Fond du Lac, the Rev. H. C. E. Costelle, who is now laboring most acceptably and successfully at Washington and Hope; from the Diocese of Central New York, the Rev. William J. Miller, now the acceptable Rector of St. Luke's, Hot Springs; from the Diocese of Minnesota, the Rev. J. L. Berne.

I have transferred by Letters Dimissory the Rev. P. A. Johnson, to the Diocese of Minnesota; the Rev. George S. Gibbs to the Missionary Diocese of Colorado, and the Rev. James A. Matthews to the Diocese of Ohio.

The Rev. I. O. Adams has removed from St. John's, Camden, to Trinity Church, Pine Bluff. The Rev. D. McManus has resigned charge of Grace Church, Phillips County, and is residing at Fort Smith, and in temporary charge of Trinity Church, Van Buren. The Rev. Edwin C. Alcorn has resigned the charge of St. Paul's Church, Batesville, and Grace Church, Newport, and is residing beyond the limits of Arkansas.

The Rev. D. L. Trimble has officiated at Camden during the past year, and very acceptably. He has begun a work among the colored people at Pine Bluff, which I trust will result in great good.

Two new Rectories have been secured— at Pine Bluff and Washington. The small Rectory at Dardanelle has been completed; the Rev. Dr. Mac-Donald is contemplating its enlargement. The interior of St. Paul's Church, Fayetteville, has been beautifully finished, and it is now awaiting the consecration to take place in a few days. St. Luke's, Hot Springs, has been much improved internally. I have no definite information, but presume that St. Andrew's Church, Marianna, is well under way. Christ Church, Little Rock, is going up rapidly, and not a moment too soon, as the Chapel in which the Parish has worshiped for some years is too small for the congregation. And lastly, I am happy to announce that the west end of the Cathedral of the Diocese, embracing the nave and aisles, with tower and baptistry, is very near its completion. The portion now built, will, when the whole plan is carried out, afford four hundred and seventy-five sittings. I am not without some hope of being able in the near future to erect the transept and chancel, and so provide for the accommodation of a thousand or more worshipers. With a Church of that capacity, our Missionary center would soon become strong and capable of furnishing more means to carry out the good work than are now derived from all external sources; and the comparatively small sum of six thousand dollars more would give Arkansas a Cathedral worthy to bear the name, by its dimensions, beauty and completeness of arrangement. If my life is spared a few years I shall complete the building I have undertaken, even though no further external aid be granted me. But I cannot bear to lose the time and the opportunities which must be, in a measure, lost, if for the next two, three or four years I am obliged to use most of the means raised by the Cathedral congregation in extending the Church edifice instead of for the extension of the Church in the Diocese. May the Giver of all good put it into the hearts of those who are able to do so, to aid me in this work, which is scarceley less than all-important to the future welfare of the Church in Arkansas.

In this connection I would suggest the inquiry whether any change is necessary in the Canons of the Diocese in order to allow the Laity worshiping at the Cathedral a representation in the Annual Council. When the Chapter is duly organized, I suppose it will be granted that such a body can exercise in this matter all the powers exercised by a Parish Vestry. But I do not wish to hurry the organizing of a Cathedral Chapter. Perhaps it might not be amiss to so shape the Canon as to allow the congregation *in Vestry assembled*, on Easter Monday, to elect Delegates to this Body. The Vestry only represents the Parish, and the Parish, or congregation, ought to have, and doubtless, in equity, has the right to do all that it can authorize and empower its agents, the Wardens and Vestrymen, to do.

One topic more I will dwell on very briefly. The Revised Prayer-Book having passed the last General Convention, will, if it pass the next General Convention, become the standard of worship for the American Church. But are we prepared for so important a step? In some respects *the proposed book* is an improvement on our present one. In not a few cases the changes made are no improvements, and in some cases they are decidedly for the worse. The Commission, for the time that they had to work in, and the restrictions under which they worked, accomplished wonders. But much of the new material set forth is in a very crude state. I should exceedingly regret to see the book adopted finally in its present condition. Had the last General Convention, after going over the volume, as it did, referred the whole matter back to the Commission, and giving them three years more to revise, improve and polish their work, I think it would have done a very wise thing, perhaps the very wisest thing. Had the Constitution been so amended as to allow the tentative use of this book, that, too, would have been a wise move. However much the Prayer-Book may be improved by the revision, it has not been brought to a state that really and fully satisfies anybody. A beginning has been made, but nothing satisfactory, as yet, accomplished. We can better afford to get on without any change for awhile, than we can afford to fasten on the American

Church, for an indefinite number of years, a book which can ill bear nice and searching examination. Do not let it harden into an unchanging form till it has been properly shaped. I advise this Council to instruct its Deputies to the next General Convention to vote and speak against the adoption of the *proposed book* in its present form as the authorized standard of our worship. Grant even that it is good, yet it is far from good enough to take the place of our old Prayer-Book. We can have something better, and we shall have something better, and that before long, if we reject this and send it back to the same, or to a new, Committee, to be perfected. Thus much I have felt it my duty to say upon this subject. I believe there are many, very many, Churchmen that feel as I do upon this matter. I hope our services may be improved and enriched, and that right soon, but I cannot accept what is offered to us as a finality.

And now, Brethren, begging your pardon for the long time I have kept you from your labors, I close abruptly my Annual Address, after begging that the Holy Paraclete may guide you into all truth, and fill you with all wisdom, that you may take such action as may lead to the good of the world, the prosperity of the Church, and the glory of God, through Him who died for our sins, and arose for our justification—our adorable Lord, Jesus Christ.

H. N. PIERCE.

NOTE.—I have omitted to mention above that at the last Council I reported a balance in my hands of $23.55, for Diocesan Missions. I subsequently received from St. Paul's, Batesville, $8.21, and from Grace, Newport, $6.79, which swelled the sum to $38.55. This money I appropriated to the Rev. Dr. McDonald, and paid over the same to him.

The following resolution proposed by the Rev. I. O. Adams, was adopted:

Resolved, That so much of the Bishop's address as relates to the revision of the Book of Common Prayer, be referred to a Special Committee, to report at the next Annual Council.

Whereupon the Bishop appointed Rev. Messrs. Adams, Vaulx and Tupper, of the Clergy, and Mr. R. V. McCracken, of the Laity.

The following resolution proposed by the Rev. I. O. Adams, was adopted:

Resolved, That the Bishop be requested to appoint one Clergyman and one Layman to assist the Rev. Dr. Fulton in his preparation of the history of the Church in the South during the existence of the Confederate Government, as suggested in his (the Bishop's) address.

The Rev. William C. Stout, of Morrillton, and Mr. J H. Van Hoose, of Fayetteville, were appointed as such Committee.

The following communication was presented by the Bishop to the Council, from the Rev. C. L. Hutchins, Secretary of the House of Deputies of the General Convention, which was referred to the Committee on Constitution and Canons:

COMMUNICATION.

THE GENERAL CONVENTION OF THE PROTESTANT EPISCOPAL CHURCH, TO THE SECRETARY OF THE COUNCIL OF THE DIOCESE OF ARKANSAS:

SIR:—In compliance with the requirements of Article IX of the Constitution, I would hereby officially make known, through you, to the Council of the Diocese of Arkansas, that the following alterations of the Constitution of the Church are proposed, to wit: those comprised in the two resolutions subjoined, said resolutions having been constitutionally adopted by a General Convention of the Protestant Episcopal Church, held in the City of Philadelphia, Pa., in October, A. D. 1883, to wit:

1.   It was, by concurrent action of the two Houses of the Convention (vide Journal of Convention, pp. 240, 263, 279, 280).

Resolved, That Articles II and III of the Constitution be amended by substituting the words "House of Deputies" for the word "Convention" in the fourteenth line of Article II of the Constitution as printed in the Digest of 1880, and that the words "House of Deputies" be, in like manner, substituted for the word "Convention" in the twelfth line of Article III, as printed above;

So that the Articles shall read as follows —:

ARTICLE II.

The Church in each Diocese shall be entitled to a representation of both the Clergy and the Laity. Such representation shall consist of not more than four Clergymen and four Laymen, communicants in this Church, residents in the Diocese, and chosen in the manner prescribed by the Convention thereof; and in all questions when required by the Clerical or Lay representation from any Diocese, each Order shall have one vote; and the majority of suffrages by Dioceses shall be conclusive in each Order, provided such majority comprehend a majority of the Dioceses represented in that Order. The concurrence of both Orders shall be necessary to constitute a vote of the House of Deputies. If the Convention of any Diocese should neglect or decline to appoint Clerical Deputies, or if they should neglect or decline to appoint Lay Deputies, or if any of those of either Order appointed should neglect to attend, or be prevented by sickness or any other accident, such Diocese shall nevertheless be considered as duly represented by such Deputy or Deputies as may attend, whether Lay or Clerical. And if, through the neglect of the Convention of any of the Churches which shall have adopted or may hereafter adopt this Constitution, no Deputies, either Lay or Clerical, should attend at any General Gonvention, the Church in such Diocese shall nevertheless be bound by the acts of such Convention.

ARTICLE III.

The Bishops of this Church, when there shall be three or more, shall, whenever General Conventions are held, form a separate House, with a right to originate and propose acts for the concurrence of the House of Deputies composed of Clergy and Laity; and when any proposed act shall have passed the House of Deputies, the same shall be transmitted to the House of Bishops, who shall have a negative thereon; and all acts of the Convention shall be authenticated by both Houses. And in all cases the House of Bishops shall signify to the House of Deputies their approbation or disapprobation (the latter with their reasons in writing), within three days after the proposed act shall have been reported to them for concurrence; and, in failure thereof, it shall have the operation of a law. But until there shall be three or more Bishops, as aforesaid, any Bishop attending a General Convention shall be a member *ex-officio*, and shall vote with the Clerical Deputies of the Diocese to which he belongs; and a Bishop shall then preside.

II. It was by concurrent action of the two Houses of Convention (*vide* Journal of Convention, pp. 130, 273, 274. 300-303),—

Resolved, That Article IV of the Constitution be amended by striking out the word "and" in the third line of said Article, and inserting in place thereof the words following:—

" *Provided*, That, when a Missionary Jurisdiction shall be organized as a Diocese, the Bishop of such Jurisdiction shall become the Bishop of the new Diocese; and

" *Provided, further*, That when a part of a Missionary Jurisdiction shall be organized as a new Diocese, the Bishop of such Jurisdiction shall become the Bishop of the new Diocese, or, at his election, remain the Bishop of that part of such Jurisdiction not included in the new Diocese;" and leaving the residue of the said Article to stand as an independent paragraph;

So that the Article shall read as follows:

ARTICLE IV.

The Bishop or Bishops in every Diocese shall be chosen agreeably to such rules as shall be fixed by the Convention of that Diocese; *provided*, that, when a Missionary Jurisdiction shall be organized as a Diocese, the Bishop of such jurisdiction shall become the Bishop of the new Diocese; and *provided*, further, that, when a part of a Missionary Jurisdiction shall be organized as a new Diocese, the Bishop of such Jurisdiction shall become the Bishop of the new Diocese, or, at his election, remain the Bishop of that part of such Jurisdiction not included in the new Diocese.

Every Bishop of this Church shall confine the exercise of his Episcopal office to his proper Diocese, unless required to ordain, or confirm, or perform any other act of the Episcopal office in another Diocese by the Ecclesiastical authority thereof.

In testimony whereof, I have this day hereunto affixed my name.

CHAS. L. HUTCHINS,
Secretary of the House of Deputies.

MEDFORD, MASS., April 14, 1884.

The Committee reported as follows:

The Committee on Constitution and Canons, to whom was referred the above, recommend their adoption by this Diocese.

Signed,   JAMES J. VAULX,
I. O. ADAMS,
M. L. BELL,
A. WASSELL,
D. McMANUS.

The Rev. J. J. Vaulx reported that, as a Committee appointed by the Eleventh Annual Council, to present to the General Convention of 1883, a memorial for the establishment of a Court of Appeals, he had performed that duty, as appears of record on pages 171 and 234 of the Journal and Digest of that Body for 1883.

The Committee on Constitution and Canons recommend the adoption of the following addition to Title I, Canon I:

Provided, That the congregation worshiping in the Cathedral Church may, on the Monday in Easter Week, or as early thereafter as practicable, elect three communicants to represent them subject to the laws and regulations governing parochial representation.

J. J. VAULX, *Chairman.*

Which was read, and passed by both Orders, thus amending the Canon to read as above.

Said Committee also recommend that the amendment offered by the Rev. Dr. Tupper, relating to the manner of choosing Deputies to the General Convention, be adopted. Whereupon the amendment so offered, being an addition to Section 3, Canon X, Title I, was read, and passed by both Orders, thus amending the Canon:

Or shall be filled by appointment of the Bishop from the Clergy Canonically connected with the Diocese, and from the Lay communicants of the Diocese.

The Committee on Unfinished Business reported as follows:—

The Committee on Unfinished Business beg leave to state that they find nothing left over from last Council, needing attention, and respectfully ask to be discharged.

Signed,   D. McMANUS,
         A. L. O'NEALE,
                 Committee.

The following report of the Committee on the State of the Church was then read and received:

To THE RT. REV. THE PRESIDENT OF THE TWELFTH ANNUAL COUNCIL OF THE DIOCESE OF ARKANSAS:

Your Committee on the State of the Church beg leave to report that, from the limited number of Parochial Reports placed in their hands, they are unable to ascertain the true condition of the Church in Arkansas, that is to be gleaned from statistics, and therefore could not make any proper estimate of what has been done in Church progress and extension without fuller information.

We feel satisfied, however, from evidence brought before us, that the Diocese is in a good and healthy condition, and presents encouraging prospects of Church growth, and that, too, within a field so poorly provided with Clergymen and the means necessary for their support and their work.

It is gratifying to know that the Bishop is building, and will at an early day occupy for services of public worship, a beautiful and substantial edifice in Little Rock, as the Cathedral Church for his Diocese, which will constitute a central point for Missionary work throughout his Diocese; and if his plans can be carried out, which he feels confident can be done if he

TABULAR STATEMENT.

Parishes Reported.	Rector or Missionary.	Baptisms. Adults.	Infants.	Total.	Marriages.	Burials.	Sunday-School. Teachers.	Scholars.	Total.	Communicants. Last Report.	Confirmed.	Removed in to Parish.	Removed from Parish.	Died.	Total.	Contributions.
St. John's, Camden	J. J. Vaulx	1		1	2		3	30	33	48	3		13		36	$112 00
St. Paul's, Fayetteville	J. J. Vaulx	1	5	6	3	4	4	70	74		4				90	
St. James', Eureka	J. J. Vaulx		2		3	13					10	2			8	269 80
St. John's, Fort Smith	J. L. Berne	6	17	23	3	13	10	100	110		10	2			104	1,504 74
St. John's, Helena	W. B. Burrows	1	12	13	6	9	9	65	74	83	5	1	5		90	1,814 75
St. Luke's, Hot Springs	W. J. Miller	2	3	5	3	1	8	65	73	24	16				30	1,125 73
Christ Church, Little Rock	T. C. Tupper	15	52	67	21	45	20	290	309	312	16	5		6	322	3,226 28
St. Andrew's, Marianna	C. A. Bruce		4	4	1	5				17		5			22	
St. Paul's, Newport				9	2	8	7	100	107		11	13	6	1	10	1,300 00
Trinity Church, Pine Bluff	I. O. Adams	2	17	19	2	8	7	100	107		11	13	6	1	68	2,429 58
Grace Church, Washington	H. C. E. Costelle	1	8	9	1	4	5	25	30		6		1	2	45	1,022 11
Total		29	120	156	41	89	9	735	801	484	55	21	27	9	820	$12,804 99
Estimated number of communicants from Parishes and Missions not reporting to Council, taking the Journal of last year as a basis															351	
Grand total															1171	

PAROCHIAL REPORTS.

ST. JOHN'S, CAMDEN.

Baptisms—

    Adults 1

    Confirmations..... 3

    Marriages (one by Rev. Mr. Tupper).................... 2

Sunday-Schools—

    Teachers 3

    Scholars 30

Communicants —

    Last reported..48

    Confirmed 3

                                      51

    Removed 15

    Present number..36

    Communion alms, including regular offertory........$52 00

    Other sources.................................... 90 00

                                      $112 00

    Convention appropriation...................$18 00

    Parochial purposes........................ 84 00—102 00

    On hand... $10 00

    The Rt. Rev. Bishop of Arkansas received one offertory. No services at the time special collections should have been made.

                                             C. H. STONE, *Junior Warden.*

ST. PAUL'S, FAYETTEVILLE.

Baptisms —

    Adults 1

    Infants... 5

    Total.. 6

    Confirmations.. 4

Communicants—

    Present number..90

    Marriages 3

    Burials.. 4

Sunday-School—

    Teachers 4

    Pupils..70

OFFERINGS.

Communion alms...............................	$45 00
Weekly offertory................................	70 00
All other sources...............................	1,075 00
Total..	$1,190 00

APPROPRIATIONS.

Domestic missions	$20 00
Missions to Jews................................	3 35

Parochial purposes, the balance.

J. L. CRAVENS, *Treasurer.*

REMARKS: The Church has been completed, and was consecrated the second Sunday after Easter, 1884.

JAMES J. VAULX, *Rector.*

ST. JAMES' MISSION, EUREKA SPRINGS.

Baptisms—

    Infants... 2

Offerings	$50 00
Other sources...................................	219 20
Total	$269 20
Appropriated for Mission purposes	269 20

J. J. VAULX, *Priest.*

N. B. We have secured a piece of ground here, with a building on it, which has been fitted up for worship.

ST. JOHN'S, FORT SMITH.

Baptisms —

    Adults 6

    Infants 17

    Total 23

    Confirmations...10

Communicants—
Present number...................................109
Marriages 3
Burials.. 13
Celebrations of the Holy Communion.................. 50
Sunday-School—
Teachers 10
Pupils...100

OFFERINGS.

Weekly offertory..................... ....$232 20
All other sources................................. 1,272 52

Total $1,504 72

APPROPRIATIONS.

Convention assessment, 1883........................$56 00
Endowment of Episcopate........................... 7 25
Sunday-School expenses............................ 46 39
Christmas expenses................................ 35 00
Salary of Rector..................................800 00
Donation 4 70
Incidental expenses...............................190 48
Organ 300 00
Music.. 39 90
Repairs.. 25 00

Total $1,504 72

C. M. BARNES, *Secretary of Vestry.*

Jos. L. BERNE, *Rector.*

ST. JOHN'S, HELENA.

Baptisms—
Adults 1
Infants 12

Total 13
Communicants—
Last reported..................................... 83
Removed into the Parish........................... 2
Removed from the Parish........................... 5
Present number................................... 80
Marriages 6
Burials.. 6

Sunday-School—

    Teachers 9

    Pupils 65

OFFERINGS.

Communion alms................................... $74 45

Weekly offertory.................................. 147 25

All other sources...............................1,593 05

Total $1,814 75

APPROPRIATIONS.

Convention assessment............................ $25 00

Endowment of the Episcopate....................... 12 65

Diocesan Missions................................. 6 75

Domestic Missions................................. 11 55

Jewish Missions.................................. 1 95

Parochial purposes...........................$1,756 85

Total $1,814 75

Jno. J. Horner, *Treasurer.*

                                   W. B. Burrows, *Rector.*

ST. LUKE'S, HOT SPRINGS.

Baptisms—

    Adults 2

    Infants... 3

    Total 5

    Confirmations.. 5

Communicants—

    Last reported...24

    Added anew.. 6

    Present number..30

    Burials.. 1

Sunday-School—

    Teachers 8

    Pupils..65

OFFERINGS.

Communion alms...................................$25 10

Weekly offertory..................................511 38

All other sources.................................589 25

Total $1,125 73

APPROPRIATIONS.

Convention assessment.............................$15 00
Diocesan Missions.................................. 32 45
Parochial purposes................................798 01

Total $845 46

J. A. POLHAMIUS, *Treasurer.*

REMARKS: The Parish was nearly eight months without a Rector. The present Rector took charge February 10, 1884.

W. J. MILLER, *Rector.*

CHRIST CHURCH, LITTLE ROCK.

Baptisms—
    Adults 15
    Infants 52

    Total...67
    Confirmations...16
Communicants—
    Last reported...312
    Added anew... 16
    Total...328
    Died 6
    Present number.......................................322
    Marriages 21
    Burials 45
Sunday-School—
    Teachers 20
    Pupils...280

    Total..300

OFFERINGS.

Communion alms................................. $210 74
Weekly offertory............................... 435 75
All other sources............................. 2,251 13
Collections, etc.............................. 328 66

Total... $3,226 28

APPROPRIATIONS.

Convention assessment...........................$ 75 00
Diocesan Missions.............................. 28 26
Offering for Prayer-Books.... .... 13 20
Easter offering of Ch. and S. S. for Ch. bd'g fund... 143 95
Ch. So. for Pro. of Christianity Amongst the Jews.. 8 25

General Missions, by individuals................... 20 00
Parochial purposes............................. 2,686 88
Melbourne and LaCrosse sufferers................. 40 00
"Pious and charitable uses," C. A................. 210 74

Total $3,226 28

R. H. PARHAM, JR., *Treasurer.*

REMARKS: Our new Church building will be ready for occupation by next Easter, we have every reason to hope. The ladies of the congregation, by their Easter festival, have made $1000, which they have turned over to the Building Committee; and the enthusiasm manifested by all interested in the growth of the Parish is sufficient to warrant our most sanguine expectations.

T. C. TUPPER, *Rector.*

ST. ANDREW'S MISSION, MARIANNA.

Baptisms—
    Infants.. 3
Communicants--
    Last reported............ 17
    Removed into the Parish............................ 5
    Total.. 22
    Present number..................................... 22
    Marriages 1

REMARKS: The ladies of the Mission have on hand about $1300 for a Church building. Three of the baptisms were in the Parish of St. John's, Helena, as also the marriage.

C. A. BRUCE, *Missionary.*

ST. PAUL'S, NEWPORT.

Baptisms 9
Burials... 5
Communicants 10
Marriages 2

L. MINOR, *Senior Warden.*

TRINITY, PINE BLUFF.

Baptisms—
    Adults 2
    Infants.. 17

    Total.. 19
    Confirmations...................................... 11

Communicants—

Last reported..20

Added anew..43

Removed into the Parish..............................13

Total...76

Removed from the Parish.............................. 6

Dropped 1

Died 1

Present number......................................68

Marriages 2

Burials... 8

Sunday-Schools—

Teachers 7

Pupils...100

Confirmed persons on roll not inc. among communicants...49

OFFERINGS.

Communion Alms.............................. $28 43

Weekly offertory............................. 32 10

All other sources............................2,369 05

Total $2,429 58

APPROPRIATIONS.

Convention assessment....................... $34 00

Endowment of the Episcopate................. 4 65

Diocesan Missions........................... 6 85

Parochial purposes.......................... 2,287 23

Jewish Missions............................. 1 75

Other expenses.............................. 95 10

Total $2,429 58

H. H. HUNN, *Treasurer.*

REMARKS: This Parish is doing well. A very handsome Rectory has been built, furnished, and is now occupied by the Rector.

INNES O. ADAMS, *Rector.*

TRINITY CHURCH, VAN BUREN.

Baptisms 9

Confirmations....................................... 2

Communicants 42

Burials... 2

Marriages 1

Sunday-Schools—

    Teachers 5

    Scholars 40

    Contributions $35 00

S. A. PERNOT, Senior Warden.

ST. MARK'S, HOPE, AND GRACE CHURCH, WASHINGTON.

Baptisms—

    Adults 1

    Infants 8

    Total.. 9

    Confirmations... 6

Communicants—

    Added anew.. 6

    Died 2

    Present number......................................45

    Marriages 1

    Burials... 4

Sunday-School—

    Teachers 5

    Pupils 25

OFFERINGS.

Communion alms........................ .... $89 21

All other sources............................... 932 90

Total $1,022 11

APPROPRIATIONS.

Convention assessment........................... $10 00

Diocesan Missions 3 20

Domestic Missions.............................. 20 00

Parochial purposes.............................. 642 06

Objects outside Diocese......................... 23 95

Other expenses, support of Missionary.............. 322 90

Total $1,022 11

REMARKS: Since last Council a house and three acres of land have been purchased at Washington for the use of the Missionary.

H. C. E. COSTELLE, Missionary.

☞ Collections required to be made :

For Diocesan Missions—On the first Sunday in Lent, and on Trinity Sunday.

For the Episcopate Fund—On the first Sunday in Advent.

In addition to these, the Clergy of the Diocese are requested to devote an offertory to the Theological Department of the University of the South, and also to make collections for the General Missions of the Church.

The Thirteenth Annual Council of the Diocese of Arkansas will be held in the City of Little Rock, on the Second Friday after Easter, A. D. 1885.

JOURNAL OF PROCEEDINGS

OF THE

THIRTEENTH ANNUAL COUNCIL

OF THE

With the Secretary's Compliments.

HELD IN CHRIST CHURCH, LITTLE ROCK, ARKANSAS, ON THE 17th, 18th AND 19th
DAYS OF APRIL, A. D. 1885.

LITTLE ROCK, ARK.
GAZETTE PRINTING COMPANY,
1885.

OFFICERS OF THE DIOCESE OF ARKANSAS.

Standing Committee:

REV. T. C. TUPPER, D. D., President.

THE REV. MESSRS. W. A. TEARNE AND INNES O. ADAMS

MESSRS. M. L. BELL, AND P. K. ROOTS, Secretary.

Deputies to the General Convention:

REV. J. J. VAULX,	MR. L. H. ROOTS,
REV. T. C. TUPPER, D. D.	MR. J. H. ROGERS,
REV. INNES O. ADAMS,	MR. M. L. BELL,

MR. W. W. SMITH.

Board of Missions:

The Rt. Rev. the Bishop of the Diocese, and the Clerical Members of the Standing Committee.

Bishop:

The RT. REV. HENRY N. PIERCE, D. D. LL.D., Little Rock.

Priests:

The REV. INNES O. ADAMS, ... Trinity, Pine Bluff

The REV. JOSEPH L. BERNE, . . . St. John's, Fort Smith

The REV. WILLIAM B. BURROWS, ... Missouri

The REV. C. A. BRUCE, ... Helena

The REV. H. C. E. COSTELLE, . . . Grace, Washington

§The REV. GEO. H. HUNT, ... St. Paul's, Newport

The REV. D. McMANUS, ... Fort Smith

†The REV. D. F. McDONALD, D. D., ... Dardanelle

The REV. W. J. MILLER, ... St. Luke's, Hot Springs

The REV. W. C. STOUT, ... Lewisburg

The REV. W. A. TEARNE, . Trinity Cathedral, Little Rock

The REV. DAVID L. TRIMBLE, , ... Pine Bluff

The REV. T. C. TUPPER, D. D., Christ Church, Little Rock

The REV. J. J. VAULX, ... St. Paul's, Fayetteville

Deacon:

†The REV. A. W. PIERCE, ... Mobile, Alabama

+ Absent from Council
§ Not canonically connected

M. L. Bell, *Chancellor.*
Arkadelphia, St. Mark's.
Augusta, St. Paul's.
Batesville, St. Paul's.
Camden, St. John's—C. H. Stone.
Dardanelle, St. Paul's.
Fayetteville, St. Paul's.
Fort Smith, St. John's—John H. Rogers.
Helena, St. John's.
Hot Springs, St. Luke's—I. W. Carhart, G. G. Latta, J. P. Mellard.
Jacksonport, Grace Church.
Lake Village, Emmanuel.
Little Rock, Christ Church—W. G. Whipple, G. H. VanEtten, W. W. Smith. Alternates—Logan H. Roots, Robt. J. Matthews, and Lt. Edward Davis, U. S. A.

Trinity Cathedral—G. W. Caruth, F. J. H. Rickon, and T. C. Gunning. Alternate—Alex. Robertson.

Newport, St. Paul's.
Phillips County, Grace Church—Jno. T. Jones.
Pine Bluff, Trinity—Mack Hammett, R. V. McCracken, Geo. E. Valliant and H. H. Hunn, Alternate.

Prescott, St. James.
Van Buren, Trinity.
Washington, Grace Church—John R. Eakin.

PROCEEDINGS

OF THE

THIRTEENTH ANNUAL COUNCIL.

CHRIST CHURCH, LITTLE ROCK, ARK., }
April 17, 1885. }

The Thirteenth Annual Council of the Diocese of Arkansas convened in Christ Church, Little Rock, Friday morning, the 17th day of April, A. D. 1885.

After divine service, participated in by the attending clergy, the Rev. Geo. H. Hunt, of Newport, preached the Convention Sermon, and the Rt. Rev. H. N. Pierce, D. D., LL.D., Bishop of Arkansas, celebrated the Holy Communion, assisted by the Rector of the Parish.

The Bishop called the Council to order, and, on calling the roll of clergy, canonically resident in the Diocese, the following answered to their names:

Bishop—Rt. Rev. H. N. Pierce, D. D., LL.D. *Priests*— The Reverend Messrs. I. O. Adams, Rector of Trinity Church, Pine Bluff; C. A. Bruce, of Helena; Geo. H. Hunt, of Newport; D. McManus, of Fort Smith; William J. Miller, Rector of St. Luke's, Hot Springs; Walter A. Tearne, Dean of Trinity Cathedral, Little Rock; David L. Trimble, Missionary, Pine Bluff; and Dr. T. C. Tupper, Rector of Christ Church, Little Rock.

On calling the roll of parishes, the following were found to be represented in the Council:

St. Luke's, Hot Springs; Christ Church, Little Rock; Trinity Cathedral, Little Rock; Trinity Church, Pine Bluff; Grace Church, Washington.

The President appointed the Rev. Messrs. I. O. Adams, and D. L. Trimble, a Committee on Credentials, who reported that "they find after due examination that the following named Lay Delegates have been duly elected to this Council, viz:

"Grace Church, Phillips County, Jno. T. Jones. Christ Church, Little Rock, William G. Whipple, Geo. H. VanEtten, W. W. Smith; Alternates, Logan H. Roots, Robert J. Matthews, and Edward Davis, U. S. A. Grace Church, Washington, John R. Eakin. Trinity Church, Pine Bluff, .R. V. McCracken, Geo. E. Valliant, Mack Hammett; Alternate, H. H. Hunn. Trinity Cathedral, Little Rock, Geo. W. Caruth, F. J. Rickon, T. C. Gunning; Alternate, Alex. Robertson. St. Luke's, Hot Springs, J. P. Mellard, I. W. Carhart, and Geo. G. Latta."

Thereupon, the roll of Lay Representatives was called and the following answered to their names:

Edward Davis, John R. Eakin, R. V. McCracken, Logan H. Roots, Geo. E. Valliant, and William G. Whipple.

On motion, the Rev. Dr. Tupper was unanimously reelected Secretary of the Council, and the Chairman declared the same duly organized and ready for the transaction and dispatch of the regular order of business and of such other matters as should properly come before it.

On motion, the Council adjourned to meet in Christ Church Chapel, at 7 o'clock, p. m.

April 17th, 7 p. m.

The Council reassembled pursuant to adjournment, the Rt. Rev. H. N. Pierce, D. D., LL.D., in the chair.

The Secretary gave notice that he had appointed as his assistant for the present Council, the Rev. H. C. E. Costelle, Rector of Grace Church, Washington.

The Rev. J. J. Vaulx, Rector of St. Paul's, Fayetteville; the Rev. Joseph L. Berne, Rector of St. John's, Fort Smith; the Rev. William C. Stout, of Morrilton; the Rev. H. C. E. Costelle, Rector of Grace Church, Washington, answered to their names and took their seats in the Council.

Hon. Jno. H. Rogers, of Ft. Smith; Mr. C. H. Stone, of Camden, and Col. Geo. G. Latta, of Hot Springs; also, Col. Geo. W. Caruth, Messrs. F. J. H. Rickon, and T. C. Gunning, of Trinity Cathedral, Little Rock, presented their credentials and were duly admitted to seats in the Council.

The Rt. Rev. President announced the following standing committees for the Thirteenth Annual Council:

ON STATE OF THE CHURCH.

Clergy.	*Lay.*
William C. Stout,	R. V. McCracken,
David L. Trimble.	J. P. Mellard,
J. L. Berne,	H. C. E. Costelle.

ON CONSTITUTION AND CANONS.

Clergy.	*Lay.*
James J. Vaulx,	John H. Rogers,
C. A. Bruce,	William G. Whipple,
I. O. Adams,	Marcus L. Bell.

ON FINANCE AND AUDITING COMMITTEE.

Mr. Logan H. Roots,	Mr. C. H. Stone,
Mr. George G. Latta,	Mr. H. H. Hunn,
Mr. George William Caruth.	

ON UNFINISHED BUSINESS.

Rev. D. McManus,	Mr. Geo. E. Valliant.

ON NEW PARISHES.

Clergy.	*Lay.*
William J. Miller,	John R. Eakin,
Dean Tearne,	Edward Davis, U. S. A.

The Bishop then read his Annual Address before the Council, being the next order of business, as follows :—

BISHOP'S ADDRESS.

Brethren of the Clergy and Laity :

To-day we are assembled in the Thirteenth Annual Council of the Diocese of Arkansas. The year past, though one full of perplexities and anxieties, on my part at least, has resulted in no little encouragement. I feel that the Diocese is gradually working its way to a more assured and firmer position, than it has hitherto attained. There are parishes and missionary stations still without pastoral care, and there are many fields white with harvests into which we have sent no laborers. But if God spares my life and prospers my efforts for a few years more, I hope to be able to report a better state of things. St. Paul's, Batesville, rendered vacant by the removal of the Rev. Walter A. Tearne to Little Rock, and St. John's, Helena, rendered vacant by the removal of the Rev. W. B. Burrows to the Diocese of Missouri, are making search for acceptable rectors, and will, I trust, soon be successful. Since our last Council the Rev. W. A. Tearne and the Rev. Geo. H. Hunt have been added to our clergy list. The former is dean of Trinity Cathedral, Little Rock; the latter is rector of St. Paul's, Newport. The Rev. Wm. B. Burrows is officiating at Nevada, Missouri, but is still canonically connected with the Diocese of Arkansas. The Rev. D. McManus is officiating regularly in Trinity Church, Van Buren. The Rev. A. W. Pierce, who has gratuitously devoted eighteen months and more of his time to furnishing the plans and drawings for the Cathedral, and most carefully superintending the work, has removed to the Diocese of Alabama, but is, as yet, canonically connected with the Diocese of Arkansas. He has passed all the examinations and is ready to be ordered priest. These are the only clerical changes to be reported. In church building the advance is no little. The Parish of St. James, at Eureka Springs, have purchased a small building and fitted it up for services. The Cathedral at Little Rock is, so far as the house and aisles are concerned, complete in all respects, save that the font is still lacking. St. Andrews, at Marianna, was covered in months ago, and I presume to say is now nearly if not quite finished.   And last, but by no means least, the new Christ Church at Little Rock, spacious and imposing, is in such a state of forwardness as leads us to hope for its speedy completion.   To these few statements I append an abstract of my Journal, as brief as I can well make it.

ABSTRACT OF JOURNAL—1884.

My last Annual Report closed on the 24th of April, 1884.

April 25: St. Mark's day ; the Annual Council of the Diocese of Arkansas met in St. Paul's Church, Fayetteville, Ark.; on that occasion, after morning service said by Rev. Messrs. Vaulx and McManus, and a sermon by the latter, I celebrated the H. E.; during this and the following day I presided at the sessions of the Diocesan Council.

April 26: I read my Annual Address.

April 27, Sunday : The second after Easter; at 11 a.m. I consecrated to the service of Almighty God, St. Paul's Church, Fayetteville, Arkansas, Rev. J. J. Vaulx read the sentence of consecration; the Rev. Messrs. Berne, Burrows, Adams and Rev. Dr. Tupper said morning prayer and litany ; Rev. Messrs. Vaulx and McManus assisted in saying the communion office ; I preached and celebrated the H. E.; I was present and took part in the evening services.

April 28, Monday : The Diocesan Council adjourned at 9 a.m., *sine die* ; at 10 a.m. I instituted the Rev. J. J. Vaulx rector of St. Paul's Church, Fayetteville, Ark.; the Rev. Messrs. Adams and Burrows said morning prayer and the Rev. J. L. Berne preached.

May 1, Thursday : St. Philip's and St. James' day ; attended services in St. Paul's Church and received the Holy Communion.

May 4, Sunday : The third after Easter; at 10 a.m. I celebrated the H. E. in St. James' Church, Eureka Springs, Ark., assisted by the Rev. J. J. Vaulx ; at 11 a.m. I assisted in saying the service and preached ; at night I assisted in saying the service and preached again ; the congregation at Eureka Springs have purchased a lot on which is a small building ; this, though cheap and rough, has been fitted up in a churchly manner; I was much pleased at being able to officiate in a church of our own; the people have shown a willingness to do for themselves, which is very commendable; the spirit exhibited gives me good hopes for the future.

May 5, Monday: I preached at evening service in St. Paul's Church, Fayetteville, and confirmed three persons (one male and two females) and made an address.

May 7, Wednesday: I assisted at evening service in St. John's Church, Ft. Smith; the Rev. J. J. Vaulx preached.

May 11, Sunday: The fourth after Easter; I assisted at morning service and preached in Christ Church, Little Rock.

May 18, Sunday: The fifth after Easter; In Christ Church, Little Rock, I assisted at morning service and preached.

May 25, Sunday: After Ascension; In Christ Church, Little Rock, I assisted at morning service and preached.

June 3, Whit-Sunday: In Christ Church, Little Rock, I celebrated the H. E., assisted by the rector, Rev. Dr. Tupper.

June 8, Saturday: Trinity Sunday; I assisted at morning service and preached in Christ Church, Little Rock.

June 15, Sunday: The first after Trinity; In St. Peter's Church, Columbia, Tenn., I assisted in saying morning service and preached.

June 20, Friday: In St. Peter's Church, Columbia, I baptized an adult, preached, and confirmed two persons (one male and one female).

June 22, Sunday: The second after Trinity; In St. Peter's Church, Columbia, I said morning and evening services, celebrated the H. E. and preached twice.

June 29, Sunday: The third after Trinity; In St. Peter's, Columbia, I said morning and evening services, celebrated the H. E. and preached twice.

July 4, Friday: At Columbia, administered the Holy Communion to a sick person, in private.

July 6, Sunday: The fourth after Trinity; In St. Peter's, Columbia, Tenn., I said morning and evening services and preached twice and celebrated the H. E.; in the afternoon, I visited a dying man and administered to him the Holy Communion.

July 8, Tuesday: I officiated at a funeral at Ashwood, Tenn.

July 13, Sunday: The fifth after Trinity; I preached twice and celebrated the H. E.; I was assisted in the services by the Rev. Dr. Pickett, of the Diocese of Mississippi.

July 22, Tuesday: The sixth after Trinity; In St. Peter's, Columbia, I celebrated the H. E.; I assisted in saying morning service; Rev. Dr. Pickett preached; at night I preached.

July 23, Wednesday: I officiated at a funeral in Columbia, Tenn.

July 27, Sunday: The seventh after Trinity; In Christ Church, Little Rock, Ark., I assisted in saying morning service and preached.

July 28, Monday: I gave my canonical consent to the consecration of the Rev. Samuel D. Ferguson, Bishop-elect of Cape Palmas, and to the consecration of the Rev. William J. Boone, Bishop-elect of Shanghai; I received the letters dimissory, transferring Rev. Walter A. Tearne, from the Diocese of Iowa to the Diocese of Arkansas.

August 3, Sunday: The eighth after Trinity; In Christ Church, Little Rock, I assisted in saying morning service, preached and celebrated the H. E.

August 10, Sunday: The ninth after Trinity; In Christ Church, Little Rock, I assisted in saying morning service and preached; at night, I confirmed in the same church two persons (two females).

August 17, Sunday: The tenth after Trinity; In Christ Church, Little Rock, I assisted at morning service and preached.

August 24, Sunday: The eleventh after Trinity; In Christ Church, Little Rock, I assisted at morning service and preached.

August 28, Thursday: Sent my annual report to the Board of Missions.

August 31, Sunday: The twelfth after Trinity; In Christ Church, Little Rock, I assisted at morning service and preached.

September 7, Sunday: The thirteenth after Trinity; In

Christ Church, Little Rock, I assisted at morning service and celebrated the H. E.

September 14, Sunday: The fourteenth after Trinity, St Matthew's Day; In Christ Church, Little Rock, I assisted a morning service and preached.

September 23, Tuesday: Gave my canonical consent to the consecration of Rev. Nelson S. Rulison, D. D., Assistant Bishop-elect of Central Pennsylvania.

September 28, Sunday: The sixteenth after Trinity; assisted in saying morning service in Christ Church, Little Rock

October 5, Sunday: The seventeenth after Trinity; In Christ Church, Little Rock, I assisted in saying morning service, preached and celebrated the H. E.

October 12, Tuesday: The eighteenth after Trinity; In St. John's Church, Helena, Ark., I assisted in saying morning service, preached and celebrated the H. E.; at night, I preached again, confirmed twelve persons (8 females and 4 males), and addressed the class, after which, I confirmed in private one o the class, unable by reason of ill health to attend the service of the church (a gentleman).

October 13, Monday: I confirmed at Helena, a gentleman this makes the number confirmed for St. John's, Helena, 14 at night, after evening service, said by Messrs. Bruce and Bur rows, I preached at Marianna, Arkansas.

October 14, Tuesday: At Marianna, Ark., I assisted in saying morning service and made a short address; the Rev Mr. Burrows preached.

October 19, Sunday: The nineteenth after Trinity; on this day Trinity Cathedral, Little Rock, was for the first time opened for services; the Rev. I. O. Adams said the prayers and the litany; I said the ante-communion; the Rev. W. A. Tearne read the epistle; I preached, and assisted by the Rev. W. A. Tearne, I celebrated the H. E.; at 4 p. m., the Rev. D. L Trimble and myself said evening service and the Rev. W. A. Tearne preached. Thus after years of planning and working of cares and anxieties, I have seen the west end of the Cathedral opened for services. Thank God for His goodness! may He

enable us to carry out in full the plans formed.   I see no great
future for Diocesan growth except through the successful working of this scheme.   This is a matter which concerns every
parish in Arkansas, much more nearly than most persons imagine.

October 20, Monday: I appointed the Rev. Walter A.
Tearne, Dean of Trinity Cathedral.

October 26, Sunday: The twentieth after Trinity; In
Trinity Cathedral, Little Rock, I attended the early celebration
and received the Holy Communion;   the Dean celebrated;
I assisted in saying morning service;   in the afternoon, I
preached.

October 28, Tuesday: Festival of St. Simon and St.
Jude; at 10 a. m., in Trinity Cathedral, Little Rock, I celebrated the H. E.; this day I accepted as a postulant for Holy
Orders, Mr. Stephen D. Lewis, of Helena, Arkansas, and notified him of the fact.

November 1, Saturday: All Saints's Day;   attended
morning service at the Cathedral and received the Holy Communion.

November 2, Sunday: The twenty-first after Trinity;
in Trinity Cathedral, Little Rock, I assisted at morning service,
preached and celebrated the H. E.; at evening service also, I
assisted.

November 9, Sunday: The Twenty-second after Trinity;
in Trinity Cathedral, Little Rock, at 7:30 a. m. attended early
celebration and received; at 9, attended at the first meeting of
the Sunday School; I assisted in saying the morning service;
at evening service, I preached.

November 10, Monday: Gave the Rev. J. B. Wicks letters dimissory from the Indian Territory to the Diocese of
Massachusetts.

November 12, Wednesday: Mr. Stephen D. Lewis, of
Helena, was this day duly admitted a candidate for Holy Orders in the Diocese of Arkansas.

Nov. 16, Sunday: The twenty-third after Trinity; In
Trinity Cathedral, Little Rock, the Rev. W. C. Stout began

morning service; I said the prayers and the ante-communion, and preached; I assisted in saying evening service, also.

November 23, Sunday: Next before Advent; In St. Paul's Church, Fayetteville, Ark., I assisted in saying morning service, preached and celebrated the H. E., assisted by the Rector, Rev. J. J. Vaulx; in the afternoon, I preached again, confirmed one person (a female), and made an address.

November 29, Saturday: In the Methodist Church, at Tahleqauh, Cherokee Nation, Indian Territory, after evening prayer, said by the Rev. J. J. Vaulx, I preached.

November 30, Sunday: The first in Advent, and St. Andrew's Day; At 11 a. m., in the Methodist Church, Tahlequah, after morning prayer, said by Rev. Mr. Vaulx, I said the communion office, preached and celebrated the H. E.; at 3 p. m., Rev. Mr. Vaulx said the litany and baptized a child, the son of the principal Chief, D. W. Bushyhead; I preached and confirmed two persons (one male and one female), and made an address; at night, I preached again.

December 1, Monday: I visited the Cherokee Female Seminary, about 4 miles from Tahlequah, and said evening service and made an address.

December 7, Sunday: The second in Advent; in the Kiowa School-House, Anadarbo, Indian Territory, I addressed the Sunday School; later, I said the service, preached and celebrated the H. E. at the church.

December 10, Wednesday: At night, made an address at the Kiowa and Camanche School.

December 14, Sunday: The third in Advent; attended a. m., the Sunday School at the Kiowa School-House; the Rev. Paul Zotow, Kiowa Deacon, addressed the children; in the afternoon, I said evening service at the church and preached.

December 21, Sunday: The fourth in Advent; In St. Paul's Church, Fayetteville, I assisted in saying morning service, preached, confirmed two persons (one male and one female), and assisted by the Rector, the Rev. J. J. Vaulx, celebrated the H. E.

December 25, Thursday: Christmas Day; In Trinity Cathedral, Little Rock, I assisted in saying the morning service, preached, and assisted by the Dean, celebrated the H. E.

December 26, Friday: St. Stephen's Day; attended the service in the Cathedral and received the Holy Communion; the Dean celebrated.

December 27, Saturday: A heavy rain; no service said at the Cathedral.

December 30, Tuesday: The first after Christmas, and Holy Innocent's Day; in Trinity Cathedral, at Little Rock, I assisted in saying morning service, preached and celebrated the H. E.; no evening service, owing to heavy rain.

ABSTRACT OF JOURNAL—1885.

January 1, Thursday: The Circumcision; attended service in the Cathedral and received the Holy Communion; Dean Tearne celebrated.

January 4, Sunday: The second after Christmas; in Trinity Cathedral, Little Rock, I assisted in saying morning service, preached and celebrated the H. E.; I said evening prayer and preached again.

January 6, Tuesday: The Epiphany; I celebrated the H. E., and lectured on the day, assisted by Dean Tearne.

January 11, Sunday: The first after Epiphany; in Trinity Cathedral, Little Rock, I assisted in saying morning service; in the afternoon, I preached.

January 18, Sunday: The second after Epiphany, attended the early celebration at the Cathedral and received the Holy Communion; at morning service I preached; I assisted in saying evening service.

January 25, Sunday: The third after Epiphany, and St. Paul's Day; in the Trinity Cathedral, Little Rock, I assisted in saying morning service, preached and celebrated the H. E.; I assisted in saying evening service, also.

February 1, Sunday: Septuagesima; In Trinity Cathedral, Little Rock, I assisted in saying morning service, and celebrated the H. C.; at the evening service I preached.

February 2, Monday: The Purification; attended service at the Cathedral and received the Holy Communion; Dean Tearne celebrated.

February 8, Sunday: Sexagesima; in the Cathedral, Litttle Rock, I attended the early celebration and received; at 11 a. m., I preached; at 2 p. m., I officiated at a funeral; at 4, I assisted in saying evening service.

February 15, Sunday: Quinquagesima; in Trinity Cathedral, I said morning service, preached and celebrated the H. E. ; at 4:30 p. m., the Rev. C. C. Johnson, of the Diocese of Toronto, said evening prayer, and I preached again.

February 18, Wednesday: Ash Wednesday; I said morning and evening service and preached in the Cathedral, Little Rock.

February 20, Friday: Said morning service in Trinity Cathedral.

February 22, Sunday: The first in Lent; In Christ Church, Little Rock, I said morning service and preached; at 4:30 p. m., I said evening prayer and preached at the Cathedral.

February 25, Wednesday: In St. Paul's Church, Batesville, Ark., Dean Tearne said evening prayer; I preached and confirmed 7 persons, and addressed the class; during the day I confirmed one person, making the eighth.

February 26, Thursday: I confirmed at Batesville, four persons more, making in all at this visitation, 12 persons (7 females and 5 males); I made an address on confirmation on this occasion; at night of the same day, in St. Paul's Church, Newport, Ark., after evening prayer, said by the Rev. Geo. H. Hunt, I preached and confirmed 7 persons (4 females and 3 males), and addressed the class.

February 27, Friday: I preached at night in the same church, after evening prayer, said by Rev. Mr. Hunt.

February 28, Saturday: Preached at night in St. Paul's Church, Newport.

March 1, Sunday: The second in Lent; in St. Paul's Church, Newport, Ark., I assisted in saying morning service.

preached and celebrated the H. E., being assisted by the Rev. Geo. H. Hunt; the confirmation on this occasion is the first I ever held at Newport; I trust the good work so auspiciously begun will grow steadily; the Rev. Mr. Hunt has cause to be encouraged with the results already reached.

March 4, Wednesday: Attended Lenten service at the Cathedral, in Little Rock.

March 8, Sunday: The third in Lent; at 11 a. m., in St. Luke's Church, Hot Springs, Ark., the Rev. Wm. J. Miller, Rector, said morning prayer; I said the communion office, preached and confirmed three persons (all females), made a brief address and, assisted by the Rector, celebrated the H. E.; the offertory on this occasion, I devoted to my missionary work, it amounted to $25.00; in the afternoon I preached again at evening prayer.

March 10, Tuesday: Attended Lenten service in the Cathedral, at Little Rock.

March 11, Wednesday: A. m. attended Lenten services at the Cathedral; at 5 p. m., in Christ Church, Little Rock, I said a short special service and introduced to the audience, Mrs. Twing, of New York, who gave a very interesting account of the women's auxiliary and its modes of working; I trust this visit of Mrs. Twing's will result in the establishing of a Diocesan Branch in Arkansas. My absence from home and much occupation, has prevented me till now to give the proper attention to this matter that I hope to be able to give soon.

March 13, Friday: Attended Lenten services at the Cathedral.

March 15, Sunday: The fourth in Lent; in Grace Church, Washington, Arkansas, at 10 a. m., I addressed the Sunday School; at 11, I assisted in saying morning service, preached and, assisted by the Rev. H. C. E. Costelle, celebrated the H. E.; at 4 p. m., in St. Mark's Church, Hope, Ark., after evening prayer, said by Rev. H. C. E. Costelle, I preached; at 8. p. m., in Grace Church, Washington, I preached again.

March 18, Wednesday: Attended Lenten services in the Cathedral, Little Rock.

March 19, Thursday: Lenten services at the Cathedral.

March 20, Friday: Lenten services at the Cathedral.

March 22, Sunday: The fifth in Lent; in St. John's Church, Ft. Smith, Arkansas, I assisted at morning service, preached and celebrated the H. E., being assisted by the Rector, Rev. J. L. Berne; at night, I preached again, confirmed nine persons (5 males and 4 females), and addressed the class.

March 23, Monday: In St. John's Church, Ft. Smith, I confirmed one person (a female); in the afternoon, I met the ladies of the congregation, who have done so much good work during the past year, and urged them to begin to build the rectory at once; I have never seen the parish at Ft. Smith so vigorous and full of life as at present.

March 24, Tuesday: At the Rector's request, I baptized at Ft. Smith, two adults.

March 25, Wednesday: Annunciation; in St. James' Church, Eureka Springs, Arkansas, after evening service, said by Rev. J. J. Vaulx, I preached.

March 26, Thursday: In St. James' Church, Eureka Springs, at 7:30, the Rev. Mr. Vaulx baptized one adult; I preached, confirmed five persons (four females and one male), and addressed the class; I have great hopes of this parish; they began right and have the right spirit.

March 27, Friday: In St. Paul's Church, Fayetteville, Ark., at night, I preached, confirmed two persons (both females), and made an address.

March 29, Sunday: Palm Sunday; in St. Paul's Church, Fayetteville, I assisted in saying morning service and preached, and received the Holy Communion; the Rector celebrated; at 4 p. m., in Trinity Church, Van Buren, Ark., after evening prayer, said by the Rev. D. McManus, I preached and confirmed one person, (a male); at 7:30, after a short service, I preached again and confirmed two persons (two females).

March 30, Monday: In Holy Week; attended 5 p. m. service in the Cathedral, at Little Rock.

March 31, Tuesday: In Holy Week; attended services at the Cathedral in the forenoon and afternoon.

April 1, Wednesday: In Holy Week; attended service at the Cathedral in the forenoon and afternoon.

April 2, Maunday Thursday: Heavy rain prevented the assembling of the congregation.

April 3, Good Friday: In the Cathedral, at Little Rock, I assisted in saying morning and evening services, and at the morning service I preached.

April 5, Sunday: Easter Day; In Trinity Cathedral, at 11 a. m., I assisted at morning service, preached and celebrated the H. E.; at 4 p. m., I confirmed six persons (five males and one female), and addressed the class; it was the first confirmed in the Cathedral; at 8 p. m., in Christ Church, Little Rock, after evening prayer, said by the Rev. Dr. Tupper, I preached, confirmed twenty-six persons (seventeen females and nine males), and addressed the class.

April 12, Sunday: The first of Easter; in Trinity Church, Pine Bluff, while morning service was being said by Rev. Messrs. Adams and Trimble, a fire broke out within a few rods of the church, and we suspended the services; in the same church, at 8 p. m., Rev. Messrs. Adams and Trimble said evening prayer, and I preached, confirmed one person (a female), and made an address.

To this abstract, I here add the following

SUMMARY.

Sermons	83
Addresses	24
Eucharists	31
Confirmations	103
Church consecrated	1
Rectors instituted	1
Adult baptisms	3
Funerals	4
Clergymen received	2
Removed but canonically resident	2

Of the baptisms, two were in Arkansas, and will be reported by the Rector of St. John's, Ft. Smith. The others were

beyond the borders of the Diocese. Of the funerals, three
were in Tennessee and one in Arkansas, and will appear in the
report of the Dean of the Cathedral. Two of the confirmations
were in the Diocese of Tennessee and two in the Indian Territory.

One person has been admitted a candidate for Holy Orders, and will soon be prepared for ordination to the Dioconate.

The number of miles traveled in performance of my duties, is 4937.

Before closing, I wish to call your attention to a few of
the many matters that I might properly bring before you.

The first is the importance of completing the Cathedral
and the Clergy-house. I place this first, because very little can
be done towards the occupying of new points by the Church
until our missionary center is strongly established. Nor can
the services be kept up at several points where we already have
church buildings. I beg the Diocese will aid me as far as they
are able, in this great work. I hereby return my heartfelt
thanks for assistance given, as also for sympathy exhibited. I
propose to furnish for this year's journal, a full statement of
moneys received and paid out in the erection and furnishing of
the Cathedral, and the sources whence they were derived. In
that document, I shall take the opportunity of returning thanks
by name, to some of my many good friends, who have aided
me by their bounty. I will add in this connection one great
reason why the Diocese as a whole, should feel a deep interest
in this matter. The time is not far distant when the Diocese
will be called on to support its Bishop. A strong Cathedral
congregation, which can be readily gathered without in the
least weakening the old mother church of this city, will render
the burden on the Diocese at large a very light one.

And this brings me to my second point, the importance of
taking active measures to increase the Episcopal fund. I would
suggest that a special committee be appointed to consider and
report on this subject at this present Council.

The third point to which I wish to direct your attention, is
the importance of our *now* beginning work among the colored

people of this Diocese. I believe the time has come for us to make a vigorous movement in this direction.

I propose that all the moneys raised for Diocesan missions by the stated collections, should be devoted to this object. The collections made at my visitations, I shall donate as I may deem most wise, to the establishment of the missionary center, to the aiding of some struggling parish, or to any work looking to the spread of the church in Arkansas. But I think it will be best to devote the semi-annual offertories provided for by canon, to the work among the colored people. I hope the sum thus raised will be very considerably increased during the coming year.

I am happy to state that the Rev. D. L. Trimble is preparing to begin this good work very soon, at Pine Bluff. Let us aid him in making it a success.

Much will depend on the outcome of our first undertaking. The fruit gathered in our first field will, if good, become the seed wherewith to plant the whole state. Let our alms and our prayers and our labors be given for awhile specially to this work.

There are many other subjects that I should like to bring forward for your consideration, but as we must confine our action at present, to a few things, it is not worth our while to deliberate on many things. Let us undertake a few and try to do them well.

Now, invoking the blessing of the Holy Trinity on you and your proceedings, I leave you to enter upon your deliberations in the fear of God and under the guidance of the Holy Ghost.

On motion, the Bishop was requested to appoint the following committee, to carry out his suggestion in the foregoing address, relating to the *Episcopate Fund*, viz:—Rev.'s Wm. J. Miller, J. J. Vaulx, and T. C. Tupper, D. D., and Messrs. P. K. Roots, John H. Rogers, and C. H. Stone.

On motion, a committee, consisting of Messrs. J. J. Vaulx,

W. C. Stout, Logan H. Roots, and John H. Rogers, was appointed to consider the subject of a Clergy-house, connected with the Cathedral, in Little Rock.

The following reports were then read and received:

REPORT OF STANDING COMMITTEE OF THE DIOCESE.

To the Rt. Rev. H. N. Pierce, D. D., LL.D., President of the Council:

The Standing Committe of the Diocese met in Little Rock, May 28, 1884, and signed testimonials of the Rev. Wm. J. Boone, Bishop-elect of the China Mission, Shanghai, and of the Rev. Samuel D. Ferguson, Bishop-elect of Cape Palmas, and parts adjacent.

Committee met in Little Rock, November 12, 1884, and signed the testimonials of the Rev. Wm. Paret, D. D., Bishop-elect of the Diocese of Maryland; also recommended Mr. Stephen D. Lewis, of Helena, to be admitted as a candidate for Holy Orders.

Respectfully submitted,

T. C. TUPPER, *President.*

REPORT OF TREASURER OF DIOCESAN AND OTHER FUNDS.

To the Rt. Rev. the President and Members of the Thirteenth Annual Council of the Diocese of the State of Arkansas:

As Treasurer of the Diocesan Fund, I would respectfully submit the following as my annual report:—

RECEIPTS.

1884.
May 17, Balance on hand, ... $ 218 85
1885.
March 15, Grace Church, Washington, ... 10 00
April 15, St. Paul's Parish, Batesville, ... 10 00
April 16, Trinity Parish, Pine Bluff, 1883, ... 16 00
"   " St. Paul's Parish, Newport, ... 5 00
"   " St. Luke's, Hot Springs, ... 20 00
April 17, Grace Church Parish, Phillips County, ... 3 00
"   " Trinity Parish, Van Buren, ... 5 00
"   " Christ Church, Little Rock, ... 75 00

April 17, St. John's, Camden,.. .... 15 50
" " Trinity, Pine Bluff,... . ...:........... .... 26 50
" " Trinity, Little Rock, ... 12 50
" " St. John's, Fort Smith 57 50

$ 474 85

DISBURSEMENTS.

1884.
July 30, The O'Neale & Stevens Co 92 29
November 17, Episcopate Fund,......... .... 81 56
1885.
February 14, Gazette Printing Co., for blank forms,................ .. .. 3 00
Balance on hand, ... 298 00

$ 471 85

As Trustee for the fund of Disabled Clergy, I would respectfully submit the following as my annual report :—

RECEIPTS, ETC.

1884.
April 20, Balance on hand,.. 22 35
January 19, St. Luke's, Hot Springs, ... 8 28

Making Balance on hand, ... $ 30 63
There has been no disbursement from this fund.

As Treasurer of the fund for Diocesan Missions, I would
respectfully submit the following as my annual report :—

RECEIPTS, ETC

1884.
April 17, Balance on hand, ... 8 20
1885.
April 17, Trinity, Pine Bluff, ... 7 70

Making total on hand,.. . . .. $ 15 90
There has been no disbursement from this fund.
All of which is respectfully submitted.

LOGAN H. ROOTS,
Treasurer of respective funds

REPORT OF TRUSTEE OF EPISCOPATE FUND.

*To the Rt. Rev. the President and Members of the Thirteenth Annual
Council of the Diocese of Arkansas :*

As Trustee of the Episcopate Fund, I submit the following
statement :—

RECEIPTS, ETC.

1884.
May 22, Balance on hand, ... 111 91
April 17, Diocesan Fund, ... 81 56
1885.
March 14, Building Association Stock ; paid in $195 and $10 premiums,. .. . 205 00
" " Logan H. Roots, ... 10 00
" " P K. Roots, ... 5 00
April 1, Wm. McIlroy, ... 5 00
" " St. John's, Fort Smith, ... 5 65

April 16, Trinity Church, Pine Bluff, ...   2 05
" " Mrs. P. D. Scott,. 1 00
" " St. John's, Camden, ...   15 55
" " Rev. W. C. Stout,. 1 00
                                                                              $ 476 75
1884.   DISBURSEMENTS.
June 16, Building Association Dues,. 25 00
July 16,   "   "   " 25 00
August 16, "   "   " 25 00
Sept. 16,   "   "   " 25 00
October 17, "   "   " 25 00
Nov. 17,   "   "   " 25 00
Dec. 1,   "   "   " 25 00
1885.
January 16,"   "   " 25 00
Feb. 16,   "   "   " 25 00
March 16,   "   "   " 20 00
April 16,   "   "   " 20 00
April 16, J. L. Bay, for recording two deeds, ...   3 50
February 25, Taxes 1884,. 29 93
                                                                              $ 298 43
         Balance on hand,. 178 32
                                                                              $ 476 75

It is with pleasure I report that the chain of title to the three lots belonging to the Diocese has been completed and made perfect, and the deed from the Bishop placed upon record. And now the funds are :
                               ASSETS, ETC.
$2000 Stock in Building Association. Amount paid in. . . . .$ 820 00
Lots 10, 11, and 12, Block 200 .   . .   .   700 00
Cash in hand. 178 32
                                                                              $ 1698 32
         All of which is respectfully submitted.
                                                    P. K. ROOTS,
                                                         Trustee.

The foregoing reports of Treasurer and Trustee of the Episcopate Fund were referred to the Auditing Committee who, after examination of same, reported to the Council as follows:—

REPORT OF AUDITING COMMITTEE.

LITTLE ROCK, ARK., APRIL 18, 1885.

Your Committee, to whom was referred the Reports of the Treasurer and Trustees, respectfully report:—They find all the funds properly accounted for and that the Treasurer presented receipts for all his disbursements, and in compliance with the standing orders of the Council, turned over to the Trustee of the Episcopate Fund, all that he had on hand over and above fifty dollars; and find further that the Trustee of the Episcopate

Fund has managed during the year to increase the value of the assets on hand and properly accounts for all received by him.

Your Committee cannot but regret that the amount received for the Episcopate Fund during the year, has not been larger.

All of which is respectfully submitted.

C. H. STONE,
For the Committee.

Lieut. Edward Davis offered the following resolution, which was adopted :

"*Resolved*, That after paying the expenses of printing the journal of the Council, etc., the sum of $100, or such sum as is needed, be appropriated out of any funds remaining in the Treasury, for the purpose of buying a new set of Episcopal robes for the Bishop; and the Bishop is hereby authorized to draw on the Treasurer for such sum."

The following report of Committee on proposed Alteration of the Book of Common Prayer, by the General Convention of 1883, was received, and the committee granted further time, as desired.

" The committee appointed at the Twelfth Annual Council, to report to this Council upon that part of the Bishop's address relating to the revision of the Book of Common Prayer, request, that inasmuch as the " proposed book " is just now presented to the Diocese for examination, and in order that they may obtain further information on the subject, they ask to be permitted to make their report at the Fourteenth Annual Council, which will convene prior to the assembling of the General Convention in 1886."

Signed :

I. O. ADAMS, ⎫ Committee
J. J. VAULX, ⎬ of the Clergy.
T. C. TUPPER, ⎭

R. V. McCRACKEN,
Committee of the Laity.

The following resolution of Lieut. Davis was referred to Committee on Canons :

"Resolved, That Title III, Canon III, Section 1, be amended to read as follows:—

"That every parish shall take up offertories for Diocesan Missions as often as the Council shall appoint, but the following offerings are required to be made and not to be diverted to other purposes except upon special authority of the Council: The first Sunday in Lent and Trinity Sunday, for the benefit of Diocesan Missions. Easter Day, for the Episcopate Fund. Christmas Day, for the aged and infirm Clergy, and widows and orphans of deceased Clergymen of the Diocese. National Thanksgiving Day, for the benefit of the Rector of the parish."

On motion, the Council adjourned until tomorrow morning, at nine o'clock.

SECOND DAY.

CHRIST CHURCH CHAPEL,
April 18, 1885, 9 o'clock, a. m.

Council met pursuant to adjournment.

Present, same as yesterday.

Rev. W. B. Burrows appeared and took his seat in Council.

Mr. Geo. H. VanEtten, Lay Delegate of Christ Church, appeared and took his seat.

The Committee on Constitution and Canons, to whom was referred the resolution of Lieut. Davis, recommended its adoption by this Council, amending the same by striking out the last clause, for which a substitute was offered by Col. Roots, to the effect "that the section of the Canon now under discussion be amended so as to recommend that each parish devote the offering at the Easter Day service to the Episcopate Fund of the Diocese," which failed to pass.

The question was then put on the report of the committee, which was lost; and then the original resolution, as offered, was adopted. The Canon, thus amended, was made to read as follows:—

Section 1 of Canon IV, Title III. "Every parish shall take up offertories for Diocesan Missions as often as the Council shall appoint, but the following offerings are required to be made and not to be diverted to other purposes, except upon special authority of the Council, viz: The first Sunday in Lent and Trinity Sunday, for the benefit of Diocesan Missions; Easter Day, for the Episcopate Fund; Christmas Day, for the fund for aged and infirm Clergy, and widows and orphans of deceased Clergymen of the Diocese; National Thanksgiving Day, for the Rector of the parish."

The committee to whom was referred that part of the Bishop's address on the completion of the Cathedral and the building of a Clergy-house, reported that "they have considered the subject and think that nothing has ever come before this Council of greater importance than this, and therefore recommend the adoption of the following resolutions:—

Resolved, That the Bishop be requested to devote the offerings at his visitations to the building of the clergy house.

Resolved, That the Bishop be requested to make an appeal, or cause the Rector to make an appeal for that object, at the same time.
JAMES J. VAULX,
W. C. STOUT,
JNO. H. ROGERS,
LOGAN H. ROOTS.

Which resolutions were adopted.

The Council then proceeded to the election of a Standing Committee of the Diocese for the ensuing year, which resulted as follows: Rev. Dr. T. C. Tupper, Rev. Innes O. Adams, Rev. W. A. Tearne, and Messrs. P. K. Roots and M. L. Bell.

The deputies to the General Convention of the Church, were then elected. The result of the ballot stood as follows: Rev. James J. Vaulx, Rev. T. C. Tupper, D. D., Rev. I. O. Adams. Of the Laity, Messrs. Logan H. Roots, John H. Rogers, M. L. Bell, W. W. Smith.

After several unsuccessful ballots for the fourth clerical deputy, it was decided to leave the appointment of the same to the Bishop of the Diocese, agreeably to Sec. 3, Canon X, Title I.

The Rev. William C. Stout was re-elected Registrar of the Diocese.

The Rev. William B. Burrows resigned the Trusteeship of the General Theological Seminary, and the Rev. Innes O. Adams, at his suggestion, was nominated for the position.

Maj. P. K. Roots was re-elected Trustee of the Episcopate Fund, and Col. Logan H. Roots re-elected Treasurer of the Contingent and Other Funds of the Diocese.

After which, the Council took a recess until 4 o'clock, p. m.

Council re-assembled at 4 o'clock, p. m., with the Bishop in the chair.

The Committee on the State of the Church made their report as follows :—

"To the Rt. Rev. Father and Brethen in the Fourteenth Annual Council, assembled:

"Your Committee on the State of the Church, having had referred to them the Bishop's annual address, and the several parochial reports submitted to the Council, beg leave to report that from a hasty examination of these several papers and from other information informally received, it appears that the Church in the Diocese of Arkansas is making steady progress. A notable increase in the number of baptisms and confirmations, indicates this progress. The parochial reports are more full, and from a larger number of parishes than have heretofore been made ; but they fail to present the whole facts in regard to the several parishes, which however, will hereafter be shown in a summary of statistics following the parochial reports, printed in the Journal of this Council.

"There has been in the past year considerable advance in church building. The first portion of the Cathedral has been completed and opened for service, wherein a good congregation has been gathered. Christ Church, Little Rock, is engaged in erecting a noble edifice of large seating capacity. Active work going on, now gives promise of its completion before the next Annual Council. When completed, it will be the noblest

House of God in the State. St. Andrew's Church, Marianna, is also nearly completed, and other improvements and repairs have been made in several other localities.

"The contributions of the faithful in the several parishes, have been reasonably liberal, in view of the great financial depression throughout the country. Thus it appears that there is ground for satisfaction with the results of the past year's labors of Bishop and Clergy.

"But Brethren, there is another aspect of the state of the Church, not so satisfactory. The State of Arkansas is large and constantly increasing in population. There is a large field and the harvests are ripe, and no laborers to be sent into the field. In all the new towns springing up over the state, there are members of the Church who have no services, no sacraments, and worst of all, no hopes of these rights of inheritance in the near future. How great this spiritual destitution is, only those who suffer can tell. ' For twelve years, I have not set my foot in a church; for twelve years, I have not received the Holy Sacrament. O God! shall it always be so?' This was the wail of a daughter of the Church, recently heard by one of your committee. There are hundreds of such cases in the state.

"For this terrible spiritual destitution of our brethren, your committee can offer no remedy. We can pray God in His infinite mercy, to send help where it is so much needed, and implore our brethren everywhere to aid us in ministering to the wants of the spiritually destitute. Children not baptised, youth uncatichised and unconfirmed, faithful men living and dying without the blessed Eucharist; all going down to their graves without one office of our Holy Religion, reveals a picture over which, not only men but angels may weep.

"Such is the State of the Church, and besides all this, there remain the heresy, irreligion, atheism and downright wickedness, that prevail throughout the land. How great indeed is the need of help to do the work that ought to be done!

"All of which is respectfully submitted.
Signed: WILLIAM C. STOUT, *Chairman*."

The Committee on Admission of New Parishes, made the following report:—

"That no parishes have made application for admission into union with this Council. The committee beg leave to add to this report that, having examined the Constitution and Canons of the Diocese for guidance in the work of the committee, find nothing on the subject. Had any parish made application, we would not have known how to act in the premises, not knowing what terms of admission were necessary to be complied with. Your committee would therefore respectfully recommend that this Council take such action as may define by canon, the terms on which new parishes shall be admitted into union with the Council.

"Your committee also recommend the adoption of the following resolution:—

"*Resolved*, That Title I, Canon I, Section 2, shall have no application to new parishes or to newly organized missions, applying for admission to the Council after their organization, and such parishes and missions shall not be required to pay the annual assessment as a condition of representation, provided they apply for admission at the first Council after organization.

Signed:

W. J. MILLER, *Chairman.*"

Which report was adopted.

On motion of Rev. H. C. E. Costelle, the Secretary was instructed to have 500 copies of the Journal printed, and to be paid for the cost of same, by the Treasurer of the Diocese.

On motion, the Revs. Innes O. Adams and David L. Trimble were appointed a committee to revise and codify the canons of the Diocese, and make their report at the next Council.

On motion of Rev. W. C. Stout, "the thanks of the Council were tendered the Rev. Dr. Tupper by a rising vote, for his faithful and efficient services as Secretary of the Diocese for the past eight years, which he has given without any remuneration."

The following report of the Committee on matter of the Episcopate Fund, referred to in the Bishop's address, was then read and received:—

"Your committee, to whom was referred the matter of taking action towards increasing the Episcopal Fund of the Diocese, beg leave to recommend the adoption of the plan of enrollment, prepared by the church at large, to raise one million dollars for endowment of the Missionary Episcopates, and several other specified objects. The plan will be found in a volume entitled, "Missionary Enrollment for 1886." The plan is briefly this: That pledges of $5.00 cash be obtained, payable in October, 1886. We recommend a like procedure on the part of this Diocese, and that each Clergyman do his best towards carrying it out. A pledge of $5.00, to be paid within eighteen months, should be no great matter to obtain. Let us try what we can do. The two-fold disposition to which the contributions made are liable, should be specified in the sub-scription books."

Signed:

REV. W. J. MILLER,
Chairman.

On motion of Rev. I. O. Adams, the thanks of the members of the Council were tendered the Rev. Dr. Tupper, Rector of Christ Church, his vestry and congregation, for the entertainment of the Clergy and Lay Delegates in attendance at the Thirteenth Annual Council of the Diocese.

On motion of Rev. J. J. Vaulx, the Fourteenth Annual Council will convene, D. V., in Trinity Church, Pine Bluff, on the second Friday after Easter, 1886.

On motion, the Council adjourned to meet in Trinity Cathedral tomorrow afternoon, immediately at the close of the evening service.

TRINITY CATHEDRAL,
                                April 19th, 5 p. m.

The Council met pursuant to adjournment.

There appearing nothing on the Secretary's table for attention, the Bishop of the Diocese made a few touching and encouraging remarks, and very feelingly alluded to the action of the Council in voting their Diocesan a new set of robes. After which, the Council was closed with appropriate prayers and benediction by the Bishop.

HENRY N. PIERCE,
                                Bishop of Arkansas.

Attest :

TULLIUS C. TUPPER, *Secretary.*

PAROCHIAL REPORTS.

ST. PAUL'S CHURCH, BATESVILLE.
DIOCESE OF ARKANSAS, 1884.

Rectorship of Rev. Walter A. Tearne and his visitations as Dean, 1885.

Baptisms—

Adults... 2

Infants.. 6
   ————
Total..8

Comfirmations....................................12

Funerals.. 2

Celebrations...................................... 9

Average Attendance...............................15

Number of services..............................28

Number of sermons...............................27

February, 1885. Visitations—

Services..10

Sermons.... 9

Celebrations...................................... 2

Sunday School—

Teachers.. 4

Pupils..30

APPROPRIATIONS.

Convention assessment.........................$ 10 00

Respectfully submitted,

EDWARD M. DICKINSON,
Senior Warden.

April 13, 1885.

ST. PAUL'S, BATESVILLE.

From August 1, to October 15, 1884.

Baptisms—

Adults.. 2

Infants.. 6

Total........... 8

Confirmations...... 12

Number of services...38

Number of celebrations................................11

Remarks: I have simply given a summary of my own acts. The parochial statistics will doubtless be furnished by the Warden.

W. A. TEARNE, *Dean.*

ST. JOHN'S, CAMDEN.

Baptisms—

Adults.. 1

Infants.. 4

Total..... 5

Communicants........ 31

Marriages... 1

D. L. TRIMBLE, *Missionary.*

ST. JAMES', EUREKA SPRINGS.

Baptisms—

Adults... 2

Infants... 3

Total...... 5

Confirmations....................................... 5

Sunday School pupils........... 40

Communicants.......................................22

Remarks : We have bought and fitted up a small building

for services. All are earnestly at work, with prospects of good growth next year.

I report at Rogers, 2 Communicants; at Bentonville, 2 Communicants, and at Huntsville, 4 Communicants.

JAS. J. VAULX, *Priest in charge.*

ST. PAUL'S, FAYETTEVILLE.

Baptisms—
 Adults... 1
 Infants........ 6
                —
  Total....................................... 7
Confirmations....................................... 8
Communicants.......................................92
Burials.. 4
Sunday School—
 Teachers....................................... 5
 Pupils...90

OFFERINGS.

Domestic missions.... ....$ 35 00
Foreign missions................................. 15 00
Mexico... 10 00
Society for promoting Christianity among Jews....... 12 35
                 —
  Total........ ....$ 72 35

Remarks: The church has been consecrated during the past year.

JAS. J. VAULX, *Rector.*

ST. JOHN'S, FT. SMITH.

Baptisms—
 Adults...12
 Infants..20
                —
  Total.......................................32

Communicants—
    Present number 115
Marriages 1
Burials 2
Celebrations of Holy Eucharist 28
Sunday School—
    Teachers 10
    Pupils 100

OFFERINGS.

Sunday School offertory	$ 50	00
Ladies' Aid Society	340	00
Sale of old organ	50	00
Weekly offertories	186	59
All other sources	770	41
Total	$ 1397	00

APPROPRIATIONS.

Convention assessment, 1884	$ 54	50
Endowment of Episcopate	5	65
Salary of Rector	734	35
Incidental expenses	151	82
Organist	50	00
Repairs on church	340	00
Sunday School expenses	50	00
Balance on hand	10	68
Total	$ 1397	00

C. M. BARNES, *Sec'y of Vestry.*

, J. L. BERNE, *Rector.*

--- —

ST. LUKE'S, HOT SPRINGS.

Baptisms—
    Adults 2
    Infants 9
    Total 11
Confirmations 5

Communicants—

Last reported.......... 30

Present number........................ 40

Marriages.. 2

Burials.................... 6

Sunday School—

Teachers....................................... 7

Pupils..85

OFFERINGS.

Communion alms....... .... $ 60 84

Weekly offertory................. .... 520 54

Rentals and subscriptions....................... 1038 20

Other sources....... .... 517 15

Total........................... $ 2136 73

APPROPRIATIONS.

Convention assessment..... .... $ 15 00

Episcopate Fund............................. 8 28

Parochial Purposes........................... 1152 38

Diocesan missions........................... 32 45

" Pious and charitable purposes," C. A............ ...... 75 84

Other purposes (improving church building)..... .. 715 14

Total........................... $ 1999 09

Value of church property................. ...$ 5000 00

Amount of insurance on church property..........$ 2200 00

J. A. POLHAMIUS, *Treasurer.*

Remarks: The above financial report is for the year ending Epiphany, 1885, and includes only a part of the moneys
raised and expended for improvements on the church building,
which has been thoroughly repaired.

W. J. MILLER, *Rector.*

117887

CATHEDRAL, LITTLE ROCK.

Baptisms—
    Adults... 1
    Infants.. 5

        Total......... 6
Confirmations....................................... 6
Communicants.......................................62
Burials... 3
Sunday School—
    Teachers....................... 4
    Pupils..37

OFFERINGS.

Weekly offertory................................$ 469 28

        Total...............................$ 469 38

APPROPRIATIONS.

Convention assessment...........................$ 12 50
Diocesan missions... .... 8 60
Jews... 3 35

        Total.............................$ 24 45
Value of church property.......................$ 7000 00
Amount of insurance on church property.........$ 2500 00
Number of services..............................74
Number of celebrations..........................35

   WILLIAM C. STEVENS, *Treas. of the Parish.*

       WALTER A. TEARNE, *Dean.*

CHRIST CHURCH, LITTLE ROCK.

Baptisms—
    Adults.. 9
    Infants...32

        Total.......................................41
Confirmations.......................................28

Communicants—

Last reported............................322

Added anew.............................. 28

Removed into the parish................. 4

Total...............................354

Removed from the parish................. 24

Died................................... 6

Present number..........................324

Marriages...................................19

Burials.....................................48

Sunday School—

Teachers................................20

Pupils..................................300

OFFERINGS.

Communion alms..........................$ 140 20

Weekly offertory........................ 409 99

Rentals and subscriptions............... 2268 34

Other sources........................... 1879 15

Total...........................$ 4697 68

APPROPRIATIONS.

Convention assessment...................$ 75 00

Parochial purposes (Rector's salary, $1800)........ 2678 33

Diocesan missions....................... 19 65

Domestic missions....................... 12 50

Foreign missions........................ 37 50

Colored missions........................ 8 00

Church institutions..................... 26 50

" Pious and Charitable Uses," C. A............... 140 20

Other purposes (Ladies' Aid Society)............ 1700 00

Total...........................$ 4697 68

Value of church property..................$ 55,000 00

A. L. O'NEALE, Esq., *Treas. of the Parish.*

Remarks: Since the last annual council, the ladies of the

parish have raised, by their festival entertainments, about $1700.00, which amount has been applied to the new church building.

T. C. TUPPER, *Rector.*

ST. ANDREW'S, MARIANNA.

Baptisms—
    Infants.. 4
                                                          —
        Total... 4
Communicants—
    Last reported 22
    Removed into the parish............................ 2
    Removed from the parish............................ 2
    Present number.....................................22
Communion alms ....$ 9 00
Value of church property...................$ 3000 00

C. A. BRUCE, *Missionary.*

ST. PAUL'S, NEWPORT.

Baptisms—
    Adults... 6
    Infants.. 2
                                                          —
        Total........ 8
Confirmations...................................... 7
Communicants—
    Added anew... 4
    Removed from the parish............................ 3
    Present number....................................24
Marriages.... 3
Sunday School—
    Teachers... 2
    Pupils..20

OFFERINGS.

Communion alms.......................	} $ 55	05
Weekly offertory.......................		
Rentals and subscriptions......................	303	65
Other sources...........................	84	00

Total...........................	$ 442	70

APPROPRIATIONS.

Convention assessment.....................	$ 5	00
Parochial purposes.....................	428	20
Diocesan missions.......................	9	50

Total...........................	$ 442	70
Value of church property....	$1300	00

GEO. K. TOZER, *Treas. of the Parish.*

Remarks: The undersigned has only been in charge of this station since October last, but he has endeavored to make this report complete for the entire year.

GEO. H. HUNT, *Priest in charge.*

GRACE CHURCH, PHILLIPS COUNTY.

Communicants—

Removed from the parish......................	2
Present number.......................	13

OFFERINGS.

Communion alms.......................	$ 5	25

Total.....	$ 5	25
Value of church property.....................	$ 2500	00

Remarks: Impossible to give full report. I have also attended two funerals in the parish of St. John's, Helena.

C. A. BRUCE, *Rector.*

TRINITY CHURCH, PINE BLUFF.

Baptisms—

Infants...........................	11

Total...........	11

Confirmations.......................... 1
Communicants—
    Last reported.............................. 68
    Added anew....................................... 3
    Removed into the parish............................ 2
                                              —
    Total................................73
    Removed from the parish......................... 4
    Present number................................69
Sunday School—
    Teachers.. 8
    Pupils... 100

OFFERINGS.

Communion alms........................ $ 29 45
Weekly offertory...............................   134 45
Rentals and subscriptions.... ....   848 51
Other sources..........................   675 85

    Total.......................... $ 1688 26

APPROPRIATIONS.

Convention assessment..................... ......$ 26 50
Episcopate Fund......... ....   2 05
Parochial purposes...........................   1601 61
Diocesan missions............................   7 70
Church institutions (Society for Promotion of Christi-
    anity Among Jews)........................   3 15
"Pious and charitable uses," C. A........ .....   29 45
Other purposes..............................   17 80

    Total.......................... $ 1688 26
Value of church property (church and rectory)....$ 15,000 00
Amount of insurance on church property (on rectory) $1000 00
H. H. HUNN, *Treas. of the Parish.*

Remarks: The parish is doing well. A fine cistern and
servants' room has been added to the rectory. The debt on
the rectory has been reduced from $660.00 to $440.00.

INNES O. ADAMS, *Rector.*

TRINITY CHURCH, VAN BUREN.

Baptisms—

Infants 7

Total 7

Confirmations, ... 3

Communicants—

Last reported 35

Added anew 3

Total 38

Removed from the parish 1

Present number 37

Marriages 1

Burials . . . . ₄

Sunday School—

Teachers 3

Pupils 30

OFFERINGS.

Communion alms . . . . }
Weekly offertory . . . . } $ 16 70

Other sources 31 20

Total . . . . $ 47 90

APPROPRIATIONS.

Convention assessment . . . . $ 6 25

Episcopate fund 3 75

Parochial purposes 10 70

Domestic missions 6 00

Other purposes 21 20

Total . . . . $ 47 90

D. McMANUS, *Rector.*

GRACE CHURCH, WASHINGTON.

Baptisms—
Adults... 2
Infants..... 5

Total.................................. 7
Communicants—
Last reported...............................33
Removed into the parish..................... 2

Total.................................35
Removed from the parish..................... 8
Died..................................... 1
Present number...............................26
Marriages... 2
Burials... 2
Sunday School—
Teachers...................................... 5
Pupils..25

APPROPRIATIONS.

Communion alms.............................$ 89 25
Subscriptions................................. 246 60
Other sources................................. 148 90

Total.............................$ 484 75

OFFERINGS.

Convention assessment.......................$ 10 00
Parochial purposes........................... 406 25
Domestic missions............................ 15 00
Other purposes............................... 13 00
Balance on hand................... 40 50

Total.............................$ 484 75

Remarks: A new roof has been put on the church, and a memorial cross procured, commemorative of Mrs. Jenkins and Mrs. Purdom.

H. C. E. COSTELLE, *Missionary.*

SUMMARY OF STATISTICS FROM PAROCHIAL REPORTS.

Baptisms...............................152
Confirmations.........................85
Marriages.............................37
Burials...............................78
Commmuicants........................950
    Estimated number from parishes and missions
       not reporting.........................316
                               ———
                             1266
Sunday School (teachers and pupils)....................1086
Offerings...........................$11,449 90

■> Collections required by canon.

For Diocesan Missions—On the first Sunday in Lent, and on Trinity Sunday.

For the Episcopate Fund—On Easter Day.

For Aged and Infirm Clergy, and Widows and Orphans of Deceased Clergymen of the Diocese—On Christmas Day.

For the Benefit of the Rector of the Parish—On National Thanksgiving Day.

The Fourteenth Annual Council of the Diocese of Arkansas will convene in Trinity Church, Pine Bluff (D. V.), on the Second Friday after Easter, A. D. 1886.

☆ THE SECRETARY

※ DIOCESE ✛ OF ✛ ARKANSAS ※

✛ JOURNAL ✛

OF THE

Fourteenth Annual Council

—⟩ 1886 ⟨—

JOURNAL

OF THE

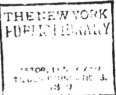

Fourteenth Annual Council

OF THE

PROTESTANT EPISCOPAL CHURCH

IN THE

Diocese of Arkansas.

HELD IN TRINITY CHURCH, PINE BLUFF, ARKANSAS, ON THE
7TH, 8TH AND 9TH DAYS OF MAY, A. D., 1886.

LITTLE ROCK ARK
KELLOGG PRINTING COMPANY
1886

THE DIOCESE OF ARKANSAS.

OFFICERS OF THE COUNCIL.

President :
THE RT. REV. HENRY NILES PIERCE, D. D. LL. D.,
Little Rock.

Secretary :
THE REV. WILLIAM J. MILLER, A. M., Hot Springs.

Treasurer :
COL. LOGAN H. ROOTS, Little Rock.

Registrar :
REV. WILLIAM C. STOUT, Morrilton.

Chancellor :
HON. M. L. BELL, Pine Bluff.

Trustee of the Episcopate Fund :
MR. P. K. ROOTS, Little Rock.

Trustees of the University of the South :
REV. JOSEPH L. BERNE,
MESSRS. W. G. WHIPPLE AND ALBERT WASSELL.

Trustee of the General Theological Seminary :
REV. INNES O. ADAMS, Pine Bluff.

Standing Committee:

Rev. T. C. TUPPER, D. D., President.

The Rev. Messrs. G. F. DEGEN and INNES O. ADAMS

Messrs. M. L. BELL, and P. K. ROOTS, Secretary.

Deputies to the General Convention:

Clergy.	Lay.
Rev. J. J. VAULX, B. D.,	Mr. R. V. McCRACKEN,
Rev. INNES O. ADAMS,	Mr. Geo. H. VanETTEN,
Rev. W. J. MILLER, A. M., ·	Mr. LOGAN H. ROOTS,
Rev. W.W. ESTABROOKE, M.D.	Mr. Geo. W. CARUTH.

Alternates:

Rev. RICHARD TOTTEN,	Mr. C. H. STONE,
Rev. WILLIAM C. STOUT,	Mr. J. J. HORNER,
Rev. D. L. TRIMBLE,	Mr. Steph. WHEELER,
Rev. G. F. DEGEN.	Mr. H. S. COLEMAN.

Committee on Constitutions and Canons to Report at the Next Annual Council:

Clergy.	Lay.
The Rt. Rev., The Bishop,	Mr. Geo. W. CARUTH,
Rev. J. J. VAULX,	Mr. R. V. McCRACKEN,
Rev. I. O. ADAMS,	Mr. Geo. VanETTEN,
Rev. Geo. F. DEGEN.	Mr. M. L. BELL.

LIST OF THE CLERGY OF THE DIOCESE.

Bishop:

The RT. REV. HENRY N. PIERCE, D. D. LL. D., Little Rock.

Priests:

The REV. INNES O. ADAMS, - - - - Trinity, Pine Bluff.

The REV. E. C. ALCORN, - - - - - - St. Louis, Mo.

The REV. JOSEPH L. BERNE, - - - - - Galveston Texas.

The REV. C. A. BRUCE, - - - - - - - - - Helena.

The REV. GEO. F. DEGEN, - Trinity Cathedral, Little Rock.

The REV. W. W. ESTABROOKE, M. D., Tr'y C'dr'l, Little Rock.

The REV. D. MCMANUS, - - - - - - - - Fort Smith.

The REV. D. F. MCDONALD, D. D., - - - - Dardanelle.

The REV. W. J. MILLER, A. M., - - St. Luke's, Hot Springs.

The REV. C. H. NEWMAN, - - - - - - - - Missouri.

The REV. W. C. STOUT, - - - - - - - - Lewisburg.

The REV. W. A. TEARNE, - - St. Paul's, Batesville, Ark.

The REV. RICHARD TOTTEN, A. M., - - - Helena, Ark.

The REV. DAVID L. TRIMBLE, - - - - - - Pine Bluff.

The REV. T. C. TUPPER, D. D., Christ Church, Little Rock.

The REV. J. J. VAULX, - - - - St. Paul's, Fayetteville.

LIST OF PARISHES AND LAY DEPUTIES.

M. L. Bell, *Chancellor.*

Arkadelphia, St. Mark's.

Augusta, St. Paul's.

Batesville, St. Paul's—H. S. Coleman.

Camden, St. John's—C. H. Stone, H. A. Millen and H. Higinbotham.

Dardanelle, St. Paul's.

Fayetteville, St. Paul's.

Fort Smith, St. John's.

Helena, St. John's.

Hot Springs, St. Luke's—I. W. Carhart, J. P. Mellard and F. Polhamius.

Jacksonport, Grace Church.

Lake Village, Emmanuel.

Little Rock, Christ Church—P. K. Roots, G. H. VanEtten, R. J. Matthews. Alternates—Logan H. Roots, A. L. O'Neale and R. H. Parkham.

Little Rock, Trinity Cathedral—G. W. Caruth, Alex Robertson and Edwin C. Gould.

Newport, St. Paul's.

Phillips County, Grace Church.

Pine Bluff, Trinity Church, R. V. McCracken, N. B. Trulock, J. S. Bell. Alternates—Geo. E. Valliant, C. T. Harding and M. Hammett.

Prescott, St. James.

Van Buren, Trinity.

Washington, Grace Church.

PROCEEDINGS .

OF THE

FOURTEENTH ANNUAL COUNCIL.

TRINITY CHURCH, PINE BLUFF, ARK., }
Friday May 7, 1886.

The Fourteenth Annual Council of the Diocese of Arkansas convened in Trinity Church, Pine Bluff, Friday morning, the 7th day of May, 1886.

Morning prayer was said by the Rev. Messrs. Estabrooke and Miller, the Litany by the Rev. J. J. Vaulx. The Holy Eucharist was celebrated by the Bishop, the Rt. Rev. H. N. Pierce, D. D. LL. D., assisted by the Rev. D. F. McDonald, D. D. and the Rev. Geo. F. Degen, Dean of the Cathedral.

At this service the Bishop delivered his annual address. See Appendix I.

At 5 o'clock p. m. the Bishop called the Council to order, and on calling the roll of Clergy canonically resident in the Diocese the following answered to their names : ·

Bishop—The Rt. Rev. H. N. Pierce, D. D., LL. D.

Priests—The Rev. Drs. T. C. Tupper, Rector of Christ Church, Little Rock, and D. F. McDonald, of St. Paul's, Dardanelle; the Rev. Messrs. Innes, O. Adams, Rector of Trinity Church, Pine Bluff; Geo. F. Degen, Dean of the Cathedral ; W. W. Estabrooke, Canon of the Cathedral ; W. J. Miller, Rector of St. Luke's Church, Hot Springs ; W. C. Stout, Lewisburg ; Richard Totten, Rector of St. John's, Helena, and J. J. Vaulx, Rector of St. Paul's, Fayetteville.

On calling the Roll of Parishes the following were found to be represented in the Council: St. Paul's, Batesville; St. John's, Camden; Trinity Cathedral and Christ Church, Little Rock; Trinity, Pine Bluff.

The President appointed the Rev. Messrs. J. J. Vaulx and W. J. Miller a committee on credentials, who reported that the following Lay Delegates have been duly elected to this Council.

St. Paul's, Batesville, H. S. Coleman; St. John's, Camden, C. H. Stone, H. A. Millen and H. Higinbotham; St. Luke's, Hot Springs, J. P. Mellard, J. W. Carhart and Frank Palhamius; Christ Church, Little Rock, P. K. Roots, Geo. H. VanEtten and R. J. Matthews; Alternates, R. H. Parkham, Logan H. Roots and A. L. O'Neal; Trinity Cathedral, Geo. W. Caruth, Edwin C. Gould and Alex Robertson; Trinity, Pine Bluff, R. V. McCracken, N. B. Trulock and M. L. Bell; Alternates, Geo. E. Valiant, C. T. Harding and Mack Hammett.

The roll of Lay Representatives being called the following answered to their names:

Messrs. H. S. Coleman, R. V. McCracken, N. B. Trulock, Geo. H. VanEtten, R. J. Matthews, Logan H. Roots, C. H. Stone, Geo. W. Caruth and Alex Robertson.

On motion, the Rev. T. C. Tupper, D. D. was unanimously re-elected Secretary of the Council. Whereupon the Chairman declared the same to be duly organized and ready for the transaction of business. The Secretary appointed the Rev. W. J. Miller as his assistant.

The Chairman appointed the committee on the State of the Church as follows:

REV. W. J. MILLER, *Chairman*,
REV. W. C. STOUT,
REV. D. F. McDONALD, D. D.,
MR. C. H. STONE,
MR. H. S. COLEMAN.

On motion Council adjourned to meet immediately after evening service.

May 7th, 9 p m.

After Evening Prayer, and sermon by the Rev. W. J. Miller, the Council met pursuant to adjournment, the Bishop presiding.

The Chairman appointed the Standing Committees as follows:

ON CONSTITUTION AND CANONS.

Clergy.	*Lay.*
Rev. J. J. Vaulx,	Mr. Geo. W. Caruth,
Rev. I. O. Adams,	Mr. R. V. McCracken,
Rev. Geo. F. Degen,	Mr. Geo. H. VanEtten.

ON FINANCE AND AUDITING COMMITTEE.

Mr. Logan H. Roots,	Mr. C. H. Stone,
Mr. N. B. Trulock,	Mr. Alex Robertson,
Mr. H. S. Coleman.	

UNFINISHED BUSINESS.

Rev. W. W. Estabrooke,   Mr. R. J. Matthews.

NEW PARISHES.

Rev. D. L. Trimble,   Mr. R. V. McCracken,
Rev. Richard Totten.

The Rev. Dr. Tupper, Chairman of the Standing Committee of the Diocese reported that no business had been transacted by the committee during the year.

Mr. Logan H. Roots, as Treasurer of the Diocesan Fund, reported the following:

REPORT AS TREASURER OF THE DIOCESAN FUND.

Balance on hand........................ ....\$298 00	
May 2, 1885, Trinity, Van Buren......	1 50
May 5, 1886, St. Luke's, Hot Springs......	30 00
" 6, St. Paul's, Newport.............................	8 00
" 7, Christ Church, Little Rock......................	75 00
" 7, Trinity, Pine Bluff.........	37 00
" 7, St. John's, Camden...........................	15 00
" 7, Trinity, Little Rock.............................	15 00

" " St. Paul's, Batesville............................. 12 50
" " St. John's, Helena...... .... 24 00
" " St. Agnes', Morrilton 2 00
    Total............ · .... ———$518 00

DISBURSEMENTS.

May 2,1885 Voucher No. 1. T. B. Coddington, T'r Gen'l Con..$ 7 50
" 25,   "   " 2. Bishop's Robes...... .... 99 33
July 3,   "   " 3. Publish'g and mail'g Con. Journal 63 35
" 3,   "   " 4. Secretary Tupper, Post. and St'ay 3 75
Jan. 30,   "   " 5. P. K. Roots, Trustee Ep'pate F'd 105 57
    Total........... .... ——$279 50

    Balance on hand. ....· $238 50

Respectfully submitted,
LOGAN H. ROOTS,
Treasurer.

Mr. Logan H. Roots, Treasurer of the Diocesan Missions and of the Fund for Disabled Clergy, read the following reports :

REPORT AS TREASURER OF THE DIOCESAN MISSION FUNDS.

Balance on hand.................................$15 90
June 3, 1885, Christ Church, Little Rock, Contribution... 13 40
Aug. 6, Trinity, Pine Bluff............................. 3 30
March 19, 1886, St. Paul's, Batesville..................... 9 00
March 22, Trinity Cathedral, Little Rock...... .... 5 00
April 9, St. Paul's, Newport......... .... 2 70
April 26, Trinity, Pine Bluff................... .... 4 20
May 7, Balance on hand.... ....,.........$53 50

REPORT AS TREASURER OF FUNDS FOR DISABLED CLERGY.

Balance on hand....................................$30 63
December 28, 1885, Christ Church, Little Rock........... 24 60
" 30, St. Paul's, Batesville...... .... 12 60
" 30, St. Luke's, Hot Springs..................... 11 95
January 4, 1886, Trinity, Little Rock..................... 7 20
April 26, Trinity, Pine Bluff............................. 8 50
May 7, Balance on hand..................... ... .$95 48

Respectfully submitted,
LOGAN H. ROOTS,
Treasurer and Trustee.

The report of Mr. P. K. Roots, Treasurer and Trustee of the Episcopate Fund was read as follows:

REPORT OF TRUSTEE OF EPISCOPATE FUND.

Balance on hand	$178 82
May 5, 1885, Trinlty, Van Buren	3 50
January 30, 1886, L. H. R., Diocesan Fund	105 57
April 26, Christ Church, Little Rock	38 90
" 27, " " Sunday School, Little Rock	10 00
" 27, St Paul's, Batesville	7 57
" 28, " " Newport	7 10
May 7, Trinity, Pine Bluff	29 75
" 7, St. John's, Helena	19 25
" 7, Rev. W. C. Stout	5 00
Total	$454 90

DISBURSEMENTS.

May 16, 1885, Building Association Dues	$20 00
June 16, " " "	20 00
July 16, " "	20 00
August 15, "	20 00
Sept. 16, "	20 00
Oct. 17, "	20 00
Nov. 16, "	20 00
Dec. 16, "	20 00
January 16, 1886 " "	20 00
Feb. 13, Taxes for 1885, Lots 10, 11 and 12	26 93
Feb. 16, Building Association Dues	20 00
March 16, " " "	20 00
April 16, " " "	20 00
Total	$266 93
May 7, Balance on hand	$188 03

Respectfully submitted,

P. K. ROOTS, *Trustee.*

On motion the foregoing reports were referred to the Auditing Committee.

The following resolution was offered by Mr. Geo. W. Caruth :

Resolved, That the Treasurer be and he is hereby directed to pay the sum of one hundred dollars to the Rev. T. C. Tupper, D. D., as an honorarium, in testimony of the grateful appreciation in which his years of faithful service as Secretary is held by this Council. Adopted.

The Council then proceeded to the election of the Standing Committee of the Diocese for the ensuing year, which resulted as follows:

Clergy.	*Lay.*
Rev. T. C. Tupper, D. D.,	Mr. P. K. Roots,
Rev. I. O. Adams,	Mr. M. L. Bell.
Rev. Geo. F. Degen.	

The Delegates to the General Convention were voted for. On the first ballot the following named persons were duly elected:

Clergy.	*Lay.*
Rev. J. J. Vaulx,	Mr. R. V. McCracken,
Rev. I. O. Adams.	Mr. Geo. H. VanEtten,
	Mr. Logan H. Roots,
	Mr. Geo. W. Caruth.

The Chairman announced another ballot for two Clerical Deputies. On the second ballot there was no election. On the third ballot, no election. On motion the Council adjourned to meet Saturday morning, May 8th, at 9:30 o'clock.

SECOND DAY.

Trinity Church, Pine Bluff,}
Saturday, May 8th, 9:30 a. m. }

The Council re-assembled pursuant to adjournment, the Bishop presiding.

A fourth ballot for two Clerical Delegates to the General Convention being taken resulted in the election of the Rev. Messrs. W. W. Estabrooke and W. J. Miller.

The Council then proceeded to the election of Alternate Delegates, and the following were elected on the first ballot:

Clergy.	Lay.
Rev. Richard Totten,	C. H. Stone,
Rev. W. C. Stout,	Jno. J. Horner,
Rev. D. L. Trimble.	Stephen Wheeler,
	H. S. Coleman.

There being one Clerical Alternate Delegate to be voted for, a second ballot was taken and the Rev. Geo. F. Degen was elected.

The committee on Unfinished Business reported as follows:

PINE BLUFF, May 8th, 1886.

To the Diocesan Council:

Your committee on Unfinished Business would respectfully report that the Rev. Messrs. D. L. Trimble and I. O. Adams were appointed a committee to revise and codify the Canons of the Diocese and to report at this Council.

Respectfully Submitted,

W. W. ESTABROOKE,
R. J. MATTHEWS.

The committee appointed on the Revision and Codification of the Canons being called on, reported as follows:

PINE BLUFF, May 8th, 1886.

To the Diocesan Council:

Your committee appointed at the last meeting of the Council, report that the amendments to the Canons are so few that a codification of the same would demand so great an expense that they have deemed it inexpedient to take action in the matter.

Respectfully submitted,

D. L. TRIMBLE,
I. O. ADAMS.

On motion of the Rev. I. O. Adams, the Rev. W. C. Stout was unanimously elected Registrar.

On motion of Mr. G. H. VanEtten, it was resolved that a committee of one be appointed to ascertain whether a vacancy existed in the Trusteeship of the University of the South. The Chairman appointed the Rev. Geo. F. Degen as such committee.

The Rev. I. O. Adams offered the following amendment to Canon VI, Sec. 1.

"*Resolved*, That Canon VI, Sec. 1, be thus amended: At the opening of every Council there shall be the celebration of the Holy Communion, and a sermon by a Priest appointed by the Bishop, when the Bishop himself does not deliver a sermon or charge. And this *may be* preceeded by Morning Prayer." Referred to the Committee on Canons.

The committee on the Revised Prayer Book made the following report, which was adopted.

PINE BLUFF, May 7, 1886.

To the Fourteenth Annual Council of the Diocese of Arkansas—

Your committee to whom was referred the Proposed Book, beg leave to submit the following report:

They have performed their duty in as faithful manner as it has been possible under the circumstances; and although they have that *love* and *veneration* for the *Book of Common Prayer* that is felt by all the Children of the Church, they are forced to confess that it admits of *improvement*; and while they appreciate the work of the committee on *Ritual* and *Liturgical* improvement appointed by the General Convention, not denying that there has been added *enrichment* and perhaps *flexibility*, they think the Proposed Book is far from being above criticism, and therefore recommend that the Deputies to the next General Convention be instructed to vote against the adoption of the Book in its present form, and recommend the following changes:

In the Communion Office omit the following Rubric—

"Then shall be said the Apostle's Creed, or this that followeth," and put in its place the following:

"Then shall be said the *Nicene Creed*," and after this should be printed the *more accurate* translation of the *true Nicene Creed*, and *not* that which is *so called*. It is eminently proper that the Eucharistic Creed be the *Nicene* and *not* the *Apostles'*, and to this end every effort should be made to obtain a *perfect* and *authentic* translation. That there must be a distinc-Creed of the Communion Office also a particular—a Creed that *must be* said whenever there is a celebration; hence, the Rubric as it now stands, permitting either of the two, or none at all, if one of them has been said at Morning Prayer is essentially wrong; and every one that obeys this Rubric will place the *Morning Prayer above* the *Holy Office*.

While your committee recommend these changes, if the Proposed Book is to be adopted, they feel that the Book of Common Prayer with a page of Rubrical directions would give all the flexibility necessary.

INNES O. ADAMS, *Chairman* ;
JAS. J. VAULX,
T. C. TUPPER,
R. V. McCRACKEN, *Layman.*

The Chairman of the Finance and Auditing Committee made the following report, which was adopted:

PINE BLUFF, May 8th, 1886.

To the Diocesan Council—

Your committee to whom was referred the reports of the Treasurer and Trustees respectfully report :

They find all the funds properly accounted for and vouchers for all disbursements. We respectfully call attention to the advisability of greater care being used in the Parochial Reports. For upon examination of the same different sums were found stated as paid into certain funds, into the hands of the various Trustees, which had oeen paid the Bishop for the Cathedral fund. Such discrepancy might create unnecessary embarass-ment, as similar errors have incited criticism in the past.

Respectfully submitted,
N. B. TRULOCK,
For the Committee.

The time having come for the election of the Treasurer of the Diocesan Fund, of Diocese Missions and of the Fund for Dis-abled Clergy, Mr. Logan H. Roots was re-elected, the Sec-retary being instructed to cast the vote for the Council. Mr. P. K. Roots was re-elected Treasurer and Trustee of the Epis-copate Fund, in the same manner.

On motion the Council adjourned to re-a-semble at 1:30 p. m.

May 8th, 1:30 *p. m.*

The Council re-assembling, and the Bishop being absent, the
Rev. W. C. Stout was elected Chairman and Mr. R. J. Matthews
was appointed Secretary *pro tem.* Mr. I. B. Daniels (colored),
a candidate for Holy Orders, was admitted to a seat on the floor
of the house as an honorary member.

On motion of Rev. Geo. F. Degen, it was resolved that the
15th Annual Council be held in' Trinity Cathedral, Little
Rock. Adopted.

The Bishop taking the chair called for the report of the
Committee on the State of the Church, which was presented and
read, as follows:

PINE BLUFF, May 8th, 1886.

To the Diocesan Council—

Your committee beg leave to make the following report:

Without doubt it is well to obey the custom, as year after
year passes away, to sum up what has been done by the Church
in this Diocese. In this vast field of ecclesiastical labor the
sheep of the fold are greatly scattered and the means of communication in many parts of the State limited and difficult.
Hence there are many hindrances to Church extension and many
discouragements to both Bishop and Clergy.

But notwithstanding the drawbacks, we are privileged to
state that from the Bishop's annual address and the reports of the
various parishes we find much to encourage. The number of
baptisms, confirmations and communicants reported is larger
this year than last, and we believe the Church in Arkansas is
putting on new strength.

From the Cathedral many new and important points have
been reached. The services of the Church have been established
in places where heretofore they had not been held, and the prospect is that thus established they will become regular and permanent. We are led to understand that two new Canons will

be added to the Cathedral staff. This increase of workers will enable the Bishop to introduce or maintain the services in a number of places in other parts of the Diocese now neglected and uncared for.

This is as it should be, and it is a source of encouragement to know that the Church in Arkansas can take up this aggressive work. We rejoice to know that the Church in this Diocese has reached that point in her history when she shall be no longer satisfied to simply exist, but to *live*, knowing that she has a mission in this great commonwealth; that she has a goodly heritage to bestow; that she has lost sheep of the House of Israel to search out, and a glorious Gospel to proclaim to the multitude around. This is her work. For this she needs earnest and self-sacrificing Clergy, a loyal and zealous people who shall realize more and more, as the years come and go, "We are laborers together with God."

For what God hath wrought in the past, for what He is now doing, we offer to Him praise and thanksgiving, and pray that He may so continue to bless us in our work "by the mighty power of the Holy Ghost that the comfortable Gospel of Christ may be truly preached, truly received and truly followed in all places to the breaking down of the kingdom of sin, Satan and death, till at length the whole of His dispersed sheep being gathered into one fold, shall become partakers of Everlasting Life."

Respectfully submitted,

W. J. MILLER, *Chairman.*
W. C. STOUT,
C. H. STONE,
H. S. COLEMAN.

On motion, the report was adopted.

The Rev. Walter A. Tearne appeared and took his seat in the Council.

The Rev. Dean Degen, committee to examine into the Trusteeship of the University of the South, reported "That there is at present no vacancy in the number of Trustees of the University of the S⟨outh." Adopted. •

On motion of the Rev. Dr. Tupper the thanks of the Council were returned by a rising vote to the Rector, Vestry and people of Trinity Church, Pine Bluff, for their very generous hospitality.

The committee on Constitution and Canons made their report, which on motion was received.

The Council taking action on the report and after certain amendments, it was adopted as follows:

PINE BLUFF, May 8th, 1886.

To the Diocesan Council—

The committee on Constitution and Canons beg leave to present the following report:

The following resolution has been presented to the committee and they recommend its adoption.

Resolved, That Title I, Canon VI, Sec. 1, be thus amended: At the opening of every Council there shall be a celebration of the Holy Communion and a sermon by a Priest appointed by the Bishop, when the Bishop himself does not deliver at that time a sermon or charge. And this *may be* preceeded by Morning Prayer."

Signed: I. O. ADAMS,
                        J. J. VAULX.

Your committee also recommend the adoption of the following resolutions.

Resolved, That a committee of three (3) Clergymen and three (3) Laymen on Constitution and Canons be appointed by the Bishop to report at the next Annual Council, whose duty it shall be to present a full digest of existing Constitution and Canons and accompanying the same with the recommendations for changes which their judgment may approve.

Resolved, That the same committee be empowered to construct blanks for the use of the Secretary for the securing of proper statistics of the Church in this Diocese, and the blanks thus prepared be furnished to the Clergy before the assembling of the 15th Annual Council.

Resolved, That hereafter all Parochial Reports be made up to and including Easter Monday, and that they be forwarded to the Bishop within three days thereafter.

Respectfully submitted,

> JAS. J. VAULX, *Chairman.*
> I. O. ADAMS,
> GEO. F. DEGEN,
> GEO. H. VaɴETTEN,
> · GEO. WM. CARUTH,
> R. V. McCRACKEN.

On motion of Mr. Logan H. Roots the Secretary was instructed to have 500 copies of the Journal printed.

On motion of Mr. Geo. H. VanEtten it was resolved that the next Annual Council meet on the second Wednesday after Easter.

On motion of Mr. Logan H. Roots it was resolved that hereafter the offerings for Diocesan Missions be subject to the order of the Bishop and left to his discretion as to their use.

On motion, the Bishop, Secretary and Assistant Secretary were appointed a committee to revise and prepare the minutes of the Council for publication.

On motion, it was resolved that the Bishop and Chancellor be added to the committee on Constitution and Canons when appointed.

On motion, the Council adjourned until Sunday, May 9th, after evening service for the purpose of final adjournment.

THIRD DAY.

TRINITY CHURCH, PINE BLUFF, }
May 9th, 9:30 p. m.

After evening prayer, and sermon by the Rev. Richard Totten, the Council met pursuant to adjournment, the Bishop presiding. The committee on Constitution and Canons to report at the next Annual Council was appointed by the Chairman as follows:

Clergy.	Lay.
Rev. J. J. Vaulx,	Mr. Geo. W. Caruth,
Rev. I. O. Adams,	Mr. R. V. McCracken,
Rev. Geo. F. Degen.	Mr. Geo. H. VanEtten,
	Mr. M. L. Bell.

After a stirring and affectionate address by the Bishop and the bestowal of his blessing the Council adjourned *sine die.*

HENRY N. PIERCE,

ATTEST: *Bishop of Arkansas.*

W. J. MILLER, *Secretary.*

PAROCHIAL REPORTS.

ST. PAUL'S CHURCH, BATESVILLE, ARK.

Baptisms—

    Adults.. 4

    Infants 10

                                             ———

        Total 14

Confirmations 12

Communicants—

Last reported..................................... 56

Added anew....................................... 12

Removed into the Parish............................ 2

                                             ———

        Total.................................. 70

Removed from the Parish............................ 1

Dropped 1

Died 1

Present number.................................... 70

Marriages 2

Burials 2

Sunday School—

    Teachers... 6

    Pupils 45

OFFERINGS.

Communion Alms............. ....$ 22 80
Weekly Offertory.............................. ...... 88 65
Vestry Ladies' Aid Society and St. Agnes' Guild.... 458 50
Salary 360 50

      Total............................:....$930 55

APPROPRIATIONS.

Convention Assessment...........................$ 12 50
Episcopate Fund................................ 7 57
Parochial purposes.............................. 779 75
Domestic Missions.............................. 7 10
" Pious and Charitable Uses," C. A., Society——..... 3 25
Other purposes——Aged Clergy·&c.............. 12 60

      Total....................... ......$822 77
Value of Church property.....................$4 500 00

HARVEY L. MINIKIN,
Treasurer of the Parish.

Remarks: My work in this Parish was begun October 21st, 1885. What has been accomplished financially has been in the parish alone. My people are attempting great things for God.

WALTER A. TEARNE, *Rector.*

ST. JOHN'S CHURCH, CAMDEN, ARK.

Confirmations 1
Communicants—
Last reported.. 31
   Removed from the parish.......................... 1
   Present number.................................. 30
Sunday School—
   Teachers.. 5
   Pupils 40

OFFERINGS

Rentals $100 00
Other sources, Alms (about) 12 00

Total............................$112 00

APPROPRIATIONS.

Convention Assessment...........................$ 15 00
Diocesan Missions, Cathedral (about)............... 12 00
Other purposes................................... 7 90

Total...............................$ 34 90
Value of Church property................ ....$1200 00
Amount of insurance on Church property........... 600 00

H. HIGINBOTHAM,
Treasurer of the Parish.

Remarks: No Rector for the past year.

C. H. STONE, *Warden.*

ST. PETER'S CHURCH, CONWAY.

OFFERINGS.

Offertory .... 60c.

APPROPRIATIONS.

Parochial purposes............................... 60c.

Remarks: Held only one service at this place April 15th,
1886. Could not obtain any data from which to form a report.
The Parish virtually defunct. Propose (D. V.) to hold services
there on Thursday preceeding the 3rd Sunday in each month.

W. W. ESTABROOKE,
Canon, Trinity Cathedral.

ST. PAUL'S CHURCH, DARDANELLE.

Baptisms—
Adults 1
Infants 14

Total............................... 15
Confirmations 7

Communicants—
    Added anew.................................... 8·
    Removed from the parish....................... 4
    Dropped 1
    Died .... 2·
    Present number................................ 11
Marriages... 1
Burials .... 2·

OFFERINGS.

Communion Alms..............................$ 10 00·
Subscriptions 200 00

      Total..................... ....$210 00·

APPROPRIATIONS.

Parochial purposes (used to finish Church)...........$210 00·
" Pious and Charitable Uses," C. A................ 20 00·

      Total............................$240 00
Value of Church property......................$500 00·

        D. F. McDONALD, *Rector.*

UNORGANIZED MISSION AT DeVALL'S BLUFF.

Communicants—
    Present number................................ 8·

OFFERINGS.

Subscriptions ....$ 43 30

APPROPRIATIONS.

Parochial purposes..............................$ 43 30

      W. W. HIPOLITE, *Treasurer.*

M. L. SOREY and THOS. M. HORSFALL, *Wardens.*

    Remarks: This report is from January 1st to May 1st, 1886. Services on the 1st Sunday in each month.

        W. W. ESTABROOKE,
          Canon, Trinity Cathedral.

ST. PAUL'S CHURCH, FAYETTEVILLE.

Baptisms—

Adults 3

Infants 15

Total........................ 18

Confirmations 9

Communicants—

Died 1

Present number...................................128

Marriages 5

Burials 5

Sunday School—

Teachers.. 9

Pupils 130

OFFERINGS.

Communion Alms.............................$ 36 00

Weekly Offertory................................. 97 75

Rentals and Subscriptions........................ 722 00

Other offerings 73 80

Total.............................$929 55

APPROPRIATIONS.

Parochial purposes.............................$ 796 00

Diocesan Missions, paid the Bishop on visitation..... 10 75

Soc. for Promoting Christianity among Jews......... 3 00

"Pious and Charitable Uses," C. A............... 36 00

Other purposes................................. 10 00

Total.............................$ 855 75

Value of Church property, about.................$6000 00

J. L. CRAVENS,

Treasurer of the Parish.

Remarks: The above report includes the number of communicants and baptisms at Eureka Springs and Bentonville and Sunday School at Eureka Springs.

JAS. J. VAULX, *Rector.*

ST. JOHN'S CHURCH, HELENA.

Baptisms—
Adults.. 5
Infants 18
                                                  —
        Total....................................... 23
Confirmations... 27
Communicants—
Last reported................................... 80
Added anew...................................... 38
Removed into the parish......................... 1
                                                  —
        Total....................................... 39
Removed from the parish......................... 4
Dropped 4
Died.. 2
Present number.................................109
Burials... 8
Sunday School—
Teachers.. 10
Pupils.. 80

OFFERINGS.

Communion Alms................................$ 37 40
Weekly Offertory............................. 1064 80
Rentals and subscriptions..................... 296 30
Other sources................................. 756 86
Left out.....................................   2 50
                                              _____
        Total.. ....$2157 86

APPROPRIATIONS.

Convention Assessment.........................$ 24 00
Episcopate Fund...............................   19 25
Parochial Purposes........................... 1361 10
Paid Bishop, Cathedral work...................   9 50
Domestic Missions.............................   37 35

"Pious and Charitable Uses," C. A........ .... 37 40
Other purposes................................. 435 36

     Total............................$2033 96
Value of Church property......................$6000 00
Amount of insurance on Church property.........$3500 00

    Remarks: My report of work dates from June 21st, 1885.
In the Treasurer's report offerings from the same date, but the
rest is for the year ending May 1st, 1886.

            RICHARD TOTTEN, *Rector.*

ST. LUKE'S CHURCH, HOT SPRINGS.

Baptisms—
    Adults.. 2
    Infants 14

     Total........................ 16
Confirmations... 13
Communicants—
    Last reported.................................. 40
    Added anew..................................... 20
    Removed from the parish........................ 8
    Dropped 1
    Died... 2
    Present number................................. 60
    Marriages 7
    Burials.. 6
Sunday School—
    Teachers 6
    Pupils... 75

OFFERINGS.

Communion Alms..............................$ 75 78
Weekly Offertory............................ 1130 18
Rentals and subscriptions................... 1158 75
Other sources............................... 987 34

     Total............................$3352 05

APPROPRIATIONS.

Convention Assessment........................... 20 00
Parochial purposes.............................. 2091 74
To the Bishop (two offerings)................... 52 76
Aged and Infirm Clergy (two offerings)......... 20 23
" Pious and Chairitable Uses," C. A............. 75 78

Total...........................$2260 51
Value of Church property, ...$8000 00
Amount of insurance on Church building..........$2200 00

J. A. POLHAMIUS,
Treasurer of the Parish.

Remarks: During the year the Church was consecrated on St. Luke's Day, 1885. The Parish is raising money for a Rectory, about $1600.00 have been secured.

W. J. MILLER, *Rector.*

CHRIST CHURCH, LITTLE ROCK.

Baptisms—
   Adults................................. 9
   Infants................................ 39

   Total.................................. 48
Confirmations.............................. 28
Communicants—
   Last reported..........................324
   Added anew............................. 28
   Removed from the parish................ 10
   Died................................... 13
   Present number.........................329
   Marriages.............................. 11
   Burials................................ 54

Sunday School—
   Teachers............................... 22
   Pupils.................................300

OFFERINGS.

Communion Alms	$ 125	75
Weekly Offertory	377	10
Rentals and Subscriptions	2395	85
Other sources	108	02
Total	$3006	72

APPROPRIATIONS.

Convention Assessment	$ 75	00
Episcopate Fund	38	90
Parochial purposes	2706	52
Diocesan Missions, P'd Bishop 13,40	26	70
W. & O. Deceased Clergymen	24	85
Jewish Missions	9	00
" Pious and Charitable Uses," C. A	125	75
Total	$3006	72
Value of Church property	$55000	00

A. L. O'NEALE,
Treasurer of the Parish.

Remarks: Private offerings for Domestic Missions not noted in this report, but acknowledged in the *Spirit of Missions.*

There is every reason to hope that the new Church edifice will be completed and ready for consecration ere the lapse of another year.

TULLIUS C. TUPPER, *Rector.*

TRINITY CATHEDRAL, LITTLE ROCK.

Baptisms—

Adults	3
Infants	11
Total	14
Confirmations	14

Communicants—

Last reported	62

Added anew...................................... 14
Removed into the Parish........................ 6

Total...................................... 82
Removed from the Parish........................ 8
Dropped 7
Present number................................. 67
Marriages..... 3
Burials.. 1

Sunday School—
Teachers....................................... 7
Pupils... 60

Parish School—
Teachers....................................... 1
Pupils... 7

OFFERINGS.

Communion Alms..............................$ 9 65
Weekly Offertory............................... 352 74
Rentals and Subscriptions, (part of Weekly Offertory). 527 85
Other sources...... .... 621 50

Total..............................$1511 24

APPROPRIATIONS.

Convention Assessment..........................$ 15 00
Episcopate Fund (not yet collected) in hand........ 1 00
Parochial purposes............................. 1398 44
Diocesan Missions............................... 5 00
Domestic Missions.............................. 5 00
Foreign Missions............................... 4 95
Colored Missions............................... 44 80
Church Institutions............................ 8 48
" Pious and Charitable Uses," C. A............. 19 65
Other Purposes................................. 9 00

Total..............................$1511 24

Value of Church property......................$7000 00
Amount of insurance on church property..........$2500 00

EDWARD C. GOULD,
Treasurer of the Parish.
REV. GEO. F. DEGEN,
Dean and Rector.

UNORGANIZED MISSION AT LONOKE.

Baptisms—
    Infants 2
Confirmations... 7
Communicants—
    Present number.................................... 14

OFFERINGS.

Other sources....................................$ 12 75

APPROPRIATIONS.

Parochial purposes...............................$ 12 75

JOHN W. SLUTE,
JOHN L. BLACK,
Wardens.

Remarks: This report is from January 1st to May 1st, 1886. Services held on the last Friday in each month.

W. W. ESTABROOKE,
Canon, Trinity Cathedral.

ST. ANDREW'S MISSION, MARIANNA.

Baptisms—
    Adults... 1
    Infants.. 2
        Total... 3
Confirmations.. 3
Communicants—
    Last reported.................................... 22
    Removed from the Parish.......................... 1
    Present number................................... 29

Burials...   ;
Sunday School—
    Teachers......................................   5·
    Pupils..............   25

OFFERINGS.

Communion Alms............ ....$ 12 70·
Other Alms including Offering to Domestic Missions..   14 25·

    Total............... ....$ 26 95·
Value of church property....,..................$3000 00·

C. A. BRUCE, *Missionary.*

ST. AGNES' CHURCH, MORRILTON.

Baptisms—
    Adults...   1
Confirmations ....   2·
Communicants—
    Present number................................   16·

OFFERINGS.

Rental and Subscriptions.........................$ 50 00
Other sources...................................   9 20·

    Total..............................$ 59 20·

APPROPRIATIONS.

Convention Assessment..........................$ 2 00·
Parochial purposes..............................   57 20

    Total..............................$ 59 20·

Wm. N. SANDLIN,
Treasurer of the Parish.

Remarks: This report is from January 1st to May 1st, 1886. Services held 3rd Sunday in each month.

W. W. ESTABROOKE,
Canon, Trinity Cathedral.

ST. PAUL'S CHURCH, NEWPORT.

Baptisms—

Adults	4
Infants	10
Total	14

Confirmations 5

Communicants—

Added anew	1
Removed into the Parish	1
Present number	26

Sunday School—

Teachers	6
Pupils	30

OFFERINGS.

Communion Alms	$ 8	55
Rentals and Subscriptions	100	00
Other sources	40	00
Total	$148	55

APPROPRIATIONS.

Convention Assessment	$ 8	00
Episcopate Fund	7	10
Parochial purposes	140	00
Diocesan Missions	2	70
Missions among the Jews	1	75
Other purposes, Sunday School &c	16	00
Total	$175	55
Value of Church property	$1500	00

FRANK W. FROST,
Treasurer of the Parish.

Remarks: This report is from January 1st to May 1st, 1886. Services are held on the 2nd and 4th Sundays in each month.

W. W. ESTABROOKE,
Canon, Trinity Cathedral.

GRACE CHURCH, PHILLIPS COUNTY.

Baptisms—
    Infants..........   4
Confirmations......   4
Communicants—
    Last reported................................... 13
    Present number................................ 13

OFFERINGS.
Communion Alms............... ....$ 5 30

APPROPRIATIONS.
Domestic Missions.............................$ 3 45
Value of Church property..... ....$2500 00

THOMAS JONES,
Treasurer of the Parish.

Remarks.   Three of the baptisms were colored.

C. A. BRUCE, *Rector.*

TRINITY CHURCH, PINE BLUFF.

Baptisms—
    Infants..   6
Confirmations......................................   6
Communicants—
    Last reported................................... 73
    Added anew...................................   7
    Removed into the Parish.........................   7
                                             ——
       Total................................. 87
    Removed from the Parish.........................   2
    Dropped...   1
    Died.....   1
    Present number................................ 83
    Marriages   3
    Burials..   9
Sunday School—
    Teachers.......................................   8
    Pupils.................. 100

OFFERINGS.

Communion Alms........................ .....$	29	25
Weekly Offertory..............................	120	83
Rentals and Subscriptions......................... ...	824	00
Other sources.................................	591	37
Total..........................$1565		45

APPROPRIATIONS.

Convention Assessment..........................$	37	00
Episcopate Fund......	29	75
Diocesan Missions.............................	7	50
Soc. Promoting Christianity among the Jews........	2	45
Domestic Missions.............................	1	50
Widows and Orphans of deceased Clergy...........	8	50
Cathedral....................................	14	15
"Pious and Charitable Uses," C. A...............	29	25
Other purposes............................	1435	35
Total.... ....,...................$1565		45
Value of Church property, about................$12 000		00
Amount of insurance on Church property........ $1 000		00

H. H. HUNN,

Treasurer of the Parish.

Remarks: The Parish is in good condition and the debt on the Rectory has been paid.

I. O. ADAMS, *Rector.*

TRINITY CHURCH, VAN BUREN.

Baptisms—

Adults...	5
Infants..	9
Total.............................	14
Confirmations..	5

Communicants—

Last reported	35
Added anew	5
Removed from the Parish	2
Total	42
Removed into the Parish	1
Present number	41
Marriages	1
Burials	4

Sunday School—

Teachers	5
Pupils	70

OFFERINGS.

Weekly Offertory	$ 52	30
Other sources, Sunday School	21	33
Total	$ 93	63

APPROPRIATIONS.

Parochial purposes $31,60, $21,25	$ 52	85
Diocesan Missions	5	40
University of the South	4	40
Domestic Missions	15	00
Total	$ 77	65

JOHN D. WHITE,
Treasurer of the Parish.

D. McMANUS, *Rector.*

SUMMARY OF STATISTICS FROM PAROCHIAL REPORTS.

Eight Parishes and Mission Stations not reporting.

Baptisms	177
Confirmations	149
Communicants	1022
Estimated number from parishes not reporting	312
Total	1364

Marriages.............. 32
Burials.. 89
Sunday School—
    Teachers and Cupils............................1044
Offerings..................................$13 955 60
see proof.

REPORT OF REV. E. C. ALCORN.

St. Louis, May 31st, 1886.

Rt. Rev. H. N. Pierce, D. D., LL. D. Bishop of Arkansas,
Little Rock, Ark.:

My Dear Bishop:

I presume I ought to have made a report ere this. I have resided in St. Louis ever since I left Arkansas and officiated at Trinity Church almost continuously, occasional Sundays elsewhere. Since March 15th I have entire charge at Trinity. I don't see my name on your clergy list as being canonically attached, though I still belong to your diocese unless you have transferred me without my knowledge.

I am glad to see that you have got the Cathedral work under way, and that you have got your "*pou sto*" at last. Hope to get some kind of a "*pou sto*" myself again one of these days.

Yours very respectfully,

E. C. ALCORN.

THE BISHOP'S ANNUAL ADDRESS.

Dear Brethren of the Clergy and Laity:

I thank God that I am permitted to meet you again in this our Fourteenth Annual Council. Notwithstanding the fact that the important Parish of St. John's Church, Fort Smith has been vacant for more than six months and the Parishes and Missions in the southern part of the Diocese have had no regular pastoral oversight for about a year, yet, the period since our last assembling has been one of decided progress. The removal from our borders of the Rev. H. C. E. Costelle and the Rev. Wm. B. Burrows and the resignation of the Rev. J. L. Berne, all efficient laborers caused me great regret. But on the other hand we have been strengthened and comforted by the incoming of the Rev. Richard Totten, now Rector of St. John's, Helena, the Rev. Geo. F. Degen, now Dean of Trinity Cathedral and the Rev. W. W. Estabrooke, M. D:, now Canon of Trinity Cathedral and doing missionary work in a wide field. They have already shown themselves workmen that need not be ashamed. The Rev. W. A. Tearne, formerly Dean of the Cathedral, has returned to Batesville much to the satisfaction of St Paul's Parish. St. Luke's Church, Hot Springs has been made complete in all respects, and has been consecrated. St. Andrew's, Marianna, will be ready for consecration as soon as a debt of a few hundred dollars now resting on it has been paid off. Work on Trinity Church, Van Buren, has progressed during the past, and Christ Church, Little Rock shows strong signs of coming to its completion before long. The Rectory of Trinity Parish has been paid for. At Fayetteville, the Rectory has been enlarged and greatly improved. At Batesville, two rooms have been built for the Rector's use which will hereafter form a part of the Rectory. At Fort Smith, the Rectory is now building. At Hot Springs, the rectory fund has attained such dimensions as to justify beginning to build, were the necessity of doing so just now pressing. The results of our Cathedral work confirm me in my opinions often expressed as to the efficiency of that system of working. With the Dean, one canon and my own purely missionary labors, there have been forty-nine candidates for confirmation presented out of the 149 confirmed. Services are now regularly held in places never before occupied by the Church. The addition of two Canons more, an addition I hope ere long to see, will enable us to open up a large number of new fields, as well as to efficiently cultivate the old fields now but poorly cared for. With the vacancy at Fort Smith filled, and two more Canons at the Cathedral the Diocese would be in much better condition than it has ever been. With this brief glance at the past and present state of the Diocese, I beg to lay before you the following abstract of my journal:

April 25, Saturday: St. Mark's Day. I received the Holy Communion in Trinity Cathedral, Little Rock. Dean Tearne was celebrant.

April 26, Sunday: The third after Easter. I said morning service in Trinity Cathedral, Little Rock, and preached; at 5 p. m. I preached again.

May 1, Friday: St. Phillips' and St. James' Day. Attended morning service at the Cathedral and received the Holy Communion.

May 3, Sunday: The fourth after Easter, a m. I preached and celebrated the Holy Eucharist in Trinity Cathedral, and assisted in saying the evening service. At 4 p. m. I confirmed

in private four persons (two males and two females), a sick
man and his relatives.   The candidates were presented by the
Rev. Dr. Tupper, and belonged to Christ Church, Little Rock.
I assisted in saying evening prayer at the Cathedral.

May 4, Monday: I confirmed in Trinity Cathedral, Little
Rock, three persons (all males) and made an address.

May 8, Friday :   Gave letters dimissory to Rev. William
B. Burrows, transferring him to the diocese of Missouri.

May 10, Sunday: The fifth   after Trinity, a. m.   I
received the Holy Communion   in Trinity Cathedral and
assisted in saying morning service.   P. M. I preached in the
same church.

May 14, Thursday :   Ascension Day.   In St. John's
Church, Fort Smith, Ark., I received the Holy Communion,.
Rev. J. L. Berne, rector, being celebrant, and I preached.

May 17, Sunday, after Ascension. In St. Johns' Church,.
Fort Smith, I celebrated the Holy Eucharist and preached.
At night I preached again and confirmed one person (one male.)·

May 24, Sunday :   Whitsunday.   In Trinity Cathedral,
Little Rock, at morning service, I preached and celebrated the
Holy Eucharist.   I assisted in saying evening prayer,

May 28, Thursday :   In the church of the Good Shepherd,.
Mobile, Ala., I ordered priest, the Rev. Abraham Wallace
Pierce, deacon, being assisted in the services by the Right
Rev. Dr. Wilmer, bishop of Alabama ; the Rev. Mr. Johnston,
rector of Trinity Church, Mobile ; the Rev. Mr. Kimball, of
Whistler, Ala., and the Rev. Dr. Tucker, rector of Christ
Church, Mobile, who presented the candidate.   I preached the
sermon and celebrated the Holy Eucharist.   I gave letters
dimissory to my son the Rev. A. W. Pierce, transferring him
to the diocese of Alabama.

May 29, Friday :   I officiated at a funeral in St. Johns'
Church, Mobile.   The deceased was a former parishioner
of mine.

May 31, Sunday: Trinity Sunday. In St. Johns' Church, Mobile, Ala., I said morning service, preached and celebrated the Holy Eucharist; at night in Christ Church, Mobile, I preached again.

June 3, Wednesday: Commencement Day at Columbia Institute, Columbia, Tenn., I addressed the graduating class and gave the diplomas.

June 5, Friday: I officiated at a funeral in St. Peter's Church, Columbia Tenn.

June 7, Sunday: The first after Trinity. I said morning and evening services, preached twice and celebrated the Holy Eucharist in St. Peter's Church, Columbia, Tenn.

June 14, Sunday: The second after Trinity. In St. Peter's, Columbia, I celebrated the Holy Eucharist and preached twice. I was assisted in the services by the Rev. M. E. Thompson of Fayetteville, Tenn.

June 16, Tuesday: In St. Peter's Church, Columbia, Tenn., I joined in Holy Matrimony Dr. Charles W. Winn and Miss Mary Polk Branch.

June 21, Sunday: The third after Trinity. In St. Peter's, Columbia, I celebrated the Holy Eucharist and preached. The Rev. M. E. Thompson assisted me in the services. A storm prevented the gathering of a congregation in the evening.

June 24, Wednesday: Nativity of St. John Baptist. I said E. P., and lectured in St. Peters', Columbia.

June 28, Sunday: The fourth after Trinity. In St. Peters' Church, Columbia, at 7 a. m., I celebrated the Holy Eucharist; at 9:45 I administered the Holy Communion in private to a sick woman; at 10:30 a. m. I said morning service and preached, and at 7 p. m. I said evening prayer and preached.

June 29, Monday: St. Peters' Day. I said morning and evening services and preached twice in St. Peter's, Columbia.

July 1, Wednesday: In Trinity Church, Nashville, Tenn., I preached at evening service and confirmed six persons (three males and three females), and addressed the class.

July 5, Sunday: The fifth after Trinity. In Trinity Cathedral, Little Rock, I preached at morning service and celebrated the Holy Eucharist.

July 11, Saturday: I officiated at a funeral in Little Rock.

July 12, Tuesday: The sixth after Trinity. I assisted in saying morning service in the Cathedral and at 5 p. m. I preached.

July 19, Sunday: The seventh after Trinity. In the Cathedral at 7 a. m. I celebrated the Holy Eucharist; 11 said morning service and preached; p. m. baptized in private a sick child; at 5 p. m. said evening prayer and preached.

July 22, Wednesday: At Morrilton, Ark., 8:30 p. m. I preached and confirmed nine persons, four males and five females and addressed the class. The candidates were presented by Dean Tearne, who had prepared the class. The services were said by Rev. W. C. Stout and Dean Tearne. This was the first confirmation ever held at this parish.

July 23, Thursday: Preached at night service at Morrilton.

July 26, Sunday: The eighth after Trinity. In St. Paul's Church, Dardanelle, I assisted in saying morning service, preached and celebrated the Holy Eucharist. P. M. I baptized an adult; at 8 p. m. I assisted in saying evening prayer, preached and confirmed six persons (one male and five females), and addressed the class. The rector, the Rev. Dr. McDonald, after much self-denial and hard labor, has succeded in finishing this beautiful church, and the prospect for church growth is more promising than it has been for years.

August 2, Sunday: The ninth after Trinity. In St. Paul's Church, Fayetteville, I preached and celebrated the Holy Eucharist at the morning service, and at 5 p. m. I preached again.

August 4, Tuesday: At 5 p. m. attended a meeting of the congregation of St. Paul's Church, Fayetteville, and made an address.

August 9, Sunday: The tenth after Trinity. In Trinity Cathedral, Little Rock, I preached at morning service ; at 3 p. m. I confirmed in private a sick woman. The candidate was presented by the Rev. Dr. Tupper, rector of Christ Church, Little Rock. At 5 p. m. I assisted in saying evening prayer in the cathedral.

August r2, Wednesday: At Little Rock I confirmed in private a sick woman, presented by Dr. T. C. Tupper, Rector of Christ Church.

August 14, Friday: At 11 a. m. in Trinity Cathedral I joined in Holy Matrimony Garnes J. Carbo and Miss Salie Walker.

August 16, Sunday: The eleventh after Trinity. In Trinity Cathedral I said morning and evening service and preached twice.

August 23, Sunday: The twelfth after Trinity. In the Cathedral, Little Rock, I said service morning and evening, celebrated the Holy Eucharist and preached twice.

August 24, Monday: St. Bartholemew's Day. Baptized in private a sick child ; at 10:30 in Trinity Cathedral, lectured on the day and celebrated the Holy Eucharist.

August 27, Thursday: I officiated at the funeral of a child in Trinity Cathedral.

August 30, Sunday: The thirteenth after Trinity. I said morning and evening service, celebrated the Holy Eucharist and preached twice in Trinity Cathedral.

September 6, Sunday: The fourteenth after Trinity. In the Cathedral, Little Rock, I said morning and evening services, celebrated the Holy Eucharist, and preached twice.

September 7, Monday: Gave letters dimissory to Rev. H. C. E. Gostelle, transferring him to the diocese of Fond du Lac.

September 9, Wednesday: At 6 p. m., in the Cathedral, Little Rock, I joined in holy matrimony James A. Surby and Mrs. Amanda Durkee.

Sept. 13, Sunday: The fifteenth after Trinity. In the Cathedral, Little Rock, I said morning and evening services and preached twice.

September 15, Tuesday: In St. Paul's Church, Batesville, Ark., after evening prayer, said by Dean Tearne, I preached and confirmed eight persons (one male and seven females), and addressed the class. The class was prepared by Dean Tearne, who has been doing missionary work here for the month past.

September 16, Wednesday: Presided at a vestry meeting of St. Paul's Parish.

September 17, Thursday: At 7:30 p. m. presided at a meeting of the congregation of St. Paul's Church, Batesville, Ark., and made an address, explaining the object of the meeting.

September 20, Sunday: The sixteenth after Trinity. In the Cathedral, Little Rock, I said the service morning and evening; celebrated the Holy Eucharist and preached twice.

September 27, Sunday: The seventeenth after Trinity. In St. Paul's Church, Newport, Ark., I said morning and evening service and preached twice.

September 28, Monday: Said evening service in St' Paul's, Newport, and preached.

September 29, Tuesday: St. Michael and All Angels. At 10:15 a. m., in St. Paul's Church, Newport, I said morning prayer and baptized a child; at 11 I celebrated the Holy Eucharist and lectured on the day.

October 4, Sunday: The eighteenth after Trinity. In the Cathedral, Little Rock, I said morning and evening service, celebrated the Holy Eucharist and preached twice.

October 11, Sunday: The nineteenth after Trinity. In the Cathedral, Little Rock, at 10:20 a. m. I celebrated the Holy Eucharist; at 11 a. m. I assisted in saying morning prayer and the Rev. Geo. F. Degen, of the Diocese of Iowa, preached; t 7:30 p. m., Dean Tearne said evening prayer and I preached.

October 18, Sunday: The twentieth after Trinity and St.
Luke's Day. I consecrated to the worship of Almighty God,
St. Luke's Church, Hot Springs. Capt. Mellard read the
Instrument of Donation and the Rector, the Rev. Wm. J.
Miller, the sentence of consecration. The Rev. Mr. Miller and
the Rev. David L. Trimble of Pine Bluff, Ark.; said Morning
Prayer. I said the communion office, Rev. Mr. Trimble reading
the Epistle and the Rev. Mr. Miller the Gospel. I preached
and assisted by the Rector, celebrated the Holy Eucharist. I
congratulated the Parish on the success which has crowned
their persistent efforts. The church is beautiful and beautifully
furnished. At 4 p. m. I preached again and confirmed two
persons (two females), and made an address to the newly confirmed.

October 22, Thursday: At 8 p. m., in Calvary Church,
Memphis, Tenn., I joined in Holy matrimony Walter M.
Farabee and Miss Sudie Pierce Jones, both of Memphis.

October 23, Friday: At 10 a. m., in Calvary Church,
Memphis, on the written request of Rev. Dr. White, the case
being one of exigency, I confirmed one person (one female.)

October 25, Sunday: The twenty-first after Trinity. In
the Cathedral, Little Rock, I said the service morning and
evening; celebrated the Holy Eucharist and preached twice.

November 1, Sunday: The twenty-second after Trinity
and All Saints' Day. In the Cathedral at Little Rock, the
Rev. Mr. Degen said Morning Prayer and preached, and I
celebrated the Holy Eucharist; at night I preached.

November 8, Sunday: The twenty-third after Trinity.
In the cathedral, Little Rock, at 10:20 a. m., I received the
Holy Communion. The Rev. George F. Degen, who entered
on his duties as Dean to-day, was celebrant; at 11 a. m. I
preached, and at night I assisted in saying evening prayer.

November 9, Monday: I confirmed in private a sick man,
the candidate was presented by the Rev. Dr. Tupper, of Christ
Church, Little Rock.

I this day accepted the letters dimissory presented by the Rev. George Frederic Degen from the Diocese of Iowa, and sent canonical notice of such acceptance.

November 15, Sunday: The twenty-fourth after Trinity. At Morrilton, Ark., I preached after morning service said by the Rev. W. C. Stout; at 4 p. m. I preached again, and after service had an informal meeting of the congregation.

November 16, Monday: Assisted by the Rev. Mr. Stout, I said the burial service over the remains of a young mother. The interment took place in Tennessee.

November 22, Tuesday: The twenty-fifth after Trinity. In St. John's Church, Fort Smith, I said the service morning and evening, celebrated the Holy Eucharist and preached twice.

November 24, Tuesday: At the residence of Major Thomas Lanigan, Fort Smith, Ark., at 7 p. m. I joined in Holy Matrimony John Calhoun Daily, M. D., and Miss Jane Eliza Whitthorne.

November 26, Thursday: National Thanksgiving. In St. John's Church, Fort Smith, the Rev. D. McManus said Morning Prayer and I said the ante-communion and preached.

November 28, Saturday: In Trinity Church, Van Buren, Ark., I assisted the Rev. D. McManus in baptizing three adults.

November 29, Sunday: The first in Advent. In Trinity Church, Van Buren, I assisted in saying morning service and preached; at night I assisted in saying Evening Prayer, preached and confirmed three persons (three females) and addressed the class.

November 30, Monday: St. Andrew's Day. I baptized at Van Buren one adult and three children.

December 6, Sunday: The second in Advent. In the Cathedral, Little Rock, I preached and celebrated the Holy Eucharist at morning service, and assisted in saying Evening Prayer.

December 13, Sunday: The third in Advent. In St. Andrews' Church, Marianna, Ark., after Morning Prayer said by Rev. C. A. Bruce, 1 preached, and celebrated the Holy Eucharist; at 7 p. m. I preached and confirmed three persons (three females), and addressed them. The church is nearly finished inside, and proper sittings, yet lacking, will be soon put in.

December 14, Monday: In St. John's Church, Helena, Ark., after Evening Prayer said by Rev. Richard Totten, rector, I preached and confirmed sixteen persons (two of them from Grace Church, Phillips County), and addressed the class.

December 15, Tuesday: After Evening Prayer said by Rev. Messrs. Totten and Bruce, I preached in St. John's Church, Helena.

December 20, Sunday: The fourth in Advent. At Morrilton, Ark., I said service morning and evening; celebrated the Holy Eucharist and preached twice.

December 21, Monday: In St. Paul's Church, Dardanelle, Ark., after Evening Prayer said by Rev. Dr. McDonald, Rector, I preached.

December 22, Tuesday: Preached at night in St. Paul's, Dardanelle.

December 23, Wednesday: I said evening service and preached at Cabin Creek, Ark. This was the first service of our Church ever held here, so far as I can learn. The services were held in the Methodist Church.

December 25, Friday: Christmas Day. In St. John's Church, Fort Smith, I said morning service; preached and celebrated the Holy Eucharist.

December 27, Sunday: The first after Christmas and St. John's Day. In St. John's Church, Ft. Smith, I said service morning and evening; preached twice and baptized four children.

December 28, Monday: Holy Innocents. In Trinity Church, Van Buren, I said Evening Prayer, baptized a young girl and preached.

December 29, Tuesday: At 10 a. m., in Trinity Church, Van Buren, I said Morning Prayer, baptized a child and lectured.

December 31, Thursday: In St. John's Church, Fort Smith, at 8 p. m., I joined together in holy matrimony Lucien Lyons Saunders and Miss Agnes Hamilton.

January 1, Friday: The Circumcision of Christ. At Cabin Creek, Ark., at 11 a. m., I said the services, preached and celebrated the Holy Eucharist. At 7 p. m. I said Evening Prayer, baptized a young man, preached, and confirmed him and made an address to the congregation on Confirmation.

January 3, Sunday: The second after Christmas. In Trinity Cathedral, Little Rock, I preached at morning service, and assisted in saying Evening Prayer.

January 10, Sunday: The first after Epiphany. In the Cathedral assisted in saying morning service, and received the Holy Communion. At night I preached.

January 17, Sunday: The second after Epiphany. In Trinity Cathedral, Little Rock, I said morning and evening service, and celebrated the Holy Eucharist, and preached twice.

January 24, Sunday: The third after Epiphany. In St. Paul's Church, Newport, Ark., I said morning and evening services and preached twice.

January 25, Monday: The Conversion of St. Paul. In St. Paul's Church, Newport, I said morning and evening services, celebrated the Holy Eucharist and preached twice.

January 31, Sunday: The fourth after Epiphany. In the Cathedral, Little Rock, I assisted in saying morning service and received the Holy Communion. At evening service I preached.

February 2, Monday: I accepted the letters dimissory presented by Rev. W. W. Estabrooke, M. D., from the Diocese of Iowa, and gave canonical notice of such acceptance. Dr. Estabrooke becomes Canon of Trinity Cathedral, and Missionary at various points on the Iron Mountain, Memphis and Little Rock and Fort Smith Railways.

February 7, Sunday: The fifth after Epiphany. In St. John's Church, Fort Smith, I said morning and evening services; preached twice, and at evening service made an address to the congregation urging them to second vigorously the efforts of the vestry to fill the vacant rectorship; p. m. I met the gentlemen of the vestry to give them my advice and counsel.

February 13, Saturday: I preached after Evening Prayer at Prairie City, Cherokee Nation, Indian Territory.

February 14, Sunday: The sixth after Epiphany. At Prairie City, Cherokee Nation, I addressed the Sunday School; celebrated the Holy Eucharist, and preached twice.

February 15, Monday: At Prairie City. Preached at night service and baptized five children.

February 16, Tuesday: At Prairie City. Preached at night service and baptized two children.

February 21, Sunday. Septuagesima. In St. Paul's Church, Fayetteville, Ark., I celebrated the Holy Eucharist, assisted by the Rector, Rev. J. J. Vaulx, and preached at morning and evening services.

February 22, Monday: Preached at night in St. Paul's Church.

February 23, Tuesday: Preached at night in St. Paul's Church.

February 24, Wednesday: St. Matthias' Day. In St. Paul's Church, Fayetteville. Attended the morning celebration at 7 a. m., and received the Holy Communion. The rector was celebrant. At 7:30 p. m. I preached and confirmed four persons (four females), and addressed the class.

February 28, Sunday: Sexagesima. In Trinity Cathedral, Little Rock, at 10:20 a. m. I received the Holy Communion, Dean Degen was celebrant; at 11 a. m. I preached and at 4 p. m. assisted in saying Evening Prayer.

March 6, Saturday: In Trinity Cathedral, Little Rock, at 6:30 p. m. I joined in Holy Matrimony Gerry Austin Lyman and Miss Elizabeth Powell Pierce, my elder daughter.

March 7, Sunday: Quinquagesma. In Christ Church, Little Rock, I assisted in saying morning service; preached and celebrated the Holy Eucharist; at 4 p. m. I preached in Trinity Cathedral.

March 10, Wednesday: Ash Wednesday. At 9 a. m. attended at Morning Prayer, in Trinity Cathedral; at 10 I celebrated the Holy Eucharist; at 7:30 p. m. I attended Lenten service, Dean Degen officiated.

March 12, Friday: In Grace Church, Washington, Ark., I said Evening Prayer and preached.

March 13, Saturday: Made a flying trip to Nashville, Ark., (my first visit there), and baptized three children ; returned to Washington p. m., and at night I said Evening Prayer and preached in Grace Church.

March 14, Sunday: The first in Lent. In Grace Church, Washington, Ark., at 10 a. m., I said Morning Prayer and baptized two children ; at 11 I said the Litany, preached, confirmed one person (young man), and celebrated the Holy Eucharist.

At 7:30 p. m. I said Evening Prayer and preached at Hope, Ark.

March 15, Monday: In St. Mark's Church, Hope, at 11 a. m., I preached and celebrated the Holy Eucharist ; at 7;30 p. m. I said Evening Prayer, preached and made an address on Confirmation, and confirmed one person (one female.)

March 17, Wednesday: In St. James' Church, Prescott, Ark., I said Evening Prayer and preached.

March 18, Thursday: I visited Arkadelphia—a visit on inspection.

March 20, Saturday: In St. John's Church, Camden, Ark., I said Evening Prayer and preached at night.

March 21, Sunday: The second in Lent. In St. John's Church, Camden, I said morning service, preached and celebrated the Holy Eucharist; at 8 p. m. I said Evening Prayer, preached, confirmed one person (one female), and made an address on Confirmation.

March 23, Tuesday: In Trinity Cathedral, Little Rock. Attended the 7 o'clock celebration and received the Holy Communion; at 9:30 a. m. and 4:30 attended Lenten services.

March 24, Wednesday: At Morrillton, Ark, 8 p m. After Evening Prayer said by Canon Estabrooke, and Rev. W. C. Stout, I preached and confirmed two persons (two females), and addressed the class.

March 28, Sunday: The third in Lent. In St. Paul's Church, Batesville, Ark., I assisted in saying morning service; preached, and celebrated the Holy Eucharist; at 5:30 p. m. I preached, and confirmed three persons (two males and one female) and addressed the class. This makes twelve persons confirmed in this Parish since the last Annual Council. Both classes have been prepared by Rev. W. A. Tearne, now Rector of the Parish.

March 29, Monday: In St. Paul's Church, Newport, Ark., after Evening Prayer said by Canon Estabrooke, I preached, and confirmed one person (one female) and made a short address.

March 31, Wednesday: In the Cathedral at Little Rock I received at the early celebration of the Holy Eucharist, and at night attended Lenten service.

April 2, Friday: In Trinity Church, Van Buren, Ark., I said Evening Prayer; preached, and confirmed two persons (two females).

April 4, Sunday: The fourth in Lent. In St. Paul's Church, Fayetteville, Ark., I assisted in saying morning service, preached, and celebrated the Holy Eucharist; at evening service I preached again.

April 5, Monday: At 5 p. m. I preached at evening service in St. Paul's Church.

April 6, Tuesday: At 5 p. m. I preached in St. Paul's Church, Fayetteville, Ark., and confirmed two persons (one male, one female.)

April 7, Wednesday: In St. Paul's Church, Fayetteville, I preached at 5 p. m., and confirmed three persone (two males and one female.)

April 8, Thursday: In St. John's Church, Fort Smith, I said evening service, preached, and confirmed one person (one ·male), a young man whom I baptized at an earlier hour.

April 11, Sunday: The fifth in Lent. In St. Luke's, Hot Springs, Ark., I assisted in saying morning service, preached, confirmed eight persons (eight females), and made a brief address. At this service I placed on the altar and consecrated a pair of brass candlesticks, a memorial gift from a bereaved mother, and explained the service in a few remarks; then proceeded to the celebration of the Holy Eucharist. At 4:30 p. m. I preached again.

April 13, Tuesday: In Christ Church, Little Rock, I assisted in saying morning service and confirmed one person (one female; at 4:30 p. m. I made an address in Trinity Cathedral, after which I confirmed in private two persons (one male and one female); the candidates were presented by Rev. Dr. Tupper, Rector of Christ Church, Little Rock.

April 14, Wednesday: At 10 a. m. I received the Holy Communion at the Cathedral, Dean Degen was celebrant; at 5 p. m. I made an address in Christ Church, Little Rock and confirmed one person (one female).

April 17, Saturday: In St. John's Church; Helena, Ark., I assisted the Rector, the Rev. Richard Totten, in saying Evening Prayer and made an address.

April 18, Sunday: Palm Sunday. In St. John's Church, Helena, Ark., I assisted in saying morning service, preached, and confirmed seven persons (three males and four females), and made a short address, after which, assisted by the Rector, the Rev. Richard Totten, I celebrated the Holy Eucharist. At night I preached.

April 19, Monday: In Holy Week. I assisted the Rector in the Communion, made an address, confirmed one person (a

- colored man), and received the Holy Communion; at night I preached in the same church, confirmed two persons (two females), and made a brief address.

April 20, Tuesday: In Holy Week. In St. John's Church, Helena, Ark., at 10:30 a. m., I made an address and confirmed one person (one female) and received the Holy Communion. At night I preached.

April 21, Wednesday: In Holy Week. In St. John's, Helena, I made an address and celebrated the Holy Eucharist.

April 22, Thursday: Maunday Thursday. In St. Paul's Church, Newport, Ark., I preached at night after Evening Prayer said by Canon Estabrooke.

April 23, Good Friday: In St. Paul's Church, Newport, Ark., I assisted in saying morning service and preached; p. m. 3 o'clock I confirmed in private a sick woman; at 4 p. m. I confirmed in private a sick man and with him his wife and his wife's sister (one male and three females).

April 24, Saturday: Easter Even. Attended and took part in service at 7:30 p. m. in Trinity Cathedral, Little Rock, at which service Dean Degen formally admitted the choristers who then sang for the first time as a surpliced choir.

April 25, Sunday: Easter Day. In Trinity Cathedral, Little Rock, at 7:30 a. m. I celebrated the Holy Eucharist; at 11 a. m. I attended the midday celebration, the Dean preached; at 4 p. m. I preached, and confirmed eleven persons (male and female) and addressed the class. This confirmation makes the whole number for the Cathedral since the last council 14; at 7:30 p. m. Christ Church, Little Rock, I preached, and confirmed seventeen persons (four males and thirteen females) and addressed the class. This makes the whole number confirmed for Christ Church since the last council 28.

April 26, Easter Monday: Attended Morning Prayer at the Cathedral.

April 27, Easter Tuesday: Attended the celebration in the Cathedral at 7 a. m., and received the Holy Communion.

April 29, Thursday: At Lonoke, Ark., after Evening. Prayer said by Canon Eastabrooke, I preached, confirmed. seven persons (males and females), and addressed the class. This was the first I ever held in Lonoke.

April 30, Friday: At Lonoke, 10 a. m., I preached and, assisted by Canon Estabrooke, celebrated the Holy Eucharist. to twelve persons.

May 2, Sunday: The first after Easter. In Trinity Church, Pine Bluff, at 11 a. m., I assisted in saying morning service and preached; at 8 p. m. I preached and confirmed six persons (two males and four females), and addressed the class.

May 5, Monday: In Van Buren, Ark., at 11 a. m. I joined in Holy Matrimony Burr K. Field and Miss Juanita A. Bourland. On the same day at 8 p. m. I administered the Holy Communion at his residence to the Rev. D. McManus, now lying very seriously ill. May the Lord raise him up.

To this abstract I append the following

SUMMARY.

Eucharist celebrated............................... 50.
Sermons preached................................. 135
Addresses .... 39.
Confirmation .... 149.
Funerals... 4
Baptisms, infants 16, adults 6—Total.................. 22.
Letters dimissory given............................ 3.
Letters dimissory accepted.......................... 2.
Ordinations...................................... 1
Church consecrated............................... 1
Marriages.. 6.

The Rev. C. H. Newman, the Rev. E. C. Alcorn and the Rev. J. L. Berne are still canonically connected with this Diocese, though resident out its limits.

I may here mention that beyond the boundaries of Arkansas I have officiated at one funeral; celebrated two marriages. and baptized seven children.

In performing these duties I have traveled 7243 miles.

Brethren, there are many things that I would like to speak ·of on this occasion that I must pass in silence. But I ask you to pray earnestly that the Church in this land may be guided .aright. I believe this year will prove the most momentous that the American Church has ever experienced. It is full of perils if we are not true to our principles. It is full of blessed ·promises if we dare do our whole duty. The next General ·Convention will be the most important one ever held. May ·God guide and enlighten every soul in it. Pray for the Church.

H. N. PIERCE.

CANONICAL OFFERINGS.

COMMUNION ALMS:—*On the First Sunday of the Month.*.

FOR DIOCESAN MISSIONS:—*On the First Sunday in Lent,. and on Trinity Sunday.*

FOR THE EPISCOPATE FUND:—*On Easter Day.* '

FOR AGED AND INFIRM CLERGY, WIDOWS AND ORPHANS OF DECEASED CLERGYMEN OF THE DIOCESE:—*On Christmas Day.*

FOR THE BENEFIT OF THE RECTOR OF THE PARISH:—*On National Thanksgiving Day.*

THE FIFTEENTH ANNUAL COUNCIL

OF THE

DIOCESE OF ARKANSAS

Will Convene in Trinity Cathedral, Little Rock,
(D. V.) on the Second Wednesday after Easter,
A. D. 1887.

→⊁DIOCESE⁕OF⁕ARKANSAS⁕←

⁕JOURNAL⁕

OF THE

Fifteenth Annual Council.

———⊱1887⊰———

CANONICAL OFFERINGS.

TITLE III. CANON IV. SECTION I.

Every Parish shall make offerings for Diocesan Missions as often as the Council shall appoint, but the following offerings are required to be made and not to be diverted to other purposes, except upon special authority of the Council, viz.:

The first Sunday in Lent and Trinity Sunday, for the Benefit of DIOCESAN MISSIONS.

Easter Day, for the EPISCOPATE FUND.

National Thanksgiving Day for the FUND FOR AGED AND INFIRM CLERGY AND WIDOWS AND ORPHANS OF DECEASED CLERGYMEN OF THE DIOCESE.

Christmas Day, for the RECTOR OF THE PARISH.

It shall be the duty of the Treasurer of the Parish at least two weeks before Christmas Day to send written notice of the last named offering to each adult member of the Parish."

JOURNAL

OF THE

PROCEEDINGS

OF THE

FIFTEENTH ANNUAL COUNCIL

OF THE

𝔇𝔦𝔬𝔠𝔢𝔰𝔢 𝔬𝔣 𝔄𝔯𝔨𝔞𝔫𝔰𝔞𝔰.

Held in Trinity Cathedral, Little Rock, on the 20th, 21st, 22d, 23d and 24th Days of April, A. D. 1887.

LITTLE ROCK, ARK.
UNION PRINTING COMPANY,
1887.

THE DIOCESE OF ARKANSAS.

ORGANIZED A. D. 1871.

DIOCESAN OFFICERS.

Bishop:
THE RT. REV. H. N. PIERCE, D. D., L.L. D.,
Little Rock.

Standing Committee:
REV. INNES O. ADAMS, PRESIDENT.
THE REV. MESSRS. W. J. MILLER AND W. W. ESTABROOKE.
MESSRS. M. L. BELL AND P. K. ROOTS, SECRETARY.

Secretary of the Council;
THE REV. W. J. MILLER, Hot Springs.

Treasurer:
COL. LOGAN H. ROOTS, Little Rock.

Registrar:
THE REV. JAS. J. VAULX, Fayetteville.

Chancellor:
THE HON. M. L. BELL, Pine Bluff.

Trustee of the Episcopate Fund:
MR. P. K. ROOTS, Little Rock.

LIST OF THE CLERGY OF THE DIOCESE.

Bishop:

Rt. Rev. Henry N. Pierce, D. D., L.L. D., Little Rock.

Priests:

Rev. Innes O. Adams............ ....Pine Bluff.

Rev. E. C. Alcorn..................................St. Louis, Mo.

Rev. Joseph L. Berne...............................Little Rock.

Rev. C. A. Bruce...................................Helena.

Rev. Wallace Carnahan...........................Little Rock.

Rev. Geo. F. Degen.................................Fort Smith.

Rev. W. W. Estabrooke...........................Little Rock.

Rev. D. F. MacDonald, D. D.......................Dardanelle.

Rev. W. J. Miller....... ....Hot Springs.

Rev. C. H. Newman..............................,........ ———

Rev. Richard Totten ....Helena.

Rev. David L. Trimble.................... ....Pine Bluff.

Rev. James J. Vaulx...............................Fayetteville.

Deacon:

Rev. H. A. L. Peabody..............................Little Rock.

CANDIDATES FOR HOLY ORDERS:

Mr. Hans A. Biejby.   Mr. Andrew Wilson.

Mr. Isaiah Daniels.

LIST OF PARISHES AND MISSIONS,

WITH THE NAMES OF LAY DELEGATES.

ARKADELPHIA, St. Marks.

BATESVILLE, St. Paul's—Mr. H. S. Coleman.*

CAMDEN, St. John's.

DARDANELLE, St. Paul's.

EUREKA SPRINGS, St. James.

FAYETTEVILLE, St. Paul's—Mr. W. R. McIlroy.

FORT SMITH, St. John's—Messrs. John H. Rogers, Milton
Boyd and S. H. Wheeler.

HELENA, St. John's—Dr. H. M. Grant and Messrs. P. O.
Thweat and S. S. Faulkner.

HOPE, St. Mark's.

HOT SPRINGS, Messrs. J. P. Mellard,* G. G. Latta and Dr.
T. B. Buchanan.

LAKE VILLAGE, Emmanuel.

LITTLE ROCK, Trinity Cathedral—Messrs. T. C. Gunning,*
Alex. Robertson and Geo. W. Caruth.*

LITTLE ROCK, Christ Church—Messrs. W. W. Smith, R. H.
Parham and R. J. Polk. *Alternates*—F. D. Clark,*
W. A. Cantrell and R. L. Goodrich.*

MARIANNA, St. Andrew's—Messrs. H. P. Rogers, S. A.
Bishop and J. M. Daggett.

MORRILTON, St. Agnes'—Dr. Scarborough.*

NASHVILLE, Church of the Redeemer.

NEWPORT, St. Paul's—Mr. L. Miner.

PHILLIPS COUNTY, Grace.

PINE BLUFF, Trinity—Messrs. R. V. McCracken,* George
E. Valliant and J. B. Trulock. *Alternates*—Dr.
Brunson and M. L. Bell.*

PRESCOTT, St. James.

VAN BUREN, Trinity.

WASHINGTON, Grace.

Services have been held with more or less regularity at the following
places: Arkansas City, Bentonville, Brinkley, Cabin Creek, Clarksville,
Conway, DeVall's Bluff, Farmdale, Forrest City, Huntsville, Loneke,
Malvern, Ozark, Russellville, Searcy, Vanndale.

*Present at the Council.

PROCEEDINGS

OF THE

FIFTEENTH ANNUAL COUNCIL.

The Fifteenth Annual Council of the Diocese of Arkansas convened in Trinity Cathedral, Little Rock, Wednesday morning, the 20th day of April, 1887.

Morning Prayer was said by the Rev. W. W. Estabrooke, the Litany by the Rev. George F. Degen. The sermon was preached by the Rev. Joseph L. Berne, from the text, St. John xvii, 21. The Holy Eucharist was celebrated by the Rt. Rev. the Bishop of the Diocese, assisted by the Rev. Messrs. Bruce and Carnahan.

The Council was called to order immediately after the service, when on the calling of the roll of the Clergy canonically resident in the Diocese, the following answered to their names:

Bishop:

The Rt. Rev. H. N. Pierce, D. D., LL. D.

Priests:

Rev. Joseph L. Berne, Canon of Trinity Cathedral.

Rev. C. A. Bruce, Rector of St. Andrew's, Marianna.

Rev. Wallace Carnahan, Rector of Christ Church, Little Rock.

Rev. Geo. F. Degen, Rector of St. John's, Fort Smith.

Rev. W. W. Estabrooke, Canon of Trinity Cathedral, Little Rock.

Rev. W. J. Miller, Rector of St. Luke's, Hot Springs.

Rev. Richard Totten, Rector of St. John's, Helena.

Deacon:

Rev. H. A. L. Peabody, Trinity Cathedral, Little Rock.

The Rev. Messrs. Estabrooke and Totten were appointed a Committee on Credentials, who reported that the following Lay Delegates had been duly elected to the Council:

Trinity Cathedral, Little Rock—Messrs. T. C. Gunning, Alex. Robertson and Geo. W. Caruth.

Christ Church, Little Rock—Messrs. W. W. Smith, R. H. Parham, jr., and R. J. Polk. Alternates, Messrs. F. D. Clark, W. A. Cantrell and R. L. Goodrich.

St. John's, Fort Smith—Messrs. J. H. Rogers, Milton Boyd and S. H. Wheeler.

St. John's, Helena—Messrs. P. O. Thweat, S. S. Faulkner and Dr. H. M. Grant.

St. Luke's, Hot Springs—Messrs. J. P. Mellard, G. G. Latta and Dr. T. B. Buchanan.

St. Paul's, Newport—Mr. L. Miner.

Trinity, Pine Bluff—Messrs. R. V. McCracken, George E. Valliant and J. B. Trulock. Alternates, Dr. R. Brunson and Mr. M. L. Bell.

On the calling of the roll of Lay Delegates, the following answered to their names:

Mr. George W. Caruth,   Mr. F. D. Clark,
Mr. T. C. Gunning,   Mr. R. L. Goodrich,
                  Mr. Alex. Robertson.

A quorum being present the Rt. Rev., the Bishop, announced that the Council was ready for organization and the transaction of business.

Nominations for Secretary being in order, the Rev. C. A. Bruce offered a resolution that Mr. Geo. W. Caruth be empowered to cast the ballot for the Council for the re-

election of the Rev. W. J. Miller as Secretary. Carried.
The ballot being cast Mr. Miller was declared to be elected.

The Rev. C. A. Bruce, Rector of St. Andrew's Church,
Marianna, read a petition from that Parish asking for admission into union with the Council, as follows :

To the Fifteenth Annual Council of the Diocese of Arkansas:

We, the undersigned, hereby declare that St. Andrew's Parish, Marianna, has been duly organized by the adoption of the Articles of Association
as prescribed by the Canons of the Diocese of Arkansas; that the number
of communicants is now thirty-six (36); that a church edifice has been
erected and, entirely free from debt, has been consecrated to the service and
worship of Almighty God in due form. and we hereby respectfully ask that
St. Andrew's Parish, Marianna, Ark., be admitted into union with the
Diocese of Arkansas. Signed,

C. A. BRUCE, Rector.

JOHN M. DAGGETT, Clerk of the Vestry.

The Rt. Rev., the Bishop, appointed Rev. Geo. F. Degen
and Mr. Geo. W. Caruth a Committee on the Admission
of New Parishes, who made the following report :

It appearing that the Canons relative to new parishes have been complied with in the case of St. Andrew's Parish, Marianna, the Committee on
New Parishes recommend its admission. Signed,

GEO. F. DEGEN,
GEO. W. CARUTH.

Whereupon the Parish was duly admitted into union
with the Council by a formal vote.

The Committee on Credentials reported that Messrs. H
P. Rogers, S. A. Bishop and J. M. Daggett had been
elected Lay Delegates to this Council from St. Andrew's
Parish, Marianna. The Secretary calling their names,
Mr. J. M. Daggett appeared and took his seat.

On motion, the Council adjourned to meet on Thursday,
April 21st, at 9:30 A. M.

SECOND DAY.

TRINITY CATHEDRAL, LITTLE ROCK, ⎱
Thursday, April 21, 1887.   ⎰

Morning Prayer was said by the Rev. D. F. MacDonald, D. D., and the Rev. W. J. Miller. After service the Council was called to order by the Rt. Rev., the Bishop.

On the calling of the roll the following answered to their names who were not present at the opening of the Council: The Rev, D. F. MacDonald, D. D., and the Rev. J. J. Vaulx. Lay Delegates, Messrs. J. P. Mellard and R. J. Polk.

The following Standing Commitees were appointed:

State of the Church:

Rev. C. A. Bruce,	Mr. Alex. Robertson,
Rev. W. W. Estabrooke,	Mr. J. P. Mellard,
Rev. D. F. MacDonald, D. D.	

Constitution and Canons:

Rev. J. J. Vaulx,	Mr. Geo. W. Caruth,
Rev. I. O. Adams,	Mr. R. V. McCracken,
Rev. Geo. F. Degen,	Mr. M. L. Bell.

Finance and Auditing Committee:

Mr. R. L. Goodrich,	Mr. H. S. Coleman,
Mr. R. J. Polk,	Mr. M. L. Bell,
Mr. J. M. Daggett.	

Unfinished Business:

Rev. W. Carnaban,	Rev. J. L. Berne,
Mr. F. D. Clarke.	

The Committee on Credentials reported that Mr. H. S. Coleman had been elected a Lay Delegate to this Council, to represent St. Paul's Parish, Batesville, who answering to his name took his seat.

The Secretary read the reports of Mr. Logan H. Roots, the Treasurer of the Diocesan Fund, the Fund for Diocesan Missions, and for Aged and Infirm Clergy. [See Appendix II.] Also the report of Mr. P. K. Roots, the Trustee of the Episcopate Fund. [See Appendix III.]

On motion, they were referred to the Auditing and Finance Committee:

The Rev. George F. Degen offered the following resolution:

Resolved, That the Treasurer of the Diocese be instructed to pay the traveling expenses of the Clerical Deputies from this Diocese to the last General Convention.

Which, on motion, was referred to the Finance Committee.

The Rev. R. Totten offered the following resolution:

Resolved, That the basis of assessment on the Parishes be changed from the number of communicants to the number of confirmed persons in the Parish, and that the Committee on Constitution and Canons be requested to take the matter into consideration and report to this Council for action.

Which, on motion, was laid on the table.

The Rev. I. O. Adams and the Rev. D. L. Trimble appeared and took their seats in the Council.

On motion, the Council took a recess until 2 P. M.

AFTERNOON SESSION.

THURSDAY, April 21st.

The Council met pursuant to adjournment, and was called to order by Rev. C. A. Bruce, the senior Presbyter of the Diocese, who in the absence of the Bishop presided.

Mr. R. V. McCracken, Lay Delegate from Trinity Church, Pine Bluff, appeared and took his seat.

The report of the Finance and Auditing Committee was read, as follows :

To the Diocesan Council:

Your Committee, to whom was referred the reports of Mr. Logan H. Roots, treasurer of the Diocesan Fund, the Fund for Disabled Clergy and of Diocesan Missions, and of Mr. P. K. Roots, trustee of the Episcopate Fund, respectfully report :

That from the partial reports submitted to us by the above officers, we find the several funds properly accounted for.

Your Committee, to whom was also referred the resolution to pay the actual expenses of the Clerical Deputies from this Diocese to the last General Convention, would also report that the fund on hand from which these expenses would be drawn is $183.68. From this amount must be deducted the expenses of this Council, which we estimate at not less than $150 00, thus leaving a balance of only $33.68. The figures speak more than words.

RALPH L. GOODRICH,

R. J. POLK,

JOHN M. DAGGETT.

On motion, the report was received and the Committee discharged.

On motion of the Rev. I. O. Adams, the Secretary was directed to cast the ballot for the Council for the re-election of Mr. Logan H. Roots as Treasurer of the Diocesan Fund, the Fund for Disabled Clergy and of Diocesan Missions. The Secretary reporting that the duty was performed, Mr. Roots was declared elected.

On motion, Mr. P. K. Roots was re-elected Trustee of the Episcopate Fund in the same manner.

On motion, the Secretary was directed to cast the ballot for the Council for the election of the Rev. J. J. Vaulx as Registrar of the Diocese.

The Bishop then read his Annual Address. [See Appendix I]

On motion of the Rev. I. O. Adams, the Rt. Rev., the Bishop, was requested to appoint a Committee to consider that portion of the Bishop's address touching upon the death of the Rev. D. McManus and the Rev. W. C. Stout, and to report to the Council at the session on Friday. The following named Clergy were appointed as such Committee: the Rev. Messrs. I. O. Adams, C. A. Bruce and J. J. Vaulx.

On motion, the Council adjourned to meet on Friday at 9:30 A. M.

THIRD DAY.

TRINITY CATHEDRAL, LITTLE ROCK, }
Friday, April 22, 1887. }

The Council reassembled pursuant to adjournment. Morning Prayer was said by the Rev. J. J. Vaulx and the Litany by the Rev. I. O. Adams. After the service the Council was called to order by the Rt. Rev., the Bishop. The Secretary calling the roll, all present as on yesterday. The Hon. M. L. Bell, the Chancellor of the Diocese, appeared and took his seat. The minutes were read and approved.

The Rev. George F. Degen, President of the Standing Committee, read the report of the Committee, as follows:

To the Diocesan Council:

The Standing Committee beg leave to submit the following report:

June 2, 1886.—Met at Little Rock, the Rev. T. C. Tupper, D. D., acting President. The Committee organized by electing the Rev. Geo. F. Degen as President, and Mr. P. K. Roots as Secretary.

The Rev. Dr. Tupper presented his resignation as a member of the Committee, which was accepted, and the Rev. W. J. Miller was elected to fill the vacancy.

Consent was given to the consecration of the Rev. Edwin Gardner Weed, S. T. D., Bishop-elect of Florida.

The following resolution was passed unanimously:

"*Resolved*, That the Standing Committee of the Diocese of Arkansas, in accepting the resignation of the Rev. Tullius C. Tupper, D. D., as a member of the Committee, place on record their regret at the necessity of his resignation, and their great appreciation of his long and faithful services. Reviewing the past, we recall his promptness, zeal and sacrifice in the dis-

charge of his duties as a member and as President of the Committee, and
we beg leave to assure him that his faithful services and wise counsel shall
be held in thankful remembrance, and that our prayers shall go with him
that God may bless and prosper him in his new field of labor.

"*Resolved*, That a copy of these resolutions be forwarded to the Rev.
Dr. Tupper, with our sincere regard and esteem."

July 27.—Met at Little Rock, the Rev. Geo. F. Degen in the Chair.

Consent was given to the translation of the Rt. Rev. Daniel Sylvester
Tuttle, D. D., Missionary Bishop of Utah, to the Diocese of Missouri.

Mr. Hans A. Beijby and Mr. Andrew Wilson, postulants, were recommended to the Bishop to be received as candidates for Holy Orders.

February 18, 1887.—Met at Little Rock, the Rev. I. O. Adams, acting
President, in the Chair.

Recommended Mr. H. A. L. Peabody to the Bishop for ordination to
the Diaconate.

April 21.—Met at Little Rock, the Rev. Geo. F. Degen in the Chair.

Consent was given to the consecration of the Rev. Elisha Smith Thomas,
D. D., assistant Bishop-elect of Kansas.

Signed,   GEORGE FREDERICK DEGEN,
                                                        President.

P. K. ROOTS, Secretary.

The Rev. Geo. F. Degen read the report of the Committee on Constitution and Canons, appointed at the last Diocesan Council, recommending certain amendments and
additions to the Constitution and Canons of the Diocese.

On motion, it was resolved that the report be received
and acted on article by article, as follows:

THE CONSTITUTION.

The Committee on Constitution and Canons recommend
the following changes:

Resolved, That the Preamble, and all of Art. I preceding the words "this Church will conform," etc., be
struck out, and that the remainder of Article I, beginning
"This Church conforms," constitute the Preamble.
Adopted.

Resolved, That Art. II be struck out. Adopted.

Resolved, That Arts. III and IV be condensed and
combined to read as follows:

ARTICLE I.
OF THE CLERGY AND LAITY.

There are three orders of the Clergy, Bishops, Priests and Deacons.

The Bishop exercises all the functions of the ministry, presides over the Church by Apostolic authority, and has the sole right to ordain, to confirm, and to pronounce judicial sentence upon offenders. He governs the Church in his own Diocese, according to the Holy Scriptures and the Canons of this Church. He does not, ordinarily, act in any important matter without the advice and consent of a Standing Committee of Priests and Laymen.

The functions of Priests and Deacons are set forth in the General Canons of the Church.

The Laity are divided and organized, according to local convenience, into Parishes and Congregations. They commit the general management of their parochial business to a portion of their own number, annually elected, and called Wardens and Vestrymen. To these belong the administration of all the secular concerns of their particular Parish; but they have no part in the spiritual government of the Church, which belongs to the Clergy alone.

Adopted.

Resolved, That Art. V be changed to read as follows:

ARTICLE II.
OF THE COUNCIL.

There shall be a Council of the Diocese annually, at such time and place as the Council may from time to time determine; and in case of its failure to do so the Bishop shall appoint the time and place. In this Council the Bishop shall preside by virtue of his office; the Clergy shall sit by right of their order, and the Laity shall be represented by delegates chosen for that purpose by the Vestry of each Congregation.

The Chancellor, Secretary and Treasurer of the Diocese shall be entitled to seats in the Council, with privilege of debate, but shall have no vote, by reason of their offices.

Special Councils may be called by the Bishop, or, in case of a vacancy in the Episcopate, by the Standing Committee, when some urgent necessity may require the action of the whole Church. Without the concurrence of the Clergy and the Laity, no rule or law of the Church can be adopted, changed or done away.

Adopted.

Resolved, That Art. VI be adopted as it stands, with the omission of the last sentence, to read Art. III. Adopted.

Resolved, That Art. VII be adopted as Art. IV. Adopted.

Resolved,   That Art. VIII shall read as follows :

ARTICLE V.
OF THE ADMINISTRATION OF JUSTICE.

The Clergy, Priests and Deacons, may be tried by an Ecclesiastical Court, composed of Presbyters chosen for that purpose. But there shall be no such trial except on due presentment, and according to the Canon for the trial of Clergymen set forth in this Diocese, and the rules of ecclesiastical law.

Adopted.

Resolved,   That the following be adopted as

ARTICLE VI.
OF THE TENURE OF CHURCH PROPERTY.

The Rector, Wardens and Vestry, or other persons in whose names the property of any Church or Parish may be vested, shall not, by deed, or any other means, without the consent of the Bishop and Standing Committee, under their hands given, grant, alienate, or otherwise dispose of any lands, messuages or hereditaments, in them vested for the use and benefit of said Church, nor charge nor encumber the same to any person whatever.

Adopted.

Resolved,   That Art. IX be adopted as Art. VII, changing the word " proposition " to " proposal." Adopted.

On motion, the Constitution as amended was adopted as a whole. [For Constitution see Appendix VII.]

On motion of Mr. Geo. W. Caruth, the Secretary was directed to have 250 copies of the Constitution as amended printed, and to distribute the same to the Parishes of the Diocese.

A communication was received from the Superintendent of the Arkansas School for the Blind, inviting the members of the Council to visit that institution.

On motion, it was resolved that the invitation be accepted with thanks, and that the Council visit the School on Saturday at 3 P. M.

The Rev. I. O. Adams read the report of the Committee on Memorials, as follows :

To *The Diocesan Council:*

Your Committee, to whom was referred that portion of the Bishop's Address that officially announced the deaths of the Rev. D. McManus and the Rev. W. C. Stout, Priests, offer the following resolution :

Resolved, That while this Council with deep sorrow hears the announcement that since its last meeting two of our brethren have been taken from us, the evidence it has that they died in the " communion of the Catholic Church, in the confidence of a certain faith, in the comfort of a reasonable, religious and holy hope," in favor with God and "in perfect charity with the world," is an assurance that they now, in the Paradise of God, rest from their labor, until *they,* with *all the faithful departed, in the glory of the Resurrection,* shall be raised to Life.

And, in testimony of this, the Secretary is requested to prepare and insert in the Journal of this Council a Memorial Page.

Signed,   C. A. BRUCE,
                                         J. J. VAULX,
                                         I. O. ADAMS.

On motion, it was ordered that the report of the Committee on Constitution and Canons be the first order of business for this afternoon.

The hour having arrived for the election of the Standing Committee of the Diocese, the Rev. W. W. Estabrooke and Mr. R. L. Goodrich were appointed tellers. The following named persons were elected on the first ballot: the Rev. Messrs. I. O. Adams, W. W. Estabrooke and W. J. Miller, and Messrs. M. L. Bell and P. K. Roots.

On motion, it was resolved that the next Annual Council meet on the second Thursday after Easter, 1888, in St. Andrew's Church, Marianna.

Mr. John M. Daggett, acting for the Rev. C. A. Bruce, chairman, read the report of the Committee on the State of the Church. [See Appendix IV.]

On motion, the Council took a recess until 2 P. M.

AFTERNOON SESSION.

FRIDAY, April 22d.

The Council reassembling, it was called to order by the Rt. Rev., the Bishop, at 2 P. M.

On motion, the Secretary was requested to cast the ballot for the Council for the Hon. M. L. Bell as Chancellor of the Diocese.

The time for the order of the day, the consideration of the report of the Committee on Constitution and Canons, having arrived, the Rev. Mr. Degen read the report, recommending certain changes and additions to the Canons, which, on motion, was acted on article by article, as follows:

CANONS.

The Committee recommend that the following changes be made in the Canons:

TITLE I.

Resolved, That Section 1, Canon I, be struck out. Adopted.

Resolved, That Sec. 1 read as follows:

The Members of the Council shall consist of the Clergy and Laity of the Diocese having the following qualifications: Every Clergyman having been admitted canonically by the Ecclesiastical authority shall be a member of the Council; but no Clergyman shall be entitled to vote at the election of a Bishop unless he shall have been canonically and actually a resident of the Diocese for six months. Every Parish, regularly organized as required by the Constitution, shall be entitled to send three delegates to the Council, and every duly organized Mission Station shall be entitled to send one delegate; provided, always, that such delegates shall be communicants of the Protestant Episcopal Church, and that no person under ecclesiastical censure or process, whether Clergyman or Layman, shall be allowed a seat in the Council.

Adopted.

Resolved, That Sec. 2 read as follows:

The first standing committee appointed by the Bishop after the Council has been duly organized, and the last to make a report, shall be a Committee on Ways and Means, consisting of one Priest and two Laymen, whose duty it shall be to consider the condition of each Parish and make an equitable assessment upon them, to be applied to the Episcopate Fund and the current expenses of the Diocese.

The Lay Delegates from each Parish to the Diocesan Council shall, as a necessary part of their credentials, present to the Council the receipt of the

Treasurer of the Diocese, or other satisfactory evidence, showing the payment of this assessment. Provided, That the Council, when formally organized, may, for good and sufficient reasons, excuse any delinquent Parish from the payment of any portion or all of this assessment.

Adopted.

Resolved, That in Sec. 1, Canon II, the word "is" be substituted for the words "may be." Adopted.

Resolved, That Sec. 1, Canon VIII, be amended to read as follows.

At every Council the presiding officer shall appoint standing committees on—

1. Credentials of Lay Delegates.
2. Ways and Means.
3. Admission of New Parishes.
4. State of the Church.
5. Auditing and Finance.
6. Unfinished Business.
7. Constitution and Canons.

And on such other subjects as he may deem requisite to put the Council in possession of properly proposed information for their action.

Adopted.

Resolved, That the following be added as—

Sec. 2. He shall also appoint a Committee, to be known as the Committee on Judiciary, to be composed of three Laymen, the Chancellor being one and to be chairman, who shall remain as members of such committee until their successors are appointed.

Adopted.

Resolved, That the following be added to Canon IX, to form—

Sec. 2. A Trustee shall be annually elected by the Council, who shall be known as the Trustee of the Episcopate Endowment Fund, and who shall be specially charged with the responsibility for the accumulation and investment of said Fund. As often as the amount received by him shall aggregate the sum of $50.00 he shall invest the same, under the supervision of the Bishop and the Standing Committee of the Diocese. It shall be the duty of said Trustee to make annual reports to the Council of the condition of said Fund and the investment thereof.

Adopted.

Resolved, That Canon X, Sec. 1, read as follows:

Deputies to the General Convention shall be chosen at each Annual Council, and shall continue in office until others are chosen.

Adopted.

Resolved, That Sec. 2 read:

Deputies to the General Convention shall be chosen by ballot, the Clergy and Laity separately electing the Deputies and substitutes of their respective orders.

Adopted.

Resolved, That Sec. 3 read:

Substitutes for Deputies shall be elected one at a time, and in the event of the resignation or inability of any Deputy, Clerical or Lay, such vacancy shall be filled by the substitutes in the order of election, and the journal must show the order of election of all substitutes, Clerical and Lay.

Adopted.

Resolved, That Sec. 4 be struck out. Adopted.

Resolved, That the following be introduced as—

CANON XIII.
OF THE CHANCELLOR OF THE DIOCESE.

There shall be elected by the Council an officer learned in the law under the title of Chancellor of the Diocese, whose duty it shall be to act as the legal counselor of the Bishop and of the Standing Committee in matters affecting the interests of the Church, as his professional counsel may be asked or required.

The Chancellor of the Diocese shall hold his office for the term of three years, and in the event of a vacancy the Annual Council next ensuing shall elect a successor for the full term of three years.

Adopted.

On motion, Sec. 2, Canon III, was referred back to the Committee.

Resolved, That in Sec. 3 of the same Canon the words "and its precincts after its consecration" be struck out. Adopted.

On motion, the Council adjourned to meet Saturday morning at 9:30.

FOURTH DAY. ·

TRINITY CATHEDRAL, LITTLE ROCK, }
Saturday, April 23, 1887. }

Morning Prayer was said by the Rev. Canon Estabrooke
and the Rev. D. L. Trimble. The Council was called to
order, the Rt. Rev., the Bishop, in the Chair.

On motion, the calling of the roll was dispensed with.
The minutes of the previous day's proceedings were read,
and after certain corrections were approved.

The Bishop appointed the Rev. I. O. Adams and Messrs.
Geo. W. Caruth and R. L. Goodrich as the Committee on
Ways and Means.

The Rev. J. J. Vaulx offered a resolution that the action
whereby Sec. 2, Canon I, Title I, had been adopted, be
reconsidered. Carried.

The Rev. J. J. Vaulx moved that Sec. 1, Canon I of
Title I, be retained as it originally stands in the Canons
of the Diocese.

The Rev. C. A. Bruce offered an amendment to Mr.
Vaulx' motion, that the Canon be amended by striking
out the words "six months." Lost.

The vote being taken on Mr. Vaulx' resolution, it was
lost.

On mo ion, the Canon, as amended, was re-enacted.

The consideration of the report of the Committee on
Constitution and Canons being resumed, the Rev. Mr. De-
gen offered the following resolution concerning Sec. 2,
Canon III, Title II, which had been referred back to the
Committee :

TITLE II.

Resolved, That Title II, Canon III, Sec. 2, be changed
to read as follows :

To the Rector belongs the control of the keys of the church, and the right to open the Church for public prayer, sermons, catechetical instructions, marriages, funerals and baptisms, and all the rites and ceremonies authorized by the Protestant Episcopal Church in America, at all times when he may deem proper.

Adopted.

Resolved, That Canon IV be struck out. Adopted.

Resolved, That Canon V be numbered Canon IV, and that Sec. 2 be changed to read as follows:

In it shall be entered the names of all persons baptized, confirmed, married and buried in the Parish. It shall contain a list of all communicants, of all families, and of all individuals not thus included, belonging to the Parish or regularly attending its services. It shall also contain a record of all collections made in the Church.

Adopted,

Resolved, That Canon VI be numbered Canon V, that Canon VII be numbered Canon VI, and that Canon VIII be numbered Canon VII. That in Canon VIII all that follows the words "express order of the Council" be struck out. Adopted.

Resolved, That Canon IX be numbered Canon VIII, and that in Sec. 2 of the same the word "Church" be changed to "Council." Adopted.

TITLE III.

Resolved, That in Title III, Canon I, the word "annually" be added at the end of Sec. 4. Adopted.

Resolved, That Canon II, Sec. 1, be changed to read: "All organized Mission Stations shall be under the control of the Bishop and Missionary Committee." Adopted.

Resolved, That these words be added at the end of Sec. 3 of the same Canon: "Who shall have the right to debate but not to vote." Adopted.

Resolved, That Canon IV be changed to read as follows:

Every Parish shall make offerings for Diocesan Missions as often as the Council shall appoint, but the following offerings are required to be made and not to be diverted to other purposes except upon special authority of the Council, viz.: The first Sunday in Lent and Trinity Sunday, for the benefit of Diocesan Missions; Easter Day, for the Episcopate Fund; National Thanksgiving Day, for the Fund for aged and infirm Clergy and widows and orphans of deceased Clergymen of this Diocese; Christmas Day, for the Rector of the Parish. It shall be the duty of the Treasurer of the Parish, at least two weeks before Christmas Day, to send written notice of the last-named offering to each adult member of the Parish. Adopted.

On motion, a recess was taken until 2 P. M.

AFTERNOON SESSION.

SATURDAY, April 23d.

The Council assembled, pursuant to adjournment, at 2 P. M. In the absence of the Secretary, the Rev. Mr. Degen was appointed Secretary *pro tem.*

The consideration of the report of the Committee on Constitution and Canons was resumed, as follows:

Resolved, That Canon V be struck out. Adopted.

Resolved, That Canon VI be changed to read as follows:

The Bishop of the Diocese shall be, ex officio, President of the Missionary Committee. The Committee shall report, through its Secretary, to the Annual Council. The Treasurer shall receive, hold and pay out funds, subject to the order of the Committee. His accounts shall be audited by the Council as a separate and distinct Fund.

Adopted.

TITLE IV.

Resolved, That in Title IV, Canon I, Sec. 4, the word " they " be inserted after the words " performance of this duty." Adopted.

Resolved, That in Canon II the following changes be made in the form of organization of new Parishes: In the Preamble change the word " Congregation " to " Parish." In Art. I omit the words " or Congregation." In Art. 4 substitute the words " baptized members " for the word " communicants," and omit all that follows the words " brought before the Easter meeting." Adopted.

Resolved, That the Order of Business of the Annual Council be amended to read as follows:

1. Calling the Roll.
2. Presentation of the Certificates of Lay Delegates.
3. Appointment of Committee on Credentials.
4. Report of Committee on Credentials.
5. Election of Secretary.
6. Appointment of Standing Committees.
7. Annual Address of the Bishop.
8. Report of the Standing Committee.
9. Reports of Special Committees.
10. Reports of Trustees of the several Funds.
11. Report of the Auditing Committee.
12. Election of Treasurer.
13. Election of the Standing Committee.
14. Report on the State of the Church.
15. Election of Deputies to the General Convention.
16. Election of Trustees of the several Funds.
17. Election of Registrar.
18. Election of Chancellor.
19. Report of Committee on Unfinished Business.
20. Miscellaneous Business.
21. Report of Committee on Ways and Means.

Adopted.

On motion of Mr. Geo. W. Caruth, the further consideration of the report was suspended until after the return of the members of the Council from their visit to the School for the Blind.

The hour having arrived for the election of Deputies to the General Convention, the Rev. W. W. Estabrooke and Mr. R. L. Goodrich were appointed tellers. The following Deputies were elected on the first ballot:

Clerical.	*Lay.*
Rev. I. O. Adams,	Mr. J. P. Mellard,
Rev. W. J. Miller,	Mr. H. S. Coleman,
Rev. W. W. Estabrooke.	Mr. Geo. W. Caruth.

There being one Clerical and one Lay Deputy remaining to be elected a second ballot was taken, which resulted in the election of

Rev. J. J. Vaulx.   Mr. J. M. Daggett.

The Council then took a recess until 4 P. M., in order to visit the State Institution for the Blind.

---

4 O'CLOCK, P. M.

The Council re-assembled, the Rt. Rev., the Bishop, in the Chair.

The election of alternate Deputies to the General Convention being in order, the following-named persons were duly elected:

ALTERNATE DEPUTIES.
[In the order of their election.]

Clerical.	Lay.
1. Rev. C. A. Bruce,	1. Mr. R. J. Polk,
2. Rev. D. F. MacDonald, D.D.	2. Mr. R. V. McCracken.
3. Rev. D. L. Trimble,	8. Mr. P. O. Thweat,
4. Rev. J. L. Berne.	4. Mr. John H. Rogers.

The election of Trustees of the University of the South resulted as follows: The Rev. Geo. F. Degen and Messrs. G. W. Caruth and F. D. Clarke.

On motion, the Secretary was directed to cast the ballot for the Council for the Rev. I. O. Adams as Trustee of the General Theological Seminary.

On motion of the Rev. I. O. Adams, the action taken on Canon IV, Title III, was reconsidered.

The Rev. Mr. Degen moved that the Canon be repealed. Lost.

On motion of the Rev. Mr. Adams, the Canon was amended by substituting the word " work" for " station."

The report of the Committee on Constitution and Canons being resumed, the report of the Committee on Title V was read.

On motion, it was resolved that the consideration of the report be postponed, and that the Council adjourn to meet at 8 P. M.

NIGHT SESSION.

SATURDAY, April 23d.

Council assembled pursuant to adjournment at 8 P. M., the Rev. C. A. Bruce in the Chair.

The Council at once took up the consideration of the report of the Committee on Constitution and Canons, on

TITLE V.

The Secretary of the Committee offered the following resolution :

Resolved, That in Title V, Sec. 3 be amended to read—

In order to bring a Clergyman to trial, a charge shall be made to the Judiciary Committee, signed by at least two communicants of the Diocese, one of whom shall be a Priest, affirming that the charge is true and that the accusers will make it good. Thereupon, it shall be the duty of the Secretary of the Committee to furnish the accused a copy of the charge, and require an answer to be filed thereto within thirty days from the date of the receipt of said copy. On the coming in of the answer, a copy of the same shall be furnished the parties making the charge, accompanied by a notice that all proof on the issue, of both parties, must be taken and filed with the Secretary within ninety days from the date of the notice. All proof must be by depositions taken before an officer authorized to administer oaths, and must be upon reasonable notice, and filed with the Secretary. Both parties have the right to be present at the taking of the depositions, and to be represented by counsel. At the end of the ninety days the hearing shall close, and thereupon the said Committee shall consider the charges, and if two members of the same shall deem the charges clearly within the scope of the Canons, and sustained by the proof, it shall be so declared in writing, and they shall file all the papers in the case with the Standing Committee of the Diocese. In case the accused is a member of the Standing Committee, the two remaining Clerical members shall choose a Priest of the Diocese to supply his place, and for the purposes of this trial the Priest so chosen shall be considered a member of the Standing Committee.

Adopted.

The Rev. Mr. Vaulx offered a resolution that when completed Title V be adopted as a whole. Carried.

The Bishop appeared and took the Chair.

The following resolutions were offered and acted on :

Resolved, That Sec. 4 be amended to read as follows :

On the receipt of the presentation and papers, it shall be the duty of the Clerical members of the Standing Committee to consider the charge, and if, in the opinion of at least two of said Clerical members, the charge be clearly within the scope of the Canons, and sustained by the proof adduced, they shall impartially select by lot seven Presbyters of the Diocese, to meet on a certain day after ninety days, at a certain place within which the accused may reside. Immediately upon their selection, the names shall be forwarded to the accused, and he shall forthwith send to the Secretary of the Standing Committee the names of those to whom he objects, if any. Three of the seven may constitute the court, and the accused shall have the right to object to any individual until the number is reduced to three. If no member is excepted to, all that assemble shall sit as a court. The court shall be judges both of law and fact.

Adopted.

Resolved, That Sec. 6 be struck out. Adopted.

Resolved, That to Sec. 7 the following words be added:

Provided, however, that all the evidence heard at the trial shall be reduced to writing at the time it is given, and signed by the witness before he leaves the room.

Adopted.

Resolved, That in Sec. 9 the words " the Bishop shall declare him indefinitely suspended. And " be struck out, and the word "degredation" changed to "deposition." Adopted.

Resolved, That in Sec. 10 the following words be struck out: " And on any new matter that the prosecution may add thereto ;" also the words, " but the judgment of guilty shall not be rendered on less evidence than is required in a civil court ;" also the words, " to the Bishop." And that the following be added at the end of this section :

Immediately upon rendering the verdict, it shall be the duty of the clerk of the court to deliver all the pleadings and evidence to the Bishop, who shall give notice to both the judge advocate and the accused, that on a day fixed he will hear the case on appeal, if the accused be found guilty. At such hearing the accused shall have the right to be represented by a Lay Communicant learned in the law, and the Bishop may call two of the neighboring Diocesans, who snall sit with him at the hearing, to assist him in arriving at a correct determination.

Adopted.

Resolved, That Sec. 11 be struck out.   Adopted.

Resolved, That in Sec. 12, the words "within twenty days," and also the words, "Furthermore, the Bishop may, at his discretion, pronounce a lighter sentence than that indicated by the court," be struck out, and that the word "degredation" be replaced by the word "deposition." Adopted.

Resolved, That in Sec. 13 the word "Bishop" be struck out, and also the words "affidavits may be received as evidence, and." Following this, that the word "may" be changed to "must.' Also, that the last sentence of the section be struck out.   Adopted.

Resolved, That in Secs. 16 and 22 the word "degredation" be replaced by "deposition."   Adopted.

Rev. Geo. F. Degen moved that Title V, as amended, be adopted as a whole.   Carried.

Rev. Mr. Degen moved that the Canons, as amended, be adopted as a whole.   Carried.   [For Canons as amended, see Appendix VII.]

The Rt. Rev., the Bishop, appointed as the Standing Committee on Judiciary, the Chancellor of the Diocese, the Hon. M. L. Bell, and Messrs. G. W. Caruth and H. S. Coleman.

The Rev. Mr. Adams, as Chairman of the Committee on Ways and Means, read its report. [See Appendix V.] Which, on motion, was adopted, and the Committee discharged.

The Rev. Mr. Degen offered the following resolution :

Resolved, That each Parish may, at its option, pay its assessment in quarterly installments.   Carried.

The following resolution was unanimously adopted :

Resolved, That the Secretary be instructed to convey to the Superintendent of the Arkansas School for the Blind the thanks of this Council for the courtesies extended to them, and to express their gratification at the evidence given them of the admirable manner in which the institution is conducted.

On motion, it was

Resolved, That the thanks of the Council be returned to the Clergy and Congregation of Trinity Cathedral, and to the Rector and people of Christ Church, for their very generous hospitality.

It was ordered that 500 copies of the Journal be printed for distribution.

On motion, the Council adjourned to meet Sunday evening, at Christ Church, after evening service.

FIFTH DAY.

CHRIST CHURCH, LITTLE ROCK, }
SUNDAY, April 24th, 8 P. M. }

Evening Prayer was said by the Rev. D. F. MacDonald, D. D., and the Rev. Messrs. Bruce and Degen. The sermon was preached by the Rt. Rev., the Bishop.

The Council being called to order immediately after the service, the Rev. Mr. Adams offered a resolution that the Committee on Constitution and Canons be discharged, and that the Rev. Mr. Degen be instructed to prepare blanks for parochial reports and other blanks that may be needed for the work of the Council. Carried.

The Rev. Mr. Carnahan, Chairman of the Committee on Unfinished Business, reported that there was nothing further demanding the attention of the Council.

The Rev. Mr. Peabody moved that the thanks of this Council be given to the Secretary for his services. Carried.

The Rev. Mr. Vaulx moved that the minutes that had not been submitted to the Council be submitted to the Bishop for his examination and approval. Carried.

After a few earnest words of encouragement by the Bishop, and the bestowal of his blessing, the Council adjourned *sine die.*

HENRY N. PIERCE,

Bishop.

ATTEST:

W. J. MILLER, *Secretary.*

In Memoriam.

THE REV. DAVID McMANUS,
PRIEST.

Born April 19th, 1815, at Carrick-on-Shannon, County Roscommon, Ireland.

Baptized and confirmed in the Roman Catholic Church, in that place.

Educated at the Royal College of Maynooth, Dublin.

Ordered Deacon there on the eve of Whitsun Day, 1841, by the Most Rev. Daniel Murray, Archbishop of Dublin, and by the same Prelate ordained Priest on the following day.

Came to the United States soon after and was appointed Chaplain of the Sisters of the Sacred Heart, New York City, under the R. C. Bishop Hughes.

While there renounced Romanism and was received into the American Church by the Rt. Rev. B. T. Onderdonk, D. D.

First took Missionary work at Van Buren, Ark. Was appointed Chaplain in the U. S. Army and stationed at Fort Gibson, Ind. Ter. During the civil war took charge of St. Paul's Church, Fayetteville, Ark. Subsequently he became Rector of St. Mary's Church, Eugene City, Oregon; St. John's Fort Smith, Ark.; Grace Church, Phillips County, Ark. During his closing years he took up his residence at Fort Smith, becoming Rector of Trinity Church, Van Buren.

Entered into rest June 17th, 1886.

JESU, MERCY.

In Memoriam.

✝

REV. WILLIAM CUMMING STOUT,

PRIEST.

Born February 18, 1824, in Green County, Tenn.

Baptized and confirmed by the Rt. Rev. Leonidas Polk, D. D.

Graduated at Kemper College, Missouri; was also a student at Nashotah and the Theological Seminary at Alexandria, Va.

Ordered Deacon by the Rt. Rev. Wm. Meade, D. D., of the Diocese of Virginia.

Ordained Priest by the Rt. Rev. Leonidas Polk, D. D.

For several years was Rector of St. Paul's Church, Fayetteville, Ark., and for one year officiated at Christ Church, Little Rock.

Owing to feeble health he had no cure for many years, but did what missionary work he was able to perform.

Since the organization of the Diocese he had occupied the office of Registrar, which office he filled at the time of his death.

For some time before his death he had charge of the infant Church at Morrilton, Ark., where he died on the 11th day of December, 1886, aged 63 years.

"Blessed are the dead who die in the LORD: even so saith the SPIRIT; for they rest from their labors.

APPENDIX I.

THE BISHOP'S ANNUAL ADDRESS.

Dear Brethren, of the Clergy and Laity:

Assembled in this Fifteenth Annual Council of the Diocese of Arkansas, we find cause both for sorrow and for comfort. Sorrow—because we miss familiar faces that were wont to greet us lovingly at our Annual Councils. Since we last met together, a scant year ago, two of our Clergy, eldest in age and residence, have been summoned from this world and gone to their reward. The Rev. David McManus—the Rev. William C. Stout. Ever since I became acquainted with Arkansas these names have been household words with me. Just before we met in Council last year, I administered the Holy Communion to the Rev. D. McManus, then lying on what proved to be, ere long, his death-bed. I found him then in patience and faith humbly waiting the manifestation of God's will, and fully reconciled to it, whether the decision were for life or for death. He had been reared in the Roman Communion, and had for some years exercised the functions of the priesthood therein. But years ago he became truly a Catholic. From time to time, strong efforts were made to draw him back into Romanism. But he was too well grounded in theology to be influenced by Roman arguments and mediæval sophistries. He died a true Catholic —without a shadow of doubt resting upon his mind as to the wisdom of the step taken by him years before, when he professed his faith in the Holy Catholic Church,

renounced allegiance to the Bishop of Rome and rejected
Rome's unauthorized additions to the Catholic faith.   Mr.
McManus was a scholar, and no mean theologian, though
sometimes in danger, in reacting against Romanism, of
leaning towards opposite errors, as great, if not as danger-
ous.   But if he sometimes leaned in that direction, he did
not fall.   He was a man of much simplicity of character,
and, till years and infirmities accumulated upon him, active in the duties of the ministry.   The few last years of
his life were labor and sorrow, and Death came to him as
a kindly messenger from the Lord, to release him from his
struggles.

The Rev. William C. Stout, prevented by his want of
health, and more especially by the uncertainty of his
health, from engaging in the steady work of the ministry,
lamented, more deeply than most persons dreamed of, what
he considered his enforced quiescence.   And it was always
a source of great regret to me that he was not of a more
vigorous constitution.   For the Church lost much by not
having the full benefit of his clear, logical head, of his well-
stored mind, of his gentle and generous heart.   Few men
were more fluent conversationalists than he.   And his talk
was not mere talk—he was full of information upon almost
all conceivable subjects.   His reading was very extensive
and very varied, and he had read nothing which he had
not digested by careful and discriminating thought, and,
so far as what was valuable was concerned, made his own
by assimilation.   He had information enough to furnish
well a dozen minds for eminent success in different depart-
ments of life.   Had he been less universal, he would have
seemed much greater to the mass of mankind.   He had a
wise head, and a loving and true heart.   He rests in peace,
and we feel his absence.   Let us cherish his memory.

The death of these two brethren is peculiarly impressive
to me personally.   Of the six Clergy resident in Arkansas
when I entered upon this field, the only one now resident

in the Diocese is the Rector of St. Andrew's, Marianna. All the rest have removed to distant regions on earth, or have entered the Paradise of God. We will soon follow— soon, though the years before us be many and long. Nothing remains in one stay, except the Kingdom of God, which, taken as one grand whole, knows no decay, but goes on ever from strength to strength. And from this glorious fact arises comfort in the midst of sorrow.

Nor is it in the advance of the grand whole alone, that our hearts are cheered. We may well feel that as a Diocese we are progressing, gradually but steadily, towards a better position. One Church, St. Andrew's, Marianna, has been consecrated during the past year. Two others are completed: Christ Church, Little Rock, the occupation of which fills my heart with joy and with gratitude to God, and Trinity Church, Van Buren. In both these Parishes I now look for new and vigorous growth. Another Church has been begun, at Nashville, and I trust will be ready for occupancy in a few months. Nashville is a new field, which has received very little culture from the Church, and which is even now bearing good fruit. I am hoping to hear every day that a new Church has been begun at Morrilton. A goodly sum has been subscribed, and I trust the work will not be delayed. New fields are opening before us every month. At Forrest City, Arkansas City and Nashville, regular though infrequent services have been established for the first time since our last Annual Council, and I am now more anxious than ever to increase our movable Clerical force, for place after place is calling for our services.

The Clerical changes have been few during the year. The Rev. T. C. Tupper, D. D., has removed to the Diocese of Kansas, and is working very successfully there. His place has been ably filled by the Rev. Wallace Carnahan, from the Diocese of Alabama. The Rev. J. L. Berne, who was for awhile residing beyond our borders, has returned to us,

3

and, as a Canon of Trinity Cathedral, is doing good service in a wide field in Southern Arkansas. The Rev. Geo. F. Degen, late Dean of the Cathedral, is now the successful Rector of St. John's Church, Fort Smith. Mr. H. A. L. Peabody, transferred as a candidate for Holy Orders from the Diocese of Wisconsin in November last, was on the 9th day of March ordained to the Diaconate. Two candidates for Deacons' Orders have been admitted within a twelve-month—Mr. H. A. Beijby and Mr. Andrew Wilson. They are now preparing themselves for the Diaconate, and I expect to see our Clerical force increased by their ordination before many months pass. I pray God that the steps taken to establish settled Pastors at Batesville and at Van Buren may ere long prove successful. With these points well filled I should feel that we had taken a long step forward. There is a need for one or more additional Clerical workers in connection with Trinity Cathedral and the missionary field supplied by the Cathedral Clergy. The opening of St. Philip's Mission, a most promising enterprise, specially calls for this increase of laborers, and I am now planning to secure such increase, if possible. Efforts are being made to build a Church for this interesting Mission, which I hope may prove successful. I commend the work to your prayers, and I ask for your aid. I must not omit to mention here that a debt of about $600 resting on the rectory of St. Paul's Church, Fayetteville, has been raised, by the diligence and energy of the Rector mainly. On the whole, I count the past year a successful one, and while it is worthy of being remembered for results already attained, it abounds in promises for the future, Time forbids me from going farther into detail, and I forbear to even mention many things I should like to discuss at length.

I submit now, for your consideration, a brief abstract of my journal. Though dry enough, it may be of use. My last report ended with May 6, 1886.

May 7, Friday: At 11 a.m., in Trinity Church, Pine Bluff, I read my Annual Address, and celebrated the Holy Eucharist, assisted by Dean Degen, at the opening services of the Fourteenth Annual Council of the Diocese of Arkansas. I presided at the sessions of the Council till its adjournment.

May 8, Saturday: Attended Morning Prayer, and presided in the Council. At night attended a reception given to the Council at Mr. R. V. McCracken's.

May 9, Sunday, the second after Easter: In Trinity Church, Pine Bluff, at 11 a.m., I celebrated the Holy Eucharist, assisted by Rev. Dr. MacDonald. At 4 p.m., I preached at a missionary meeting and made an address. At night, after evening service and sermon, I made a brief address and declared the Fourteenth Annual Council of the Diocese of Arkansas adjourned *sine die.*

May 10, Monday: In Trinity Church, Pine Bluff, at 7 a.m., I celebrated the Holy Eucharist, assisted by the Rev. J. J. Vaulx.

May 16, Sunday, the third after Easter: At 11 a.m., in Grace Church, Phillips county, Ark., I preached, confirmed two persons, (one male and one female,) and, assisted by the Rev. C. A. Bruce, celebrated the Holy Eucharist.

May 23, Sunday, the fourth after Easter: At 11 a.m., in St. Andrew's Church, Marianna, Ark., I preached and, assisted by the Rev. C. A. Bruce, celebrated the Holy Eucharist. At 8 p.m., I preached, confirmed five persons, (four males and one female,) and addressed the class.

May 24, Monday: I said Evening Prayer and preached at Forrest City, and baptized four children.

May 30, Sunday, the fifth after Easter: At 11 a.m., in Camden, Ark., I said morning service, preached, and celebrated the Holy Eucharist. At 8 p.m., I said Evening Prayer, preached, confirmed two persons, (two females,) and addressed them.

June 3, Thursday, Ascension Day: At 10:30 a.m., in Trinity Cathedral, Little Rock, I preached, and received the Holy Communion, Dean Degen being celebrant. Gave letters dimissory to the Rev. Joseph L. Berne, to the Diocese of Texas.

June 6, Sunday after Ascension: In the Cathedral, Little Rock, I said morning and evening services, celebrated the Holy Eucharist, and preached twice.

. June 7, Monday: Gave letters dimissory to Rev. Tullius C. Tupper, D. D., to the Diocese of Kansas.

June 9, Wednesday: Attended the Commencement exercises of Columbia Institute, Columbia, Tenn., and delivered the diplomas to the graduating class and made a brief address. Attended a meeting of the trustees of the Institute.

June 13, Sunday, Whitsunday: At 7:30 a.m., in St. Peter's Church, Columbia, Tenn., I celebrated the Holy Eucharist. At 11 a.m., I attended morning service in the same Church.

June 20, Trinity Sunday: At 10:30 a.m., in St. Paul's Church, Dardanelle, Ark., I assisted in saying morning service, preached, and, assisted by Rev. Dr. MacDonald, celebrated the Holy Eucharist. I assisted in saying Evening Prayer and preached again.

June 27, Sunday, the first after Trinity: I said morning service and preached in Christ Church, Little Rock. At 5:30 I preached in Trinity Cathedral.

June 29, Tuesday, St Peter's Day: At 8 p.m., in Grace Church, Washington, Ark., I said Evening Prayer and preached.

July 4, Sunday, the second after Trinity: At 11 a.m., in St. Paul's Church, Fayetteville, I preached and, assisted by the Rev. J. J. Vaulx, celebrated the Holy Eucharist.

July 8, Thursday: In St. James' Church, Eureka Springs, Ark., after Evening Prayer said by the Rev. J. J. Vaulx, I preached.

July 9, Friday: Preached at night in St. James' Church, Eureka Springs.

July 10, Saturday: At Eureka Springs, I confirmed in private one person, a lady, sick. At night attended a meeting of the communicants of the Parish.

July 11, Sunday, the third after Trinity: At 11 a.m., in St. James' Church, Eureka Springs, Ark., I assisted in saying morning service, preached and, assisted by Rev. J. J. Vaulx, celebrated the Holy Eucharist. At 8 p.m., I preached, confirmed eight persons, (two males and six females,) and addressed the class.

July 18, Sunday, the fourth after Trinity: At 11 a.m., in St. Paul's Church, Fayetteville, Ark., I preached. At 5:30 p.m., I preached and confirmed four persons, (one male and three females,) and addressed the class. At 8 p.m., I preached again.

July 25, Sunday, the fifth after Trinity and St. James' Day: At 11 a.m., in Christ Church, Little Rock, I assisted in saying the morning service, preached, and celebrated the Holy Eucharist. At 5:30 I preached in Trinity Cathedral.

July 27, Tuesday: This day Mr. Hans Adolph Beijby and Mr. Andrew Wilson were admitted as candidates for Deacon's Orders in the Diocese of Arkansas.

August 1, Sunday, the sixth after Trinity: At 11 a.m., in St. John's Church, Fort Smith, Ark., I said morning service, preached, and celebrated the Holy Eucharist.

August 3, Tuesday: At 10:30 a.m., in St. John's Church, Fort Smith, I joined in Holy Matrimony Lorion Miller, of Albuquerque, New Mexico, and Miss Wrenetta G. Bostick, of Fort Smith.

August 8, Sunday, the seventh after Trinity: At 10:30 a.m., in St. Peter's Church, Columbia, Tenn., I said morning service, preached, and celebrated the Holy Eucharist. At 5 p.m., I baptized a child, and made an address on Holy Baptism.

August 10, Tuesday: At Col. Bethel's residence, six miles from Columbia, Tenn., I joined in Holy Matrimony Hugh M. Neely, of Memphis, Tenn., and Mrs. Mary B. McCown.

August 11, Wednesday: I baptized two children at Columbia, Tenn.

August 15, Sunday, the eighth after Trinity: At 7 a.m., in St. Peter's Church, Columbia, I celebrated the Holy Eucharist. At 10:30 I preached.

August 22, Sunday, the ninth after Trinity: At 7 a m., in St. Peter's Church, Columbia, Tenn., I celebrated the Holy Eucharist. At 10:30 I said morning service and preached. At 5 p.m., in the same Church, I joined in Holy Matrimony Albert W. Warren and Miss Ella N. Nix.

August 24, Tuesday, St. Bartholomew's Day: At 10:30, in St. Peter's Church, Columbia, I preached and celebrated the Holy Eucharist.

August 27, Friday: At 8 p.m., I preached in the Church of St. Mary Magdalene, Fayetteville, Tenn.

August 29, Sunday, the tenth after Trinity: At 10:30 I preached in St. Peter's Church, Columbia, Tenn.

September 4, Saturday: I buried from Trinity Cathedral, Little Rock, my second son, Henry Walker Pierce, being assisted in the service by my son, the Rev. A. W. Pierce, of Mobile, Ala. Accepted letters dimissory of Rev. Wallace Carnahan, from the Diocese of Alabama.

September 5, Sunday, the eleventh after Trinity: At 11 a.m., in Trinity Cathedral, I celebrated the Holy Eucharist, assisted by Dean Degen. At 5:30 p.m., I preached.

September 8, Wednesday: Made my annual report to the Board of Missions.

September 9, Thursday: Sent the Bishop of Alabama canonical notice of my acceptance of Rev. Wallace Carnahan's letters dimissory.

September 12, the twelfth after Trinity: At 11 a.m., I preached in Trinity Cathedral. At 5:30 p.m., I assisted in saying Evening Prayer.

September 19, Sunday, the thirteenth after Trinity. At 11 a.m., in St. Andrew's Church, Marianna, Arkansas, I preached, confirmed four persons, (three males and one female,) addressed the class and, assisted by the Rev. C. A. Bruce, celebrated the Holy Eucharist. At 7:30 I preached again and confirmed one person, (one female).

September 20, Monday: At 8:30 a.m., I attended a meeting of the congregation, and made an address exhorting them to pay off the church debt.

September 26, Sunday, the fourteenth after Trinity: At 11 a.m., in Grace Church, Washington, Ark., I said morning service, preached, and celebrated the Holy Eucharist. At 4:45 p.m., I said Evening Prayer and preached again.

September 27, Monday: At 4:30 p.m., in St. Mark's Church, Hope, Ark., I said Evening Prayer, baptized a child and preached.

October 3, Sunday, the fifteenth after Trinity: At 11 a. m., in Christ Church, Little Rock, the Rector, Rev. Wallace Carnahan, said the Litany and read the Epistle. I said the communion office, preached and, assisted by the Rector, celebrated the Holy Eucharist. At 4 p.m., I preached in Trinity Cathedral.

October 6, Wednesday: At 10:30 a.m., in St. James' Church, Chicago, Ill., I attended the opening of the General Convention and assisted in the services.

October 7, Thursday : In attendance on the sessions of the House of Bishops.

October 8, Friday : Made an address at the Board of Missions.

October 9, Saturday : At the House of Bishops.

October 10, Sunday, the sixteenth after Trinity : At 10:30 attended Divine service at St. Mark's Church, Chicago, and heard a very fine missionary address from Bishop Thompson of Mississippi. The following week was spent in attendance at the House of Bishops and the Board of Missions.

October 17, Sunday, the seventeenth after Trinity : I preached at morning service in St. Mark's Church, Chicago. The week following I was in daily attendance at the House of Bishops, etc.

October 23, Saturday : Attended the celebration of the Holy Eucharist in St. James' Church, Chicago, and took part in the election of two missionary bishops, one for Utah and Nevada, the other for Wyoming and Idaho.

October 24, Sunday, the eighteenth after Trinity : In the Cathedral at Davenport, Iowa, at 7:30 a.m., I celebrated the Holy Eucharist. At 11 a.m. I preached in the same Church. At 5 p.m., after Evening Prayer said, I lectured at St. Katharine's School. At 7:30 p.m., I preached again at the Cathedral.

October 25, Monday : In daily attendance at the sessions of House of Bishops till October 28th, when the General Convention adjourned *sine die.*

October 31, Sunday, the nineteenth after Trinity : At 11 a.m., in Trinity Cathedral, Little Rock, I preached and, assisted by Canon Berne, celebrated the Holy Eucharist. At 4 p.m., I preached again.

November 1, Monday, All Saints' Day : In Trinity Cathedral, I preached and celebrated the Holy Eucharist at

10 a.m. I was assisted in the services by Canons Estabrooke and Berne.

November 7, Sunday, the twentieth after Trinity: At
11 a.m., in the Cathedral, Little Rock, I celebrated the
Holy Eucharist. Preached at 4 p.m.

November 10, Wednesday: At Little Rock, I joined in
Holy Matrimony Andrew J. Martin, of Alabama, and Mrs.
Katie B. Ashley.

November 14, Sunday, the twenty-first after Trinity:
In the Cathedral, Little Rock, I said morning service,
preached; and celebrated the Holy Eucharist. At 4 p.m.,
I said Evening Prayer and preached.

November 17, Wednesday: At 11 a.m., assisted by
Canon Estabrooke, I buried from the Cathedral, Halfdan
Vassal Degen, son of the Dean. In connection with the
funeral rites I celebrated the Holy Eucharist.

November 21, Sunday, next before Advent: In Trinity
Cathedral, at 11 a.m., I celebrated the Holy Eucharist, assisted by Dean Degen. Preached at 4 p.m.

November 25, Thursday, Thanksgiving Day: I celebrated the Holy Eucharist in the Cathedral, Little Rock.

November 26, Friday: Sent the Bishop of Wisconsin
notice of my acceptance of letters dimissory of Mr. H. A.
L. Peabody, a candidate for Holy Orders.

November 28, Sunday, the first in Advent: At 11 a.m.,
in the Cathedral, Little Rock, I celebrated the Holy Eucharist. At 7 p.m., in the Knights of Honor Hall, at Forrest City, Ark., after Evening Prayer said by Canon Estabrooke, I preached and confirmed two persons, (one male
and one female,) and addressed the class.

November 30, Tuesday, St. Andrew's Day: At 11 a.m.,
I consecrated to the service and worship of Almighty God,
St. Andrew's Church, Marianna, Ark. Rev. R. Totten
and Canon Estabrooke said Morning Prayer. Major Rag-

land read the instrument of donation. The Rev. C. A. Bruce read the sentence of consecration. I preached and celebrated the Holy Eucharist, assisted by the Rev. C. A. Bruce.

December 1, Wednesday: In St. Andrew's I preached at morning service.

December 5, Sunday, the second in Advent: In Trinity Cathedral, Little Rock, at 11 a.m., I celebrated the Holy Eucharist. Preached at 4 p. m.

December 12, Sunday, the third in Advent: At 11 a.m., in St. David's Church, Austin, Texas, I preached. At 4 p. m., I preached again.

December 19, Sunday, the fourth in Advent: I preached at 11 a.m. and again at 4:30 p.m., in St. David's Church, Austin, Texas.

December 25, Saturday, Christmas Day : In the Cathedral, Little Rock, Ark., at 7:30 a.m., I celebrated the Holy Eucharist. At 10:30 I said morning service, preached and celebrated the Holy Eucharist.

December 26, Sunday, the first after Christmas and St. Stephen's Day: At 10:30 a.m., in the Cathedral, Little Rock, I said morning service, preached, and celebrated the Holy Eucharist. At 4 p.m., I said Evening Prayer and preached.

December 27, Monday, St. John's Day: In the Cathedral, I celebrated the Holy Eucharist and lectured on the day.

December 28, Tuesday, Holy Innocents : At 10:30 a.m., in the Cathedral, Little Rock, I celebrated the Holy Eucharist. At 2 p.m., I officiated at a funeral in Little Rock.

January 1, 1887, Saturday, the Circumcision: At 10:30 a.m., in the Cathedral, Little Rock, I celebrated the Holy Eucharist and lectured on the day.

January 2, Sunday, the second after Christmas: At 11

a.m., in the Cathedral, Little Rock, I said morning service, preached and celebrated the Holy Eucharist. At 7 p.m. I said Evening Prayer and preached.

January 6, Thursday, the Epiphany: At 11 a.m., in St. Luke's Church, Hot Springs, Ark., I preached, confirmed four persons, (four females,) and addressed the class; after which, assisted by the Rector, the Rev. William J. Miller, I celebrated the Holy Eucharist. At 3:30 p.m., I confirmed in private two persons, (one male and one female).

January 9, Sunday, the first after Epiphany : At 11 a. m., in Grace Church, Washington, Ark., I preached, confirmed two persons, (one male and one female,) and addressed the class; after which, assisted by Canon Berne, I celebrated the Holy Eucharist. At 7:30 p.m., I preached again.

January 10, Monday: In the Methodist Church, Nashville, Ark., at 7:30 p.m., after Evening Prayer, said by Canon Berne, I preached, and confirmed eight persons, (two males and six females,) and addressed the class.

January 11, Tuesday: Assisted by Canon Berne, I celebrated the Holy Eucharist at Nashville. In the afternoon, at Center Point, Ark., I baptized a child, and confirmed a young man prevented by ill health from reaching Nashville. At 7:30 I preached again in the Methodist church at Nashville.

January 16, Sunday, the second after Epiphany: At 11 a.m., in Grace Church, Newport, Ark., I preached and, assisted by Canon Estabrooke, celebrated the Holy Eucharist. At 7 p.m. I preached again, confirmed nine persons, (three males and six females,) and addressed the class.

January 17, Monday: At 7 p.m., in St. Paul's Church, Batesville, Ark., after Evening Prayer said by Canon Estabrooke, I preached.

January 18, Tuesday: Assisted by Canon Estabrooke, I celebrated the Holy Eucharist in St. Paul's, Batesville, Ark. At 7 p.m. I confirmed in private one person, (a fema'e). The candidate was presented by Canon Estabrooke.

January 19, Wednesday: Accepted letters dimissory of Rev. J. L. Berne, from the Diocese of Texas, and gave Canonical notice of acceptance.

January 23, Sunday, the third after Epiphany : At 7:30, in the Cathedral, Little Rock, I celebrated the Holy Eucharist. At 11, I said morning service, preached, and again celebrated the Holy Eucharist. At 4:30 I said Evening Prayer and preached.

January 25, Tuesday, the Conversion of St. Paul: At 10:30, in the Cathedral, Little Rock, I lectured on the day, and celebrated the Holy Eucharist.

January 30, Sunday, the fourth after Epiphany: At 11, in Trinity Church, Pine Bluff, I preached at morning service and, assisted by the Rector, Rev. I. O. Adams, celebrated the Holy Eucharist. At 7:30 I preached, confirmed three persons, (one male and two females,) and addressed the class.

February 2, Wednesday, the Purification: At 10:30, in the Cathedral, Little Rock, I lectured on the day, and celebrated the Holy Eucharist assisted by Canon Berne.

February 6, Sunday, Septuagesima: At 7:30 a.m., in Cathedral, Little Rock, I celebrated the Holy Eucharist. At 11 I said morning service, preached, and celebrated the Holy Eucharist. At 2:45, at St. Philip's Mission, I said Evening Prayer and preached. At 4:30, in the Cathedral, I said Evening Prayer and preached.

February 13, Sunday, Sexagesima: At 11 a.m., in St. John's Church, Helena, Ark., I preached, confirmed four persons, (four females,) and, assisted by the Rector, Rev.

Richard Totten, celebrated the Holy Eucharist. At 7:30, I preached again.

February 14, Monday: At 7:30 p.m., in St. Andrew's Church, Marianna, Ark., after Evening Prayer said by the Rev. C. A. Bruce, I preached and confirmed two persons, (two females,) and addressed the class.

February 15, Tuesday: At 7:30 p.m., in St. Andrew's Church, I preached.

February 20, Sunday, Quinquagesima: At 11 a.m., in the Cathedral, Little Rock, I celebrated the Holy Eucharist. At 2:45 I said Evening Prayer and preached at St. Philip's Mission. At 4:30 I preached in Trinity Cathedral.

February 23, Ash Wednesday: At 10:30 I said the ante-communion and preached in Trinity Cathedral.

February 25, Thursday, St. Matthias' Day: After Morning Prayer in Trinity Cathedral, said by Canons Estabrooke and Berne, I lectured on the day and celebrated the Holy Communion.

February 25, Friday: I said Morning Prayer and Litany in the Cathedral.

February 27, Sunday, the First in Lent; At 7:30 a.m., in the Cathedral, Little Rock, I celebrated the Holy Eucharist. At 11, the Rev. D. L. Trimble said Morning Prayer and Litany ; I preached, and celebrated the Holy Eucharist assisted by the Rev. Mr. Trimble. At 2:45, I said Evening Prayer and preached at St. Philip's Mission. At 4:30, I said Evening Prayer and preached in the Cathedral.

March 1, Tuesday: At 8 p.m., in St. John's Church, Camden, Ark., after Evening Prayer said by Canon Berne, I preached, confirmed seven persons, (six males and one female,) and addressed the class.

March 3, Thursday: At 10 a.m., in Trinity Cathedral, Little Rock, I assisted in saying morning service and gave a short lecture.

March 6, Sunday, the second in Lent: At 7:30 a.m., in the Cathedral, Little Rock, I celebrated the Holy Eucharist, At 11, I preached and celebrated the Holy Eucharist. At 2:45, I preached at St. Philip's Mission. At 5, I preached in the Cathedral.

March 9, Wednesday: In Trinity Cathedral, Little Rock, Ark., I ordained to the Diaconate Henry Amos Lamson Peabody. Canon Estabrooke said Morning Prayer. The Rev. Wallace Carnahan, Rector of Christ Church, Little Rock, preached the sermon. Canon Berne read the Epistle. Canon Estabrooke presented the candidate. I said the rest of the service and celebrated the Holy Eucharist, unaided, as the rubric seems to require.

March 11, Friday: At 7:30 p.m., in St. Paul's Church, Fayetteville, Ark., after evening prayer said by Rev. J. J. Vaulx, I preached.

March 13, Sunday, the third in Lent: In St. Paul's, Fayetteville, at 11 a.m., I preached and, assisted by the Rector, Rev. J. J. Vaulx, celebrated the Holy Eucharist. At 7:30 I preached again, confirmed four persons, (one male and three females,) and addressed the class.

March 15, Tuesday: At 8 p.m., in St. James' Church, Eureka Springs, Ark., I preached and confirmed three persons, (three females,) and addressed the class.

March 16, Wednesday: At 7:30 a.m., in St. Paul's Church, Fayetteville, Ark., I preached and confirmed one person, (one female).

March 19, Saturday: I baptized two children in Van Buren, Ark.

March 20, Sunday, the fourth in Lent: In Trinity Church, Van Buren, at 11 a.m., I assisted in saying morning service and preached. At 7:30 p.m., in St. John's Church, Fort Smith, after Evening Prayer said by Rev. G. F. Degen and Dr. MacDonald, I preached, confirmed sixteen persons, (four males and twelve females,) and addressed the class.

March 22, Tuesday: In Trinity Church, Van Buren, Ark., Rev. Dr. MacDonald saying Evening Prayer, I baptized a young girl, preached, confirmed three persons and addressed the class. After service I met the Vestry of Trinity Parish, and consulted with them as to their having a resident Clergyman.

March 23, Wednesday: At 7:30 p.m., at Morrilton, Ark., after Evening Prayer said by Rev. Dr. MacDonald, I preached.

March 27, Sunday, the fifth in Lent: At 11 a.m., in Trinity Cathedral, Little Rock, I preached and celebrated the Holy Eucharist. At 2:45 I preached at St. Philip's Mission, and at 5 I preached in the Cathedral.

April 3, Sunday, the sixth in Lent: At 11 a,m., in Trinity Cathedral, Little Rock, the Rev. H. A. L. Peabody said Morning Prayer and Litany and read the Epistle. The Rev. Henry T. Heister, of the Diocese of Chicago, preached, and I celebrated the Holy Eucharist assisted by Rev. Mr. Heister. At 2:45, at St. Philip's Mission, the Rev. Mr. Peabody said Evening Prayer and preached, and I baptized two adults. At 5 p.m., I preached in the Cathedral.

April 10, Sunday, Easter Day: At 7:30 a.m., in Trinity Cathedral, Little Rock, I celebrated the Holy Eucharist. At 11 I preached in the Cathedral. Rev. Mr. Heister celebrated the Holy Eucharist. At 2:45, at St. Philip's Mission, Rev. Mr. Peabody said Evening Prayer, Rev. Mr. Heister preached. I confirmed six persons, (five males and one female,) and addressed the class. At 5 p.m., in the Cathedral, Little Rock, Rev. Mr. Peabody said Evening

Prayer and preached, and I confirmed three persons, (three females,) and addressed the class. At 7:30 p.m., in Christ Church, Little Rock, I preached and confirmed twenty-six persons, (four males and twenty-two females,) and addressed the class.

April 11, Monday in Easter week: At 10:30 a.m., in the Cathedral, Little Rock, I celebrated the Holy Eucharist and presided at the Easter Monday meeting.

April 17, Sunday, the first after Easter: At 11 a.m., in Trinity Cathedral, Little Rock, I celebrated the Holy Eucharist, assisted by Rev. Mr. Peabody. Canon Berne preached. At 5 p.m., I preached.

To this fleshless skeleton of my record, I here append a still more condensed

SUMMARY:

Sermons.. 128
Addresses 33
Eucharists.. 71
Confirmed.. 143
Baptisms (children 12, adults 3,)........................... 15
Marriages 4
Funerals 3
Candidates for Holy Orders—
    Admitted...... 2
    Received by transfer... 1
Ordinations, to Diaconate.................................... 1
Churches consecrated. 1
Letters dimissory given.. 2
Letters dimissory received.................................... 2
Number miles traveled.....................................8890

All of the baptisms, marriages and funerals are recorded in the different parishes where the services were performed and need not be taken into account by the Committee on the State of the Church in making up the statistics of the Diocese.

I cannot close this address without a single word in regard to the General Convention held in Chicago in October last. No General Convention ever showed so catholic a spirit. None has ever been so fraught with grand, glorious consequences, as I believe will follow that of 1886.

Now, I will detain you no longer from the important duties before you, but will close with the earnest prayer that the Holy Spirit will guide you into a knowledge of what you ought to do, and will give you grace to enable you to faithfully perform the same.

H. N. PIERCE, *Bishop.*

APPENDIX II.

REPORT OF THE TREASURER OF THE DIOCESE.

THE DIOCESAN FUND.

RECEIPTS.

Balance on hand..	$238 50
June 14, 1886, St. John's, Fort Smith.................	27 00
April 19, 1887, St. Paul's, Newport	10 00
" St. Luke's, Hot Springs...............	40 00
April 21, St. John's, Fort Smith..........................	52 00
" Christ Church, Little Rock	75 00
" Trinity Cathedral, Little Rock..............	20 00
" St. John's, Helena.............................	41 00
" St. Paul's, Batesville..........................	12 50
" Trinity, Pine Bluff..............................	84 00
Total..	$550 00

DISBURSEMENTS.

May 11, 1886, T. C. Tupper	$100 00	
May 18, Secretary's expenses....................	2 75	
July 1, Secretary's expenses....................	14 10	
July 2, Kellogg Prtg Co., prtg Proceedings	66 50	
Nov. 26, W. W. Astor, Gen'l Conv. Assmnt	39 00	
Nov. 16, Episcopate F'd, P. K. Roots, treas.	41 97	
Total......................................	——$264 32	
Balance on hand.......:...............................	$285 68	

DIOCESAN MISSION FUND.

RECEIPTS.

Balance on hand	$ 53 50
March 25, 1887, Newport	1 45
April 4, Pine Bluff	5 05
April 12, Christ Church, Little Rock	49 05
April 21, Christ Church, Little Rock	108 13
Total	$217 18

DISBURSEMENTS.

Oct. 2, 1886, Dean Degen	$30 00	
Feb. 8, 1887, Bishop Pierce	23 50	
Total		$ 53 50
Balance on hand		$163 68

FUND FOR DISABLED CLERGY.

Balance on hand	$ 95 48
December 29, 1886, St. Luke's, Hot Springs	12 00
Jan. 7, 1887, Pine Bluff	5 50
Balance on hand	$112 78

LOGAN H. ROOTS,
Treasurer and Trustee.

APPENDIX III.

REPORT OF TRUSTEE OF EPISCOPATE FUND.

RECEIPTS.

Balance on hand..	$138	03
Nov. 16, 1886, From Diocesan Fund......................	41	97
Jan. 24, 1887, Logan H. Roots.........	10	00
Jan. 24, P. K. Roots..	10	00
Feb. 1, St. Luke's, Hot Springs..........................	29	40
April 12, Missions of Nashville and Washington...	18	20
April 21, Christ Church, Little Rock...................	110	40
April 21, St. John's, Helena...............................	24	00
April 21, Trinity, Pine Bluff.............................	19	20
April 22, Trinity, Little Rock............................	9	15
Total	$410	35

DISBURSEMENTS.

May 15, 1886, Building Association Dues.....$20	00
June 16, Building Association Dues............ 20	00
July 17, Building Association Dues............ 20	00
Aug. 16, Building Association Dues............ 20	00
Sept. 16, Building Association Dues............ 20	00
Oct. 16, Building Association Dues.............. 20	00
Nov. 16, Building Association Dues............ 20	00
Dec. 16, Building Association Dnes............ 20	00
Jan. 15, 1887, Building Association Dues..... 20	00
Feb. 10, Taxes 1886, lots 10, 11, 12, block 200 25	99

Feb. 16, Building Association Dues............ 20 00
March 16, Building Association Dues........... 20 00
April 16, Building Association Dues 20 00
    Total ....——$265 99

    Balance on hand............................ ......$144 36.

ASSETS OF THE FUND.

The expenditures required for the ensuing twelve months are as follows :

To complete Building Association payments........$240 00
To pay taxes on the lots, about............ .... 40 00
Total necessary disbursements during next twelve
   months....................... .... 280 00
From which deducting cash on hand 144 36
Leaves to be raised this year.......................... ... 135 64

By raising this small additional amount, our funds in May, 1888, will amount to $3500, as follows :

Lots 10, 11, 12, block 200, 14th and Spring sts.....$1500 00
Building Association stock............................. 2000 00

    Total $3500 00

P. K. ROOTS, Trustee.

APPENDIX IV.

REPORT OF COMMITTEE ON THE STATE OF THE CHURCH.

LITTLE ROCK, ARK., April 22, 1887.

To the Diocesan Council:

Your Committee on the State of the Church beg leave to submit the following report:

Although we have many reasons for profound gratitude for the condition of our Diocese, we have cause for deep sorrow in that we have lost two of our most venerable and beloved Priests since the assembling of our last Council. The Diocese, we have no doubt, will cherish their memories and award every godly sympathy to their bereaved families. We would say more were it not that this subject has been referred to a special committee of this Council.

Your Committee can offer the most unqualified congratulations for the unwearied, effective and most encouraging labors of our Bishop. Never before in the history of the Diocese have so many points been reached by the services of the Church, nor in any one year have there been such numbers of baptisms, and of communicants added, as in this. These solid indications of prosperity are largely due to the Cathedral system organized by the Bishop, enabling the Church to introduce her services into places which could not otherwise be reached.

As one of the indications above-mentioned, we might name a number of Parishes that have erected churches and rectories and liquidated all debts thereon. Also there are other points which have but recently been reached by the Church, that either seriously contemplate or are actually taking steps to do likewise.

But owing to the difficulty of properly supporting a sufficient number of Clergy in the field, the Church must necessarily feel very much crippled in what she desires to accomplish. Nevertheless, we bless God, there are earnest and efficient laborers among the laity, who are holding services at different points, under the direction of the Bishop and Canons of the Cathedral and other Clergy, thus keeping alive the Church, and causing her not to be a stranger any longer among the people. By this instrumentality one strong Parish (if not more) has been built up in this Diocese. We would therefore earnestly recommend that the number of these Lay workers may be multiplied and tendered every encouragement possible.

We must not fail to commend the important work that is being accomplished among the colored people in this city by the Cathedral Clergy. St. Philip's Mission has been successfully established, inasmuch as six persons have been already confirmed, and promises greater success in the future.

There is an unprecedented movement at present, which must continue, in the development of the State; population is increasing at an amazing rate; new railroads are building and more are projected; and new towns are springing up along the lines, opening up a vast work for the Church; we hear the Macedonian cry on every side— " Who will come over and help us?"

The impending and most vital question is, therefore, whence shall come the means?

In the meantime, amid these difficulties, let us abate not our courage, but, with the help of God, continue to preach the Gospel to the poor, and feed the scattered flock of Christ, in the abiding hope that at no distant day this Diocese will reap a harvest pleasing to the Head of the Church and honorable to herself.

C. A. BRUCE, *Chairman.*
W. W. ESTABROOKE,
DAVID F. MacDONALD,
J. P. MELLARD,
ALEX. ROBERTSON.

APPENDIX V.

REPORT OF COMMITTEE ON WAYS AND MEANS.

To the Diocesan Council:

Your Committee, having in view the ability and size of the various Parishes, report the following—

SCHEDULE OF PAROCHIAL ASSESSMENT:

Batesville, St. Paul's	$ 20 00
Camden, St. John's	10 00
Dardanelle, St. Paul's	5 00
Fayetteville, St. Paul's	20 00
Fort Smith, St. John's	100 00
Helena, St. John's	50 00
Hope, St. Mark's	5 00
Hot Springs, St. Luke's	40 00
Little Rock, Trinity Cathedral	25 00
Little Rock, Christ Church	160 00
Marianna, St. Andrew's	15 00
Newport, St. Paul's	10 00
Phillips County, Grace	5 00
Pine Bluff, Trinity	45 00
Van Buren, Trinity	10 00
Washington, Grace	5 00
Total	$525 00

Respectfully submitted,

I. O. ADAMS,
GEO. W. CARUTH,
RALPH L. GOODRICH.

APPENDIX VI.

PAROCHIAL REPORTS.

ST. MARK'S CHURCH, ARKADELPHIA.

No report.

UNORGANIZED MISSION, ARKANSAS CITY.

Baptisms: infants, 2.   Communicants, 4.

OFFERINGS.

Subscriptions...$ 50 00

APPROPRIATIONS.

Mission purposes.. 50 00

Mrs. J. G. WARFIELD, *Treasurer.*

REMARKS—This report is from March 10, 1887, at which time services were commenced. Services are held on the second Sunday in each month.

W. W. ESTABROOKE,
Canon Trinity Cathedral.

ST. PAUL'S CHURCH, BATESVILLE.

No report.

ST. JOHN'S CHURCH, CAMDEN.

Baptisms: infants, 2. Confirmations, 7. Communicants: added anew, 7; present number, 37. Sunday School: teachers, 5; pupils, 25.

REMARKS—I have celebrated the Holy Eucharist about four or five times since I took the Mission charge of this Church.   J. L. BERNE,
Priest in Charge.

ST. PAUL'S CHURCH, DARDANELLE.

Baptisms: infants, 2. Communicants: last reported, 12; added anew, 2; present number, 14. Marriages, 1. Burials, 2. Sunday school: teachers, 3; pupils, 25.

OFFERINGS.

Communion alms...$ 4 00
Value of Church property............................$2,500 00

REMARKS—The Church property is in perfect repair and entirely free from debt. The Parish meets with strong opposition from the various sects, but still it wholesomely grows.

DAVID F. MacDONALD,
Rector.

ST. JAMES' CHURCH, EUREKA SPRINGS.

Baptisms: adults, 8; infants, 2; total, 10. Confirmations, 12. Communicants: present number, 30. Marriages, 2. Burials, 1. Sunday school: teachers, 3.

OFFERINGS.

Offerings...$ 67 95
Other sources..   27 60
                                                            _____
    Total ....$ 95 55

APPROPRIATIONS.

Mission purposes... $67 95
On hand... 27 60

Total $95 55
Value of Church property................................$100 00

JAS. J. VAULX,
Priest in Charge.

ST. PAUL'S CHURCH, FAYETTEVILLE.

Baptisms: adults, 1; infants, 12; total, 13. Confirmations, 9. Communicants: present number, 109. Marriages, 2. Burials, 4. Sunday school: teachers, 3.

OFFERINGS.

Communion offerings......................................$ 115 63
Weekly offertory... 57 87
Other sources... 899 72

Total $1,072 72

APPROPRIATIONS.

Parochial purposes, Rector's salary, etc............ $1,015 47
Jewish Missions 3 60
Charleston sufferers...................................... 10 15
"Pious and charitable uses," C. A.................... 43 50
Total 1,072 72

Value of Church property........................$6,000 00

W. R. McILROY,
Treasurer of the Parish

REMARKS—In the above is included work done and communicants at Bentonville and Huntsville. Our Rectory is now out of debt, and I hope next year to report more contributions to outside purposes.

JAS. J. VAULX, *Rector.*

UNORGANIZED MISSION, FORREST CITY.

Baptisms: infants, 2. Confirmations, 2. Communicants, 7.

OFFERINGS.

Communion alms	$	1 80
Subscriptions	101	30
Other sources, Ladies' Guild	50	00
Total	$153	10

APPROPRIATIONS.

Mission purposes	101	30
Other purposes	50	00
" Pious and charitable uses," C. A.	1	80
Total	$153	10

Mrs. JOHN GATLING,
Treasurer of the Mission.

REMARKS—This report is from June, 1886, to Easter, 1887. Services are held on the fourth Sunday of each month.　　W. W. ESTABROOKE,
Canon Trinity Cathedral.

ST. JOHN'S CHURCH, FORT SMITH.

Baptisms: adults, 10; infants, 16; total, 26. Confirmations, 16. Communicants: last reported, 110; added anew, 16; removed into the Parish, 24; present number, 150. Marriages, 1. Burials, 7. Sunday school: teachers, 11. pupils, 114.

OFFERINGS.

Communion alms	$	57 20
Weekly offertory	710	25
Rentals and subscriptions	285	15
Other sources	1,825	31
Total	$2,877	91

Convention assessment.................................$ 52 00
Parochial purposes....................................... 2,685 35
Diocesan Missions, paid to Bishop........... ....   11 10
Colored Missions 66 91
" Pious and charitable uses," C. A....................   57 20
Other purposes..   5 35

Total..$2,877 91
Value of Church property...........................$15,000 00

M. N. BLAKEMORE,
Treasurer of the Parish.

REMARKS—A commodious rectory has been built during the year. This report covers only the last four months of the year, since the present Rector took charge, except $876.00 of the offerings paid on the rectory.

GEORGE FREDERIC DEGEN,
Rector.

ST. JOHN'S CHURCH, HELENA.

Baptisms: infants, 10. Confirmations, 4. Communicants: last reported, 109; added anew, 4; removed into the Parish, 5; total, 118; removed from the Parish, 4; present number, 114. Marriages, 1. Burials, 4. Sunday school: teachers, 10; pupils, 90.

Communion alms...$ 49 15
Weekly offertory... 1,302 85
Other sources... 542 95
Convention assessment.....................................   41 00

Total...$1,935 95

APPROPRIATIONS.

Convention assessment...................................$ 41 00
Episcopate Fund 24 00
Parochial purposes.. 1,581 43
Domestic Missions..   17 55
Foreign Missions..   4 10
Jewish Missions...   4 45
" Pious and charitable uses," C. A..................   78 40

Total $1,750 93
Value of Church property............................$12,000 00
Amount of Insurance ou Church property........ 3,200 00

RICHARD TOTTEN,
Rector.

P. O. THWEATT, Senior Warden; GREENFIELD
QUARLES, Junior Warden; S. S. FAULKNER, Secretary;
S. S. FAULKNER, Treasurer.

ST. MARK'S, HOPE.

Baptisms: infants, 1. Communicants: removed from
the Parish, 1; died, 1; present number, 10. Burials, 2.

REMARKS—This Parish has been dead for years. It is
lately picking up. A number of repairs on the Church
building have been made, new platforms for the altar, and
a very pretty vestry or sacristry has been added by making
partitions. The people have awakened to renewed interest
by the mercy of Almighty God. I have celebrated the
Holy Eucharist, and taught them all I could of Church
doctrine.   J. L. BERNE,
Priest in Charge.

ST. LUKE'S CHURCH, HOT SPRINGS.

Baptisms: adults, 1; infants, 8; total, 9. Confirmations,
6. Communicants: last reported, 60; added anew, 20;

present number, 80. Marriages, 5. Burials, 5. Sunday School: teachers, 7; pupils, 65.

OFFERINGS.

Communion alms...$	64	80
Weekly offertory...	423	43
Rentals and subscriptions...............................	908	30
Other sources........	205	72
Total..$1,602		25

APPROPRIATIONS.

Convention assessment...................................	40	00
Episcopate Fund...	29	40
Parochial purposes...... 1,267		62
Diocesan Missions..	6	82
Domestic Missions........	23	22
Bible and Prayer-Book Society..	5	00
Aged and infirm Clergy	12	00
"Pious and charitable uses," C. A....................	64	80
Other purposes...	100	50
Total...$1,549		36
Value of Church property....................$11,000		00
Amount of insurance on Church property........ 2,200		00

J. A. POLHAMIUS,
Treasurer of the Parish.

REMARKS—During the year the Parish completed the Rectory Fund,' and has now in its treasury $2,500.00. A handsome sterling silver paten and chalice have been purchased, also a full set of vestments. The robing room has been furnished at an expense of $30.00 or $40.00, so that the Church building is now complete in all of its appointments. W. J. MILLER,
Rector.

EMMANUEL CHURCH, LAKE VILLAGE.
No report.

TRINITY CATHEDRAL, LITTLE ROCK.

Baptisms: adults. 3; infants, 21; total, 24. Confirmations, 9. Communicants: last reported, 63; removed into the Parish, 2; total, 65; removed from the Parish, 20; present number, 45. Marriages, 1. Burials, 3. Sunday school: teachers, 4; pupils, 30.

OFFERINGS.

Weekly offerings	$ 962	98
Other sources	545	22
Total	$1,508	20

APPROPRIATIONS.

Convention assesment	20	00
Episcopate Fund	8	00
Parochial purposes	1,476	70
Other purposes	3	35
Total	$1,508	20

H. A. L. PEABODY,
Treasurer of the Parish.
W. W. ESTABROOKE,
Senior Canon.

CHRIST CHURCH, LITTLE ROCK.

Baptisms: adults, 8; infants, 10; total, 18. Confirmations, 26. Marriages, 4. Burials, 10. Communicants: last reported, 329; present number, 460. Sunday school: teachers, 23; pupils, 232; total, 255.

OFFERINGS.

Church building	$11,547	00
Parish expenses	2,417	00
Communion alms	132	90
Gifts to the Rector	205	00
Council assessment	75	00

Episcopate Fund	110	90
Diocesan Missions	178	28
Domestic Missions	110	00
Foreign Missions	114	40
Widows and Orphans of deceased Clergy	33	00
University of the South	50	00
Conversion of the Jews	12	00
American Church Building Fund	5	00
Total	$14,990	48

REMARKS—This report covers only the period of my charge, seven and one-half months, except for the items of Church Building and Parish Expenses, which cover the Council year. On Easter Day was held the first service in the new Church, an occasion of Thanksgiving to God.

WALLACE CARNAHAN,

——

Rector.

ST. ANDREW'S CHURCH, MARIANNA.

Baptisms: adults, 4; infants, 8; total, 12. Confirmations, 12. Communicants: last reported, 29; added anew, 12; total, 41; removed from the Parish, 4; dropped, 1; present number, 36. Marriages, 3. Sunday school: teachers, 5; pupils, 30.

OFFERINGS.

Communion alms	$23	00
Weekly offerings, since Nov. 30, 1886	19	25
Total	$42	25

APPROPRIATIONS.

Parochial purposes	19	25
" Pious and charitable uses," C. A.	23	00
Total	$42	25

H. P. ROGERS,
Treasurer of the Parish.
C. A. BRUCE,
Rector.

ST. AGNES' CHURCH, MORRILTON.

Communicants—
    Present number... 28

OFFERINGS.

Communion alms...$5 00

REMARKS—I can render no full account of this Parish, because I have only twice visited the point. However, the people are to build a Church this summer. They have the money on hand to finish it throughout. The building will cost about $1,300.00.

D. F. MacDONALD,
Priest in Charge.

CHURCH OF THE REDEEMER, NASHVILLE.

Baptisms: adults, 5. Confirmations, 10. Communicants: last reported, 3; added anew, 10; present number, 13. Sunday school: teachers, 4; pupils, 12.

OFFERINGS.

Weekly offerings...$5 00

APPROPRIATIONS.

Episcopate Fund $5 00

M. LEE,
Treasurer of the Parish.

REMARKS—The Holy Eucharist has been celebrated twice since I took charge. Besides the ten baptisms which I have administered at the Mission I have baptized two others, making twelve in all.

J. L. BERNE,
Priest in Charge.

ST. PAUL'S CHURCH, NEWPORT.

Baptisms: adults, 1; infants, 4; total, 5. Confirmations, 10. Communicants: last reported, 26; added anew, 10; removed into the Parish, 2; total, 38; removed from the Parish, 5; died, 1; present number, 32. Marriages, 2. Burials, 1. Sunday school: teachers, 6; pupils, 36.

OFFERINGS.

Communion alms	$ 11 75
Subscriptions	358 95
Other sources	59 25
Total	$429 95

APPROPRIATIONS.

Convention assessment	10 00
Parochial purposes	415 50
Diocesan Missions	1 45
Domestic Missions	3 00
Total	$429 95

W. L. MADDOCK,
Treasurer of the Parish.

REMARKS—Services are held on the first and third Sundays in each month.

W. W. ESTABROOKE,
Priest in Charge.

GRACE CHURCH, PHILLIP'S COUNTY.

No report.

TRINITY CHURCH, PINE BLUFF.

Baptisms: adults, 2; infants, 3; total, 5. Confirmations, 3. Communicants: last reported, 87; added anew, 8; died, 4; present number, 91. Marriages, 4. Burials, 10. Sunday school: teachers, 8; pupils, 100.

OFFERINGS.

Communion alms...$	19	62
Weekly offertory..	132	15
Rentals and subscriptions.................................	891	75
Other sources.................	117	37
Total...	1,160	89

APPROPRIATIONS.

Convention assessment..............................—....	34	00
Episcopate Fund...	19	65
Parochial purposes......................... ....…	1,048	02
Diocesan Missions..	7	35
University of the South	9	00
Domestic Missions...	4	10
Foreign Missions...	4	00
Widows and Orphans of deceased Clergy............	5	60
Church Institutions.......................................	6	35
"Pious and charitable purposes," C. A.................	19	62
For the Jews...	8	20
. Total..	1,160	89
Value of Church property........ ....$12,000		00
Amount of insurance on Church property......... 1,000		80

REMARKS—The Parish is active and the Church is grow-ing. " The Brotherhood of St. Andrew " are doing splen-did service.   INNES O. ADAMS,

Rector.

ST. JAMES' CHURCH, PRESCOTT.

No report.

TRINITY CHURCH, VAN BUREN.

Baptisms: adults, 1. Confirmations, 3. Communicants:

last reported, 43; added anew, 3; present number, 46. Marriages, 1. Sunday school: teachers, 6; pupils, 67.

OFFERINGS.

Communion alms..$7 00

Value of Church property....................................$4,000 00

REMARKS—The Congregation of this Parish is about occupying their new and handsome building; also, they are about calling a resident Clergyman. The Parish is growing stronger every day.

DAVID F. MacDONALD,
Priest in Charge.

GRACE CHURCH, WASHINGTON.

Baptisms: infants, 3. Confirmations, 2. Communicants: last reported, 8; added anew, 2; present number, 10. Burials, 1. Sunday school: teachers, 3; pupils, 14.

OFFERINGS.

Weekly offerings........................... ....$13 20

APPROPRIATIONS.

Episcopate Fund... 13 20

REMARKS—The Holy Eucharist has been celebrated here about six or seven times.

J. L. BERNE,
Priest in Charge.

ADDITIONAL REPORTS.

REPORT OF THE REV. D. F. MacDONALD, D. D.

Rt. Rev. H. N. Pierce, D. D., LL. D., Bishop of the Diocese of Arkansas:

MY DEAR BISHOP—There are a number of other points, in addition to those mentioned elsewhere, in which I have

opened Missions. I give Clarksville one Sunday in every
month, where there are large and interested congregations
that attend the services of the Church. There is strong as
well as reasonable talk of erecting a Church building at
this point. There were five children to be baptized there
at my last visit, but sickness prevented their coming. The
baptisms will take place, I hope, at my next service.
From the five Missionary points, outside the organized
Parishes, in which I hold stated services, I have eight (8)
candidates preparing for Confirmation in the newly opened
Missions. I give Russellville services as often as my time
and means can possibly permit. At this point I have had
three baptisms. So far as I can judge, the Church in this
portion of the Diocese is steadily gaining ground. There
is every reason for abiding encouragement.

   Faithfully yours,

     DAVID F. MacDONALD.

REPORT OF THE REV. W. W. ESTABROOKE,

SENIOR CANON OF TRINITY CATHEDRAL.

My Dear Bishop:

In addition to the reports I have made according to the
printed form, I would respectfully add, that I held services
in Camden from June 26th to September 26th, on one
Sunday in each month, and baptized five infants and one
adult.

Several services at Brinkley, and baptized three infants
and one adult

Several services at DeVall's Bluff, and baptized two infants.

Several services at Lonoke, and baptized one infant and
one adult.

Also occasional services at Conway, Searcy and Vann-ale.

Your obedient servant,

W. W. ESTABROOKE.

REPORT OF THE REV. J. L. BERNE,

CANON OF TRINITY CATHEDRAL.

To the Rt. Rev. H. N. Pierce, D. D., LL. D., Bishop of Arkansas:

RT. REV. FATHER IN GOD—Besides the charge of Hope, Camden and Washington, I have, at your request, visited Prescott once, and hope to go regularly hereafter. There are two other places that ought to have the Church's over-sight, Rocky Comfort and Center Point, and, if possible, I will give them services.

The people of Camden are all alive to work for the Church, which I can also say for the people of my other Missions. The Camden Church people are to put in a new Altar, so that the Holy Communion can be properly celebrated. They are doing the same at Hope.

The Church at Nashville when completed will be an ornament to the village. The building will be Gothic, (no east window,) but a proper receptacle for God's Altar. Instead of wasting money on poor glass called "stained," they will darken the windows either with paint or ground glass. The Chancel proper will be put in when the size of the Congregation demands it.

The people everywhere I go are thirsting for Catholic Truth. Sectarianism has burnt over all of them, and they are tired of its negative teaching.

Faithfully, your Son in Christ,

J. L. BERNE.

TABLE OF PAROCHIAL STATISTICS.

PARISHES AND MISSIONS.	BAPTISMS.			Confirmations.	Communicants.	Marriages.	Burials.	SUNDAY SCHOOLS		Offerings.	Value of Church Property.
	Adults.	Infants.	Total.					Teachers.	Pupils.		
Arkadelphia, St. Mark's											$ 1,200 00
Arkansas City, Mission...		2	2		4					$ 50 00	4,500 00
Batesville, St. Paul's......		1	1		70						
Brinkley, Mission...........	1	3	4	1							
Camden, St. John's........	5	3	8	9	37			5	25		1,200 00
Center Point, Mission.....		1	1	1							
Dardanelle, St. Paul's.....		2	2		14	1	2	3	25	4 00	2,500 00
DeVall's Bluff, Mission.....		2	2		8						
Eureka Spgs, St. James'	8	2	10	12	30	2	1	3	30	95 00	100 00
Fayetteville, St. Paul's...	1	12	13	9	109	2	4	3	100	1,072 72	6,000 00
Forrest City, Mission		6	6	2	7					153 10	
Fort Smith, St. John's...	10	16	26	16	150	1	7	11	114	2,877 91	15,000 00
Helena, St. John's........		10	10	4	114	1	4	10	96	1,935 95	12,000 00
Hope, St. Mark's..........		1	1		10		2				1,200 00
Hot Springs, St. Luke's.	1	8	9	6	80	5	5	7	65	1,602 25	11,000 00
Lake Village, Emmanuel											1,200 00
Little Rock, Cathedral...	3	21	24	9	45	1	3	4	30	1,508 20	7,000 00
Little Rock, Christ	8	10	18	26	460	4	10	23	232	14,990 48	55,000 00
Lonoke, Mission...........	1	1	2		14						
Marianna, St. Andrew's..	4	8	12	12	36	3		5	30	42 25	3,000 00
Morrilton, St. Agnes.......					23					5 00	
Nashville, Ch. Redeemer	5	7	12	10	13			4	12	5 00	2,000 00
Newport, St. Paul's.......	1	4	5	10	22	2	1	6	36	429 95	1,500 00
Phillips County, Grace...				2	13						2,500 00
Pine Bluff, Trinity........	2	3	5	3	91	4	10	8	100	1,160 89	12,000 00
Prescott, St. James'.......											1,200 00
Russellville, Mission......		3	3								
Van Buren, Trinity	1		1	3	46	1		6	67	7 00	4,000 00
Washington, Grace.........		3	3	2	10		1	3	14	13 20	2,000 00
Total	51	129	18[0]	143	1406	27	50	101	976	$25,902 80	$146,100 00

CONSTITUTION AND CANONS.

CONSTITUTION,

As Proposed at the Fifteenth Annual Council at Little Rock, April 20, 1887, and to be finally acted on at the Sixteenth Annual Council.

PREAMBLE.

This Church conforms to the Constitution and Canons of the Protestant Episcopal Church in the United States of America, as set forth by the General Convention of the same; to which Constitution and Canons this Church hereby accedes and subordinates herself, according to the rules of ecclesiastical law.

ARTICLE I.

Of the Clergy and Laity.

There are three orders of the Clergy: Bishops, Priests and Deacons.

The Bishop exercises all the functions of the ministry, presides over the Church by Apostolic authority, and has the sole right to ordain, to confirm, and to pronounce judicial sentence on offenders. He governs the Church in his own Diocese, according to the Holy Scriptures and the Canons of this Church. He does not, ordinarily, act in any important matter without the advice and consent of a Standing Committee of Priests and Laymen.

The functions of Priests and Deacons are set forth in the General Canons of the Church.

The Laity are divided and organized, according to local convenience, into Parishes or Congregations. They commit the general management of their parochial business to a portion of their own number, annually elected, and called Wardens and Vestrymen. To these belong the administration of all the secular concerns of their particular Parish; but they have no part in the spiritual government of the Church, which belongs to the Clergy alone.

ARTICLE II.

Of the Council.

There shall be a Council of the Diocese annually, at such time and place as the Council may, from time to time, determine; and, in case of its failure to do so, the Bishop shall appoint the time and place. In the Council the Bishop shall preside by virtue of his office. The Clergy shall sit by right of their order, and the Laity shall be represented by Delegates chosen for that purpose by the Vestry of each Congregation.

The Chancellor, Secretary and Treasurer of the Diocese shall be entitled to seats in the Council, with privilege of debate, but shall have no vote by reason of their offices.

Special Councils may be called by the Bishop, or, in case of a vacancy in the Episcopate, by the Standing Committee, when some urgent necessity may require the action of the whole Church.

Without the concurrence of the Clergy and Laity, no rule or law of the Church can be adopted, changed or done away.

ARTICLE III.

Of the Organization of Congregations.

All Congregations and Parishes represented in the Primary Convention, shall be deemed duly organized; and thereafter, the organization of all Parishes shall be in the form provided by Canon, and subject to the will of the Council. And no Parish shall have an organic existence, or corporate life in this Church, unless acknowledged by the Council and approved by the Bishop.

ARTICLE IV.

Of the Support and Advancement of the Church.

All Christian men are bound to bear their just share of the burdens which duty imposes.

The Council, by Canon and resolution, may establish special funds:

First—For the support of the Episcopate.

Second—For the support of Missionaries.

Third—For the support of aged and infirm Clergymen.

Fourth—For Church building.

Fifth—For education of men for the Ministry; and take all other measures necessary for the advancement of Christ's Kingdom: *Provided*, that this Article does not imply any power to make any assessment except for the necessary expenses of the Diocese.

ARTICLE V.

Of the Administration of Justice.

The Clergy, Priests and Deacons may be tried by an Ecclesiastical Court, composed of Presbyters chosen for that purpose. But there shall be no such trial except on due presentment, and according to the Canon for the trial of Clergymen set forth in this Diocese, and the rules of ecclesiastical law.

ARTICLE VI.

Of the Tenure of Church Property.

The Rector, Wardens, and Vestry, or other persons in

whose names the property of any Church or Parish may be vested, shall not, by deed or any other means, without the consent of the Bishop and Standing Committee, under their hands given, grant, alienate, or otherwise dispose of any lands, messuages, or hereditaments in them vested for the use and benefit of said Church, nor charge, nor encumber the same to any person whatever.

ARTICLE VII.

Of Amending the Constitution.

A proposal to amend this Constitution must be laid before the Council in writing, and, if approved, shall lie over until the next annual Council, and, in the meantime, shall be notified to the Parishes: and then, if it be approved by the Bishop, and by two-thirds of the Clergy, and by two-thirds of the Laity present, voting by orders, the proposed amendment shall become a part of the Constitution.

THE CANONS

Enacted by the First Annual Council, A. D. 1872–Revised by
the Fifteenth Annual Council, A. D. 1887.

TITLE I.

OF THE COUNCIL OF THE DIOCESE.

CANON I.

OF THE COUNCIL.

SECTION 1. The Members of the Council shall consist of
the Clergy and Laity of the Diocese having the following
qualifications: Every Clergyman having been admitted
canonically by the ecclesiastical authority shall be a Member of the Council; but no Clergyman shall be qualified to
vote at the election of a Bishop unless he shall have been
canonically and actually a resident of the Diocese for six
months. Every Parish regularly organized as required by
the Constitution shall be entitled to send three Delegates
to the Council, and every duly organized Mission Station
shall be entitled to send one Delegate; *provided always:*
that such Delegates shall be communicants of the Protestant Episcopal Church, and that no person under ecclesiastical censure or process, whether Clergyman or Layman,
shall be allowed a seat in the Council.

SEC. 2. The first standing committee appointed by the
Bishop, after the Council has been duly organized, and the
last to make a report, shall be a Committee on Ways and
Means, consisting of one Priest and two Laymen, whose

duty it shall be to consider the condition of each Parish
and Mission, and to make an equitable assessment upon
them, to be applied to the Episcopate Fund and the current expenses of the Diocese. The Lay Delegates from
each Parish to the Diocesan Council shall, as a necessary
part of their credentials, present to the Council the receipt
of the Treasurer of the Diocese, or other satisfactory evidence, showing the payment of this assessment. *Provided* :
That the Council, when formally organized may, for good
and sufficient reasons, excuse any delinquent Parish or
Mission from the payment of any portion or all of this
assessment.

SEC. 3. The Council shall, ordinarily, deliberate and
vote without any distinction of orders ; but any member
may call for a division upon any question, and if this call
is sustained by two other members, then the question shall
be put first to the Clergy and next to the Laity, who shall
vote by Parishes; and in such case a majority of both orders shall be necessary to constitute an affirmative vote of
the Council.

SEC. 4. The Bishop presides in Council by virtue of his
office, and has the right to express his opinion upon every
subject that may come before the Council. In the absence
of the Bishop, the Council shall elect a Chairman from
the Clergy present. At each Council a Secretary and
Treasurer shall be elected by a joint ballot of the whole
body.

SEC. 5. When a Bishop is to be elected the Council
shall always vote, by orders, in this wise: The Clergy
shall make a nomination by ballot, and a majority of Lay
Delegates, voting by Parishes, shall concur by ballot, in
order to constitute an election.

SEC. 6. When any great necessity shall arise, the
Bishop, or, if there be no Bishop, the President of the
Standing Committee, may call a special Council. In such

case, four weeks' notice shall be given to every Clergyman and to one of the Wardens in every Parish in the Diocese, stating the time, place and objects of the special Council ; and no other matters shall be proposed or acted upon than those specified in the call of said special Council.

CANON II.

OF THE SECRETARY AND TREASURER.

SECTION 1. The Secretary of the Council shall keep, in a fit book, full and exact records of all its acts, and shall preserve all papers, documents, memorials, etc., belonging to the same, duly indorsed and filed in such way that they may be easily consulted whenever recourse to them may be necessary. He shall also prepare, under the direction of the Bishop, at least one week before the meeting of the Council, a list of all the Ministers canonically resident in the Diocese, annexing their respective stations, distinguishing Priests from Deacons, but not inserting the name of any Clergyman who is suspended from the Ministry. The list thus prepared shall be laid before the Council immediately after it shall be called to order, and the names of the clerical members shall be called therefrom. Nevertheless, the Council has power immediately to order the correction of any errors or omissions.

SEC. 2. The Treasurer shall have charge of the General Fund of the Diocese, and all other funds the Council may commit to his care, and shall keep a strict account of the same in a fit book, with a distinct place therein for all proper entries. He shall keep a regular account with all funds and with all persons and Parishes concerned, and shall annually exhibit a balance sheet to the Auditing Committee. He shall indorse and file away all warrants, orders, or other papers belonging to his department, and shall have his accounts audited at each Council by the Finance Committee.

Sec. 3.   When a vacancy occurs in the office of Secretary or Treasurer the ecclesiastical authority shall appoint a fit person to fill the vacancy, who shall receive all records, funds and papers, from the hands of the former officer or his legal representatives, and such appointee shall continue in office and perform all the duties thereof until the ensuing Council shall have elected some one to fill the same.

CANON III.

OF THE REGISTRAR.

Section 1.   A Registrar shall be elected by the Council, into whose keeping shall be committed all documents pertaining to the history of the Church in the Diocese of Arkansas, that are now, or may hereafter become the property of the Council.   It shall be the duty of said Registrar to preserve all the documents herein referred to, in some suitable place of deposit, and to hold them subject to such regulations as the Council may, from time to time, prescribe.

Sec. 2.   Said Registrar shall hold his office for one year and until another shall be chosen in his place.

CANON IV.

OF REGULAR ATTENDANCE AT COUNCIL.

Section 1.   Every Clergyman in the Diocese shall attend the Annual Council, unless he has a satisfactory excuse; and it is the duty of every Parish to send Lay Delegates, and it shall be the duty of the Vestry to make provision for their representation.   A satisfactory excuse will be required for every failure.

Sec. 2.   No member of the Council shall leave the same during the session without having obtained leave of absence from the Council.

CANON V.

OF THE NUMBER NECESSARY TO CONSTITUTE A QUORUM.

SECTION 1. A quorum for ordinary business at the Annual Council shall consist of such Clergy and Delegates from the Parishes as may be present; but, if the Bishop be not present, such quorum shall have power only to receive reports of Committees and Parishes, and to refer the same; to elect the ordinary officers and committees, and to fix the time and place for the next Council. In the election of a Bishop, two-thirds of the Clergy and a majority of all the Parishes shall be present before the Council proceed to elect. At any *called* Council, other than as provided for in Article II of the Constitution, a quorum shall consist of a majority of all the Clergy entitled to seats, and Lay Delegates from four or more Parishes.

CANON VI.

OF THE OPENING OF THE COUNCIL.

SECTION 1. At the opening of every Council there shall be a celebration of the Holy Communion, and a sermon by a Priest appointed by the Bishop when the Bishop himself does not deliver at that time a sermon or charge. And this *may* be preceded by Morning Prayer.

CANON VII.

OF THE STANDING COMMITTEE OF THE DIOCESE.

SECTION 1. At every Annual Council there shall be elected three Priests and two Laymen, by ballot, as a Standing Committee for the ensuing year. They shall elect, from their own body, a President and Secretary. They shall meet on the summons of the President. To constitute a quorum two Priests must be present, and when required they shall vote by orders.

6

Sec. 2.   It shall be the duty of the Secretary to keep a regular record of their proceedings, in a book which shall belong to the Diocese, and which, together with all papers in the possession of the Committee, shall be open to the inspection of the Committee, or the Council, when required.

Sec. 3.   The Standing Committee shall be summoned on the requisition of the Bishop, whenever he shall wish their advice; and they may meet, of their own accord and agreeably to their own rules, when they may be disposed to advise the Bishop.   And the President shall call a meeting at any time, on the request in writing of any two members, or when he may deem it necessary.

Sec. 4.   When the Diocese is vacant, through any cause, it shall be the duty of the Standing Committee to call a meeting forthwith, and, after consultation as to the time and place, to summon a Special Council of the Diocese, to elect a successor, with all convenient speed; *provided:* that if such vacancy occur within less than six months before the Annual Council there shall be no Special Council, but the election of a Bishop shall be deferred until the Annual Council; and during the vacancy, the Standing Committee shall exercise all the powers of the ecclesiastical authority consistent with their character as the administrators of the Diocese under the Council.

CANON VIII.

OF THE APPOINTMENT OF STANDING COMMITTEES.

Section 1.   At every Council the presiding officer shall appoint standing committees on—

1.   Credentials of Lay Delegates.
2.   Ways and Means.
3.   Admission of New Parishes.
4.   State of the Church.

5. Auditing and Finance.
6. Unfinished Business.
7. Constitution and Canons.

And on such other subjects as he may deem requsite to put the Council in possession of properly proposed information for their action.

SEC. 2. He shall also appoint a committee to be known as the Committee on Judiciary, to be composed of three Laymen, the Chancellor to be one and to be chairman, who shall remain as members of such committee until their successors are appointed.

CANON IX.

OF THE ELECTION OF TRUSTEES.

SECTION 1. Every Council shall elect Trustees for all Funds that may be created.

SEC. 2. A Trustee shall be annually appointed by the Council, who shall be known as the Trustee of the Episcopate Endowment Fund, and who shall be specially charged with the responsibility for the accumulation and investment of said fund. As often as the amounts received by him shall aggregate the sum of $50.00 he shall invest the same, under the supervision of the Bishop and Standing Committee of the Diocese. It shall be the duty of the said Trustee to make annual reports to the Council of the condition of said fund and the investment thereof.

CANON X.

OF DEPUTIES TO THE GENERAL CONVENTION.

SECTION 1. Deputies to the General Convention shall be chosen at each Annual Council, and shall continue in office until others are chosen.

SEC. 2. The Deputies to the General Convention shall

be elected by ballot, the Clergy and Laity separately electing the Deputies and Substitutes of their respective orders.

Sec. 3. Substitutes for Deputies shall be elected one at
a time, and, in the event of the resignation or inability of
any Deputy, Clerical or Lay, such vacancy shall be filled
by the substitutes in the order of election, and the Journal
must show the order of election of substitutes, Clerical and
Lay.

CANON XI.

OF PUBLISHING THE JOURNAL.

Section 1. The proceedings of the Council shall be
published by the Secretary, under the supervision of the
Bishop, and duly distributed, unless the Council shall otherwise order.

CANON XII.

OF FAILURE TO ELECT OFFICERS.

Section 1. In all cases of failure to elect officers, whether
in the Council or in a Parish, the persons last elected shall
continue to serve with full power until their successors are
elected.

CANON XIII.

OF THE CHANCELLOR OF THE DIOCESE.

Section 1. There shall be elected by the Council an
officer learned in the law, under the title of Chancellor of
the Diocese, whose duty it shall be to act as the legal
counselor of the Bishop and of the Standing Committee,
in matters affecting the interests of the Church, as his
professional counsel may be asked or required. The Chancellor of the Diocese shall hold his office for the term of

three years, and, in the event of a vacancy, the Annual Council next ensuing shall elect a successor for the full term of three years.

ORDER OF BUSINESS.

1. Calling the Roll.
2. Presentation of the Certificates of Lay Delegates.
3. Appointment of Committee on Credentials.
4. Report of Committee on Credentials.
5. Election of Secretary.
6. Appointment of Standing Committees.
7. Annual Address of the Bishop.
8. Report of the Standing Committee.
9. Reports of Special Committees.
10. Reports of Trustees of the several Funds.
11. Report of the Auditing Committee.
12. Election of Treasurer.
13. Election of the Standing Committee.
14. Report on the State of the Church.
15. Election of Deputies to the General Convention.
16. Election of Trustees of the several Funds.
17. Election of Registrar.
18. Election of Chancellor.
19. Report of Committee on Unfinished Business.
20. Miscellaneous Business.
21. Report of Committee on Ways and Means.

TITLE II.

OF PARISHES AND PARISH MINISTERS.

CANON I.

SECTION 1. All vacant Parishes shall be under the pastoral care of the Bishop. He shall provide for public worship, as far as he can, by occasional services of the Clergy, and by fit persons appointed as Lay readers.

CANON II.

Section 1. When any Parish shall have elected a Rector and he shall have accepted the call, it shall be the duty of the Vestry to file with the Bishop a minute of their proceedings, including the particular agreement on their part and the acceptance of the elected Minister, showing that he accepts on the terms and agreements stipulated by the Vestry. The Bishop shall make record thereof, and the same shall be binding on the parties concerned, and held as a firm contract.

CANON III.

Section 1. The Rector shall preside at all Vestry meetings, if present, and open the same with prayer, and may advise, but not vote, on any question.

Sec. 2. To the Rector belongs the control of the keys of the Church, and the right to open the Church for public prayer, sermons, catechetical instruction, marriages, funerals, baptisms, and all rites and ceremonies authorized by the Protestant Episcopal Church in America, at all times when he may deem proper.

Sec. 3. The Church building shall never be used for any secular or profane purpose.

CANON IV.

Section 1. Every Parish Minister shall keep a Parish Register, which shall be a well-bound book, and, as far as may be, uniform throughout the Diocese.

Sec. 2. In it shall be entered the names of all persons baptized, confirmed, married and buried in the Parish. It shall contain a list of all the communicants, of all families, and of individuals not thus included, belonging to the Parish, or regularly attending its services. It shall also contain a record of all collections made in the Church.

Sec. 3. From this Register shall the annual parochial reports be made to the Council, under all the heads that may be required by the Council or Canons.

CANON V.

Section 1. It shall be the duty of the Vestry to report, annually, to the Council, by their Delegates, a full statement of their financial condition, according to general order of the Council. This statement shall contain the amount and value of their property and the net income of their Parish.

CANON VI.

Section 1. It shall be the duty of the Vestry to make a full exhibit to the Bishop at the time of his annual visitation, if he shall so require, of all their affairs, and receive from him counsel and advice for the conduct of the affairs of the Parish.

CANON VII.

Section 1. The organization of a new Parish shall be forthwith notified to the Bishop, and, if approved by him, the Parish may elect a Rector, and send Delegates and apply for admission to the Council.

Sec. 2. But if the new Parish proposed to be organized be within the territorial bounds of any existing Parish, the Bishop shall notify the Rector and Wardens thereof, and, if objection be made thereto, notice shall be given to both parties, and the Bishop, within thirty days thereafter, shall hear the same before the Standing Committee, and the decision of the Standing Committee, approved by the Bishop, shall determine the case; *provided,* that no Parish within any city shall be divided for the purpose of forming a new and independent Parish within its boundaries, except by express order of the Council.

CANON VIII.

SECTION 1. Congregations, Parishes, and the members thereof, shall never recognize any suspended Clergyman, otherwise than as declared by the ecclesiastical authority.

SEC. 2. If any Parish, or the members thereof, shall take part with a contumacious Clergyman, they shall forfeit their rights in the Council.

SEC. 3. All parochial property is held by a tenure subject to this rule.

SEC. 4. In case any Congregation should be so far forgetful of the honor of GOD's Church as to transgress in this matter, it shall be the duty of the Treasurer of the Diocese, or of the Trustees of the General Fund, to proceed at once to recover all the Church's property in such contumacious Parish, and to reduce it to the control of the Diocese.

SEC. 5. The organization of every Parish shall recognize this rule, and, if it be not expressed in the Articles of Association, their admission into union with the Council shall bind them to this law.

TITLE III.

OF CONVOCATIONS, DIOCESAN MISSIONS AND CHURCH EXTENSION.

CANON I.

SECTION 1. The Bishop may divide the Diocese into Districts, naming the town in each District which shall be the center of a Missionary work; and every Clergyman in the Diocese, and every Parish and Missionary Station, shall be assigned to one or the other of the Missionary centers.

SEC. 2. The Clergy and Laity of each District, when organized, shall constitute a Convocation, and have charge of the Missionary work in the field assigned by the Bishop.

SEC. 3. The Bishop shall appoint one of the Clergy in each District as Dean of Convocation. The Convocation shall elect a Secretary, who shall be a Clergyman, and a Treasurer, who shall be a Layman.

SEC. 4. The Convocation shall be governed by such rules as they shall adopt, with the Bishop's approval, and each shall report, through its Dean, to the Bishop annually.

SEC. 5. The Deans of Convocation shall constitute the Missionary Committee of the Diocese. Until such time as the Bishop shall divide the Diocese into Districts, the Bishop and the Clerical members of the Standing Committee shall constitute said Missionary Committee.

SEC. 6. Every Parish shall, by its Vestry, appoint one Delegate to Convocation.

SEC. 7. In Missionary Stations, the Missionary in charge or Dean of Convocation shall appoint the Lay Delegate.

CANON II.

SECTION 1. All organized Mission Stations shall be under the control of the Bishop and Missionary Committee.

SEC. 2. All Missionaries shall be appointed by the Bishop.

SEC. 3. Missionary Stations duly organized shall report to the Annual Council the same as Parishes, and shall be entitled to send one Delegate, who shall have the right to debate but not to vote.

CANON III.

In any community where there are twelve baptized adults, one of whom shall be a male communicant, desirous of organizing a Mission Station, they shall assemble themselves —their own Missionary being present, or, if they have no Missionary, any Clergyman of the Diocese being present and consenting—and adopt the following form of organization, affixing their signatures thereto, and sending a copy of the same to the Bishop of the Diocese for his approval:

" We, whose names are hereunto subscribed, desirous of enjoying the privileges of religious worship and instruction of the Holy, Catholic and Apostolic Church, according to the forms and doctrines of the Protestant Episcopal Church in the United States of America, have, this ——— day of ———, A. D. ——, at ———, in the State of Arkansas, formed ourselves into a Congregation, and adopted the following Articles of Association:

"Article I. This Association or Congregation shall be known by the name of the ——— Mission.

"Article II. This Association acknowledges, accedes to, and will be governed by. the Constitution, Canons, doctrines, discipline and worship of the Protestant Episcopal

Church in the United States, and the Constitution and Canons of the Protestant Episcopal Church in the Diocese of Arkansas.

"Article III. When any person uniting with this Association shall disclaim or refuse conformity to the authorities mentioned in the preceding Article, he shall cease to be a member of the Association, and shall no longer enjoy the privilege of voting in the election of officers, of being elected an officer, or of exercising any function concerning or connected with the said Association; *but this exclusion shall not affect the spiritual standing of the excluded.*

"Article IV. In this Mission, regular attendants at the services of the Church shall be entitled to vote for officers and on all matters brought before the Easter meeting.

"Article V. The officers of this Association shall be: The Minister in charge as President *ex officio;* a Warden, who must be a male communicant, and appointed by the Minister; a Secretary and a Treasurer, elected by ballot annually the Monday in Easter week, or as soon thereafter as possible, due notice having been given of time and place of election.

"Article VI. The duties of these officers shall be the same as those of like officers in organized Parishes.

"Article VII. All lands, tenements, or other property, real or personal, of this Association, shall vest in the Bishop of this Diocese, or under whose supervision it may for the time be, and his canonical successors, to be by him and them held in trust for the benefit of the Mission.

"Article VIII. We promise to pay the sum of $—— per annum, for the support of the Missionary whom the Bishop or Missionary Committee may send to us."

CANON IV.

SECTION 1. Every Parish shall make offerings for Dio-cesan Missions as often as the Council shall appoint, but the following offerings are required to be made and not to be diverted to other purposes, except upon special authority of the Council, viz: The first Sunday in Lent and Trinity Sunday, for the benefit of Diocesan Missions; Easter Day, for the Episcopate Fund; National Thanksgiving Day, for the Fund for aged and infirm Clergy, and widows and orphans of deceased Clergymen of the Diocese; Christmas Day, for the Rector of the Parish. It shall be the duty of the Treasurer of the Parish, at least two weeks before Christmas Day, to send written notice of the last-named offering to each adult member of the Parish.

CANON V.

SECTION I. The Bishop of the Diocese shall be *ex officio* President of the Missionary Committee. The Committee shall report, through its Secretary, to the Annual Council. The Treasurer shall receive, hold, and pay out funds, subject to the order of the Committee. His accounts shall be audited by the Council as a separate and distinct fund.

TITLE IV.

OF VESTRIES AND WARDENS AND THEIR DUTIES, ETC.

CANON I.

SECTION 1. Annually, at a meeting on Easter Monday, or as soon thereafter as may be, the members of the Parish entitled to vote shall elect not less than three nor more than eleven Vestrymen, of whom the Rector or Minister shall appoint one as Senior Warden and the Vestry shall elect another as Junior Warden. *Provided:* That the Congregation worshiping in the Cathedral Church may, on the Monday in Easter week, or as early thereafter as practicable, elect three communicants to represent them, subject to the laws and regulations governing parochial representation.

Sec. 2. Notice of the election shall be given on Easter Day, or at the service last* preceding the election, after morning prayer, and the congregation duly warned of the importance of the election.

Sec. 3. The Vestry elect shall meet within ten days thereafter, and organize by the election of the Junior Warden, Treasurer and Secretary. As soon as the offices are filled the Secretary and Treasurer, if not re-elected, shall pass over to their successors the books, papers, accounts and moneys in their hands. The Vestry shall then proceed to elect Delegates to represent the Parish in the next Council of the Diocese, and the Secretary of the Vestry, or the Rector, shall give the Delegates elect certificates to that effect.

Sec. 4. It is, in general, the duty of the Wardens and Vestrymen to consider and determine upon the election of a Minister when the Parish is vacant ; to see that the Minister is well and properly supported, sufficiently and punctually paid ; to make and execute all contracts for the erection of church edifices, rectories, and other Church buildings ; to provide for their furnishing and repair and due preservation ; to have and to hold all Church property as trustees of the Parish, and as such generally to transact all the temporal and financial business of the Parish.

Sec. 5. It is the special duty of the Wardens to see that the Church edifice be kept from unhallowed uses ; that it be kept clean and in good repair, duly lighted and warmed; to provide a sufficient supply of books and eccle-siastical vestments to be used in the public ministrations by the Minister, and to provide proper elements for the celebration of the Holy Communion and preserve due order during service.

SEC. 6.   In the absence of the Rector the Wardens pre-side at Parish and Vestry Meetings.

SEC. 7.   In the absence of the Wardens their duties de-volve on the Vestrymen.

SEC. 8.   It is the duty of the Secretary to attend all the meetings of the Vestry, and perform the proper func-tions of his office.

SEC. 9.   It shall be the duty of the Treasurer to receive all moneys collected under authority of the Vestry; to collect all moneys due the Vestry or Congregation, and to pay them out on the order of the Vestry in the manner they shall provide.   Two weeks before Easter, every year, the Treasurer shall present to the Vestry a full statement of all his accounts, and the Vestry shall audit the same, and, if found correct, order the annual balance to be made up in accordance therewith.

SEC. 10.   The Minister may call meetings of the Vestry whenever he shall desire, and shall call a meeting when requested by any two members of the Vestry, of which he shall give due notice: but meetings may be held at regular periods by regulation of the Vestry.   At every meeting the minutes of the former meeting shall be read and ap-proved, or corrected and approved.

SEC. 11.   It shall be the special duty of the Vestry, at the time of public service, or other meeting in the Church, to see that the congregation is properly seated, and in the performance of this duty they shall give special attention to strangers.

CANON II.

NEW PARISHES—FORM FOR ORGANIZATION OF NEW PARISHES.

Hereafter, all new Parishes shall be organized by the adoption of the following form of organization :

" We, whose names are hereunto subscribed, desirous of enjoying the privileges of religious worship and instruction of the Holy, Catholic and Apostolic Church, according to the forms and doctrines of the Protestant Episcopal Church in the United States of America, have, this —— day of ——, A. D. ——, at ———, in the State of Arkansas, formed ourselves into a Parish, and adopted the following articles of association :

"Article 1. This Association shall be known by the mame of ' The Rector, Wardens and Vestry of ——— Church.'

"Article 2. This Association acknowledges, accedes to, and will be governed by, the Constitution, Canons, doctrine, discipline and worship of the Protestant Episcopal Church in the United States, and the Constitution and Canons of the Protestant Episcopal Church in the Diocese of Arkansas.

"Article 3. When any person, uniting with this Association, shall disclaim or refuse conformity to the authorities mentioned in the preceding Article, he shall cease to be a member of the Association, and shall no longer enjoy the privilege of voting in the election of Vestrymen, of being elected a Vestryman, or of exercising any function concerning or connected with the said Association ; *but this exclusion shall not affect the spiritual standing of the excluded.*

"Article 4. In this Parish all baptized members of the Church, who are duly registered as members of this Congregation, shall be entitled to vote for Vestrymen and on all matters brought before the Easter meeting.

"Article 5.   The Vestrymen of ——— Church shall be elected annually, on the Monday in Easter week, or as soon thereafter as may be, by a majority of the voters assembled for that purpose, notice to that effect having been given publicly to the Congregation on the preceding Sunday.   The Vestrymen so elected shall continue in office one year or until their successors are chosen.

"Article 6.   The Rector of ——— Church shall be elected by the Wardens and Vestrymen in open meeting, which shall be duly convened for that purpose, they having due regard in all such elections to the previously ascertained wishes of the Congregation, and *especially* of the *communicants* of the Church.

"Article 7.   No person shall be chosen Rector or Minister, or Associate Rector or Assistant Minister, of ——— — Church, or be allowed to exercise any of the functions of the Sacred Ministry in the same, unless he be recognized by the Bishop having charge of this Diocese, or. if there be no Bishop. by the Standing Committee of the same, as an ordained Minister of the Protestant Episcopal Church, in good standing; provided, that nothing in this article shall prevent the Wardens and Vestry from inviting any Clergyman of the Protestant Episcopal Church, in good standing, to officiate occasionally in the Church, or interfere with the performance of the usual services by Lay Readers, duly appointed to so officiate in the absence of the Rector or Minister.

"Article 8.   The annual rents, contributions and other revenues raised by this Congregation, shall be applied by the Wardens and Vestry to the maintenance and support of the Rector or Minister, and to such other objects as are connected with the well-being of the Church, and to no other purpose whatever.

"Article 9. This Association, or the Rector, Wardens and Vestry, or other persons in whose name the property of —— Church may be vested, shall not, by deed or any other means, without the consent of the Bishop of the Diocese, under his hand given, grant, alienate, or otherwise dispose of, any lands, messuages or hereditaments, in them vested for the use and benefit of said Church, nor charge nor encumber the same to any person whatever.

"Article 10. In case of the dissolution or extinction of this Association, for any cause whatever, the lands, tenements and other estates, real or personal, if such there be, shall vest in the Bishop of the Protestant Episcopal Church in this Diocese, or under whose supervision it may for the time be, and his canonical successors, to be by him and them held in trust for the benefit of a future Congregation of the Protestant Episcopal Church which may be formed in the same place or its vicinity, and upon the same principles as the present Church and Association.

CANON III.

SECTION 1. Clergymen and Laymen shall exercise due care in signing the papers of candidates for the Ministry, and shall not sign except upon personal knowledge or reasonable evidence. And if any fraud or concealment may have been used to obtain certificates, the signers, on evidence of the facts, may revoke their recommendation. And if they shall rashly or unadvisedly, without due care and caution, or through favor, or with corrupt purpose, sign the recommendation of candidates, whereby unworthy or unfit persons may be admitted to the Ministry, whether they be Clergymen or Laymen, they shall be subject to ecclesiastical censure.

TITLE V.

TRIAL OF MINISTERS.

SECTION 1. Every Clergyman in this Diocese shall be liable to presentment and trial for the following offenses, to-wit:

First—Crime and immorality.

Second—Holding and teaching, publicly or privately and advisedly, any doctrine contrary to that expressly and generally set forth in the standards of the Protestant Episcopal Church in the United States.

Third—Violation of the Constitution and Canons of the General Convention, or of the Constitution and Canons of the Diocese of Arkansas.

SEC. 2. If a Minister of this Church shall be found guilty of any of the offenses enumerated in the foregoing section, he shall be admonished, suspended or degraded.

SEC. 3. In order to bring a Clergyman to trial, a charge shall be made to the Judiciary Committee, signed by at least two of the communicants of the Diocese, one of whom shall be a Priest, affirming that the charge is true and that the accusers will make it good. Thereupon it shall be the duty of the Secretary of the Committee to furnish the accused a copy of the charge, and require an answer to be filed thereto within thirty days from the date of the receipt of said copy. On the coming in of the answer, a copy of the same shall be furnished the parties making the charge, accompanied by a notice that all proof on the issue, of both parties, must be taken and filed with the Secretary within ninety days from the date of the notice. All proof must be by deposition, taken before an officer authorized to administer oaths, and must be upon reasonable notice. Both parties have the right to be pres-

ent at the taking of the depositions and to be represented
by counsel.

At the end of the ninety days the hearing shall close,
and thereupon the said Committee shall consider the
charges, and if two members of the same shall deem the
charges clearly within the scope of the Canons, and sustained by the proof, it shall be so declared in writing, and
they shall file all the papers in the case with the Standing
Committee of the Diocese.

In case the accused is a member of the Standing Committee, the two remaining Clerical members shall choose a
Priest of the Diocese to supply his place, and for the purposes of this trial the Priest so chosen shall be considered
a member of the Standing Committee.

SEC. 4. On the receipt of the presentation and papers,
it shall be the duty of the Clerical members of the Standing Committee to consider of the charge, and if in the
opinion of at least two of said Clerical members the charge
be clearly within the scope of the Canons, and sustained
by the proof adduced, they shall impartially select by lot
seven Presbyters of the Diocese, to meet on a certain day
after ninety days, at a certain place, within which the accused may reside. Immediately upon their selection, the
names shall be forwarded to the accused, and he shall
forthwith send to the Secretary of the Standing Committee
the names of those to whom he objects, if any. Three of
the seven may constitute the Court, and the accused shall
have the right to object to any individual until the number
is reduced to three. If no member is excepted to, all that
assemble shall sit as a Court. The Court shall be judges
both of law and fact.

SEC. 5. The Standing Committee shall be prosecutors
in the case, and shall appoint a judge-advocate, who shall
be a Priest of this Diocese. The Standing Committee
shall give the accused sixty days' notice of the time and
place of trial, and shall, also, deliver to him, at the same

time, a copy of the charges preferred against him; and i
shall not be required to answer to anything not contain
in the presentment.

SEC. 6.   At the time fixed for the trial, the members
the Court shall assemble at the place designated, ai
choose a President and Clerk from their own numbe
and they shall, before they proceed, adopt and declare tl
rules by which the trial shall be conducted, if rules
ecclesiastical trial have not already been set forth by a
thority. *Provided*, however, that all the evidence heard
the trial shall be reduced to writing at the time it is give
and signed by the witness before he leaves the room.

SEC. 7.   The accused shall be allowed counsel, whom l
may choose from among the Priests of the Church, and l
may also advise with a Lay communicant learned in tl
law.   If the accused decline to choose counsel, the Cou
shall appoint counsel for him from the Priests of the Di
cese.

SEC. 8.   If the accused shall not appear for trial, witho
assigning sufficient cause, the Court shall proceed again
him for contempt, and he shall be suspended by the Bishc
from the exercise of all Clerical functions for the space
six months.   And if, in the six months, he shall not appl
for trial, at any time afterwards, with the consent and a
vice of the Standing Committee, the Bishop may procee
to pronounce upon the recusant the sentence of depositic
from the Ministry.

SEC. 9.   But if, in the six months above-named, tl
accused shall appear for trial, the Court may proceed c
the presentment originally made, and shall adjudge hi:
guilty or not guilty, according to the evidence.   The Cou
shall render their verdict; and if it shall be guilty, the
shall designate the penalty or degree of censure which, i
their judgment, ought to be pronounced against hin

which the Bishop shall not exceed, though he may modify it.

Immediately upon rendering the verdict, it shall be the duty of the Clerk of the Court to deliver all the pleadings and evidence to the Bishop, who shall give notice to both the judge-advocate and the accused that on a day fixed he will hear the case on appeal, if the accused be found guilty. At such hearing, the accused shall have the right to be represented by a Lay communicant learned in the law, and the Bishop may call two of the neighboring Diocesans, who shall sit with him at the hearing, to assist him in arriving at a correct determination.

SEC. 10. The Clerk of such Ecclesiastical Court shall keep a record of all the proceedings, which shall contain a copy of the presentment, the specifications under particular charges, the notice to the accused, his answer, his plea or pleas, a clear statement of the evidence for and against, both oral and written, and the judgment of the Court. An attested copy of this record shall be forthwith delivered to the Bishop.

SEC. 11. The Bishop shall proceed to declare the decision of the Court, and pronounce sentence, if he approve the findings ; but, if he disapprove, he may order a new trial, stating in the order the grounds and reason of his decision. And when the sentence is less than deposition, the Bishop may, for satisfactory reasons, reprieve or wholly pardon the condemned. But this extraordinary power shall be exercised only in extraordinary cases, and, in such a case, the Bishop shall report his action to the next Annual Council for approval.

SEC. 12. Every summons, notice or citation, mentioned in the proceedings, shall be deemed to be duly served by the delivery of a written notice to the person to be summoned, notified or cited, or by leaving it or a certified copy at his residence or last known residence, by a person duly appointed in writing by the Standing Committee or Court, as the case may require. Depositions must be taken according to the rules of law.

SEC. 13. The Court may adjourn from day to day, or to a day certain, for the purpose of allowing parties to obtain evidence that they may affirm to be necessary to the maintenance of their cause; but to obtain a postponement of trial for more than three days the party making the motion shall solemnly affirm that such postponement is sought, not for delay, but that justice may be done, and that he expects thereby to obtain evidence which is material to his cause, and which he cannot now produce.

SEC. 14. Suspension from the exercise of the functions of the Ministry shall, *ipso facto*, sever the connection between a Clergyman and his Parish.

SEC. 15. If any Clergyman shall be contumacious when suspended, and attempt to perform any of the functions of the sacred Ministry, the Bishop shall at once cite him before the Standing Committee; and, if the alleged facts be admitted or proven by sufficient evidence, on having been duly cited, such suspended Clergyman shall not appear or give reasons for not appearing, the Bishop, with the consent of the Standing Committee, may proceed at once to pronounce upon said recusant the grave sentence of deposition from the Ministry.

SEC. 16. No Clergyman shall be suspended, or receive any public censure from the Ecclesiastical authority of the Diocese, without having been adjudged thereto in the manner provided in this Canon.

SEC. 17. If an accused Clergyman shall, to avoid notice or citation, remove himself out of the Diocese, he may be duly served with all notices by publication in some newspaper published at the capital of the State, or the Church-newspaper which the Bishop shall have adopted as the official organ of the Diocese.

SEC. 18. If there shall be a necessity for the trial of a Clergyman, at any time when the Episcopate of the Diocese is vacant, the Bishop of some neighboring Diocese may, at the request of the Standing Committee, perform all the acts assigned by this Canon to the Bishop of the Diocese.

SEC. 19. Any resort to a civil court on the part of the accused, for the purpose of impeding, delaying, or avoiding trial, shall be treated as contumacy, and shall be sufficient cause to suspend such Clergyman from the exercise of the Ministry for contumacy, until he shall appear and demand a trial.

SEC. 20. No Clergyman under trial, or suspension, or against whom charges have been presented by the Standing Committee, can be transferred to any other Diocese, or be received therefrom. And if charges are made against a Clergyman who has already obtained letters dimissory, said charges shall be sent to the Diocese to which the letters were taken, within six months after the date of said letters, and not later. And if such letters have not been presented and received at the time, the party shall be remanded to his Diocese for trial, and his letters dimissory thereby revoked.

SEC. 21. All rights, claims and privileges, which any Clergyman may enjoy, or have a right to enjoy or receive, in the Diocese, by virtue of her general law, or by particular Canon, are, by the sentence of suspension or deposition, *ipso facto*, forfeited and rendered void; and every Clergyman shall hold his Ecclesiastical rights subject to this tenure.

INDEX.

ANNOUNCEMENT.

The Sixteenth Annual Council of the Diocese of Arkansas will be held (D. V.) in St. Andrew's Church, Marianna, Ark., on the second Thursday after Easter, April 12th, A. D. 1888.

THE SECRETARY
DIOCESE OF ARKANSAS

JOURNAL

OF THE

Sixteenth Annual Council

* * * 1888 * * *

·Special·Offerings·

RECOMMENDED BY THE COUNCIL.

DIOCESAN MISSIONS, on the first Sunday in Lent and on Trinity Sunday.

EPISCOPATE FUND, on Septuagesima Sunday or on Easter Day.

AGED AND INFIRM CLERGY AND WIDOWS AND ORPHANS OF DECEASED CLERGY OF THE DIOCESE, National Thanksgiving Day.

UNIVERSITY OF THE SOUTH, on the first Sunday in Advent.

JOURNAL

OF THE

‑ ‑ PROCEEDINGS ‑‑

OF THE

SIXTEENTH ANNUAL COUNCIL

OF THE

Dioçese of Arkansas,

Held in St. Andrew's Church, Marianna, on the 12th, 13th, 14th, 15th and 16th Days of April, A. D 1888.

LITTLE ROCK, ARK.·
PRESS PRINTING COMPANY.
1888.

THE DIOCESE OF ARKANSAS,

ORGANIZED A. D. 1871.

DIOCESAN OFFICERS.

Bishop :
THE RT. REV. H. N. PIERCE, D. D., LL. D.

Standing Committee :
REV. INNES O. ADAMS, PRESIDENT.
THE REV. MESSRS. W. J. MILLER AND W. W. ESTABROOKE,
MESSRS. M. L. BELL AND P. K. ROOTS.

Secretary of the Council :
THE REV. W. J. MILLER, Hot Springs.

Treasurer :
MR. LOGAN H. ROOTS, Little Rock.

Registrar :
MR. GEO. H. VANETTEN, Little Rock.

Chancellor :
THE HON. M. L. BELL, Pine Bluff.

Trustee of the Episcopate Fund :
MR. P. K. ROOTS, Little Rock.

Trustees of the University of the South:

THE REV. GEO. F. DEGEN,

MESSRS. GEO. W. CARUTH AND F. D. CLARKE.

Trustee of the General Theological Seminary:

THE REV. INNES O. ADAMS.

Deputies to the General Convention:-

Clerical.	*Lay.*
REV. I. O. ADAMS,	MR. LOGAN H. ROOTS,
REV. W. J. MILLER,	MR. H. P. ROGERS,
REV. W. W. ESTABROOKE,	MR. STEPHEN WHEELER,
REV. J. J. VAULX,	MR. GEO. W. CARUTH.

Supplemental Deputies to General Convention:

[In the order of their election.]

Clerical.	*Lay.*
1. REV. GEO. F. DEGEN,	1. MR. M. L. BELL,
2. REV. CHAS. H. PROCTOR	2. MR. P. O. THWEAT,
3. REV. L. F. GUERRY,	3. MR. L. MINER,
4. REV. D. L. TRIMBLE,	4. MR. J. P. MELLARD.

Committee on Judiciary:

THE HON. M. L. BELL, Chancellor.

MESSRS. GEO. W. CARUTH AND H. S. COLEMAN.

Preacher of Council Sermon:

THE REV. RICHARD TOTTEN, A. M.

LIST OF THE CLERGY OF THE DIOCESE.

Bishop:

RT. REV. HENRY N. PIERCE, D. D., L.L. D., Little Rock.

Priests:

Rev. INNES O. ADAMS, Rector of Trinity..........Pine Bluff

Rev. E. C. ALCORN*........................St. Louis, Mo.

Rev. FRANK M. BAYNE, Rector of St. Agnes.......Morrilton

Rev. JOSEPH L. BERNE*........................———

Rev. C. A. BRUCE, Rector of St. Andrew's.........Marianna

Rev. WALLACE CARNAHAN, Rector of Christ Church, Little Rock

Rev. GEO. F. DEGEN, Rector of St. John's.......Fort Smith

Rev. W. W. ESTABROOKE, Canon, Trinity Cathedral,Little Rock

Rev. L. F. GUERRY,* Rector of Trinity..........Van Buren

Rev. R. S. JAMES, D. D., Rector of St. Paul's.....Dardanelle

Rev. D. F. MacDONALD, D. D.*...............Witcherville

Rev. W. J. MILLER, Rector of St. Luke's.......Hot Springs

Rev. C. H. NEWMAN*...........................———

Rev. D. S. C. M. POTTER, D. D., Rector of St. James,
Eureka Springs

Rev. CHAS. H. PROCTOR,* Trinity Cathedral.....Little Rock

Rev. RICHARD TOTTEN, Rector of St. John's..........Helena

Rev. DAVID L. TRIMBLE*......................Pine Bluff

Rev. JAMES J. VAULX, Rector of St. Paul's......Fayetteville

*Not present at the Council.

LIST OF PARISHES AND MISSIONS,

WITH NAMES OF LAY DELEGATES.

ARKADELPHIA, St. Mark's.

ARKANSAS CITY, Mission.

BATESVILLE, St. Paul's.

CAMDEN, St. John's.

DARDANELLE, St. Paul's.

EUREKA SPRINGS, St. James.

FAYETTEVILLE, St Paul's.

FORT SMITH, St. John's—Messrs. Stephen Wheeler, Edwin Shelby* and Walter Naish.

HELENA, St. John's—Messrs. Janus W. Richens, S. S. Faulkner* and P. O. Thweat.*

HOPE, St. Marks.

HOT SPRINGS, St. Luke's—Messrs. James P. Mellard,* George G. Latta* and Dr. T. B. Buchánan.*

LAKE VILLAGE, Emmanuel.

LITTLE ROCK, Trinity Cathedral, Messrs. Logan H. Roots, Wm. G. Whipple* and Geo. W. Caruth.* *Alternates—* T. C. Gunning, Alex. Robertson* and —— Finney.*

LITTLE ROCK, Christ Church—Messrs. John D. Adams,* W. W. Smith* and Dr. L. R. Stark.* *Alternates—*R. L. Goodrich,* R. J. Polk* and G. S. Brack.

MAMMOTH SPRING, St. Andrew's.

MARIANNA, St. Andrew's—Messrs. Wm. H. Clark, H. P. Rogers and John M. Daggett.

MORRILTON, St. Agnes—Messrs. Wm. M. Scarborough,* Wm. Sandlin* and James Scarborough.*

NASHVILLE, Church of the Redeemer.

NEWPORT, St. Paul's—Messrs. Lancelot Miner,* Wm. Magoffin* and Gustave Jones.*

PHILLIPS COUNTY, Grace.

PINE BLUFF, Trinity—Messrs. Rufus V. McCracken, Marcus L. Bell and N. B. Trulock.* *Alternates—*Chas. H. Harding,* Geo. E. Valliant* and M. S. Trulock.*

PRESCOTT, St. James.

VAN BUREN, Trinity.

WASHINGTON, Grace.

WITCHERVILLE, Mission.

*Not present at the Council.

PROCEEDINGS

OF THE

SIXTEENTH ANNUAL COUNCIL.

The opening service of the Sixteenth Annual Council of the Diocese of Arkansas was held in St. Andrew's Church, Marianna, on Thursday, April 12, 1888, at 11 o'clock a. m.

Morning Prayer was said by the Rev. Messrs. Vaulx, Degen and Carnahan. The sermon was preached by the Rev. W. J. Miller, who took for his text, Acts I, verse 3: "To whom also He showed Himself alive after His Passion by many infallible proofs, being seen of them forty days, and speaking of the things pertaining to the Kingdom of God." The Holy Eucharist was celebrated by the Rt. Rev., the Bishop, assisted by the Rev. C. A. Bruce, Rector of the Parish.

After the service the Council was called to order by the Bishop. The Secretary was requested to call the roll of the Clergy canonically connected with the Diocese, when the following answered to their names:

Bishop:

The Rt. Rev. Henry N. Pierce, D. D., LL. D.

Priests:

Rev. I. O. Adams,	Rev. R. S. James, D. D.
Rev. Frank M. Bayne,	Rev. W. J. Miller,
Rev. C. A. Bruce,	Rev. D. S. C. M. Potter, D. D.
Rev. W. Carnahan,	Rev. Richard Totten,
Rev. Geo. F. Degen,	Rev. J. J. Vaulx,

Rev. W. W. Estabrooke.

The Rev. Messrs. Adams and Carnahan were appointed a Committee on Credentials, who reported that the following Lay Delegates had been duly elected to the Council:

Trinity Cathedral, Little Rock—Messrs. Logan H. Roots, Wm. G. Whipple, Geo. W. Caruth. Alternates, T. C. Gunning and Alex. Robertson.

Christ Church, Little Rock—Messrs. John D. Adams, W. W. Smith, Dr. L. R. Stark. Alternates, R. L. Goodrich, R. J. Polk and G. S. Brack.

St. John's, Helena—Messrs. J. W. Richens, S. S. Faulkner and P. O. Thweat.

St. Andrew's, Marianna—Messrs. Wm. H. Clarke, John M. Daggett and H. P. Rogers.

St. Agnes, Morrilton—Messrs. Wm. M. Scarborough, Wm. N. Sandlin and James Scarborough.

Trinity, Pine Bluff—Messrs. R. V. McCracken, M. L. Bell, N. B. Trulock. Alternates, Chas. T. Harding, M. S. Trulock and Geo. E. Valliant.

St. Luke's, Hot Springs—Messrs. J. P. Mellard, Geo. G. Latta and Dr. T. B. Buchanan.

St. John's, Fort Smith—Messrs. Stephen Wheeler, Edwin Shelby and Walter Naish.

On calling the roll the following answered to their names:

Hon. M. L. Bell, Chancellor.

Stephen Wheeler,	J. W. Richens,
Walter Naish,	T. C. Gunning,
M. L. Bell,	Wm. H. Clarke,
R. V. McCracken,	John M. Daggett,
Logan H. Roots,	H. P. Rogers.

On motion of the Rev. C. A. Bruce, the Rev. W. J. Miller was unanimously re-elected Secretary.

On motion the Council took a recess until 5 o'clock p. m.

AFTERNOON SESSION.

THURSDAY, April 12th.

The Council re-assembled at 5 o'clock p. m., the Bishop in the chair. The following Standing Committees were appointed:

Ways and Means:

Rev. R. Totten, Chairman.
Messrs. John M. Daggett and Logan H. Roots.

Admission of New Parishes:

Rev. Wallace Carnahan.
Mr. R. V. McCracken.

State of the Church:

Rev. C. A. Bruce, Chairman.

Rev. W. W. Estabrooke,	Mr. T. C. Gunning,
Rev. Geo. F. Degen,	Mr. J. W. Richens,

Mr. John M. Daggett.

Auditing and Finance:

Mr. M. L. Bell, Chairman.

Mr. H. P. Rogers,	Mr. S. S. Faulkner,
Mr. Stephen Wheeler,	Mr. John D. Adams.

Unfinished Business:

Rev. R. S. James, D. D.,	Rev. D. S. Potter, D. D.

Mr. Walter Naish.

Constitution and Canons:

Rev. J. J. Vaulx, Chairman.

Rev. I. O. Adams,	Mr. M. L. Bell,
Rev. Geo. F. Degen,	Mr. J. M. Daggett,
Rev. W. Carnahan,	Mr. R. V. McCracken.

The Secretary read the application of St. Agnes' Church, Morrilton, for admission into union with the Council, as follows:

To the Sixteenth Annual Council of the Diocese of Arkansas:

We, the undersigned, hereby declare that St. Agnes' Parish, Morrilton, has been duly organized by the adoption of the Articles of Association as prescribed by the Canons of the Diocese of Arkansas; that the number of communicants is now thirty (30); that a church edifice has been erected, and we hereby respectfully ask that St. Agnes' Parish, Morrilton, Ark., be admitted into union with the Diocese of Arkansas. Signed,

FRANK M. BAYNE, Minister in Charge.

CARROLL ARMSTRONG, Secretary of the Vestry.

MORRILTON, ARK., April 4, 1888.

The above application was referred to the Committee on the Admission of New Parishes, who made the following report:

To the Diocesan Council:

The Committee on the Admission of New Parishes has examined the application of St. Agnes' Church, Morrilton, and find from their papers that the Parish has complied with the requirements of the Canons.

The committee accordingly recommend the admission of that Parish and offer the following resolution:

Resolved, That St. Agnes' Church, Morrilton, be admitted into union with the Council of the Diocese of Arkansas.

Signed,   WALLACE CARNAHAN.

R. V. McCRACKEN.

Whereupon, the Parish was duly admitted by a formal vote.

The Rev. Geo. F. Degen, as committee on the blank form for Parochial Reports, submitted his report, which, on motion, was referred back to the committee for further consideration.

The Rev. I. O. Adams read the report of the Standing Committee of the Diocese. (See Appendix II.)

Col. Logan H. Roots read his report as Treasurer of the Diocese, of the Diocesan Mission Fund and of the Fund for Aged and Infirm Clergy and Widows and Orphans of Deceased Clergymen of the Diocese. (See Appendix III.) Also, the report of Mr. P. K. Roots as Treasurer of the Episcopate Fund. (See Appendix IV.)

On motion, these reports were referred to the Auditing and Finance Committee.

On motion, the Council adjourned to meet Friday, April 13, at 9 a. m.

SECOND DAY.

St. Andrew's Church, Marianna, Ark., }
Friday, April 13, 1888. }

The Council reassembled pursuant to adjournment. The Litany was said by the Rev. Dr. Potter. After service the Council was called to order by the Rt. Rev., the Bishop. The minutes of yesterday's proceedings were read and approved.

The Bishop then read his annual address. (See Appendix I.)

The Rev. R. Totten offered the following resolution, seconded by the Rev. J. J. Vaulx:

"*Resolved*, That in the Parochial Reports the number of actual communicants, the number of confirmed persons, and the number of registered baptized persons in the Parish shall be stated." Which on motion was referred to the Committee on Parochial Reports.

The Rev. R. S. James, D. D., read the report of the Committee on Unfinished Business, as follows :

To the Diocesan Council:

Your committee respectfully suggest that according to Article VII of the Constitution the amendments to the same, adopted by the Fifteenth Annual Council, should be further approved by the Council before final adoption.

Signed,   RICHARD S. JAMES,
          DANIEL S. C. M. POTTER,
          WALTER NAISH.

The Hon. M. L. Bell read the report of the Auditing and Finance Committee, as follows :

To the Diocesan Council:

Your committee respectfully report that we have examined the reports of the Treasurer of the Diocese and the Trustee of the Episcopate Fund and find them correct. The Treasurer, Mr. Logan H. Roots, has procured a suitable book and made a very interesting compilation of the finances of the Diocese from its organization in 1871 down to date.

Credit is due to Mr. P. K. Roots, Trustee of the Episcopate Fund, for the manner in which he has fostered the small amounts coming into this Fund from the time he commenced, by advancing the money to redeem the lots in Little Rock for-

Resolved, That the Bishop be, and is hereby, requested to appoint a committee to draft a memorial to the Lambeth Conference asking the setting forth by it of a correct translation of the Creed of the undivided church as set forth by the last of the Ecumenical Councils, and begging them to recommend its use in the Communion Office. Adopted.

The Bishop appointed the following committee: The Rev. Messrs. J. J. Vaulx, I. O. Adams and C. A. Bruce.

The committee on blank form for Parochial Reports made its report, which, on motion, was adopted and the committee discharged.

The time having arrived for the election of Deputies to the General Convention, the Council proceeded to vote. On the first ballot the following were elected:

Clerical:	*Lay:*
Rev. I. O. Adams,	Mr. Logan H. Roots,
Rev. W. J. Miller,	Mr. H. P. Rogers.

There remaining two Clerical and two Lay Deputies to be voted for, a second ballot was taken, which resulted as follows:

Clerical:	*Lay:*
Rev. J. J. Vaulx,	Mr, Stephen Wheeler,
Rev. W. W. Estabrooke,	Mr. Geo. W. Caruth.

The election for Supplemental Deputies resulted as follows:

Clerical:	*Lay:*
1. Rev. Geo. F. Degen,	1. Mr. M. L. Bell,
2. Rev. Chas. H. Proctor,	2. Mr. P. O. Thweat,
3. Rev. L. F. Guerry,	3. Mr. L. Miner,
4. Rev. D. L. Trimble.	4. Mr. J. P. Mellard.

On motion, the Council adjourned to meet Saturday morning at 9 o'clock.

THIRD DAY.

St. Andrew's Church, Marianna, Ark., }
Saturday, April 14, 1888. }

Morning Prayer was read by the Rev. Messrs. Vaulx and Miller. After service the Council was called to order, the Rt. Rev., the Bishop, in the chair. The minutes of the previous day's proceedings were read and approved.

The Committee on Credentials reported that Messrs. L. Miner, Wm. Magoffin and Gustave Jones had been duly elected as delegates from St. Paul's Church, Newport, to this Council.

The Chairman of the Committee on Constitution and Canons moved the adoption of the following resolution:

Resolved, That the Constitution, as proposed at the last Diocesan Council, be adopted. Carried.

The Rev. Geo. F. Degen offered the following resolution:

Resolved, That the Constitution as adopted be amended by changing Article I to read as follows:

There are three orders of the Clergy.

First—The Bishop, who exercises all the functions of the Ministry, presides over the Church by Apostolic Authority and has the sole right to ordain, to confirm, and to pronounce judicial sentence on offenders; and governs the Church in his Diocese according to the Holy Scriptures and the Canons of this Church.

Second—The Priests or Presbyters, who preach the Word, administer the Sacraments of the Church, and have the oversight and pastoral care of the Laity in their several Congregations. They also have the right to advise their Bishop and to share in the government of the Church, according to the Canons.

Third—The Deacons, who having received limited office in the general Ministry, serve in the same where they may be appointed by the Bishop They are subject to the orders of the Bishop, cannot take the Rectorship of a Church and must be under the supervision and care of some Priest, who shall direct them in their work.

The Laity are divided and organized, according to local convenience, into Parishes or Congregations. They commit the general management of their parochial business to a portion of their own number, annually elected, and called Wardens and Vestrymen. To these belong the administration of all the secular concerns of their particular Parish; but they have no part in the spiritual government of the Church, which belongs to the Clergy alone.

Adopted.

The Hon. M. L. Bell offered a resolution that Article IV, of the Constitution, as adopted, be amended by adding the words "which shall include all current expenses and proper provision for the Episcopate Fund." Adopted.

The Rev. Mr. Carnahan moved and the Rev. Mr. Adams seconded the adoption of the following resolution :

Resolved, That the election of Trustees of the University of the South, and other Trustees not specified, be made the seventeenth order of business and that the items following be numbered accordingly. Carried.

The Rt. Rev., the Bishop, laid before the Council a communication from St. Andrew's Mission at Mammoth Springs, Ark., and announced that it had been admitted as an organized mission.

The Rev. Mr. Totten moved and the Rev. Mr. Degen seconded the adoption of the following resolution :

Resolved, That the Council directs the Treasurer of the Diocese to transfer to the Trustee of the Episcopate Fund, whatever funds of the Diocese above fifty (50) dollars that are in his hands after paying the cost of printing and mailing the Journal of Proceedings and the payment of the assessment of the General Convention. Adopted.

On motion, a recess was taken until 2 o'clock p. m.

AFTERNOON SESSION,

SATURDAY, April 14th.

The Council reassembled, the Rt. Rev., the Bishop, in the chair.

The report of the Missionary Committee of the Diocese was read as follows:

To the Diocesan Council :

The Missionary Committee of the Diocese, as required by Canon V, Section 1, Title III, report that it met in the city of Little Rock on the 19th day of October, 1887, when it acted as a council of advice to the Bishop, according to the Missionary

Canon, and authorized the Bishop to draw one hundred (100) dollars from the Diocesan Mission Fund for the colored work.

Signed,   W. J. MILLER, Sec'y.

The Rev. Mr. Adams offered the following resolution, which was adopted by a rising vote :

Resolved, That the thanks of this Council be returned to the Rector and congregation of St. Andrew's Parish and the citizens of Marianna for their generous hospitality.

The Rev. Mr. Carnahan offered the following resolution :

Resolved, That this Council has heard with much pleasure the expression of the Bishop's intention of attending the approaching Lambeth Conference, and that it is the earnest hope of the Council that the Bishop's visit may prove conducive to his health and happiness and to the glory of God and the edification of the Church. Adopted by a rising vote.

The Rev. Mr. Carnahan having read a communication from the Vestry of Christ Church, Little Rock, inviting the Council to hold its next meeting in that Parish, Col. Logan H. Roots moved that the Seventeenth Annual Council of the Diocese be held in Christ Church, Little Rock, on the second Thursday after Easter, May 2, 1889. Carried.

On motion, the Secretary was authorized to have printed 500 copies of the journal and 1,000 copies each of Certificates of Lay Delegates and of the blank forms for Parochial Reports.

The Rev. Mr. Degen read the report of the Committee on the State of the Church (See Appendix V), which, on motion, was received.

The report of the Committee on Ways and Means was then read by the Secretary, which, after certain changes, was adopted and the Committee discharged. (See Appendix VI.)

The Rev. C. A. Bruce offered the following resolution :

Resolved, That the Secretary be instructed to send one month before the meeting of the Council to each Parish in union with the Diocese and to all Mission Stations, a form of Parochial Report, with the request that they report to the Bishop five (5) days before the meeting of the Council. Adopted.

On motion, the Council adjourned to meet Monday, April 16th, at 9 a. m.

SUNDAY.

St. Andrew's Church, Marianna, Ark., }
Second Sunday after Easter, 1888. }

Divine service was held at 11 o'clock a. m., at which the Rev. Daniel S. C. M. Potter, D. D., LL. D., Deacon, the Rev. Richard S. James, D. D., Deacon, and the Rev. Frank M. Bayne, Deacon, were admitted to the Sacred Order of Priests. The Ordination Sermon was preached by the Rev. Wallace Carnahan, Rector of Christ Church, Little Rock, from the text, Colossians I, verse 17: "And He is before all things and by Him all things consist." The candidates were presented by the Rev. Messrs. Bruce, Degen and Estabrooke, the Clergy present uniting in the Laying on of Hands. The Holy Eucharist followed, being celebrated by the Rt. Rev., the Bishop.

At 4 o'clock p. m. a second service was held, at which the Rt. Rev., the Bishop, delivered a discourse on the general subject: "Why the Providence of God permits divisions among Christian people."

Evening Prayer was said at 8 o'clock p. m. by the Rev. Messrs. Bayne and Estabrooke. The preacher for the evening was the Rev. Geo. F. Degen, Rector of St. John's Church, Fort Smith, who took for his text, Genesis XXIX, verse 20: "And Jacob served seven years for Rachel; and they seemed unto him but a few days, for the love he had to her." After the sermon the Rector of the Parish presented one candidate for Confirmation. The closing prayers were read and the benediction pronounced by the Rt. Rev., the Bishop.

CLOSING SESSION.

St. Andrew's Church, Marianna, Ark., ⎫
Monday, April 16, 1888. ⎭

The Holy Eucharist was celebrated by the Rt. Rev., the Bishop, assisted by the Rev. C. A. Bruce.

After the service the Council was called to order, the Bishop in the chair.

The minutes of Saturday's proceedings were read and approved.

The Rev. Richard Totten was appointed to preach the sermon at the opening of the next annual Council.

The Rev. C. A. Bruce offered the following resolution:

Resolved, That the Council respectfully request the Bishop to furnish a copy of the sermon preached by him on the subject of "Divisions Among Christians," for publication. Adopted.

There being no further business, on motion, the Council, after prayers by the Rt. Rev., the Bishop, adjourned *sine die.*

H. N. PIERCE,

Attest: *Bishop of Arkansas.*

W. J. MILLER,
Secretary.

APPENDIX I.

THE BISHOP'S ANNUAL ADDRESS.

Brethren of the Clergy and Laity:

It is with a heart filled with devout thankfulness to the Giver of all good gifts that I greet you at this, our Sixteenth Annual Council.

I bless God's holy Name for all His mercies vouchsafed to us, that we are again permitted to assemble, and under auspices in many respects more favorable than those of previous years; that the number of Clergy is increasing; that the vacant places are being filled with able workmen; that our feeble Parishes are growing stronger; that the houses of God are becoming more numerous; that new fields are opening before us; that the calls for the services of the Church are becoming more frequent and more urgent; that we can look forward with hope of ere long seeing this once very feeble Diocese a power · in the land.

The number of Clergy now at work in the Diocese is greater than ever before. Of the laborers in this portion of the vineyard a year ago, only one has been lost to us. The Rev. H. A. L. Peabody was deposed from the Ministry in the Church of God on the 1st day of February last, in less than one year from the date of his admission to the Diaconate. Never before had I been called upon to perform so painful a duty. Yes! so exceedingly painful, that I pray God to spare me a repetition of the agony I then suffered.

The Rev. Joshua B. Whaling, made a Deacon on the 4th day of August last, was about a month later transferred to the

Diocese of Southern Dakota. I regretted to lose him, but the Rev. Dr. Potter, Deacon, from the Diocese of Massachusetts, has become the first settled Pastor of St. James Church, Eureka Springs, now become a Parish instead of a Mission, and is working there with great acceptance. The Rev. Charles H. Proctor, also from the Diocese of Massachusetts, has been added to the Cathedral Clergy staff, to my great comfort. The Rev. Le Grande F. Guerry, from the Diocese of South Carolina, has just taken charge of Trinity Church, Van Buren. With the Church building completed, new life has appeared there, so that I look for rapid growth in that quarter. I trust the above may be so marked in another year that I can safely reduce the Missionary appropriation to that field, since the same is much needed for other and newer missions.

Mr. Frank M. Bayne, formerly a Preacher among the followers of the late Dr. Cummings, deposed from the Ministry when Assistant Bishop of Kentucky, was transferred to Arkansas, as a candidate for Holy Orders, from the Diocese of New Jersey. He has already been made a Deacon and is now working at Morrilton successfully. Dr. Richard S. James, lately a prominent Minister of the Baptist denomination, has likewise been made a Deacon and is laboring successfully at Dardanelle. Both of these Deacons have already presented classes for confirmation; and as they are men of established character, as well as of experience in parochial work, I propose, with the canonical consent of the Standing Committee, to raise them in a few days to the Priesthood. There seems to be in these cases no need of the customary and generally wise delay. The Rev. Mr. Galbraith, a Deacon canonically connected with the Diocese of Northern Texas, has shown himself in his position of Assistant Minister in Christ Church, Little Rock, a good workman.

We may now glance at the material improvements of the past twelve months. Besides the completion of the Church at Van Buren, we can report the completion of a small, but very churchly building at Nashville. Never has a little labor borne more abundant fruits than may be seen in the Church of the Redeemer, Nashville. The like may be said in regard to Morrilton. In the summer of 1885, less than three years ago, I made my first visitation of that place. Now, the Parish of St. Agnes there, rejoices in the possession of a beautiful Church, and is making a noble effort to make itself self-supporting. To these must be added St. Philip's Church at Little Rock. A neat edifice has been erected, and the work is developing so rapidly that its capacity may require enlargement before long. These three Churches are an outgrowth from the Cathedral. Had it not been built, these Churches would not, so far as we can see, now exist, and this is but the beginning of what the Cathedral system in Arkansas will, by God's blessing, accomplish. It is feeble yet—in its infancy—but the providence of God will give it strength, for there is a great work for it to do.

Through the zeal and energy of Mr. P. P. B. Hynson, formerly a member of St. Paul's Church, Batesville, a Church and rectory are being built at Mammoth Spring, a new and thriving town on the Kansas City and Memphis Railway. A most noble spirit has been exhibited there. May God bless the efforts now made. A new Church, very much needed, will be soon begun at Camden, and at Hot Springs a new and larger Church will soon appear. Lots have been secured for Churches at Arkansas City and at Rocky Comfort. I must not forget to speak of our acquisition, on most favorable terms, of Buckner College, of which I shall have more to say hereafter. Besides the new Churches, great improvements have been made in those already built. Grace Church, Washington, St. Paul's, Batesville, Trinity Cathedral, and most conspicuously St. Andrew's, Marianna, have been much improved in various ways. Indeed, the one last mentioned, the Church in which we are now assembled, is a proof of what can be effected by patience and zeal. Few Parishes in the country are so feeble in members, and fewer still have done so much in proportion to their members. If it progresses as it has done, it will become indeed a pattern Parish. Christ Church, Little Rock, is making a noble effort to extend the Church in that city. In fact the material growth is an outgrowth of increasing spiritual energy everywhere manifesting itself throughout the Diocese. I could go into particulars and illustrate this statement largely. But want of time forbids. I can only sum up many interesting details in the assertion, that never have the prospects of the Church in Arkansas appeared so bright; never has her future seemed so full of hope. But I must hasten on to an account of my own doings and I here add an abstract of my journal. I would have made it shorter, but I present even now a mere skeleton of the whole.

ABSTRACT OF MY JOURNAL.

I closed my last Annual Address with a report of my official acts to April 19, 1887, the eve of the day appointed for the meeting of the Fifteenth Annual Council of the Diocese of Arkansas.

April 20: At the opening services of the Fifteenth Council of this Diocese, in Trinity Cathedral, Little Rock, the Rev. J. L. Berne, Canon of Trinity Cathedral, preached, and I celebrated the Holy Eucharist, assisted by the Senior Priest of the Diocese, the Rev. C. A. Bruce, Rector of St. Andrew's Church, Marianna.

April 21: I read my Annual Address. I presided at the sessions of the Council until its final adjournment.

April 24, the second Sunday after Easter: At 11 a.m., in Trinity Cathedral, Little Rock, I consecrated a beautiful Altar Cross of brass, the gift of Rev. George F. Degen, Rector of St. John's Church, Fort Smith; and a memorial of his young son, Halford V. Degen, the first acolyte of Trinity Cathedral. I celebrated the Holy Eucharist, assisted by the Rev. George F. Degen and the Rev. David L. Trimble. At 2:45 p.m., I preached at St. Philip's Mission, Little Rock. At 8 p.m., I preached in Christ Church, Little Rock, made a brief address, and adjourned the Council *sine die*.

April 25, St. Mark's day: In the Cathedral, I celebrated the Holy Eucharist. After the services, at a meeting of the Clergy, I presided, and after free discussion, it was decided to take no steps towards forming a branch of the Church Unity Society.

May 1, Sunday, the third after Easter, and the Feast of Sts. Philip and James: At 7 a.m. and 11 a.m., I celebrated the Holy Eucharist in Trinity Cathedral. At 2:45 p.m., at St. Philip's Mission, I baptized two children and preached. At 5 p.m. I preached in the Cathedral.

May 4, Wednesday: In Newport, Ark., at 4:30 p.m., I confirmed in private a sick woman. At 8 p.m., in St. Paul's Church, Newport, after evening service said by Canon Estabrooke, I preached, confirmed five persons (1 male, 4 female) and addressed the class.

May 8, Sunday, the fourth after Easter: In the Cathedral, Little Rock, at 7:30 a.m., I celebrated the Holy Eucharist. At 11 a.m., I assisted in saying the morning service, preached and celebrated the Holy Eucharist a second time. At 8 p.m., in Trinity Church, Pine Bluff, I preached, confirmed two persons (1 male, 1 female) and addressed the class.

May 11: I gave my written official consent to the exchange of the site of St. Luke's Church, Hot Springs, for a larger lot in a more eligible situation.

May 13: Presided at a meeting of the Cathedral Chapter.

May 15, Sunday, the fifth after Easter: In the Cathedral, Little Rock, at 11 a.m., I assisted in saying morning service, preached, and celebrated the Holy Eucharist. At 2:45 p.m., at St. Philip's Mission, I said Evening Prayer and preached. At 5 p.m., I assisted in saying Evening Prayer in the Cathedral.

May 17: I gave my written official consent to placing a mortgage on Christ Church, Little Rock, in order to fund the debt of the Parish.

May 19, Thursday, Ascension Day: In the Cathedral, Little Rock, at 10 a.m., assisted by Canon Berne, I said the

Communion Office, preached and celebrated the Holy Eucharist.

May 22, Sunday after the Ascension: In the Cathedral, Little Rock, at 7:30., a.m., I celebrated the Holy Eucharist. At 11 a.m., I said the Communion Office, preached, and celebrated the Holy Eucharist again. At 6 p.m., I assisted in saying Evening Prayer.

May 25 : At the residence of Mr. George H. Hyde, Little Rock, I joined in holy matrimony, Mr. Frank Wittenberg and Miss Ruth Hyde.

May 29, Whitsun-Day: In the Cathedral, Little Rock, at 11 a.m., I said the Communion Office, preached, and celebrated the Holy Eucharist. At 3 p.m., at St. Philip's Mission, I said Evening Prayer and preached. At 6 p.m., in the Cathedral, I said Evening Prayer.

May 30, Monday in Whitsun-Week : I said the Communion Office, lectured on the day and celebrated the Holy Eucharist.

May 31, Tuesday in Whitsun-Week : I said the Communion Office, lectured and celebrated the Holy Eucharist in the Cathedral.

June 5, Trinity Sunday : At 7:30 a.m., in the Cathedral, at Little Rock, I celebrated the Holy Eucharist. At 11 a.m., I said the Communion Office, preached, and celebrated the Holy Eucharist. At 6 p.m., I preached again.

June 8: In Christ Church, Little Rock, I joined in holy matrimony, Mr. Abraham Ellis Carroll and Miss Carrie Estelle Cohen.

June 11, Saturday, St. Barnabas' Day : In the Cathedral, Little Rock, at 11 a.m., I said the Communion Office, lectured on the day, and celebrated the Holy Eucharist.

June 12, Sunday, the first after Trinity : At 11 a.m., in the Cathedral, Little Rock, I said the Communion Office, preached, and celebrated the Holy Eucharist. At 6 p.m., I preached again.

June 19, Sunday, the second after Trinity: I preached at morning service, and again at evening service, in St. Peter's Church, Columbia, Tenn.

June 26, Sunday, the third after Trinity: In St. Peter's Church, Columbia, Tenn., I preached at morning service.

July 3, Sunday, the fourth after Trinity, in St. Peter's Church, Columbia, Tenn.: I preached at morning service.

July 6: I attended a meeting of the Nashville Convocation, held in the Church of the Messiah, Pulaski, Tennessee, and made a short address.

July 7, in the Church of the Messiah, Pulaski, Tenn.: At 11 a. m. I celebrated the Holy Eucharist. At 6 p. m. I assisted the Rt. Rev. Dr. Garrett, Bishop of Northern Texas, in laying the corner-stone of the new Church. At night I attended a service held in the opera house, Pulaski, and heard an able sermon from Bishop Garrett.

July 8: P. M. attended a session of the Convocation and made a short address. At night I preached at the opera house.

July 10, Sunday, the fifth after Trinity, in St. Peter's Church, Columbia, Tenn.: I attended the morning service and preached at the evening service.

July 12: I assisted at the funeral services of a young lady in Columbia, Tenn.

July 17, Sunday, the sixth after Trinity, in St. Peter's Church, Columbia, Tenn.: I attended the early celebration and received. At 6 p. m. I baptized a child. At night I preached.

July 20: At 5 p. m. I said Evening Prayer in St. Peter's, Columbia, I baptized two children, and made an address.

July 24, Sunday, the seventh after Trinity, in St. Peter's, Columbia: At 7 a. m. I celebrated the Holy Eucharist. At 10:30 I baptized a young girl, assisted in saying morning service and preached.

July 31, Sunday, the eighth after Trinity, in Trinity Cathedral, Little Rock: At 11 a. m. I said the Communion Office, preached and celebrated the Holy Eucharist, assisted by the Rev. A. W. Pierce, of the Diocese of Alabama. At 6 p. m. I preached again.

August 4, in Trinity Cathedral, Little Rock, Arkansas: At 10 a. m. the Rev. H. A. L. Peabody said Morning Prayer, the Rev. A. W. Pierce, of the Diocese of Alabama, reading the Lessons. I preached. The Rev. J. L. Berne presented the candidate, the Rev. A. W. Pierce read the Epistle, and I made a Deacon of Mr. Joshua Brown Whaling. I celebrated the Holy Eucharist and administered to both Clergy and Laity, as the rubric requires.

August 7, Sunday, the ninth after Trinity, in the Cathedral at Little Rock: At 11 a. m. I said the Communion Office, preached and celebrated the Holy Eucharist. At 6 p. m. I said Evening Prayer.

August 14, Sunday, the tenth after Trinity, in Christ Church, Little Rock: At 11 a. m. the Rev. J. B. Whaling said Morning Prayer, I read the Epistle, I baptized an infant, said the Communion Office and preached. At 6 p. m. I preached in Trinity Cathedral.

August 16: I administered the Holy Communion, in private, to a sick person.

August 18: I confirmed, in private, a sick man and his wife, and there being several persons present, I made an address on Confirmation. The candidates were members of St. Philip's Mission.

August 21, Sunday, the eleventh after Trinity, in the Cathedral, Little Rock: At 11 a. m. I celebrated the Holy Eucharist, assisted by Canon Berne.

August 24, St. Bartholomew's Day, in the Cathedral, Little Rock: I said the Communion Office, lectured on the day and celebrated the Holy Eucharist, assisted by Canon Berne. This day I wrote to Dr. Richard S. James, late a minister of the Baptist denomination, at Witcherville, Sebastian county, Arkansas, accepting him as a postulant for Holy Orders. Dr. James comes to us after long and diligent study of the claims of the Church, and with a thorough conviction of the validity of those claims.

August 26: I administered the Holy Communion, in private, to the sick.

August 27: I said the Burial Service, and made a funeral address over the remains of an old and esteemed friend. The services were held in the First Presbyterian Church, Little Rock.

August 28, Sunday, the twelfth after Trinity, in the Cathedral, Little Rock: At 11 a. m. I said the Communion Office, preached, and celebrated the Holy Eucharist, assisted by the Rev. A. W. Pierce. At 6 p. m. I took part in the evening service.

August 29: At 9 a. m. I said Morning Prayer in the Cathedral.

August 30: At 9 a. m. I said Morning Prayer in the Cathedral.

August 31: I said Morning Prayer and Litany in the Cathedral.

September 1: I said Morning Prayer in the Cathedral. I this day gave my official consent to the forming of a Parish at Eureka Springs, Ark.

September 2: I said Morning Prayer and Litany.

September 3: Said Morning Prayer.

September 4, Sunday, the thirteenth after Trinity, in the Cathedral, Little Rock: I said the Communion Office, preached, and celebrated the Holy Eucharist. At 6 p. m., I preached again.

September 11, Sunday, the fourteenth after Trinity: In the Cathedral, Little Rock, I said the Communion Office, preached, and celebrated the Holy Eucharist, assisted by the Rev. J. B. Whaling. At 4 p. m., at St. Philip's Mission, I said Evening Prayer and preached.

September 12 : I this day gave the Rev. Joshua Brown Whaling letters dimissory to the Missionary Diocese of Southern Dakota.

September 18, Sunday, the fifteenth after Trinity : In the Cathedral at Little Rock, at 11 a. m., I said the Communion Office, preached, and celebrated the Holy Eucharist, assisted by the Rev. A. W. Pierce. At 3 p. m., at St. Philip's Mission, I said Evening Prayer, and preached. At 6 p. m., I took part in the evening service at the Cathedral.

September 19 : I said Morning Prayer in the Cathedral.

September 20 : Said Morning Prayer in the Cathedral.

September 21, St. Matthew's Day : In the Cathedral, at 11 a. m., I said the Communion Office, preached, and celebrated the Holy Eucharist.

September 22 : I said Morning Prayer.

September 23 : Said Morning Prayer and Litany.

September 24 : I gave this day my written official consent to place a mortgage on the Buckner College property in order to secure the $1000 loan obtained from the Church Building Fund.

September 25, Sunday, the sixteenth after Trinity : In the Cathedral, Little Rock, at 11 a. m., I said the Communion Office, preached, and celebrated the Holy Eucharist. At 5:30, at the Cathedral, I confirmed one person belonging to the Parish of Grace Church, Washington, Arkansas.

September 28 : In the Church of the Redeemer, Nashville, Arkansas, I joined in holy matrimony, Mr. Willie L. Delony and Miss Ellie Sypert.

October 2, Sunday, the seventeenth after Trinity : In the Cathedral, Little Rock, at 11 a.m., I said the Communion Office, preached, and celebrated the Holy Eucharist. At 5 p. m. I preached again.

October 3: I said Morning Prayer in the Cathedral.

October 4: Said Morning Prayer.

October 5: Said Morning Prayer and Litany.

October 6: Said Morning Prayer.

October 7: Said Morning Prayer and Litany.

October 8: Said Morning Prayer.

October 9, Sunday, the eighteenth after Trinity: In the Cathedral, Little Rock, at 11 a. m., I said the Communion Office, preached, and celebrated the Holy Eucharist. At 3:30 p. m., I officiated at a funeral. At 5 p. m., I preached at the Cathedral.

October 12, in St. John's Church, Fort Smith: At 8 p. m., I preached, and confirmed one person (female).

October 13, in the Union Church, Witcherville, Arkansas: At 8 p. m., after Evening Prayer, said by Rev. Dr. MacDonald and Rev. Geo. F. Degen, I preached, and confirmed eleven persons (nine males and two females), and addressed the class: This occasion was one of great interest, for among the confirmed was Dr. Richard S. James, an eminent Baptist divine, who was seeking the ministry in the Church. I had the pleasure of laying hands upon him, his wife and two of his sons. This was my first visit to Witcherville, and my first opportunity of inspecting Buckner College, which has recently come into the hands of our Church on such favorable terms that it will be a disgrace to us should we fail to retain it and make it a great missionary center for Western Arkansas. The Church school there opened is now flourishing beyond the expectations of the most sanguine friends of the enterprise. I recommend it to the Churchmen of Arkansas and the neighboring Dioceses as an institution where their sons and daughters may receive a sound education, and on terms cheaper than I have ever known elsewhere. It is situated in a portion of the State famous for its healthfulness and surrounded by a country of exceeding beauty. Buckner College will do a great work if well sustained by patronage and a very limited degree of liberality in gifts to establish it on a firm basis.

October 16, Sunday, the nineteenth after Trinity, in the Cathedral, Little Rock: At 11 a. m., I said the Communion Office, addressed the congregation concerning Buckner College and my visit there, preached, and celebrated the Holy Eucharist. At 5 p. m., I took part in the evening service.

October 17: I said Morning Prayer in the Cathedral.

October 18, St. Luke's Day, in the Cathedral: At 11 a. m., I said the Communion Office, lectured on the day and celebrated the Holy Eucharist.

October 19. I said Morning Prayer in the Cathedral.

October 25: I attended officially the opening services of the Missionary Council in the Church of St. James, Philadelphia, Pa.

October 26: Attending the Missionary Council.

October 27: Attended officially the opening services of the House of Bishops, in the Church of St. James.

October 28: Attending the House of Bishops, which adjourned at 5 p. m.

October 30, Sunday, the twenty-first after Trinity, in the Church of the Nativity, Philadelphia: At 10:30 a. m., I preached and made an appeal for the Church work in Arkansas. At 3 p. m., I addressed the Sunday School. At 4:30 p. m., I preached in St. Mark's Church, Philadelphia, and followed with an appeal. At 8 p. m., I preached in St. Clement's Church, Philadelphia, and made an appeal for Arkansas.

October 31: At 11:30 a. m., I attended the Monday "Clericus," and being called upon, made a short address on Church Mission, the subject under discussion.

November 1, All-Saints' Day: I visited Ogantz Institute near Philadelphia, and at night made an address to the young ladies assembled in the school room. I was charmed with my visit to this school, which is doing noble work for God among the daughters of the wealthiest of the land.

November 2: I preached at night in the Church of the Nativity, Philadelphia.

November 5: At 4 p. m., at the Church of the Epiphany, in Philadelphia, I expounded the Sunday School lessons to several hundred teachers from the different city Parishes.

November 6, Sunday, the twenty-second after Trinity: At 10:30 I visited the flourishing Sunday Schools of the Church of the Mediator, Philadelphia, and made missionary addresses in the infant department, and in the general school. At 11 a. m., I made a missionary address in the Church, and, assisted by the Rector, the Rev. Dr. Appleton, celebrated the Holy Eucharist. At 4 p. m., I preached in St. Andrew's Church, and made an appeal for Arkansas. At 8 p. m., I preached in the Church of the Holy Comforter, and made a missionary address.

November 9: Preached in the Church of the Nativity, Philadelphia, at night.

November 13, Sunday, the twenty-third after Trinity: At 10:30 a. m., I preached and made an appeal in the Church of the Crucifixion, Philadelphia. At 2:30 p. m., I addressed the Sunday School in St. Jude's Church. At 7:45 p. m., I preached and made an appeal in All-Saints' Church. This was my last Sunday in Philadelphia, and I take this opportunity of expressing my thanks for the kindness shown me by many of the city Clergy, and of acknowledging my great indebtedness in every way to the Rector of the Church of the Nativity, the Rev. Dr. Jefferis.

November 20, Sunday, the next before Advent: I preached at both morning and evening services, and made an appeal for Arkansas in St. Paul's Church, Rahway, New Jersey.

November 24, Thanksgiving Day: I attended service in Trinity Church, Norwich, Conn.

November 27, Sunday, the first in Advent: In St. Paul's Church, Rahway, New Jersey, I preached at both morning and evening service.

December 3, at the Institute, Columbia, Tenn.:   I addressed the young ladies and the teachers assembled in the study hall. I am more and more impressed by the excellence of this school every visit I make to it.   The proposed enlargement of the Institute building will make it one of the grandest schools in the land, north or south.

December 4, Sunday, the second in Advent, in St. Peter's Church, Columbia, Tenn.:   I preached at morning service, and, assisted by the Rector, the Rev. Dr. Becketts, celebrated the Holy Eucharist.   At night I preached again.

December 7:   I lectured in study hall at the Institute.

December 8:   Lectured again, as above.

December 11, Sunday, the third in Advent, in the Cathedral, Little Rock: I said the Communion Office, preached, and celebrated the Holy Eucharist.   At 7:30 p. m., I preached again.

December 16:   I officiated at the funeral of a child at Little Rock.

December 18, Sunday, the fourth in Advent, in the Cathedral, Little Rock: At 11 a. m., I said the Communion Office, preached, and celebrated the Holy Eucharist, assisted by Canon Berne.   At 7:30 I assisted in saying Evening Prayer.

December 19, in Trinity Church, Van Buren, Arkansas: Rev. Canon Estabrooke said Evening Prayer and baptized four adults.   I preached, and confirmed twenty-three persons (twelve males and eleven females), and addressed the class. This was the first time I ever officiated in the new Church, and it was indeed a fine beginning.   The Parish at Van Buren, after many delays, has now a very cheering prospect of growth. I will add here that the Rev. Mr. Guerry, from the Diocese of South Carolina, took charge of the same at Easter.   Owing to his so recent removal, he has not found it possible to meet us in Council, where we would all be so glad to welcome him.

December 21, St. Thomas' Day, in the Cathedral, Little Rock: At 11 a. m., I preached on the Gospel for the day, and celebrated the Holy Eucharist, assisted by Canon Estabrooke. I this day wrote to Mr. P. P. B. Hynson, Mammoth Spring, Fulton connty, Arkansas, and sent my official consent to the organizing a Parish at that point. Mammoth Spring is very near the Missouri line. A Church and a rectory are now going up. I gave my approval also to the design of the little band, who are working so nobly, of calling in a Clergyman of the Diocese of Missouri, to give them partial services, till they are strong enough to sustain a Rector of their own.

December 25, Christmas Day, in the Cathedral, Little Rock: At 11 a. m., I said morning and evening service, preached, and celebrated the Holy Eucharist. At 7:30 p. m., I said Evening Prayer and preached.

December 26, St. Stephen's Day: In the Cathedral, Little Rock, at 11 a. m., I celebrated the Holy Eucharist. At 8 p. m., in St. Paul's Church, Newport, Arkansas, after Evening Prayer said by Canon Estabrooke, I preached, and confirmed two persons (two females), and addressed the class.

December 28: I this day accepted the letters dimissory presented by the Rev. Daniel S. C. M. Potter, D. D., from the Diocese of Massachusetts, and notified the Rt. Rev. Dr. Paddock of my acceptance.

December 30: At 4:30, in the Cathedral, Little Rock, I confirmed one person (one female.) The candidate is properly registered at the Church of the Redeemer, Nashville, Ark.

January 1,1888, Sunday,The Circumcision: In the Cathedral, Little Rock, Ark., I said full morning service, preached, and celebrated the Holy Eucharist. At 7:30 I said Evening Prayer and preached.

January 6, The Epiphany: In the Cathedral, at 11 a.m., I said the Communion Office. Canon Berne read the Epistle, and assisted me.   Canon Estabrooke preached and I celebrated the Holy Eucharist.

January 8, Sunday, the first after Epiphany: In the Cathedral, Little Rock, I said full morning service, preached and celebrated.   At 7:30 I said Evening Prayer and preached.

January 15, Sunday, the second after Epiphany: In the Cathedral, Little Rock, I said full morning service and, assisted by Canon Berne, celebrated the Holy Eucharist.   At 3 p. m., in St. Philip's Church, Little Rock, Canon Estabrooke said Evening Prayer and I preached.   This was the first service in the newly erected Church.   Though the weather was exceedingly cold, the congregation was good.   It was an occasion that made my heart glad.   I thank God that He has permitted me to see this good beginning of work among the colored population of Arkansas.   At 4:30 I attended a missionary meeting at Christ Church, Little Rock, where the Rev. Mr. Woodman and Miss Sybil Carter, Agents of the Board of Missions, gave, in elegant terms, much interesting information.

January 22, Sunday, the third after Epiphany: In the Cathedral, Little Rock, I said full morning service, preached, and celebrated the Holy Eucharist.   At 3 p.m., I said Evening Prayer and preached in St. Philip's Church.   At 7:30 I preached at the Cathedral, after Evening Prayer said by the Rev. D. L. Trimble, of Pine Bluff.

January, 29, Septuagesima: At 11 a.m., in the Cathedral, Little Rock, I said the Communion Office, preached, and celebrated the Holy Eucharist, assisted by Canon Berne, who said the rest of the morning service.

February 1, one of the saddest days of my whole life: At 4 p.m., in Trinity Cathedral, Little Rock, Arkansas, in the presence of Rev. Wallace Carnahan, Rector of Christ Church, Little Rock, and of Rev. W. W. Estabrooke, M. D., Canon of Trinity Cathedral, I pronounced the sentence of deposition from the Ministry of the Church of God, on the Rev. Henry Amos Lamson Peabody, acting according to the requirements of Title II, Canon 5, Section 1, of the Digest. This was the first time I have ever been impelled to pronounce the sentence of deposition, or even the sentence of suspension, on a brother Clergyman.

February 2, The Purification: I celebrated the Holy Eucharist. Canon Estabrooke preached and Canon Berne assisted me.

February 5, Sunday, Sexagesima: In Trinity Church, Pine Bluff, I said the Communion Office, preached, and, assisted by the Rector, Rev. I. O. Adams, celebrated the Holy Eucharist. At 7:30 p.m., I preached, confirmed 6 persons (5 males and 1 female), and addressed the class.

February 6, in the Court House at Arkansas City: After Evening Prayer said by Canon Estabrooke, I preached, confirmed 5 persons (5 females), and addressed the class.

February 12, Sunday, Quinquagesima: In the Cathedral, Little Rock, I said full morning service, preached, and celebrated the Holy Eucharist. At 3:30 I preached in St. Philip's Church. At 7:30 assisted in saying Evening Prayer at the Cathedral.

February 15, Ash Wednesday: I assisted in saying morning and evening service in the Cathedral. Canon Estabrooke preached.

February 16: Assisted in saying morning and evening service in the Cathedral, and read a lecture.

February 17: I said Morning Prayer. Canon Estabrooke said the Litany. I said Evening Prayer and lectured.

February 18: I said Morning Prayer.

February 19, Sunday, the first in Lent: In the Cathedral, Little Rock, I said full morning service, preached, and celebrated the Holy Eucharist. At 3:30 in St. Philip's I said Evening Prayer and preached. At 7:30 I assisted in saying Evening Prayer in the Cathedral. Canon Berne preached.

February 20: I said Morning Prayer in the Cathedral.

February 21 : I said Morning Prayer in the Cathedral.

February 22: I said Morning Prayer. Also, Evening Prayer and lectured.

February 23: I said Morning Prayer in the Cathedral. I said Evening Prayer, baptized two adults and lectured.

February 24, St. Matthias' Day : In the Cathedral, assisted by Canon Estabrooke, I lectured on the day and celebrated the Holy Eucharist. At 5 p.m., I said Evening Prayer and lectured.

February 25 : In the Cathedral, I assisted in saying Morning Prayer. Rev. W. Carnahan presented and I confirmed one person (1 female). The candidate belonged to Christ Church, Little Rock.

February 26, Sunday, the second in Lent: In the Cathedral I said full morning service, preached, and celebrated the Holy Eucharist. At 3:30 I said Evening Prayer and preached in St. Philip's Church. At 7:30 I said Evening Prayer and preached in the Cathedral.

February 27 : Said Morning Prayer and Evening Prayer and lectured.

February 28: Said Morning Prayer and Evening Prayer and lectured.

February 29: I said Morning Prayer and assisted in saying Evening Prayer, and lectured.

March 1: Said Evening Prayer and lectured in the Cathedral.

March 2: Said Morning Prayer and Litany and Evening Prayer and lectured.

March 3: Said Morning Prayer.

March 4, Sunday, the third in Lent: In the Cathedral, Little Rock, said full morning service, preached, and celebrated the Holy Eucharist. At 3:30, in St. Philip's, said Evening Prayer and preached. At 7:30, in the Cathedral, the Rev. J. H. Galbraith said Evening Prayer and I preached.

March 5: Said Morning and Evening Prayer and lectured.

March 6: Said Morning and Evening Prayer and lectured.

March 7: Said Morning Prayer, Litany and Evening Prayer and lectured.

March 8: Said Morning and Evening Prayer and lectured. Sent to the Bishop of Massachusetts notice of my acceptance of letters dimissory, presented by Rev. Charles H. Proctor.

March 9: Said Morning Prayer in the Cathedral.

March 10: In St. Paul's Church, Batesville, Arkansas, I said Evening Prayer and preached.

March 11, Sunday, the fourth in Lent: In St. Paul's, Batesville, I said Morning Prayer and baptized one adult and two children. At 11 a. m., I said the Litany and Communion Office, preached, and confirmed one person (one male), and celebrated the Holy Eucharist. At 7:30 p. m., in St. Paul's Church, Newport, after Evening Prayer, said by Canon Estabrooke, I preached, confirmed seven persons (one male, six female), and addressed the class.

March 13: At 5 p. m., in the Cathedral, Little Rock, I said Evening Prayer. During the day I conducted the examinations of Dr. Richard S. James and Mr. Frank M. Bayne for Holy Orders.

March 14: I said Evening Prayer. During the day conducted the examination of the candidates for Holy Orders.

March 15: In the Cathedral, Little Rock, Ark., Morning Prayer having been duly said at 9 a.m., at 11 a.m. I held an Ordination. The Rev. Charles H. Proctor, Canon of Trinity Cathedral, preached the sermon; the Rev. W. W. Estabrooke, M. D., Canon of Trinity Cathedral, presented the candidates; the Rev. Wallace Carnahan, Rector of Christ Church, Little Rock, read the Epistle; the Rev. J. L. Berne, Canon of Trinity Cathedral, acted as Server, and I admitted to the Sacred Order of Deacons Richard S. Jones, D. D., and Mr. Frank Morris Bayne. I celebrated the Holy Eucharist, and administered in both kinds to all who received. The Rev. Mr. Galbraith was present. At 5 p.m., Rev. Mr. Bayne said Evening Prayer; the Rev. Wallace Carnahan pronounced the Absolution, and presented three persons (3 females) for confirmation, and I confirmed the same. This makes four confirmed recently at the Cathedral for Christ Church, Little Rock.

March 18, Sunday, the fifth in Lent: In St. Paul's Church, Fayetteville, Ark., I said the Communion Office, preached, and confirmed three persons (1 male, 2 female), addressed the class, and celebrated the Holy Eucharist. At 7:45 p.m., I said Evening Prayer and preached.

March 23: At 7:30 p.m., in St. Paul's Church, Fayetteville, I preached, confirmed four persons (3 male, 1 female), and addressed the class.

March 24: In St. John's Church, Fort Smith, at 8 a.m., I celebrated the Holy Eucharist.

March 25, Sunday, the sixth in Lent: In Trinity Cathedral, in Little Rock, at 11 a.m., I celebrated the Holy Eucharist. At 2 p.m., I said the Burial Service over Margaret Russell Degen, youngest daughter of Rev. George F. Degen, Rector of St. John's Church, Fort Smith, a second time sorely afflicted since he came to the Diocese. May God bind up the wounded hearts.

March 26, Monday, in Holy Week: At 7:45 p.m., in St. Paul's Church, Dardanelle, after Evening Prayer, said by the Rev. Dr. James, I preached, confirmed five persons (2 males, 3 females), and addressed the class.

March 27, Tuesday, in Holy Week: At 9 a.m., in St. Paul's Church, Dardanelle, I said the Communion Office, lectured, and, assisted by the Rev. Dr. James, celebrated the Holy Eucharist.

March 28, Wednesday, in Holy Week: In Hot Springs, Ark., I baptized one adult. At 11 a.m., in St. Luke's Church, I assisted in saying morning service. At 4:30 p.m., I preached and confirmed ten persons (2 males, 8 females), and addressed the class.

March 29, Maunday Thursday: At 11 a.m., in St. Luke's Church, Hot Springs, I lectured on the Holy Communion, and celebrated the Holy Eucharist, assisted by the Rev. Wm. J. Miller, Rector, and Canon Estabrooke. At 3 p.m., by the Rector's request, I baptized a lady in private, and confirmed her and her sick daughter.

March 30, Good Friday: I preached at morning services, Hot Springs.

April 1, Easterday: At 11 a.m., in the Cathedral, Little Rock, I preached and celebrated the Holy Eucharist. At 3:30 p.m., in St. Philip's Church, I preached and confirmed seven persons (1 male, 6 females), and addressed the class. At 5 p.m., in Trinity Cathedral, I confirmed four persons (1 male, 3 females), and addressed the class. At 7:30 p.m., in Christ Church, Little Rock, I preached, confirmed thirty-four persons (9 males, 25 females), and addressed the class.

April 2, Easter Monday: In St. John's Church, Fort Smith, at 8 p.m., I preached, confirmed eleven persons (3 males, 8 females), and addressed the class.

April 3, Easter Tuesday: In St. Agnes' Church, Morrilton, at 7:30, after Evening Prayer, said by the Rev. Mr. Bayne, I preached, and confirmed five persons (3 male, 2 female), and addressed the class. This was my first service in the beautiful new church.

April 4: In St. Agnes' Church, Morrilton, I preached, and, assisted by the Rev. Mr. Bayne, celebrated the Holy Eucharist.

April 5: Sent to the Bishop of South Carolina notice of the acceptance of letters dimissory, presented by Rev. L. F. Guerry.

April 8, Low Sunday: In St. John's Church, Helena, at 10.30 a.m., I assisted in saying morning service, preached, con-

firmed five persons (3 male, 2 female), and addressed the class;
assisted by the Rector, the Rev. R. Totten, celebrated the
Holy Eucharist. At 7:45 p.m., I preached again.

April 9: In St. Andrew's Church, Marianna, I preached
at night.

April 10: In the same church I preached at night.

April 11: In St. Andrew's Church, Marianna, I preached
at night, and confirmed one person (1 male).

SUMMARY.

Sermons 116
Lectures and addresses............................. 70
Holy Eucharists celebrated........................ 67
Confirmations 163
Baptisms: Infants, 8; adults, 6.................... 14
Funerals... 4
Marriages.. 3
Deacons ordained 3
Letters dimissory given—a deacon.................. 1
Letters dimissory accepted: Priests, 1; deacon, 1...... 2
Candidates for Holy Orders........................ ..
Miles traveled 7608

The baptisms are all registered where they were performed,
as also the marriages and the funerals.

In presenting to you this abstract and summary, I must again
remind you how inadequately they represent the work actually
performed during the past year. My journal in full would
give the merest outline of my real life, and the abstract given
is but a mere sketch of my journal.

And now, brethren, I must bring this address to a close.
But I ought not to do so without announcing to you my purpose of attending the Lambeth Conference, which is to meet
in England on the third day of July next. I shall not take
this voyage to Europe for recreation. I am not going for the
pleasure of sight-seeing, nor that I may gaze upon the home

of my ancestors. I go from a sense of duty and in order to place before the assembled Episcopate of the Anglican Communion a subject second in importance to none that will be considered by that august assembly. I go to try to secure some action by that body on the commonly-called Nicene Creed, by which I mean the Creed of the Catholic Church, the one undivided Church of God. The question is simply this: Is the Creed printed in our Morning and Evening Prayer, under the heading "Or This," in any true sense ever the commonly-called Nicene Creed? I answer: No! The Church in England has, so far as I have been able to discover, never called that the Nicene Creed, nor has the Church in the United States of America done so. Wherever in their formularies they print THIS Creed they do not call it the *Nicene Creed*. Wherever they speak of the *Nicene Creed*, they do not print this Creed, for which I know no better, and indeed no other name than our, "OR THIS." I believe that in all this matter the Divine Providence has, through the influence of the Holy Ghost, guided the Anglican Communion. Whether the revisers of the Prayer Book in this country did or did not, in their carelessness, rather than their ignorance, *mean* the "Or This" when they framed the rubric in the Communion Office, allowing the use there of *the Nicene Creed*, I know not and I care less. Perhaps they, as many others have done under the secret guidance of the Holy Ghost, "builded wiser than they knew." It is enough for me to know what they did and what they said, and to know also that all law is to be interpreted literally where such interpretation gives an intelligent and proper meaning, and above all a meaning in exact accordance with well-known, generally-acknowledged and firmly-established principles. Therefore I say that the rubric, as it stands in the Communion Office of our Church, fully authorizes every priest in the American Church to use the pure, unchanged Creed of the undivided Church of God as set forth by the undisputed Ecumenical Councils. And, I may add, that there is no expressed authority for using the "Or This" in the Communion Office. The rubric says : The Apostles' Creed, or the Nicene Creed; and no one will pretend to say that the "Or This" is the Nicene Creed; and no one, that has examined the subject, will maintain that the Church in this land has ever declared it so to be. Being well assured of these facts, I told the House of Bishops in 1883 that the rubric as it stands authorizes any priest to recite the Nicene Creed after the Gospel for the Day; and I asked that an authoritative translation be made and set forth. I waited with patience for years, and used the Apostles' Creed instead of that fuller statement of the Faith which the Holy Catholic Church orders me to use. I waited in vain, and at last, urged by the highest sense of duty and the dictates of conscience, I made the most exact and faithful translation I could of the Catholic Creed as set forth by the last of the Ecumenical Councils that took action on this matter—the Council of Chalcedon. I shall be glad to see a better and more faithful rendering of the same than I have been able to give. for I am, above all things, anxious to follow, not mere mediævalism, but the instructions of the Church Catholic; and herein I feel and know that I am treading in the very footsteps of the fathers of the English reformation and the great doctors of the Anglican Church. They constantly appealed to the primitive Church and to the undivided Church of God in vindication of their action, their belief and their usages. It was on this line of defence that Jewell and all the great apologists and ablest divines of the Anglican Communion placed themselves in meeting and triumphing over the attacks of the Church of Rome. Even if they erred at times as to matters of fact, they never wavered as to the principle that our only reliable guide, after the Holy Scriptures and even in the interpretation of the word of God itself, is the voice of the one, holy, Catholic and Apostolic Church—the only Church in which any of us profess to believe even to this day. And that this appeal to the authority of that Church is the only true and sound one was clearly recognized by English law. For Blackstone tells us, in commenting on the Statute (1 Eliz., Ch. 1), that nothing thereafter was to be accounted heresy: "But only such tenets which have been heretofore so declared: 1. By the words of the Canonical Scriptures. 2. By the first four General Councils, or such others as have only used the words of the Holy Scriptures." As to the third specification given by Blackstone, viz.: "Which shall hereafter be so declared by the Parliament, with the assent of the Clergy in Convocation," I have only two things to say: First, The very wording implies that there had been the desire of conforming to these standards to that date, and a belief that the aim had been attained. Second, That few in this generation will think that Convocation and Parliament combined can create new articles of the Faith. Though we acknowledge six General Councils, but four are here mentioned, because these only touched the Creed. Nor was it merely for the time and under the pressure of peculiar circumstances that the Anglican Communion assumed the position referred to. It is the position professedly held to-day. In evidence I need but adduce the declaration of the first Lambeth Conference, twenty-one years ago. There, after citing the prayer of our blessed Lord, "That all believers in Him might be one, even as He was one with the Father," the assembled Bishops, representing every branch of the Anglican Communion, proceed as follows: "Lastly, we do here solemnly record our conviction that unity will be most effectually promoted by maintaining the *Faith in its purity and integrity, as taught in the Holy Scriptures, held by the Primitive Church, summed up in the Creeds, and affirmed by the undisputed General Councils."* This declaration of the Lambeth Conference was, in 1868, heartily indorsed by the General Convention of the Church in the United States.

Moreover, the House of Bishops, in 1886, at the last General Convention, reiterated, or if you will, re-echoed the sentiments of the first Lambeth Conference in the most emphatic manner. For, in the report of the Committee on Christian Unity, a report that was adopted with great unanimity, they say: "As essential to the restoration of unity among the divided branches of Christendom, we account the following, to-wit: 1. The Holy Scriptures of the Old and New Testament as the revealed Word of God. 2. The Nicene Creed as the sufficient statement of the Christian Faith." · I pass over the third point, which relates to the two great Sacraments, and the fourth, which relates to the Historic Episcopate, and repeat the second. "*The Nicene Creed* as the sufficient statement of the Christian Faith." I can testify that by the *Nicene Creed* here, is meant not the "Or This," which every Bishop present, so far as I could judge, acknowledged NOT to be the Nicene Creed, but the Creed set forth by the whole Church acting through the undisputed General Councils. I say: "So far as I could judge," for the question was presented when the report was under consideration, and no Bishop's voice was raised against the above-given interpretation of the words. From what has been laid before you, it seems certain that the Anglican Communion is as much committed to the principle that nothing should be required of any Christian in the matter of the Faith save what has been set forth by the undisputed General Councils as the Faith, as she is to the principle that the Holy Scriptures are the revealed Word of God.

Now, what have the undisputed General Councils so set forth? The Council of Chalcedon, the last that took action on this matter, concludes thus: "These things, then, having been expressed by us with all possible precision and carefulness, the Holy and Ecumenical Synod decrees that it shall be unlawful for any one to produce, or write, or compose, or devise or teach any other *Faith*. But those who presume to compose, or propound, or teach, or deliver any other CREED to persons desirous of turning to the acknowledgment of the truth from heathenism, or Judaism, or any heresy whatever, if they be Bishops or Clergymen, shall be deposed, Bishops from the Episcopate and Clergymen from the Clergy; and, if they be Monks or Laymen, they shall be anathematized." Now of what Creed does Chalcedon thus speak? I give it here and in as literal a translation as I can make in correct English:

THE NICENE CREED.

" We believe in one GOD, the FATHER, Almighty, Maker of heaven and earth, and of all things visible and invisible;

"And in one LORD JESUS CHRIST, the only begotten Son of God, Begotten of the Father before all worlds, Light of Light, very God of very God, Begotten, not made, Being of one substance with the Father; By whom all things were made; Who, for us men, and for our salvation, came down from heaven, And was incarnate of the Holy Ghost and the Virgin Mary, And was made man, And was crucified for us under Pontius Pilate, and suffered, and was buried, And the third day rose again according to the Scriptures. And ascended into heaven, And sitteth on the right hand of the Father, And cometh again with glory to judge the quick and the dead; Of whose kingdom there shall be no end;

"And in the HOLY GHOST, the LORD, and the Giver of life; Who proceedeth from the Father; Who with the Father and the Son is together worshipped and glorified; Who spake by the prophets;

"And in One, Holy, Catholic and Apostolic Church. We acknowledge one Baptism, for the remission of sins; We look for the resurrection of the dead, and the life of the world to come. Amen."

The General Council of Ephesus had previously declared that no one should be required to profess any other *Faith* than that set forth at Nicea and Constantinople, the same as Ephesus and Chalcedon, laid down as fundamental. But Chalcedon goes beyond Ephesus and demands, not only that we profess the Catholic Faith, but that we profess it as it is precisely formulated in this Creed. And in this fact we find a crushing reply to the elaborate argument of a learned American Professor in favor of the " Or This." He attempts to show that

the addition of the so-called "FILIOQUE" clause was allowa-
ble by pointing out the well-known fact that there were great
variations in formulas setting forth the Faith in the early Church.
True enough; and if it was just because such variations and
freedom of statement were leading to mistatements concerning
the *Faith*, that the Catholic Church was impelled to formulate
the Faith in precise words, and her perfected formula I have
just cited in full.   Now, the Church Catholic had rightful authority to bind Christians down to the use of this "form of
sound words;" or, she had no such authority.   If the former
supposition be true, then no *inferior* authority, whether a
Spanish Provincial Council, an English Convocation, nor an
American General Convention, has a shadow of right to add
to or to alter or to take from that Creed a single word, much
less to add what is virtually another article of the Faith.   If
such right exist anywhere it must be in another true, Ecumenical Council; for no inferior body can claim it.   Yet, "Was
incarnate BY the Holy Ghost OF the Virgin Mary," is not,
"Was incarnate of the Holy Ghost AND the Virgin Mary;"
"Who proceedeth from the Father AND THE SON" is more
than, "Who proceedeth from the Father;" and "One Catholic
and Apostolic Church" is less than, "One HOLY, Catholick and
Apostolick Church."   Let human ingenuity try to twist the
truth as it will, these changes in the Creed of the Catholic
Church have no more authority than the latest additions from
the Vatican.   The FILIOQUE clause may indeed contain less
pernicious error than the pretended articles relating to the
Immaculate Conception and Papal Infallibility, but it has no
more right in the Creed than either of them has.   And whatever truth may be implied in that interpretation cannot be
fundamental truth, else would the Catholic Church, "the pillar
and the ground of the truth," have made it an article of the
Creed.   Moreover the whole Anglican Communion has acknowledged that these changes have no authority by the reiterated declaration that nothing, as touching the Faith, should
be required of a Christian man, except what has been set forth

as such by the undisputed General Councils. But let us go back, and take the other horn of the dilemma. Suppose the Church Catholic, acting through her Ecumenical Councils, had no rightful authority to formulate the Faith and bind men down to the use of a precise form of words, what then follows? Obviously this: No inferior Council can so bind you and me. We are then still left to that freedom, which, according to the opinion of the aforementioned learned American professor, the early Christians exercised when they enjoyed the blessed privilege of making each man his own Creed. If, then, we are left thus untrammeled, who will blame us if we choose to use the very Creed set forth by the undivided Church, rather than rashly risk making a Creed of our own? We certainly show our modesty, if not our wisdom, in so doing. The united Anglican Episcopate is pledged to require, in the matter of belief, no more than this from any man. It has promised to unite with all Christians on this platform. It remains to be seen whether the Anglican branch of the Church will grant to her own faithful children what she so liberally offers to others. If we believe that the Protestant Episcopal Church has less authority than the one Holy Catholic and Apostolic; if we believe that the Church in England, Ireland or Scotland is also inferior to the same Catholic Church, the Anglican Communion must remember that we are but reciting to the world the lesson we learned at her knee. She has taught us true Catholicity; she cannot blame us if we are truly Catholic. If, brethren, I speak warmly, it is because the interest at stake is to me of vital importance. With me it is the Holy Catholic Church, or no Church; Catholicity, or perfect individualism. Logically there is no third position to take; and, in my heart, I find no other position to desire.

You see, brethren, why I wish to be in England on the third of July. But it will be asked, what do I expect to accomplish by being present at the Lambeth Conference? Do I expect that body to legislate on this subject? I answer, No! It does not assume to have any such power. It cannot alter

4

the Creed as it is used in the English, Irish, Scotch, American,
and the many Colonial Churches. But it can declare that
every Christian Bishop, Priest, Deacon and Layman has a
right to recite the Creed of the Holy Catholic Church in the
Communion Office; and it can give to the world the most accurate translation of that Creed of which our mother English
tongue is capable—in its purity and in its entirety. And these
two things I shall humbly ask the assembled Bishops to do.
I say, "In the COMMUNION OFFICE." For while a National
Church may have the right to insert into her daily offices
many things which are merely provincial, she has no right to
introduce into the Eucharistic Services anything not absolutely
Catholic. Because every Christian is not bound to attend
Morning and Evening Prayer; but every Christian is bound
to receive the Holy Communion. And no Christian body can
put into the divine Liturgy aught un-Catholic and thus bar the
way to the Holy Table, without being guilty of something like
the sin of schism.

Brethren, I have done. Never have I uttered words under
a deeper sense of my responsibility to God than I have felt in
speaking to-day. Pray ye earnestly that the Holy Ghost may
lead the Church of God into all truth, keep it from all harm,
and make it outwardly one, as it is one in Christ Jesus, in spite
of human weakness and human wickedness. May the Divine
Head so bless His Church that we may be able to add to St.
Paul's "One Lord, one Faith, one Baptism," one Eucharist
also. "O pray for the peace of Jerusalem! they shall prosper that love thee."

I have detained you long. But I could say no less and
quiet my conscience.

I will not longer keep you from other though minor
matters May God guide you in all your deliberations.

                                        H. N. PIERCE.

APPENDIX II.

REPORT OF THE STANDING COMMITTEE.

To the Diocesan Council:

The Standing Committee of the Diocese beg leave to submit the following report:

The committee met at Little Rock, in the Cathedral, on April 22, 1887, and organized by electing Rev. Innes O. Adams President, and Mr. P. K. Roots Secretary. Canonical consent was given to the consecration of the Rev. Elisha Smith Thomas, D. D., as Assistant Bishop of the Diocese of Kansas.

Met at Pine Bluff, July 8, 1887, and recommended Mr. Joshua B. Whaling to the Bishop for ordination to the Diaconate; and gave its consent to the transfer of the Rt. Rev. Wm. Forbes Adams to the Diocese of Easton.

Met at Little Rock, October 19, 1887, and recommended Dr. Richard S. James to the Bishop as a candidate for Holy Orders; also, gave its consent to the sale of certain lots in the city of Little Rock, belonging to the Episcopate Fund, to the Bishop, for the consideration of $1500, the same being secured by real estate in the city of Little Rock.

Met at Little Rock, November 29, 1887, when consent was given to the consecration of the Rev. Abiel Leonard as Missionary Bishop of Nevada and Utah, and of the Rev. James S. Johnston as Missionary Bishop of Western Texas.

Met at Little Rock January 24, 1888, but there being no business before the committee, nothing was transacted.

Met at Pine Bluff March 6, 1888, when it recommended the Rev. Daniel S. C. M. Potter, D. D., LL. D., Deacon, to

the Bishop for admission to the Sacred Order of Priests; and
Dr. Richard S. James and Mr. Frank M. Bayne for ordination
to the Diaconate.

Met at Little Rock April 11, 1888, and recommended the
Rev. Richard S. James, D. D., and the Rev. Frank M. Bayne,
Deacons, to the Bishop for admission to the Sacred Order of
Priests within the time fixed by the Canons.

Respectfully submitted,

I. O. ADAMS,
President.

APPENDIX III.

REPORT OF THE TREASURER OF THE DIOCESE.

THE DIOCESAN FUND.

RECEIPTS.

Balance on hand........................$285 68	
March 14, 1888, St. Paul's, Newport............	10 00
March 20, St. John's, Camden...................	20 00
March 30, St. Luke's, Hot Springs...............	40 00
April 7, Christ Church, Little Rock..............	160 00
April 11, St. John's, Fort Smith.................	100 00
April 12, St. John's, Helena....................	50 00
" Trinity, Pine Bluff.....................	45 00
" St. Andrew's, Marianna................	15 00
" Trinity, Little Rock...................	25 00
" St. Paul's, Fayetteville.................	20 00

Total......   . ...$770 68

DISBURSEMENTS.

July 12, 1887, Prtg Coun. Pro. and Constitution.$156 40	
July 21, 1887, Mailing " " "	15 98
Feb. 8, Book for Treasurer's Accounts........	1 50
April 11, Episcopate Fund...	61 80
Total disbursements.................——$235 68	

Balance on hand........................$535 00

Balance on hand........................	$163 68
June 9, 1887, St. John's, Fort Smith...............	5 85
June 17, Trinity, Pine Bluff......................	4 00
June 21, Trinity, Pine Bluff.......................	6 00
June 21, St. John's, Camden......................	3 20
June 22, St. Andrew's, Marianna............	2 40
March 5, 1888, St. John's, Fort Smith.............	10 75
April 7, Christ Church, Little Rock...............	82 73
" St. John's, Helena.................	11 00
Total.............................	$289 61

DISBURSEMENTS.

Feb. 22, 1888, Bishop Pierce................$100 00	
Mar. 5, Buckner Coll. (by order Bishop Pierce). 10 75	
April 12, To the Bishop................... 11 00	
Total...............................———$121 75	
Balance $167 86	

FUND FOR DISABLED CLERGY.

RECEIPTS.

Balance on hand.........................	$112 98
Nov. 26, 1887, St. Luke's, Hot Springs............	3 85
Jan. 31, 1888, Trinity, Pine Bluff.................	8 05
April 7, Christ Church, Little Rock...............	10 70
Total on hand...........................	$135 58

All of which reports are respectfully and fraternally sub-

LOGAN H. ROOTS,

APPENDIX IV.

REPORT OF TRUSTEE OF EPISCOPATE FUND.

RECEIPTS.

Balance on hand	$144	36
Dec. 22, 1887, Part on Lots 10, 11 and 12, Block 200.	100	00
March 5, 1888, Part on Lots 10, 11 and 12, Block 200.	100	00
April 4, St. John's, Helena	27	80
April 4, Trinity, Pine Bluff	52	60
April 6, Logan H. Roots	10	00
April 6, P. K. Roots	10	00
April 7, St. Luke's, Hot Springs	20	00
April 9, Trinity, Pine Bluff	5	00
April 11, Diocesan Fund	61	80
April 11, St. John's, Fort Smith	9	00
" St. Andrew's, Marianna	16	75
" Trinity Cathedral, Little Rock	10	00
Total	$567	31

DISBURSEMENTS.

May 16, 1887, Building Association Dues	$20	00
June 16, Building Association Dues	20	00
July 16, Building Association Dues	20	00
Aug. 16, Building Association Dues	20	00
Sep. 16, Building Association Dues	20	00
Oct. 17, Building Association Dues	20	00
Nov. 16, Building Association Dues	20	00
Dec. 16, Building Association Dues	20	00
Jan. 16, Building Association Dues	20	00
Feb. 16, Building Association Dues	20	00
March 16, Building Association Dues	20	00
Total disbursements	$220	00
Balance on hand	$ 347	31.
Value int. in Lots 10, 11 and 12, Blk. 200, Little Rock	1,300	00
Building Association Stock value	1,980	00
Total present value of Assets of the Fund	$3,627	31

P. K. ROOTS,

Trustee.

APPENDIX V.

REPORT OF THE COMMITTEE ON THE STATE OF THE CHURCH.

To the Diocesan Council:

Your Committee on the State of the Church beg leave to submit the following report:

It is with profound gratitude that we congratulate the Diocese on the advancement which the Church has made during the past year. Her Clergy list has increased from 14 to 17. The Parochial reports show an increase of twelve and a half per cent in the number of confirmations and of communicants, while the amount of offerings and value of Church property has made an advance of twenty per cent. When we consider that the year from Easter to Easter has been a short one, the increase is still more marked.

The successful working of the Cathedral system for Church Extension, which was reported upon a year ago by our predecessors, has been as marked the past year as heretofore, and its results are beginning to show in increased interest in Church services, in the erection of new Church edifices and in Mission Parishes seeking permanent relations with the Council. The seeds so patiently and carefully sown have budded, and are beginning to blossom and bear fruit.

It should be a matter of congratulation to Church people at Little Rock and throughout the Diocese that St. Philip's Colored Mission has met with such remarkable success during the past year. No aid has been received for it from the Board of Missions or any Missionary Fund. The entire labor has been performed and the work directed by the Bishop's family. It is firmly established and will doubtless be the center of a great missionary work.

The prospect of the successful establishment of a Diocesan School is a matter for great congratulation. A magnificent property, valued, on the most moderate estimate, at $8000, has come into the hands of the Church at an outlay of less than $1000, or practically for nothing. The school has enrolled fifty-eight students during this its first year, but it is to be noted with grave reprehension that scarcely any of these are from Church families. The Church people of Arkansas have failed wholly to manifest any interest in this splendid opportunity which is thrown at their feet. Neither by money nor by patronage have they, to any appreciable extent, aided in the establishment or encouragement of this school. Expenses have been incurred in adapting the building to our needs, and in furnishing it, to the amount of about $1500. A dollar from every communicant in the State would pay it off. Must we ask for it in vain? It will be to the everlasting disgrace of the Church in Arkansas, if, after all the labor, and anxiety, and personal expenditure of money, that have been bestowed upon it by a few disinterested Churchmen, this property is lost, and the enterprise suffered to die out.

As one result of increased vigor, your Committee desire to note the establishment at Fort Smith of a Parochial Hospital, which has been in successful operation for nearly a year, ministering to the necessities of suffering humanity. It is true that it is not yet what it should be, nor what it is hoped it will become when such an institution shall be properly appreciated, and receive the support it merits. Donations have been received from some parts of the State and from abroad, and it is hoped that a suitable building will ere long be erected, with ample accommodations and appliances for such medical and surgical aid as may be required.

While we note with joy, and with gratitude to GOD, who

has permitted us to see this increase for our poor labor, these
signs of progress of Church life, your Committee feel most
solemnly the duty that is laid upon them of calling your attention to the fact that this good showing of growth and activity
is only *comparative*.   Our offerings are *larger*, our workers are
more in number, a few *more* points are supplied with Church
services than before.   But the aggregate offerings, the number
of workers, and the number of Parishes and Missions are still
pitifully small.   If, instead of comparing the present status o
the Church with that of a year ago, we compare it with what
remains undone, as shown by a glance at the map of the State,
instead of being filled with gratulation we may well beat our
breasts and say, "Unprofitable servants are we."   The opportunities that are opening up to the Church every day, in all
sections of the Diocese, are many and great.   But if we fail
to improve them to the full extent of our ability, it had been
better for us in the Day of Judgment to have lacked the opportunities.   In the judgment of your Committee, the time is
ripe for the carrying out of some systematic plan for the extension of the Church throughout those portions of the State
where it is yet unknown.   Arkansas has attracted more attention during the past year from people in the North and East
seeking a mild climate and profitable fields of investment than,
perhaps, any other State in the Union.   The population of the
State has increased, and is still increasing, at a marvelous
rate, especially in the northeast and southwest, both of which
sections are to the Church almost *terra incognita*.   Some provision should be made for ministering to the spiritual needs of
these immigrants, and keeping pace in Church matters with the
great advance of material development.   Title III, Canon 1,
of our Diocesan Canons, provides that the Bishop may divide
the State into Missionary Convocations for this very purpose.
And we respectfully recommend that the Bishop be requested
to make this division as soon as possible ; and that, if, in his
judgment the time has not come for carrying this out completely, *i. e.*, with reference to the whole State, at least a be-

ginning be made at once, and one or two sections be set apart and the experiment fairly tried during the coming Conciliar year in such sections. Your Committee have made a careful study of such statistics as are at hand in regard to the increase of population and development of material resources of the several portions of the State, and they respectfully suggest a division on the following lines: For the Northeast Convocation, the northern and eastern boundaries to be the State line and the Mississippi river; for the western and southern boundaries, the counties of Fulton, Sharp, Independence, White, Woodruff, Cross, and Crittenden. For the Southwest Convocation, the boundary lines to be the western State line and the counties of Sebastian, Logan, Yell, Montgomery, Pike, Howard and Little River. If this, or any division is made, they recommend that all the Clergy should make an earnest effort to increase the contributions of their people for Diocesan Missions, and that all funds given for this purpose, and not specified for Cathedral work shall be applied to the development of aggressive work in the Missionary Convocations. If these recommendations be adopted and acted on, even for one solitary Convocation, your Committee feel assured that a report can be made to the next Council of Church advance such as has never before been chronicled in this Diocese.

We cannot close this report without calling the attention of the Council and of the Diocese to the pressing need of an increase to the Episcopate Fund. Some means should be devised by which the Fund can be, and should be, more rapidly augmented than in the past.

C. A. BRUCE,
W. W. ESTABROOKE,
GEORGE F. DEGEN,
JAS. W. RICHENS,
J. M. DAGGETT.

APPENDIX VI.

PAROCHIAL ASSESSMENTS.

REPORT OF COMMITTEE ON WAYS AND MEANS.

To the Diocesan Council:

Your Committee on Ways and Means respectfully report that after a careful and earnest effort to consider the condition of each Parish and Mission and to make an equitable assessment upon them to be applied to the necessary expenses of the Diocese, respectfully recommend the following assessments:

Batesville, St. Paul's	$ 20 00
Camden, St. John's	15 00
Dardanelle, St. Paul's	10 00
Eureka Springs, St. James'	10 00
Fayetteville, St. Paul's	20 00
Fort Smith, St. John's	125 00*
Helena, St. John's	60 00
Hope, St. Mark's	5 00
Hot Springs, St. Luke's	50 00
Little Rock, Trinity Cathedral	25 00
Little Rock, Christ Church	250 00
Marianna, St. Andrew's	15 00*
Morrilton, St. Agnes'	10 00
Nashville, Church of the Redeemer	5 00
Newport, St. Paul's	10 00
Phillips County, Grace	5 00
Pine Bluff, Trinity	60 00*

Van Buren, Trinity............................... 10 00
Washington, Grace 10 00
Witcherville......... .... 5 00

    Total..$720 00

*Amount increased at the request of the Delegates.

The Committee respectfully call attention to the fact that these assessments are payable aside from and in addition to the receipts from offerings for other specific purposes.

Respectfully submitted,

RICHARD TOTTEN,
LOGAN H. ROOTS,
JOHN M. DAGGETT,
Committee.

APPENDIX VII.

PAROCHIAL REPORTS,
For Year Ending Easter Monday, 1888.

ST. MARK'S CHURCH, ARKADELPHIA.
No report.

UNORGANIZED MISSION, ARKANSAS CITY.
Rev. W. W. ESTABROOKE, Minister.

Number of families, 12; whole number of souls, 30. BAPTISMS, 4. Confirmations, 5. COMMUNICANTS: Admitted, 5; received, 1; total added, 6; removed, 2; total lost, 2; present number, male 1, female 8; total, 9. Marriages, 1. PUBLIC SERVICES, Sundays, 24; other days, 2; total, 26.

OFFERINGS.

PAROCHIAL: Communion alms, $1.50; Rector's salary, $200; Parish expenses, $15; Bible and Prayer Book Society, $1.50; Organ fund, $80; total, $298.

ST. PAUL'S CHURCH, BATESVILLE.

No report.

ST. JOHN'S CHURCH, CAMDEN.
Rev. J. L. BERNE, Minister.
C. H. STONE, J. R. YOUNG, Wardens

Number of families, 20; whole number of souls, 80. BAPTISMS: Infants, 5. COMMUNICANTS: Removed, 1; present

number, male 12, female 25 ; total, 37. Marriages, 1. PUBLIC
SERVICES: Sundays, 24 ; other days, 1 ; total, 25. SUNDAY
SCHOOL: Teachers, male 2, female 3 ; pupils, males 18, females
24. Church sittings, 150.

OFFERINGS.

PAROCHIAL· Communion alms, $46.55 ; Rector's salary,
$200 ; Parish expenses, $100 ; Ladies Guild, $1653.75 ; Sunday
school, $107 ; S. S. Birthday Box, $13. Total, $2000.43.

DIOCESAN: Diocesan assessment, $20 ; Diocesan Missions,
$3.20 ; for charitable purposes, $50. Total, $73.20.

Total offerings, $2180.63.

Estimated value of Church and grounds, $2500.

ST. PAUL'S CHURCH, DARDANELLE.

Rev. RICHARD S. JAMES, D. D., Minister.

W. E. DeLONG, W. S. SMITH, Wardens.

Number of families, 8. BAPTISMS: Infants, 2. Confirmations,
5. COMMUNICANTS: Admitted, 5 ; received, 6 ; total added, 11 ;
removed, 2 ; died, 1 ; total lost, 3 ; present number, male 8,
female 14 ; total, 22. Burials, 1. PUBLIC SERVICES: Sundays,
8 ; other days, 1 ; total, 9. SUNDAY SCHOOL: Teachers, males
2, females 2 ; pupils, males 10, females 15. Rectory.

OFFERINGS.

Cathedral work.................................$ 2 45
Estimated value of church and grounds........... 2500 00

REMARKS.—I have been in charge but four weeks, holding
services twice on Sunday during that time. The Sunday school
has been in operation but three of these Sundays. I find no
complete account of the history of the Parish previous to
entering upon my duties.

R. S. JAMES.

ST. JAMES' CHURCH, EUREKA SPRINGS.

Rev. D. S. C. M. POTTER, D. D., LL. D., Minister.

G. W. MALCOLM, Junior Warden.

Number of families, 30; whole number of souls, 60 or 70. BAPTISMS: Infants, 2. COMMUNICANTS: Present number, males 4, females 30; total, 34. Burials, 2. SUNDAY SCHOOL: Teachers, male 2, female 3; pupils, male 10, female 20. Church sittings, 50.

OFFERINGS.

PAROCHIAL: Balance on hand November 1, $78.90. Communion alms, $51.75; Rector's salary, $185.45; donations, $25; other means, $33.50. Total, $374.60.

Estimated value Church and grounds, $200.

. ST. PAUL'S CHURCH, FAYETTEVILLE.

Rev. J. J. VAULX, Rector.

GEO. F. DEANE, J. L. CRAVENS, Wardens.

BAPTISMS: Infants, 5; adults, 3; total, 8. Confirmations, 7. COMMUNICANTS: Present number, 112. Marriages, 3. Burials, 3. SUNDAY SCHOOL: Teachers, 5; pupils, —. Rectory.

OFFERINGS.

PAROCHIAL: Communion alms, $110.92; Rector's salary, $450; Parish expenses, $52.40; miscellaneous, $177.15. Total, $770.47.

DIOCESAN: Assessment, $20; Cathedral work, $3.16. Total, $23.16.

EXTRA DIOCESAN: Miscellaneous, $7.25. Total, $7.25.

Total offerings, $844.04.

Estimated value of Church and grounds...........$4000 00
Estimated value of Rectory..................... 2000 00

Total.......................................$6000 00

ST. JOHN'S CHURCH, FORT SMITH.

Rev. Geo. F. Degen, Rector.

Stephen Wheeler, Cassius M. Barnes, Wardens.

Number of families, 99; whole number of souls, 421. Baptisms: Infants, 19; adults, 11; total, 30. Confirmations, 12. Communicants: Admitted, 12; received, 44; total added, 56. Removed, 3; died, 2; total lost, 5. Present number, male 63, female 138; total, 201. Marriages, 7. Burials, 12. Public Services: Sundays, 163; other days, 102; total 265. Sunday School: Teachers, male 1, female 10; pupils, male 54, female 69. Church sittings, 200 Rectory.

OFFERINGS.

Parochial: Communion alms, $84.17; Rector's salary, $1000; Parish expenses, $409.34; miscellaneous, $660; St. John's Hospital, $1074. Total, $3227.50.

Diocesan: Diocesan assessment, $109; Diocesan Missions, $31.40; miscellaneous, $8.65; Buckner College, $104.60; Cathedral work, $6. Total, $253.65.

Extra Diocesan: Domestic Missions, $48.76.

Total offerings, $3529.91.

Estimated value of Church and grounds $10,000 00
Estimated value of Rectory.................... 1,800 00
Estimated value other Church property.......... 640 00

Total $12,440 00
Amount of indebtedness on Church property........ $750 00

ST. JOHN'S CHURCH, HELENA.

Rev. Richard Totten, Rector.

P. O. Thweat, S. S. Faulkner, Wardens.

Number of families, 69; whole number of souls, 294. Baptisms: Infants, 2; adults, 1; total, 3. Confirmations, 5. Communicants: Admitted, 5; received, 3; total added, 8.

5

Removed, 3. Present number, male 26, female 93. Total, 119.
Marriages, 1. Burials, 6. PUBLIC SERVICES: Holy Communion, 76; Sundays, 125; other days, 120; total, 245.
SUNDAY SCHOOL: Teachers, male 2, female 9. Pupils, male
and female, 80. Church sittings, 400.

OFFERINGS.

PAROCHIAL: Communion alms, $56.20; miscellaneous,
$450; weekly, $1274.35. Total, $1780.55.

DIOCESAN: Assessment, $50; Cathedral work, $11; Episcopate Fund $27.80. Total, $88.80.

EXTRA DIOCESAN: Domestic Missions, $35.60; Conversion
of the Jews, $7.50. Total, $43.10.

Total offerings, $1912.45.

Estimated value Church and grounds............$12,000 00

ST. MARK'S CHURCH, HOPE.

No report.

ST. LUKE'S CHURCH, HOT SPRINGS.

Rev. W. J. MILLER, Rector.

JAS. P. MELLARD, GEO. G. LATTA, Wardens.

Number of families, 60. BAPTISMS: Infants, 8; adults, 3
total, 11. Confirmations, 12. COMMUNICANTS: Admitted, 12
received, 1; total added, 13. Removed, 8; died, 3; total lost
11. Present number, 82. Marriages, 1. Burials, 4. PUBLIC
SERVICES: Sundays, 73; other days, 52; total, 125. SUNDAY
SCHOOL: Teachers, 8; pupils, 65. Church sittings, 180.

OFFERINGS.

PAROCHIAL: Communion alms, $74.06; Rector's salary
$1000; Parish expenses, $360.40; Church building fund
$1427.70; miscellaneous, $85.30. Total, $2947.46.

DIOCESAN: Assessment, $40; Cathedral work, $17.25; Aged and Infirm Clergy, $3.85; Episcopate fund, $20; total, $81.10.

EXTRA DIOCESAN: University of the South, $20.55; American Church Building Fund, $12.05; Conversion of the Jews, $6.15; Mission to Deaf Mutes, $25.65; total, $64.40.

Total offerings, $3092.96.

Estimated value Church and grounds............$11,000 00

EMMANUEL CHURCH, LAKE VILLAGE.

No report.

CHRIST CHURCH, LITTLE ROCK.

Rev. WALLACE CARNAHAN, Rector.
Rev. J. E. H. GALBRAITH, Assistant Minister.
R. H. PARHAM, W. W. SMITH, Wardens.

Number of families, 331; whole number of souls, 1628. BAPTISMS: Infants, 40; adults, 17; total, 57. Confirmations, 38. COMMUNICANTS, 508. Marriages, 7. Burials, 18. SUNDAY SCHOOLS: Teachers 41, pupils 365.

OFFERINGS.

PAROCHIAL: Communion alms, $333.20; Rector's salary, $2332.90; salary of assistant minister (seven months), $493.35; rent of Rectory, $587.50; Church carpet and furniture, $1318; insurance on Church, $498.15; other Parish expenses, $1402.32. Total, $10,770.21.

DIOCESAN: Assessment, $160; Aged and Infirm Clergy, $10.70; Diocesan Missions, $82.73; Episcopate Fund, $72.49. Total, $325.92.

EXTRA DIOCESAN: Domestic Missions, $269.09; Foreign Missions, $100.78; Conversion of Jews, $13.50; American

Church Building Fund, $12.60; New York Bible and Prayer Book Society, $10; University of the South, $50. Total, $455.97.

Total offerings, $11,552.10.

Estimated value Church and grounds............$60,000 00

TRINITY CATHEDRAL, LITTLE ROCK.

Rt. Rev. H. N. PIERCE, D. D., LL. D., Bishop.

Rev. W. W. ESTABROOKE, Senior Canon.

GEO. W. CARUTH, ALEX. ROBERTSON, Wardens.

Number of families, 37; whole number of souls, 118; BAPTISMS: Infants, 3. Confirmations, 4. COMMUNICANTS: Admitted, 4; received, 5; total added, 9; removed, 6. Present number, male 12, female 36; total, 48. Marriages, 3. Burials, 2. PUBLIC SERVICES: Sundays, 104; other days, 160; total, 264. SUNDAY SCHOOL: Teachers, 5; pupils, male 12, female 12. Church sittings, 300.

OFFERINGS.

PAROCHIAL: Weekly offertory, $654.28.

DIOCESAN: Assessment, $25; Episcopate Fund, $10; total, $35.

Total offerings, $689.28.

Estimated value Church and grounds..............$8000 00
Estimated value other Church property (St. Philip's). 3000 00

Total $11,000 00
Amount of indebtedness on Church property (St.
    Philip's)................................ 1300 00

REMARKS—At St. Philips' Mission we report 32 (infants) baptisms and 9 confirmations.

This report simply embraces the Cathedral work performed in Little Rock. The work performed elsewhere will be found in reports made by Canons Estabrooke and Berne.

ST. ANDREW'S MISSION, MAMMOTH SPRING.

Number of families, 1. BAPTISMS: Infants, 1. PUBLIC SERVICES: Sundays, 10; other days, 10; total, 20.

OFFERINGS.

Parish expenses.................................$ 200 00
Estimated value of Church and Rectory........... 2000 00

P. P. B. HYNSON,
Treasurer.

ST. ANDREW'S CHURCH, MARIANNA.

Rev. C. A. BRUCE, Rector.

F. H. GOVAN, S. A. BISHOP, Wardens.

Number of families, 14. BAPTISMS: Infants, 3. Confirma-tions, 1. COMMUNICANTS: Admitted, 2. Removed, 5; died, 1; total lost, 6. Present number, 32. Burials, 1. PUBLIC SERVICES, Sundays, 100. SUNDAY SCHOOL: Teachers, male 2, female 2; pupils, 25. Church sittings, 110.

OFFERINGS.

PAROCHIAL: Communion alms, $22.20; Parish expenses, $62.70; Sunday school, $10; Church improvement, $801.55; Altar improvement, $12.10. Total, $908.55.

DIOCESAN: Assessment, $15; Diocesan Missions, $2.40; Episcopate Fund, $16.75; Cathedral work, $2.35; miscellane-ous, $3. Total, $39.50.

EXTRA DIOCESAN: Domestic Missions, $14.65; Domestic Missions (S. S.), $3.60. Total, $18.25.

Total offerings, $966.35.

Estimated value of Church and grounds...........$4000 00

ST. AGNES' CHURCH, MORRILTON.

Rev. FRANK M. BAYNE, Deacon in Charge.

WM. M. SCARBOROUGH and WM. M. SANDLIN, Wardens.

Number of families, 11; whole number of souls, 30. BAPTISMS: Infants, 1; adults, 1; total, 2. Confirmations, 5. COMMUNICANTS: Admitted, 5; received, 2; total added, 7. Present number, male 8, female 22; total, 30. PUBLIC SERVICES: Sundays, 12; other days, 40; total, 52. Church sittings, 150.

OFFERINGS.

PAROCHIAL: Communion alms, $3.40; Parish expenses, $139.40. Total, $142.80.

DIOCESAN: Assessment, $10; Cathedral work, $6.60; total, $16.60.

Total offerings, $159.40.

Estimated value of Church and grounds...........$2766 80

Amount of indebtedness on Church property....... 1221 97

CHURCH OF THE REDEEMER, NASHVILLE.

See Additional Reports.

ST. PAUL'S CHURCH, NEWPORT.

Rev. W. W. ESTABROOKE, Priest in Charge.

Number of families, 30; whole number of souls, 110. BAPTISMS: Infants, 9; adults, 9; total, 18. COMMUNICANTS: Admitted, 7. Removed, 3; died, 1; total lost, 4. Present number, male 4, female 31; total, 35. Marriages, 4. Burials, 1. PUBLIC SERVICES: Sundays, 97; other days, 15; total, 112. SUNDAY SCHOOL: Teachers, male 2, female 3; pupils, male 20, female 26. Church sittings, 175.

OFFERINGS.

PAROCHIAL: Communion alms, $50; Rector's salary, $400; Parish expenses, $150; Ladies' Guild, $97.60; Sunday school, $52.35. Total, $749 95.

DIOCESAN: Assessment, $10.

EXTRA DIOCESAN: Bible and Prayer Book Society, $2.50; American Church Building Fund (S. S. Lenten offering), $2.75. Total, $5.25.

Total offerings, $765.20.

Estimated value Church and grounds..............$2500 00

GRACE CHURCH, PHILLIPS COUNTY.

No report.

TRINITY CHURCH, PINE BLUFF.

Rev. INNES O. ADAMS, Rector.
M. L. BELL, R. V. McCRACKEN, Wardens.

Number of families, 75; whole number of souls, 316. BAPTISMS: Infants, 9. Confirmations, 8. COMMUNICANTS: Admitted, 8; received. 16; total added, 24; Died, 2. Present number, male 21. female 88; total, 109. Marriages, 9. Burials, 6. PUBLIC SERVICES: Sundays, 104; other days, 44; total, 148: SUNDAY SCHOOL: Teachers, males 3, females 6; pupils, males 45, females 55. Church sittings, 450. Rectory.

OFFERINGS.

PAROCHIAL: Communion alms, $25.35; Rector's salary, $900; Parish expenses, $198; Christmas day and S. S., $68.40; new organ (S. S. offering), $19.25; Trinity Church Association, $580. Total, $1701.65.

DIOCESAN: Assessment, $45; Diocesan Missions, $16.40; Aged and Infirm Clergy, $8; Episcopate Fund, $57.60; Cathedral work, $6.30. Total, $127.

EXTRA DIOCESAN: Domestic Missions, $5.55; Colored Missions, $4.70, American Church Building Fund, $8.70; Conversion of the Jews, $6.45. Total, $25.40.

Total offerings, $1854.05.

Estimated value of Church and grounds..........$12,000 00
Estimated value of Rectory 3,500 00

Total $15,500 00

ST. JAMES' CHURCH, PRESCOTT.

No report.

TRINITY CHURCH, VAN BUREN.

See Additional Reports.

GRACE CHURCH, WASHINGTON.

See Additional Reports.

UNORGANIZED MISSION, WITCHERVILLE.

Rev. D. F. MacDonald, D. D., Minister.

Number of families, 5; whole number of souls, 29. BAPTISMS: Infants, 1; adults, 3; total, 4. Confirmed, 11. COMMUNICANTS: Admitted, 3. Removed, 3. Present number, male 9, female, 6; total, 15. PUBLIC SERVICES: Sundays, 48; other days, 12; total, 60. SUNDAY SCHOOL: Teachers, male 2, female 2; pupils, male 9, female 6. Church sittings, 50.

OFFERINGS.

PAROCHIAL: Communion alms, 8: Parish expenses, $30. Total, $38.

EXTRA DIOCESAN: Domestic Missions, $3; American Church Building Fund, $1.20. Total, $4.20.

Total offerings, $42.20.

Estimated value Church and grounds............$9,000 00·
Amount of indebtedness on Church property...... 1,800 00

ADDITIONAL REPORTS.

REPORT OF THE REV. J. L. BERNE,

CANON OF TRINITY CATHEDRAL.

Rt. Rev. H. N. Pierce, D. D., LL. D.:

DEAR BISHOP—I resigned Camden in January, 1888, being there as Mission Priest one year and three months. I have done my best, every time I made my visits there, to encourage the people to build a new Church, as the one used there is not much better than a barn. The people are at work, I hear, to commence a proper building. I have baptized five infants, married one couple and celebrated the Holy Eucharist several times.

ST. MARK'S CHURCH, HOPE—I resigned this Parish in February, 1888, being there one year and four months. The people could not or would not pay the promised salary, so I stopped going to them. They are now in debt to me over *four* months or thereabout. I have baptized one adult and two infants and read the Burial Service over two. I have had the Church altered so as to make it very attractive, a new and pretty altar, foot paces, rail and lectern, all new. The seats are made comfortable and the windows stained.

GRACE CHURCH, WASHINGTON—I resigned the charge of this Parish Easter Monday, April 2, 1888. This little Church is renovated, new lectern, new stove, the entire Church painted and the chancel arch put in. The people at Washington have been faithful workers and have paid for all the alterations and owe me nothing. I have read service and preached there once every month, and celebrated the Holy Eucharist several times.

At Nashville the Church of the Redeemer is finished and ready for benediction. The people there have been faithful and are struggling hard to keep up the services with the help of the faithful Lay Reader, Mr. Lee. They keep up a Sunday school and Sunday morning service. The little Church is an ornament to the village. The interior is very pretty, seats are in, a beautiful altar of white and gilt, reading desk, and all for Church services complete. I baptized one man and one child there, and celebrated the Holy Eucharist four times. I resigned my work there Easter Monday, 1888.

Very respectfully,

J. L. BERNE,
Mission Priest.

REPORT OF THE REV. L. F. GUERRY,

·RECTOR OF TRINITY CHURCH, VAN BUREN.

Dear Bishop :

I herewith send you an official statement of my acts since becoming a Clergyman of this Diocese, and regret very much that on account of the short time that I have been in charge of this Parish my report is not fuller.

Services held on Sunday, 4; week services, 2; total, 6. Celebration of Holy Communion: Public, 1. Burials, 1. Easter offering, including Sunday school, $38.

Faithfully yours,

L. F. GUERRY.

REPORT OF THE REV. W. W. ESTABROOKE,

SENIOR CANON OF TRINITY CATHEDRAL.

My Dear Bishop:

In addition to reports I have made, according to the printed form, I would respectfully add the following record of work performed during the Conciliar year:

At Van Buren: Held two services, preached two sermons, baptized ten adults, presented twenty-three for confirmation, celebrated Holy Communion once.

At Green Back: Two services and two sermons.

At Pendleton: Two services, two sermons, one baptism (infant) and one celebration.

At Portia: One service, one sermon, one marriage.

At Forrest City: Six services, six sermons, three baptisms (infants) and two celebrations.

At St. Phillip's Chapel: One service.

At Trinity Cathedral: Thirty-four services, fourteen celebrations and eleven sermons.

Your obedient servant,

WILLIAM WILMOT ESTABROOKE.

REPORT OF THE REV. D. F. MacDONALD, D. D.

Dear Bishop:

Witcherville as a center of Missionary operations can safely be viewed as second only to the Cathedral in Little Rock. I could give a young Deacon his education gratis, and at the very lowest board, in order that he might visit the surrounding towns and villages and give occasional services. Until the College is firmly on its legs, and until I am relieved somewhat from its petty details, it is grievous to admit that my own visitations to various points have been intermittent.

We require another man here. I can partially support him.
Whence comes the man, and whence can come the rest of his
support? He and I, between us, could open the way for more
extended operations. We have already secured building lots
in the towns of Mansfield and Huntington; and, in the latter
town, we are making preparations for the building of a neat
little Chapel. All this property is to be deeded to the Bishop
and his successors. To sum the thing up: All the surrounding localities are requesting our services; but, to my great
sorrow, I cannot obey all these calls. All I can say is that
there is a great field right here for the Church, and that I can
only put in the wedge and feebly strive to send it home by my
ineffectual hammer. Should any member of the Council know
of a reputable young man properly desiring Holy Orders, I
could promise him free instruction and nominal board if the
Bishop give him authority as lay reader. This beginning,
though small, would surely be an earnest of something hidden
in the future, of which this Diocese might be laudably proud.

Here there is no lack of work—no necessity for a strike.
We need men and means. If the Bishop had the means there
could be no question about the man. I cannot close this
report without saying that, in no other day in the history of
Arkansas, has a Bishop needed so much the liberality of our
Domestic Board. Even another $1000 added to the present
apportionment of the Diocese would make his right arm very
strong. In the meantime let us be thankful that pathways are
opening to the feet of her, known as the "Woman of the
wandering and bleeding foot," and that God, in good time,
will bring her where she can find rest.

DAVID F. MacDONALD,
Missionary.

BUCKNER COLLEGE.

WITCHERVILLE, April 9, 1888.

To the Bishop of Arkansas:

I am here only since October last—making six months.
After being here a few weeks the charge of the College was
thrown on my hands. We commenced with five teachers and

seven pupils; since then two of the faculty have retired, but our students have increased to an enrollment of fifty-eight, including thirteen boarders. It would be useless to name the number and variety of our discouragements. The incisive battle is fought and the victory is, day by day, becoming more assured and complete. Instead of spreading, in the body of this report, a detailed statement of the difficulties surrounding *Buckner College*, I would feel under an imperishable obligation should the Rev. Mr. Degen present its claims and condition to the Diocesan Council. He knows all that the Bishop and Diocese would desire to know about it. I do hope the Bishop and Council will give him an opportunity to do so. My own plan is first to relieve the College of debt, by going north after next June, with the consent of the Bishop, and collect money sufficient to pay the debt of $1800, or at all events, to break the backbone of the debt. This, of course, will secure this valuable property to the Diocese. Until this is done all other things must turn out mere futilities. The Diocese can aid most materially in the matter. She may or may not see fit to aid *Buckner College*, but I humbly submit that a Diocesan School,with as plendid and valuable property already within her grasp, ought to call up a spirit of timely and substantial sympathy—a sympathy that would not waste itself in the vapor of words—but one that expresses itself in gifts which make sympathy effective. *Buckner College* needs this sympathy *now* from the Church at large and from this Diocese.

I cannot leave the College for an hour—this is my excuse for my non-attendance at the Council. My presence here every hour seems absolutely necessary. I will, therefore, end this very incomplete report by expressing the simple and honest hope that the Diocese in Council will, in some way, come to the aid of *Buckner College* and assist us in relieving the institution from a burden which may swamp her. I write this hurriedly and with many cares upon my mind. Brethren, I would help you if I could. Please do what in you lies in this matter to the honor of God and the furtherance of His Church upon the earth; and let the glory be to Him to whom alone the glory belongs.

DAVID F. MacDONALD.

TABLE OF PAROCHIAL STATISTICS.

PARISHES AND MISSIONS.	BAPTISMS. Adults	Infants	Total	Confirmations	Communicants	Marriages	Burials	SUNDAY SCHOOL Teachers	Pupils	OFFERINGS Parochial	Diocesan	Extra Diocesan	Total	Value of Church Property.
Arkadelphia, St. Mark's	1		4	5	9			5	42	298 00			298 00	1,000 00
Arkansas City, Mission		2	3	1	70			1	25					
Batesville, St. Paul's		2	5	5	57	1		5	30	2,000 43	73 20		2,180 63	4,500 00
Camden, St. John's		2	2		22						2 45		2 45	2,500 00
Dardanelle, St. Paul's	1	2	2	7	34	3		4	40	374 60			374 60	2,500 00
Eureka Springs, St. James'		3	8		112			5		770 47	23 16	7 25	844 04	200 00
Fayetteville, St. Paul's	3													6,000 00
Forrest City, Mission	11	19	30	12	201	7	12	11	123	3,227 30	253 65	48 70	3,529 91	12,440 00
Fort Smith, St. John's	1	2	3	5	119	1	6	11	80	1,780 55	88 80	43 10	1,912 45	12,000 00
Helena, St. John's	1	2	3		10	1	2							1,200 00
Hope, St. Mark's	3	8	11	12	82		4	8	65	2,947 46	81 10	64 40	3,093 96	11,000 00
Hot Springs, St. Luke's														1,000 00
Lake Village, Immanuel		3	3	4	48	3	2	5	24	654 28	35 00		689 28	8,000 00
Little Rock, Cathedral	17	40	57	38	508	7	18	41	365	10,770 21	325 92	455 97	11,552 10	60,000 00
Little Rock, Christ Church		32	32	9	14									3,000 00
Little Rock, St. Philip's														
Lonoke, Mission		1	1	1	32			4	25	200 00			200 00	2,000 00
Mammoth Spring, Mission	1	1	3	5	30	1				908 55	39 50	18 25	946 80	4,000 10
Marianna, St. Andrew's	1	1	2	1	35					142 80	16 60		159 40	2,766 80
Morrilton, St. Agnes'	9	9	18	15	13			5	46					2,040 00
Nashville, Church of the Redeemer	1	1	1		109		2			749 95	10 00	5 25	765 20	2,500 00
Newport, St. Paul's														
Pendleton, Mission														
Phillips County, Grace		9	9	8		9	6	9	100	1,701 65	127 00	25 40	1,854 05	2,500 00
Pine Bluff, Trinity						1								15,500 00
Portia, Mission			10	23	69									
Prescott, St. James'	10				10					38 00			38 00	1,000 00
Van Buren, Trinity		1	4	11	15		1	4	15	38 00		4 20	42 20	4,000 00
Washington, Grace	3													2,000 00
Witcherville, Mission														9,000 00
Total	61	155	216	163	1,599	37	59	117	980	$26,545 45	$1,076 38	$672 52	$28,294 85	$172,606 80

APPENDIX VIII.

ORDER OF BUSINESS FOR COUNCIL PROCEEDINGS.

1. Calling the Roll.
2. Presentation of the Certificates of Lay Delegates.
3. Appointment of Committee on Credentials.
4. Report of Committee on Credentials.
5. Election of Secretary.
6. Appointment of Standing Committees.
7. Annual Address of the Bishop.
8. Report of the Standing Committee.
9. Reports of Special Committees.
10. Reports of Trustees of the several Funds.
11. Report of the Auditing Committee.
12. Election of Treasurer.
13. Election of the Standing Committee.
14. Report on the State of the Church.
15. Election of Deputies to the General Convention.
16. Election of Trustees of the several Funds.
17. Election of Trustees of the University of the South and other Trustees not specified.
18. Election of Registrar.
19. Election of Chancellor.
20. Report of Committee on Unfinished Business.
21. Miscellaneous Business.
22. Report of Committee on Ways and Means.

117890

INDEX.

✳ Announcement ✳

* * *

The Seventeenth Annual Council of the Diocese of Arkansas will be held (D. V.) in Christ Church, Little Rock. Ark., on the second Thursday after Easter, May 2d, A. D. 1889.

W. J. MILLER, Secretary.

The Secretary

DIOCESE OF ARKANSAS

JOURNAL

OF THE

Seventeenth Annual Cou

* * *1889* * *

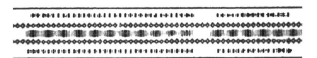

Z

·Special·Offerings·

Recommended by the Council, and the Dates on which they Shall be Made.

DIOCESAN MISSIONS, on the First Sunday in Lent, and on Trinity Sunday.

EPISCOPATE FUND, on Septuagesima Sunday, or on Easter Day.

AGED AND INFIRM CLERGY, AND WIDOWS AND ORPHANS OF DECEASED CLERGY OF THE DIOCESE, on National Thanksgiving Day.

UNIVERSITY OF THE SOUTH, on the First Sunday in Advent.

JOURNAL

OF THE

$\Longrightarrow$PROCEEDINGS$\Longleftarrow$

OF THE

SEVENTEENTH ANNUAL COUNCIL

OF THE

Diocese of Arkansas,

Held in Christ Church, Little Rock, on the 2d, 3d, 4th and 5th Days
of May, A. D. 1869.

LITTLE ROCK, ARK :
PRESS PRINTING COMPANY.
1889.

THE DIOCESE OF ARKANSAS.

ORGANIZED A. D. 1871.

DIOCESAN OFFICERS.

Bishop:

THE RT. REV. H. N. PIERCE, D. D., LL. D.

Standing Committee:

THE REV. INNES O. ADAMS, PRESIDENT.
THE REV. MESSRS. W. J. MILLER AND J. J. VAULX,
MESSRS. M. L. BELL AND P. K. ROOTS.

Secretary of the Council:

THE REV. W. J. MILLER, Hot Springs.

Treasurer:

MR. LOGAN H. ROOTS, Little Rock.

Registrar:

MR. GEORGE H. VANETTEN, Little Rock.

Chancellor:

THE HON. M. L. BELL, Pine Bluff.

Trustee of the Episcopate Fund:

MR. P. K. ROOTS, Little Rock.

LIST OF THE CLERGY OF THE DIOCESE.

Bishop:

RT. REV. HENRY N. PIERCE, D. D., LL. D., Little Rock.

Priests:

Rev. INNES O. ADAMS, Rector of Trinity..........Pine Bluff

Rev. C. A. BRUCE, Rector of St. Andrew's.........Marianna

Rev. WALLACE CARNAHAN, Rector of Christ Church, Little Rock

Rev. J. E. CURZON, Assistant at the Cathedral....Little Rock

Rev. GEORGE F. DEGEN, Rector of St. John's......Fort Smith

Rev. W. W. ESTABROOKE.....................Chicago, Ill

Rev. L. F. GUERRY, Rector of Trinity............Van Buren

Rev. R. S. JAMES, D. D., Rector of St. Paul's......Dardanelle

Rev. D. F. MacDONALD, D. D...........Diocese of Albany

Rev. W. J. MILLER, Rector of St. Luke's........Hot Springs

Rev. D. S. C. M. POTTER, D. D..........Mattapoisatt, Mass

Rev. CHAS. H. PROCTOR, Dean of Trinity Cathedral, Little Rock

Rev. B. W. TIMOTHY, Rector of St. Philip's......Little Rock

Rev. D. L. TRIMBLE, Mission at Pendleton........Pine Bluff

Rev. JAMES J. VAULX, Rector of St. Paul's.......Fayetteville

LIST OF PARISHES AND MISSIONS,

WITH NAMES OF LAY DELEGATES.

ARKADELPHIA, St. Mark's.

ARKANSAS CITY, Mission.

BATESVILLE, St. Paul's—Messrs. Ed. M. Dickinson, J. C. Fitzhugh. *Alternates*—W. B. Lawrence, J. T. Warner.

CAMDEN, St. John's.

DARDANELLE, St. Paul's—Messrs. W. E. DeLong,* A. P. James and Henry Barnett.

EUREKA SPRINGS, St. James.

FAYETTEVILLE, St. Paul's.

FORT SMITH, St. John's—Messrs. Edwin Shelby,* Talbot Stillman, Bleecker Luce. *Alternates*—Andrew Jackson, Guy Barton.*

HELENA, St. John's—Messrs. H. M. Grant* and S. S. Faulkner.

HOPE, St. Mark's.

HOT SPRINGS, St. Luke's—Messrs. J. P. Mellard, G. G. Latta* and Richard Bancroft.*

LAKE VILLAGE, Emmanuel.

LITTLE ROCK, Trinity Cathedral—Messrs. George W. Caruth, William G. Whipple and Logan H. Roots. *Alternates*—Alexander Robinson, Robert J. Matthews and W. C. Finney.

LITTLE ROCK, Christ Church—Messrs John D. Adams, R. H. Parham and L. R. Stark. *Alternates*—G. S. Brack, R. J. Polk and F. D. Clarke.

LITTLE ROCK, St. Philip's—Messrs. J. O. W. Alexander, W. W. Logan and Oscar W. Shaw.*

MAMMOTH SPRING, St. Andrew's Mission—Mr. P. P. B. Hynson.

MARIANNA, St. Andrew's—Messrs. H. P. Rogers, S. A. Bishop and J. M. Daggett.

MORRILTON, St. Agnes—Messrs. Wm. M. Scarborough, Chas. D. James and G. N. Paine *Alternate*—Wm. N. Sandlin.

NASHVILLE, Church of the Redeemer.

NEWPORT, St. Paul's—Messrs. Launcelot Minor and Gustave Jones.* *Alternates*—Charles Minor,* B. Bond* and F. Doswell.*

PHILLIPS COUNTY, Grace.

PINE BLUFF, Trinity—Messrs. M. L. Bell, R. V. McCracken and George E Valiant. *Alternates*—Randolph Brunson, Frank M. Roane and T. P. Stoney.

PRESCOTT, St. James.

VAN BUREN, Trinity—Messrs. John Flitz, John White* and S. A. Pernot.* *Alternates*—P. D. Scott,* H. A. Meyer* and James A. Kearney.*

WASHINGTON, Grace.

WITCHERVILLE, Mission.

---

*Not present at the Council.

PROCEEDINGS

OF THE

SEVENTEENTH ANNUAL COUNCIL.

The Seventeenth Annual Council of the Diocese of Arkansas convened in Christ Church, Little Rock, on the second Thursday after Easter, May 2d, 1889.

Divine service was held at 11 a.m., at which the Rt. Rev., the Bishop, read a portion of his Annual Address (see Appendix 1) and celebrated the Holy Eucharist, being assisted by the Rev. C. A. Bruce, the Senior Presbyter of the Diocese, and the Rev. Wallace Carnahan, Rector of the Parish.

After the service the Council assembled for the purpose of organizing, being called to order by the Rt. Rev., the Bishop of the Diocese. On the Secretary calling the roll of the Clergy canonically connected with the Diocese, the following answered to their names:

Bishop:

Rt. Rev. Henry Niles Pierce, D. D., LL. D.

Priests:

Rev. I. O. Adams,	Rev. R. S. James, D. D.
Rev. C. A. Bruce,	Rev. W. J. Miller,
Rev. W. Carnahan,	Rev. Charles H. Proctor,
Rev. J. E. Curzon,	Rev. B. W. Timothy,
Rev. G. F. Degen,	Rev. D. L. Trimble,
Rev. L. F. Guerry,	Rev. J. J. Vaulx.

The Revs. Messrs. Adams and Guerry were appointed the Committee on Credentials, who reported that the following

Lay Delegates had been duly elected and were entitled to seats in this Council :

St. John's, Helena—Dr. H. M. Grant, and Mr. S. S. Faulkner.

St. Luke's, Hot Springs—Messrs. J. P. Mellard, G. G. Latta and Richard Bancroft.

Trinity Cathedral, Little Rock—Messrs. Geo. W. Caruth, Wm. G. Whipple, Logan H. Roots. Alternates, Alex Robertson, R. J. Matthews and Wm. C. Finney.

St. Andrew's, Mammoth Spring—Mr. P. P. B. Hynson.

St. Andrew's, Marianna—Messrs. H. P. Rodgers, S. A. Bishop and J. M. Daggett.

St. Agnes', Morrilton—Messrs. Wm. M. Scarborough, Charles D. James, G. N. Paine. Alternate, W. N. Sandlin.

Trinity, Pine Bluff—Messrs. M. L. Bell, R. V. McCracken, Geo. E. Valiant. Alternates, F. M. Roane, T. P. Stoney and Dr. Randolph Brunson.

Trinity, Van Buren, Messrs. John Flitz, John White, S. A. Pernot. Alternates, P. D. Scott, H. A. Meyer and James A. Kearney.

The Committee also reported that they had received certificates of the election of Delegates from Christ Church, Little Rock, with a communication objecting to the payment of the assessment made on that Parish, and therefore could not report them as entitled to seats in this Council.

On calling the roll of Lay Delegates the following answered to their names :

James P. Mellard,	J. M. Daggett,
H. P. Rodgers,	Charles D. James,
S. A. Bishop,	R. V. McCracken,
G. W. Caruth,	S. S. Faulkner,
Wm. G. Whipple,	P. P. B. Hynson,
Logan H. Roots,	Wm. M. Scarborough.

being present for the transaction of busin

The Rev. J. J. Vaulx offered a resolution that Christ Church, Little Rock, be excused from paying the amount assessed on that Parish. The Rev. Dr. James moved that the resolution be amended by substituting for the word "excused," the words, "that the offer of Christ Church be accepted." A vote being taken on the amendment, it was lost. A vote being taken on the original motion and the yeas and nays being called for, resulted as follows: Yeas 8, nays 9. The motion was lost.

On motion the Council adjourned to meet Friday morning, May 3d, at 9:30 o'clock.

SECOND DAY.

CHRIST CHURCH, LITTLE ROCK, }
Friday, May 3, 1889. }

The Council reassembled pursuant to adjournment, the Rt. Rev., the Bishop, in the chair.

The minutes of yesterday's proceedings were read and approved.

The Committee on Credentials read a supplemental report as follows:

To *the Diocesan Council:*

The Committee on Credentials have received certificates of election of Lay Delegates from the following Parishes, and report that they are entitled to seats in this Council:

St. Paul's, Batesville—Messrs. Ed. M. Dickinson, J. C. Fitzhugh. Alternates, W. B. Lawrence and J. T. Warner.

St. Paul's, Newport—Messrs. L. Minor, Gustave Jones. Alternates, Charles Minor, B. Bond and F. Doswell.

St. John's, Fort Smith—Messrs. Edwin Shelby, Talbot Stillman, Bleecker Luce. Alternates, Andrew Jackson and Guy Barton.

[Signed],   I. O. ADAMS,
L. F. GUERRY.

On the calling of the roll, the following answered to their names:

Launcelot Minor,	Talbot Stillman,
Ed. M. Dickinson,	Bleecker Luce,
J. C. Fitzhugh,	Andrew Jackson.

The Rev. Mr. Miller offered a resolution that all visiting clergymen and candidates for Holy Orders now in the city, and the members of the Vestry of Christ Church, be cordially invited to seats in this Council. Carried. Under this resolution the Rev. Mr. Rowden, of the Diocese of Louisiana, and several members of the Vestry of Christ Church, were welcomed by the Council.

The Bishop appointed the following standing committees

Ways and Means:

Rev. J. J. Vaulx, Chairman.

S. S. Faulkner and J. M. Daggett.

New Parishes:

Rev. R. S. James, D. D., Chairman.

S. A. Bishop,	Talbot Stillman,

Charles D. James.

State of the Church:

Rev. W. Carnahan, Chairman.

Rev. Chas. H. Proctor,	Mr. Bleecker Luce,
Rev. L. F. Guerry,	Dr. H. M. Grant,

Mr. Geo. W. Caruth.

Auditing and Finance:

Mr. H. P. Rodgers, Chairman.

Wm. M. Scarborough,	R. V. McCracken,
Andrew Jackson,	P. P. B. Hynson.

Constitution and Canons:

Rev. C. A. Bruce, Chairman.

Rev. G. F. Degen,	Mr. M. L. Bell,
Rev. I. O. Adams,	Mr. W. G. Whipple,
Rev. D. L. Trimble,	Mr. L. Minor,

Mr. P. O. Thweat.

Unfinished Business:

Rev. W. J. Miller, Chairman.

Rev. J. E. Curzon,   Mr. S. S. Faulkner,
Rev. G. F. Degen,   Mr. A. P. James.

Rev. I. O. Adams, as President of the Standing Committee of the Diocese, read its report of business transacted during he past year. (See Appendix II).

Mr. A. P. James, Delegate from St. Paul's Church, Dardaielle, appeared and took his seat.

Mr. Launcelot Minor offered the following resolution, econded by Mr. Logan H. Roots.

WHEREAS, the Rector, Wardens and Vestry of Christ Church, Little Rock, :em the assessment laid upon them unconstitutional, and demur to its payment erefore,

Resolved, That this Council hereby remits said assessment and admits the elegation of Christ Church, Little Rock, to seats in this Council.

Carried by the following vote: Yeas 22; nays 6. Wherepon the Delegates from Christ Church appeared and took ieir seats.

The Rev. J. J. Vaulx read the following communication ·om St. Paul's Parish, Fayetteville:

'o the Diocesan Council:

At a meeting of the Vestry of St. Paul's Parish, Fayetteville, held on Monday in :aster week, 1889, the following resolution was entered on the Minutes:

" *Resolved*, That St. Paul's Parish, in Vestry assembled, hereby requests the)iocesan Council about to convene to amend Title IV, Canon I, section 1, by in-:rting after the words 'nor more than eleven Vestrymen,' these words '*who hall be communicants of the Parish in good standing.*'

"*Resolved*, That the Secretary of this meeting be required to furnish the Rector rith a copy of the above resolution to be presented to the Diocesan Council."

[Signed],   J. J. VAULX,
                              Rector St. Paul's Church, Fayetteville.

On motion, the above communication was referred to the Committee on Constitution and Canons.

Applications for admission into union with the Diocese vere made by St. Philip's Church, Little Rock, and the Church of the Redeemer, Nashville, which on motion were re-'erred to the Committee on the Admission of New Parishes.

The Rev. Mr. Carnahan offered an amendment to Title V of the Canons, which on motion was referred to the Committee on Constitution and Canons.

The Rt. Rev., the Bishop, then delivered the remainder of his Annual Address, in which he formally announced that he here and now accepted the Episcopate of the Diocese of Arkansas, to which he had been elected eighteen years ago. This acceptance was duly acknowledged with thanks by a rising vote of the Council, the question being put by the Secretary

Mr. P. K. Roots read his report as Trustee of the Episcopate Fund (See Appendix IV), which on motion was referred to the Auditing and Finance Committee.

Mr. Logan H. Roots read his reports of the various Funds of which he is Treasurer (See Appendix III), which were referred to the Auditing and Finance Committee.

The Hon. M. L. Bell moved that the amendment to the Constitution proposed at the Sixteenth Annual Council, providing for the addition to Article IV of the words "which shall include all current expenses and proper provision for the Episcopate Fund," be adopted. Carried.

Mr. John Flitz, Delegate from Trinity Church, Van Buren, appeared and took his seat.

On motion, a recess was taken until 3 p.m.

AFTERNOON SESSION.

FRIDAY, 3 p.m.

The Council re-assembled and was called to order by the Rt. Rev., the Bishop of the Diocese.

The Rev. Mr. Adams offered a resolution that so much of the Bishop's address relating to the death of the Rev. Richard Totten, late Rector of St. John's Church, Helena, be referred to a committee of three clergymen to report at the morning session of the Council on Saturday. Adopted.

The Bishop appointed the Rev. Messrs. Bruce, Vaulx and Miller as such committee.

The Rev. Mr. Adams moved that the amendment proposed at the last Council to Article I of the Constitution be adopted. Carried by the following vote: Clergy 9, Lay 12.

Mr. R. V. McCracken read the following report of the Auditing and Finance Committee:

To the Diocesan Council:

Your committee respectfully report that they have carefully examined the reports of Mr. Logan H. Roots as Treasurer of the Diocese, of the Diocesan Missionary Fund and of the Fund for Disabled Clergy of the Diocese. We find the statements made in the same to be correct, and the items of disbursements stated therein are accompanied by properly authenticated vouchers.

We have also examined the report of Mr. P. K. Roots, as Trustee of the Episcopate Fund, and find that he is deserving the thanks of the Diocese for the careful and helpful manner in which he has assisted in having this very important fund cared for and increased. Two thousand dollars having been received by maturity of building association stock, the money has been reinvested, and for the money while in his hands during the time that elapsed from the maturity of the building association stock to reinvestment thereof, he has allowed and charged himself with interest on the money thus awaiting investment.

[Signed],   H. P. RODGERS,
         R. V. McCRACKEN,
         A. JACKSON,
         P. P. B. HYNSON.

On motion, the report was received and the Rev. Mr. Bruce moved that the thanks of this Council be returned to Mr. P. K. Roots for the faithful manner in which he has managed the Fund entrusted to him. Carried.

The time having arrived for the election of the Treasurer of the Diocese, the Rev. Mr. Bruce nominated Mr. Logan H. Roots and the Rev. Mr. Carnahan nominated Mr. Samuel D. Adams. The vote being taken by ballot, the tellers made the following report: Number of votes cast 32; necessary to a choice 17; of which Mr. Logan H. Roots received 20 votes and Mr. S. D. Adams 12. Whereupon the Chair declared Mr. L. H. Roots duly elected.

The Council then proceeded to the election of the Standing Committees of the Diocese. The vote being called for by orders, the first ballot resulted in the election of Messrs. M. L. Bell and P. K. Roots. A second ballot being taken, the Rev.

Messrs. Adams and Miller were elected as clerical members.
There remaining one clerical member to be voted for, and
after several ballots had been cast the Rev. J. J. Vaulx was
duly elected. The Chair then announced the members of the
Standing Committee for the ensuing year to be the Rev.
Messrs. Adams, Miller and Vaulx. Lay, Messrs. M. L. Bell
and P. K. Roots.

Mr. Geo. H. Van Etten read his report as Registrar of the
Diocese, as follows:

To the Diocesan Council:

It is my pleasure to report to the Council assembled that I have received from
the Bishop valuable papers and deeds belonging to the Diocese of Arkansas. I
have placed all these papers in a drawer in the Safety Deposit Vaults of the First
National Bank of Little Rock, which was kindly donated by Col. Logan H. Roots
for one year for this purpose.

I have also received from the Secretary of the Diocese a large box containing
Journals of different Dioceses throughout the United States, which, together with
those of Arkansas from its organization, are carefully stored away.

There are five complete sets of the Journals of the Diocese of Arkansas which
I would recommend to have bound and distributed in the following manner : One
set for the Bishop, a set for the Standing Committee, one for the Secretary, one for
the Chancellor and one to be kept by the Registrar.

Several applications have been made to me for back numbers of the Journals,
to which I have not yet responded, having received no authority to give the same
away or to make exchanges. I would recommend that the next Registrar be fully
instructed on this point.

When the Cathedral is completed there will doubtless be a room where these
valuable archives will be conveniently placed so that they will be accessible to the
Clergy of the Diocese at any time. Respectfully submitted,

G. H. VAN ETTEN,

Registrar.

On motion of Mr. L. H. Roots, the report was received
and the Registrar empowered to carry out his recommendations so far as they meet with the approval of the Standing
Committee of the Diocese.

The Rev. Mr. Adams offered a resolution that the wording
of Canon I, Section 2, be restored so as to correspond to
Article IV of the Constitution, as amended at this morning's
session. Adopted.

Mr. Bleecker Luce read a memorial from the Trustees of Buckner College, the consideration of which was, on motion, made the order of business for Saturday morning at 10 o'clock.

The Hon. M. L. Bell offered the following resolution :

Resolved, That the necessary expenses of the Clerical members of the Standing Committee, in attending the regular meetings, be paid by the Treasurer of the Diocese, on the certificate of the Secretary of the Committee.

Adopted.

The Rev. Mr. Miller having conveyed to the Council an invitation from the Rector, Wardens and Vestry of St. Luke's Church, Hot Springs, to hold its next meeting in that Parish, offered the following resolution :

Resolved, That when this Council adjourns, it adjourn to meet in St. Luke's Church, Hot Springs, on the second Thursday after Easter, 1890.

The Rev. Mr. Bruce moved that the resolution be amended by substituting for the words, "St Luke's Church, Hot Springs," the words, "Trinity Cathedral, Little Rock." Carried.

The vote being taken on the original resolution as amended, it was adopted.

The Rev. Geo. F. Degen offered the following preamble and resolution :

WHEREAS, The Rector and Lay Delegates of St. John's Church, Fort Smith, consider the assessment made upon them and paid to the Council flagrantly unjust, as being out of all proportion to the demand made upon the next largest Parish in the Diocese;

Resolved, That one hundred dollars of said assessment be remitted and returned to said Parish.

The resolution was lost by the following vote : Yeas, 11 ; nays, 13.

The Rev. Dr. James read the following report from the Committee on New Parishes:

To the Diocesan Council:

The Committee on New Parishes would respectfully report that the applications of two new parishes, viz., St. Philip's, Little Rock, and the Church of the Redeemer, Nashville, have been referred to it. On examination of the Articles of Association,

2

and other evidence of their Canonical organization, your Committee are satisfied that all has been done in accordance with the Canons, and accordingly recommend their admission as regular Parishes into the Diocese.

[Signed],   R. S. JAMES,
                                                  TALBOT STILLMAN,
                                                  C. D. JAMES.

The report being adopted, the two Parishes were duly admitted by a formal vote.

On motion, the Council adjourned to meet Saturday morning at 9:30 o'clock.

THIRD DAY.

CHRIST CHURCH, LITTLE ROCK, }
Saturday, May 4, 1889.   }

The Council reassembled at 9:30 a. m., and after prayers by the Bishop, was called to order. The minutes of the previous day were read and approved.

The Committee on Credentials made the following additional report :

To the Diocesan Council :

St. Philip's Parish, Little Rock, having been admitted into union with the Diocese, your Committee have received the certificate of the election of Messrs. J. O. W. Alexander, W. W. Logan and Oscar W. Shaw as Delegates to this Council from this Parish, and report that they are entitled to seats.

[Signed],   I. O. ADAMS,
                                                  L. F. GUERRY.

The Rev. Mr. Vaulx, from the Committee appointed to consider a portion of the Bishop's Address, read the following report :

To the Diocesan Council :

Your committee, to whom was referred that portion of the Bishop's Address announcing officially the death of the Rev. Richard Totten, sometime Rector of St. John's Church, Helena, offer the following resolution :

Resolved, That while we mourn our loss in the death of our brother, we thank God for the life of this earnest Priest, and pray God to give us grace so to follow his good example that with him we may be partakers of His Heavenly Kingdom.

We recommend that the Secretary be requested to prepare and insert in the Journal of this Council a Memorial Page.

[Signed],

C. A. BRUCE,
J. J. VAULX,
W. J. MILLER.

The report was adopted by a rising vote.

The Rev. D. L. Trimble offered an amendment to Canon I, Section 1, Title I, which, on motion, was referred to the Committee on Constitution and Canons.

Mr. W. G. Whipple, from the Committee on Constitution and Canons, made the following report:

Gentlemen of the Council:

Your committee, to whom was referred the proposition to amend the Canons so as to provide as a necessary qualification of a Vestryman that he shall be a communicant, beg leave to report that they have had the same under consideration, and are of opinion that, while such a qualification would be very desirable, and would naturally tend, other things being equal, to insure in Vestrymen greater zeal, interest in the Church and general efficiency, would be right on principle and in harmony with the fitness of things; yet, on the other hand, under the real necessities of the situation, as Parishes in our Diocese are obliged to be constituted and organized, the same would be inexpedient and impracticable. In certain Parishes it is ascertained that there are not enough male communicants to compose a Vestry, in some instances actually existing not more than one or two, and in other cases there are now among the Vestry non-communicants who are of the highest degree of usefulness and value to the maintenance of the Parish. Moreover, there are instances, some within recent experience, of persons whose position on the Vestry has led to their confirmation. In some cases there would be no alternative but to disband the Parish organization or constitute the Vestry of ladies. The latter course we do not recommend. It is untried in our Diocesan system, and would at least be experimental. We think the secular duties devolving on the Vestrymen, especially that paramount one of regulating the finances of the Parish, can best be performed by men.

We therefore respectfully recommend that the proposed change be not made.

Respectfully submitted,

C. A. BRUCE,
GEO. F. DEGEN,
I. O. ADAMS,
D. L. TRIMBLE,
M. L. BELL,
WM. G. WHIPPLE,
Committee.

On motion, the report was adopted.

Mr. Whipple also read the following report:

Gentlemen of the Council:

The Committee on Constitution and Canons, to whom was referred the proposition to substitute for Title V of the Canons, entitled, "Trial of Ministers," an entirely new Canon providing a different mode of trial, beg leave to report that they have had the same under advisement, and have carefully compared the proposed method of trial of Ministers with that provided in the existing Canon of the Diocese.

The present method has been established only two years, and has not been long enough in operation, or under observation, to develop any serious defects. It is very carefully devised to insure deliberation and thoroughness in the presentation of charges against clergymen, the trial of them, the sifting of the evidence of guilt or innocence, and the conviction or acquittal as the truth may thus be disclosed. The plan provided should secure a correct result—the disclosure of guilt or protection of innocence. The method virtually embraces four steps or proceedings, each a separate investigation, viz.:

First—A trial before laymen, the Judiciary Committee.

Second—Before the clerical members of the Standing Committee.

Third—Before a Court of Presbyters; and,

Fourth—Before the Bishop or Bishops.

Each step or trial is carefully guarded, is fair and impartial, and should not be tedious, and on the whole the ordeal thus laid down is perhaps the best of any Diocese in the land. By it accused innocence is scrupulously protected, while guilt should be sure of complete and prompt retribution.

If it be alleged that guilt should be more rapidly punished, it should be remembered that it has passed into a proverb that it is better that many guilty should escape than that one innocent should suffer. The greatest merit, perhaps, that this system can claim is that by thus dividing the responsibility of conviction, it relieves the judges, to a great extent, of the oppressive and sometimes fatal responsibility which in other Jurisdictions has proven so fraught with unhappy results.

The proposed canon is noticeable chiefly in this, that it substitutes expedition for thoroughness, and aims rather more at quick than unerring results. At all events its merits are not such that your committee are prepared to so soon abandon the methods of our new Canon in order to make way for it.

Respectfully submitted,

C. A. BRUCE,
I. O. ADAMS,
GEORGE F. DEGEN,
D. L. TRIMBLE,
M. L. BELL,
WM. G. WHIPPLE,
Committee on Constitution and Canons.

On motion, the report was adopted.

The order for the day having been reached, Mr. Bleecker Luce offered the following resolution :

WHEREAS, A memorial has been presented to this Council setting forth certain facts, among others, that Buckner College, a very desirable school property, estimated to be worth $5000, could be secured for the use of the Diocese by the assumption of an indebtedness of not exceeding $1400 ; and,

WHEREAS, Speedy action, if any be desirable, seems required—

Resolved, That a committee of three, to be composed of at least two laymen, be appointed by the Chairman of the Council to inquire into this matter immediately, and they are directed, should they find the facts as stated in said memorial, to take such steps as may be necessary, and that they report their findings and conclusions to the Standing Committee of the Diocese, who are hereby directed to co-operate with such committee of three in all necessary steps and in such manner as they may find most suitable and feasible for the purpose of securing such property to the Diocese. And that this Council hereby ratifies, confirms and adopts as the act of the Diocese such action of the committees aforesaid.

Adopted.

The Chair appointed the following named persons as such committee : Messrs. L. H. Roots, Talbot Stillman and G. H. Van Etten

The Rev. Mr. Carnahan read the report of the Committee on the State of the Church (see Appendix V), which, on motion, was received.

The Rev. Mr. Adams offered the following resolution, which was seconded by Mr. J. M. Daggett :

Resolved, That inasmuch as this Diocese has no official organ, and as it will be well for it to have one, it now appoints a committee of two priests and one layman to make all the necessary arrangements for the selection of an editor, and the publication of a paper to be named " *The Diocese of Arkansas*," and to be the authorized official organ of the Diocese.

Adopted.

The Bishop appointed the Rev. Messrs. Degen and Miller, and Mr. George H. Van Etten, as such committee.

The Rev. Mr. Degen offered the following resolution :

Resolved, That the Diocese of Arkansas, in Council assembled, expresses its profound sympathy with the Bishop of Lincoln in the prosecution to which he has been lately subjected, and its earnest hope that his present trouble may be overruled by God to the glory of His Name, the welfare of His Church, and the establishment of His servants in the enjoyment of that liberty wherewith Christ hath made us free.

Resolved, That the Secretary of the Diocese be, and is hereby, instructed to convey to Bishop King this expression of its feeling.

Adopted.

Col. Logan H. Roots offered the following resolution :

WHEREAS, The fostering of the Episcopate fund is an important duty ; be it,_ *Resolved*, That the Council hereby directs the Treasurer of the Diocese after paying the cost of printing and destributing the Journal of Proceedings and paying assessment of the General Convention, to transfer to the Trustee of the Episcopate Fund whatever, if any, Diocesan funds are remaining in his hands, excepting and reserving only $50 for incidental expenses and such additional amount as the President of the Standing Committee may estimate will be required . for paying expenses of clerical members attending meetings of such committee.

Adopted.

The Rev. Mr. Adams read the report of the Board of Missions, as follows :

To the Diocesan Council:

The clerical members of the Standing Committee met with the Bishop in Marianna as the Board of Missions of the Diocese on April 16th, 1888, and authorized the Rev. W. J. Miller, Secretary, to print and send out to the Clergy of the Diocese a circular letter urging increased offerings for Diocesan missions.

It also authorized the Bishop to draw on the Treasurer of the Diocesan Missionary Fund for the sum of $125 for the work of missions in the Diocese.

[Signed],   I. O. ADAMS, *President.*

On motion the report was received.

On motion the Council took a recess until 7:30 p.m.

EVENING SESSION.

SATURDAY, May 4.

The Council reassembled at 7:30 p.m., the Bishop in the chair.

Messrs. J. O. W. Alexander and W. W. Logan, Lay Delegates from St. Philip's Parish, Little Rock, appeared and took their seats.

Mr. W. G. Whipple read the following report of the Committee on Constitution and Canons :

Gentlemen of the Council:

The Committee on Constitution and Canons, to whom was referred the proposition to amend the Canons so as to more perfectly provide for the representation in the Council of the Cathedral, beg leave to report that they have had that matter under advisement, and respectfully recommend that Title I, Canon I, entitled, " Of the Council," be amended by inserting in Section 1 of said Title and Canon immediately after the words, " Every Parish regularly organized as required by the Constitution," these words, " and the Cathedral Chapter," so that the said section shall read, " Every Parish regularly organized, as required by the Constitution and the Cathedral Chapter, shall be entitled to send three delegates to the Council," etc.

Your committee further recommend that Title IV, Canon I, be amended by striking out the proviso to Section 1 of said Title and Canon, and inserting in lieu thereof the following: " Provided that the congregation worshiping in the Cathedral Church may on the Monday in Easter week, or as early thereafter as practicable, elect not less than three nor more than eleven members of the Chapter, who shall choose delegates to represent the Cathedral in the next Council of the Diocese."

Respectfully submitted,   GEO. F. DEGEN,
                                           I. O. ADAMS,
                                           D. L. TRIMBLE,
                                           WM. G. WHIPPLE,
                                           M. L. BELL,
                                                      Committee.

On motion the above report was adopted.

The Rev. Mr. Degen, as Trustee of the University of the South, read the following report :

To the Diocesan Council:

During the past year the work of the University has been eminently successful, considering the circumstances under which it has been conducted.

The fact cannot be too often repeated to the various Dioceses from which the University draws its principal patronage, and to which it looks principally for support, that no institution of higher learning can be permanently conducted without endowment. The question is often asked why the Grammar Schools of our Church are so successful, and why our Colleges and Universities seem to drag out a miserable existence.

The answer is simple. It is, that the Preparatory Schools are more than self-supporting, while Colleges, apart from endowment or State subsidy, cannot possibly support themselves.

The support of the University of the South so far has been from the surplus of its very flourishing Grammar School Department But this state of affairs cannot last much longer. There is even now a crying need for decent buildings to house our students for educational and spiritual purposes. We sorely need better class rooms and better chapel accommodations.

A step is being taken in this direction, through the agency of Mr. Silas McBee, under the order of the Board of Trustees at its meeting in August, 1888. Mr McBee, it is understood, has subscriptions looking towards permanent endowment of the University to the amount of about fifty thousand dollars, but this is scarcely the beginning of the endowment that is actually needed to make a complete success of this valuable institution. The effort in this direction should not begin to cease until a quarter of a million of dollars has not only been subscribed, but has been actually collected.

In lieu of a vested endowment for the support of the Theological Department, the various dioceses interested in the work at Sewanee have undertaken to subscribe enough each year to support this Department. The Theological Department submits a statement of receipts up to date, and respectfully requests your Convention to carefully consider the same. As little interest has been manifested by many Parishes and some Dioceses in the matter of the support of the Theological Department, the present plan of support has nevertheless proved itself an entirely practicable one. The Professors have never received the full amount of salaries promised them, but they have succeeded in living upon what they have received, and they feel that all that is required to enable them to do so with less anxiety and more comfort is only that what is being done should be done with a little more certainty and regularity. We have the right to ask that the Church shall assure itself whether the Department is not faithfully and loyally discharging the trusts committed to it; and if it is doing so, then that the obligation to support it shall be remembered and met. No very great increase of even the present interest and efforts in its behalf is needed to very materially lighten its difficulties and increase its efficiency; and we pray your Convention and the individual members of it to exert themselves to that end.

Receipts from the Diocese of Arkansas to date..............$ 72 50
Receipts from all Dioceses................. .... 2,310 82
Amount of assessment of the Diocese of Arkansas 150 00
Amount of assessment of all the Dioceses.................. 5,000 00

It will be seen that this Diocese has contributed a little less than one half of the very small sum apportioned to it for the support of the Theological School. I beg leave, therefore, to offer the following resolution :

"*Resolved*, That the Rectors or Delegates of the various Parishes represented in this Council, be asked to pledge on the floor of this body a given sum to make up the deficit in our assessment, or $77.50, and also like pledges for the whole assessment for next year."

[Signed],   GEORGE FREDERICK DEGEN.

On motion, the report was received and the resolution adopted.

The roll being called for pledges to make up the deficit in the assessment for last year, the following pledges were received :

Christ Church, Little Rock......... ... .$ 25 00
St. John's, Fort Smith........................ .. 15 00
Trinity, Pine Bluff..... .... 10 00
St Paul's, Dardanelle........................... 2 50
St. Luke's, Hot Springs...................... ..... 10 00
St. Andrew's, Marianna............. .... 5 00
Trinity Cathedral................................ 10 00
St. Agnes', Morrilton............................ 2 50
St. John's, Helena 10 00
Trinity, Van Buren............................. 2 00
St. Paul's, Batesville........................... 10 00
St. Philip's, Little Rock........................ 5 00

Total....................................$118 00

The roll being called a second time for pledges for the assessment for the University of the South for the next year, the following response was made:

St. Paul's, Newport........... ....$ 5 00
St. Paul's, Dardanelle........................ ..... 2 50
St. Luke's, Hot Springs...................... .... 25 00
St. Andrew's, Marianna......................... 10 00
Trinity Cathedral............,................ 15 00
St. Agnes', Morrilton........................ . 10 00
Trinity, Pine Bluff.......... .... 10 00
St. John's, Helena.. .... 10 00
Trinity, Van Buren...... .... 5 00
Christ Church, Little Rock...................... 75 00
Church of the Redeemer, Nashville.... .... 2 50
Grace, Washington............................. 2 50
St. Mark's, Hope.............................. 2 50
St. Philip's, Little Rock........................ 5 00

Total.......................................$180 00

Mr. Geo. E. Valiant, Delegate from Trinity Church, Pine Bluff, appeared and took his seat.

The time having arrived for the election of Deputies to the General Convention, the Chair appointed as tellers for the

Clerical vote the Rev. Messrs. Trimble and Curzon, and for the Lay vote, Messrs. Daggett and Faulkner. A ballot being taken, the tellers reported that the Rev. Messrs. Adams, Miller and Vaulx were elected Clerical Deputies, and Mr. Logan H. Roots as Lay Deputy.

There being one Clerical and three Lay Deputies to be voted for, a second ballot was made, when Messrs. John D. Adams, H. P. Rodgers and Geo. W. Caruth were declared to be elected. No election of Clerical Deputy. On the fourth ballot the Rev. Chas. H. Proctor was elected. Whereupon, the Chair announced that the following members had been elected to represent this Diocese in the General Convention :

Clerical:	*Lay* :
Rev. I. O. Adams,	Mr. Logan H. Roots,
Rev. W. J. Miller,	Mr. John D. Adams,
Rev. J. J. Vaulx,	Mr. H. P. Rogers,
Rev. Chas. H. Proctor.	Mr. Geo. W. Caruth.

The Council then proceeded to the election of Supplementary Deputies, when the following were elected in the order given :

Clerical :	*Lay :*
Rev. Geo. F. Degen,	Mr. G. H. Van Etten,
Rev. D. L. Trimble,	Mr. Bleecker Luce,
Rev. J. E. Curzon,	Mr. R. V. McCracken,
Rev. C. A. Bruce.	Dr. H. M. Grant.

The election of Trustee of the Episcopate Fund followed, when the ballot being made, Mr. P. K. Roots was declared to be elected.

The Council then proceeded to the election of Registrar, . when Mr. Geo. H. Van Etten was elected.

The Rev. Mr. Bruce moved that the thanks of the Council be returned to Christ Church and Trinity Cathedral for their kind hospitality. Carried.

The Rev. Mr. Adams moved that the Treasurer of the Diocese be instructed to pay to the Sexton of Christ Church

he sum of ten dollars ($10) for his care of the building during
he sessions of the Council. Carried.

It was moved and seconded that the thanks of the Council
e returned to the Managers of the Missouri Pacific Railroad
nd of the Memphis and Little Rock Railroad for their kind-
ess in granting to the members of the Council reduced rates.
:arried.

On motion, the Secretary was instructed to have printed
oo copies of the Journal.

Mr. J. M. Daggett read the report of the Committee on
Vays and Means (see Appendix VI), which, on motion, was
dopted and the committee discharged.

An opportunity was then given to the Rectors and Dele-
ates present to voluntarily increase their assessments, that a
arger amount might be transferred to the Episcopate Fund.
'he roll was called, with the following result:

1ission at Pendleton	$ 20 00
'rinity Cathedral	50 00
it. John's, Helena	30 00
it. Paul's, Fayetteville	10 00
it. John's, Fort Smith	75 00
it. Mark's, Hope	3 00
:hurch of the Redeemer, Nashville	3 00
it. Paul's, Batesville	10 00
1ission at Witcherville	2 50
Total	$203 50

On motion, the Council adjourned to meet on Sunday,
fter evening service.

SUNDAY.

CHRIST CHURCH, LITTLE ROCK, }
Second Sunday After Easter, 1889. }

After evening service, at which addresses were made on
he subject of "Missions," by the Bishop and the Rev.

Messrs. Carnahan, Vaulx and Guerry, and the Rev. Dr.
the Council was called to order by the Rt. Rev., the Bis
the Diocese.

There being no further business, on motion, the C
after prayers by the Bishop, adjourned *sine die*.

H. N. PIERC

Bishop of Arka

ATTEST:

W. J. MILLER,
   Secretary.

IN MEMORIAM.

THE REV. RICHARD TOTTEN, A. M.,

PRIEST.

Born at Hartford, Conn., December 14, 1842.

Baptized in Christ Church, Hartford, by the Rev. Geo. Burgess, D. D., May, 1843.

Confirmed July 6, 1859, in Bruton Parish Church, Williamsburg, Va., by Bishop Johns.

Educated partly at William and Mary College, Va., and partly at the Iowa State University, where he graduated with the degree of A. B. The degree of A. M., was an honorary degree conferred upon him by Trinity College while he was pursuing his theological studies at Middletown, Conn.

Ordered Deacon Oct. 24, 1869, in Christ Church, Lexington, Ky., by Bishop Smith.

Assistant in St. John's Church, Cincinnati, Ohio, from March 20, 1869 to July 18, 1870.

Minister in charge of St. James', Goshen, and St. John's, Elkhart, Ind., from Aug. 1, 1870, to Dec. 12, 1871.

Ordained Priest Nov. 17, 1870, in St. James' Church, Goshen, by Bishop Talbot.

Supplied St. Peter's Church, Paris, Ky., from Jan. 1, 1872 to Aug. 30, 1872.

Rector of St. Paul's, Jeffersonville, Ind., from Sept. 1, 1872, to July 20, 1874.

Rector of All Saints Church, Talbot County, Md., from March 12, 1875, to Aug. 1, 1876.

Invalided from Aug. 1, 1876, to Dec. 1, 1877.

Took temporary charge Christ Church, Lexington, Ky., from Dec. 1, 1877, to March 1, 1878.

Rector of St. Luke's Church, Cannelton, Ind., from May 18, 1878, to Nov. 20, 1882.

At Christ Church Seminary, from Nov. 21, 1882, to Sept. 7, 1883.

Head Master of Otey School, Mount Pleasant, Tenn.. from Sept. 10, 1883, to Jan. 18 1885

Rector of St. John's Church, Helena, Ark., from June 18, 1885, to Jan. 9, 1889.

Died at Helena, Jan. 9, 1889.

" Forever with the Lord,
Amen   So let it be."

APPENDIX I.

THE BISHOP'S ANNUAL ADDRESS.

Brethren of the Clergy and Laity:

We have assembled again in Annual Council as a Diocese for the seventeenth time, and I believe that the past year has shown, and every succeeding year will more fully show, the wisdom of the clergy and laity who in convocation assembled at Little Rock on the 14th day of May, 1871, decided that a complete organization of the Church in Arkansas was then desirable, and requested me to summon the Primary Convention on St. Bartholomew's Day of that same year. That move towards the formation of a Diocese was no instigation of mine In fact, I was very doubtful as to its expediency. I was convinced that the step would arouse jealousies and chill the sympathies of many who are influenced more by words than by things, and thus deprive us in a great degree of the financial aid so sorely needed in this great field. I knew there was a glamour about the name "Missionary Jurisdiction" which is not felt where a "Diocese" is spoken of, as there is likewise about a quarter of a million of Indians compared with thirty times as many colored people. A taste for the romantic is not confined to school girls; few consider which is the greater, nobler and more important work to be done. But the members of that Convocation considered that since the consecration of Bishop Leonidas Polk, the first Missionary Bishop of Arkansas, thirty-three years had elapsed; that Bishop George Washington Freeman and Bishop Henry Champlin Lay, both men of marked ability and indefatigable in labor, had succeeded Bishop Polk. And yet when the last of these left the field, there was in Arkansas only six church edifices (or seven if we count the diminutive building then at Van Buren), only six clergymen, and only one self-supporting Parish, Christ Church, Little Rock; and if this was the result of thirty-three years' labor in a missionary jurisdiction, they believed that the Church in Arkansas had not a hopeful future before it working on that plan. It seemed to them necessary to rouse the churchmen of Arkansas to do something for themselves, and they thought that preliminary to that an organization should be effected and steps taken which would render it impossible for them to have another Missionary Bishop. It was a bold step, but they took it, and the Rubicon was crossed, and I believe they took it wisely, and such I believe will be the opinion of all who compare the progress of the past eighteen years with that made in the preceding thirty-three years. Still more convincing will be the evidence when it is considered that during the first six or seven years of my Episcopate the condition of the State of Arkansas was not favorable to the growth of the Church, or of any great institutions. We were recovering from the effects of the war and had not started on the new career which will eventually place Arkansas in the front rank of States.

When Arkansas applied for admission as a Diocese at the General Convention of 1871, held in Baltimore, my fears were realized. She was but coldly received and she had ample proof that she was no longer a favorite field in which were to be dispersed the gifts of churchmen in the older Dioceses. Yet what offense had she committed? She had simply avowed her resolution to gradually place herself in a position where she would not be dependent on the charities of others; her resolution to relieve the Church at large after my decease of the support of her Episcopate; her resolution to force her children into activity, so as to provide for themselves in the inevitable future. Methinks she acted generously, if not prudently, when I look a few years onward and see that our General Board of Missions will ere long become richer by her action then taken, by the amount pledged to my support.

The Diocese has not as energetically carried into effect these resolutions as she ought to have done. This we are bound to confess. But the fact that our Episcopate Fund has now attained a value very near, if not quite up to $8000,' shows that she has not been wholly negligent of her duty. A little more time, and a little more vigorous effort will bring us to the time, for which I heartily pray—the time when the Diocese of Arkansas will be self-supporting. But even then we shall not be quite forgiven unless we cease to vote in the General Convention, or vote as other people wish us to. For the cry is now, in some quarters, for proportionate representation in our National Council. If such be the wish of the Church at large, my vote will never be recorded against that proposed change of the Constitution. But I think these Dioceses who are asking for this change, should first apply the principle to their Diocesan Conventions and admit representatives according to the size of the Parishes, and then remember that the apparently unjust inequality complained of existed in the General Convention from the very beginning in this country.

In the session of 1792 the number of clergy in the different Dioceses was as follows: Virginia, 60; Maryland, 34; Connecticut, 22; New York, 19; South Carolina, 15; Pennsylvania, 14; Massachusetts (in 1799), 10; New Jersey, 9; New Hampshire (in 1799), 3; Delaware, 3; Rhode Island, 2. The whole number (if I am right in my count), was 191. Of these Maryland and Virginia together had 94, nearly one-half. Neither Pennsylvania nor Massachusetts then was as strong in clergy as Arkansas is now, yet great Virginia and great Maryland were generous enough to give an equal voice to little Pennsylvania and little Massachusetts. Cannot great Pennsylvania and great Massachusetts be equally generous to her younger and smaller sisters?

These Dioceses had had then the fostering care of the Church of England for more years than Arkansas has been fostered, and had attained to but a feeble growth. Please to give the Western Dioceses ninety years more, and the question under consideration will no longer be of importance.

3

For some of the older States have nearly all the population they can sustain. The newer States are larger in extent and increasing rapidly in population. In less than fifty years the strength of this people will be in the South and West, and in less than one hundred years the strength of the Church may be there also.

The evils of the present state of things, if any there be, time will gradually correct. But if the change proposed commends itself to the American Church, I will vote for it, for in the end, and that not far distant, it will matter nothing to us. In such a case, however, the right to call for a vote by Dioceses and orders must be preserved and its use restricted, so as to prevent action merely, thus giving the weaker Dioceses the equivalent of a veto power for their self-protection. This much I have said here, because in all the discussions on this subject, Arkansas has been cited as the illustration of a small Diocese, exercising a disproportionate power. I trust the churchmen of Arkansas will work with such energy that the disputants may be forced to seek their illustration elsewhere in 1892. I shall probably return to the general topic here considered, the relation of the Diocese of Arkansas to the Church in the United States, before I close, and speak of it in another connection. Meanwhile let me consider some of the signs of increased vigor in the Diocese.

Beginning in the Northwest, I am too glad to say that the Parish of St. John's, at Eureka Springs, has secured a larger and better place of worship. St. Paul's, at Fayetteville, has enlarged the Rectory by the addition of a second story, and the debt thereby accrued is nearly if not quite extinguished. The Church, its surroundings and its furniture have all been improved. The Parish is in fine condition and much stronger than ever before. Trinity Church, Van Buren, under its new Rector, the Rev. L. F. Guerry, is united and gaining in strength daily. Having completed and paid for their Church, now ready for consecration, they are taking steps to secure the next necessity, a Rectory, and with every pros-

pect of speedy success. St. John's, Fort Smith, under its un-
tiring and progressive Rector, is showing an immense amount
of work and a growth proportionate. The number of communicants is more than double what the Rev. Mr. Degen found
there when he took charge about two and one-half years ago.
St. John's Hospital, concerning which I have been far from
sanguine, I now think bids fair to become a permanency and
a blessing to coming generations, as well as to the present. I
believe the Rector will now be able to announce that the debt
on the Rectory is nearly or quite paid off.

At Dardanelle, the building put up by the Rev Dr. Mc-
Donald has, by the good management of the Rev. Dr. James
passed into the hands of the Parish. I visited St. Paul's,
Dardanelle, at Whitsuntide, last year. The Rector asked me
to postpone my visitation to a later date, as he was not quite
ready for me yet. But the prospects there are hopeful The
same may be said of St. Agnes', Morrilton, to which Dr.
James gives one-half of the Sundays each month. Both
Parishes are making steady headway against much prejudice
and opposition. Besides these two Parishes mentioned, Dr.
James has begun hopeful missionary work at Conway.

Christ Church, Little Rock, is flourishing in all respects.
The confirmations there during the past year are more than
were ever before reported from that Parish. I am glad to say
that the debt incurred for completing the Church is being
steadily, and I may say rapidly, extinguished. I hope we may
have the pleasure of consecrating this handsome edifice to
Almighty God in another year.

St. Philip's is progressing more than satisfactorily under
the Rev. Mr. Timothy. It is pleasant to remember that though
work began in the smallest way, only two and one-half years
ago, and which has had the benefit until very recently of an
afternoon service only on Sundays for about two years, has
already given thirty-two candidates for confirmation. The
congregation are exerting themselves nobly, and require careful fostering for a year or two more, to become a strong
congregation.

The Cathedral has been, during the past year, by the energy of Dean Proctor, seconded by the Chapter and Congregation, enlarged to its proposed proportions, and though the addition is yet unfinished in the interior, it is now opened for service. I am sure that the Diocesan Council, which gave its approval and full recognition to my Cathedral scheme at its inception, will now show increased interest in it as it approaches its completion. The future of the Diocese is more closely connected with this work than shallow thinkers generally suppose. The number confirmed at the Cathedral the past year is unusually small, but as there is quite a large class, so the very reverend, the Dean, informs me, now in preparation, there is a prospect that the coming year will make a better showing. The Rev. John E. Curzon, of the Cathedral clergy, has been with us but a few months, but he is doing a noble work at Newport, at Hope, Washington and Nashville, giving two Sundays in the month to Newport, and the other Sundays to the three other points. No man in this Diocese is working harder or more acceptably.

There is yet a vacancy on our Cathedral staff, which I hope will be soon filled; then our operations will be more extensive. Mr. Curzon is doing all that one man can do, and indeed more than I feel right to lay on him longer than necessity compels.

St. Luke's, Hot Springs, is making a very important move onward. A new lot has been secured, in size and site much superior to the old one; an excellent foundation laid for a beautiful brick church, much larger than the present frame building. The work will be pressed forward as fast as possible to completion. The Rev. Mr. Miller's success, in what was once considered a difficult field, has been very marked.

In Pine Bluff, Trinity Church, under the pastorate of the Rev. I. O. Adams, is enjoying a prosperity hitherto unknown. The parish is united and working as one man. A new and excellent pipe organ; a new porch at the entrance of the church; various improvements in the interior; now beautifully lighted by electricity; an increase of the Rector's salary,

and a steady growth of communicants, and not a cent of debt
on Church and Rectory. All these things prove that Mr.
Adams is doing his duty faithfully, and that the congregation
appreciates his labors.

Next we proceed to Marianna, where a few years ago the
Church began her work under circumstances by no means
promising. There labors, the Rev. Mr. Bruce, the only sur-
vivor of the little band of clergy whom I found on my entrance
into this field, who still remains here. The one more who is
yet this side of the river of death, is Rev. P. G. Jenkins, now
of the Diocese of South Carolina. As in Dardanelle, so in
Marianna, the Church advances in the face of prejudice, opposition and constant misrepresentation ; but God be praised,
she does advance, and is taking firm hold of one family after
another under the guidance of her able and well-read pastor.
Every year sees some progress, and prejudices are gradually
dying out. Considering that less than ten years have passed
since the first services were held there, and that it was several
years later that we began to hold services regularly, the handsome and well-furnished house of worship, with its churchly
services, is a monument of a victory won. Only time is required to make that victory complete.

St. John's Church, Helena, reminds us of the great loss the
Diocese has felt during the past few months. On the 9th day
of January last, the Rev. Richard Totten, Rector of that parish, ceased from his labors and entered into his rest. Of this
earnest and devoted Priest of God, it is scarcely possible to
speak too highly. Only those that knew him well and were
acquainted with the work he did, and the way he did it, can
know how much the Church in Arkansas has lost by his removal to Paradise. Never was a man more gentle and patient
under opposition, or more unyielding where principle was involved. For his own will and wishes he cared little or nothing ; for the will of God and His Church he cared everything.
He was ready to be all things to all men, if thereby he could
bring them to Christ, and make them faithful and devout

children of the Church, and a congregation better instructed and better trained than he has left, one would have to travel far to find. He won all hearts. By gentleness and sound arguments he overcame all prejudices, and the whole community mourned for him as for a friend and a brother. He has left upon the parish and city such an impress for good as time can hardly erase. I thank God for the remembrance he has left to us, for it is precious. Nothing shows the thoroughness of his instructions so well as the present spiritual energy shown by his parish. His death did not paralyze those who loved him so well; they seem endowed with new power, as if his mantle had fallen back upon them as he took his flight. The class of fifteen confirmed there on the fifth Sunday in Lent shows that he being dead yet speaketh.

I am glad to say that this important Rectorship is not to remain vacant long. The Rev. C. H. Lockwood, from the Diocese of Alabama, has already accepted a call to it, and will enter on his labors about the middle of this month. I had the pleasure of meeting him in Helena during my visitation, and feel that I can congratulate both the Parish and the Diocese on this acquisition to our clerical force. St. John's, Helena, will soon follow the example of St. Luke's, Hot Springs, and erect a larger and more permanent church. The present site has become very valuable and will find a ready sale. Meanwhile the ladies of the Parish have secured a larger lot, well situated and nearly paid for. They talk of building a Rectory upon it within the next few months, and I have little doubt they will do so.

Besides the points we have mentioned there are others where the services are partly suspended, owing to vacancies in the rectorship.

St. James, Eureka Springs, is vacant, but the Rev. J. J. Vaulx is rendering them such service as he can find time for. I trust this vacancy will soon be filled. Had not the great fire there greatly crippled the means of the leading members of the parish, I feel confident this would have been done very

speedily. Besides the services at Eureka, Mr. Vaulx is holding services at three or four points in the neighborhood of
Fayetteville, or at greater distances, and thus laying the foundation for several future Parishes.

The Rev. Mr. Guerry has a week-day appointment in
Alma at stated periods.

St. Paul's, Batesville, has made several calls, but has not,
as yet, succeeded in securing a Rector. I hope they may be
successful soon, and obtain a man after God's own heart.

St. John's Camden, has had no regular services for several
months, as there was no place in which to hold services. But
the new church is now nearly, or quite finished, and provision
will soon be made to resume the work under improved
conditions.

The Rev. David L. Trimble is holding stated services at
Pendleton, and with good hopes for the future. He speaks
very encouragingly of that field.

Arkansas City, Lake Village and Monticello have been
considering the question of securing a clergyman to divide his
time between them; and had it not been for some unfortunate
circumstances, I think they would have done so, and I am not
without hope that the arrangement may even yet be effected.
The churchmen at Arkansas City have a lot, and they are
moving for the erection of a small Church thereon, a Church
so planned as to be capable of being enlarged as the circumstances may demand.

I take this opportunity to return my thanks to the Rev. R.
W. Anderson, of the Diocese of Northern Texas, and Rector
of St. James', Texarkana, who has generously held services
for the little band at Rocky Comfort. They have a lot and
are accumulating funds to build a church. I had made an
agreement with Mr. Anderson to visit there and confirm a
class about the beginning of this year; but my long illness
prevented me, much to my regret, from keeping my appointment. I hope now to visit them very soon.

I must not omit to mention here the noble work done by a
handfull of churchmen at Mammoth Springs during the past

two years. A Church and a Rectory have been completed
and paid for, with the exception of a debt of $300, or less,
and this young vine has already borne fruit, for on the 4th
of February last the Rev. Dr. Tuttle, Bishop of Missouri, acting at my request, confirmed in that Church nine persons
(three male and six female).

A Parish in Missouri lies within a few miles of Mammoth
Springs, and the Bishop of Missouri has invited me to visit
that point when I make my visitation of St. Andrew's. By
this kindly interchange of services both Parishes may be much
benefited.

The Rev. Galbraith B. Perry prepared the above mentioned
class, spending a week or two there previous to Bishop Tuttle's
visit. I owe him many thanks for his valuable services. These
neighboring Parishes will be served by the same Priest, and I
have promised them some assistance from our Diocesan missions. I hope the Treasury is, or will be in condition to
enable me to redeem my promise, and also to redeem a pledge
of like tenor, which I have made to the Mission at Rocky
Comfort. Two hundred dollars will be required for these
purposes.

I am extremely desirous of starting anew our services at
Prescott and at Arkadelphia, and as soon as I can increase the
Cathedral staff of clergy I shall make the attempt. I trust
the time may be near at hand.

Having taken a survey of the whole field I have but to add
here a statement of the clerical changes during the past year.
The Rev. Joseph L. Berne has been transferred to the Diocese
of Springfield in the Province of Illinois.   The Rev. E. C. Alcorn has been transferred to the Diocese of Missouri.   Three
clergymen canonically connected with the Diocese, are now
residing beyond its borders.   The Rev. Dr. MacDonald in the
Diocese of Albany; the Rev. W. W. Estabrooke, M. D., in the
Diocese of Chicago, Province of Illinois; the Rev. Dr. Potter,
in the Diocese of Massachusetts; the Rev. Richard Totten and
the Rev. C. H. Newman (the latter long absent from Arkan-

sas), are dead; the Rev. Frank Morris Bayne (Priest,) has been deposed from the ministry in the Church of God; the Rev. John E. Curzon has been received from the Diocese of Fond du Lac, and is on the Cathedral staff; the Rev. B. W. Timothy has been received from the Diocese of Maryland, and is in charge of St. Philip's, Little Rock, working very acceptably and successfully. I have been daily expecting to receive the Letters Dimissory of the Rev. C. H. Lockwood, but they have not yet reached me.

I herewith present to you

AN ABSTRACT OF MY JOURNAL.

I closed my last report on April 11, 1888.

April 12, 1888: Thursday, at 11 o'clock a. m. in St. Andrew's Church, Marianna, Arkansas, Rev. Messrs Vaulx, Degen and Carnahan said Morning Prayer. I said the Communion Office; the Rev. C. A. Bruce read the Epistle; the Rev. Wm. J. Miller preached, and I *celebrated* the Holy Eucharist, assisted by the Rector, the Rev. C. A. Bruce. After the close of the Services the Sixteenth Annual Council of the Diocese of Arkansas was called to order, duly organized and proceeded to business. I presided.

April 13: Friday, I attended Litany Services at 9 a. m., presided in the Council all day and delivered my Annual Address, and attended every service at night.

April 14: Saturday, attended Morning Prayer; presided in the Council; held a meeting of the Missionary Committee— *i. e.*, of the Clerical members of the Standing Committee.

April 15: Sunday, the second after Easter. In St. Andrew's Church, Marianna, at 9 a. m. I *addressed* the Sunday School; at 11 a. m. the Rev. Wallace Carnahan preached; the Rev. C. A. Bruce presented the Rev. Daniel S. C. M. Potter, D. D., Deacon; the Rev. W. W. Estabrooke, M. D., presented the Rev. Richard S. James, D. D., LL. D., Deacon, and the Rev. George F. Degen presented the Rev. Frank M. Bayne, Deacon, and I *ordered* the three Deacons Priests. The Rev. I. O. Adams read the Epistle and the Rev. J. J. Vaulx the

Gospel. I *celebrated* the Holy Eucharist alone, as the Rubric requires. At 4 p. m., the Rev. C. A. Bruce said a special short service and I *preached* a sermon on Church Unity; at 8 p. m., Rev. Messrs. Bayne and Estabrooke said Evening Prayer; the Rev. G. F. Degen preached and I *confirmed one* person. (female).

April 16: Monday, at 9 a. m., in St. Andrew's Church, Marianna, I *celebrated* the Holy Eucharist, assisted by the Rev. C. A. Bruce, and in place of the sermon delivered an *address*, after which the Council was called to order, and adjourned *sine die*.

April 19: Thursday, I presided at a meeting of the Trinity Chapter, and appointed the Rev. Charles H. Proctor, Dean of Little Rock.

April 22: Sunday, the third after Easter, at 11 a. m., in Trinity Cathedral, Little Rock, the Rev. Mr. Galbraith, Deacon of the Diocese of Western Texas, said Morning Prayer, the Rev. C. H. Proctor reading the lessons and saying the Prayers, the Rev. George F. Degen preached, and I *instituted* the Rev. Charles Haydon Proctor, Rector of the Cathedral congregation, and *installed* him Dean of the Cathedral. The Very Reverend the Dean celebrated the Holy Eucharist as the office requires, assisted by the Rev. Mr. Galbraith. At 3:30 p. m., I said Evening Prayer, and *preached* in St. Philip's Church, Little Rock.

April 25: Wednesday, at 8:30 p. m., in Trinity Cathedral, Little Rock, I *joined* in holy matrimony William Porter Stone (Lieutenant in the United States Army) and Miss Martha E. Williams.

April 29: Sunday, the fourth after Easter, at 11 a. m., in the Cathedral, Little Rock, I assisted in saying Morning Service, and *celebrated* the Holy Eucharist. At 3:30 p. m., I said Evening Prayer, and *preached* in St. Philip's Church.

May 1: Tuesday, Feast of St. Philip and St. James, I *celebrated* the Holy Eucharist and *lectured* in the Cathedral.

May 6: Sunday, the fifth after Easter, I assisted in saying Morning Service and *celebrated* the Holy Eucharist in the

Cathedral, Little Rock. In the evening I said Evening Prayer and *preached* in St. Philip's.

May 7: Monday, Rogation Day, I said Morning Prayer and *lectured* in the Cathedral.

May 8: Tuesday, Rogation Day, I said Morning Prayer in the Cathedral.

May 9: Wednesday, Rogation Day, I said Morning Service in the Cathedral.

May 10: Thursday, Ascension Day, in the Cathedral, Little Rock, Canon Estabrooke said Morning Prayer. I said the Communion Office, *preached* and *celebrated* the Holy Eucharist.

May 13: Sunday after Ascension, in Trinity Church, Pine Bluff, Ark., I catechised the Sunday-school. At 10:30 a. m., at St. Michael's Mission, Pine Bluff, the Rev. D. L. Trimble said the Litany, read the Epistle, and assisted me in the Holy Communion. I said the Communion Office, *preached* and *celebrated* the Holy Eucharist. At 8 p. m., in Trinity Church, Pine Bluff, I *preached, confirmed* four persons (females), and *addressed* the class.

May 20: Sunday, Whitsun-Day, in the Cathedral, Little Rock, I *baptized* a child, said the Communion Office, *preached* and *celebrated* the Holy Eucharist, assisted by Dean Proctor. At 5:30, in the Cathedral, I said Evening Prayer, assisted by the Dean, and *baptized* two children.

May 21: Monday, in Whitsun Week, in St. Paul's Church, Dardanelle, after Evening Prayer, said by Rev. Dr. James, I *preached* and *confirmed* two persons (females).

May 21: Tuesday, in Whitsun Week, in St. John's Church, Fort Smith, I *preached* at Evening Service, and *confirmed* twelve persons and *addressed* the class. I had before service *confirmed* a sick man at St. John's Hospital—making thirteen in all (four males and nine females).

May 27: Trinity Sunday, in the morning, I *celebrated* the Holy Eucharist in the Cathedral, Little Rock, assisted by Dean Proctor. In the evening I *preached*.

May 30: Wednesday, at 9:30 a. m., in Trinity Cathedral, I *celebrated* the Holy Eucharist and *lectured*.

June 1 : Friday, I assisted in saying Morning Prayer in St. John's Church, St. Louis, Mo.

June 3: Sunday, the first after Trinity, in St. Peter's Church, Columbia, Tennessee, I assisted in saying the Morning Service, *preached* and *celebrated* the Holy Eucharist. At night I *preached* again.

June 6: Wednesday, I attended the commencement exercises of Columbia Institute, delivered the diplomas and *addressed* the graduating class.

June 10: Sunday, the second after Trinity, I *preached* at Morning Service in St. Peter's Church, Columbia, Tennessee.

June 17: Sunday, the third after Trinity, I *preached* at Morning Service in Christ Church, Norwich, Connecticut.

June 23: Saturday, I sailed in the steamship Umbria from New York for Liverpool.

June 24: Sunday, the fourth after Trinity, at 3 p. m., attended divine service on shipboard. The Rt. Rev., the Bishop of Pennsylvania officiated.

July 1 : Sunday, the fifth after Trinity, arrived in Liverpool, England, and at 11 a. m. attended services in the pro-Cathedral, and saw a class of 175 confirmed by the Bishop of Liverpool. In the afternoon I attended Evening Prayer in Chester Cathedral.

July 2 : Monday, at 7 p. m., I was present in robes at the opening service of the Lambeth Conference, in Westminster Abbey, London, England, and listened with pleasure to the Archbishop of Canterbury's very able sermon.

July 3 : Tuesday, in Lambeth Chapel, attended the actual opening of the Lambeth Conference. The Bishop of Minnesota preached the sermon and the Archbishop of Canterbury was the celebrant. All the Bishops, about 146 in number, were present in their robes. The business meeting followed. The first week was spent in the presentation of the topics to be considered. After the *appointed* speakers had made their speeches there was little or no time left for free discussion. Therefore the consideration given to the different subjects was very far from full. I trust, if there is to be another Lambeth Conference, there will be much more time given for discussion and much less time allowed for committee work. I attended all the sessions during the first week.

July 8 : Sunday, the sixth after Trinity, attended divine service morning and evening, and heard the Bishop of Zululand preach at St. Paul's Cathedral, at the Evening Service.

July 10 : Tuesday, attended the meeting of the Committee on Standards of Doctrine and Worship at Ely House, London. The Bishop of Ely presided.

July 12 : Thursday, meeting of the Committee on Standards of Doctrine and Worship.

July 15 : Sunday, the seventh after Trinity, at 10:30 a. m., I *preached* in All Saints Church, Margaret street, London.

July 18 : Wednesday, visited Cambridge University with members of the Conference. We were most hospitably entertained, and had an enjoyable day, closing with a grand dinner at St. John's College

July 19: Thursday, visited Ely, and were indebted to the Bishop of Ely and Lady Alwin Compton, his consort, for most kindly hospitality at his palace. We attended Evening Prayer in their beautiful Cathedral, one of the most nearly perfect in England.

July 22 : Sunday, the eighth after Trinity, at 11 a. m., I *preached* in St. Paul's Church, Milton Place, London. At 7 p. m , I *preached* in St. Andrew's Church, Hertford.

July 24 : Tuesday, at the session of the Lambeth Conference. This week was devoted to the reception of the reports of the various committees, and to discussions thereon. But the important subjects presented required much more time than the five days allotted to them. I was in attendance every day except Monday, on which day I was late in getting back from Hertford. From Monday evening till Wednesday evening I was a guest at Lambeth Palace, and I shall ever remember with pleasure the kindness of His Grace, the Archbishop and of Lady Benson.

July 28 : Saturday, attended in robes the closing services of the Lambeth Conference in St. Paul's Cathedral. The Archbishop of York preached a sermon worthy of the great occasion. I must here express my great indebtedness to the Rev. Wm. J. Jefferies, D. D., of Philadelphia, Penn., who kindly acted as my chaplain during the Conference. I owe him a debt of lasting gratitude for thousands of kindnesses.

July 29 : Sunday, the ninth after Trinity, I *preached* at Morning Service in St. Peter's Church, Belieze Park, London. The Rev. F. W. Tremlet, D. D., the Vicar of this Parish, is well known to Southern churchmen, on account of his interest in the University of the South and the great services he has rendered it. I was glad to meet him face to face.

July 31 : Tuesday, I visited Canterbury Cathedral. It would take pages to tell what I saw, and volumes to tell what I thought and felt.

August 5 : Sunday, the tenth after Trinity, at 11 a. m., I attended the Madeleine, in Paris, France, and for the first time saw the Roman Catholic service in a Roman Catholic country. A fine Anglican Service is much more imposing and impressive.

August 12 : Sunday, attended services morning and evening, and visited several churches in Rome, Italy.

August 19 : Sunday, I attended service and visited several of the churches in Venice, Italy.

As this is my Annual Address and not a lecture on my travels, I pass unmentioned the many things of deepest interest which I saw in Genoa, Pisa, Rome, Naples, Pompei, Florence, Venice and Milan. Every day was crowded with work, and I brought back unnumbered memories which make my life all the richer in thoughts and emotions. If any doubts of the deadening influence of the Papacy, he has but to catch a glimpse of the new Italy that is springing into energetic life. Now that the Papal and foreign yoke has been cast off, we behold in the changing present evidences of a dismal past.

At Lucerne, Switzerland, I met the Rt. Rev. Dr. Knickerbocker, Bishop of Indiana, and we traveled to Geneva in company, much to my satisfaction. From him I learned the sad news of the death of the Bishop of Michigan, the Rt. Rev. Dr. Harris, a death very unexpected and widely regretted.

August 26 : Sunday, the thirteenth after Trinity, I spent in Paris, France.

August 31 : Friday, at Tilbury, England, acting at the re-quest of the Bishop of St. Albans, conveyed to me through the Rev. Mr. Naish, I *confirmed* sixteen persons (ten male, six female), and *addressed* the class, after which I made a missionary *address.* At this confirmation no Evening Service was said, and so far as my observations at Liverpool, and my subsequent inquiries could inform me, I learned that it was not the custom in England to connect Morning or Evening Prayer with the Confirmation. This custom I greatly approve, and I have resolved to follow it generally in Arkansas. You doubtless have observed that there is no Rubric which requires the Confirmation Office to be mixed with any other service.

September 1 : Saturday, I visited Rochester Cathedral, also Cobham Church, both places of interest.

September 2 : Sunday, the fourteenth after Trinity, I attended divine service in Foundling Hospital Chapel, London.

September 5 : Wednesday, sailed in the steamship, "City of New York," from Liverpool for New York.

September 9 : Sunday, the fifteenth after Trinity, at 11 a. m., on shipboard, I assisted the Rt. Rev., the Bishop of Pennsylvania, in saying the Morning Service.

September 16 : Sunday, the sixteenth after Trinity, in St. Paul's Church, Rahway, New Jersey, I *preached* at morning Service and *preached* again at Evening Service.

September 23 : Sunday, the seventeenth after Trinity, in Trinity Cathedral, Little Rock, I said the Communion Office, read the Lambeth Evangelical Letter instead of a sermon, and *celebrated* the Holy Eucharist, assisted by Dean Proctor. At 4 p.m., I said Evening Prayer and *lectured* in St. Philip's Church.

September 29 : Saturday, St. Michael and All Angels, at 11 a.m., in Christ Church, Little Rock, the Rev. Wallace Carnahan said the ante-Communion Service. I read the Gospel and *lectured* on the day.

September 30 : Sunday, the eighteenth after Trinity, at 11 a.m., in the Cathedral, Little Rock, I assisted in saying

Morning Service, *preached* and *celebrated* the Holy Eucharist, assisted by Dean Proctor. At 4 p. m., in St. Philip's, I said Evening Prayer and *preached*.

October 7: Sunday, the nineteenth after Trinity, at 11 a.m., in the Cathedral, Little Rock, I assisted in saying the Morning Service and *celebrated* the Holy Eucharist. At 4 p. m. in St. Philip's I said Evening Prayer and *preached*.

October 14: Sunday, the twentieth after Trinity, at 7:30 a.m., in the Cathedral, Little Rock, I *celebrated* the Holy Eucharist. At 11 a. m., I said Morning Prayer and Litany and *preached*. At 3:30 p. m., in St. Philip's, I said Evening Prayer and *preached*. At 5 p., m. I said Evening Prayer in the Cathedral.

October 16: Tuesday. I officiated at a funeral in Little Rock.

October 21: Sunday, the twenty-first after Trinity, at 11 a.m., in the Cathedral, Little Rock, I said Morning Service, *preached*, and *celebrated* the Holy Eucharist. At 5 p. m., I said Evening Prayer.

October 28: Sunday, the twenty-second after Trinity, at 7:30, in the Cathedral, Little Rock, I *celebrated* the Holy Eucharist. At 11 I said Morning Prayer and Litany, and *preached*. At 3:30 p.m. I said Evening Prayer and *preached* in St. Philip's. At 5 p.m. I said Evening Prayer in the Cathedral.

October 29: Monday, at 7:30 p.m., in St. Paul's Church, Newport, Ark., after Evening Prayer said by Canon Estabrooke, I *preached*, *confirmed* three persons, and *addressed* the class. I *confirmed* also one person in private. Total, four (three female, one male).

October 30: Tuesday, in St. Paul's, Newport, I *confirmed* one person.

October 31: Wednesday, visited Searcy and tried to arrange for an exchange of the Church lot there for one more eligibly situated.

November 1: Thursday, All Saint's Day, I *celebrated* the Holy Eucharist in Trinity Cathedral, Little Rock, assisted by Canon Estabrooke, who preached the sermon.

November 4: Sunday, the twenty-third after Trinity, in Trinity Cathedral, I said Morming Service and *preached*, and *celebrated* the Holy Eucharist. At 3:30 p. m. I said Evening Prayer and *preached* in St. Philip's. At 5 p. m. I said Evening Prayer in the Cathedral.

November 9: Friday, I gave Letters Dimissory to the Rev. J. L. Berne to the Diocese of Springfield, Province of Illinois.

November 11: Sunday, the twenty-fourth after Trinity, at 7:30 a. m., in the Cathedral, Little Rock, I *celebrated* the Holy Eucharist. At 11 a. m. I said Morning Prayer and Litany, and *preached*. At 3 p. m. I' said Evening Prayer and *preached* in St. Philip's. At 4:30 p. m. I said Evening Prayer in the Cathedral.

November 18: Sunday, the twenty-fifth after Trinity, in the Cathedral, I said Morning Service, *preached* and *celebrated* the Holy Eucharist. In St. Philip's, at 3 p. m., I said Evening Prayer, and *preached*. In the Cathedral, at 4:30, I said Evening Prayer.

November 22: Thursday, I held a meeting of the Rector, Vestry and Congregation of St. James' Parish, at Eureka Springs, and tried to adjust matters between the Vestry and Rector.

November 23: Friday, I *preached* in St. Paul's Church, Fayetteville, at night, and *confirmed* seven persons (four male, three female) and *addressed* the class.

November 25: Sunday, the next before Advent, in Trinity Church, Van Buren, at 11 a. m., I assisted in saying the Morning Service, *preached*, *confirmed* six persons (one male, five female) and *addressed* the class; after which, I *celebrated* the Holy Eucharist, assisted by the Rector, the Rev. L. F. Guerry. At 7 p. m., I *preached* again.

November 26: Monday, I *preached* at night in St. John's Church, Fort Smith.

November 29: Thursday, National Thanksgiving, in the Cathedral, Little Rock, after Morning Prayer, said by Rev.

John E. Curzon, Deacon of the Diocese of Fond du Lac, I said the ante-Communion and *preached*. In the evening, I *baptized* a child.

December 2: Sunday, the first in Advent, at 11 a. m., in the Cathedral, Little Rock, I assisted in saying the Morning Service, *preached* and *celebrated* the Holy Eucharist, assisted by the Rev. Mr. Curzon. At 3 p. m., I *preached* in St. Philip's and *baptized* five adults. At 5 p. m., I assisted in saying Evening Prayer in the Cathedral.

December 6: Thursday, at 11 a. m., I *baptized* two adults belonging to St. Philip's Congregation. The service was in the Cathedral. At 4:30 p. m., I *confirmed* one person in the Cathedral (one female).

December 9: Sunday, the second in Advent, in the Cathedral, at 7:30 a. m., I *celebrated* the Holy Eucharist. At 11 a. m , I assisted in saying Morning Service, and the Rev. Mr. Curzon preached. At 3 p. m., in St. Philip's, Little Rock, I *preached* and *confirmed* seven persons (males and females) and *addressed* the class.

December 14: Friday, in St. Mark's Church, Hope, Arkansas, after a short service, said by the Rev. Mr. Curzon, I *preached, confirmed* eight persons (two male, six female) and *addressed* the class.

December 16: Sunday, the third in Advent, at 11 a. m., assisted by the Rev. Mr. Curzon, I *consecrated* to the worship of Almighty God the Church of the Redeemer at Nashville, Arkansas. I *preached* and *celebrated* the Holy Eucharist. At 7 p. m. I *preached* again, *baptized* one person, a lady, hypothetically, and *confirmed* one person (one male).

December 23: Sunday, the fourth in Advent. This was the fourth Sunday in all my ministry that I was unable through sickness to attend to my ministerial duties.

December 25 Tuesday, I received the Holy Communion in my sick chamber.

December 30: Sunday after Christmas, confined to my sick room. From this date till Epiphany, 1889, I was too weak to officiate. This severe illness was the most protracted I ever experienced.

January 6, 1889: Sunday, Epiphany, at 11 a. m., in the Cathedral, Little Rock, I *celebrated* the Holy Euchari-t, assisted by Dean Proctor, who took the rest of the service and preached. At 3 p. m. I said Evening Prayer in St. Philip's and *preached*.

January 10: Thursday, I wrote to the Rev. Dr. Potter, Eureka Springs, Arkansas, declaring a dissolution of the pastoral relation between himself and the Parish of St. James. I this day sent notice to the Ecclesiastical Authority of the Diocese of Maryland of my acceptance of the Letters Dimissory presented by the Rev. B. W. Timothy, Priest.

January 13: Sunday, the first after Epiphany, I *preached* at Morning Service in the Cathedral, Little Rock.

January 20: Sunday, the second after Epiphany, at 11 a. m., in Trinity Church, Pine Bluff, after Morning Prayer and Litany, said by Rev. I. O. Adams and the Rev. D. L. Trimble, I said the Communion Office, the Rev. Mr. Trimble reading the Epistle and the Rev. Mr. Adams, the Rector, the Gospel, and I *preached* and *celebrated* the Holy Eucharist, assisted by the Rector. At 7:30 p. m. I *preached* again and *confirmed* five persons (five female) and *addressed* the class.

January 23: Wednesday, I this day gave notice of my *acceptance* of the Letters Dimissory presented from the Diocese of Fond du Lac by the Rev. John E. Curzon, Deacon. I also gave, this day, my canonical *consent* to the consecration of all the Bishops-elect now awaiting consecration.

January 27: Sunday, the third of the Epiphany, in the Cathedral, Little Rock, I assisted in saying Morning Service, *preached* and *celebrated* the Holy Eucharist, assisted by the Very Reverend, the Dean.

February 3: Sunday, the fourth after Epiphany, at 11 a. m., in the Cathedral, Little Rock, I assisted in saying Morning Service, *preached* and *celebrated* the Holy Eucharist. At 5 p. m. I assisted in saying Evening Prayer.

February 4: Monday. I this day *licensed* Mr. Walter Naish to act as Lay-reader at Arkansas City.

February 10: Sunday, the fifth after Epiphany, I assisted in saying Morning Service in the Cathedral, *preached* and *celebrated* the Holy Eucharist. I assisted in saying Evening Prayer also.

February 11: Monday, I examined the Rev. John E. Curzon, Deacon, for Priest's Orders, assisted by Revs. Messrs. Adams and Trimble.

February 12: Tuesday, I continued Mr. Curzon's examination.

February 13: Wednesday, at 10 a. m., I attended Morning Prayer in the Cathedral, after which, in the presence of I. O. Adams, the Very Rev. C. H. Proctor, and the Rev. D. L. Trimble, I *pronounced* the sentence of deposition from the Ministry in the Church of God on the Rev. Frank Morris Bayne, Presbyter, according to Title II, Canon 5, Section 1, of the Digest. God only knows how painful the performance of this sad duty was. At 11 a. m, I *preached* and *ordered priest* the Rev. John Edward Curzon, Deacon. The candidate was presented by the Rev. I O. Adams; the Epistle was read by the Rev. Wallace Carnahan, the Gospel by the Very Rev. C. H. Proctor, and the Rev. Messrs. Adams, Proctor, Carnahan and Trimble united in the imposition of hands. I *celebrated* the Holy Eucharist and administered alone as the Rubric demands.

February 17: Sunday, Septuagesima, in St. Peter's Church, Columbia, Tenn., I said Morning Service, *preached* and *celebrated* the Holy Eucharist. At night, I said Evening Prayer and *preached* again.

February 24: Sunday Sexagesima, in St. Peter's Church, Columbia, Tenn., I assisted in saying Morning Service and *preached* at 7. p. m. After Evening Prayer said by the Rector, the Rev. Dr. Beckett, I *preached* again.

March 3: Tuesday Quinguagesima, at 11 a. m., in St. John's Church, Fort Smith, I *preached, confirmed* eight per sons (one male, seven females) and *addressed* the class. At 7:30 p. m. I *preached, confirmed* four persons (one male, three females) and *addressed* the class.

March 4: Monday, in St. John's, Fort Smith, I *confirmed* two persons (one male, one female).

March 6: Ash Wednesday, at 10 a. m., in St. Paul's Church, Fayetteville, Ark., I assisted in saying Morning Service, *preached* and *celebrated* the Holy Eucharist, assisted by the Rector, Rev. J. J. Vaulx.

March 10: Sunday, the first in Lent, in St. Paul's Church, Fayetteville, I assisted in saying Morning Service, *preached* and *celebrated* the Holy Eucharist. At 8 p. m. I *preached* again, *confirmed* four persons (one male, three females) and *addressed* the class.

March 11: Monday at 7:30 p. m. I assisted in saying Evening Prayer, and *preached* in St. Paul's.

March 12: Tuesday, in St. Paul's, Fayetteville, at 10 a. m. I said Morning Prayer. At 7:30 I *preached*.

March 13: Wednesday, at 7:30 p. m. in St. Paul's Church, Fayetteville, I *preached* and *confirmed* one person (one male).

March 14: Thursday in Trinity Church, Van Buren, Ark., at 7:30 p. m., after Evening Prayer said by the Rector, the Rev. L. F. Guerry, I *preached* and *confirmed* four persons, and *addressed* the class.

March 15: Friday forenoon I assisted the Rev. L. F. Guerry in saying the funeral service in Van Buren. At 7:30 p m. I *preached* in Trinity Church.

March 17: Sunday, the second in Lent, in St. Agnes' Church, Morrilton, Ark., I assisted in saying Morning Service and *preached*. At 7:30 p.m. I *preached* again and *confirmed* one person (one female).

March 24: Sunday, the third in Lent, in St. Paul's Church, Newport, Arkansas, at 11 a. m., I assisted in saying Morning Service, *preached* and *celebrated* the Holy Eucharist, assisted by the Rev. J. E. Curzon. At 7:30 p. m., I *preached* again, *confirmed* five persons (three male, two female) and *addressed* the class.

addressed the class.   At 8 p. m., I *preached* in Christ Church, Little Rock, and *confirmed* forty-eight persons (twenty-two males, twenty-six females), and *addressed* the class.

April 22:   Easter Monday. at 9:30 a. m , I attended Morning Service in the Cathedral, and later presided at the meeting for the election of members of the Chapter.

April 25:   Thursday, St. Mark's Day, at 11 a. m , in Christ Church, Little Rock, I *confirmed* four persons (one male, three females), and *addressed* the class.

April 28:   Sunday, the first after Easter, I *preached* in the Cathedral, Little Rock, at Morning Service.   At 8 p. m., in Trinity Church, Pine Bluff, I *preached, confirmed* three persons (three females), and *addressed* the class; after which I dedicated the organ, which is made a memorial of Rev. Robert Wilson Trimble LL. D., the first Rector of the Parish, and of his wife, Elmira.   " Blessed are the dead who die in the Lord."

To this abstract I add the following:

SUMMARY.

Sermons	93
Lectures and addresses	36
Celebrations	41
Confirmations 191, and by Bishop Tuttle 9—200 for Arkansas for the year ; besides 16 confirmed in England, making the whole number confirmed by myself, personally	207
Ordinations (to the Priesthood)	4
Institutions	1
Churches consecrated..............................	1
Corner-stone laid..................................	1
Baptisms—infants, 7 ; adults, 12. Total..............	19
Marriages..	1
Funerals......................	2
Letters Dimissory given............................	2
Letters Dimissory accepted.........................	2
Depositions (a Priest)................................	1
Miles traveled 17,758

of which 9913 were on the ocean and in Europe, and 7845 in the United States.

The baptisms are recorded where they were administered, ✤ and will appear in the Parochial Reports.

In continuance of my address, I now approach a subject which deeply concerns myself, personally, and scarcely less concerns the Diocese of Arkansas. In the Primary Convention of this Diocese, as the minutes show, I was unanimously elected, by both Orders, Bishop of the Diocese of Arkansas. I copy from the Journal what followed: "The Rev. Messrs. Stout and Ruth, and Messrs. McCracken and Stone were appointed a committee to wait upon the Bishop and inform him of his election. The committee retired, and after a time reported that they had performed the duty assigned them, and that the Bishop would respond in person. The Bishop, having entered and resumed the chair, addressed the Council in regard to the Episcopate; declaring that, though at this time he was not prepared to accept or decline the office of Bishop of the Diocese of Arkansas, he would not leave his present field of labor until the Diocese of Arkansas was prepared to sustain a Bishop."

In the year 1871 the Diocese of Arkansas was duly admitted into connection with the General Convention, and her Deputies, clerical and lay, were admitted to seats in that body. In the first Annual Council of the Diocese of Arkansas, assembled in Christ Church, Little Rock, May 9, 1872, I spoke in my Annual Address as follows:

"At our Primary Council I was elected Bishop of Arkansas. I asked time to consider before I accepted or declined. My reason for doing so was, that I might obtain a definite opinion from the General Convention as to the interpretation of Paragraph 5, Section 7, Canon 13, Title I, concerning the meaning of said Canon. I have not the shadow of a doubt in my own mind, as I am personally acquainted with the history of its enactment, and the object aimed at. Indeed, I was one of the parties who procured its passage. During the General Convention I raised the question in reference to the Diocese of Nebraska, the position of which was precisely the same as that

of Arkansas ; but owing to the press of business before the
house, and owing to the fact that the question involved did
not seem to require an immediate solution, no satisfactory and
definite response was returned.   I am, not, therefore, even
now, prepared to accept the office of Diocesan of Arkansas.
Should the Council, however, desire to settle the matter before
the assembling of the next General Convention, I will not im-
pede any action that it may now wish to take.   I will decline
at once, and leave it as perfectly free as it was before my election.   If, on the other hand, I still reserve my answer, it must
be with the express understanding that the election continues
in as full force as it had on the day it was made, and that I
have the time till the next General Convention in which to
make my answer, unless I may deem it expedient to accept
sooner.   I leave the decision of this matter in the hands of
this Council, and will be guided by its wishes.   Meanwhile, I
cannot but urge you to take steps looking to the future support of the Episcopate of Arkansas.   The measures proposed
at our Primary Council have, so far, proved abortive.   I feel
that I can urge this subject upon your consideration with all
the more freedom, inasmuch as it does not concern myself
personally."

Thus far I quote from the Journal of the Council of 1872.
In response to this, the Council gave me, not merely what I
asked for, the time till the meeting of the next General Convention, but all the time I chose to take, As the Journal shows
the matter was left wholly in my hands.   The Canon, or part
of the Canon referred to, is cited by its old numbers as they
stood in 1868, and also in 1871.   Its present number is [7],
Section 6, Canon 15, Title 1, but the law itself is unchanged

Now, for the clearer understanding of what I have to
say, I quote the words of the Canon in full   It reads thus
" Any Bishop or Bishops elected and consecrated under th
section shall be entitled to a seat in the House of Bishoj
and shall be eligible to the office of Diocesan Bishop in a
organized Diocese within the United States.   And whene

a Diocese shall have been organized within the jurisdiction of such Missionary Bishop, if he shall be chosen Bishop of such Diocese, he may accept the office without vacating his Missionary appointment; *Provided*, that he continue to discharge the duties of Missionary Bishop within the residue of his original jurisdiction, if there be such residue." Such was the law of this Church when I was elected Bishop of Arkansas; such is the law of this Church now, and you will observe there is no limitation as to the time within which the Bishop's acceptance is to take place. That depends on the Bishop himself and the Diocese to which he is elected Diocesan.

The history of the later portion of the Canon cited is as follows: In 1853 the Diocese of Texas, formed 1849, and admitted to the General Convention 1853, elected as Diocesan Rt. Rev. George Washington Freeman, D. D., then Missionary Bishop of Arkansas, the Indian Territory and Texas. Bishop Freeman, knowing the weakness of the Church in Texas, was unwilling to give up his Missionary appointment and trust for his support to the feeble Diocese of Texas. The Diocese of Texas therefore instructed its Deputies to the General Convention, which met that year in New York City, to procure, if possible, such a change of the then existing Canon as would render it possible for Bishop Freeman to accept the Episcopate of Texas and yet receive his support from the Board of Missions, according to the original contract between himself as Missionary Bishop and said Board of Missions.

I was a member of the Diocesan Convention that elected Bishop Freeman, and I was a Deputy from the Diocese of Texas to the General Convention of 1853. When that body proceeded to business, the Texas Deputation had an interview with the Rev. William Cooper Mead, D. D., then and for a long time afterwards Chairman of the Committee on Canons. We told Dr. Mead what we wished to effect. He informed us that his committee had that very subject then under consideration, for the relation of Bishop Kemper to the Diocese of Wisconsin was a case precisely like that presented by the

Diocese of Texas.   To meet the cases of Texas and Wisconsin and to enable Bishops Freeman and Kemper to become Diocesans without forfeiting their salaries as Missionary Bishops the Canon was changed and took the form it now has. The law has undergone no alteration since.   As to its meaning, the circumstances of its passage and the definiteness of its wording leaves no room for a doubt.   "Without vacating his Missionary appointment" is a pledge that the Bishop's retaining his salary as guaranteed to him at the time of his appointment as Missionary Bishop, is a matter at his own option, for there is no peculiar advantage in such a position except the pecuniary benefit which can be secured to him by these words.   The proviso added is just and simply requires the Bishop to perform his duty in all the jurisdiction originally assigned him.   The last clause of the proviso qualifies the proviso only and not the body of the Canon.   This refers to cases where the jurisdiction is twofold or more; as Oregon and Washington Territory formerly under Bishop Morris; as Colorado and Wyoming, formerly under Bishop Spalding; as Arkansas, the Indian Territory and Texas, formerly under Bishop Freemen.   In case the Missionary jurisdiction is simple, as Northern Texas, as Western Texas, as Northern California, as Montana, and as Oregon at this time, then the proviso has no application.   They, under this and other Canons, may become Dioceses whenever they deem such action desirable, and the Missionary Bishops, if elected, may become Diocesans without "vacating their Missionary appointments."

Furthermore, should Wyoming become a Diocese, and the Missionary Bishop become the Diocesan therefor, and should the House of Bishops, acting under (2) Section 6, Canon 15, Title I, subsequently separate Idaho and make it the jurisdiction of a new Missionary Bishop, the rights of Bishop Talbot would in nowise be affected.   He would remain Diocesan of Wyoming, "without vacating his Missionary appointment, and be entitled to draw his salary as such."

And, in like manner, if the House of Bishops should next October place the Indian Territory under any of the Missionary Bishops now in the field, or under a new Missionary Bishop as his single jurisdiction, the rights that have accrued to me under this law of the Church would by such action be in nowise affected.

The House of Bishops has, by the Canon just cited, the right to take such action, and it has had the right these many years past, and they are the sole judges as to the time when they will exercise it. But, I repeat it, such action cannot invalidate my rights under the pre-existing contract. And under this Canon law of the Church, and on the conditions here laid down, I now and hereby accept the Episcopate of Arkansas and become your Diocesan. I have set forth this matter fully, not to instruct the House of Bishops or the Board of Missions, both of whom know the law of the Church, and my rights under it, as well as I do, but because some of our Church papers have so spoken on this subject as to indicate a general ignorance sadly needing instruction.

And now, brethren, in this connection, let me exhort you to take the proper steps and to put forth vigorous efforts to increase your growing Episcopate fund. In the course of nature you cannot expect to have my services for any long period. A man on the verge of three-score and ten has not many years to look forward to, and the support of your next Bishop will fall wholly upon yourselves. You must be prepared for the coming emergency, for you know not when it may arise. Energy and concert of action may so hasten the time of your being self-supporting that I may myself have the great satisfaction of thanking the Board of Missions for their kindly aid in the past, and of releasing them from any obligation to support the Episcopate of Arkansas in the future. For your own sakes, and for my sake also, I beg you to use all diligence to attain so desirable an end.

I have so long detained you that I have time to add but a word concerning the Lambeth Conference. That good will grow out of that large gathering of Bishops I believe ; but I feel that but little was done toward the attainment of the most important aim of this century—the union, or outward unity of the Holy Catholic Church.

It does comparatively little good to gather together and intensify mere Anglicanism. The struggle to secure and maintain an absolute uniformity in all branches of the Anglican Communion is by no means wholesome or praiseworthy. Difference in minor things and agreement in Catholic principles, and complete harmony and full intercommunion under such conditions, would be in accordance with primitive usage, and would give to the world the great lesson it just now needs. For centuries the Church has labored for uniformity, forgetting that what we most need is Catholicity, Catholic comprehensiveness, and more of the Catholic spirit. I hope the next conference, whether at Lambeth or elsewhere, will bring together the representatives of all believers, who are ready to meet and to unite on the broad basis of primitive Christianity as held by the undivided Church of God.

From such a gathering good results might flow. All has been attained that can be attained, unless we merge the Anglican Conference into something wider and more comprehensive, and endeavor to manifest the God-given unity by the first of resultant duties—visible union and cordial unison.

But I will detain you no longer. May the Holy Spirit teach us what we ought to do and enable us to do it.

May the blessing of God the Father, the Son and the Holy Ghost, the eternal I AM, rest upon you and remain with you ever.

H. N. PIERCE,
Bishop of Arkansas.

APPENDIX II.

REPORT OF THE STANDING COMMITTEE.

To the Diocesan Council:

The Standing Committee met in St. Andrew's Church, Marianna, on Friday, April 13, and organized by electing the Rev. Innes O. Adams, President, and the Rev. W. J. Miller Secretary *pro tem.* On motion of the Rev. W. J. Miller, Mr. P. K. Roots was elected Secretary.

The Committee then adjourned to meet on call of the President.

The Committee met at noon of Tuesday, July 22, 1888, in the City of Little Rock. All the members were present.

A letter from the Bishop was read, dated June 22, 1888, stating that he would be absent from the Diocese for several months on a visit to England, and consequently he transferred the Ecclesiastical Authority to the Standing Committee during his absence.

The Committee gave its unanimous consent to the consecration of the Rev. Leighton Coleman, S. T. D., as Bishop of Delaware, and the consecration of the Rev. Geo. McClellan Fiske as the Bishop of Fond du Lac.

The Committee declined to give its consent as the Ecclesiastical Authority of the Diocese, to the Vestry of St. John's, Fort Smith, permitting them to mortgage their Church property for the sum of $1500.

The following resolution was offered and unanimously adopted: "That the Standing Committee of the Diocese of Arkansas, do hereby authorize and direct the Trustee of the Episcopate Fund of said Diocese, to use such funds as he may have in his hands, in purchasing the claims or mortgages on the McMurray property in Pine Bluff, which has been devised to said fund by the late James McMurray; and also to pay off such legacies as may be against said property so as to prevent a premature sale of said property at a loss; and to purchase such debts or claims against said estate as he may be able to purchase at a discount, or that may be necessary to prevent the sale of said property at a loss. And if the said Trustee should find, on consultation with the executor of the will of said McMurray and the Chancellor of the Diocese, that it would be of material benefit to said fund to pay off all claims against said estate, he, the Trustee of the Episcopate fund, is authorized and empowered to make said payments and take said real estate property as it stands, and collect the rents for the use of said Episcopate Fund; and this power and authority shall extend and continue for one year from this date."

The Committee met in Pine Bluff in November, 1888, and recommended Mr. C. M. Humphreys to the Bishop as a candidate for Holy Orders.

The Committee met in Pine Bluff on the 18th of December, 1888, and gave its unanimous consent to the consecration of the Rev. C. C. Grafton as Bishop of Fond du Lac; also the Rev. Boyd Vincent as Assistant Bishop of Southern Ohio, and the Rev. J. Mills Kendrick, as Missionary Bishop of Arizona and New Mexico.

The resignation of the Rev. W. W. Estabrooke as a member of the Committee, was read and accepted.

The Committee met in Little Rock on the 10th of January, 1889, and gave its consent to the consecration of the Rev. Cyrus F. Knight as Bishop of Milwaukee.

The Committee met in Little Rock on the 10th of February, 1889, and recommended the Rev. John Edward Curzon, Deacon, to the Bishop, to be advanced to the Sacred Order of Priests.

The Rev. Chas. H. Proctor was elected to fill the vacancy in the Committee caused by the resignation of the Rev. Dr. Estabrooke.

All of which is respectfully submitted.

INNES O. ADAMS,
President Standing Committee.

POSTSCRIPT.

I desire to state to the Council that in June, 1888, Mr. James McMurray, a communicant of the Church, and of Trinity Parish, Pine Bluff, died, leaving to P. K. Roots, Trustee of the Episcopate Fund, and his successors in office, his estate, after the debts and several bequests are paid, for the benefit of the Episcopate Fund.

That said estate, when the debts and bequests are paid, will be worth about $3000.

And further, that I borrowed from P. K. Roots, Trustee of the Episcopate Fund, the sum of $865.85 to pay off certain mortgages, claims, etc., that might prevent a forced or premature sale of the property, and transferred said claims and mortgage to P. K. Roots, Trustee of the Episcopate Fund.

The property is now bringing rents at the rate of $40 per month, and I hope by twelve months from next June, after I have made my final settlement, to turn it over to the Episcopate Fund free of debt.   Respectfully submitted.

INNES O. ADAMS,

Executor.

APPENDIX III.

REPORT OF THE TREASURER OF THE DIOCESE.

THE DIOCESAN FUND.

RECEIPTS.

Balance on hand	$535	00
May 2, 1889, Trinity Cathedral....	25	00
" Trinity, Pine Bluff................	60	00
" St. Luke's, Hot Springs...	50	00
" St. John's, Helena............	60	00
" St. Andrew's Mission....	15	00
" St. Paul's, Dardanelle.........	10	00
" St. Paul's, Fayetteville........	20	00
" St. James', Eureka Springs.......	10	00
" St. Agnes', Morrilton	10	00
" Trinity, Van Buren............	10	00
" St. Paul's, Batesville...........	20	00
" St. John's, Fort Smith..........	125	00
" St. Paul's, Newport............	10	00
Total.............................	$960	00

DISBURSEMENTS.

April 17, 1888, W. W. Astor, Treas. Gen'l. Conv	$ 13	00
June 5, Press Printing Co. (Journal).........	112	20
June 9, Mailing Journal..................	11	51
June 11, Sentinel, Hot Springs (printing Reports)	9	50
December 26, Episcopate Fund.............	340	00
Total	$486	21
Balance on hand.......................	$473	79

DIOCESAN MISSION FUND.

RECEIPTS.

Balance on hand.................. ....$167 86	
May 29, 1888, St. Andrew's, Marianna......	8 80
" St. Paul's, Newport..................... .	2 00
" 30, Trinity, Van Buren......	3 55
" 31, St. Luke's, Hot Springs..................	20 00
June 2, Trinity, Pine Bluff......................	4 40
" 6, St. Luke's, Hot Springs........	1 00
" 18, St. James', Eureka Springs...............	3 57
" 23, St. John's, Camden.....,..	3 00
July 5, St. John's, Helena..................	7 85
March 2, 1889, Trinity, Pine Bluff........	7 25
" 13, St. Luke's, Hot Springs.................	17 85
" 19, St. Andrew's, Marianna.................	3 50
April 23, St. Philip's, Little Rock..........	5 00

Total..................................$256 13

DISBURSEMENTS.

June 8, 1888, Rev. D. F. MacDonald............$127 00

Balance on hand....... ....$129 13

FUND FOR DISABLED CLERGY, ETC.

RECEIPTS.

Balance on hand $135 58	
Dec. 1, 1888, St. Luke's, Hot Springs........... .	8 30
" 5, Trinity, Van Buren......................	2 00
" 11, Trinity, Van Buren...................	4 85
" 12, Trinity Cathedral......................	4 55
April 23, 1889 St. Philip's, Little Rock............	2 00

Total on hand........................ .$157 28

All of which reports are respectfully submitted.

LOGAN H. ROOTS,

Treasurer.

APPENDIX IV.

REPORT OF TRUSTEE OF EPISCOPATE FUND.

RECEIPTS.

Balance on hand.....	$ 347 31
April 25, 1888, Building Association..............	2000 00
May 25, part interest on lots 10, 11 and 12, block 200	75 00
May 30, balance Building Association.......... ...	3 00
Dec. 1, balance 1888, interest on lots 10, 11 and 12, block 200.............................	65 00
Dec. 26, Diocesan Fund	34.) 00
Feb. 19, 1889, St. Luke's, Hot Springs	24 50
April 4, part principal on lots 10, 11 and 12, blk 200	100 00
April 9, Logan H. Roots.......................	10 00
April 9, P. K. Roots	10 00
April 23, Trinity, Pine Bluff.....................	61 75
April 23, St. Philip's, Little Rock.................	3 00
April 26, Grace Church, Washington.............	10 80
April 26, St. John's, Helena Sunday-School........	27 05
May 1, interest.........................	94 50
May 3, Rev. Mr. C. A. Bruce	10 00
Total.....................	$318 1 91

DISBURSEMENTS.

April 19, 1888, balance due on old Building Association ....$	10 00
Sept. 29, invested in the McMurray estate, through Rev. I. O. Adams	865 60
Jan. 17, 1889, recording mortgage on lots 10, 11 and 12, block 200........	2 25
Jan. 22, invested in new Building Ass'n...	1781 25
April 27, total dues paid to new Building Association to date..............	102 00
Total disbursements......... .	$2761 10

Balance on hand..............	420	81
Balance due on lots 10, 11 and 12, block 200...................	1200	00
Invested in McMurray bequest ...	865	60
Invested in Building Association..	1883	25
Total present value of assets of the fund...................	$4369	66
Value of fund last report	3627	31
Increase of fund during the year.	$ 742	35

Some months since I was informed by Rev. I. O. Adams, of Pine Bluff, that Mr. James McMurray of that city, before he died, had bequeathed to me and my successors in office, as Trustees of the Episcopate Fund, the whole of his estate that remained after the payment of his debts and bequests to others, which I am informed will likely increase our fund about $2000.

Subsequently the Standing Committee, on the 22d day of June, 1888, acting as the Ecclesiastical Authority of the Diocese, passed a resolution directing the purchase of such claims, mortgages. legacies, etc., as would prevent a premature sale of the property, which resolution is fully recited in the record of the proceedings of the Standing Committee.

After this action by the Committee, Rev. I. O. Adams, executor of the estate of James McMurray, made application approved by Chancellor M. L. Bell for $865.60, to be applied in compliance with the provisions of said resolution.

This amount was sent to the executor, and there was received in return therefor mortgage and claims against the estate that have been transferred to me as Trustee of the Episcopate Fund, aggregating $865.87.

All of which report is respectfully and fraternally submitted.

P. K. ROOTS,

Trustee.

APPENDIX V.

REPORT OF THE COMMITTEE ON THE STATE OF THE CHURCH.

Your Committee on the State of the Church respectfully make the following report:

We rejoice, and thank God that we are able to report marked progress since last Council. Not only has there been a larger number confirmed during the past year than in any previous year, but there is evidence of increased zeal upon the part of our Clergy, and a corresponding co-operation on the part of the Laity which manifestly accounts for the unusual growth; but far more important to note is the *improved spiritual tone* of the Diocese. Never before has the Church in this State been able to put forth her claims with such hopes of a hearing as she now enjoys. Much remains to be done in order to give the Church her natural position in this great State; but we are cheered by recent improvement, and we feel that the Diocese can now go forward with buoyant steps to accomplish her great mission. To this end we earnestly recommend the revival of the Diocesan Board of Missions, which, co-operating heartily with the Bishop, can, we believe, greatly advance the work of the Diocese by encouraging activity amongst the Missionaries, by inducing the reinforcement of our laborers, and by stimulating the collection of means to carry on the work.

The Bishop's announcement that he accepts the Episcopate of the Diocese to which he was elected eighteen years ago, is received with gratitude and delight. We feel that this act of the Bishop marks an era in the Diocese; and we trust that it may prove the signal for renewed effort to demonstrate our affection for the Bishop, and our hearty desire to help and in him in his arduous work. Especially ought the Bishop's acceptance of the Diocese encourage the accumulation of an Episcopate Fund, by which we shall be enabled to offer the Bishop our active support without the aid of the Board of Missions.

A remarkable feature in the history of the Diocese during the past year has been the unprecedented growth of the Church in the City of Little Rock. An aggressive work, resulting in the presentation of seventy-four candidates for confirmation and ninety two for baptism, the Cathedral building an accomplished fact, St. Philip's colored Mission organized with a settled Rector, provision made for the two adjunct Mission Sunday-Schools of Christ Church—almost new Missions in themselves, and certain foundation of two new Parishes in the near future—all harbingers of bright days for Arkansas, and an encouragement for renewed effort.

The report of St. John's Hospital at Fort Smith indicates that God is blessing a work in which we are particularly interested, and for which we record our thanks to Him.

In conclusion, we beg leave to remind the brethren of the Clergy and Laity that the only true basis for the real prosperity of the Church is a life consecrated to God. Without the sincere cultivation of personal holiness, without a true imitation of the example of our beloved Lord and Saviour, no numerical growth, no financial success can avail for the promotion of Christ's kingdom on earth.

WALLACE CARNAHAN,
CHARLES H. PROCTOR,
L. F. GUERRY,
GEORGE W. CARUTH,
BLEECKER LUCE.

APPENDIX VI.

PAROCHIAL ASSESSMENTS:

REPORT OF COMMITTEE ON WAYS AND MEANS.

To the Diocesan Council:

Your Committee respectfully report that after a careful examination of the condition of each Parish and Mission, they have made the following assessments :

	ASSESSMENT.	AD'NAL. PLDG'D.
St. Paul's, Batesville	$ 20 00	$ 10 00
St. John's, Camden	15 00	
St. Paul's, Dardanelle	10 00	
St. John's, Eureka Springs	10 00	
St. Paul's, Fayetteville	40 00	10 00
St. John's, Fort Smith	125 00	75 00
St. John's, Helena	60 00	30 00
St. Mark's, Hope	5 00	3 00
St. Luke's, Hot Springs	50 00	
Trinity Cathedral	75 00	50 00
Christ Church, Little Rock	275 00	
St. Philip's, Little Rock	10 00	
St. Andrew's, Mammoth Springs	5 00	
St. Andrew's, Marianna	15 00	
St. Agnes', Morrilton	15 00	
Church of the Redeemer, Nashville	5 00	3 00
St. Paul's, Newport	15 00	
Mission at Pendleton	10 00	20 00
Grace, Phillips County	5 00	
Trinity, Pine Bluff	60 00	
Trinity, Van Buren	20 00	
Grace, Washington	10 00	
Mission at Witcherville	5 00	2 50
Total	**$860 00**	**$203 50**
		$1063 50

The Committee suggest that the amount available for the Episcopate Fund from this assessment will fall far below the amount that should be added to that fund the coming year, and would therefore urge upon the Parishes special efforts for the increase of the fund by offerings and subscriptions.

Respectfully submitted,

J. J. VAULX,
S. S. FAULKNER,
J. M. DAGGETT,
Committee.

APPENDIX VII.

PAROCHIAL REPORTS
For the Year Ending Easter Monday, 1889.

ST. MARK'S CHURCH, ARKADELPHIA.
No report.

UNORGANIZED MISSION, ARKANSAS CITY.
No report.

ST. PAUL'S CHURCH, BATESVILLE
Ed. M. Dickinson, Senior Warden.

Number of families, 40; whole number of souls, 102; number of baptized persons, 90, Baptisms: Infants, 6; adults, 2; total, 8. Confirmations, 1. Died, 1. Actual Communicants: Present number, male 20, female 20; total, 40. Number of confirmed persons, 60. Burials, 4. Public Services, 6. Holy Communion: Public, 3. Sunday School: Teachers, 6; pupils, 61.

OFFERINGS:

Diocesan: Aassessment, $20; miscellaneous, $12.50; Bishop's visit for Cathedral, $12.20. Total, $44.70.

Total offerings, $44.70.

Estimated value of Church and grounds...........$2500 00
Estimated value of Rectory..................... 500 00
Estimated value of other Church property......... 500 00

Total......................................$3500 00
Amount of indebtedness on Church property.....$ 242 00

REMARKS: The above report is correct, so far as I have been able to ascertain from the records of the Church during the past year. Having had no Rector since the 1st of last March, one year ago, our Church has been at a standstill, with the exception that we have kept up the Sunday School service very regularly. Respectfully submitted,

ED. M. DICKINSON,
Senior Warden.

ST. JOHN'S CHURCH, CAMDEN.

REV. WM. WILMOT ESTABROOKE, Minister.

Number of families, 26; whole number of souls, 80; number baptized persons, 74. BAPTISMS: Infants, 4. ACTUAL COMMUNICANTS: Received, 7; present number, male 14, female 30; total, 44. Number of confirmed persons, 46. PUBLIC SERVICES: Sundays, 15. HOLY COMMUNION: Public, 6.

OFFERINGS.

PAROCHIAL: Communion alms, $12.60; Rector's salary and Parish expenses, $100; miscellaneous, $4.55. Total,$117.15.
DIOCESAN: Diocesan missions, $3.
Total offerings, $123.10.
NOTE: The above report is for the time from Easter Monday to December 1, 1888.

ST. PAUL'S CHURCH, DARDANELLE.

REV. RICHARD S. JAMES, D. D., LL. D., Rector.

W. E. DeLONG, HENRY BARNETT, Wardens.

Number of families, 9. Confirmations, 2. ACTUAL COMMUNICANTS: Admitted, 5; received, 2; total added, 7; removed, 1; total withdrawn, 4; total lost, 5; present number, male 8, female 16; total, 24. Marriages, 1. Burials, 2. PUBLIC SERVICES: Sundays, 50; other days, 19; total, 69. HOLY COMMUNION: Public, 12. SUNDAY SCHOOL: Teachers, 5; pupils, 28. Church sittings, 150. Rectory? Yes.

PAROCHIAL: Communion alms, $9.50; Rector's salary and Parish expenses, $150; miscellaneous, $4.90. Total, $164.40.

DIOCESAN: Diocesan assessment, $10; Bishop's visit for Cathedral, $2. Total, $12.

Total offerings, $176.40.

Estimated value of Church and grounds..... .....$2500 00
Estimated value of Rectory..... .... 325 00

Total... ....$2825 00
Amount of indebtedness on Church property. ... 325 00

ST. JAMES' CHURCH, EUREKA SPRINGS.

No report.

ST. PAUL'S CHURCH, FAYETTEVILLE.

REV. JAS. J. VAULX, Rector.

W. R. WELCH, M. D., J. F. SIMONDS, PH. D., Wardens.

Number of families, 50. BAPTISMS: Infants, 9; adults, 7; total, 16. Confirmations, 12. Actual communicants, 128. Number of confirmed persons, 132. Marriages, 2. Burials, 6. PUBLIC SERVICES: Sundays, 156; other days, 138; total, 294. HOLY COMMUNION: Public, 90; Private, 3; total, 93. SUNDAY SCHOOL: Teachers, 4. Church sittings, 250. Rectory? Yes.

OFFERINGS.

PAROCHIAL: Communion alms, $59.00; Rector's salary, $500; weekly offertory, $60.72; Easter offerings, $126.40; raised by St. Paul's Guild, $716.02. Total, $1462.14.

DIOCESAN: Diocesan assessment, $20; Bishop's visit to Cathedral, $16.07; paid to the Bishop money loaned for building Church, $75. Total, $111.07.

EXTRA DIOCESAN: Domestic Society for promoting Christianity among the Jews, $4.80; yellow fever sufferers, $26.40. Total, $31.20.

Total offerings, 1604.41.

Estimated value of Church and grounds...........$3000 00

Estimated value of Rectory.................... 3000 00

Total...............................$6000 00

The above report includes communicants in Washington, Benton and Madison counties, as far as known to the Rector of St. Paul's Church, all under his care.

ST. JOHN'S CHURCH, FORT SMITH.

REV. GEORGE FREDERIC DEGEN, Rector.

STEPHEN WHEELER, WILLIAM M. MELLETTE, Wardens.

Number of families, 162; whole number of souls, 644; number baptized persons, 604. BAPTISMS: Infants, 46; adults, 9; total, 65. Confirmations, 36. ACTUAL COMMUNICANTS: Admitted, 36; received, 41; total added, 77; removed, 17; died, 2; withdrawn, 1; total lost, 20; present number, male 8; female 182; total, 260. Number confirmed persons, 260. Marriages, 6. Burials, 12. PUBLIC SERVICES: Sundays, 168; other days, 191; total, 359. HOLY COMMUNION: Public, 110; private, 3; total, 113. SUNDAY SCHOOLS: Teachers, 13; pupils, 158. Church sittings, 200. Rectory? Yes.

OFFERINGS.

PAROCHIAL: Communion alms, $97.65; Rector's salary and Parish expenses; $1610.21; miscellaneous, $1430.23; St. John's Hospital, $2068.66; building fund, $400. Total, $5606.75.

DIOCESAN: Diocesan assessment, $125; Buckner College, $569.88; Cathedral (Bishop's visit), $24.46; total, $719.34.

EXTRA DIOCESAN: Domestic missions, $86.15; foreign missions, $14.35; miscellaneous, $27.40. Total, $127.90.

Total offerings, $6453.99.

Estimated value of Church and grounds.........$10,000 00
Estimated value of Rectory 1,800 00
Estimated value of other Church property 680 00

Total $12,480 00
Amount of indebtedness on Church property...... 150 00

ST. JOHN'S CHURCH, HELENA.

P. O. THWEATT, G. QUARLES, Wardens.

Number of families, 74; whole number of souls, 283. BAPTISMS: Infants, 3; adults, 3; total, 6. Confirmations, 15. ACTUAL COMMUNICANTS: Admitted, 15; received, 1; total added, 16; removed, 3; died, 1; total lost, 4; present number, male 34; female, 96; total, 130. Number of confirmed persons, 145. Marriages, 2; Burials, 6. SUNDAY SCHOOL: Teachers, 13; pupils, 92; Church sittings, 400.

OFFERINGS:

PAROCHIAL: Rector's salary and Parish expenses, $800; Miscellaneous, $920; of miscellaneous amount $340.50 was for burial of Rector. Total, $1720.

DIOCESAN: Diocesan assessment, $60; Episcopate Fund from Sunday School, $27.05; Bishop's visit for Cathedral, $23.60. Total, $110.65.

EXTRA DIOCESAN: University of the South, $8.70. Total, $8.70.

Total offerings, $1839.35.

Estimated value of Church and grounds.........$12,000 00
Estimated value of other Church property 1,500 00

Total...................................$13,500 00
Amount of indebtedness on Church property..... 400 00

S. S. FAULKNER,
Treasurer of Parish.

ST. MARK'S CHURCH, HOPE.

REV. J. E. CURZON, Minister.

Number of families, 7; whole number of souls, 32; number of baptized persons, 27. BAPTISMS: Infants, 7; adults, 3; total, 10. Confirmations, 8. ACTUAL COMMUNICANTS: Received, 8; total added, 8; removed, 1; died, 1; total lost, 2; present number, male, 6; female 11; total, 17. Burials, 2. PUBLIC SERVICES: Sundays, 2; other days, 13; total, 15. HOLY COMMUNION: Public, 5. SUNDAY SCHOOL: Teachers, 5; pupils, 35. Church sittings, 130.

OFFERINGS.

PAROCHIAL: Communion alms, $8.10; Rector's salary and Parish expenses, $128.45; miscellaneous, $2. Total, $138.55. Total offerings, $138.55.

Estimated value of Church and grounds.........$300 00

NOTE (by the Secretary): The above is the combined report of the Rev. Dr. Estabrooke and the Rev. J. E. Curzon.

———

ST. LUKE'S CHURCH, HOT SPRINGS.

REV. W. J. MILLER, Rector.

JAMES P. MELLARD, GEORGE G. LATTA, Wardens.

Number of families, 70. BAPTISMS: Infants, 6; adults, 4; total, 10. Confirmations, 6. ACTUAL COMMUNICANTS; Admitted, 10; received, 5; total added, 15; removed, 9; died, 4; total lost, 13; present number, 90. Marriages, 5. Burials, 7. PUBLIC SERVICES: Sundays, 83; other days, 67; total, 150. HOLY COMMUNION: Public, 24; private, 4; total, 28. SUNDAY SCHOOL: Teachers, 6; pupils, 70.

OFFERINGS.

PAROCHIAL: Communion alms, $85.13; Rector's salary and Parish expenses, $1295.84; miscellaneous, $93.25; additional alms, $62; Church building fund, $3019.54; total, $4555.76.

DIOCESAN: Diocesan assessment, $50; Diocesan missions, $39.35; aged and infirm clergy, $8.40; Episcopate Fund, $24.50; St. James', Eureka Springs, $2; Buckner College, $6; St. John's Hospital (Sunday-school offering), $22.56; Cathedral work among colored people, $6.75; total, $159.56.

EXTRA DIOCESAN: Domestic Missions, $20.65; University of the South, $12.15; conversion of the Jews, $5.67; total, $38.47.

Total offerings, $4753.79.

Estimated value of Church and grounds..........$12,000 00
Estimated value of other Church property... ....   2,500 00

Total $14,500 00

EMMANUEL CHURCH, LAKE VILLAGE.
No report.

CHRIST CHURCH, LITTLE ROCK.
REV. WALLACE CARNAHAN, Rector.

R. H. PARHAM, JR., AND DR. W. A. CANTRELL, Wardens.

Number of families, 334; number of communicants, 557; number of souls, (about) 1600. BAPTISMS: Infants, 30; adults, 8; total, 38. Confirmations, 53. Marriages, 9. Burials, 24. SUNDAY SCHOOLS: Teachers, 42; pupils, 378; total, 420.

OFFERINGS.

PAROCHIAL: Communion alms, $376.55; other expenditures, $11,238.50. Total, $11,615.05.

DIOCESAN: For Cathedral and Cathedral work, $32.70 missionary box, $175. Total, $207.70.

EXTRA DIOCESAN: Domestic missions, $179.59; yello' fever sufferers, $78.75; foreign missions, $25; University the South, $25. Total, $308.34.

Aggregate offerings, $12,131.09.

Value of Church edifice and grounds..... ......$58,000 00
Value of Rectory and ground................ ..... 8,000 00
Value of Mission Chapel and lot.... .. .. 1,500 00

Total value of Church property............$67,500 00

ST. PHILIP'S CHURCH, LITTLE ROCK.

Rev. Benjamin W. Timothy, Rector.

John O. W. Alexander, London W. Walker, Wardens.

Number of families, 20; whole number of souls, 75; number of baptized persons, 50. Baptisms: Adults, 2; total, 2. Confirmations, 16. Actual Communicants: Admitted, 16; received, 1; total added, 17; present number, male, 10; female 21; total, 31. Public Services: Sundays, 46; other days, 32; total, 78. Holy Communion: Public, 6. Sunday School: Teachers, 4; pupils, 50. Church sittings, 200.

OFFERINGS:

Parochial: Communion alms, 85 cents; Rector's salary and Parish expenses, $210.35; Chancel furniture, etc., $55. Total, $266.20.

Diocesan: Diocesan Missions, $5; aged and infirm Clergy, $2; Episcopate Fund, $3. Total, $10.

Extra Diocesan: Domestic missions, $1; foreign missions, $1; colored missions, $1; Indian missions, $1; Jewish missions, $1. Total, $5.

Total offerings, $281.20.

Estimated value of Church and grounds..........$1900.00

This report covers only the period of my charge, three and one half months. B. W. TIMOTHY,

Rector.

TRINITY CATHEDRAL, LITTLE ROCK.

THE VERY REV. C. H. PROCTOR, Dean.

REV. J. E. CURZON, Assistant Minister.

G. W. CARUTH, WILLIAM G. WHIPPLE, Wardens.

BAPTISMS: Infants, 53; adults, 1; total, 54. Confirmations, 5. Communicants, 150. Marriages, 1. Burials, 5. SUNDAY SCHOOL: Teachers, males, 9; pupils 125.

OFFERINGS.

PAROCHIAL: Communion alms, $24.50; Rector's salary and Parish expenses, $1121.58; miscellaneous, $479.50; miscellaneous, $1445,00; Sunday School and clubs, $272.50. Total, $3343.08.

DIOCESAN: Diocesan assessment, $25; aged and infirm Clergy, $4.55; miscellaneous, $2125.60. Total, $2155.15.

Total offerings, $5498.23.

Estimated value of Church property.............$18,000 00

NOTE: The Cathedral report covers less than one year of work, and includes only the personal report of the Dean. In many statistics called for, it is not possible to make an accurate record, and for that reason they have been left blank altogether. An imperfect communicant list of about twenty-five members, a year ago, has been corrected, and the present approximate number, somewhat less than the actual list on the Rector's visiting book, is submitted. The confirmed includes a small class presented at St. Philip's, in December, by the Assistant Minister; but the communicant list does not include any who are entitled to be registered at St. Philip's, now that it is organized.

The sum total of offerings does not include the pledges that have been made for building. These sums will be reported as they are received.

The Cathedral Parish is in reality in the process of formation, and the routine of an established Parish is practically an impossibility at the present stage of its history. It is the time of seed-sowing; the promise of an abundant harvest is a stimulus which a Divine Providence has placed in our hands. With this blessing the Cathedral may hope to present a report in the near future, in which the whole Diocese may rejoice.

C. H. PROCTOR,

Dean, etc.

ST. ANDREW'S CHURCH, MAMMOTH SPRING.

P. P. B. HYNSON, Warden.

Number of families, 4; whole number of souls, 28; number baptized persons, 28. BAPTISMS: Infants, 6; adults, 4; total, 10. Confirmations, 9. ACTUAL COMMUNICANTS: Total added, 1; removed, 3; present number, male, 5; female, 11; total, 16. Number of confirmed persons, 16. PUBLIC SERVICES, 57. HOLY COMMUNION, 4. SUNDAY SCHOOL: Teachers, 7; pupils, 40.

OFFERINGS.

PAROCHIAL: Communion alms, $58.25; Rector's salary and Parish expenses, $125; miscellaneous, $221. Total, $404.25.
DIOCESAN: Miscellaneous, $9.50. Total, $9.50.
EXTRA DIOCESAN: Miscellaneous, $23. Total, $23.
Total offerings, $436.25.

Estimated value of Church and grounds........... $1000 00
Estimated value of Rectory..................... 1000 00

Total....................................... $2000 00
Amount of indebtedness on Church property....... $300 00

ST. ANDREW'S CHURCH, MARIANNA.

REV. C. A. BRUCE, Rector.

F. H. GOVAN, SAMUEL A. BISHOP, Wardens.

Number of families, 16; whole number of souls, 72. Number of baptized persons, 60. BAPTISMS: Infants, 5; total, 5.

Confirmations, 3. ACTUAL COMMUNICANTS: Admitted, 3; received, 1; total added, 4; removed, 4; died, 1; total lost, 5; present number, male, 10, female 21; total, 31. Number of confirmed persons, 33. Marriages, 2. Burials, 1. PUBLIC SERVICES: Sundays, 130; other days, 8; total, 138. HOLY COMMUNION: Public, 47. SUNDAY SCHOOL: Teachers, 5; pupils, 30. Church sittings, 115.

OFFERINGS.

PAROCHIAL: Communion alms, $29.70; Parish expenses, $380.35; miscellaneous for Church, $128.05. Total. $538.10.

DIOCESAN: Diocesan assessment, $15; Diocesan missions, $12.30; Arkansas City Mission, $11; the Bishop, for Cathedral, $4.10. Total, $42.40.

EXTRA DIOCESAN: Domestic missions, $15; total, $15.

Total offerings, $595.50.

Estimated value of Church and grounds $3000 00

ST. AGNES' CHURCH, MORRILTON.

REV. RICHARD S. JAMES, D. D., Rector.

W. M. SCARBOROUGH, W. P. STOUT, Wardens.

Number of families, 12. BAPTISMS: Infants, 2. Confirmations, 1. ACTUAL COMMUNICANTS, 34. Marriages, 1. Burials, 1. PUBLIC SERVICES: Sundays, 38; other days, 3; total, 41. HOLY COMMUNION, 10. Church sittings, 150.

OFFERINGS.

PAROCHIAL: Rector's salary and Parish expenses, $223.90.

DIOCESAN: Diocesan assessment, $10; Bishop's visit for Cathedral, $1.15. Total, $11.15.

Total offerings, $235.05.

Estimated value of Church and grounds $2766 80

Amount of indebtedness on Church property 1187 02

CHURCH OF THE REDEEMER, NASHVILLE.

Rev. John Edward Curzon, Mission Priest.

Number of families, 7; whole number of souls, 27; number of baptized persons, 27. BAPTISMS: Infants, 3; adults, 2 total, 5. Confirmations, 1. ACTUAL COMMUNICANTS: Admitted, 1; present number, males, 6; females, 12; total, 18. Number of confirmed persons, 18. Burials, 1. PUBLIC SERVICES Sundays, 3; other days, 12; total, 15. HOLY COMMUNION: Public, 7; private, 3; total, 10. SUNDAY SCHOOL: Teachers, 4; pupils, 16. Church sittings, 125.

OFFERINGS.

PAROCHIAL: Communion alms, $11.85; Rector's salary and Parish expenses, $141.15; miscellaneous, $22.50; total, $175.50.

Total offerings, $175.50.

Estimated value of Church and grounds.............$700 00

NOTE (by the Secretary): The above is the combined report of the Rev. Dr. Estabrooke and the Rev. J. E. Curzon.

ST. PAUL'S CHURCH, NEWPORT.

Rev. J. E. Curzon, Minister.

Lancelot Minor, J. S. Jones, Wardens.

Number of families, 35; whole number of souls, 116; number of baptized persons, 100. BAPTISMS: Infants, 3; adults, 1; total, 4. Confirmations, 18. ACTUAL COMMUNICANTS: Admitted, 18; total added, 18; removed, 2; died, 2; total lost, 4; present number, male 5, female 38; total, 43. Number of confirmed persons, 45. Marriages, 2. Burials, 4. PUBLIC SERVICES: Sundays, 50; other days, 42; total, 92. HOLY COMNUNION: Public, 21; private, 1; total, 22. SUNDAY SCHOOL: Teachers, 7; pupils, 75. Church sittings, 175.

PAROCHIAL: Communion alms, $32.30; Rector's salary and Parish expense, $836.35. Total, $868.65.

DIOCESAN: Diocesan missions, $2; miscellaneous, $1.45; Bishop's visit for Cathedral, $2.60. Total, $6.05.

EXTRA DIOCESAN: Sunday-school for American Church building fund, $2.75.

Total offerings, $877.45.

Estimated value of Church and grounds $2500 00

NOTE (by the Secretary): The above is the combined report of the Rev. Dr. Estabrooke and the Rev. J. E. Curzon.

GRACE CHURCH, PHILLIPS COUNTY.
No report.

TRINITY CHURCH, PINE BLUFF.
REV. INNES O. ADAMS, Rector.
M. L. BELL, R. V. McCRACKEN, Wardens.

Number of families, 107; whole number of souls, 370; number of baptized persons, 24. BAPTISMS: Infants, 12; adults, 4; total, 16. Confirmations, 12. ACTUAL COMMUNICANTS: Admitted, 29; received, 21; total added, 50; removed, 3; died, 3; withdrawn, 1; total lost, 7; present number male, 26, female 125; total, 151. Number of confirmed persons, 18. Marriages, 6. Burials, 9. PUBLIC SERVICES: Sundays, 164; other days, 44; total, 208. HOLY COMMUNION: Public, 20; private, 2; total, 22. SUNDAY SCHOOL: Teachers, 9; pupils, 100. Church sittings, 450. Rectory? Yes.

PAROCHIAL: Communion alms, $48.96; Rector's salary and Parish expenses, $1189.20; miseellaneous, 3464.55. Total, $4702.71.

DIOCESAN : Diocesan assessment, $60; Diocesan missions, $11.65; aged and infirm clergy, $4.85; Episcopate fund, $61.75; Cathedral, Bishop's visitation, $6. Total, 144.25.

EXTRA DIOCESAN : University of the South, $3.35; Church building fund, $6.75; conversion of the Jews, $2.65. Total, $12.75.

Total offerings, $4859.71.

Estimated value of Church and grounds $12,0C0 00
Estimated value of Rectory 3,500 00
Estimated value of other Church property...... . 1,000 00

Total $16,500 00

Amount of indebtedness on Church property, none.

NOTE: This Parish is in splendid shape. An elegant pipe organ has been purchased and set up in the Church as a memorial to Dr. Trimble and his wife, a suitable marble tablet has been placed thereon, and the Bishop has dedicated it. A handsome vestibule has been built and presented to the Parish by Vestryman J. B. Trulock. The Church has, through the efforts of Trinity Church Association, been greatly improved and beautified in the interior with paint and kalsomine, and handsomely carpeted throughout. A brick curb wall has been placed in front of the pavement. The altar raised three steps above the sanctuary floor, a re-table and reredos placed on it. Two elegant brass vases have been presented for the altar by a class of boys in the Sunday school ; and another class, of young girls, have bought and presented to the Sunday school a fine library. The Young Ladies' Guild have erected a very beautiful rail and curtains on brass rods around the organ, presented $55.70 to the organ fund, and have purchased two annunciators for the hymns and services of the Church. The salary of the Rector has been increased. Two valuable lots for mission work have been donated by Vestryman McCracken and his wife. The Parish is free from debt. The offerings are more than double what they were last year. And while we have lost seven from the list of communicants, we have added thereto forty-two, and many who have never before received the communion have this year received the benefit and bless-ing. For all of which the *Rector thanks God*.

I. O. ADAMS,
Rector.

ST. JAMES' CHURCH, PRESCOTT.
No Report.

TRINITY CHURCH, VAN BUREN.

REV. LeGRAND F. GUERRY, Rector.

CHAS. RIBLING and JAS. A. KEARNEY, Wardens.

Number of families, 28 ; whole number of souls, 140 ; number of baptized persons, 130. BAPTISMS : Infants, 1 ; adults, 3 ; total, 4. Confirmations, 10. ACTUAL COMMUNICANTS : Admitted, 10; received, 2; total added, 12 ; removed, 4 ; died, 2 ; total lost, 6; present number, male, 6; female, 41 ; total, 47. Number of confirmed persons, 67. Marriages, 5. Burials, 4. PUBLIC SERVICES : Sundays, 110 ; other days, 70 ; total, 180. HOLY COMMUNION : Public, 16 ; total 16. SUNDAY SCHOOL : Teachers, 7 ; pupils, 50. Church sittings, 250.

OFFERINGS.

PAROCHIAL : Communion alms, $50.57 ; Rector's salary and Parish expenses, $762.95 ; miscellaneous, $9.65 ; offerings at Easter, $187.25. Total, $1010.42.

DIOCESAN : Diocesan missions, $3.55 ; aged and infirm clergy, $2 ; Bishop's visit for Cathedral, $3.25. Total, $8.80.

EXTRA DIOCESAN : Foreign missions, $3.55 ; University of the South, $2.40. Total, $5.95.

Total offerings, $1025.17.

Estimated value of Church and grounds........$3000 00

In addition to services above reported, I have officiated twice in the town of Alma, nine miles distant, and with encouraging results. It is my hope to establish a congregation at this point. The spirit of my charge in Van Buren, I am thankful to say, is improving daily. My people are becoming more and more united, and are working nobly in the cause of the Church.

GRACE CHURCH, WASHINGTON.

Rev. J. E. Curzon, Minister.

Number of families, 12; whole number of souls, 47; number of baptized persons, 44. BAPTISMS: Infants, 3. ACTUAL COMMUNICANTS: Removed, 2; total lost, 2; present number, male, 5, female 19; total, 24. Number of confirmed persons, 24. Marriages, 3. PUBLIC SERVICES: Sundays, 12, other days, 14; total, 26. HOLY COMMUNION: Public, 7. SUNDAY SCHOOL: Teachers, 4; pupils, 14. Church sittings, 175.

OFFERINGS.

PAROCHIAL: Communion alms, $20.93; Rector's salary and Parish expenses, $226.25; miscellaneous, $81.75. Total, $328.93.

Estimated value of Church property.............$500 00

NOTE (by the Secretary): The above is the combined report of the Rev. Dr. Estabrook and the Rev. J. E. Curzon.

ADDITIONAL REPORTS.

REPORT OF THE REV. R. S. JAMES, D. D., LL. D.

DARDANELLE, ARK., April 27, 1889.

The Rt. Rev. H. N. Pierce, D. D., LL. D., Bishop of Arkansas:

Besides my regular Sunday services at Dardanelle and Morrilton, I have preached at Russellville, Conway and Judsonia. In the last named, I found eight communicants, who, as soon as possible, will be organized into a Mission. At Conway I found the remnants of St. Peter's Parish, which had not held services for several years. I was privileged to baptize four there, two adults and two infants. Another adult is waiting my next visit to be baptized. At my second visit to Conway, Col. A. P. Robinson authorized me to select two lots on the public square for the use of the Church. These he is ready to deed to the Bishop or a Vestry, whenever one is elected. Illness, on two occasions, has prevented my carrying out all my plans in reference to Conway, but I hope before many weeks have passed to show still better results.

Faithfully yours,

RICHARD S. JAMES,

Missionary.

REPORT OF THE REV. D. S. C. M. POTTER, D. D., LL. D.

MATTAPOISETT, PLYMOUTH COUNTY, MASSACHUSETTS, ⎫
April 23, 1889.   ⎭

The Rt. Rev. H. N. Pierce, D. .D., LL. D., 1700 Center Street, Little Rock, Ark.:

MY DEAR BISHOP : Since my temporary departure from your Diocese in January, I have participated in the services of our Holy Catholic Church in Ascension Church, Mount Sterling, Ky.; in St. Luke's Church, Buffalo, N. Y.; in Christ Church, Rochester, N. Y.; in St. Paul's Church, Syracuse, N. Y., and in St. Paul's Church, Boston, Mass. I will be in this Diocese for a brief period, and perhaps in Central New York, but hope by the favor of Divine Providence, that I will be called to a field of labor, in your Diocese, at an early season, where I may devote myself wholly to the work of the Ministry of Christ Jesus, our Lord. With much love to the brethren ministering to the Churches in Arkansas, and to yourself as my spiritual father in the Holy Catholic Apostolic Church, in which God has appointed you an overseer, I remain your faithful servant in Christ,

REV. DANIEL S. C. M. POTTER, D. D.

TABLE OF PAROCHIAL STATISTICS.

PARISHES AND MISSIONS.	No. Families.	BAPTISMS Infants.	BAPTISMS Adults.	BAPTISMS Total.	Confirmations.	Communicants.	Marriages.	Burials.	SUNDAY SCHOOLS Teachers.	SUNDAY SCHOOLS Pupils.	OFFERINGS Parochial.	OFFERINGS Diocesan.	OFFERINGS Extra Diocesan.	OFFERINGS Total.	Value of Church Property.
Arkadelphia, St. Mark's	40	6	2	8	1	9						44 70		44 70	$ 1,000 00
Arkansas City, Mission	26	4		4											3,500 00
Batesville, St. Paul's		2	2	4											2,500 00
Camden, St. John's			2		2	40	1	4	6	61	117 15		8 00	120 15	
Conway, [Mission]	9					44			5	28					2,825 00
Dardanelle, St. Paul's		9	7	16		24	2	6	4	40	164 40	12 00		176 40	200
Eureka Springs, St. James'	50	46	19	65	12	128	6	12	12	158	452 14	111 07	31 20	1,604 41	6,000 00
Fayetteville, St. Paul's	162	3	8	15	36	260	2	6	13	92	5,606 75	719 34	127 90	6,458 99	12,480 00
Fort Smith, St. Jo's	71	7	3	10	16	130	6	2	6	35	1,720 00	110 65	8 70	1,880 35	13,500 00
Helena, St. John's	7	6	4	10	6	17	2	5	6	70	138 55			138 55	800
Hope, St. M[ark's]	70				8	90	5				4,565 76	159 56	38 47	4,758 79	14,500 00
Hot Spring, St. [Luke's]															1,000
Lake Village, Immanuel															
Little [Rock], Christ Church	324	30	8	38	53	557	9	24	42	378	11,615 05	207 70	306 34	12,181 09	67,560 00
[Li]ttle Rock, St. Philip's	20		2	2	16	31		5	9	50	266 20	10 15	5 00	281 20	1,900
Little Rock, Trinity Cathedral		53	1	54	5	150			9	125	3,343 08	2,155 15		5,498 23	18,000 00
[Hot] Spring, Mission	4					16									3,000
Marianna, St. Andrew's	16	6	4	10	9	31	1	1	7	40	538 10	42 40	20 00	595 50	2,766 80
Morrilton, St. Agnes'	12	5		5	3	34		2	5	30	228 90	11 15	15 00	235 05	2,600
Nashville, Church of the Redeemer	7	3		2		18	1		4	16	175 50			176 50	2,500 00
Newport, St. Paul's	35	3	2	5	1	43	1	4	7	75	868 65	6 05	2 75	877 45	
Phillips County, Grace						13									
Pine Bluff, Trinity	107	12		16	18	151	6	5	9	100	4,702 71	144 26	12 75	4,859 71	16,500 00
Prescott, St. James	28			4	12	47	5	8	7	50					1,000
Van Buren, Trinity	12	1	1	4	10	24			4	14	1,010 42	8 80	5 95	1,025 17	3,000 00
Washington, Grace		1	3	3		10					328 98			328 93	500
Witcherville, Mission															9,000 00
Total	1079	201	65	266	200	1965	45	90	145	1862	$37,241 54	$3,752 82	$579 06	$41,572 92	$188,671 80

APPENDIX VIII.

ORDER OF BUSINESS FOR COUNCIL PROCEEDINGS.

1. Calling the Roll.
2. Presentation of the Certificates of Lay Delegates.
3. Appointment of Committee on Credentials.
4. Report of Committee on Credentials.
5. Election of Secretary.
6. Appointment of Standing Committees.
7. Annual Address of the Bishop.
8. Report of the Standing Committee.
9. Reports of Special Committees.
10. Reports of Trustees of the several Funds.
11. Report of the Auditing Committee.
12. Election of Treasurer.
13. Election of the Standing Committee.
14. Report on the State of the Church.
15. Election of Deputies to the General Convention.
16. Election of Trustees of the several Funds.
17. Election of Trustees of the University of the South and other Trustees not specified.
18. Election of Registrar.
19. Election of Chancellor.
20. Report of Committee on Unfinished Business.
21. Miscellaneous Business.
22. Report of Committee on Ways and Means.

INDEX.

The Domestic and Foreign Missionary Society of the Protestant Episcopal Church in the United States of America.

The Society asks for stated offerings as follows, and on the dates given when possible :

. Domestic Missions, the First Sunday in Advent.

Foreign Missions, the Second Sunday after the Epiphany.

Missions to colored people, the Third Sunday after the Epiphany.

Missions to Indians, the Fourth Sunday after Easter.

The Treasurer is now MR. GEORGE BLISS, to whom all remittances should be sent, at his office,

22 Bible House, New York City.

ANNOUNCEMENT.

The Eighteenth Annual Council of the Diocese of Arkansas will be held (D. V.) in Trinity Cathedral, Little Rock, on the second Thursday after Easter, April 17th, 1890.

W. J. MILLER, Secretary.

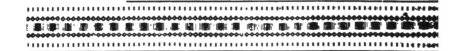

THE SECRETARY

Diocese of Arkansas

JOURNAL

OF THE

Eighteenth Annual C

..1890...

REPORT OF THE COMMITTEE

APPOINTED BY THE

EIGHTEENTH ANNUAL COUNCIL

OF THE

DIOCESE OF ARKANSAS,

TO INVESTIGATE CERTAIN CHARGES MADE AGAINST THE COUNCIL,
TOGETHER WITH A STATEMENT OF THE ACTION
TAKEN THEREON.

PRINTED BY ORDER OF THE COUNCIL.

1890.

Report.

To The Diocesan Council:

The Committee to whom was referred that portion of the Bishop'
address relating to certain charges made against the Diocesan Counci
for the years 1888 and 1889 have the following to offer as their report.

The Committee held its first meeting at Trinity Cathedral, Littl
Rock, Arkansas, at two o'clock p. m., April 18, 1890, at which time th
Bishop of the Diocese, the Right Rev Henry A. Pierce, referred t
it a number of copies of the *"Arkansas Churchman,"* a paper edited an
controlled by the Rev. Wallace Carnahan, wherein, we were informed
could be found the articles and statements, which were the basis of tha
part of his address above mentioned.

Upon examining the papers presented to us, we found printed the
in, editorials and communications over the signature of the editor, fro
which the following extracts are taken:

"That Parish (Christ's) intends now to quietly wait and see wha
the other Parishes propose to do. If a majority of the Parishes of thi
Diocese wish to have the infamous record of the last Council repeated
Christ Church of Little Rock will give them the fullest opportunity t
assume all the responsibility for it."—*Churchman. March, 1890.*

"A majority of the Council has for more than two years been tryin
to spite Christ Church; Little Rock, because of the reformatory work tha
Parish and Rector have been carrying on. * * * Now, however, th
lay men all over the Diocese are arousing themselves and seem determine
that in the future, the disgrace of the Council making spiteful war on th
only strong Parish in the Diocese shall be wiped out."—*Churchma
August, 1889.*

"The whole trouble is told in one sentence. Christ Church, Little Rock
is bent on the reformation of the Diocese, the moral status of which ha
been a stench in the nostrils of decent people; and the powers tha
have governed the Diocese are bent on punishing Christ Church for th'
reformatory work.—*Churchman. August, 1889.*

"The General Convention would be justified in refusing him a sea
in that body; and in passing a resolution rebuking the brazen insolenc
of our Council."—*Churchman. October, 1889.*

"The Council has misrepresented you for years."—*Churchman
October, 1889.*

"For years, most of the best and strongest laymen have ignored th
Diocesan Council. Whether this withdrawal of many of our best me
from participation in Diocesan affairs has been the result of disgust at th
prevailing corruption."—*Churchman. October, 1889.*

"It is known as the Diocese, that never tries a minister for immorality
Unsavory reputation makes Arkansas attractive to corrupt ministers."
Churchman. May, 1889.

"Plutocracy rules the Diocese of Arkansas. A corrupt layman wit
his safes stuffed with stolen gold, has for years governed this Dioces
with as absolute sway as an Oriental Nabob rules his slaves."—*Church
man. June, 1889.*

"Here is a question in ethics. Is the privilege of borrowing a dred dollars without security from a bad man, a sufficient reas voting for that bad man for a Diocesan office?"—*Churchman. June,*

"And yet so subtle and powerful is the unscrupulous use of m that this man is still able to foist himself on the Church as a Dio officer."—*Churchman. June, 1889.*

"Can the General Convention do anything for a diocese tha sunk into moral degradation, and seems to be irreformable from w Ought a deputy who was elected by trickery be allowed a seat house?"—*Churchman. August, 1889.*

"That Parish (Christ) will certainly never again seem to sha responsibility of such infamous proceedings as have characterized th three Councils of the Diocese."—*Churchman. April, 1890.*

"At one time it was evident that certain persons would certain defeated, there being a majority of one against them. Two negro gates were brought in toward the close of the Council, the antici majority was overcome and the obnoxious persons were ele —*Churchman. February, 1890.*

"We understand that individuals, (presumably the evil doers Diocese,) have been doing some sly confidential lying abou reform work of Christ Church, Little Rock, and its rector. We this means, as the only available means, of branding those cowardly hoods. No Churchman of Arkansas will dare over his signature, to licly deny a single statement of this paper in the last October numb in any other issue. And if any one to whom the denials have made privately, will give evidence, we promise to convict the pe denying our statements, in the criminal courts of the sta *Churchman. March, 1890.*

The Committee then adjourned to meet again at room 25, C Hotel, Little Rock, at 8 o'clock p. m., of the same day, and instruct Secretary to notify the Rev. Mr. Carnahan, in writing, of the tim place of said meeting, and to invite him to be present and produc proof as he deemed necessary in support, or explanation.

The Secretary performed that duty by delivering to Mr. Carna written notice of the Committee meeting aforesaid, in which noti incorporated that portion of the Bishop's address referred to the mittee, together with the names of the individual members Committee, and the resolution providing for its creation; a cc which notice is made a part of this report and marked Exhibit "A.

When the notice aforesaid was delivered to Mr. Carnahan Secretary, he expressed his inability to attend the meeting of the mittee at the time mentioned in the notice, or upon the fol morning and declined to fix a time and place where he would m Committee; stating that it would take weeks and probably mont him to get ready to present his testimony.

The Committee assembled at 8 o'clock p. m. at the Capitol H aforesaid, and, Mr. Carnahan not appearing in person, or by represen proceeded to hear testimony as to whether the charges set forth Bishop's address had been made, and if so by whom. After liste a number of witnesses, the Committee adjourned to meet again at Trinity Cathedral, at 10:30 o'clock a. m , April 19, 1890, and instructed the Secretary to again notify Mr. Carnahan of the time and place of said meeting, which was done by delivering to him a written notice thereof, which notice is made a part of this report, marked Exhibit "B."

Upon the assembling of the Committee at Trinity Cathedral, Mr. Carnahan not appearing, other testimony was heard upon the same subject as the first. The Committee endeavored to secure the statement of every delegate present at this meeting of the Council, who had been present at either of the three preceding annual Councils of the Diocese, and, with a very few exceptions, did so. These statements were reduced to writing, and are filed herewith and made part of this report. Notably among the exceptions mentioned, is the Rev. Dr. James, who refused to appear before the Committee, as shown by his letter, made a part of this report, marked Exhibit "C."

The Committee very much desired a statement from Dr. James, as he was Chairman of the Committee on New Parishes at the Council of 1889, when the negro delegates from St. Philip's church were admitted. The three delegates of Christ Church in the Annual Council of 1889 were requested to appear before the Committee and make statements, but only one responded, viz: Mr. F. D. Clarke.

After hearing all the testimony, the Committee arrived at the following conclusions:

First. That the charges referred to in the Bisbop's Address had been made.

Second. That the charges had been published in the columns of the *"Arkansas Churchman,"* a paper edited and controlled by the Rev. Wallace Carnahan.

Third. That said charges were un-Christianlike utterances, wantonly and recklessly made, and so far as the investigation of this Committee have extended, are neither in whole, or in part sustained by the truth. All of which is respectfully submitted. (Signed.)

JAMES J. VAULX,
D. S. C. M. POTTER,
W. M. MELLETTE,
W. B. WELSH.

Upon motion of Mr. Geo. W. Caruth, the foregoing report was received and filed, and two thousand copies ordered printed for distribution

Exhibit "A."

To the Rev. Wallace Carnahan, Rector of Christ Church, Little Rock, Arkansas:

Whereas, the Diocesan Council of the Protestant Episcopal Church, duly assembled at the City of Little Rock, Arkansas, April 18th, 1890, adopted the following resolution, to-wit:

Resolved, That a committee of clergy and laymen, be appointed, to which shall be referred that portion of the Bishop's address read this

And the following persons were appointed upon said committee Rev. D. S. C. M. Potter, Rev. James J. Vaulx, Dr. W. B Welch, Dickinson and W. M. Mellette. And whereas that portion of the op's address referred to in the above resolution is as follows, to-wit:

For some time back, and specially during the past year, there been not merely insinuations, but bold and reiterated assertions, th Diocesan Councils ot 1888, and in a greater degree that of 1889, w famous in character, and guilty of crooked, partial, and corrupt that a majority of its members were under the absolute control of man; that they were influenced by bribery; that they from spite taxe Parish unjustly, and exorbitantly; that they treated said Parish discourtesy and insult; that they admitted a new Parish into conne with the Council, and allowed its representatives to take their seats selfish and partisan motives: that such Parish was organized on th or during the session of the Council for a special purpose, and to s the votes of the representatives for carrying certain measures "

And it having come to the knowledge of this Committee th charges above referred to in the Bishop's address, were made by yo by publishing the same in a certain paper under your control, calle *"Arkansas Churchman,"* you are hereby invited and notified t present at a meeting of said Committee to be holden at the C Hotel, room 25, City of Little Rock, Arkansas, April 18, 1890, 8 o' p. m., and there produce such testimony as you may deem necessa support, or explanation of the same.

D. S. C. M. POTTER,   W. M. MELLETTE.
Chairman of Committee.   *Secret*

Exhibit "B."

REV. WALLACE CARNAHAN, *Rector Christ Church,*
                Little Rock, Arkansas.

DEAR SIR: The special Committee of the Diocesan Coun Arkansas, to whom was referred that portion of the Bishop's addre lating to certain charges made against said Council, will again session at Trinity Cathedral, April 19, 1890, at 10: 30 o'clock a. which session of the Committee you are invited to be present, and to such proof as you may desire, touching upon the matters set forth i Bishop's address.   Respectfully,

W. M. MELLETTE, *Sec'y. of Com.*

The Committee requests an answer to this notice in writi agreeable to you.   W. M. MELLETTE, *Sec'y*

Exhibit "C."

No. 1213 W. 3d St., Little Rock, Ark.

MR. MELLETTE,

DEAR SIR: When I consented to meet the Committee to have been referred certain portions of the Bishop's address, it was the supposition that Christ Church would have full opportunity to a etc. This you remember was the agreement in the Council. But I

Testimony.

STATEMENT OF REV. GEO. F. DEGEN.

Have been a member of the fifteenth, sixteenth and seventeen annual Councils of the Diocese of Arkansas. ● do not know of any c rupt methods pursued in either of these Councils, or of any undue infl ence brought to bear upon any one, to obtain votes, or to turn the acti of the Council in any particular direction, except such as is referred to the following instances: 1. Upon a question which was violentl opposed (in the seventeenth Council,) by the rector of Christ Church Little Rock, one clerical member refused to vote; and afterwar stated, in my hearing, that while he was not opposed to the resolutio he did not feel at liberty to vote for it because he was under personal o ligation to the Rector of Christ Church. I also heard indignatio freely expressed by members of that Parisn in attendance upon the Coun cil, but not members of it, because the said member had not vote against the resolution, on the ground that they had furnished him wit certain supplies just prior to the meeting of the Council.

2. Shortly before Easter, of 1889, a member of my own Paris St. John's, Fort Smith, received a letter from the Rector of Christ Churc Little Rock, urging him to attend the Easter Monday Parish meeting my Church, and to influence the selection of delegates to the seventeen Council in such a way as to secure the election of men opposed to t re-election of the then Treasurer of the Diocese. Copies of this lett and the reply sent, in which the request was refused, were placed in m possession by the person addressed, and I still have them.

(*For letter referred to see Exhibit "D."*)　　GEORGE FREDERIC DEGEN.

STATEMENT OF D. S. C. M. POTTER.

I attended the Council of 1888, at Marianna, Ark., and had knowledge, or belief of any improper proceedings during the session said Council.

D. S. C. M. POTTER.
Rector of St. Agnes' Church, Morrillto

STATEMENT OF REV. J. J. VAULX.

I, James J. Vaulx, Rector of St. Paul's Church, Fayetteville, was member of the last three Diocesan Councils, and attended their sessio regularly. I saw nothing during said sessions that indicated improp influence being used by any person, or persons upon others, to contr their votes. To the best of my knowledge and belief, there were corrupt methods used; and had there been, I would have denounced the then and there. I read the letters referred to in Mr. Degen's testimon

they were as he stated. These Councils were conducted as properly
every respect as those of any other Diocese that I have ever attended.

Jas. J. Vaulx.

STATEMENT OF REV. W. J. MILLER.

I, W. J. Miller, Rector of St. Luke's Church, Hot Springs, Ark., and
member of the seventeenth annual Council of the Diocese of Arkansas,
ch met in Christ Church, Little Rock, do testify that I was in attend-
e at said Council, and, to the best of my knowledge and belief, there
no undue influence used, or attemped to be used, by any individual
individuals, to procure the election of any person or the passage of
measure. As far as I could see or hear, the course of the proceed-
was not different from those of other Councils I have attended,
er in this Diocese or in any other Diocese of which I have been a
mber.

W. J. Miller.

STATEMENT OF REV. B. W. TIMOTHY.

I am Rector of St. Philip's Parish, Little Rock. The Parish was organ-
ed in the regular way, in January prior to the meeting of Council of
pril, 1889. The Parish was not organized for any purpose except
vancement in religious matters. No one ever approached me on the
subject of voting in a certain way.

Benj. W. Timothy.

STATEMENT OF REV. I. O. ADAMS.

I was chairman of the Committee on Credentials at the Council of
1889. As such, I passed upon the credentials of St. Philip's Church, and
found them correct and regular. I made the examination of their papers
after the Committee on Admission of new Parishes had recommended the
admission of this Parish, and it had been admitted by vote of the Council.
I knew nothing, and heard nothing, of these delegates being admitted for
any improper purpose, or to carry any certain points. I did not see the
occurrence of anything to render the last three Councils infamous.

Innes O. Adams.

STATEMENT OF MR. TALBOT STILLMAN.

I was a member of the Committee on Admission of new Parishes, in
he Council of 1889. The Articles of Association of St. Philip's Church
were presented, and being found regular in every respect the report on
he admission of the Parish was favorable. I was not approached by
ny one, in any manner, with regard to the admission of this Parish into
he Council for any improper or for any certain or specific purpose or
urposes.

Talbot Stillman.

STATEMENT OF MR. J. O. W. ALEXANDER.

I reside in the city of Little Rock; I was a lay member of the Coun-
il of 1889, and represented St. Philip's Church, Little Rock. I do not
now the exact date of the organization of the vestry. I was confirmed
n Easter Day, 1889. St. Philip's was an organized Parish at the time.
participated in the proceedings of the last Council when present. I
was not influenced by any one in my voting upon any matters that came
efore the Council. I saw no proceedings inconsistent with a Christian

Council, during my attendance on the same. I never saw anything in the *Arkansas Churchman* relating to this matter.

J. O. W. ALEXANDER.

STATEMENT OF VERY REV. CHAS. H. PROCTOR.

I was a member of the Diocesan Council of the State of Arkansas, in the year 1889. I have no knowledge, information, or belief that anything was done at the meetings of that Council other than in the regular way, or that any undue influence was used by any individual member of that Council, to carry out any particular measure or policy pending before said Council. The proceedings of that Council were, I believe, governed by a true Christian spirit, and a sincere desire to uphold the dignity and purity of the Diocese.   C. H. PROCTOR, Dean of Little Rock.

STATEMENT OF MR. GEO. W. CARUTH.

I have read the statement of Dean Proctor, and concur in the same. I have been a member of the last three Councils, and, so far as I know the statements therein made would apply to all. GEO. WM. CARUTH.

STATEMENT OF MR. F D. CLARKE.

I was a member of the Diocesan Councils of 1887 and 1889, representing Christ Church, Little Rock. In the Council of 1889 I remember an interruption in the election of officers. Some were elected, and then other business was taken up, and I think possibly something like two days intervened before the remainder of the officers were elected. This struck me as peculiar, but I saw nothing that would indicate any improper influence as being used. I do not know whether this delay was according to parliamentary rules or not.   F D. CLARKE.

STATEMENT OF REV. C. A. BRUCE.

I am Rector of St. Andrew's Church, Marianna. I was in attendance at the Council of 1889, and participated in its proceedings. No undue influence was used, to my knowledge, in any of its proceedings.

C. A. BRUCE.

STATEMENT OF MR. J. C. FITZHUGH.

I was a lay member of the last Council, from St. Paul's Church, Batesville. I neither saw nor heard anything in the proceedings of the Council, during the time I was in attendance, that would lead me to infer that undue influence was used, or attempted to be used, in any of its proceedings.   J. C. FITZHUGH.

STATEMENT OF MR. ANDREW JACKSON.

I was an alternate lay delegate and attended as such, representing St. John's Church, Fort Smith, at the Diocesan Council of 1889. During the time of my attendance at said Council, I observed no evidence of undue influence used, or attempted to be used by any individual or individuals, in any of the proceedings of said Council.   A. JACKSON.

STATEMENT OF MR. J. P. MELLARD.

I reside at Hot Springs, Ark., and was a lay delegate, representing St. Luke's Church of said town, in the Council of 1889. During the time

I attended said Council, from my knowledge of the proceedings, I have no reason to believe that there were any undue influences used upon any person, or persons, in regard to any of the proceedings of said Council.

J. P. MELLARD.

STATEMENT OF MR. WM. G. WHIPPLE.

I was a delegate to the Council of 1889, from Trinity Cathedral. I have no knowledge, information, belief, or suspicion that at said session of the Council any undue influence was used by any individual or individuals, to carry through any particular measures. The Rev. Wallace Carnahan is the editor and proprietor of the *Arkansas Churchman*, or, at least, universally recognized as such It is generally understood that all editorial matter appearing in a paper is chargeable to the editor of said paper.

WM. G. WHIPPLE.

STATEMENT OF REV. D. L. TRIMBLE.

I am the minister in charge of St. Mary's Mission, Pendleton, Desha County, Ark. I was in attendance on the Councils of the Diocese of Arkansas of 1888 and 1889, and participated in their deliberations. No undue influence of any kind was used, to my knowledge, to influence any member of said Councils in the discharge of his duty as a member.

STATEMENT OF MR. GEO. E. VALLIANT.

I was a lay delegate from Trinity Church, Pine Bluff, to the Diocesan Councils of 1888 and 1889. To my knowledge, there was no undue influence of any kind used to influence or bias the mind of any member, in the discharge of his duty as a member.

GEO. E. VALLIANT.

STATEMENT OF MR. R. J. MATHEWS.

I was an alternate delegate from Trinity Cathedral, in the Councils of 1888 and 1889, and frequently exercised the functions of my principals. I know of no undue influence, financial or otherwise, brought to bear upon any delegate or alternate to said Council. The proceedings of these two Councils were in all manner conducted with proper dignity and Christian spirit.

R. J. MATHEWS.

STATEMENT OF MR. ED. M. DICKINSON.

I attended at the last Council, for the year 1889, and, during the time I was at its meetings, to the best of my knowledge and information, no undue influence was used during the proceedings of said Council.

ED M. DICKINSON.

Minority Report.

Mr E. M. Dickinson filed the following as a minority report:

As evidence has been introduced, referring to the action of certain parties in this matter, the undersigned would respectfully suggest that final action thereon be postponed until they can have time to consider, and present such evidence in this behalf as they desire. To the end that peace and harmony may prevail and that justice may be done.

E. M. DICKINSON.

JOURNAL

OF THE

PROCEEDINGS

OF THE

EIGHTEENTH ANNUAL COUNCIL

OF THE

Diocese of Arkansas,

Held in Trinity Cathedral, Little Rock, on the 17th, 18th and 19th Days of April, A. D., 1890.

LITTLE ROCK, ARK.:
PRESS PRINTING COMPANY.
1890.

THE DIOCESE OF ARKANSAS.

ORGANIZED A. D. 1871.

DIOCESAN OFFICERS.

Bishop:

THE RT. REV. H. N. PIERCE, D. D., LL. D.

Standing Committee:

THE REV. INNES O. ADAMS, PRESIDENT.
THE REV. MESSRS. W. J. MILLER AND J. J. VAULX,
MESSRS. M. L. BELL AND P. K. ROOTS.

Secretary of the Council:

THE REV. W. J. MILLER, Hot Springs.

Treasurer:

MR. LOGAN H. ROOTS, Little Rock.

Registrar:

MR. GEORGE H. VANETTEN, Little Rock.

Chancellor:

THE HON. M. L. BELL, Pine Bluff.

Trustee of the Episcopate Fund:

MR. P. K. ROOTS, Little Rock.

LIST OF THE CLERGY OF THE DIOCESE.

Bishop:

RT. REV. HENRY N. PIERCE, D. D. LL. D., Little Rock.

Priests:

REV. INNES O. ADAMS, Rector of Trinity . . . . Pine Bluff

REV. C. A. BRUCE, Rector of St. Andrew's . . . . Marianna

REV. WALLACE CARNAHAN, Rector of Christ Church, Little Rock

REV. GEORGE F. DEGEN, Rector of St. John's . . . . . Fort Smith

REV. J. E. H. GALBRAITH, Assistant at Christ Church, Little Rock

REV. L. F. GUERRY, Rector of Trinity . . . . Van Buren

REV. R. S. JAMES, D. D., Rector of St. Paul's . . . . . Dardanelle

REV. C. H. LOCKWOOD, Rector of St. John's . . . . Helena

REV. D. F. MACDONALD, D. D . . . . Diocese of Albany

REV. W. J. MILLER, Rector of St. Luke's . . . . Hot Springs

REV. D. S. C. M. POTTER, D. D., Rector of St. Agnes', Morrilton

REV. CHAS. H. PROCTOR, Dean of Trinity Cathedral, Little Rock

REV. B. W. TIMOTHY, Rector of St. Philip's . . . . . Little Rock

REV. D. L. TRIMBLE, Mission at Pendleton . . . . Pine Bluff

REV. JAMES J. VAULX, Rector of St. Paul's . . . . . . Fayetteville

REV. J. B. WHALING, Missionary in charge of Washington, Hope and Nashville . . . . P. O., Hope

LIST OF PARISHES AND MISSIONS,

WITH NAMES OF LAY DELEGATES.

ARKADELPHIA, St. Mark's.

ARKANSAS CITY, Mission.

BATESVILLE, St. Paul's—Messrs. Ed. M. Dickinson, John C. Fitzhugh, Harry L. Minnikin. *Alternates*—Dr. W. B. Lawrence, Lee D. Stone and James B. Fitzhugh.

CAMDEN, St. John's.

DARDANELLE, St. Paul's.

EUREKA SPRINGS, St. James'.

FAYETTEVILLE, St. Paul's—Messrs. J. L. Cravens,* J. M. Whitham* and Dr. W. B. Welch.

FORT SMITH, St. John's—Messrs. Wm. M. Mellette, Andrew Jackson, Jno. M. Keith.* *Alternates*—Talbot Stillman, Chas. T. Breedlove* and S. F. Lowther.*

HELENA, St. John's—Messrs. P. O. Thweatt,* Greenfield Quarles and S. S. Faulkner.

HOPE, St. Mark's.

HOT SPRINGS, St. Luke's—Messrs. J. P. Mellard, Geo. G. Latta* and R. B. Bancroft.*

LAKE VILLAGE, Emmanuel.

LITTLE ROCK, Trinity Cathedral—Messrs. Geo. W. Caruth, Logan H. Roots, Wm. G. Whipple. *Alternates*—Robert J. Matthews, Alex Robinson* and S. S. Wassell.*

LITTLE ROCK, Christ Church.

LITTLE ROCK, St. Philip's—Messrs. J. O. W. Alexander,* Samuel Spight and Dr. R. W. Granger.

MAMMOTH SPRING, St. Andrew's—Messrs. P. P. B. Hynson,* Chas. T. Arnett* and Chas. E. Elmore. *Alternates*—Chas. D. James* and Alfred P. James.

MARIANNA, St. Andrew's—Messrs. H. P. Rodgers,* J. P. Dunham and W. H. Clark, Jr.

MORRILTON, St. Agnes'—Messrs. Wm. Magoffin, G. N. Paine*
and Wm. N. Sandlin.* *Alternates*—T. P. Stout* and R.
W. Ray.*

NASHVILLE, Church of the Redeemer.

NEWPORT, St. Paul's—Mr. L. Minor.

PENDLETON, St. Mary's.

PHILLIPS COUNTY, Grace.

PINE BLUFF, Trinity—Messrs. M. L. Bell, N. B. Trulock, Geo.
E. Valliant. *Alternates*—T. P. Stoney, John Temple,
and Will Jordan.

PRESCOTT, St. James.

VAN BUREN, Trinity—Messrs. P. D. Scott,* John Fritz,* Jas.
A. Kearney.* *Alternates*—S. A. Pernot,* Chas. Ribling*
and H. A. Mayer.*

WASHINGTON, Grace.

WITCHERVILLE, Mission.

Services are held with more or less regularity at the following places:

Altheimer,	Rocky Comfort,	Winslow,
Huntington,	Richmond,	Bentonville,
• Huntsville,	Boonsboro,	Conway.

*Not present at the Council.

PROCEEDINGS

OF THE

EIGHTEENTH ANNUAL COUNCIL.

The Eighteenth Annual Council of the Diocese of Arkansas assembled in Trinity Cathedral, Little Rock, on the second Thursday after Easter, April 17, 1890.

The Holy Communion was celebrated at 11 a. m., by the Rt. Rev., the Bishop of the Diocese, assisted by the Rev. Messrs C. A. Bruce and James J. Vaulx. At this service, the Bishop read a portion of his Annual Address. (See Appendix I.)

The Council was called to order immediately after the service, when on calling the roll of the Clergy canonically resident in the Diocese, the following answered to their names:

Bishop:

Rt. Rev. H. N. Pierce, D. D., LL. D.

Priests:

Rev. I. O. Adams,	Rev. W. J. Miller,
Rev. C. A. Bruce,	Rev. D .S. C .M. Potter, D. D.,
Rev. L. F. Guerry,	Rev. Chas. H. Proctor,
Rev. R. S. James, D. D.,	Rev. B. W. Timothy,
Rev. C. H. Lockwood,	Rev. D. L. Trimble,

Rev. J. J. Vaulx.

The Rev. Messrs. Bruce and Timothy were appointed a Committee on Credentials, who reported that the following Lay Delegates had been duly elected and were entitled to seats in this Council:

St. Paul's Church, Fayetteville—Messrs. J. L. Cravens, J. M. Whitham and Dr. W. B. Welch.

Trinity Church, Pine Bluff—Messrs. M. L. Bell, N. B. Trulock, Geo. E. Valliant. Alternates, T. P. Stoney, John Temple and Will Jordan.

St. Paul's Church, Batesville—Messrs. Ed. M. Dickinson, J. C. Fitzhugh, W. L. Minnikin. Alternates, L. D. Stone, J. B. Fitzhugh and Dr. W. B. Lawrence.

St. Philip's Church, Little Rock—Messrs. J. O. W. Alexander, Samuel Spight and Dr. W. R. Granger.

St. John's Church, Helena—Messrs. P. O. Thweatt, Greenfield Quarles and S. S. Faulkner.

Trinity Cathedral, Little Rock—Messrs. Geo. W. Caruth, Logan H. Roots, Wm. G. Whipple. Alternates, R. J. Matthews, Alex. Robinson and S. S. Wassell.

Trinity Church, Van Buren—Messrs. P. D. Scott, John Fritz, Jas. A. Kearney. Alternates, S. A. Pernot, Chas. Ribling and H. A. Mayer.

St. Andrew's, Marianna—Messrs. H. P. Rodgers, J. P. Dunham and W. H. Clark, Jr.

St. Andrew's Mission, Mammoth Spring—Mr. Chas. E. Elmore.

St. Paul's Church, Newport—Mr. L. Minor.

On calling the roll of Lay Delegates the following answered to their names:

Dr. W. B. Welch.

Mr. M. L. Bell,

Mr. N. B. Trulock,

Mr. Ed. M. Dickinson,

Mr. H. L. Minnikin,

Mr. Samuel Spight,

Dr. W. R. Granger,

Mr. Greenfield Quarles,

Mr. S. S. Faulkner,

Mr. W. G. Whipple,

Mr. Logan H. Roots,

Mr. R. J. Matthews,

Mr. J. P. Dunham,

Mr. Chas. E. Elmore,

Mr. L. Minor.

A quorum being present the Rt. Rev., the Bishop, announced that the Council was ready for organization, and called for nominations for the office of Secretary.

The Rev. Dr. James moved that the Rev. Dr. Potter be empowered to cast the ballot for the Council for the re-election of the Rev. W. J. Miller as Secretary. Carried.

The ballot being cast, Mr. Miller was declared to be duly elected.

On motion a recess was taken until 3 p. m.

AFTERNOON SESSION.

THURSDAY, 3 p. m.

The Council reassembled, the Rt. Rev., the Bishop, in the chair. The first order of business being the appointment of the Standing Committees, they were appointed by the Bishop, as follows:

Ways and Means:

Rev. Charles H. Proctor,
Messrs. Greenfield Quarles and L. Minor.

On New Parishes:

Rev. L. F. Guerry,   Mr. H. L. Minnikin,
Mr. J. P. Dunham,   Mr. N. B. Trulock.

On State of the Church:

Rev. C. A. Bruce,   Mr. Geo. W. Caruth,
Rev. R. S. James, D. D.,   Dr. W. B. Welch,
Rev. Dr. Potter,   Mr. Ed. M. Dickinson,
Mr. N. B. Trulock.

Constitution and Canons:

Rev. J. J. Vaulx,   Mr. M. L. Bell,
Rev. I. O. Adams,   Mr. W. G. Whipple,
Rev. D. L. Trimble,   Mr. S. S. Faulkner,
Rev. C. H. Lockwood,   Mr. Charles E. Elmore.

Auditing and Finance:

Mr. N. B. Trulock,   Dr. W. R. Granger,
Mr. J. C. Fitzhugh,   Mr. Wm. Magoffin.

The Rev. J. B. Whaling, Mr. J. C. Fitzhugh, Lay Delegate from St. Paul's Church, Batesville, and Mr. George W. Caruth, Lay Delegate from Trinity Cathedral, appeared and took their seats.

The Rev. Mr. Vaulx read the following communication :

To the Council of the Diocese of Arkansas:

At a meeting of the Vestry of St. Paul's Church, Fayetteville, held April 10, 1890, the following resolution was adopted :

Resolved, That the Council about to convene be requested to amend Title IV, Canon I, Section 1, by inserting after, "nor more than eleven Vestrymen," the words, " who shall be communicants of the Parish in good standing."

J. M. WHITHAM,
Secretary St. Paul's Parish.

On motion, the above communication was referred to the Committee on Constitution and Canons.

The Rev. Dr. James read the application of St. Andrew's Church, Mammoth Spring, for admission as a Parish as follow :

To the Diocesan Council:

We, the undersigned, hereby declare that St. Andrew's Parish, Mammoth Spring, has been duly organized by the adoption of the Articles of Association, as prescribed by the Canons of the Diocese of Arkansas ; that the number of communicants is now twenty-two (22); that a church edifice has been erected, and we hereby respectfully ask that St. Andrew's Parish, Mammoth Spring, Ark., be admitted into union with the Council of the Diocese of Arkansas.

R. S. JAMES,
A. P. JAMES,   *Minister in charge.*
Secretary of Vestry.

The application, on motion, was referred to the Committee on New Parishes.

Mr. Logan H. Roots read his reports as Treasurer of the Diocesan Fund, the Fund for Diocesan Missions and for Aged and Infirm Clergy (see Appendix III), which, on motion, were referred to the Committee on Auditing and Finance.

The Treasurer, in the course of his reports, stated that he had received a communication from the Treasurer of Christ Church, Little Rock, enclosing a check for $50 in payment for dues of that Parish for the year 1888-89, and asked for instruction from the Council.

Mr. M. L. Bell moved that the communication, with enclosure, be referred to the Committee on Finance.

Mr. L. Minor moved as an amendment that the check for $50 be accepted.

Mr. William G. Whipple moved as an amendment to the amendment that the check be returned to Christ Church, inasmuch as the dues of that Parish for the year 1888–89 had been remitted by the action of the Seventeenth Annual Council.

A vote being called for by orders, Mr. Whipple's amendment was lost by the following vote: Clerical, ayes 6, nays 5; Lay, ayes 2, nays 6.

Mr. George W. Caruth offered the following resolution as a substitute for the original motion and its proposed amendments:

Resolved, That the Treasurer of the Diocese be directed to give to the Treasurer of Christ Church a receipt to be worded as follows: "Received from the Treasurer of Christ Church, Little Rock, fifty dollars, being amount contributed by Christ Church towards the payment of the Diocesan expenses for 1888-89."

Carried.

On motion, the Council adjourned to meet Friday morning at 9:30 o'clock.

SECOND DAY.

TRINITY CATHEDRAL, LITTLE ROCK, }
Friday, April 18, 1890. }

The Council reassembled pursuant to adjournment. Morning Prayer and Litany were said by the Rev. D. L. Trimble and the Rev. Dr. Potter, after which the Council was called to order by the Rt. Rev., the Bishop.

The roll being called, the Rev. Geo. F. Degen and Messrs. Wm. M. Mellette, Andrew Jackson and Talbot Stillman, Delegates from St. John's Church, Fort Smith, answered to their names, who were not present at the preceding day's session.

The minutes were read and approved.

The Rev. Mr. Adams read the report of the Standing Committee of the Diocese (See Appendix II).

The Rev. L. F. Guerry read the following report from the Committee on New Parishes:

To the Diocesan Council:

The Committee on New Parishes respectfully report that they have received the application of but one Parish, viz.: St. Andrew's, Mammoth Spring, Ark , and that having examined the Articles of Association and other evidence of the canonical organization of this Parish, and finding all in accordance with the Canons of the Diocese, hereby recommend the admission of St. Andrew's as a regular Parish into union with the Diocese.

Respectfully submitted,

L. F. GUERRY,
J. P. DUNHAM,
H. L. MINNIKIN,
N. B. TRULOCK,
Committee.

On motion, the report was received and its recommendation adopted, whereupon the Parish was admitted by a formal vote.

The report of Mr. P. K. Roots as Trustee of the Episcopal Fund was read (See Appendix IV), and on motion was referred to the Auditing and Finance Committee.

The Bishop then read the remainder of his Annual Address.

The Rev. C. A. Bruce read a report of the Committee on Credentials, stating that St. Andrew's Church, Mammoth Spring, having been admitted as a Parish, was entitled to representation in this Council, and that the committee had received the certificates of election of Messrs. P. P. B. Hynson, Chas. T. Arnett and Chas. E. Elmore.

The Secretary calling their names, Mr. Chas. E. Elmore appeared and took his seat.

The following communication was received from the Rector, Warden and Vestry of Christ Church, Little Rock :

To the Diocesan Council:

The Rector, Warden and Vestry of Christ Church, Little Rock, respectfully represent to the Eighteenth Annual Council of the Diocese of Arkansas, as an explanation of the absence of Delegates from this Parish in Council, that the introduction of negro Delegates into Council has, in the judgment of the members of this Parish, destroyed the value of moral influence in Council and indefinitely postpones the hope of that reform in the Diocese which is so desperately needed. This fact has already been demonstrated; for at the last, the Seventeenth Annual Council, when it was apparent that there was a majority of the Lay vote favorable to reform, negro Delegates were introduced and that majority was neutralized.

Knowing the negro character as we do, we have no reason to doubt that any number of negro Delegates could be brought into the Council for the purpose of defeating reform.

We oppose the introduction of negro Delegates into Council in no spirit of unfriendliness to the negro. On the contrary, we earnestly favor the utmost effort of the church to evangelize the negro race in a legitimate and honorable way. Indeed, one ground of our objection to the admission of negroes into our Council is the notorious fact that such action inevitably injures the cause of the negro evangelization by antagonizing the best element of the white race.

But we confess that our chief reason for opposing the retention of negro Delegates in Council is the fact of their conspicuous incapacity for the difficult task of ecclestiastical legislation and their susceptibility to manipulation.

We feel that it would be useless and degrading for us to enter the Council until a constitutional amendment is enacted that shall confine representation in Council to the white race.

[Signed]

WALLACE CARNAHAN,
JOHN D. ADAMS,
W. A. CANTRELL,
R. H. PARHAM, JR.,
G. S. BRACK,
L. R. STARK,
RALPH L. GOODRICH,
J. H. HANEY,
RUFUS J. POLK,
SAM B. ADAMS,
JOHN W. GOODWIN,
T. C. POWELL.

Mr. N. B. Trulock moved that the above communication be laid on the table. Carried.

Mr. N. B. Trulock again moved that the communication from Christ Church do not appear in the minntes of the Council. A vote being taken, the motion was lost and the communication ordered to be printed in the Journal.

Mr. Launcelot Minor moved that the Bishop's address referring to certain charges made against the members of the Seventeenth Annual Council be referred to a committee of three laymen, to report to this Council.

The Rev. Mr. Bruce offered as an amendment, that the committee consist of two clergymen and three laymen. Carried.

A vote being taken on the original motion as amended, it was adopted.

The Chairman appointed the committee as follows: Rev. D. S. C. M. Potter, D. D., the Rev. J. J. Vaulx, Messrs. Wm. M. Mellette, Ed. M. Dickinson and Dr. W. B. Welch.

The Rev. Mr. Lockwood moved that the committee be authorized to employ a stenographer to expedite its work. Carried.

On motion a recess was taken until 3:30 p. m.

AFTERNOON SESSION.

FRIDAY, 3 p. m.

The Council re-assembled, and was called to order by the Rt. Rev., the Bishop.

The Rev. Mr. Bruce, from the Committee on Credentials, reported that the certificate of Delegates from St. Luke's Church, Hot Springs, had been received, and that that Parish was entitled to representation. The Secretary calling the roll, Mr. Jas. P. Mellard appeared and took his seat.

The Committee on Unfinished Business was appointed, as follows:

Rev. Geo. F. Degen,	Mr. Talbot Stillman,
Rev. J. B. Whaling,	Mr. J. P. Mellard.

The Secretary read the following report of the Registrar of the Diocese:

To the Diocesan Council:

I have to report that five volumes of the Journal of the Diocese of Arkansas have been bound and delivered as follows: One to the Bishop, one to the Secretary, one to the Chairman of Standing Committee, one to the Chancellor and one to the Registrar.

I have made a complete inventory of Journals of the Diocese of Arkansas and of other Dioceses in my possession, a copy of which is hereto attached.

There are numerous calls for copies of the Journal of the Fifteenth Convention, 1887, as it contains the Constitution and Canons as amended, but there is only one copy remaining.

Respectfully submitted,

G. H. VAN ETTEN,

Registrar.

CATALOGUE OF JOURNALS OF THE DIOCESE OF ARKANSAS IS APPENDED FOR READY REFERENCE.

Annual Conventions.	Year.	Number of Copies.
Primary	1872	112
2d, 3d and 4th	1873-75-76	100
5th	1877	67
6th	1878	62
7th	1879	29
8th	1880	62
9th	1881	21
10th	1882	170
11th	1883	40
12th	1884	49
13th	1885	45
14th	1886	92
15th	1887	1
16th	1888	13
17th	1889	57

NOTE.—The Catalogue of Journals of other Dioceses is not given here from want of space, but can be seen in the Registrar's office.

On motion, the report was received and the thanks of this Council returned to Mr. Van Etten for his very valuable services.

The time having arrived for the election of Chancellor of the Diocese, the Rev. Mr. Vaulx nominated Mr. M. L. Bell for re-election to that office.

The Rev. Mr. Degen moved that the Secretary be instructed to cast the ballot for the Council. Carried.

The ballot being cast, Mr. Bell was declared to be duly elected.

2 D

The Chairman appointed the Committee on Judiciary as follows:

Mr. M. L. Bell.

Mr. Wm. G. Whipple,   Mr. Wm. M. Mellette,

The Rev. Mr. Vaulx offered the following resolution:

Resolved, That when this Council adjourns, it adjourn to meet in St. Paul's Church Fayetteville, on the second Thursday after Easter, April 9, 1891.

Adopted.

Mr. Wm. G. Whipple read the following report of the Committee on Constitution and Canons:

Gentlemen of the Council:

Your committee to whom was referred the proposition to amend the Canons so as to provide as a necessary qualification of a Vestryman, that he shall be a communicant, beg leave to report that the same identical proposition was at the last Annual Council introduced and referred to the Committee on Constitution and Canons, by them taken under advisement, and unanimously reported upon; which report was adopted by the Seventeenth Annual Council.

As the grounds of their conclusion embodied in the said report of that committee are entirely satisfactory to us, and appear to us conclusive of the subject, we take the liberty to adopt their report, which is as follows:

"That while such a qualification would be very desirable, and would naturally tend, other things being equal, to insure in Vestrymen greater zeal, interest in the Church, and general efficiency; would be right on principle and in harmony with the fitness of things; yet, on the other hand, under the real necessities of the situation, as Parishes in our Diocese are obliged to be constituted and organized, the same would be inexpedient and impracticable. In certain Parishes it is ascertained that there are not enough male communicants to compose a Vestry; in some instances actually existing not more than one or two, and in other cases there are now among the Vestry, non-communcants who are of the highest degree of usefulness and value in the maintenance of the Parish. Moreover, there are instances, some within recent experience, of persons whose position on the Vestry has led to their confirmation. In some cases there would be no alternative but to disband the Parish organization or constitute the Vestry of ladies. The latter course we do not recommend. It is untried in our Diocesan system, and would at least be experimental. We think the secular duties devolving on the Vestrymen, especially that paramount one of regulating the finances of the Parish, can best be performed by men."

We, therefore, respectfully recommend that the proposed change be not made.

Respectfully submitted,

I. O. ADAMS,
D. L. TRIMBLE,
M. L. BELL,
S. S. FAULKNER,
WM. G. WHIPPLE,
Committee on Constitution and Canons.

On motion, the above report was received and its recommendation adopted.

Mr. Whipple also read the following amendments to Title V of the Canons, recommended by the Committee on Constitution and Canons:

Gentlemen of the Council:

Your committee having had under consideration Title V of the Canons, on the subject of the Trial of Ministers, beg leave unanimously to recommend the following changes in the same, as follows:

At the close of Section 1 of said Title add the following words: "Fourth. Any act which involves a breach of his ordination vows." In Section 3 of said Title, after the word "good" where it occurs in said section at the end of the first sentence thereof add the following: "*Provided*, That in the case of a clergyman of an organized Parish the charge may also be made by the Wardens thereof affirming as aforesaid." In Section 4 of said Title, in lieu of the word "seven" wherever it occurs in said section, insert the word "five," and in lieu of the word "ninety" where it occurs in the first sentence of the said Section 4, insert the word "thirty." In Section 5 of the same Title, in lieu of the word "ninety" where it occurs in second sentence of said section, insert the word "thirty." In Sections 8 and 9, in lieu of the word "six" wherever it occurs in said section insert the word "three."

Respectfully submitted,

Committee on Constitution and Canons.

The consideration of the above was, on motion, postponed until the meeting of the next Annual Council.

Mr. A. P. James, Delegate from St. Andrew's Church, Mammoth Spring, appeared and took his seat.

The Rev. Mr. Degen, from the Committee on Unfinished Business, reported that a committee had been appointed at the last Council to consider the affairs of Buckner College and to report at this Council.

On motion, the Council proceeded to the election by ballot of the Standing Committee of the Diocese. The Chairman appointed the Rev. Dr. Potter and Mr. J. P. Mellon as tellers, who reported the following vote cast:

Number of votes cast 22, necessary to a choice, 12.

CLERICAL MEMBERS.

Rev. I. O. Adams, 17.   Rev. Dr. James, 1.

Rev. J. J. Vaulx, 14.   Rev. George F. Degen, 8.

Rev. W. J. Miller, 19.   Rev. C. H. Lockwood, 1.

Rev. Mr. Carnahan, 4

LAY MEMBERS.

Mr. P. K. Roots, 22.   Mr. M. L. Bell, 17.

Mr. John D. Adams, 4.

The Chairman announced the Standing Committee of the Diocese for the ensuing year to be as follows:

Rev. I O. Adams,   Mr. M. L. Bell,

Rev. J. J. Vaulx,   Mr. P. K. Roots,

Rev. W. J. Miller.

Mr. N. B. Trulock read the report or the Committee on Auditing and Finance, as follows:

To the Diocesan Council:

Your committee respectfully report that they have examined the reports of Mr. Logan H. Roots, as Treasurer of the various Diocesan Funds, and of Mr. P. K. Roots, Trustee of the Episcopate Fund, and find them correct.

We find that the latter has carried out the suggestions of the last Council, which advised the re-investment of the funds in the stock of the building association, and we recommend that the same policy be continued. We also recommend that the Fund for Disabled Clergy be similarly invested.

We also file herewith the report of the Rev. Innes O. Adams, executor of the estate of James McMurray, deceased, which shows that it is being so managed as to make the bequest likely to net about $3000 to the Episcopate Fund.

Respectfully submitted,

N. B. TRULOCK,

J. C. FITZHUGH,

W. R. GRANGER,

Committee.

On motion, the report was received and the committee discharged.

On motion, the Council adjourned to meet Saturday morning at 9:30 o'clock.

THIRD DAY.

TRINITY CATHEDRAL, LITTLE ROCK, }
Saturday, April 18, 1890. }

Morning Prayer was said by the Rev. Mr. Adams, after which the Council was called to order by the Bishop.

The minutes of the preceding day were read and approved.

The Rev. Mr. Trimble moved that hereafter all names voted for by ballot appear in the Journal.
Carried.

The Rev. Mr. Adams moved that the Constitution and Canons, as amended to date, be printed with the Journal of this Council.
Carried.

The time having arrived for the election of Registrar, the Rev. Mr. Adams moved that the Secretary be directed to cast the ballot for the Council for the re-election of Mr. Geo. H. VanEtten.
Carried.

The ballot being cast, Mr. VanEtten was declared to be duly elected.

The Rev. Mr. Vaulx offered the following resolution :

Resolved, That Title IV, Canon II, be, and is hereby amended thus, after the article numbered 7, the following be inserted : "Article 8. No person shall be eligible as a Vestryman unless he be a communicant in good standing."

Resolved, That the Articles now numbered 8, 9 and 10 be numbered 9, 10 and 11.

. [Signed] J. J. VAULX,
I. O. ADAMS.

On motion, the above was referred to the Committee on Constitution and Canons.

Mr. William Magoffin, Delegate from St. Agnes' Church, Morrilton, appeared and took his seat.

The Rev. Mr. Degen made a verbal report as Trustee of the University of the South, and urged that pledges be made for the ensuing year.

The election of Trustees of the University of the South being in order, the following members were elected: Rev. D. L. Trimble, Mr. George W. Caruth, Mr. R. V. McCracken.

On motion, the Rev. George F. Degen was elected Trustee of the General Theological Seminary.

On motion of Mr. M. L. Bell, the Secretary was directed to cast the ballot for the Council for the re-election of Mr. Logan H. Roots, as Treasurer of the Diocese.

Carried.

The ballot being cast, Mr. Roots was declared to be duly elected.

Mr. Bell also moved that the Secretary cast the ballot for the Council for the re-election of Mr. P. K. Roots, as Trustee of the Episcopate Fund.

Carried.

The ballot being cast, Mr. P. K. Roots was declared to be duly elected.

The Rev. Mr. Degen read the following report of the Committee on the Diocesan paper :

To the Diocesan Council:

The Special Committee appointed by the Council to make arrangements for the publication of a Diocesan paper, respectfully report that they met immediately after adjournment of Council and elected the Rev. W. J. Miller as editor and publisher.

The first number was issued in the following September, and the paper has since appeared regularly at monthly interval.   The paper has a circulation of 1000 copies, but we regret to say that the paid subscription list is small.   We respectfully represent that the paper has been conducted in a manner creditable to the Diocese, its policy having been to avoid controversy, to disseminate news of the church work being carried on in the Diocese, and to instruct the people in the history and doctrine of the church.   In carrying out this policy we think the editor has been singularly successful, and we beg leave to recommend the adoption of the following resolutions:

Resolved, That this Council heartily approves the conduct of the paper known as "The Diocese of Arkansas," and recognizes the said paper as its official organ; that it urges upon the Clerical and Lay Delegates the duty of taking active measures to secure its financial support.

Resolved, That the thanks of the Council be, and are hereby, extended to the

Rev. W. J. Miller for his able conduct of the paper, and his self-denying efforts for its successful establishment.

GEORGE F. DEGEN,
G. H. VAN ETTEN,
Committee.

On motion, the report was received and the resolutions appended adopted.

On motion, a recess was taken until 3:30 p. m.

AFTERNOON SESSION.

SATURDAY, 3:30 p. m.

The Council re-assembled, and was called to order by the Rt. Rev., the Bishop of the Diocese.

Mr. N. B. Trulock read the report of the Committee on the State of the Church. (See Appendix V.)

On motion, the report was received and the resolution offered by the Committee adopted and referred to the Committee on Constitution and Canons.

The Rev. C. A. Bruce offered the following resolution:

Resolved, That this Council proceed to elect a Clergymen to preach the Council Sermon at the next Council, at such time as the Bishop shall appoint.

Adopted.

Rev. Mr. Trimble nominated the Rev. Chas. H. Lockwood, as Preacher at the next Council. The vote being taken, Mr. Lockwood was elected and the Rev. L. F. Guerry as Alternate.

The Rev. Mr. Adams read the following report from the Standing Committee of the Diocese:

To the Diocesan Council:

After a careful consideration of the report of the Special Committee in regard to the affairs of Buckner College, the Standing Committee do not find that the Diocese is in any way pledged, by good faith or otherwise, to see the Buckner College indebtedness paid, but we do recommend that the Council ask for pledges from all the Parishes and Missions of the Diocese to make donations toward paying the same.

INNES O. ADAMS, *President.*

P. K. ROOTS, *Secretary.*

On motion of Mr. L. Bell, the consideration of the amendment of Title IV was postponed until the next Council.

On motion, the vote fixing the next meeting of the Council at Fayetteville, was reconsidered and the words "Trinity Cathedral, Little Rock," were substituted.

The time having arrived for the election of Delegates to the General Convention, the Council proceeded to ballot for the same. The Rev. Mr. Trimble and Mr. J. P. Mellard were appointed tellers, who reported the following members elected on the first ballot:

Clerical.	*Lay.*
Rev. I. O. Adams,	Mr. Logan H. Roots,
Rev. W. J. Miller,	Mr. John D. Adams,
Rev. J. J. Vaulx,	Mr. Geo. W. Caruth,
Rev. C. A. Bruce.	Mr. H. P. Rodgers.

The Council then proceeded to the election of Supplementary Delegates, when the following were elected in the order given:

Clerical.	*Lay.*
Rev. Geo. F. Degen,	Mr. Talbot Stillman,
Rev. D. L. Trimble,	Mr. N. B. Trulock,
Rev. Chas. H. Proctor,	Mr. G. Quarles,
Rev. C. H. Lockwood.	Mr. W. G. Whipple.

Rev. Mr. Bruce offered the following resolution:

Resolved, That the Treasurer of the Diocese pay to the sexton of Trinity Cathedral, $10 for his services during the sessions of the Council.

Adopted.

The Secretary read a communication from Mr. Geo. H. Van Etten, tendering his resignation as Registrar, which on motion, was not accepted.

The Rev. Mr. Adams offered the following resolution:

Resolved, That the thanks of this Council be hereby conveyed to the Dean and congregation of Trinity Cathedral for their kind, courteous and hospitable entertainment of the members of the Council.

Adopted.

Mr. M. L. Bell offered the following resolution:

Resolved, That the Council hereby directs the Treasurer of the Diocese, after paying the costs of printing and distributing the Journal of Proceedings and paying assessment of the General Convention, to transfer to the Trustee of the Episcopate Fund whatever, if any, Diocesan funds are remaining in his hands, excepting and reserving only $50 for incidental expenses, and such additional amount as the President of the Standing Committee may estimate will be required for paying expenses of clerical members attending meetings of such committee.

Adopted.

On motion, the Secretary was directed to have 500 copies of the Journal printed.

On motion, a recess was taken until 7:30 p. m.

NIGHT SESSION.

SATURDAY, 7:30 p. m.

The Council re-assembled, and was called to order by the Bishop.

Mr. Wm. M. Mellette, as Secretary of the committee to whom was referred that portion of the Bishop's Address referring to certain charges made against members of the Seventeenth Annual Council, read its report.

On motion, the report was received, ordered to be filed and 2000 copies to be printed, and the committee discharged.

The Secretary read the report of the Committee on Ways and Means (See Appendix VI) which, on motion, was received and the committee discharged.

On motion of Mr. Geo. W. Caruth, the sum of $25 was voted to the Secretary in recognition of his services.

On motion of the Rev. Mr. Degen. the roll of Parishes was called for pledges for the relief of Buckner College, and pledges were received as follows :

St. Paul's, Fayetteville .... $ 10 00
Trinity, Pine Bluff..... .... 20 00
St. Paul's, Batesville 10 00
Trinity Cathedral 20 00
St. John's, Fort Smith 50 00

There being no further business, the Council, on motion, and after a beautiful and touching address and prayers by the Bishop, adjourned *sine die*.

W. J. MILLER,
Secretary.

Attest: H. N. PIERCE,
Bishop of Arkansas.

APPENDIX I.

THE BISHOP'S ANNUAL ADDRESS.

Brethren of the Clergy and Laity:

Another year has passed, and we are assembled in Annual Council for the eighteenth time. On the whole, the past year has been one of advances, though to me personally, dashed with no little grief and disappointment.

Most of the Parishes have improved in numbers and in working power, but several points, where there is ability to support the services of the Church, either wholly or in large part, are still vacant. To some of these Parishes I have made liberal offers of aid, but as yet have met with no responsive action on their part. There ought to be some remedy where a Vestry presistently month after month refuse or neglect to fill a vacant pastorate. Several ways of meeting this great evil have occurred to my mind, but the fairest and most feasible would be to let the Parish, under certain circumstances, be (to use the old English term Easter Monday meeting) " in Vestry assembled," and act by their inherent authority directly, instead of through their usual representatives and agents, for such only are the Vestry of any Parish. I think such a measure would in some cases be efficient for good, but I pray God that He will stir up the hearts of His children that they may no longer allow God's heritage to lie waste through indifference or carelessness. All concerned should remember that they have a great responsibility before God in the offices they hold. I have spoken more or less fully as to the condition of many of the Parishes in the abstract of my journal and need add nothing farther here. The following changes, clerical and otherwise, have taken place during the year past: The

Rev. C. H. Lockwood has presented Letters Dimissory from the Diocese of Alabama, and he is now working with great acceptance and success as the Rector of St. John's Church, Helena.

The Rev. J. B. Whaling, having presented Letters Dimis-- sory from the Diocese of South Dakota, as a Deacon, has been advanced to the priesthood, and has lately taken charge of the Parishes at Hope, Washington and Nashville, with his resi— dence at Hope.

The Rev. J. E. Galbraith, having presented Letters Di- missory from the Diocese of Western Texas, is doing good work as the Assistant Minister of Christ Church, Little Rock.

The Rev. D. S. C. M. Potter, D. D., who had been for some time out of the Diocese as to actual residence, has, much to my satisfaction, returned, and is now Rector of St. Agnes' Church, Morrilton.

The Rev. R. S. James, D. D., who last year occupied this post, has become Rector of St. Andrew's Church, Mammoth Spring. Ark., and is working well.

I have given Letters Dimissory to the Rev. W. W. Esta- brooke. M. D., to the Diocese of Springfield, in the Province of Illinois, and to the Rev. J. E. Curzon, to the Diocese of Pitts- burg, Pa. Both of these clergymen did noble work for the Church in Arkansas.

I have ordered two Deacons, Priests ; the Rev. J. B. Whaling and the Rev. Edward C. M. Rawdon. The latter was priested at the request of the Bishop of Central Pennsylvania, in which Diocese he was continually resident. He continued only a few weeks in Arkansas and then removed to Pennsyl- vania.

Of the General Convention, which I attended in New York in October last, I have said somewhat in the abstract of my Journal which follows, and I have to add but little more here ; the Prayer-Book revision occupied most of the attention of the Convention. The principal improvements have been in the way of flexibility, and abridgment where necessity requires. The change of Rubric concerning the use of the Creed in the Communion, allows now of the use of the Toledo Creed, generally called the *or this*. after the gospel, but it has empha- sized the importance of the Nicene Creed by making it obli- gatory on certain great festivals. For the Toledo Creed has not yet been called by the Church in this country or in En- gland the Nicene Creed, nor can any one, acquainted with the subject, deem it to be so.

It has been erroneously supposed that the General Conven- tion made the use of the Toledo Creed absolutely binding, but, thank God, it failed to do this, as it seems to me a great wrong, and of forcing upon the children of the Church what she freely offers to all Christians not now in her communion the lib- erty of dispensing with.

There are other matters that I wish to call your attention to before the close of this Council, but the consideration of which I postpone for the present.

I herewith present to you

AN ABSTRACT OF MY JOURNAL.

May 2, 1889: At the opening of the Diocesan Council in Christ Church, Little Rock, I read a portion of my Annual Address and celebrated the Holy Eucharist.

May 3: I presided in the Council and delivered the re- mainder of my Annual Address.

May 5: Sunday, the second after Easter. I *celebrated* the Holy Eucharist in Trinity Cathedral. Little Rock. At night I presided at a Missionary meeting in Christ Church, Little Rock, and made the opening address. At the close I made a brief address and the Council adjourned *sine die*.

May 12: Tuesday, the third after Easter. At Pendleton, Arkansas, I *preached*, *confirmed* three persons (two males, one female), *addressed* the class and *celebrated* the Holy Eucharist. The Rev. D L. Trimble, who is doing a fine work at this missionary point, assisted me.

May 19: Sunday, the fourth after Easter. In the Cathe- dral, at Little Rock, I *preached* and *celebrated* the Holy Eucharist in the morning, and also assisted in saying Evening Prayer.

May 26: Sunday, the fifth after Easter, I *preached* at morning service and again at night in St. Peter's Church, Columbia, Tennessee.

May 30: Ascension Day, I *preached* and *celebrated* the Holy Eucharist, in St. Peter's, Columbia, assisted by the Rector, Rev. Dr. Beckett.

June 2: Sunday, after Ascension, morning I *celebrated* the Holy Eucharist in St. Peter's, Columbia. At night I *preached* and *confirmed* four persons (one male, three females), and addressed the class. This confirmation was administered by permission and at the request of the Rt. Rev., the Bishop of Tennessee. One of the candidates was *confirmed* for St. Paul's Parish, Newport, Arkansas.

June 5: I attended the commencement exercises of the Columbia Institute. I *addressed* the graduating class and delivered the diplomas.

June 9: Sunday, Whitsunday, in Trinity Cathedral, Little Rock, Ark., at 11 a. m., I *preached*, *confirmed* eleven persons (male and female), *addressed* the class and *celebrated* the Holy Eucharist, assisted by the Very Rev., the Dean. At 3 p. m., I *confirmed* in private a sick man. The candidate was presented by the Rev. Wallace Carnahan, Rector of Christ Church, Little Rock.

June 16: Trinity Sunday, I *preached* at morning service in the Cathedral, Little Rock, and *celebrated* the Holy Eucharist.

June 19: St. Mark's Church, Hope, Arkansas. At night I *baptized* an adult and a child, *preached*, *confirmed* six persons (four males, two females), and addressed the class. The candidates were presented by the faithful missionary, the Rev. J. E. Curzon.

June 23: Sunday, the first after Trinity, at 11 a. m., in the Cathedral, Little Rock, I *celebrated* the Holy Eucharist. At 8 p. m. in Trinity Church, Pine Bluff, Ark., I *preached* and con-

firmed ten person (six males, four females), and addressed the class.

June 26: I started on my visitation of the Indian Territory. I went by Fayetteville and the Rev. J. J. Vaulx accompanied me on the trip. We left Fayetteville June 27th at 4 o'clock p. m. and arrived at Guthrie, Oklahoma, Indian Territory, Saturday afternoon, June 29.

June 30: The second Sunday after Trinity, at 11 a. m., in the Hall of the Board of Arbitration, Guthrie, I said the Communion office, and the Rev. Mr. Vaulx *preached* and I *celebrated* the Holy Eucharist. At 2:30 p. m. the Rev. Mr. Vaulx said the Litany and I *preached*. After the services a meeting was called of persons desirous of organizing a Parish at Guthrie. After the matter was opened and the necessary committees appointed, the meeting adjourned till Tuesday evening at 8 o'clock. At 7:30 p. m. I *joined* in holy matrimony David M. Haines and Mrs. Irene Jester. At 8 p. m. the Rev. Mr. Vaulx said Evening Prayer and I *preached* again. The afternoon and night services were held in the Masonic Hall, kindly placed at our disposal for the occasion. The following day was spent in making calls, hunting up church people. Among those who received the Holy Communion on Sunday morning was Lieut. Elliott, of the United States Army, and a son of the much lamented Bishop of Western Texas.

July 2: The day was spent much the same as yesterday; at night the adjourned meeting of the congregation was held. The day and evening were very rainy and the attendance consequently small. We, however, adopted the Articles of Association in the forms prescribed by the Canons of the Diocese of Arkansas, and appointed committees to inquire about church lots and to consider the subject of erecting a small church capable of being enlarged till it could seat 800 or 1000 worshippers. I showed them how it was possible, by framing the building rightly in the beginning, not only to greatly increase the size but also to turn their wooden edifice, as they enlarged it, into a brick or stone one, if they so desired, with very little loss of the money already expended. It is my judgment that very few churches should be so built that they cannot be enlarged so as to seat 800 persons.

I must here express my wonder at what we found at Guthrie. The place was just seventy days, that is, ten weeks old, yet here was a population of at least 10,000 souls. Many of the streets were graded, and almost every branch of business as well represented as in older towns; stores of all kinds were established and filled with large and varied stocks of goods; electric lights and electric street railways were looked forward to as things of the near future; good order prevailed through-— out, and the law was as thoroughly enforced as you find it in any of the cities in the old States; except quite a number of gambling houses and the temporary character of many of the buildings, there was little to indicate that Guthrie might not be fifty years old, and yet it was born on the 22d day of April, last. The great body of the people are of such intelligence and character as are seldom seen in frontier towns. I do not believe that this or any other age ever saw anything to compare with the settlement of Guthrie, and what I say of Guthrie may be said of other towns of the newly opened territory of Oklahoma. Oklahoma City has five or six thousand population and is in all respects a town or city. It is amazing to see what has been accomplished in so short a time. Frisco, El Reno and Reno City and several other places, though much smaller, all show an energy that I have never elsewhere seen. That all of these towns will receive a temporary check and even dwindle away, is a foregone certainty, for they have already outgrown the surrounding country. But the fact that the land office at Guthrie has already issued the papers for considerably more than four thousand homesteads, shows that the Oklahoma District will soon be well settled, and, with the settlement of the country, will cause the revival and growth of the towns.

July 3: At 10 a. m., the Rev. Mr. Vaulx, who had been of great aid to me so far on this trip, took the train for Kansas on his way home, and in the afternoon I took the train for Oklahoma City, thirty-two miles south of Guthrie. There I found the whole town astir preparing for a grand celebration of the Fourth of July. I had a note of introduction to a gentleman whose wife was reported to be a communicant of the Church, but calling on him I found that his family had not yet arrived I could hear of no other church people.

July 4: As the town was likely to be crowded by thousands of people from Texas and Kansas to attend a three day's fete, and as nothing could be done in the prevailing excitement, I resolved to take the stage for Darlington. I went to the Oklahoma City Gazette office and left a notice for publication, asking churchmen and friends of the church to leave their names and addresses at the Gazette office in order that I might call upon them on my return some weeks later. At 10 a. m., I took the stage for Darlington. I dined on the way at Frisco, where among the frame buildings and tents, a store of considerable size was going up in the red sandstone which abounds in the neighborhood. About 4:30 p. m., we reached El Reno, where a grand celebration of the Fourth was in pro‑ gress. A thousand whites and about fifteen hundred Arrapa‑ hoes and Cheyenne Indians were on the ground all in gala costume. The bright red, yellow and blue blankets of the Indians presented a very picturesque scene. Foot-races, horse-races, ball-play, etc., were the amusements of the hour. but everything was very orderly for such a large crowd. Quite a number of soldiers, officers and their families were present from Fort Reno, only four miles distant. At El Reno I changed horses and vehicle, after about three-quarters of an hour delay. I met while I was waiting a Col. McDonald from Florida, a Mr. Chalmers from Virginia, both churchmen They promised to secure a church lot at El Reno. I reached Darlington late in the afternoon and put up at the Darlington Hotel, which was my headquarters during my stay at that place. I proceeded at once after my thirty-two miles ride to hunt up the Rev. David Okahater, our clergyman Indian, but did not find him there.

3 D

July 5: Went to Fort Reno, one mile and a half from Darlington; called on Col. Wade, the Commandant, and made arrangements for services on Sunday; called also on Mrs. Elliott, wife of Lieut. Elliott. Returning to Darlington, I called on Col. Ashley, the Indian Agent, and found Deacon David P. Okahater; made several calls.

July 6: In making calls in Darlington I found Mr. Simpson and his wife, communicants of the Church, and charming people. Mr. Simpson is the principal of the Arapahoe school.

July 7: Third Sunday after Trinity. Our Cheyenne Deacon, the Rev. David P. Okahater, drove me over to Fort Reno where I *baptized* the infant daughter of Lieut. Stephen Habersham and Catherine Walker, *nee* Otey, his wife. This baptism was one of peculiar interest to mel as I knew so well the much lamented grandfather, the late Bishop of Western Texas, and the venerated great grandfather, the former Bishop of Georgia. The occasion recalled many events in a long line of by-gone years. At 10:30, in the hall or Chapel at Fort Reno, I said the Morning Service; *preached* and *celebrated* the Holy Eucharist. I dined at Col. Wade's and had the pleasure of making the acquaintance of his charming household. At 3 p. m. I said Evening Prayer and *preached* in the Cheyenne Church at Darlington to a small congregation of Indians and whites; at 8 p. m. I said Evening Prayer and *preached* at the Arapahoe school-house. The congregation was composed principally of whites, with a few Indians.

July 8: Was spent in calling, gathering information, etc. I found that the Cheyenne Deacon had been faithful in performing such duties as he could. At my request he gave me a list of the Indians confirmed here several years ago. In this list he specified those that had died and the present residence of all that have survived. He is a faithful and good man, and has the confidence of all, both Indians and whites, but a Deacon of limited education can do but little, unless guided by a Priest, and the meagre appropriation made to this territory by the Board of Missions has rendered impossible for me to maintain even a single Priest in this territory, but I have hopes now, with the assistance of the few churchmen in Darlington and its neighborhood, to be able to place a Priest at Darlington very soon. He will give a portion of his time to Anadarko also.

July 9: At the Arapahoe school-house at 11 a. m. I *baptized* a young girl, *preached* and *celebrated* the Holy Eucharist. Among the communicants were three Cheyennes.

July 11: I started for Anadarko, forty miles south of Fort Reno, where is the Indian Agency of the Comanche, Kiowa, Wichita, Apache and Cado Indians. The vehicle was a short buck-board, without top and in a very shaky condition. My small steamer trunk was lashed on behind, but proved to be too great a weight for the freight carriage. Before we got half way to our journey's end, we had to bind the buck-board together with ropes to prevent breaking down, and being left on foot in the wide prairies. Besides the anxiety as to our means of locomotion, I had to endure the rays of a scorching sun. There was too strong a prairie breeze blowing to admit of my raising an umbrella and had it been calm, I could hardly have done so, because both hands were required to secure me from tumbling out of the lop-sided and half broken-down vehicle. Thus we went our forty miles and more under a cloudless sky and a burning sun with the thermometer at 101. When I reached Anadarko at 5 p. m. I was more of a red man than any unpainted Indian I ever saw. But at Anadarko I found a solace for the discomforts of travel in the hospitable reception given me by Col. Ford and his charming family, whose kindness I shall ever hold in grateful remembrance.

July 12: I called on Col. Myers, the Indian agent at Anadarko, a very agreeable gentlemen and a man of remarkable sound common sense to guide his large intelligence. I talked with him about the Kiowa Deacon, Paul Zotom, of whom I have very unsatisfactory accounts. I ascertained that Paul was near Fort Sill and had been there for months. He had not received the notice of my coming sent to him several weeks before. Col. Myers kindly offered to send out a scout to bring him in. I found there had been some unauthorized (I mean unauthorized by any one who had authority to act in the premises) attempt to sell the Episcopal Church at Anadarko. To prevent any such attempts in the future, I deposited with the agent a written order to deliver no property belonging to the Church here, of whatever kind, to any person, except he or they had my written permission to receive the same.

July 14: The fourth Sunday after Trinity, in the Episcopal Church, at Anadarko, at 11 a. m., I said Morning Service, *preached* and *celebrated* the Holy Eucharist; at 8 p. m. I said Evening prayer and *preached* again. From this date to one following I was engaged in making calls, gaining information, etc. The thermometer for more than a week has ranged from 100° to 106°.

July 17: Today the Rev. Paul Zotom, who has been since Monday afternoon in the neighborhood, made his first appearance, and his costume differed in no essential respect from that worn by the Indians in camp. It is true that his face was not painted, and this was about the only thing which distinguished him from the great body of the Kiowas. He has evidently left the "white man's road," and returned to the Indian path. I had a long and very unsatisfactory talk with him. I am more than afraid—I feel quite assured that his life is far from a correct one. I have strong evidence, not only of his having fallen into bad habits but of his having habitually made, during the past year and more, reports of services never performed by him. Indeed I have strong reasons for believing that he has done no missionary or ecclesiastical work for many months. The testimony received came from both Indians and whites. His reputation is very bad. Under these circumstances I have dropped his name from the list of Missionaries and expect ere long to have the evidence in regard to him in such shape as will lead to his deposition from the ministry. Perhaps Paul's position would be now quite different had he been under the direction and oversight of a Priest; that he has not been is no fault of mine. Let it rest where it should, and let those in fault answer for it before God.

I intended to leave Anadarko for Fort Reno on Thursday of this week, but could get no safe conveyance. Col. Myers offered to send me in his hack on Saturday, and it was my best opportunity.

I had intended to visit Fort Sill before returning northward, but I learned from the army officers from there that the post was just then nearly deserted, the soldiers being nearly all of them in the field.

July 20: Went to Fort Reno, where I was very kindly received by Lieut. J. A. Penn, who, with his comrade, Lieut. J. M. Jenkins, made my stay at Reno very pleasant. I had desired to get back to Darlington so as to spend a day or two there, and go on to Kingfisher, Oklahoma, for Sunday. Finding that I could not do that, I concluded to hold services at Reno or Darlington Sunday morning, and then take the stage twenty-eight miles to Kingfisher for a night service. Here again I was baffled, for the stage line was no longer running. So I reluctantly gave up design of visiting at present that new and vigorous town, born like several others April 22, 1889.

July 21: Tuesday at Fort Reno, at 10 a. m., I said the Morning Service and *preached*. In afternoon Col. Wade, the commandant, called and told me he was going to Oklahoma City in his ambulance and offered to take me with him. So late in the day we started, and I was landed at the hotel in Oklahoma City near midnight.

July 22: Made an unsuccessful hunt for churchmen, but met with no success. No names had been left at the Gazette office. At night, however, I had the pleasure of falling in with an old friend, Mr. Thomas Watson, of Newport, Ark., who is establishing an ice factory at Oklahoma City.

July 23: At 8:43 a. m., I took the train for Guthrie. On this day I received the Letters Dimissory of the Rev.' C. H Lockwood, Rector of St. John's, Helena, Ark., from the Dio-

cese of Alabama, and sent notice of my acceptance of the same.
During the rest of the week I was at Guthrie visiting, consulting, advising and planning.   I renewed the offer I had made to
the churchmen at Guthrie, that I would send them a clergyman
and see that he was supported in full for six months, on condition that they would obtain a lot and build a church.   I can
now (September 2) report that the Rev. H. B. Jefferson is
already at work at Guthrie, and letters received this morning
encourage me to think that the other part of our contract will
soon be well underway toward its fulfillment.

July 28:   Sunday, the sixth after Trinity, at 11 a. m., I said
Morning Service and *preached* at 4 p. m.   I presided at a meeting of the congregation which, after some deliberation, was
adjourned till after the Evening Service.   At 8 p. m. I said
Evening Prayer and *preached*, after which I presided at the
meeting of the congregation, and the organization of the Parish
was perfected.   I had intended to go from Guthrie to Fort
Gibson, but a letter from Post Chaplain Siebold, in reply to
one of mine, led me to infer that a visit there at this season
would be lost time, or nearly so.   I therefore postponed my
visit to Gibson, Tahlequah, Muscogee and Prairie City till
cooler weather, and resolved to return directly to Arkansas,
and on the morrow I started for Fayetteville *via* Wichita, Kan.,
and Marietta, Mo.

August 4:   Sunday, the seventh after Trinity.   In St.
Paul's Church, Fayetteville, Ark., I *preached* and *celebrated* the
Holy Eucharist, assisted by the Rector, the Rev. J. J. Vaulx.
At 8 p. m. I *preached* and *confirmed* six persons (two males and
four females).   This Parish is in fine condition and full of good
works.

August 6.   The Feast of the Transfiguration.   At 7 a. m.
I *celebrated* the Holy Eucharist in St. John's Church, Fort
Smith, Ark.

August 11:   Sunday, the eighth after Trinity.   At 11 a. m.,
in Trinity Cathedral, Little Rock, I *preached* and *celebrated* the
Holy Eucharist, assisted by the Rev. Mr. Rowdon.   At 5:3
p. m., I attended Evening Prayer.

August 13: At 8 p. m., in St. John's Church, Helena, Ark., I *preached* and *confirmed* seven persons (five males and two females) and addressed the class. This Parish, under the new Rector, the Rev. C. H. Lockwood, is full of life. A large lot has been purchased and paid for. A fine Rectory is now going up, the cost of which is to be $3000. The lot is large enough for the new church, which will be needed in the comparatively near future.

August 15: I *confirmed*, in Christ Church, Little Rock, one person (one female).

August 18: Sunday, the ninth after Trinity. At 11 a.m., in Trinity Cathedral, Little Rock, I *confirmed* one person (one male). At 5:30 I attended Evening Prayer.

August 23: At 8 p. m., in St. Agnes' Church, Morrilton, Ark., I *preached*, *confirmed* three persons (one male and two females), and addressed the class. The Rev. Dr. James presented the class.

August 24: St. Bartholomew's Day. In St. Agnes' Church, Morrilton, I *baptized* an infant.

August 25: Sunday, the tenth after Trinity, at 11 a. m., in Trinity Cathedral, Little Rock, I *preached* and *celebrated* the Holy Eucharist, assisted by the Rev. Mr. Rowdon. At 5:30 I said Evening Prayer, Rev. Mr. Rowdon reading the lessons.

August 27: At 8 p. m., in St. Paul's Church, Newport, I *joined* in holy matrimony, Mr. Gustave Jones and Miss Julia Stevens.

August 28: At 8 p. m., in St. Paul's Church, Batesville, Ark., I *preached* and *confirmed* two persons (two males) and addressed the class.

August 29: At 9 a. m., in St. Paul's Church, I *confirmed* one person (one male). At 8 p. m., in St. Paul's Church, Newport, I *baptized* two adults and one infant, *preached* and *confirmed* six persons (one male and five females) and addressed the class. The candidates, both at Batesville and Newport, were presented by the Rev. R. T. Jefferson, who is officiating temporarily at Batesville.

September 1 : Sunday, the eleventh after Trinity, at 11 a. m., in the Cathedral, Little Rock, I *preached* and *celebrated* the Holy Eucharist, assisted by the Rev. Mr. Rowdon. At 5:30 p. m. I attended Evening Prayer. At 8 p. m., at Little Rock, I *joined* in holy matrimony, Mr. Wm. Adams and Miss Elminia Payton.

September 8: Tuesday, the twelfth after Trinity. At 11 a. m., in Trinity Cathedral, Little Rock, the Rev. J. B. Whaling preached, I said the Communion office and *celebrated* the Holy Eucharist, assisted by the Rev. J. E. Curzon, who said the rest of the Morning Service. At 5:30 p. m., I *attended* Evening Prayer.

September 11 : Wednesday, I this day accepted the Letters Dimissory presented by the Rev. Joshua B. Whaling, B. D., Deacon, from the missionary jurisdiction of South Dakota, and sent the canonical notice of acceptance.

September 15 : Sunday, the thirteenth after Trinity, at 11 a. m., in the Cathedral, Little Rock, I said the Communion office and *preached*: the rest of the Morning Service was said by the Rev. C. H. Proctor, Dean.

September 18: Wednesday, examined the Rev. J. B. Whaling and the Rev. Edward C. M. Rowdon, Deacons for Priest's orders, assisted by the Rev. I. O. Adams and the Rev. J. E. Curzon.

September 19: Continued and completed the examination of Rev. Messrs. Whaling and Rowdon.

September 21 : Saturday, St. Matthew's Day, in Trinity Cathedral, Little Rock, Arkansas, at 11 a. m. Morning Prayer having been said at 9 a. m., I ordered Priests, the Rev. Joshua Brown Whaling, B. D., and the Rev. Edward Charles Mortimer Rowdon, B. D., Deacons. The Rev. John E. Curzon, B. D., preached the sermon and presented the candidates. The Very Rev. C. H. Proctor, Dean, read the epistle, and both presbyters united in the imposition of hands. I *celebrated* and administered alone as the Rubric requires. Mr. Rowdon belongs to the Diocese of Central Pennsylvania and was presented to me at the authority of the Rt. Rev. M. A. DeWolf Howe, D. D., etc.; p. m., at the Cathedral, I *confirmed* one person (male).

September 22: Sunday, the fourteenth after Trinity. In the Cathedral, Little Rock, 11 a. m. Dean Proctor said the Litany, I said the Communion office (Rev. Mr. Whaling reading the Epistle) and *preached* and *celebrated* the Holy Eucharist, assisted by the Rev. Mr. Rowdon ; p. m., I attended Evening Service.

September 29: Sunday, the fifteenth after Trinity, at 11 a. m., in St. Peter's Church, Columbia, Tenn., I assisted in saying the Morning Service and *preached*. At 7:30 I *preached* again.

October 2: Wednesday, in St. George's Church, Stuyvesant Square, New York City, I attended officially, in robes, the opening services of the Triennial General Convention, and received the Holy Communion; afterwards attended the sessions of the House of Bishops, and the General Convention sitting as the Board of Missions, during the week. On Friday I made an address in the Board, telling of the little work done in the Indian Territory and reminding the Church of the inadequacy of the appropriations to that field: No great results can be looked for where almost no means are supplied to work with. $1500 to the largest Indian field, and $20,000 to one much smaller, certainly presents quite a contrast no wonder there should be a contrast in results also.

October 6: Sunday, the sixteenth after Trinity. The morning was spent at the summer residence on Staten Island, of my honored friend, the Rev. Dr. Beckett of Columbia, Tenn. Very heavy rains prevented our attending service at the Church, some miles distant. Late in the afternoon, I returned to New York, and at night I *preached* in the Church of St. Edward the Martyr, 109th street, New York City.

During the week I was constant in my attendance on the General Convention, in the House of Bishops and in the Board of Missions. On the 8th of October the sad news of the death of Bishop Vail of Kansas reached us. The death of one so universally beloved, and so highly esteemed, produced

a very profound impression.   This, as far as I can recollect, is
the first death among our Bishops occurring during the session
of a General Convention.   Bishop Vail was on his way to
New York, when taken ill in Pennsylvania.   The Church has
sustained a great loss.   At 3 p. m., on Wednesday, October
9, the time when the funeral services were taking place in
Philadelphia, a very impressive Memorial Service was attended
by both Houses of the General Convention in St. George's
Church.

October 13:   Sunday, the seventeenth after Trinity.   At
10:15 a. m., in St. Paul's Church, 170th street, New York City,
I received the Holy Communion.   At 10:45, after Morning
Prayer and Litany, said by the Rector, the Rev. Dr. Harris, I
preached.

At 7:30 p. m., in the Church of the Good Shepherd, Brook-
lyn, Long Island, after Evening Prayer, said by the Rector,
Rev. Dr. Cornwall, and by my old friend, Rev. Dr. Townsend,
of Washington City, D. C., I *preached*.   During the week, in
attendance on the General Convention, etc.

October 20:   Eighteenth Sunday after Trinity.   At 10:30
a. m. in St. Paul's Church Duncan avenue, Jersey City Heights
I assisted the Rector, the Rev. Mr. Brush, in saying the Morning Service and *preached*.   At 7:30 p. m., I *preached* again,
During my stay in Jersey City, I was the guest of my friends
of many years and former parishioners, Col. Jacob Anderson
and family.   During the days following, attended the General
Convention.

October 24:   Thursday, at 8 p. m., in St. George's Church,
I attended in robes the closing services of the General Convention of 1889, a Convention memorable for the admirable
Christian spirit exhibited in both houses and for the absence
of everything like partisan feeling.   Doubtless much more
good could have been accomplished than there actually was.
We might have taken several grand steps towards absolute
catholicity, and I think we erred in not doing so.   But there
was so little harm done I am devoutly thankful.

I have been asked, how far is a Clergyman of the Church bound to adopt in practice, the changes now made in portions of the Prayer Book? I give my answer to this question thus: Every clergyman has a RIGHT to use all additions and amendments as have been made, but no one is BOUND to use them; for the STANDARD PRAYER BOOK heretofore set forth is not repealed, and is sufficient authority to follow until another Standard Prayer Book is set forth. Such is my judgment and I believe this position is tenable from sound reasons. If I am wrong, I am willing here, as in all things, to be corrected.

October 25: Friday. Attended a Council of the Bishops in the See House, New York, and at 5 p. m. took the boat for Norwich, Conn.

October 27: Nineteenth Sunday after Trinity. I attended Morning Service in Christ Church, Norwich, Conn.

October 29: Tuesday. Went to Providence, R. I.

October 31: Thursday. I arrived at 7 a. m. in New York, and, after making several calls, at 6:30 p. m. I took the train homeward, via, St. Louis, Mo., reaching home Saturday at midnight, November 2.

November 3: Sunday, the twentieth after Trinity. At 11 a. m., in the Cathedral, Little Rock, I *preached* and *celebrated* the Holy Eucharist.

November 10: Sunday, the twenty-first after Trinity. At 11 a. m., in the Cathedral, Little Rock, after Morning Service said by Dean Proctor and the Rev. Mr. Rowdon, I read the "Pastoral Letter of the House of Bishops." At 4:40 attended Evening Prayer.

November 17: Sunday, the twenty-second after Trinity. I attended Morning Service in Trinity Cathedral. Owing to the new plastering, the church was very damp, and the Service was necessarily made very brief.

November 19: I attended a meeting of ladies for the purpose of organizing a DIOCESAN branch of the Woman's Auxiliary, and made an address. I hope to see parochial branches of the same established in every Parish in Arkansas. The

Clergy of Arkansas owe much to the Woman's Auxiliary. Justice, to say nothing of gratitude, demands that we make this diocesan branch strong and active. Proper instructions as the formation of parochial branches can be obtained of the President, Mrs. Logan H. Roots, Little Rock.

November 24: Sunday, the next before Advent. In the Cathedral, Little Rock, I *preached* at Morning Service and attended Evening Prayer at 4:30 and closed the service.

November 28: Thursday, Thanksgiving Day. In the Cathedral, Little Rock, I said full Morning Service and *preached.*

December 1: Sunday, the first in Advent. In the Cathedral, Little Rock, at 11 a. m. After Litany said by Dean Proctor, I *preached* and *celebrated* the Holy Eucharist, assisted by the Rev. J. E. Curzon. At 3:30 I attended Evening Prayer and closed the service.

December 8: Sunday, the second in Advent. At 11 a m., in the Cathedral, Little Rock, I assisted in saying the Morning Service, and at 4:30 p. m. attended Evening Prayer

December 15: Sunday, the third in Advent. In the Cathedral, Little Rock, at 11 a. m., I *preached* and *celebrated* the Holy Eucharist. At 3 p. m., in St. Philip's Church, Little Rock, I *preached* and *confirmed* one person (one male), and *addressed* the candidate.

December 18: This day I *accepted* the Letters Dimissory presented by the Rev. J. E. H. Galbraith, from the Missionary Jurisdiction of Western Texas and sent notice of my acceptance to the Ecclesiastical Authority of the same.

December 22: The fourth Sunday in Advent. At 11 a m., in St. Luke's Church, Hot Springs, Ark., the Rev. Wm. J Miller, Rector, said Morning Prayer, read the Epistle and assisted me in the Holy Communion. I said the Communion Office, *preached, confirmed* seven persons (two males and five females), and *addressed* the class, after which I *celebrated* the Holy Eucharist. At 3 p. m., the Rev. Mr. Miller said Evening Prayer and baptized several children, and I *preached.*

. These were the first services held in the new St. Luke's Church. I had the pleasure of holding the first services in the former wooden church, which has been succeeded by this substantial and large brick one. It was a great satisfaction to be present at the opening of this new chnrch, which shows the grand advances made under the present efficient Rector. There is still a debt on the church, but I am confident that this will soon be disposed of by the energy which has erected this beautiful temple of God. As a description of this edifice has already appeared in THE DIOCESE OF ARKANSAS, it is needless for me to say more on that point; but I most heartily congratulate pastor and people on the success that has crowned their efforts. During my stay at Hot Springs I enjoyed the charming hospitality of Col. and Mrs. Rugg, of the Plateau Hotel.

December 25: Wednesday, Christmas day. At 11 o'clock a. m., I *preached* and *celebrated* the Holy Eucharist, assisted by the Very Rev. Dean Proctor. At 3 p. m., in St. Philip's Church, Little Rock, I *preached* and *confirmed* one person (one male).

December 29: The first Sunday after Christmas. At 11 a. m., in Trinity Cathedral, I *preached* and *celebrated* the Holy Eucharist, assisted by Dean Proctor. At midnight I took the train for Texarkana and Rocky Comfort.

December 31: Tuesday, in Rocky Comfort, Ark.: After Evening Prayer, said by the Rev. R. W. Anderson, Rector of St. James', Texarkana, Tex., I *preached*.

1890, January 1, Wednesday, The Circumcision. The incessant rain prevented our holding the services announced for this day.

January 2: Thursday, p. m. I *confirmed* one person in private, she being hindered from attending at Church by reason of delicate health and the bad weather. At 7 p. m. I *preached* and *confirmed* eight persons (five males and three females), and addressed the class.

January 3: Friday, at 10 a. m., I *confirmed* in private a person who, on account of her infirmity, and bad weather, was unable to be at the church last night. This makes the num·

ber confirmed at Rocky Comfort ten (five males and five females). The churchmen at this point have secured a lot and
raised several hundred dollars toward building a small church.
They have shown that they deserve to be aided by the church
at large. At 7 p. m., at Richmond, Ark. After service, said
by the Rev. R. W. Anderson, I *preachad* and *confirmed* one
person (one female).

January 4: Saturday, at Richmond, at night. The Rev.
Mr. Anderson said Evening Prayer and I *preached*.

January 5, Sunday, the second after Christmas, at Richmond, at 11 a. m. Rev. Mr. Anderson said Morning Service,
and I *preached* and *confirmed* three persons (one male and two
females), and addressed the class. This raises the number
confirmed at Richmond to four. At 7 p. m., Rev. Mr. Anderson said Evening Prayer and I *preached* again. I cannot speak
too highly of the noble work done in Southwestern Arkansas by the generous and able Rector of St. James', Texarkana.

January 6: Monday, the Epiphany. Mr. Anderson and
myself, having been detained by high water, were constrained
to spend this great feast on our way by hack to Texarkana.

January 7: Tuesday, at 7:30 p. m., I *preached* in Grace
Church, Washington, Ark., and *confirmed* four persons (four
females), the candidates being presented by the Rev. J. E.
Curzon. This church has been much improved since I saw it
last. God bless the noble band of women there.

January 8, Wednesday, at Hope, Ark., at 5 p. m., I met
the Vestry of St. Mark's Church, and we planned for the better supply of services at Hope, by settling here a clergyman,
to have charge of Hope, Washington and Nashville.

January 12: Sunday, the first after Epiphany, at 11 a. m ,
in Trinity Church, Pine Bluff, Ark. The Rev. I. O. Adams
said the Litany, read the Epistle, and assisted at the Holy
Communion. I said the Communion office, *preached* and *celebrated* the Holy Eucharist. At 7:30 p. m., I *preached* and *confirmed* ten persons (seven males and three females), and *ad-*

dressed the class. This makes the number *confirmed* in this Parish since the last Diocesan Council, twenty.

January 16: Thursday, at 8 p. m., in Christ Church, Little Rock, I joined in holy matrimony Edward Coy Longharne and Miss Matilda Sevier Churchill, daughter of Gen. Churchill, ex-Governor of Arkansas.

January 19: Sunday, the second after Epiphany, at 11 a. m., in Texarkana, Texas. The Rev. R. W. Anderson, Rector, said the Morning Prayer and read the Epistle. I said the Litany and the Ante-Communion and *preached*. At 7:30 p. m. I *preached* and *confirmed* one person (one male), and made an address. This candidate was *confirmed* at the request of the Bishop of Northern Texas, conveyed to me through the Rev. Mr. Anderson.

January 23: Thursday, in Batesville, Ark. I *baptized* an adult, a gentleman and child. At 7 p. m., in St. Paul's Church I *preached* and *confirmed* two persons (two males) and *addressed* the class. This makes the number *confirmed* since the last Council, four. After service I attended a meeting of the Vestry, and consulted with them as to filling the long existing vacancy in the Rectorship of this important Parish.

January 24: Friday, at 2 p. m. I officiated at a funeral in St. Paul's Church, Batesville.

January 25: Saturday, at 7 p. m., in St. Andrew's Church, Mammoth Springs, Ark. After Evening Prayer, said by the Rector, the Rev. Dr. James, I *preached*.

January 26: Sunday, the third after Epiphany, at 11 a. m., in St. Andrew's Church, Mammoth Springs, assisted by the Rev. Dr. James, I said the Communion office, *preached*, *confirmed* three persons (two males and one female), and *addressed* the class, after which I *celebrated* the Holy Eucharist. At 7:30 I *preached* again. This was my first visit to this young Parish, and I cannot but admire the beautiful church and the commodious Rectory, and greater becomes my admiration when I consider that, by God's blessing, so much has been accomplished by a mere handful of Churchmen. Would all our

Parishes work as they have done, we should soon have a strong Diocese.

   January 28: At 7 p. m., in St. James' Church, Eureka Springs, Ark. After Evening Prayer, said by the Rev. J. J. Vaulx, I *preached*. This Parish still continues vacant, though I am glad to say that the Vestry have made efforts to secure a Pastor, and are still trying to fill the vacancy.

   February 2: Septuagesima Sunday and the Feast of the Purification. At 11 a. m., in St. Paul's Church, Fayetteville, the Rev. J. J. Vaulx, Rector, said the Litany, read the Epistle and assisted in the Holy Communion. I said the Communion office, *preached* and *celebrated* the Holy Eucharist. At 7:30 p. m., I *preached* and *confirmed* four persons (one male and three females) and addressed the class.

   February 3: Monday, I *preached* at night in the same church.

   February 4: Tuesday, I *preached* at night in the same church.

   February 5: Wednesday, I *preached* at night in the same church.

   February 7: I *confirmed*, in private, one person (one male). This makes the number confirmed at St. Paul's, Fayetteville, since the last Diocesan Council, eleven. The Parish is now admirably organized and working nobly. I have asked the Rector to write a statement of his system for THE DIOCESE OF ARKANSAS.

   February 9: Sexagesima Sunday, at 10:30 a. m., in Trinity Church, Van Buren, the Rev. Mr. Guerry, Rector, read the Epistle and assisted in the Holy Communion. I said the Communion office, *preached* and *confirmed* three persons (one male and three females), and addressed the class, after which I *celebrated* the Holy Eucharist. At 7 p. m., I *preached* again. This Parish is growing steadily. The Rectory, added lately, is a great step onward.

   February 13: I was present at the marriage in St. John's Church, Fort Smith, of the Rev. J. L. Berne, my old friend and former presbyter, and Miss Clara Maidlow. May God bless them. After the marriage, which was celebrated by the Rector, the Rev. Geo. F. Degen, assisted by the Rev. J. J. Vaulx, I attended the elegant reception given the bridal couple, by the ladies of the Parish, at the residence of General Stephen Wheeler. It was a happy assembly.

February 16: Sunday, Quinquagesima, at 11 a. m., in St. John's Church, Fort Smith. The Rev. G. F. Degen, Rector, read the Epistle and assisted at the Holy Communion. I said the Communion office, *preached*, *confirmed* four persons (three males and one female), and *celebrated* the Holy Eucharist. At 7:30 p. m., I *preached* again. The small number confirmed is due to much sickness in the Parish, as well as to the recent illness of the Rector. A much larger class is expected later in the season. Under the ministry of its indefatigable pastor, St. John's, Fort Smith, has grown to be a strong Parish. In communicants, I think, it stands second in the Diocese, Christ Church, Little Rock, being the first.

February 19: Ash Wednesday, at 10:30 a. m., in Trinity Cathedral, Little Rock, Dean Proctor said Morning Prayer and the Litany, and read the Epistle and assisted in the Holy Communion. I said the Communion office, *preached* and *celebrated* the Holy Eucharist.

February 20: At 10:30 I said Morning Prayer in Trinity Cathedral.

February 21: In Trinity Cathedral, at 10:30 a. m., I said Morning Prayer and the Litany and at 5 p. m., Evening Prayer.

February 22: This day I gave Letters Dimissory to the Rev. W. W. Estabrooke, M. D., transferring him to the Diocese of Springfield in the Province of Illinois.

February 23: First Sunday in Lent. In Trinity Cathedral, Little Rock, at 11 a. m., I said the Litany and the Communion office, *preached* and *celebrated* the Holy Eucharist. In the evening I said Evening Prayer and *baptized* a child.

February 24: St. Matthias' Day. In Trinity Cathedral, at

4 D

11 a. m., I *celebrated* the Holy Eucharist and *lectured* on the day. At 5 p. m., I said Evening Prayer.

February 25 :   At 5 p. m., I said Evening Prayer in the Cathedral.

February 26 :   In Trinity Cathedral, Little Rock, at 11 a. m., I said Morning Prayer and Litany. A heavy rain prevented the assembling of a congregation at 5 p. m.

February 27 :   At 5 p. m., I said Evening Prayer in Trinity Cathedral.   ·

February 28 :   In Trinity Cathedral at 11 a.m., I said Morning Prayer and Litany and gave a short lecture.

March 1 :   In St. John's Church, Helena, Ark., at 5 p. m., after Evening Prayer said by the Rector, Rev. C. H. Lockwood, I *preached*.

March 2 :   Second Sunday in Lent. In St. John's Church, Helena, at 10 a. m.. I addressed the Sunday School.   At 11 a. m., I said the Communion office, the Rector reading the Epistle.   I *preached* and *confirmed* twenty-four persons (nine males and fifteen females), and addressed the class, after which, assisted by the Rector, I *celebrated* the Holy Eucharist, and, I believe, all the newly confirmed received the Holy Communion.   At 7:30 p. m., I *preached* again.

March 3 :   At 7:30 p. m., I *preached* in St. John's Helena.

March 4 :   I attended a meeting of the Vestry and gave them my counsel on several matters, and especially in regard to building a new church, which is contemplated in the near future.   The Parish is in fine condition, full of life and harmonious action.   The Rev. Mr. Lockwood is doing a grand work. It was a pleasure to be his guest in the new and beautiful Rectory.   A heavy rain prevented the assembling of a congregation at 7:30 p. m.

March 5 :   At 7:30, I *preached* in St. John's Church, Helena, Ark., and *confirmed* one person (male).   This makes the whole number confirmed in this Parish since the last Diocesan Council, thirty-two.

March 6: At 8 p. m., in St. Andrew's Church, Marianna, after Evening Prayer said by Rev. C. A. Bruce, I *preached*.

March 7: In St. Andrew's, Marianna, at 8 p. m., I *preached*.

March 8: At 8 p. m., I *preached* again.

March 9: Third Sunday in Lent. In St. Andrew's Church, Marianna, I said the Communion office, Rev. Mr. Bruce reading the Epistle. I *preached, confirmed* one person (female) and, assisted by the Rector, *celebrated* the Holy Eucharist At 8 p. m., I *preached* again. St. Andrew's has been very much improved internally since my last visit to it. The church here progresses slowly against strong opposition, but it still lives and grows.

March 11: In Trinity Cathedral, Little Rock, at 5 p. m., I said Evening Prayer and *lectured*.

March 12: In Trinity Cathedral, I said Morning Prayer and Litany and *lectured*. At 5 p. m., I said Evening Prayer and *lectured*.

March 13: In the Cathedral, at 5 p. m., I said Evening Prayer.

March 14: At 11 a. m., in the Cathedral, I attended Morning Prayer and Litany, Dean Proctor officiating.

March 16: Fourth Sunday in Lent. In St. John's Church, Camden, Ark., I said Morning Prayer and the Communion office, *preached*, and *celebrated* the Holy Eucharist. At 4 p. m., I said Evening Prayer, *baptized* a child and *preached*. After the service I met several members of the Vestry (no quorum) and discussed measures for supplying the Parish with services. I officiated for the first time in the beautiful new church. With some slight changes in the chancel the church will be very complete. Camden has suffered greatly, year after year, from removals and deaths. The number of communicants that have left St. John's would form a strong Parish, could they all be gathered in one place.

March 18: At 5 p. m., in the Cathedral, Little Rock, I said Evening Prayer and *lectured*.

March 19:   In Trinity Cathedral, at 11 a. m., I said Morning Prayer and Litany, and at 5 p. m., I said Evening Prayer.

March 20:   At 5 p. m., I said Evening Prayer in Trinity
Cathedral and *lectured*.

March 21:   In Trinity Cathedral, I attended Morning
Prayer and Litany service, Dean Proctor officiating.

March 22:   In St. Luke's Church, Hot Springs, Ark., at
4:30 p. m., after Evening Prayer said by the Rector, the Rev.
Wm. J. Miller, I *lectured* on Confirmation.

March 23:   Fifth Sunday in Lent.   In St. Luke's Church,
Hot Springs, Ark., the Rector said the Litany, read the Epistle
and officiated at the Holy Communion.   I said the Communion office, *preached* and *celebrated* the Holy Eucharist.
At 7:30 the Rector said Evening Prayer, I *preached, confirmed*
three persons (one male and two females), and *addressed* the
class.   This makes the number confirmed since the last Council, ten.   St. Luke's has been much beautified within since my
last visit, and the full set of chancel furniture which the Rector hopes to receive by Easter will still further improve its
appearance and make it a most attractive church.   In due
time handsome memorial windows will give additional beauty.
The Parish is in a very fine condition.

March 25:   In Trinity Cathedral, Little Rock, at 5 p. m., I
said Evening Prayer and *lectured*.

March 36:   At 11 a. m., in Trinity Cathedral, I said Morning Prayer and Litany.   At 5 p. m., I said Evening Prayer.

March 28:   I attended Morning Prayer and Litany in
Trinity Cathedral.

March 29:   At 7:30 p. m., in St. Agnes' Church, Morrilton, Ark., I *preached*; the Rector, the Rev. Dr. Potter, presented and I *confirmed* two persons (two males), and I *addressed* the class.

March 30:   Sunday, the sixth in Lent.   In St. Agnes'
Church, Morrilton, at 10:30 a. m., I *preached* and *celebrated*
the Holy Eucharist, assisted by Rev. Dr. Potter.   Dr. Potter
has been but a few months in this Parish, but he is doing good

work and is highly appreciated. At 12 noon, I took the train to Fort Smith, and at 7:30 p. m., the Rev. Mr. Degen said Evening Prayer, I *preached, confirmed* six persons (three males and three females), and *addressed* the class.

April 1 : Tuesday in Holy Week. At 7 a. m., I received the Holy Communion; at 7:30 p. m., in Trinity Church, Van Buren, Ark., I *preached* and *confirmed* one person (one male), after Evening Prayer said by the Rev. Mr. Guerry.

April 3 : Thursday in Holy Week. At 11 a. m., in Trinity Cathedral, Little Rock, I said Morning Prayer and *lectured*; at 5 p. m., I said Evening Prayer and *lectured*.

April 4 : Good Friday. At 11 a. m., in the Cathedral, Dean Proctor said Morning Prayer and Litany and read the Epistle; I said the Communion office and *preached*. At 5 p. m., I said Evening Prayer.

April 5 : Easter Eve. I *confirmed* in private for Trinity Cathedral (peculiar circumstances requiring it), three persons (two males, one female) This day I gave to Rev. J. E. Curzon, Letters Dimissory to the Diocese of Pittsburgh.

April 6 : Easter Day. At 11 a. m., in Trinity Cathedral, Little Rock, Dean Proctor said Morning Prayer and read the Epistle and assisted at Holy Communion; I said the Communion office, *confirmed* nineteen persons (five males and fourteen females), and *addressed* the class and *celebrated* the Holy Eucharist. At 3 p. m., in St. Philip's Church, Little Rock, I *preached* and *confirmed* two persons (one male, one female) and *addressed* the class. At 7:30 p. m., in Christ Church, Little Rock, I *preached* and *confirmed* thirty persons (twenty-eight females and two males). This makes thirty-two confirmed for this Parish since the last Council.

April 7 : Easter Monday, at 11 a. m., in Trinity Cathedral, I said Morning Service and presided at a meeting of the Parish " in Vestry assembled."

April 8 : Easter Tuesday. At 8 p. m., in St. Andrew's Church, Marianna, Ark., I *preached, confirmed* five persons (one male, four females), and *addressed* the class.

April 13: First Sunday after Easter. In the Cathedral at Little Rock, at 11 a. m., I *preached* and *celebrated* the Holy Eucharist, assisted by Dean Proctor, who said the Litany also· At 3 p. m., I *baptized* by immersion one person (one male). I am indebted to the Rev. Dr. Shelton for the use of the baptismal tank in the church of which he is Pastor. At 7 p. m. in the Cathedral, Little Rock, I *confirmed* eleven persons (three males and eight females) and *addressed* the class. This makes the number confirmed for the Cathedral since the last Council, forty-six.

To this abstract I·add the following:

SUMMARY.

Sermons and adresses		150
Confirmations—In Arkansas 222		
Elsewhere	4	226
Marriages—In Arkansas,	4	
In Indian Ty.,	1	5
Funerals		1
Baptisms—In Arkansas, (adults)	4	
(infants)	4	
In Indian Ty., (adults)	1	
(infants)	1	10
Ordinations (to the Priesthood)		2
Letters Dimissory accepted, 2 Priests, 1 Deacon		3
Letters Dimissory given, 2 Priests		2
Miles traveled		9880

All baptisms, marriages and funerals by myself in the Diocese, are recorded in the Parishes where the acts were performed, and will be reported by the same.

And now I come to a topic equally painful for me to speak of, and for you to hear, but which it is my duty to present to your attention, because it concerns the honor of the Diocesan Council as a body. For some time back, and specially during the past year, there have been, not merely insinuations, but bold and reiterated assertions that the Diocesan Council of 1888, and in a greater degree that of 1889, was infamous in character, and guilty of crooked, partial and corrupt acts; that a majority of its members were under the absolute control of one man; that they were influenced by bribery; that they from spite taxed one Parish unfairly and exorbitantly; that they treated said Parish with discourtesy and insult; that they admitted a new Parish into connection with the Council and allowed its representatives to take their seats, from selfish and partisan motives, that such Parish was organized on the eve or during the session of the Council for a special purpose and to secure the votes of the representatives for carrying certain measures, etc., etc., besides all the enormities that may be involved in the term *infamous*, freely used in reference to this matter. Now, if these accusations are based upon facts, they are such as I have not the faintest knowledge or suspicion of, but the charges are of so serious a nature that they demand a thorough investigation, and the making of this investigation is no less a duty to the accuser or accusers than to yourselves as a body. For if these charges can be established by evidence, whoever has been guilty should be reprobated by this Council. If the accusing party does not make good his averments, then this Council is bound in its own defense to demand a retraction and an apology, as full and as public as the accusations have been. And in order to get at the truth in this matter, I suggest that a committee be raised to report to this Council the facts in the case, and that this committee be authorized to summon before them all persons having or supposed to have knowledge bearing on the truth or falsity of the above-mentioned allegations against the honor and reputation of this Council. As to such allegations having been made, there can be no doubt, as they have been set forth and are preserved in print. Let this matter be sifted thoroughly, and let justice be done to all. If a wrong has been done to any Parish, or any individual, let it be righted at once. If a false accusation has been made let it be promptly retracted and apologized for. Simply justice, as well as the gospel of Christ requires thus much at all hands. I would further suggest that all evidence be taken down in writing, and that the record be open to the inspection of any member of the Council.

In presenting the *resume* of the charges made against this Council I have not designed to quote verbally, but to give the general bearing and scope of the words used.

I have now done my best by presenting this subject fairly before you.   It is for you to examine impartially and ascertain where the truth lies.   If you make no examination you virtually confess that as a body you are guilty of all that has been alleged against you.   I leave the matter in your hands.

May God guide us in all our ways, by the Holy Spirit, and make our lives to reflect as best they can the personal Christ, the Divine Word incarnate.

H. N. PIERCE,
Bishop of Arkansas.

CONFIRMATIONS.

From Easter Monday, April 22, 1889, to Easter Monday, April 7, 1890 :

Batesville, St. Paul's 5
Fayetteville, St. Paul's 11
Fort Smith, St. John's 10
Helena, St. John's 32
Hope, St. Mark's 6
Hot Springs, St. Luke's 10
Little Rock, Trinity Cathedral 46
Little Rock, Christ Church 32
Little Rock, St. Philip's 4
Mammoth Spring, St. Andrew's 3
Marianna, St. Andrew's 6
Morrilton, St. Agnes' 5
Newport, St. Paul's 7
Pendleton, St. Mary's 3
Pine Bluff, Trinity 20
Richmond, Mission 4
Rocky Comfort, Mission 10
Van Buren, Trinity 4
Washington, Grace 4
                                                                        ——
    Total 222

APPENDIX II.

REPORT OF THE STANDING COMMITTEE.

To the Diocesan Council:

The Standing Committee of the Diocese met in Christ Church, Little Rock, May 4, 1889, for the purpose of organizing.

The Rev. Innes O. Adams was elected President, and Mr. P. K. Roots Secretary.

The Committee then adjourned to meet subject to the call of the President.

The Committee met in the City of Little Rock, Thursday, September 19, 1889, and recommended the Rev. Joshua Brown Whaling, Deacon, to the Bishop to be advanced to the Sacred Order of Priests.

The following amounts as expenses of the clerical members were allowed and ordered paid: Rev. I. O. Adams, $2 ; Rev. J. J. Vaulx, $11.20.

On motion of the Rev. J. J. Vaulx, the authority conferred by resolution of this Standing Committee on June 22, 1888, in regard to the property left to the Episcopate Fund by James McMurray's request, was revived and renewed, to continue in full force and effect until the 30th day of September, 1890.

The Committee met in Trinity Cathedral, Little Rock, Thursday, April 17, 1890, and gave its consent to the consecration of the Rev. William Ford Nichols, as Assistant Bishop of the Diocese of California.

All of which is respectfully submitted.

INNES O. ADAMS,
President.

APPENDIX III.

REPORT OF THE TREASURER OF THE DIOCESE.

DIOCESAN FUND.

RECEIPTS.

May 2, 1889, balance on hand		$ 473	79
May 11, W. J. Miller, Sec'y Col. Opening Council		7	83
February 26, 1890, St. Philip's, Little Rock		10	00
April 11, St. Andrews, Marianna		15	00
"	Trinity' Cathedral	125	00
April 18, St. John's, Helena		91	80
"	St. John's, Fort Smith	125	00
"	St. Paul's, Newport	15	00
"	St. Agnes', Morrilton	10	00
"	Trinity, Pine Bluff	60	00
"	St. Paul's, Fayetteville	40	00
"	Trinity, Van Buren	11	50
"	St. Paul's, Batesville	20	00
"	St. Mary's, Pendleton	20	00
"	St. Andrew's, Mammoth Springs	5	00
April 19, St. Luke's, Hot Springs		50	00
	Total	$1,079	92

DISBURSEMENTS.

May 6, 1889, Janitor, Council	$ 10	00
July 10, W. J. Miller, Seciy, postage, etc.	16	02
July 12, Expense Book and Record, Hot Springs	1	25
July 23, printing Proceedings	120	50
September 6, P. K. Roots, Trustee Episcopate Fund	208	85

September 19, I. O. Adams, expense
    Standing Committee............... 2 00
September 19, J. J. Vaulx, expense
    Standing Committee............... 11 20
October 21, assessment General Con-
    vention 57 00
April 17, 1890, expense Journals Gen-
    eral Convention................. . 6 25   433 07

      Balance on hand.............................$646 85

FUND FOR DISABLED CLERGY, ETC.

April 23, 1889, balance on hand.....................$157 28
November 29, St. Philip's, Little Rock.............. 1 50
December 4, Trinity, Pine Bluff... .. .. 5 00
December 14, Trinity Cathedral.................... 6 10
December 31, Trinity, Guthrie, I. T............... 2 50

      Total on hand.......................$172 38

DIOCESAN MISSION FUND.

RECEIPTS.

April 23, 1889, balance on hand...................$129 13
May 7, Christ Church, Little Rock.... .... 15 25
June 18, Trinity, Pine Bluff....................... 5 00
June 20, St. Luke's, Hot Springs.............. .... 8 30
February 26, 1890, Trinity, Pine Bluff............. 5 20
March 4, St. Luke's, Hot Springs.......... .... 19 00
April 5, St. Andrew's, Marianna................... 8 60
April 8, St. Philip's, Little Rock................. 1 06

      Total............................... ....$191 48

DISBURSEMENTS.

November 14, 1889, Rt. Rev. H. N. Pierce..$ 50 00
November 20, 1889, Rt. Rev. H. N. Pierce.. 100 00   150 00

      Balance on hand...................... $ 41 48

All of which are respectfully submitted.

        LOGAN H. ROOTS,
          Treasurer.

APPENDIX IV.

REPORT OF TRUSTEE OF EPISCOPATE FUND.

RECEIPTS.

May	4, 1889, Balance on hand............	$420 81
May	7, Int. lots 10 and 11, block 200........	65 00
June	24, Part prin. lots 10, 11 and 12, block 200..	100 00
Sept.	6, Transfer from Diocesan fund..........	208 85
Nov.	14, Interest on three notes to Nov. 5......	55 00
Dec.	16, Lots 10, 11 and 12, block 200........	101 12
Feb.	8, 1890, St. Luke's, Hot Springs........	7 75
Feb.	18, Logan H. Roots....................	15 00
Feb.	18, P. K. Roots......................	10 00
March	18, Building Association, No. 6, series.....	250 00
April	3, St. Philip's........................	1 00
April	10, Trinity, Pine Bluff.................	46 60
April	11, St. Andrew's, Marianna	6 70
	Total	$1287 83

DISBURSEMENTS.

Building Association.

Sept.	18, Purchased 10 shares, No. 7...	$ 94 00
Sept.	18, Purchased 10 shares, No. 2...	223 50
Nov.	11, Purchased 5 shares, No. 7...	50 50
Feb.,1890, Purchased 20 shares, No. 6...		219 22
April	15, Purchased 10 shares, No. 7...	163 00
	Total paid purchase ($250 ret.).	$750 22
	Total paid monthly dues.....	479 00
	Balance on hand	58 61
		$1287 83

PRESENT VALUE OF ASSETS.

Balance on hand	$ 58
Bal. due on lots 10, 11 and 12 block 200....	1000
Invested in McMurray bequest.	865 6
Invested in Building Ass'n....	2862 4
Total	$4786 68
Value of funds last report.....	4369 66
Increase of fund during year..	$ 417 02

Respectfully submitted.

P. K. ROOTS,
Trustee Episcopate Fund.

REPORT OF INNES O. ADAMS, EXECUTOR OF THE ESTATE OF JAMES McMURRAY, DECEASED.

To P. K. Roots, Trustee Episcopate Fund :

Easter Monday, 1889, to Easter Monday, 1890.

ASSETS.

Value of the property................		$4000 00
Balance from rents, 1889.........	$ 96 00	
Rents 1889–90.......................	414 00	
Rents due, 1890–91	432 00	
Receipts from judgments gained........	50 00	992 00
Total.		$4992 00

LIABILITIES.

Debts, 1889–90	$317 80	
Taxes	27 50	
Insurance	15 75	$361 05
Debts due 1890–91	$140 00	
Special bequests.............	150 00	290 00

Episcopate Endowment:

Money borrowed	$865 85		
2 years' interest on same	173 16	1039 01	
Taxes, 1890		27 50	
Insurance, 1890		15 75	
Water Privilege, 1890		26 00	$1759 31
Balance			$3232 69

APPENDIX V.

REPORT OF COMMITTEE ON THE STATE OF THE CHURCH.

To the Diocesan Council:

Your Committee·on the State of the Church respectfully make the following report:

The growth of this Diocese the past two years gives us great encouragement. We find we now rate third in the point of increase in the confirmations to the average of the clergy in the Diocese of the United States.

We recommend that the Bishop be empowered by canon to call the members in any vacant Parish (which vacancy occurs six months or more), to fill said vacancies by an election held by the members of said Parishes.

St. Luke's, of Hot Springs, has built a beautiful church during the past year. It is an ornament to the city, and a monument to the zeal of the Rector and Vestry of said Parish.

St. John's Church, at Helena, under the administration of its admirable Rector, Rev. Chas. H. Lockwood, has so largely increased in members, in baptisms and confirmations that they now contemplate building a church at a cost of about twenty-five thousand dollars. Its Sunday-school has a regular attendance of about 120 members. They have built a beautiful Rectory, and furnished it throughout. This is one of the best organized Parishes in the State.

At Fayetteville the Parish is prospering under the administration of its energetic Rector.

At Fort Smith (while we regret to say), this Parish has lost about fifty communicants who have removed elsewhere, it is still fruitful in good works under its present Rector, and ad·mirable wife, who has devoted a large share of her time to the care of the distressed and afflicted at St. John's Hospital.

At Van Buren the Parish has purchased a Rectory.

Most Parishes that we have reports from are doing good work, and increasing in numbers and prosperity, all of which will be seen by the Bishop's address. The increase in confirmations has been twenty-two over and above last year. This in face of the large falling off of confirmations in some Parishes.

We find the fund to the Episcopate, and contributions to the Diocesan Mission are not increasing as they should. We ask more energetic action on the part of the Rectors and members throughout the Diocese, to secure larger contributions. The hands of the Bishop are tied .for the want of means to carry out this glorious work in the cause of Christ.

In summing up all the facts, the remarkable growth and interest in the church throughout the whole Diocese is very encouraging, and we beg this renewed interest will still continue and increase. In closing this report the committee beg to offer the following resolution:

Resolved, The Committee on Constitution and Canons be requested to take under consideration the subject of vacant Parishes, and devise some measure by which the Rectorships shall be filled.

> C. A. BRUCE, *Chairman*,
> D. S. C. N. POTTER,
> W. B. WELCH,
> ED. M. DICKERSON,
> N. B. TRULOCK.

5 D

APPENDIX VI.

PAROCHIAL ASSESSMENTS.

REPORT OF COMMITTEE ON WAYS AND MEANS.

To the Diocesan Council:

Your committee respectfully report that after a careful examination of the condition of each Parish and Mission, they have made the following assessments:

St. Paul's, Fayetteville .... $ 40 00
St. John's, Fort Smith 125 00
Trinity, Van Buren 20 00
Trinity, Pine Bluff 60 00
St. Paul's, Newport 10 00
St. Agnes', Morrilton 15 00
St. John's, Helena 100 00
St. Andrew's, Marianna 15 00
Trinity Cathedral 125 00
St. Andrew's, Mammoth Spring 10 00
St. Mary's, Pendleton 10
St. Philip's, Little Rock 10
St. Paul's, Batesville 20
St. John's, Camden 15
St. John's, Eureka Springs 10
St. Mark's, Hope 10
St. Luke's, Hot Springs 50
Grace Church, Washington 10
Christ Church, Little Rock 275
Mission, Witcherville 8 00

If from the sum total of these assessments the expenses of the Council are paid, there will be too little remaining for the usual donation to the Episcopate Fund, to be worthy of record

· the benefit of the Diocese, therefore, it is respectfully sug-
ted that extra sums be secured by pledges, offerings or sub-
ptions in the several Parishes, and added to the assessment.
;ome instances this has already been done, and with praise-
·thy generosity. We commend the good example with a
·e that it may be followed by every Parish as far as possible.
Respectfully submitted,

C. H. PROCTOR,
L. MINOR,
GREENFIELD QUARLES,
Committee.

APPENDIX VII.

PAROCHIAL REPORTS,

FOR YEAR ENDING EASTER MONDAY, 1890.

ST. MARK'S CHURCH, ARKADELPHIA.

No report.

UNORGANIZED MISSION, ARKANSAS CITY.

No report.

ST. PAUL'S, BATESVILLE.

ED. M. DICKINSON, SR., J. C. FITZHUGH, Wardens.

Number of families, 40. Whole number of souls, 102. BAPTISMS: Infants, 2; adults, 1; total, 3. CONFIRMATIONS: 5. ACTUAL COMMUNICANTS: Removed, 1; died, 2; present number of males, 20; present number of females, 20; total, 40. Number of confirmed persons, 62. Marriages, 2. Burials, 5. PUBLIC SERVICES: Sundays, 39. HOLY COMMUNION: Public, 3. SUNDAY SCHOOL: Teachers, 6; pupils, 62.

OFFERINGS.

PAROCHIAL: Rector's salary and Parish expenses, $190; total, $190.

DIOCESAN: Diocesan assessment, $20; miscellaneous, $10; total, $30.

Total offerings, $220.

ST. JOHN'S CHURCH, CAMDEN.
No report.

ST. PAUL'S CHURCH, DARDANELLE.
No report.

ST. JAMES' CHURCH, EUREKA SPRINGS.
No report.

ST. PAUL'S CHURCH, FAYETTEVILLE.
JAMES J. VAULX, Rector.
W. B. WELCH, M. D., COL. J. L. CRAVENS, Wardens.

Number of families, 51. BAPTISMS: Infants, 14; adults, 2; total, 16. Confirmations, 11. ACTUAL COMMUNICANTS: 127.* Number of confirmed persons, 130. Marriages, 3. Burials, 3. PUBLIC SERVICES: Sundays, 145; other days, 105; total, 250. HOLY COMMUNION: Public, 77; private, 6; total, 83. SUNDAY SCHOOL: Teachers, 7; pupils, about 90. Church sittings, 240. Rectory? Yes.

OFFERINGS.

PAROCHIAL: Communion alms, $66.55; Rector's salary and Parish expenses, $911.75; miscellaneous, $568.62. Total, $1547.22.

DIOCESAN: Assessment, $40; Cathedral, $11.20; for chapel in the country, $70. Total, $121.20.

EXTRA DIOCESAN: Johnstown sufferers, $6.40; society for Christianizing Jews, $3.20. Total, $9.60.

Total offerings, $1678.02.

Estimated value Church and grounds..............$3,500 00
Estimated value Rectory....................... 3,000 00

Total $6,500 00
Amount of indebtedness on Church property........$ 56 95

*This includes the Communicants at Bentonville, Huntsville, Boonsboro and Winslow, which are under my pastoral care.

ST. JOHN'S CHURCH, FORT SMITH.

Rev. George Frederick Degen, Rector.

Stephen Wheeler, Wm. M. Mellette, Wardens.

Number of families, 142. Whole number of souls, 540.
Number of baptized persons, 508. Baptisms: Infants, 37;
adults, 13; total, 50. Confirmations: 10. Actual Communicants: Admitted, 10; received, 20; total added, 30; removed,
45; died, 6; withdrawn, 3; total lost, 54; present number of male
76; female, 161; total, 237. Number of confirmed persons, 237.
Marriages, 4. Burials, 17. Public Services: Sundays, 156;
other days, 123; total, 279. Holy Communion: Public, 92;
private, 3; total, 95. Sunday Schools: Teachers, 9; pupils,
129. Church sittings, 200. Rectory? Yes.

OFFERINGS.

Parochial: Communion alms, $67.35; Rector's salary
and Parish expenses, $1361.84; miscellaneous, $878.68; St.
John's Hospital, $1481.02; total, $3788.89.

Diocesan: Diocesan assessment, $125; Diocesan missions,
$19,25; total, $144.25.

Extra Diocesan: Domestic missions, $80.57; University
of the South, $7 70; miscellaneous, $18.80; total, $107.07.

Total offerings, $4040.21.

Estimated value Church and grounds $10,000 00
Estimated value Rectory........................   1,800 00
Estimated value other Church property 680 00

Total $12,480 00

Amount of indebtedness on Church property, none.

ST. JOHN'S CHURCH, HELENA.

Rev. C. H. Lockwood, Rector.

P. O. Thweatt, G. Quarles, Wardens.

Number of families, 87; whole number of souls, 395;
number of baptized persons, 361. Baptisms: Infants, 22;
adults, 11; total, 33. Confirmations, 32. Actual Communi-

CANTS: Admitted, 50; received, 14; total added, 64; removed, 1; died, 2, withdrawn, 1; total lost, 4; present number, male, 57; female, 133; total, 190. Number of confirmed persons, 212; Burials, 5. PUBLIC SERVICES: Sundays, 92; other days, 122; total, 214. HOLY COMMUNION: Public, 47; total, 47. SUNDAY SCHOOL: Teachers, 17; pupils, 139. Church sittings, 400. Rectory? Yes.

OFFERINGS.

PAROCHIAL: Communion alms, $25.10; Rector's salary and Parish expenses, $1553.34; miscellaneous, $2008 43; Lenten offering, Sunday School, $201.30; Easter offering, disposition of Rector, $104.70. Total, $3893 87.

DIOCESAN: Diocesan assessment, $60; Episcopate fund, $31.80; for Cathedral, $7.75. Total, $99.55.

EXTRA DIOCESAN: Domestic missions, $31.60; University of the South, $20.00; conversion of the Jews, $7; Johnstown sufferers, $28. Total, $86.60.

Total offerings, $4079.02.

Estimated value of Church and grounds..........$16,000 00
Estimated value of Rectory.................... 6,000 00
   Total 22,000 00
Amount of indebtedness on Church property.... 2,800 co

The above report covers a period of ten months and six days' work, from June 1st, 1889, to Easter Monday, 1890.

ST. MARK'S CHURCH, HOPE.
No report.

EMMANUEL CHURCH, LAKE VILLAGE.
No report.

ST. AGNES' CHURCH, MORRILTON.
No report.

ST. LUKE'S CHURCH, HOT SPRINGS.

Rev. William James Miller, Rector.

James P. Mellard, George G. Latta, Wardens.

Number of families, 72. Baptisms: Infants, 9; adults, 2; total, 11. Confirmations, 10. Actual Communicants: Admitted, 10; received, 6; total added, 16; removed, 7; died, 2; total lost, 9; present number, 97. Burials, 4. Public Services: Sundays, 77; other days, 80; total, 157. Holy Communion: Public, 34; private, 2; total, 36. Sunday School: Teachers, 7; pupils, 80.

OFFERINGS.

Parochial: Communion alms, $25; Rector's salary and Parish expenses, $1212.12; Church building fund, $7542.04; raised by King's Daughters, $300; chancel furniture, $1500. Total, $10,579.16.

Diocesan: Diocesan assessment, $50; Diocesan missions, $8.50; aged and infirm Clergy, $19.80; Episcopate fund, $7.75; Cathedral work, $42.92. Total, $128.97.

Extra Diocesan: Domestic missions, $15.15; foreign missions, $11.43; University of the South, $35. Total, $61.58.

Total offerings, $10,749 71.

Estimated value of Church and grounds.... ....$25,000
Amount of indebtedness on Church property........ 4,000

For seven months Parish work was very much interrupted by reason of the old Church being torn down before the new was ready for use. The new Church was occupied on the Fourth Sunday in Advent, December 22, 1889.

CHRIST CHURCH, LITTLE ROCK.

Rev. Wallace Carnahan, Rector.

Rev. J. E. H. Galbraith, Assistant Minister.

Major John D. Adams, Senior Warden, Dr. Wm. A. Cantrell, Junior Warden.

Number of families, 352; number of communicants, 612; number of souls (about), 1700. Sunday Schools: Teachers,

36; pupils, 400; total, 436. BAPTIZED: Adults, 7; infants, 33; total, 40. Confirmed, 32. Married, 5. Buried, 23.

OFFERINGS.

PAROCHIAL: Current expenses, $3793.77; Church debt, $2714.10; communion alms, $257.15; Church furniture, $129.90; miscellaneous, $546.43. Total, $7441.35.

DIOCESAN: City missions, $715.00; Mammoth Spring, $31.50. Total, $746.50.

EXTRA DIOCESAN: Domestic missions, $161.65; work amongst the negroes, $20.00; work amongst the Jews, $15.00; work amongst the deaf-mutes, $17.65. Total, $241.30.

Aggregate, $8429.15.

VALUE OF CHURCH PROPERTY.

Church edifice and grounds.................$60,000 00
Rectory and grounds........................ 8,500 00
St. Paul's Chapel and lot.................... 1,500 00

Total $70,000 00

TRINITY CATHEDRAL, LITTLE ROCK.

THE VERY REV. C. H. PROCTOR, Dean.

G. W. CARUTH, WM. G. WHIPPLE, Wardens.

Number of families, about 200. BAPTISMS: Infants, 19; adults, 15; total, 34. Confirmations, 46. COMMUNICANTS, 150. Marriages, 3. Burials, 9. SUNDAY SCHOOL: Teachers, 7; pupils, 80.

OFFERINGS.

PAROCHIAL: Communion alms, $41.85; Rector's salary and Parish expenses, $1389.04; miscellaneous, $198.78. Total, $1587.82.

DIOCESAN: Diocesan assessment, $125; aged and infirm clergy, $6.10; miscellaneous, $10. Total, $141.10.

EXTRA DIOCESAN: University of the South, $10; miscellaneous—for the Jews, $4.20. Total, $24.20.

Total offerings, $1783.12.

Estimated value of Church property $18,000 00
Amount of indebtedness on Church property..... 2,950 00·

NOTE—This report is only partial, and by no means covers the work done in the Cathedral Parish during the year. The growth of the Parish has been remarkable, and the grea building is repeatedly well-filled at its various services. The actual number of families under parochial care is given approximately, and the number of communicants demanding the services of the Rector, is reported in the same manner.

· The financial statement is from the report of the Church Treasurer, and does not include various sums held by individuals and Parish organizations for church work.

The whole report is presented with reluctance, because it does not show fairly the legitimate results of a year of successful effort.

C. H. PROCTOR,
Dean, etc.

ST. PHILIP'S CHURCH, LITTLE ROCK.

THE REV. BENJAMIN W. TIMOTHY, Rector.

JOHN O. W. ALEXANDER, LONDON W. WALKER, Wardens.

Number of families, 22; whole number of souls, 83; number of baptized persons, 55. BAPTISMS: Adults, 2; total, 2. Confirmations, 4. ACTUAL COMMUNICANTS: Admitted, 4; received, 1; total added, 5; removed, 1; died, 2; total lost, 3; present number, male, 12; female, 21; total, 33. Number of confirmed persons, 34. Marriages, 2. PUBLIC SERVICES: Sundays, 131; other days, 5; total, 136. HOLY COMMUNION: public, 20. SUNDAY SCHOOL: Teachers, 3; pupils, 54. Chnrch sittings, 200.

OFFERINGS.

PAROCHIAL: Communion alms, $2; Rector's salary and Parish expenses, $191.30; Rectory fund, $25; Cathedral, Bishop's visit, $7.25; total, $225.55.

DIOCESAN: Diocesan assessment, $10; Diocesan missions,

$1 ; aged and infirm clergy, $1.50; Episcopate fund, $1 ; miscellaneous, $6 ; total, $19.50.

EXTRA DIOCESAN: Domestic missions, 75 cents; foreign missions, 75 cents; miscellaneous, Indian, 75 cents; colored, 75 cents; Jews, $1 ; total, $4.

Total offerings, $249.05.

Estimated value of church and grounds $1900

ST. ANDREW'S CHURCH, MAMMOTH SPRING.

REV. RICHARD S. JAMES, D. D., LL. D., Rector.

P. P. B. HYNSON, E. R. HOPKINS, Wardens.

Number of families, 10; whole number of souls, 51 ; number of baptized persons, 46. BAPTISMS: Infants, 3 ; total, 3. Confirmations, 3. ACTUAL COMMUNICANTS: Admitted, 3; received, 7; total added, 10; removed, 2; died, 2; total lost, 4; present number of males, 9; female, 13; total, 22, Number of confirmed persons, 22. Marriages, 1. Burials, 4. PUBLIC SERVICES: Sundays, 98; other days, 15 ; total, 114. HOLY COMMUNION: Public, 10. SUNDAY SCHOOL: Teachers, 8; pupils, 40. Church sittings, 120. Rectory? Yes.

OFFERINGS.

PAROCHIAL: Communion alms, $12.15; Rector's salary and Parish expenses, $240 ; miscellaneous, $432 ; total, $684.15.

DIOCESAN: Diocesan assessment, $5 ; Episcopate fund, $8.51. Total, $13 51.

Total cfferings, $697.66.

Estimated value of Church and grounds..............$1,250
Estimated value of Rectory.................. 1,000
Estimated value of other Church property............ 250

Total $2,500

Amount of indebtedness on Church property......... $325

ST. ANDREW'S CHURCH, MARIANNA.

THE REV. C. A. BRUCE, Rector.

JAMES P. DUNHAM, F. H. GOVAN, Wardens.

Number of families, 19; whole number of souls, 72; number baptized persons, 66. BAPTISMS: Infants, 3; adults, 1; total, 4. Confirmations, 6. ACTUAL COMMUNICANTS: Admitted, 6; received, 2; total added, 8; removed, 1; withdrawn, 1; total lost, 2; present number, male, 12; female, 25; total, 37. Number confirmed persons, 40. Marriages, 1. PUBLIC SERVICES: Sundays, 130; other days, 8; total, 138. HOLY COMMUNION: Public, 47. SUNDAY SCHOOL: teachers, 5; pupils, 30. Church sittings, 115.

OFFERINGS.

PAROCHIAL: Communion alms, $24; Rector's salary and Parish expenses, $399.35; miscellaneous,* $500; total, $923.35.

DIOCESAN: Diocesan assessment, $15; Diocesan missions, $8.60; Episcopate fund, $6.70; Cathedral, $12 05; total, $42.35.

EXTRA DIOCESAN: University of the South, $5; Prayer-book Society, $4.25; total, $9.25.

Total offerings, $974.95.

Estimated value Church and grounds $3,000

*This offering was a gift to the Parish and expended in paying the balance of a debt, and in furnishing the Church.

CHURCH OF THE REDEEMER, NASHVILLE.

No report.

ST. PAUL'S CHURCH, NEWPORT.

L. MINOR, JAMES S. JONES, Wardens.

Number of families, 35; whole number of souls, 118; number of baptized persons, 100. BAPTISMS: Infants, 2; total, 2. Confirmations, 7. ACTUAL COMMUNICANTS, 45.

PAROCHIAL: Miscellaneous, $274.65; Sunday School fund, $15.95; Easter offerings, $18. Total, $308.60.

Estimated value of Church and grounds............$2,500

GRACE CHURCH, PHILLIPS COUNTY.

No report.

TRINITY CHURCH, PINE BLUFF.

REV. INNES O. ADAMS, Rector.

M. L. BELL AND N. B. TRULOCK, Wardens.

Number of families, 102; whole number of souls, 356. Number baptized persons, 24. BAPTISMS: Infants, 15; adults, 3; total, 18. Confirmations, 20. ACTUAL COMMUNICANTS: Admitted, 20; received, 3; total added, 23; removed, 3; withdrawn, 1; total lost, 4; present number, male, 42; female, 128; total, 170. Number confirmed persons, 16. Marriages, 4. Burials, 11. PUBLIC SERVICES: Sundays, 164; other days, 46; total, 210. HOLY COMMUNION: Public, 25; private, 2; total, 27. SUNDAY SCHOOL: Teachers, 8; pupils, 100. Church sittings, 450. Rectory? Yes.

OFFERINGS.

PAROCHIAL: Communion alms, $40.20; Rector's salary and Parish expenses, $1174.80; miscellaneous, $446.20; total, $1651.20.

DIOCESAN: Diocesan assessment, $60; Diocesan missions, $10.20; aged and infirm clergy, $5; Episcopate fund, $46.60; miscellaneous, $25; total, $146.80.

EXTRA DIOCESAN: University of the South, $24.80; conversion of the Jews, $3; church building fund, $7.05; total, $34.85.

Total offerings, $1842.85.

Estimated value Church and grounds............$12,000 00
Estimated value Rectory....................... 3,500 00
Estimated value other Church property.... ..... 1,000 00

Total ....,........$16,500 00
Amount of indebtedness on church property, none.

GRACE CHURCH, WASHINGTON.
No report.

ST. MARY'S CHURCH, PENDLETON.
REV. D. L. TRIMBLE, Minister.

Number of families, 6; whole number of souls, 18. BAP-
TISMS: Adults, 2; total, 2. Confirmations, 3. ACTUAL COM-
MUNICANTS: Present number, male 3; female, 7; total, 10.
Number confirmed persons, 10. PUBLIC SERVICES: Sundays,
16. HOLY COMMUNION: Public, 6. SUNDAY SCHOOLS: Teachers,
5; pupils, 36. Church sittings, 150.

OFFERINGS.

PAROCHIAL; Parish expenses, $42; miscellaneous, $216.50.
Total, $258.50.

DIOCESAN: Assessments, $20 00.

Total offering, $278.50.

Estimated value of Church and grounds............$1,200 00
Estimated value of Rectory............. .... 100 00

Total..................................$1,300 00

TRINITY CHURCH, VAN BUREN.
REV. L. F. GUERRY, Rector.

S. A. PERNOT, JOHN FRITZ, Wardens.

Number of families, 28; whole number of souls, 140; number of baptized persons, 137; BAPTISMS: Infants, 5; adults,
2; total, 7. Confirmations, 4. ACTUAL COMMUNICANTS: Ad-

mitted, 4; received, 1; total added, 5; died, 1; total lost, 1; present number, male, 6; female, 45; total, 51.   Number of confirmed persons, 71.   Marriages, 3.   Burials, 5.   PUBLIC SERVICES: Sundays, 81; other days, 45; total, 126. HOLY COMMUNION: Public, 25; total, 25. SUNDAY SCHOOL: Teachers, 7; pupils, 50.   Church sittings, 250.   Rectory?   Yes.

OFFERINGS.

PAROCHIAL: Communion alms, $25.30; Rector's salary and Parish expenses, $649.50; miscellaneous, $5.90; Easter offering for debt on Rectory, $60.85.   Total, $741.55.

DIOCESAN: Diocesan assessment, $20; miscellaneous, $7.85; Cathedral work, $5.60.   Total, $33.45.

EXTRA DIOCESAN: Domestic missions, $2.25; foreign missions, $2.25; University of the South, $3.75; missions to Jews, $1.65.   Total, $9.90.

Total offerings, $784.90.

Estimated value of Church and grounds $3000 00
Estimated value of Rectory 1000 00

    Total $4000 00
Estimated indebtedness on Church property (Rectory) 750 00
    Paid on Rectory 250 00
    Cash on hand for next payment 144 38

Since the meeting of the last Council I have officiated without the Diocese five times, and administered the Holy Communion once.   In addition also to services reported in this Parish I have held service seven times at Winslow (Boston Mountain) and celebrated the Holy Communion twice.   In reference to this point, I am glad to say that here there is a valuable nucleus of church people around which to build a congregation.   On my last visit, which was in March, I found a well-organized Sunday school (mostly of children not belonging to church families), faithfully worked by an earnest layman, assisted by two ladies, all communicants of the church. A monthly service at this point by a clergyman would be a great blessing and help, and I am endeavoring to make arrangements to do this, and hope it can be successfully effected. Altogether then, while in my work of the past year, there have been some things to discourage, I feel that those which have encouraged and cheered have been greater in number, for which I thank God most heartily, and pray for a more abundant outpouring of His Holy Spirit.

TABLE OF PAROCHIAL STATISTICS.

PARISHES AND MISSIONS.	No. Families.	BAPTISMS. Infants	BAPTISMS. Adults	BAPTISMS. Total	Confirmations.	Communicants.	Marriages.	Burials.	SUNDAY SCHOOLS. Teachers.	SUNDAY SCHOOLS. Pupils.	OFFERINGS. Parochial.	OFFERINGS. Diocesan.	OFFERINGS. Extra Dio-cesan.	OFFERINGS. Total.	Value of Church Property.
Arkadelphia, St Mark's	40	2				9	2	2	6	62					$ 1,000 00
Arkansas City Mission	26		1	3	5	40	5	5			$ 190 00	$ 30 00		$ 220 00	
Batesville, St Paul's						41									3,500 00
Camden, St John's						8									2,500 00
Conway, Mission	9					24			5	28					
Dardane e, St Paul's						34									2,825 00
Eureka Springs, St James'	51	14	2	16	11	127	3	3	7	90	1 547 22	121 20	$ 9 60	1,678 02	200 00
Fayetteville, St Paul's	142	37	13	50	10	237	4	17	9	129	8 788 89	144 25	107 07	4,040 21	6,540 00
Fort Smith, St John's	87	22	11	33	32	190	5	5	17	139	3,892 87	99 55	86 60	4 079 02	12,480 00
Helena, St John's						17			5	35					22,000 00
dfe, St Mark's	72	9	2	11	10	97	4	4	7	80	10,579 16	128 97	61 58	10,749 71	800 00
Hot Sp ngs, St Luke's	200	19	15	34	46	150	9	9	80	80	1,587 82	141 10	24 20	1,783 12	25,000 00
Lake Village, Emmanuel	352	7	53	32	32	612	5	28	36	400	7,441 85	746 50	241 87	8,421 15	1,000 00
Little Rock, Trinity Cathedral	22		2		4	22	2	1	8	54	225 55	19 50	4 00	249 01	18,000 00
Little Rock, Christ Church	10	3		3	3	37	1		8	40	684 15	13 51		697 66	70,000 00
Little Rock, St Philip's	19	3	1	3	6	21			5	30	923 35	42 85	9 25	974 95	1,900 00
Ma mh Springs, St aw's	12			4	5	34									2,500 00
Marianna, St Andrew's	7					18									3,000 00
Morrilton, St Agnes	35	2	2	2	2	45	3		4	16	308 60			3 8 60	2,766 80
asthville, sh of the Redeemer	6			2	3	10			5	75	258 50	20 00		278 50	2,500 00
Newport, St Paul's						13				36					1,800 00
Pendleton, St Mary's	102	15	3	18	20	170	4	4	8	100	1 661 20	146 80	34 85	1,842 85	1,000 00
Phillips County, Grace						4									16,600 00
Pine Bluff, Trinity					4	10									1,000 00
Prescott, St James	24	5	2	7	10	51	3	6	7	50	741 55	33 45	9 90	784 90	
Richmond, Mission	12				4	28			4	14					4,100 00
Rocky Comfort, Mission					4	10									700 00
Van Buren, Trinity															500 00
Washington, Grace															9,000 00
Wincherville, Mission															
Total	1289	138	87	225	222	2074	28	86	150	1488	$ 33,830 21	$ 1,687 18	$ 586 85	$ 36,205 74	$ 211,971 80

6 D

APPENDIX VII.

CONSTITUTION AND CANONS.

CONSTITUTION,

As Proposed at the Fifteenth Annual Council at Little Rock, April 20, 1887, and finally Adopted by the Sixteenth Annual Council.

PREAMBLE.

This Church conforms to the Constitution and Canons of the Protestant Episcopal Church in the United States of America, as set forth by the General Convention of the same; to which Constitution and Canons this Church hereby accedes and subordinates herself, according to the rules of ecclesiastical law.

ARTICLE I.

Of the Clergy and Laity.

There are three orders of the Clergy :*

First—The Bishop, who exercises all the functions of the Ministry, presides over the Church by Apostolic Authority, and has the sole right to ordain, to confirm, and to pronounce judicial sentence on offenders; and governs the Church in his Diocese according to the Holy Scriptures and the Canons of this Church.

Second—The Priests or Presbyters, who preach the Word, administer the Sacraments of the Church, and have the oversight and pastoral care of the Laity in their several Congrega-

---

*Amended by the Sixteenth Annual Council to read as here given. Confirmed by action of the Seventeenth Annual Council.

ones. They also have the right to advise their Bishop and to share in the government of the Church, according to the Canons.

Third—The Deacons, who having received limited office in the general Ministry, serve in the same where they may be appointed by the Bishop. They are subject to the orders of the Bishop, cannot take the Rectorship of a Church, and must be under the care and supervision of some priest, who shall direct them in their work.

The Laity are divided and organized, according to local convenience, into Parishes or Congregations. They commit the general management of their parochial business to a portion of their own number, annually elected, and called Wardens and Vestrymen. To these belong the administration of all the secular concerns of their particular Parish; but they have no part in the spiritual government of the Church, which belongs to the Clergy alone.

ARTICLE II.

Of the Council.

There shall be a Council of the Diocese annually, at such time and place as the Council may, from time to time, determine; and, in case of its failure to do so, the Bishop shall appoint the time and place. In the Council the Bishop shall preside by virtue of his office. The Clergy shall sit by right of their order, and the Laity shall be represented by Delegates chosen for that purpose by the Vestry of each Congregation.

The Chancellor, Secretary and Treasurer of the Diocese shall be entitled to seats in the Council, with privilege of debate, but shall have no vote by reason of their offices.

Special Councils may be called by the Bishop, or, in case of a vacancy in the Episcopate, by the Standing Committee, when some urgent necessity may require the action of the whole Church.

out the concurrence of the Clergy and the Laity, no

rule or law of the Church can be adopted, changed or done away.

ARTICLE III.

Of the Organization of Congregations.

All Congregations and Parishes represented in the Primary Convention, shall be deemed duly organized; and thereafter, the organization of all Parishes shall be in the form provided by the Canon, and subject to the will of the Council. And no Parish shall have an organic existence, or corporate life in this Church, unless acknowledged by the Council and approved by the Bishop.

ARTICLE IV.

Of the Support and Advancement of the Church.

All Christian men are bound to bear their just share of the burdens which duty imposes.

The Council, by Canon and resolution, may establish special funds:

First—For the support of the Episcopate.

Second—For the support of Missionaries.

Third—For the support of aged and infirm Clergymen.

Fourth—For Church building.

Fifth—For education of men for the Ministry; and take all other measures necessary for the advancement of Christ's Kingdom: *Provided*, That this article does not imply any power to make any assessment except for the necessary expenses of the Diocese, *"which shall include all current expenses and proper provision for the Episcopate Fund."

ARTICLE V.

Of the Administration of Justice.

The Clergy, Priests and Deacons, may be tried by an Ecclesiastical Court, composed of Presbyters chosen for that purpose. But there shall be no such trial except on due pre-

---

*Amended by the Sixteenth Annual Council by adding the words in quotation marks. Confirmed by action of the Seventeenth Annual Council.

sentment, and according to the Canon for the trial of Clergymen set forth in this Diocese, and the rules of Ecclesiastical
law.

ARTICLE VI.

Of the Tenure of Church Property.

The Rector, Wardens, and Vestry, or other persons in
whose names the property of any Church or Parish may
be vested, shall not, by deed or any other means, without the
consent of the Bishop and Standing Committee, under their
hands given, grant, alienate, or otherwise dispose of any lands,
messuages, or hereditaments in them vested for the use and
benefit of said Church, nor charge, nor encumber the same to
any person whatever.

ARTICLE VII.

Of Amending the Constitution.

A proposal to amend this Constitution must be laid before
the Council in writing, and, if approved, shall lie over until the
next annual Council, and in the meantime, shall be notified to
the Parishes ; and then, if it be approved by the Bishop, and
by two-thirds of the Clergy, and by two-thirds of the Laity
present, voting by orders, the proposed amendment shall become a part of the Constitution.

THE CANONS

Enacted by the First Annual Council, A. D. 1872—Revised by the Fifteenth Annual Council, A. D. 1887.

TITLE I

OF THE COUNCIL OF THE DIOCESE.

CANON I.

OF THE COUNCIL.

SECTION 1. The Members of the Council shall consist of the Clergy and Laity of the Diocese having the following qualifications: Every Clergyman having been admitted canonically by the ecclesiastical authority shall be a member of the Council; but no Clergyman shall be qualified to vote at the election of a Bishop unless he shall have been canonically and actually a resident of the Diocese for six months. Every Parish regularly organized as required by the Constitution shall be entitled to send three Delegates to the Council, and every duly organized Mission Station shall be entitled to send one Delegate; *provided always:* That such Delegates shall be communicants of the Protestant Episcopal Church, and that no person under ecclesiastical censure or process, whether Clergyman or Layman, shall be allowed a seat in the Council.

SEC. 2. The first standing committee appointed by the Bishop, after the Council has been duly organized, and the last to make a report, shall be a Committee on Ways and Means, consisting of one Priest and two Laymen, whose duty it shall be to consider the condition of each Parish and Mis-sion, and to make an equitable assessment upon them, to be

sentment, and according to the Canon for the trial of Clergy-men set forth in this Diocese, and the rules of Ecclesiastical law.

ARTICLE VI.

Of the Tenure of Church Property.

The Rector, Wardens, and Vestry, or other persons in whose names the property of any Church or Parish may be vested, shall not, by deed or any other means, without the consent of the Bishop and Standing Committee, under their hands given, grant, alienate, or otherwise dispose of any lands, messuages, or hereditaments in them vested for the use and benefit of said Church, nor charge, nor encumber the same to any person whatever.

ARTICLE VII.

Of Amending the Constitution.

A proposal to amend this Constitution must be laid before the Council in writing, and, if approved, shall lie over until the next annual Council, and in the meantime, shall be notified to the Parishes ; and then, if it be approved by the Bishop, and by two-thirds of the Clergy, and by two-thirds of the Laity present, voting by orders, the proposed amendment shall become a part of the Constitution.

be proposed or acted upon than those specified in the call of said special Council.

CANON II.

OF THE SECRETARY AND TREASURER.

SECTION 1.   The Secretary of the Council shall keep in a fit book, full and exact records of all its acts, and shall preserve all papers, documents, memorials, etc., belonging to the same, duly indorsed and filed in such way that they may be easily consulted whenever recourse to them may be necessary. He shall also prepare, under the direction of the Bishop, at least one week before the meeting of the Council, a list of all the Ministers canonically resident in the Diocese, annexing their respective stations, distinguishing Priests from Deacons, but not inserting the name of any Clergyman who is suspended from the Ministry.   The list thus prepared shall be laid before the Council immediately after it shall be called to order, and the names of the clerical members shall be called therefrom. Nevertheless, the Council has power immediately to order the correction of any errors or omissions.

SEC. 2.   The Treasurer shall have charge of the General Fund of the Diocese, and all other funds the Council may commit to his care, and shall keep a strict account of the same in a fit book, with a distinct place therein for all proper entries.   He shall keep a regular account with all funds and with all persons and Parishes concerned, and shall annually exhibit a balance sheet to the Auditing Committee.   He shall indorse and file away all warrants, orders, or other papers belonging to his department, and shall have his accounts audited at each Council by the Finance Committee.

SEC. 3.   When a vacancy occurs in the office of Secretary or Treasurer, the ecclesiastical authority shall appoint a fit person to fill the vacancy, who shall receive all records, funds and papers from the hands of the former officer or his legal representatives, and such appointee shall continue in office and perform all the duties thereof until the ensuing Council shall have elected some one to fill the same.

CANON III.

OF THE REGISTRAR.

SECTION 1.   A Registrar shall be elected by the Council, into whose keeping shall be committed all documents pertaining to the history of the Church in the Diocese of Arkansas, that are now, or may hereafter become the property of the Council.   It shall be the duty of said Registrar, to preserve all documents herein referred to, in some suitable place of deposit, and to hold them subject to such regulations as the Council may, from time to time, prescribe.

SEC. 2.   Said Registrar shall hold his office for one year and until another shall be chosen in his place.

CANON IV.

OF REGULAR ATTENDANCE AT COUNCIL.

SECTION 1.   Every Clergyman in the Diocese shall attend the Annual Council, unless he has a satisfactory excuse ; and it is the duty of every Parish to send Lay Delegates, and it shall be the duty of the Vestry to make provision for their representation.   A satisfactory excuse will be required for every failure.

SEC. 2.   No member of the Council shall leave the same during the session without having obtained leave of absence from the Council.

CANON V.

OF THE NUMBER NECESSARY TO CONSTITUTE A QUORUM.

SECTION 1.   A quorum for ordinary business at the Annual Council shall consist of such Clergy and Delegates from the Parishes as may be present; but, if the Bishop be not present, such quorum shall have power only to receive reports of committees and Parishes, and to refer the same; to elect the ordinary officers and committees, and to fix the time and place for the next Council.   In the election of a Bishop, two-thirds of the Clergy and a majority of all the Parishes shall be present before the Council proceed to elect. At any *called* Council, other than as provided for in Article II of the Constitution, a quorum shall consist of a majority of all the Clergy entitled to seats, and Lay Delegates from four or more Parishes.

CANON VI.

OF THE OPENING OF THE COUNCIL.

SECTION 1. At the opening of every Council there shall be a celebration of the Holy Communion, and a sermon by a Priest appointed by the Bishop when the Bishop himself does not deliver at that time a sermon or charge. And this *may* be preceded by Morning Prayer.

CANON VII.

OF THE STANDING COMMITTEE OF THE DIOCESE.

SECTION 1. At every Annual Council there shall be elected three Priests and two Laymen, by ballot, as a Standing Committee for the ensuing year. They shall elect, from their own body, a President and Secretary. They shall meet on the summons of the President. To constitute a quorum two Priests must be present, and when required they shall vote by orders.

SEC. 2. It shall be the duty of the Secretary to keep a regular record of their proceedings, in a book which shall belong to the Diocese, and which, together with all papers in the possession of the Committee, shall be open to the inspection of the Committee, or the Council, when required.

SEC. 3. The Standing Committee shall be summoned on the requisition of the Bishop, whenever he shall wish their advice ; and they may meet, of their own accord and agreeably to their own rules, when they may be disposed to advise the Bishop. And the President shall call a meeting at any time, on the request in writing of any two members, or when he may deem it necessary.

SEC. 4. When the Diocese is vacant, through any cause, it shall be the duty of the Standing Committee to call a meeting forthwith, and, after consultation as to the time and place, to summon a special Council of the Diocese, to elect a successor, with all convenient speed; *provided:* That if such vacancy occur within less than six months before the Annual Council there shall be no special Council, but the election of a Bishop shall be deferred until the Annual Council; and during the vacancy, the Standing Committee shall exercise all the powers of the ecclesiastical authority consistent with their character as the administrators of the Diocese under Council.

CANON VIII.

OF THE APPOINTMENT OF STANDING COMMITTEES.

SECTION 1.   At every Council the presiding officer shall appoint standing committees on—

1.   Credentials of Lay Delegates
2.   Ways and Means.
3.   Admission of New Parishes.
4.   State of the Church.
5.   Auditing and Finance.
6.   Unfinished Business.
7.   Constitution and Canons.

And on such other subjects as he may deem requisite to put the Council in possession of properly proposed information for their action.

SEC. 2.   He shall also appoint a committee to be known as the Committee on Judiciary, to be composed of three Layman, the Chancellor to be one and to be chairman, who shall remain as members of such committee until their successors are appointed.

CANON IX.

OF THE ELECTION OF TRUSTEES.

SECTION 1.   Every Council shall elect Trustees for all funds that may be created.

SEC. 2.   A Trustee shall be annually appointed by the Council, who shall be known as the Trustee of the Episcopate

Endowment Fund, and who shall be specially charged with the responsibility for the accumulation and investment of said fund. As often as the amounts received by him shall aggregate the sum of $50 he shall invest the same, under the supervision of the Bishop and Standing Committee of the Diocese. It shall be the duty of the said Trustee to make annual reports to the Council of the condition of said fund and the investment thereof.

CANON X.
OF DEPUTIES TO THE GENERAL CONVENTION.

SECTION 1. Deputies to the General Convention shall be chosen at each Annual Council, and shall continue in office until others are chosen.

SEC. 2. The Deputies to the General Convention shall be elected by ballot, the Clergy and Laity separately electing the Deputies and Substitutes of their respective orders.

SEC. 3. Substitutes for Deputies shall be elected one at a time; and, in the event of the resignation or inability of any Deputy, Clerical or Lay, such vacancy shall be filled by the substitutes in the order of election, and the Journal must show the order of election of substitutes, Clerical and Lay.

CANON XI.
OF PUBLISHING THE JOURNAL.

SECTION 1. The proceedings of the Council shall be published by the Secretary, under the supervision of the Bishop, and duly distributed, unless the Council shall otherwise order.

CANON XII.
OF FAILURE TO ELECT OFFICERS.

SECTION 1. In all cases of failure to elect officers, whether in the Council or in a Parish, the persons last elected shall continue to serve with full power until their successors are elected.

CANON XIII.
OF THE CHANCELLOR OF THE DIOCESE.

SECTION 1. There shall be elected by the Council an officer earned in the law, under the title of Chancellor of the Diocese,.

whose duty it shall be to act as the legal counselor of the Bishop and of the Standing Committee, in matters affecting the interests of the Church, as his professional counsel may be asked or required. The Chancellor of the Diocese shall hold his office for the term of three years, and, in the event of a vacancy, the Annual Council next ensuing shall elect a successor for the full term of three years.

ORDER OF BUSINESS.

1. Calling the Roll.
2. Presentation of the Certificates of Lay Delegates.
3. Appointment of Committee on Credentials.
4. Report of Committee on Credentials.
5. Election of Secretary.
6. Appointment of Standing Committees.
7. Annual Address of the Bishop.
8. Report of the Standing Committee.
9. Reports of Special Committees.
10. Reports of Trustees of the several Funds.
11. Report of the Auditing Committee.
12. Election of Treasurer.
13. Election of the Standing Committee.
14. Report on State of the Church.
15. Election of Deputies to the General Convention.
16. Election of Trustees of the several Funds.
17. *Election of Trustees of the University of the South and other Trustees not specified.
18. Election of Registrar.
19. Election of Chancellor.
20. Report of Committee on Unfinished Business.
21. Miscellaneous Business.
22. Report of Committee on Ways and Means.

*Amended in Sixteenth Annual Council in meeting after 17.

TITLE II.

OF PARISHES AND PARISH MINISTERS.

CANON I.

SECTION I. All vacant Parishes shall be under the pastoral care of the Bishop. He shall provide for public worship, as far as he can, by occasional services of the Clergy, and by fit persons appointed as Lay readers.

CANON II.

SECTION I. When any Parish shall have elected a Rector and he shall have accepted the call, it shall be the duty of the Vestry to file with the Bishop a minute of their proceedings, including the particular agreement on their part and the acceptance of the elected Minister, showing that he accepts on the terms and agreements stipulated by the Vestry. The Bishop shall make record thereof, and the same shall be binding on the parties concerned, and held as a firm contract.

CANON III.

SECTION I. The Rector shall preside at all Vestry meetings, if present, and open the same with prayer, and may advise, but not vote, on any question.

SEC. 2. To the Rector belongs the control of the keys of the Church, and the right to open the Church for public prayer, sermons, catechetical instruction, marriages, funerals, baptisms, and all rights and ceremonies authorized by the Protestant Episcopal Church in America, at all times when he may deem proper.

SEC. 3. The Church building shall never be used for any secular or profane purpose.

CANON IV.

SECTION I. Every Parish Minister shall keep a Parish Register, which shall be a well-bound book, and, as far as may be, uniform throughout the Diocese.

whose duty it shall be to act as the legal counselor of the
bishop and of the Standing Committee, in matters affecting
the interests of the Church, as his professional counsel may b
asked or required. The Chancellor of the Diocese shall hol
his office for the term of three years, and, in the event of
vacancy, the Annual Council next ensuing shall elect a suc
cessor for the full term of three years.

ORDER OF BUSINESS.

1. Calling the Roll.
2. Presentation of the Certificates of Lay Delegates.
3. Appointment of Committee on Credentials.
4. Report of Committee on Credentials.
5. Election of Secretary.
6. Appointment of Standing Committees.
7. Annual Address of the Bishop.
8. Report of the Standing Committee.
9. Reports of Special Committees.
10. Reports of Trustees of the several Funds.
11. Report of the Auditing Committee.
12. Election of Treasurer.
13. Election of the Standing Committee.
14. Report on State of the Church.
15. Election of Deputies to the General Convention.
16. Election of Trustees of the several Funds.
17. *Election of Trustees of the University of the Sou
and other Trustees not specified.
18. Election of Registrar.
19. Election of Chancellor.
20. Report of Committee on Unfinished Business.
21. Miscellaneous Business.
22. Report of Committee on Ways and Means.

*Amended by Sixteenth Annual Council by inserting order 17.

be divided for the purpose of forming a new and independent Parish, within its boundaries, except by express order of the Council.

CANON VIII.

SECTION 1. Congregations, Parishes, and the members thereof, shall never recognize any suspended clergyman, otherwise than as declared by the ecclesiastical authority.

SEC. 2. If any Parish, or the members therof, shall take part with a contumacious Clergyman, they shall forfeit their rights in the Council.

SEC. 3. All parochial property is held by a tenure subject to this rule.

SEC. 4. In case any Congregation should be so far forgetful of the honor of God's Church as to trangress in this matter, it shall be the duty of the Treasurer of the Diocese, or of the Trustees of the General Fund, to proceed at once to recover all the Church's property in such contumacious Parish, and to reduce it to the control of the Diocese.

SEC. 5. The organization of every Parish shall recognize this rule, and, if it be not expressed in the Articles of Association, their admission into union with the Council shall bind them to this law.

TITLE III.

OF CONVOCATIONS, DIOCESAN MISSIONS AND CHURCH EXTENSION.

CANON I.

SECTION 1. The Bishop may divide the Diocese into Districts, naming the town in each District which shall be the center of a Missionary work ; and every Clergyman in the Diocese of every Parish and Missionary Station, shall be assigned to one or the other of the Missionary centers.

7 D

Sec. 2. The Clergy and Laity of each District, when organized, shall constitute a Convocation, and have charge of the Missionary work in the field assigned by the Bishop.

Sec. 3. The Bishop shall appoint one of the Clergy in each District as Dean of Convocation. The Convocation shall elect a Secretary, who shall be a Clergyman, and a Treasurer, who shall be a Layman.

Sec. 4. The Convocation shall be governed by such rules as they shall adopt, with the Bishop's approval, and each shall report, through its Dean, to the Bishop annually.

Sec. 5. The Deans of Convocation shall constitute the Missionary Committee of the Diocese. Until such time as the Bishop shall divide the Diocese into Districts, the Bishop and the Clerical members of the Standing Committee shall constitute said Missionary Committee.

Sec. 6. Every Parish shall, by its Vestry, appoint one Delegate to Convocation.

Sec. 7. In Missionary Stations, the Missionary in charge or Dean of Convocation shall appoint the Lay Delegate.

CANON II.

Section 1. All organized Mission Stations shall be under the control of the Bishop and Missionary Committee.

Sec. 2. All Missionaries shall be appointed by the Bishop.

Sec. 3. Missionary Stations duly organized shall report to the Annual Council the same as Parishes, and shall be entitled to send one Delegate, who shall have the right to debate but not to vote.

CANON III.

In any community where there are twelve baptized adults, one of whom shall be a male communicant, desirous of organizing a Missionary Station, they shall assemble themselves— their own Missionary being present, or, if they have no Missionary, any Clergyman of the Diocese being present and consenting—and adopt the following form of organization, affixing their signatures thereto, and sending a copy of the same to the Bishop of the Diocese for his approval :

" We, whose names are hereunto subscribed, desirous of enjoying the privileges of religious worship and instruction of the Holy, Catholic and Apostolic Church, according to the forms and doctrines of the Protestant Episcopal Church in the United States of America, have, this —— day of ——, A. D. ——, at ——, in the State of Arkansas, formed ourselves into a Congregation, and adopted the following Articles of Association :

"Article I. This Association or Congregation shall be known by the name of the —— Mission.

"Article II. This Association acknowledges, accedes to, and will be governed by, the Constitution, Canons, doctrine, discipline and worship of the Protestant Episcopal Church in the United States, and the Constitution and Canons of the Protestant Episcopal Church in the Diocese of Arkansas.

"Article III. When any person uniting with this Association shall disclaim or refuse conformity to the authorities mentioned in the preceding Article, he shall cease to be a member of this Association, and shall no longer enjoy the privilege of voting in the election of officers, of being elected an officer, or of exercising any function concerning or connected with the said Association ; *but this exclusion shall not affect the spiritual standing of the excluded.*

"Article IV. In this Mission, regular attendants at the services of the Church shall be entitled to vote for officers and on all matters brought before the Easter meeting.

"Article V. The officers of this Association shall be : The Minister in charge as President *ex officio;* a Warden, who must be a male communicant, and appointed by the Minister ; a Secretary and a Treasurer, elected by ballot annually the Monday in Easter week, or as soon thereafter as possible, due notice having been given of time and place of election.

SEC. 2.   The Clergy and Laity of each District, when organized, shall constitute a Convocation, and have charge of the Missionary work in the field assigned by the Bishop.

SEC. 3.   The Bishop shall appoint one of the Clergy in each District as Dean of Convocation. The Convocation shall elect a Secretary, who shall be a Clergyman, and a Treasurer, who shall be a Layman.

SEC. 4.   The Convocation shall be governed by such rules as they shall adopt, with the Bishop's approval, and each shall report, through its Dean, to the Bishop annually.

SEC. 5.   The Deans of Convocation shall constitute the Missionary Committee of the Diocese. Until such time as the Bishop shall divide the Diocese into Districts, the Bishop and the Clerical members of the Standing Committee shall constitute said Missionary Committee.

SEC. 6.   Every Parish shall, by its Vestry, appoint one Delegate to Convocation.

SEC. 7.   In Missionary Stations, the Missionary in charge or Dean of Convocation shall appoint the Lay Delegate.

CANON II.

SECTION 1.   All organized Mission Stations shall be under the control of the Bishop and Missionary Committee.

SEC. 2.   All Missionaries shall be appointed by the Bishop.

SEC. 3.   Missionary Stations duly organized shall report to the Annual Council the same as Parishes, and shall be entitled to send one Delegate, who shall have the right to debate but not to vote.

CANON III.

In any community where there are twelve baptized adults one of whom shall be a male communicant, desirous of organizing a Missionary Station, they shall assemble themselves their own Missionary being present, or, if they have no Missionary, any Clergyman of the Diocese being present and con-

communicants to represent them, subject to the laws and regulations governing parochial representation.

SEC. 2. Notice of the election shall be given on Easter Day, or at the service last preceding the election, after Morning Prayer, and the Congregation duly warned of the importance of the election.

SEC. 3. The Vestry elect shall meet within ten days thereafter, and organize by the election of the Junior Warden, Treasurer and Secretary. As soon as the offices are filled the Secretary and Treasurer, if not re-elected, shall pass over to their successors the books, papers, accounts and moneys in their hands. The Vestry shall then proceed to elect Delegates to represent the Parish in the next Council of the Diocese, and the Secretary of the Vestry, or the Rector, shall give the Delegates-elect certificates to that effect.

SEC. 4. It is, in general, the duty of the Wardens and Vestrymen to consider and determine upon the election of a Minister when the Parish is vacant ; to see that the Minister is well and properly supported, sufficiently and punctually paid ; to make and execute all contracts for the erection of Church edifices, rectories, and other Church buildings ; to provide for their furnishing and repair and due preservation ; to have and to hold all Church property as trustees of the Parish, and as such generally to transact all temporal and financial business of the Parish.

SEC. 5. It is the special duty of the Wardens to see that the Church edifice be kept from unhallowed uses ; that it be kept clean and in good repair, duly lighted and warmed ; to provide a sufficient supply of books and ecclesiastical vestments to be used in the public ministrations by the Minister, and to provide proper elements for the celebration of the Holy Communion and preserve due order during service.

SEC. 6. In the absence of the Rector the Wardens preside at Parish and Vestry Meetings.

SEC. 7. In the absence of the Wardens their duties devolve on the Vestrymen.

"Article VI.   The duties of these officers shall be the same as those of like officers in organized Parishes.

"Article VII.   All lands, tenements, or other property, real or personal, of this Association, shall vest in the Bishop of the Diocese, or under whose supervision it may for the time be, and his canonical successors, to be by him and them held in trust for the benefit of the Mission.

"Article VIII.   We promise to pay the sum of $—— per annum for the support of the Missionary whom the Bishop or Missionary Committee may send to us."

CANON IV.

SECTION I.   The Bishop of the Diocese shall be *ex officio* President of the Missionary Committee.   The Committee shall report, through its Secretary, to the Annual Council. The Treasurer shall receive, hold, and pay out funds, subject to the order of the Committee.   His accounts shall be audited by the Council as a separate and distinct fund.*

TITLE IV.

OF VESTRIES AND WARDENS AND THEIR DU— TIES, ETC.

CANON I.

SECTION I.   Annually, at a meeting on Easter Monday or as soon thereafter as may be, the members of the Parish entitled to vote shall elect not less than three nor more than eleven Vestrymen, of whom the Rector or Minister shall appoint one as Senior Warden and the Vestry shall elect another as Junior Warden.   *Provided:* That the congregation worshipping in the Cathedral Church may, on the Monday in Easter week, or as early thereafter as practicable, elect three

---

*By the action of the Sixteenth Annual Council, Canon IV, as originally proposed, was repealed and Canon V ordered to be numbered IV.

" Article 1. This association shall be known by the name of 'The Rector, Wardens and Vestry of ———— Church.'

"Article 2. This Association acknowledges, accedes to, and will be governed by the Constitution, Canons, doctrine, discipline and worship of the Protestant Episcopal Church in the United States, and the Constitution and Canons of the Protestant Episcopal Church in the Diocese of Arkansas.

" Article 3. When any person, uniting with this Association, shall disclaim or refuse conformity to the authorities mentioned in the preceding Article, he shall cease to be a member of the Association, and shall no longer enjoy the privilege of voting in the election of Vestrymen, of being elected a Vestryman, or of exercising any function concerning or connected with the said Association ; *but this exclusion shall not effect the spiritual standing of the excluded.*

" Article 4. In this Parish all baptized members of the Church, who are duly registered as members of this Congregation, shall be entitled to vote for Vestrymen and on all matters brought before the Easter meeting.

" Article 5. The Vestrymen of ———— Church shall be elected annually, on the Monday in Easter week, or as soon thereafter as may be, by a majority of the voters assembled for that purpose, notice to that effect having been given publicly to the Congregation on the preceding Sunday. The Vestrymen so elected shall continue in office one year or until their successors are chosen.

"Article 6. The Rector of ———— Church shall be elected by the Wardens and Vestrymen in open meeting, which shall be duly convened for that purpose, they having due regard in all such elections to the previously ascertained wishes of the Congregation, and *especially* of the *communicants* of the Church.

" Article 7. No person shall be chosen Rector or Minister, or Associate Rector or Assistant Minister, of ———— Church, or be allowed to exercise any of the functions of the Sacred Ministry in the same, unless he be recognized by the Bishop having charge of this Diocese, or, if there be no Bishop, by the Standing Committee of the same, as an ordained Minister of the Protestant Episcopal Church, in good standing. *Provided*, *That nothing* in this article shall prevent the Wardens and Vestry from inviting any Clergymen of the Protestant Episcopal Church, in good standing, to officiate occasionally in the Church, or interfere with the performance of the usual services by the Lay Readers, duly appointed to so officiate in the absence of the Rector or Minister.

" Article 8. The annual rents, contributions and other revenues raised by this Congregation, shall be applied by the Wardens and Vestry to the maintenance and support of the Rector or Minister, and to such other objects as are connected with the well-being of the Church, and to no other purpose whatever.

"Article 9. This Association, or the Rector, Wardens and Vestry, or other persons in whose name the property of —— —— Church may be vested, shall not, by deed or any other means, without the consent of the Bishop of the Diocese, under his hand given, grant, alienate, or otherwise dispose of, any lands, messuages or hereditaments, in them vested for the use and benefit of said Church, nor charge nor encumber the same to any person whatever.

"Article 10. In case of the dissolution or extinction of this Association for any cause whatever, the lands, tenements and other estates, real or personal, if such there be, shall vest in the Bishop of the Protestant Episcopal Church in this Diocese, or under whose supervision it may for the time be, and his canonical successors, to be by him and them held in trust for the benefit of a future Congregation of the Protestant Episcopal Church which may be formed in the same place or vicinity, and upon the same principles as the present Church and Association."

CANON III.

SECTION 1. Clergymen and Laymen shall exercise due care in signing the papers of candidates for the Ministry, and shall not sign except on personal knowledge or reasonable evidence. And if any fraud or concealment may have been used to obtain certificates, the signers, on evidence of the facts, may revoke their recommendation. And if they shall rashly or unadvisedly, without due care and caution, or through favor, or with corrupt purpose, sign the recommendation of candidates, whereby unworthy or unfit persons may be admitted to the Ministry, whether they be Clergymen or Laymen, they shall be subject to ecclesiastical censure.

TITLE V.

TRIAL OF MINISTERS.

SECTION I. Every Clergymen in this Diocese shall be liable to presentment and trial for the following offenses, to-wit:

First—Crime and immorality.

Second—Holding and teaching, publicly or privately and advisedly any doctrine contrary to that expressly and generally set forth in the standards of the Protestant Episcopal Church in the United States.

Third—Violation of the Constitution and Canons of the General Convention, or of the Constitution and Canons of the Diocese of Arkansas.

SEC. 2. If a Minister of this Church shall be found guilty of any of the offenses enumerated in the foregoing section, he shall be admonished, suspended or degraded.

SEC. 3. In order to bring a Clergyman to trial, a charge shall be made to the Judiciary Committee, signed by at least two of the communicants of the Diocese, one of whom shall be a Priest, affirming that the charge is true and that the accusers will make it good. Thereupon, it shall be the duty of the Secretary of the Committee to furnish the accused a copy of the charge, and require an answer to be filed thereto within thirty days from the date of the receipt of said copy. On the coming in of the answer, a copy of the same shall be furnished the parties making the charge, accompanied by a notice that all proof on the issue, of both parties must be taken and filed with the Secretary within ninety days from the date of the notice.   All proof must be by deposition, taken before an officer authorized to administer oaths, and must be upon reasonable notice.   Both parties have the right to be present at the taking of the depositions and to be represented by counsel.

At the end of the ninety days the hearing shall close, and thereupon the said committee shall consider the charges, and if two members of the same shall deem the charges clearly within the scope of the Canons, and sustained by the proof, it shall be so declared in writing, and they shall file all the papers in the case with the Standing Committee of the Diocese.

In case the accused is a member of the Standing Committee, the two remaining Clerical members shall choose a Priest of the Diocese to supply his place, and for the purposes of this trial the priest so chosen shall be considered a member of the Standing Committee.

SEC. 4.   On the receipt of the presentation and papers, it shall be the duty of the Clerical members of the Standing Committee to consider of the charge, and if in the opinion of at least two of said Clerical members the charge be clearly within the scope of the Canons, and sustained by the proof adduced, they shall impartially select by lot seven Presbyters of the Diocese, to meet on a certain day after ninety days, at a certain place, within which the accused may reside.   Immediately upon their selection, the names shall be forwarded to the accused, and he shall forthwith send to the Secretary of the Standing Committee the names of those to whom he objects, if any.   Three of the seven may constitute the Court, and the accused shall have the right to object to any individual until the number is reduced to three.   If no member is objected to, all that assemble shall sit as a court.   The court shall be judges both of law and fact.

SEC. 5.   The Standing Committee shall be prosecutors in the case, and shall appoint a Judge Advocate, who shall be a Priest of this Diocese.   The Standing Committee shall give the accused sixty days' notice of the time and place of trial, and shall, also, deliver to him, at the same time a copy of the charges preferred against him ; and he shall not be required to answer to anything not contained in the presentment.

SEC. 6. At the time fixed for the trial, the members of the court shall assemble at the place designated, and choose a President and Clerk from their own number ; and they shall, before they proceed, adopt and declare the rules by which the trial shall be conducted, if rules of ecclesiastical trial have not already been set forth by authority. *Provided, however,* That all the evidence heard at the trial shall be reduced to writing at the time it is given, and signed by the witness before he leaves the room.

SEC. 7. The accused shall be allowed counsel, whom he may choose from among the Priests of the Church, and he may also advise with a Lay communicant learned in the law. If the accused decline to choose counsel, the court shall appoint counsel for him from the Priests of the Diocese.

SEC. 8. If the accused shall not appear for trial, without assigning sufficient cause, the court shall proceed against him for contempt, and he shall be suspended by the Bishop from the exercise of all Clerical functions for the space of six months. And if, in the six months, he shall not apply for trial, at any time afterwards, with the consent and advice of the Standing Committee, the Bishop may proceed to pronounce upon the recusant the sentence of deposition from the Ministry.

SEC. 9. But if, in the six months above named, the accused shall appear for trial, the Court may proceed on the presentment originally made, and shall adjudge him guilty or not guilty, according to the evidence. The Court shall render their verdict ; and if it shall be guilty, they shall designate the penalty or degree of censure which, in their judgment, ought to be pronounced against him ; which the Bishop may not exceed, though he may modify it.

Immediately upon rendering the verdict, it shall be the duty of the Clerk of the Court to deliver all the pleadings and

all proof on the issue, of both parties must be taken and filed with the Secretary within ninety days from the date of the notice. All proof must be by deposition, taken before an officer authorized to administer oaths, and must be upon reasonable notice. Both parties have the right to be present at the taking of the depositions and to be represented by counsel.

At the end of the ninety days the hearing shall close, and thereupon the said committee shall consider the charges, and if two members of the same shall deem the charges clearly within the scope of the Canons, and sustained by the proof, it shall be so declared in writing, and they shall file all the papers in the case with the Standing Committee of the Diocese.

In case the accused is a member of the Standing Committee, the two remaining Clerical members shall choose a Priest of the Diocese to supply his place, and for the purposes of this trial the priest so chosen shall be considered a member of the Standing Committee.

SEC. 4. On the receipt of the presentation and papers, it shall be the duty of the Clerical members of the Standing Committee to consider of the charge, and if in the opinion of at least two of said Clerical members the charge be clearly within the scope of the Canons, and sustained by the proof adduced, they shall impartially select by lot seven Presbyters of the Diocese, to meet on a certain day after ninety days, at a certain place, within which the accused may reside. Immediately upon their selection, the names shall be forwarded to the accused, and he shall forthwith send to the Secretary of the Standing Committee the names of those to whom he objects, if any. Three of the seven may constitute the Court, and the accused shall have the right to object to any individual until the number is reduced to three. If no member is objected to, all that assemble shall sit as a court. The court shall be judges both of law and fact.

SEC. 5. The Standing Committee shall be prosecutors in the case, and shall appoint a Judge Advocate, who shall be a Priest of this Diocese. The Standing Committee shall give

for more than three days, the party making the motion shall solemnly affirm that such postponement is sought, not for delay, but that justice may be done, and that he expects thereby to obtain evidence which is material to his cause, and which he cannot now produce.

SEC. 14. Suspensions from the exercise of the functions of the Ministry shall, *ipso facto*, sever the connection between a Clergyman and his Parish.

SEC. 15. If any Clergyman shall be contumacious when suspended, and attempt to perform any of the functions of the Sacred Ministry, the Bishop shall at once cite him before the Standing Committee; and, if the alleged facts be admitted or proven by sufficient evidence, on having been duly cited, such suspended Clergyman shall not appear or give reasons for not appearing, the Bishop, with the consent of the Standing Committee, may proceed at once to pronounce upon said recusant the grave sentence of deposition from the Ministry.

SEC. 16. No Clergyman shall be suspended, or receive any public censure from the ecclesiastical authority of the Diocese, without having been adjudged thereto in the manner provided in this Canon.

SEC. 17. If an accused Clergyman shall, to avoid notice or citation, remove himself out of the Diocese, he may be duly served with all notices by publication in some newspaper published at the capital of the State, or the Church-newspaper which the Bishop shall have adopted as the official organ of the Diocese.

SEC. 18. If there shall be a necessity for the trial of a Clergyman, at any time when the Episcopate of the Diocese is vacant, the Bishop of some neighboring Diocese may, at the request of the Standing Committee, perform all the acts assigned by this Canon to the Bishop of the Diocese.

SEC. 19. Any resort to a civil court on the part of the accused, for the purpose of impeding, delaying, or avoiding trial, shall be treated as contumacy and shall be sufficient cause.

to suspend such Clergyman from the exercise of the Ministry for contumacy, until he shall appear and demand a trial.

SEC. 20. No Clergyman under trial, or suspension, or against whom charges have been presented by the Standing Committee, can be transferred to any other Diocese, or be received therefrom. And if charges are made against a Clergyman who has already obtained Letters Dimissory, said charges shall be sent to the Diocese to which the letters were taken, within six months after the date of said letters, and not later. And if such letters have not been presented and received at the time, the party shall be remanded to his Diocese for trial, and his Letters Dimissory thereby revoked.

SEC. 21. All rights, claims and privileges, which any Clergyman may enjoy, or have a right to enjoy or receive, in the Diocese, by virtue of her general law, or by particular Canon, are, by the sentence of suspension or deposition, *ipso facto*, forfeited and rendered void ; and every Clergyman shall hold his Ecclesiastical rights subject to this tenure.

INDEX.

Domestic Missions, the first Sunday in Advent.

Foreign Missions, the Second Sunday after the Epiphany.

Missions to colored people, the Third Sunday after the Epiphany.

Missions to Indians, the Fourth Sunday after Easter.

The Treasurer is now MR. GEORGE BLISS, to whom all remittances should be sent, at his office,

23 Bible House, New York City.

ANNOUNCEMENT.

The Nineteenth Annual Council of the Diocese of Arkansas will be held (D. V.) in Trinity Cathedral, Little Rock, on the second Thursday after Easter, April 9th, 1891.

W. J. MILLER, Secretary.

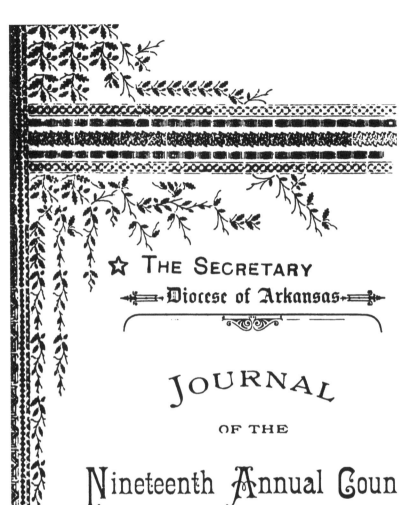

☆ THE SECRETARY

Diocese of Arkansas

JOURNAL

OF THE

Nineteenth Annual Coun

* * 1891 * *

THE DIOCESE OF ARKANSAS.

ORGANIZED A. D. 1871.

— —-

DIOCESAN OFFICERS.

Bishop:

THE RT. REV. H. N. PIERCE, D. D., LL. D.

Standing Committee:

THE REV. INNES O. ADAMS, PRESIDENT.
THE REV. MESSRS. W. J. MILLER AND J. J. VAULX,
MESSRS. M. L. BELL AND P. K. ROOTS.

Secretary of the Council:

THE REV. W. J. MILLER, Hot Springs.

Treasurer:

MR. LOGAN H. ROOTS, Little Rock.

Registrar:

MR. GEORGE H. VANETTEN, Little Rock.

Chancellor:

THE HON. M. L. BELL, Pine Bluff.

Trustee of the Episcopate Fund:

MR. N. B. TRULOCK, Pine Bluff.

Trustees of the University of the South:

THE REV. D. L. TRIMBLE,

MESSRS. GEORGE W. CARUTH AND R. V. McCRACKEN.

Trustee of the General Theological Seminary :

THE REV. GEORGE F. DEGEN.

Deputies to the General Convention :

Clerical.	*Lay.*
REV. I. O. ADAMS,	MR. LOGAN H. ROOTS,
REV. W. J. MILLER,	MR. S. S. FAULKNER,
REV. C. H. LOCKWOOD,	MR. M. L. BELL,
REV. J. J. VAULX,	MR. GEO. W. CARUTH.

Supplementary Deputies to the General Convention :

[In the order of their election.]

Clerical.	*Lay.*
1. REV. GEO. F. DEGEN,	1. ....
2. REV. W. C. RODGERS,	2. DR. W. B. WELCH,
3. REV. J. B. WHALING,	3. MR. W. G. WHIPPLE,
4. REV. C. A. BRUCE,	4. MR. GEO. H. VANETTEN.

Committee on Judiciary :

THE HON. M. L. BELL, PRESIDENT.

MESSRS. WM. M. MELLETTE, AND WM. G. WHIPPLE.

Preacher of Council Sermon:

THE REV. L. F. GUERRY.

LIST OF THE CLERGY OF THE DIOCESE.

Bishop.

RT. REV. HENRY N. PIERCE, D. D. LL. D., Little Rock.

Priests:

REV. INNES O. ADAMS, Rector of Trinity............ ....Pine Bluff

REV. H. J. BROADWELL, Rector of St. John's....... ....Camden

REV. C. A. BRUCE, Rector of St. Andrew's........ .... Marianna

REV. WALLACE CARNAHAN, Rector of Christ Church, Little Rock

REV. GEORGE F. DEGEN, Rector of St. John's....... Fort Smith

REV. J. E. H. GALBRAITH, Ass't at Christ Church, Little Rock

REV. L. F. GUERRY, Rector of Trinity............. ....Van Buren

REV. WM. B. GUION, Rector of St. Paul's........ .... Newport

REV. R. S. JAMES, D.D., Rector St. Andrew's, Mammoth Spring

REV. WM. JONES, Rector of St. Paul's..... ....Batesville

REV. C. H. LOCKWOOD, Rector of St. John's.......... .... Helena

REV. D. F. MACDONALD, D. D .... Diocese of Albany

REV. W. J. MILLER, Rector of St. Luke's ....Hot Springs

REV. D. S. C. M. POTTER, D. D., Rector St. Agnes', Morrilton

REV. WM. C. RODGERS, Dean of Trinity Cathedral, Little Rock

REV. B. W. TIMOTHY............. ....West Indies

REV. D. L. TRIMBLE, Mission at Pendleton .... Pine Bluff

REV. JAMES J. VAULX, Rector of St. Paul's... .... Fayetteville

REV. J. B. WHALING, Missionary in charge of Washington,
   Hope and Nashville............. .... P. O., Hope

Deacon:

REV. PALIN SAXBY, Minister at St. Philip's............... Little Rock

LIST OF PARISHES AND MISSIONS,

WITH NAMES OF LAY DELEGATES.

ARKADELPHIA, St. Mark's.

ARKANSAS CITY, Mission.

BATESVILLE, St. Paul's—Messrs. E. M. Dickinson, J. C. Fitz-hugh, H. S. Coleman.* *Alternates*—John T. Warner,* Wm. R. Ramsey,* W. F. Nelson.*

CAMDEN, St. John's.

DARDANELLE, St. Paul's.

EUREKA SPRINGS, St. James.

FAYETTEVILLE, St. Paul's—Dr. W. B. Welch.

FORT SMITH, St. John's—Messrs. George H. Briscoe, John H. Rogers,* Talbot Stillman.* *Alternates*—Andrew Jackson, John M. Keith, Milton P. Boyd.*

HELENA, St. John's—Messrs. G. Quarles,* S. S. Faulkner, E. C. Horner.

HOPE, St. Mark's—Mr. Edward Thomas.

HOT SPRINGS, St. Luke's—Messrs. J. P. Mellard, G. G. Latta,* Richard Bancroft.* *Alternates*—George W. Colby,* Wm. A. Collins.*

LAKE VILLAGE, Emmanuel.

LITTLE ROCK, Trinity Cathedral—Messrs. George W. Caruth, Wm. G. Whipple, Robert J. Matthews. *Alternates*— Logan H. Roots, P. K. Roots, Arthur Adams.

LITTLE ROCK, Christ Church.

LITTLE ROCK, St. Philip's—Messrs. J. O. W. Alexander, Samuel Spight, Oscar W. Shaw.

MAMMOTH SPRING, St. Andrew's.

MARIANNA, St. Andrew's—Messrs. E. D. Ragland,* James P. Dunham,* Wm. H. Clark, Jr.

MORRILTON, St. Agnes'.

NASHVILLE, Church of the Redeemer.

NEWPORT, St. Paul's—Messrs. L. Minor,* Gustave Jones, Henry A. Ridley. *Alternates*—T. D. Kinman, Jr.,* John T. Flinn,* Board Bond.*

PENDLETON, St. Mary's.

PHILLIPS COUNTY, Grace.

PINE BLUFF, Trinity—Messrs. M. L. Bell, N. B. Trulock, Thos. P. Stoney.* *Alternates*—George E. Valiant,* John Temple,* W. C. Jordan.*

PRESCOTT, St. James'.

VAN BUREN, Trinity—Messrs. H. A. Mayer,* P. D. Scott.*

WASHINGTON, Grace.

WITCHERVILLE, Mission.

Services are held with more or less regularity at the following places:

Altheimer,	Rocky Comfort,	Winslow,
Huntington,	Richmond,	Bentonville,
Huntsville,	Boonsboro,	Conway.

*Not present at the Council.

PROCEEDINGS

OF THE

NINETEENTH ANNUAL COUNCIL.

The Nineteenth Annual Council of the Diocese of Arkansas assembled in Trinity Cathedral, Little Rock, on the second Thursday after Easter, April 9, 1891.

The Holy Communion was celebrated by the Rt. Rev., the Bishop of the Diocese, assisted by the Rev. I. O. Adams and the Rev. J. J. Vaulx. The Council sermon was preached by the Rev. Charles H. Lockwood, from the text, "Ye are witnesses of these things." St. Luke, xxiv : 48.

The Council was called to order immediately after the service, by the Bishop. On calling the roll of the Clergy canonically resident in the Diocese, the following answered to their names:

Bishop:

Rt. Rev. H. N. Pierce, D. D., LL. D.

Priests:

Rev. I. O. Adams,	Rev. R. S. James, D. D.
Rev. H. J. Broadwell,	Rev. C. H. Lockwood,
Rev. W. Carnahan,	Rev. W. J. Miller,
Rev. Geo. F. Degen,	Rev. Wm. C. Rodgers,
Rev. J. E. H. Galbraith,	Rev. J. J. Vaulx,

Rev. Wm. B. Guion.

Deacon:

Rev. Palin Saxby.

The Rev. Dr. James and the Rev. I. O. Adams were appointed a Committee on Credentials, who reported that the following Lay Delegates had been duly elected and were entitled to seats in this Council :

St. Andrew's, Marianna—Messrs. E. D. Ragland, James P. Dunham and William H. Clark, Jr.

Trinity Cathedral—Messrs. George W. Caruth, William G. Whipple, Robert J. Matthews. Alternates, Logan H. Roots, P. K. Roots, Arthur Adams.

St. Philip's, Little Rock—Messrs, J. O. W. Alexander, Samuel Spight and Oscar W. Shaw.

St. John's, Fort Smith—Messrs. George H. Briscoe, John H. Rogers, Talbot Stillman. Alternates, Andrew Jackson, John M. Keith and Milton P. Boyd.

Trinity, Pine Bluff—Messrs. M. L. Bell, N. B. Trulock, T. P. Stoney. Alternates, George E. Valiant, John Temple and W. C. Jordan.

St. Paul's, Fayetteville—Dr. W. B. Welch.

St. John's, Helena—Messrs. G. Quarles, S. S. Faulkner and E. C. Horner.

St. Luke's, Hot Springs—Messrs. J. P. Mellard, George G. Latta, Richard Bancroft. Alternates, George W. Colby, William A. Collins.

St. Paul's, Newport—Messrs. L. Minor, Gustave Jones, Henry A. Ridley. Alternates, T. D. Kinman, Jr., John T. Flinn, Board Bond.

St. Mark's, Hope—Mr. Edward Thomas.

St. Paul's, Batesville—Messrs. Ed M. Dickinson, J. C. Fitzhugh, H. S. Coleman. Alternates, John T. Warner, William Ramsey, W. T. Nelson.

Trinity, Van Buren--Messrs. H. A. Mayer and P. D. Scott.

The Secretary calling the roll, the following answered to their names :

Mr. Wm. G. Whipple, Mr. Robt. J. Matthews,
Mr. Logan H. Roots, Mr. Geo. H. Briscoe,
Mr. Andrew Jackson, Mr. John M. Keith,
Mr. E C. Horner, Mr. S. S. Faulkner,
Dr. W. B. Welch, Mr. M. L. Bell,
Mr. N. B. Trulock, Mr. Wm. H. Clark, Jr.,
Mr. Gustave Jones, Mr. Henry A. Ridley.

There being a quorum of both orders present, the Council proceeded to the election of a Secretary.

The Rev. Mr. Guion nominated the Rev. W. J. Miller for re-election. The vote being taken, Mr. Miller was duly elected.

On motion, a recess was taken until 3 o'clock p. m.

AFTERNOON SESSION.

Thursday, April 9.

The Council reassembled at 3 p. m., the Rt. Rev., the Bishop, presiding.

On calling the roll, the following Delegates answered to their names, who were not present at the morning session:

Mr. J. P. Mellard, St. Luke's, Hot Springs.

Mr. Edward Thomas, St. Mark's, Hope.

Mr. Samuel Spight, St. Philip's, Little Rock.

The first order of business being the appointment of the Standing Committees, they were appointed by the President, as follows:

Committee on Ways and Means.

Rev. Wallace Carnahan,
Mr. Logan H. Roots, Mr. John M. Keith.

On State of the Church.

Rev. C. H. Lockwood,
Rev. R. S. James, D. D., Mr. J. C. Fitzhugh,
Rev. J. B. Whaling, Mr. Robt. J. Matthews,
Mr. Gustave Jones, Mr. Geo. H. Briscoe.

On New Parishes.

The Very Rev. W. C. Rodgers,

Rev. J. E. H. Galbraith,   Mr. Andrew Jackson,   ·

Rev. H. J. Broadwell,   Mr. E. C. Horner.

On Constitution and Canons.

Rev. J. J. Vaulx,

Rev. Geo. F. Degen,   Mr. M. L. Bell,

Rev. I. O. Adams,   . Mr. Wm. G. Whipple,

Rev. Wm. B. Guion,   Mr. S. S. Faulkner,

Dr. W. B. Welch.

On Auditing and Finance.

Mr. N. B. Trulock,

Mr. J. P. Mellard,   Mr. E. C. Horner,

Mr. Henry A. Ridley,   Mr. Edward Thomas.

On Unfinished Business.

Rev. Palin Saxby,   Mr. Wm. H. Clark, Jr.

The Bishop then read his Annual Address. (See Appendix I.)

Mr. S. S. Faulkner moved that those portions of the Bishop's Address touching upon the support of the Episcopate, the Canons of the Diocese and the review of Diocesan year, be referred, respectively, to the Committee on Ways and Means, the Committee on Constitution and Canons, and the Committee on the State of the Church. Carried.

The Rev. William Jones, Rector of St. Paul's Church, Batesville; the Rev. J. B. Whaling, Rector of St. Mark's Church, Hope, and Mr. J. C. Fitzhugh, Lay Delegate from St. Paul's Church, Batesville, appeared and took their seats.

The Rev. Mr. Degen offered the following resolution :

Resolved. That the Bishop be requested to set off a portion of the Diocese as a Convocation District and that all money contributed during the year for Diocesan Missions be devoted to work in that Convocation.

Adopted.

Mr. N. B. Trulock offered the following resolution :

Resolved, That Title IV, Canon I, be amended by striking out the words, "The members of the Parish entitled to vote," and inserting in lieu thereof the words, "the male members of the congregation who are either communicants or owners or renters of pews, or parts of pews, who have during the previous twelve months subscribed towards the expenses of the Parish."

On motion, the above was referred to the Committee on Constitution and Canons.

The Rev. Mr. Vaulx offered the following resolution:

Resolved, That Title IV, Canon I, Section 1, be amended as follows: That after the words " eleven Vestrymen " there be inserted these words, " who shall be communicants of the Church."

On motion, the above was referred to the Committee on Constitution and Canons by the following vote: Yeas, 17; nays, 4.

On motion, the Council adjourned to meet Friday morning at 9 o'clock.

SECOND DAY.

TRINITY CATHEDRAL, LITTLE ROCK, ⎫
Friday, April 10, 1891. ⎭

Morning Prayer was said by the Very Rev. William C. Rodgers, Dean. Immediately after the service, the Council was called to order by the Rt. Rev., the Bishop of the Diocese.

The roll being called, the Rev. L. F. Guerry, Rector of Trinity Church, Van Buren and Mr. Ed. M. Dickinson, Lay Delegate from St. Paul's, Batesville, answered to their names, who were not present at the preceding day's sessions.

The minutes were read and approved.

The Rev. Mr. Adams read the report of the Standing Committee. (See Appendix II.)

On motion, the report of the Trustee of the McMurray estate, which accompanied the report, was referred to the Committee on Auditing and Finance.

The Rev. Mr. Carnahan, having tendered his resignation as a member of the Committee on Ways and Means, and it being accepted, the Rev. William Jones was appointed to take his place.

Mr. Logan H. Roots read his reports as Treasurer of the Diocesan Fund, Diocesan Missions and the Fund for Aged and Infirm Clergy of the Diocese (see Appendix III), which, on motion, were referred to the Auditing and Finance Committee.

The report of Mr. P. K. Roots, as Trustee of the Episcopate Fund, was read (see Appendix IV), and on motion was referred to the Committee on Auditing and Finance.

The Committee on Constitution and Canons recommended the following changes in the Canons:

Resolved, That Title I, Canon I, Section 2, be amended by inserting therein before the word "provided," the words, "and that their Parish is not in arrears on any prior assessment."

Adopted.

Resolved, That Title V, Section 1, be amended by adding thereto at the close thereof, the words: "Fourth. Any act that involves a breach of his ordination vows."

Adopted.

Resolved, That Title V, Section 9, be amended by adding after the words, "The court shall render their verdict," the words "before separation."

Adopted.

The Committee also reported that having considered the proposed amendment to Canon I, Title IV, they did not recommend its adoption.

The Secretary having read a communication from the Superintendent of the School for the Blind, inviting the members of the Council to visit that institution, Mr. William H. Clark, Jr., moved that the invitation be accepted, with thanks, and that the Secretary be instructed to inform Mr. Dye that the members of the Council will visit the school on Saturday, April 11th, at 3:30 p. m. Carried.

The time having arrived for the election of the Standing Committee, the Council proceeded to the election of the same. Nominations being in order, Mr. S. S. Faulkner nominated the Rev. C. H. Lockwood; the Rev. Mr. Galbraith nominated the Rev. Mr. Miller; the Rev. Mr. Degen nominated the Very Rev. W. C. Rodgers, and the Rev. Mr. Jones nominated the Rev. J. E. H. Galbraith. The President appointed the Rev. Mr. Saxby and Mr. Wm. H. Clark, Jr., as tellers, who reported the following vote:

Number of votes cast, 33; necessary to a choice, 17.

Rev. J. J. Vaulx, 15.	Rev. Dr. James, 1.
Rev. W. J. Miller, 26.	Rev. W. Carnahan, 2.
Rev. I. O. Adams, 18.	Rev. Wm. B. Guion, 1.
Rev. Wm. C. Rodgers, 15.	Mr. M. L. Bell, 23.
Rev. George F. Degen, 3.	Mr. P. K. Roots, 19.
Rev. J. E. H. Galbraith, 2.	Mr. George W. Caruth, 9.
Rev. C. H. Lockwood, 10.	Mr. George H. VanEtten, 2.
Rev. Wm. Jones, 2.	Mr. W. G. Whipple, 2.
Rev. C. A. Bruce, 1.	Mr. S. S. Faulkner, 1.

The President announced that the Rev. I. O. Adams, the Rev. W. J. Miller, and Messrs. M. L. Bell and P. K. Roots were elected, and directed the Council to proceed to the election of one clerical member.

The tellers reported the following vote on the second ballot :

Number of votes cast, 32; necessary to a choice, 17.

Rev. W. C. Rodgers, 16.   Rev. J. J. Vaulx, 8.
        Rev. C. H. Lockwood, 8.

No election.

On the announcement of the vote the Rev. Mr. Lockwood's name was withdrawn.

A third ballot being taken, the tellers reported the follow-ing vote:

Number of votes cast, 30 ; necessary to a choice, 16.
Rev. J. J. Vaulx, 15.   Rev. W. C. Rodgers, 13.
                Rev. C. H. Lockwood, 2.

No election.

A fourth ballot being taken the following vote was re-ported:

Number of votes cast, 28 ; necessary to a choice, 15.
Rev. J. J. Vaulx, 16.   Rev. Wm. C. Rodgers, 10.
                Rev. C. H. Lockwood, 2.

Whereupon, the President announced that the Rev. J. J. Vaulx was duly elected.

On motion, a recess was taken until 3 o'clock p. m.

AFTERNOON SESSION.

FRIDAY, April 10.

The Council reassembled at 3 p. m., the Bishop presiding.

Mr. Oscar W. Shaw, Lay Delegate from St. Philips, Little Rock, appeared and took his seat.

The Rev. Mr. Adams moved that the portion of the Bishop's address relating to the death of the Very Rev. Charles H. Proctor, late Dean of Trinity Cathedral, be referred to a committee of three clergymen to report to this Council.   Carried.

The President appointed the Rev. Messrs. Adams, Vaulx and Degen as such Committee.

The Committee on Constitution and Canons recommended the following amendments to the Canons :

Resolved, That Section 3, Title V, be amended to read as follows:

SEC. 3.   In order to bring a clergyman to trial a charge or charges with specifications shall be made to the Judiciary Committee, signed by at least two male communicants of the church, affirming that the same is true and that the accusers will make the charge or charges good.   Should the Bishop have reason to believe that a clergyman is guilty of any or all of the above-named offences he shall notify the Standing Committee of the fact and the clerical members of the Standing Committee shall at once proceed to an investigation of the case, and should they be convinced of the guilt of the clergyman they shall make the charges to the Judiciary Committee, affirming as above. Thereupon, etc.

Adopted.

Resolved, That Section 4, of Title V, be amended by substituting therefor the following:

"SEC. 4. On the receipt of the presentation and papers, it shall be the duty of the clerical members of the Standing Committee to consider of the charge, and if, in the opinion of at least two of said clerical members, the charge be clearly within the scope of the Canons, and sustained by the proof adduced, they shall cite the accused to appear before them, either in person or by representative, together with the Chancellor of the Diocese; and in their presence they shall select by lot, seven Presbyters of the Diocese, to meet on a certain day after thirty days, at a certain place within which the accused may reside. Immediately upon their selection, the accused shall strike off one name from the list of seven drawn; the Judge Advocate shall then strike off a second name; the accused shall then strike off a third name; and lastly, the Judge Advocate shall strike off a fourth, and the three remaining shall constitute the Court. Should the accused refuse to exercise his right of striking off the names as proposed, then the members of the Standing Committee present, shall draw by lot from the seven names first chosen, three to constitute the Court. In case the accused, or his representative, should not appear, then the drawings shall proceed without him. The Court shall be judges both of law and fact."

Adopted.

Resolved, That Sections 8 and 9, of Title V, be amended by inserting the word "three," in lieu of the work "six," wherever it occurs in said sections.

Adopted.

Resolved, That the last paragraph of Section 9, Title V, be amended to read as follows:

"Immediately upon rendering the verdict, it shall be the duty of the Clerk of the Court to notify the Bishop of the action of the Court, delivering to him all the pleadings and evidence in the case, and he shall, at the end of ten days, pronounce sentence, unless the condemned have appealed to him from the verdict of the Court. In case of appeal, the Bishop shall give notice, etc.," striking out the words, "if the accused be found guilty."

Adopted.

Resolved, That Section 11, of Title V, be changed to read as follows:

D 2.

SEC. 11.   On hearing the case on appeal the Bishop, or the Bishop and his assessors, shall confirm the decision of the Court and at once pronounce sentence; or, order a new trial, stating in order the reason and grounds of such decision, in which case, a new Court shall be formed after the same manner as before; or, reverse the decision of the Court according to the finding in the case, and shall declare him innocent accordingly.   When the sentence of the Court is less than deposition, the Bishop may, for reasons satisfactory to him, reprieve, or wholly pardon the accused."   Striking out the words: " But this extraordinary process shall be exercised only in extraordinary cases, and in such a case the Bishop shall report his action to the next Annual Council for approval."

Adopted.

The Committee also offered the following resolution :

Resolved, That the following resolution referred to the Committee on Constitution and Canons, be continued over until the next Annual Council, and that it be considered by them, viz.: " *Resolved*, That Title IV, Canon I, Section 1, be amended by inserting after the words, " eleven Vestrymen," the words, " who shall be communicants."

Adopted.

Mr. N. B. Trulock read the report of the Committee on Auditing and Finance, as follows :

To the Diocesan Council:

Your Committee respectfully report that they have examined the reports of Mr. Logan H. Roots, as Treasurer of the various Diocesan Funds, and of Mr. P. K. Roots, Trustee of the Episcopate Fund, and find them correct.

We regret the resignation of Mr. P. K. Roots, as Trustee of the Episcopate Fund, who has so long and faithfully taken care of this fund.

We are glad to state that the Fund for Disabled Clergy of the Diocese has been invested in accordance with the recommendation of the Committee at the last Council, leaving now on hand uninvested a balance of $73.03.

We file herewith the report of the Rev. I. O. Adams, executor of James Mc-Murray, deceased.

We are sorry to state that some of the Parishes have not responded to the different funds recommended by the Council, and would respectfully urge that they give it their attention in the future.

Respectfully submitted,

N. B. TRULOCK,
E. C. HORNOR,
H. A. RIDLEY,
J. P. MELLARD.
Committee.

On motion, the report was received.

In accordance with the recommendation of the Committee, the Rev. Mr. Jones offered the following resolution :

Resolved, That the Treasurer of each of the Funds be, and is hereby, requested to send to the Wardens of the Parishes a fortnight's notice of each special offering recommended by the Council.

Adopted.

Mr. P. K. Roots having tendered his resignation as Trustee of the Episcopate Fund, and it having been accepted, Mr. J. P. Mellard offered the following resolution :

Resolved, That the thanks of this Council be, and are hereby, returned to Mr. P. K. Roots for his long, able and efficient services as Trustee of the Episcopate Fund.

Adopted by a rising vote.

The Rev. I. O. Adams, President of the Standing Committee, having asked permission to withdraw the report of the Standing Committee for correction, it was, on motion, granted.

The time having arrived for the election of the Treasurer of the Diocese, the Council proceeded to cast ballots for the same. The tellers made the following report:

Number of votes cast, 32; necessary to a choice, 17.

Mr. Logan H. Roots, 28. Mr. S. S. Faulkner, 4.

Whereupon, the President declared Mr. Logan H. Roots duly elected.

On motion, the election of Deputies to the General Convention was made the first order of business for Saturday morning.

On motion, the Council adjourned until 9 o'clock the next morning.

THIRD DAY.

TRINITY CATHEDRAL, LITTLE ROCK, {
Saturday, April 11, 1891.

Morning prayer was said by the Very Rev. Dean Rodgers.

The Council was called to order. by the Rt. Rev., the Bishop.

The minutes of the preceding day were read, and after certain corrections, were approved.

The Rev. Mr. Adams read the revised report of the Standing Committee, which was adopted.

The Rev. Mr. Adams read the following report:

To the Diocesan Council:

Your Committee, to whom was referred that part of the Bishop's Address that officially announces the death of the Very Reverend Charles H. Proctor, late Dean of Trinity Cathedral, Little Rock, Ark., offer the following resolution:

Resolved, That inasmuch as this Council has heard with great sorrow and regret the announcement of the death of our beloved brother, and while we deplore his departure from us, we take comfort in the hope that he has gone before "in the confidence of a certain faith, in the comfort of a reasonable, religious and holy hope;" therefore, the Secretary is requested to prepare and publish in the Journal of the Council a memorial page in testimony thereof.

I. O. ADAMS,
JAMES J. VAULX,
GEORGE FREDERICK DEGEN,
Committee.

On motion, the above report was adopted.

The Rev. Mr. Saxby read the report of the Committee on Unfinished Business, as follows:

To the Diocesan Council:

The Committee on Unfinished Business report that all matters left over from the Eighteenth Council have been disposed of during the Nineteenth, except as follows:

1. A recommendation by the Committee on Constitution and Canons (see page 19 of the Journal), that a change be made in Title V, Section 4, of the Canons, striking out the word "seven" and inserting "five."

2. A recommendation made at the same time, and reported on the same page of the Journal, that the word "ninety" be changed to "thirty," in Section 5, of Title V. (There is no such word as "ninety" in this section, but the word "sixty," in the fourth line is probably the word intended.)

PALIN SAXBY,

W. H. CLARK, JR.,

Committee.

On motion, the report was received and the Committee discharged.

The time having arrived for the election of Deputies to the General Convention, the Council proceeded to cast ballots for the same.

The tellers reported the following vote :

Clerical Deputies.

Number of votes cast, 13 ; necessary to a choice, 7.

Rev. I. O. Adams, 9.	Rev. W. J. Miller, 10.
Rev. Dr. James, 2.	Rev. Wallace Carnahan, 3.
Rev. C. H. Lockwood, 6.	Rev. J. E. H. Galbraith, 3.
Rev. Wm. Jones, 2.	Rev. George F. Degen, 3.
Rev. L. F. Guerry, 1.	Rev. J. J. Vaulx, 6.
Rev. C. A. Bruce, 4	Rev. Wm. C. Rogers, 2.

Rev. D. L. Trimble, 1.

Lay Deputies.

Number of votes cast, 17 ; necessary to a choice, 9.

Mr. Andrew Jackson, 2.	Mr. J. M. Keith, 4.
Mr. S. S. Faulkner, 10.	Mr. Logan H. Roots, 10.
Mr. John D. Adams, 8.	Mr. W. G. Whipple, 2.
Mr. E. C. Horner, 2.	Dr. Welch, 2.
Mr. M. L. Bell, 4.	Mr. J. C. Fitzhugh, 2.
Mr. E. M. Dickinson, 1.	Mr. Wm. H. Clark, Jr., 1.
Mr. George H. Briscoe, 2.	Mr. N. B. Trulock, 3.

Mr. J. P. Mellard, 5.

The President announced the following elected :

Clerical.	*Lay.*
Rev. I. O. Adams,	Mr. Logan H. Roots,
Rev. W. J. Miller.	Mr. S. S. Faulkner.

The President then directed the Council to proceed to the election of two Clerical and two Lay Deputies.

A second ballot being taken, the tellers reported the following vote :

Clerical Deputies.

Number of votes cast, 13 ; necessary to a choice, 7.

Rev. C. H. Lockwood, 7.	Rev. L. F. Guerry, 2.
Rev. J. J. Vaulx, 6.	Rev. George F. Degen, 3.
Rev. J. E. H. Galbraith, 2.	Rev. Wm. Jones, 1.
Rev. Wm. C. Rodgers, 3.	Rev. Dr. James, 1.

Rev. C. A. Bruce, 1.

The Rev. Mr. Lockwood elected.

Lay Deputies.

Number of votes cast, 16 ; necessary to a choice, 9.

Mr. George W. Caruth, 6.	Mr. John D. Adams, 6.
Mr. M. L. Bell, 7.	Mr. J. P. Mellard, 3.
Dr. W. B. Welch, 3.	Mr. H. A. Ridley, 1.
Mr. E. M. Dickinson, 1.	Mr. W. M. Mellette, 1.
Mr. J. M. Keith, 2.	Mr. George H. Briscoe, 1.

Mr. Andrew Jackson, 1.

No election.

THIRD BALLOT.

Clerical Deputies.

Number of votes cast, 13; necessary to a choice, 7.

Rev. Dr. James, 1.	Rev. J. J. Vaulx, 5.
Rev. W. C. Rodgers, 1.	Rev. J. E. H. Galbraith, 3.

Rev. George F. Degen, 3.

No election.

Lay Deputies.

Number of votes cast, 16; necessary to a choice, 9.

Mr. M. L. Bell, 12.	Mr. George W. Caruth, 7.
Mr. John D. Adams, 6.	Mr. W. M. Mellette, 1.
Mr. J. P. Mellard, 1.	Dr. W. B. Welch, 1.
Mr. J. M. Keith, 2.	Mr. Andrew Jackson, 1.

The President announced that Mr. M. L. Bell was elected.

FOURTH BALLOT.

Clerical Deputies.

Number of votes cast, 12; necessary to a choice, 7.

Rev. Dr. James, 1.	Rev. J. J. Vaulx, 5.
Rev. George F. Degen, 3.	Rev. J. E. H. Galbraith, 2.
	Rev. W. C. Rodgers, 1. .

No election.

Lay Deputies.

Number of votes cast, 17; necessary to a choice, 9.

Mr. George W. Caruth, 10.   Mr. John D. Adams, 6.
Mr. N. B. Trulock, 1.

The President announced that Mr. Caruth was elected, and directed the Clergy to cast their ballots for one Clerical Deputy.

FIFTH BALLOT.

Clerical Deputies.

Number of votes cast, 13; necessary to a choice, 7.

Rev. J. J. Vaulx, 7.	Rev. George F. Degen, 2.
Rev. J. E. H. Galbraith, 2.	Rev. W. C. Rodgers, 2.

Rev. Mr. Vaulx elected.

Whereupon, the President announced the Deputies to the General Convention to be as follows :

Clerical.	*Lay.*
Rev. I. O. Adams,	Mr. Logan H. Roots,
Rev. W. J. Miller,	Mr. S. S. Faulkner,
Rev. C. H. Lockwood,	Mr. M. L. Bell,
Rev. J. J. Vaulx,	Mr. George W. Caruth.

The Council then proceeded to the election of Supplementary Deputies. On the ballot being cast, the tellers reported the following vote :

Clerical Alternates.

Number of votes cast, 11 ; necessary to a choice, 6.

Rev. George F. Degen, 7.   Rev. J. E. H. Galbraith, 1.
Rev. Dr. James, 1.   Rev. J. B. Whaling, 1.
Rev. W. C. Rodgers, 1.

Rev. Mr. Degen elected.

Lay Alternates.

Number of votes cast, 17 ; necessary to a choice, 9.

Dr. W. B. Welch, 3.   Mr. John D. Adams, 5.
Mr. W. M. Mellette, 2.   Mr. Edward Thomas, 1.
Mr. W. G. Whipple, 2.   Mr. J. P. Mellard, 1.
Mr. E. M. Dickinson, 2.   Mr. J. C. Fitzhugh, 1.
No election.

SECOND BALLOT.

Clerical Alternates.

Number of votes cast, 11 ; necessary to a choice, 6.

Rev. W. C. Rodgers, 7.   Rev. J. B. Whaling, 1.
Rev. Dr. James, 1.   Rev. J. E. H. Galbraith, 1.
Rev. D. L. Trimble, 1.

Rev. Mr. Rodgers elected.

Lay Alternates.

Number of votes cast, 17 ; necessary to a choice, 9.

Mr. John D. Adams, 8.   Mr. J. P. Mellard, 2.
Mr. W. G. Whipple, 4.   Mr. E. M. Dickinson, 1.
Dr. W. B. Welch, 2.

No election.

THIRD BALLOT.

Clerical Alternates.

Number of votes cast, 11 ; necessary to a choice, 6.

Rev. J. B. Whaling, 4.   Rev. J. E. H. Galbraith, 4.
Rev. L. F. Guerry, 1.   Rev. Dr. James, 1.
Rev. Mr. Saxby, 1.

No election.

Lay Alternates.

Number of votes cast, 17; necessary to a choice, 9.

Mr. John D. Adams, 8.   Mr. W. G. Whipple, 6.
Mr. N. B. Trulock, 1.   Dr. W. B. Welch, 2.

No election.

FOURTH BALLOT.

Clerical Alternates.

Number of votes cast, 11; necessary to a choice, 6.

Rev. J. B. Whaling, 6.   Rev. J. E. H. Galbraith, 4.
Rev. L. F. Guerry, 1.

Rev. Mr. Whaling elected.

Lay Alternates.

Number of votes cast, 16; necessary to a choice, 9.

Mr. John D. Adams, 7.   Mr. W. G. Whipple, 8.
Mr. E. C. Hornor, 1.

No election.

FIFTH BALLOT.

Clerical Alternates.

Number of votes cast, 11; necessary to a choice, 6.

Rev. C. A. Bruce, 7.   Rev. J. E. H. Galbraith, 3.
Rev. L. F. Guerry, 1.

Rev. Mr. Bruce elected.

Lay Alternates.

Number of votes cast, 15; necessary to a choice, 8.

Mr. John D. Adams, 9.   Mr. W. G. Whipple, 6.
Mr. John D. Adams elected.

SIXTH BALLOT.

Lay Alternates.

Number of votes cast, 13; necessary to a choice, 7.

Dr. W. B. Welch, 8.   Mr. W. G. Whipple, 4.
Mr. J. P. Mellard, 1.
Dr. Welch elected.

SEVENTH BALLOT.

Lay Alternates.

Number of votes cast, 10; necessary to a choice, 6.
Mr. J. P. Mellard, 3.   Mr. W. G. Whipple, 4.
Mr. George H. VanEtten, 3.
No election.

EIGHTH BALLOT.

Lay Alternates.

Number of votes cast, 10; necessary to a choice, 6.
Mr. W. G. Whipple, 6.   Mr. George H. VanEtten, 4.
Mr. Whipple elected.

NINTH BALLCT.

Lay Alternate.

Number of votes cast, 8; necessary to a choice, 5.
Mr. George H. VanEtten, 5.   Mr. J. B. Mellard, 3.

The balloting completed, the President announced the Supplementary Deputies, in the order of their election, to be as follows:

Clerical.	Lay.
1. Rev. George F. Degen,	1. Mr. John D. Adams,
2. Rev. W. C. Rodgers,	2. Dr. W. B. Welch,
3. Rev. J. B. Whaling,	3. Mr. W. G. Whipple,
4. Rev. C. A. Bruce.	4. Mr. George H. VanEtten.

Mr. Robert J. Matthews read the report of the Committee on the State of the Church (see Appendix V), which, on motion was received.

Mr. J. O. W. Alexander, Lay Delegate from St. Philip's Church, Little Rock, appeared and took his seat.

The Rev. George F. Degen offered the following resolution:

Resolved, That this Council has heard with sorrow of the recent bereavement of their brother, the Rev. Dr. Potter, in the death of his wife and that we tender him our sincere sympathy in his loss.

Resolved, That the Secretary of the Council be and is hereby requested to forward to the Rev. Dr. Potter a copy of the above resolution.

Adopted by a rising vote.

The Very Rev. Dean Rodgers offered the following resolution :

Resolved, That in the opinion of this Council it is desirable to form a " Diocesan Church Choir Association" for the promotion of a high order of music in the worship of the sanctuary in this Diocese, and that we approve of measures being taken before the adjournment of the Council for the formation of the Society.

Adopted.

The Rev. Mr. Lockwood offered the following resolution :

Resolved, That the Council notes with pleasure the interest that Dean Rodgers takes in the advancement of church music in the Diocese of Arkansas, and extend to him our approval, and request him to call to his assistance in this work the Rev. Mr. Saxby.

Adopted.

The Rev. Mr. Adams offered the following resolution :

Resolved, That Section 2, Canon IX, Title I, be amended by adding the words, " The said Trustee shall execute a bond with the State of Arkansas, for the use of the Diocese of the State, in such sum as may l e required by the Council each year, to be approved by the said Standing Committee and filed there for the faithful discharge of the duties of his office.

Adopted.

Mr. Logan H. Roots moved that a bond of five thousand dollars ($5000) be required of the Trustee of the Episcopate Fund. Carried.

The time having arrived for the election of the Trustee of the Episcopate Fund, and nominations being in order, Mr. P. K. Roots nominated Mr. N. B. Trulock; Mr. Trulock nominated Mr. S. S. Faulkner; Mr. Matthews nominated Mr. George H. VanEtten; Mr. Logan H. Roots nominated Mr. J. P. Mellard. The ballots being cast, the tellers reported the following vote :

Number of votes cast, 31 ; necessary to a choice, 16.

Mr. N. B. Trulock, 13.   Mr. S. S. Faulkner, 8.

Mr. George H. VanEtten, 6.   Mr. Vaile, 3.

Mr. J. P. Mellard, 1.

No election.

A second ballot being taken, resulted as follows:

Number of votes cast, 32; necessary to a choice, 17.

Mr. N. B. Trulock, 17   Mr. S. S. Faulkner, 13.

Mr. Geo. H. VanEtten, 2.

The President then announced that Mr. N. B. Trulock was duly elected.

Mr. Logan H. Roots offered the following resolution :

Resolved, That Section 3, Canon II, Title I, be amended by inserting after the word "Treasurer" in the second line, the words "or Trustee of any Fund."

Adopted.

Mr. M. L. Bell offered the following resolution :

Resolved, That the members of the Council, in addressing the presiding officer, shall address him as "Mr. President," and that this title be given him in the Journal of the Proceedings.

Adopted.   .

Nominations being in order for the office of .Registrar, Mr. Logan H. Roots nominated Mr. George H. VanEtten for re-election to that office.   The vote being taken, Mr. VanEtten was unanimously elected.

On motion a recess was taken until 3 o'clock p. m.

AFTERNOON SESSION.

SATURDAY, April 11.

The Council reassembled, the Bishop presiding.

The Rev. Mr. Jones read the report of the Committee on Ways and Means (See Appendix VI), which, on motion, was adopted.

The Rev. Mr. Degen moved that when this Council adjourns it adjourn to meet in St. Luke's Church, Hot Springs, on the second Thursday after Easter, April 28, 1892.   Carried.

Mr. Logan H. Roots moved that ten ($10) dollars be paid to the sexton of Trinity Cathedral for his services during the Council. · Carried.   .

The Rev. Mr. Adams offered the following resolution:

Resolved, That the thanks of this Council be hereby conveyed to the Dean of Trinity Cathedral and citizens of Little Rock for their kind, courteous and hospitable entertainment of the members of the Council.

Adopted.

On motion of the Rev. Mr. Lockwood, the sum of fifty ($50) dollars was voted to the Secretary, in recognition of his services.

It was moved that the words " ninety " and " sixty " in Sections 3 and 5 of Title V, be changed to read "thirty." Carried.

.   Mr. Logan H. Roots offered the following resolution:

Resolved, That the Council hereby directs the Treasurer of the Diocese, after paying the costs of printing and distributing the Journal of Proceedings and paying assessment of the General Convention, to transfer to the Trustee of the Episcopate Fund whatever, if any, Diocesan Funds are remaining in his hands, excepting and reserving only $50 for incidental expenses, and such additional amount as the President of the Standing Committee may estimate will be required for paying expenses of clerical members attending meetings of such Committee.

Adopted.

On motion, the Secretary was directed to have 500 copies of the Journal printed for distribution

On motion a recess was taken until 5 o'clock, that the members of the Council might visit the School for the Blind.

On reassembling, the Council was called to order, the Bishop presiding.

The Rev. Mr. Jones offered the following resolution:

Resolved, That Section 1, Canon IV, Title I, be amended by adding the words: " In case of failure to make such satisfactory excuse on the part of any Parish, such Parish shall be deemed contumacious and subject to the penalty prescribed in Section 4, Canon VIII, of Title II."

The resolution was lost by the following vote : Yeas, 4; nays, 5.

The Rev. Mr. Vaulx, cffered the following resolution :

Resolved, That the Constitution and Canons as amended be printed with the Journal.

Adopted.

A communication from Mr. John D. Adams was read, in which he declined his election as Supplementary Deputy to the General Convention, which, on motion, was accepted.

The Rev. Mr. Jones moved that the Parishes be required to comply with the provisions of Canon IV, Title I. Lost by the following vote : Yeas, 6; nays, 8.

The Rev. Mr. Lockwood offered the following resolution :

Resolved, That any communicant who shall neglect for twelve months successively to receive the Holy Communion, having opportunity, may, at the discretion of the Rector, be stricken from the list of communicants, unless satisfactory reasons for such neglect be assigned to the Rector.

On motion, the consideration of the above was postponed to the next Annual Council.

The Very Rev. Dean Rodgers offered the following resolution :

Resolved, That this Council put on record its opinion that the Missionary work of the Diocese would be fostered and new work done by the appointment of a general Missionary, and suggests that this matter be brought forward at an early day in the next Annual Council.

Adopted.

There being no further business, on motion, the Council, after prayers by the Bishop, adjourned *sine die*.

H. N. PIERCE,

Bishop of Arkansas.

Attest: W. J. MILLER,

         Secretary.

In Memoriam

THE VERY REVEREND

CHARLES H. PROCTOR

PRIEST

April 19, 1888, appointed Dean of Trinity Cathedral, Little Rock.

April 22, 1888, was instituted into his office by the Bishop of the Diocese.

June 25, 1890, at Pine Bluff, Ark., after a brief illness, entered into rest.

"IN THE COMMUNION OF THE CATHOLIC CHURCH; IN THE CONFIDENCE OF A CERTAIN FAITH; IN THE COMFORT OF A REASONABLE, RELIGIOUS, AND HOLY HOPE."

JESU, MERCY.

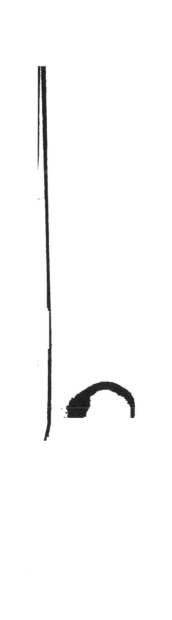

APPENDIX I.

THE BISHOP'S ADDRESS TO THE NINETEENTH ANNUAL COUNCIL.

Brethren of the Clergy and Laity:

I welcome you today to your seats in the Nineteenth Annual Council of the Diocese of Arkansas. Never have we assembled under auspices so favorable and. so encouraging to the friends of the Catholic Church in this State. God has blessed our efforts and rewarded, as He will yet more highly reward in days not now remote, our patient endurance under trials.

When misrepresented and traduced the Diocese has kept on in the even tenor of her ways, without returning evil for evil, and railing for railing; not seeking to avenge herself for wrongs done to her, being well assured that vengeance is the Lord's and that He will in His own good time duly avenge all them that trust in Him.

Extreme forbearance even is neither callousness, weakness nor cowardice, as some vainly suppose. Swift justice may result in a more speedy vindication of the innocent; but a patient and wise delay often secures some great good, which hasty action might destroy, and would certainly jeopardize. That God's mill grinds slowly, because it grinds so very small, is an old adage to the truth of which each century and year adds fresh testimony.

But in glancing at some of the adverse conditions under which the Church in Arkansas has been making advances during the year past, we are turning your attention from the real progress made.   Some of the indications of this progress call for a brief mention.

The increase in our clerical force is encouraging, both as to members and as to *material*.   Three vacancies at important points, which caused us much sorrow and anxiety a year ago, have been well filled.   St. Paul's Church, Batesville, has now as its Rector, the Rev. William Jones, from the Missionary Jurisdiction of Western Texas.   St. John's Church, Camden, has now as its Rector the Rev. Homer J. Broadwell, M. D., from the Diocese of Central Pennsylvania.   St. Paul's Church, Newport, has now as its Rector, the Rev. William B. Guion, from the Diocese of Kansas.   Two other vacancies that have occurred since our last Council have been also well filled :   St. Philips, Little Rock, made vacant by the resignation and the removal to the West Indies of the Rev. B. W. Timothy, is now faithfully served by the Rev. Palin Saxby, who was by me made a Deacon in the Cathedral Church of the Holy Trinity, Little Rock, Ark., on the 20th of November, 1890. There will be found a more detailed account of this ordination in the abstract of my journal under the above date.   Mr. Saxby was formerly a candidate for Holy Orders in the Diocese of Nebraska; and had been duly transferred to this jurisdiction some months before his ordination.

The other vacancy caused by the much-regretted death of the Very Rev. Charles H. Proctor, in June last, has been filled by the Very Rev. William C. Rodgers, who, coming to us from the Diocese of Pittsburg, Pa., became Dean of Trinity Cathedral, Little Rock, on January 1, 1891, and entered on his duties early in the February following.

I conclude what I have to say on this topic by mentioning that on my late visit to St. James' Church, Eureka Springs, I found such signs of fresh life and activity as gave me great hopes that the long vacancy there may soon be filled.

While the increase of the clergy is a source of great encouragement, the condition of the Parishes is not less encouraging.   There are everywhere signs of new life and exi.ibitions of new energy.   One indication of this is seen in the increased number of services and the larger attendance on them during the past Lenten season.   The whole number of persons confirmed since the last Council is somewhat less than in the year previous.   But this fact can be readily accounted for by other causes than a decrease of church life and a want of energy and faithfulness on the part of the Clergy.   Sickness in his own family prevented the Rector of St. Paul's, Fayetteville, from preparing his class in due time for my visitation ; therefore the confirmation was postponed to a later date, which the early falling of Easter this year forbade to be before the meeting of this Council.   The class confirmed at Trinity Cathedral was necessarily small since the Dean has had barely time to become well acquainted with his field.

In a thickly settled neighborhood about four miles west of Fayetteville, where the Rev. Mr. Vaulx has held services at regular periods for some years past, the foundation of a small Church has been laid and the building is in progress.   The Church of St. Mark's at Hope has been much improved in the interior and handsomely seated.   The improvements made in Grace Church, Washington, also have been marked.   The fine chancel furniture placed in St. Luke's Church, Hot Springs, has rendered complete this beautiful house of the Lord; and the large organ, costing $2000, contracted for several months ago, will add greatly to the beauty of the worship.   I am rejoiced to say that a surpliced choir has been introduced into this Church, and I rejoice the more because the attendant circumstances show that many Parishes now deprived of this adjunct to the worship may have it by energetic and well-directed effort ; for this choir, a good one, had been trained by two ladies, to whom the congregation owes many thanks for this and other good works.

A surpliced choir has been introduced into Trinity Church, Pine Bluff, also, and with great success.   The vested choir in

D—3.

St. Philip's Church, Little Rock, originally the second in order of time in the Diocese, after having been disbanded for many months, has been revived again. We have, therefore, four vested choirs in Arkansas. In every case good results in various ways have followed their introduction, and I shall be glad to see the number increased; for this is the best means of securing congregational singing in our Churches. All who can sing will soon add their voices in this important part of public worship, when such a choir leads.

In Trinity Cathedral, Little Rock, something towards finishing the interior has been done, at a cost of about $400. We are looking forward to a continuance of the work at an early date.

One thing I think we may greatly congratulate ourselves upon—very few of the Parishes in Arkansas are in debt, and none of them heavily so. Those that owe the most have their indebtedness well in hand and easy to manage; and during the past year decided advances have been made toward the ex-tinguishment of debts. In a few years I hope we may be able to pay as we go, and to owe no man anything, save love, which we shall always owe, since we can never repay to His children the love that God has shown to us.

I have by implication given an account of the clerical changes in this Diocese since we last assembled, but I repeat them here :

The Rev. William Jones has been received from the Missionary Jurisdiction of Western Texas; the Rev. Homer J. Broadwell, M. D., from the Diocese of Central Pennsylvania; the Very Rev. William C. Rodgers, from the Diocese of Pittsburg, Pa.; the Rev. William B. Guion, from the Diocese of Kansas. The whole number of Priests received by Letters Dimissory is four. Mr. Palin Saxby has been made a Deacon in this Diocese, so that the Clergy added are five in number. The Rev. D. F. MacDonald, D. D., and the Rev. B. W. Timothy are residing beyond the limits of Arkansas, but are still canonically connected with it, as they have not asked for Letters Dimissory. Mr. Charles T. Arnett has been admitted a candidate for the Diaconate in this Diocese. Mr. Palin Saxby was received as a candidate for Holy Orders by Letters Dimissory from the Diocese of Nebraska, and has become a Deacon. Mr. Charles L. Mellard has been received as a candidate for Holy Orders on Letters Dimissory from the Diocese of New York.

We have lost one clergyman by death. On the 25th of June last, while many miles away from Arkansas, I received a telegram informing me that the Very Rev. Charles H. Proctor, Dean of Trinity Cathedral, Little Rock, was lying critically ill at Pine Bluff. This, my first intimation of his illness, was speedily followed by a telegraphic announcement of his death at 3:15 p. m. of the same day. This death, so unexpected, and to me so sudden, was a source of great regret to me on many accounts. I was more than four hundred miles distant, and found, by consulting the time tables of the railroads, that it would be impossible for me to reach Pine Bluff, or even Little Rock, in time for the funeral services, which fact added to my regrets. I learned that the services were said in the Cathedral, and his remains were taken to the home of his childhood, Derby, Connecticut. I have some reasons to believe that had the nature of his disease been better understood at the incipiency of his sickness he might still be among living men in this world of trials, toils and sorrows. We trust he rests in peace.

To this brief sketch of the affairs of the Diocese during the conciliar year just closed I append, as usual, a brief

ABSTRACT OF MY JOURNAL.

My last report closed with the 16th of April, 1890.

April 17: Thursday, in Trinity Cathedral, Little Rock, Arkansas, at 11 a. m., I said the Communion Office, the Rev. J. J. Vaulx reading the Epistle and the Rev. C. A. Bruce reading the Gospel. I delivered a part of my annual *address* and *celebrated the Holy Eucharist.* After the service the Eighteenth Annual Council was called to order, organized and proceeded to business. I presided all day. At 8 p. m. I said Evening Prayer and Rev. Mr. Vaulx preached.

April 18: Friday, at 9:30 a. m., I attended Morning Prayer. I delivered the remainder of my annual *address* and presided in the council all day.

April 19: Saturday I presided in the Council all day. At the evening session, 7:30, the Council adjourned *sine die.*

April 20: Sunday, the second after Easter. At 11 a. m., in Trinity Cathedral, Dean Proctor said Morning Prayer, the Rev. G. F. Degen reading the lessons. I said the Communion, the Rev. D. L. Trimble reading the Epistle, and the Rev. I. O. Adams the Gospel. The Rev. Mr. Degen preached, and I *celebrated the Holy Eucharist,* assisted by Rev. Messrs. Adams and Trimble. At 4 p. m. I attended Evening Prayer.

April 22: Tuesday, I presided at a meeting of the Chapter of Trinity Cathedral.

April 27: Sunday, the third after Easter. At 11 a. m., in St. David's Church, Austin, Texas, after Morning Service, said by the Rector, the Rev. T. B. Lee, I *preached.* At 7:30 p. m. I *preached* again.

May 1: Thursday, St. Philip's and St. James' Day. In St. David's, Austin, I *celebrated* the Holy Eucharist, assisted by the Rector.

May 4: Sunday, the fourth after Easter. At 11 a. m., in St. David's, Austin, Texas, I *preached* and *celebrated the Holy Eucharist,* assisted by the Rector. At 8 p. m. I *preached* again.

May 7: Wednesday, I presided at a meeting of Trinity Cathedral Chapter, at Little Rock.

May 11: Sunday, the fifth after Easter. At 11 a. m., in Trinity Cathedral, Little Rock, I assisted in saying the Morning Service, and *preached.* At 4:30 I assisted in saying Evening Prayer.

May 13: Tuesday, I gave my *canonical consent* to the consecration of Rev. William Ford Nichols, D. D., to be Assistant Bishop of the Diocese of California.

May 15: Thursday, Ascension Day. At 10 a. m., in Trinity Church, Pine Bluff, Ark., I *preached, confirmed* seven persons (females), and *addressed* the class; after which I *consecrated* a brass cross for the altar, *in memoriam* of the Rt. Rev. Henry Champlin Lay, my predecessor in this jurisdiction. Then, assisted by the Rev. I. O. Adams, Rector, I *celebrated the Holy Eucharist.*

May 18: Sunday after Ascension. At 11 a. m., in Trinity Cathedral, Little Rock, I assisted in saying Morning Service, *preached* and *celebrated the Holy Eucharist.* At 4:30 I assisted in saying Evening Prayer.

May 21: Wednesday, I preached at a meeting of Trinity Cathedral Chapter.

May 25: Sunday, Whitsun-day. In Trinity Cathedral, Little Rock, I assisted in saying Morning Service, *preached* and *celebrated the Holy Eucharist.*

May 26: Monday, in Whitsun-week. At 11 a. m., in Trinity Cathedral, I assisted in saying the morning service.

May 27: Tuesday, in Whitsun-week, I said Morning Service in the Cathedral.

May 29: Thursday, at 8:30 p. m., in St. Mark's Church, Hope, Arkansas, I *preached* and *confirmed* eleven persons (five males and six females), and *addressed* the class.

June 1: Sunday, Trinity, at 10:30 a. m., in Trinity Cathedral, Little Rock, I *preached* and *celebrated* the Holy Eucharist.

June 4: Wednesday, at 10 a. m., at Columbia, Tenn., I took part in the Commencement Exercises of the Columbia Female Institute, and delivered the diplomas to the graduating class and *addressed* them. I again commend this admirable school to the people of Arkansas. As a trainer of young ladies, intellectually, morally and socially, it has no superior in this country.

June 8: Sunday, the first after Trinity, at 10:30 a. m., in St. Peter's Church, Columbia, Tennessee, I assisted in saying Morning Service and *preached*.

June 15: Sunday, the second after Trinity, at 10:30 a. m., in St. Peter's Church, Columbia, Tennessee, I took part in the Morning Service, *preached* and *celebrated the Holy Eucharist*, assisted by the Rev. E. Warren Clarke.

June 22: Sunday, the third after Trinity. At 10:30 a. m., assisted by the Rev. E. W. Clarke, I *preached* and *celebrated the Holy Eucharist* in St. Peter's Church, Columbia.

June 24: Tuesday, St. John the Baptist's day. At 10:30 a. m., in St. Peter's Church, I *lectured* on the day and *celebrated the Holy Eucharist*.

June 25: Wednesday. This day I received from Pine Bluff, Ark., a telegram informing me that the Rev. Charles H. Proctor, Dean of Trinity Cathedral, Little Rock, was lying seriously ill at that place. This was soon followed by another announcing his death at 3:15 this afternoon. It was impossible for me to reach Arkansas in time to attend his funeral, else I should have been here. This death was one that caused me unfeigned sorrow. It was very unexpected.

June 26: Thursday, I officiated at the funeral of a child.

June 29: Sunday, the fourth after Trinity. I *preached* and *celebrated the Holy Eucharist* at the Advent Chapel, Columbia, Tennessee.

July 6: Sunday, the fifth after Trinity. In St. Peter's Church, Columbia, Tennessee, I said the Morning Service; *preached* and *celebrated the Holy Eucharist*.

July 13: Sunday, the sixth after Trinity. In St. Peter's Church, Columbia, Tenn., I said Morning Service, *preached*, and *celebrated the Holy Eucharist*.

July 20 : Sunday, the seventh after Trinity. In St. Peter's, Columbia, I said Morning Service, *preached* and *celebrated the Holy Eucharist.*

July 23 : Wednesday, I *administered the Holy Communion* to a sick person.

July 25 : Friday, St. James the Apostle's day. In St. Peter's, Columbia, I said Morning Service, *lectured* on the day and *celebrated the Holy Eucharist.*

July 27 : Sunday, the eighth after Trinity. In St. Peter's, Columbia, I said Morning Service, *preached* and *celebrated the Holy Encharist.*

July 31 : Thursday, I officiated at a *funeral* at Columbia.

August 3 : Sunday, the ninth after Trinity. In St. Peter's, Columbia, Tenn., I said Morning Service, *preached* and *celebrated the Holy Eucharist.*

August 6 : Wednesday, the Transfiguration. In St. Peter's, Columbia, I said Morning Service, *preached* and *celebrated the Holy Eucharist.*

August 10 : Sunday, the tenth after Trinity. In St, Peter's Church, Columbia, Tenn., at 10:30 the Rev. Dr. Dalzell, of Louisiana, said Morning Prayer, read the Epistle and preached. I said the Communion Office and, assisted by the Rev. Dr. Dalzell, *celebrated the Holy Eucharist.*

August 17 : Sunday, the eleventh after Trinity. In St. Peter's, Columbia, I said the Morning Service, *preached* and *celebrated the Holy Eucharist.*

August 20 : Wednesday, in St. Peter's Church, Columbia, I *baptized* and *confirmed* a lady from Osceola, Ark., visiting here for a few weeks; both the baptism and confirmation are registered in Arkansas.

August 23 : Saturday, I officiated at a *funeral* in Columbia, Tenn.

August 24 : Sunday, the twelfth after Trinity. In St. Peter's Church, Columbia, Tenn., I said Morning Service, *preached* and *celebrated the Holy Eucharist.* This closed my

visit to Columbia, and my summer's vacation—the longest one
I have taken in twenty years. It was much needed, and
proved to be very beneficial to me.

August 31 : Sunday, the thirteenth after Trinity. In Trinity
Cathedral, Little Rock, I said Morning Service, *preached* and
celebrated the Holy Eucharist. At 4:30 I said Evening Prayer.

September 7 : Sunday, the fourteenth after Trinity. At
11 a. m., in the Cathedral, Little Rock, I said Morning Service,
preached and *celebrated the Holy Eucharist.* At 4:30 p. m , I
said Evening Prayer.

September 14: Sunday, the fifteenth after Trinity. In
Trinity Cathedral I said Morning Service and Evening Prayer,
preached and celebrated the Holy Eucharist.

September 21 : Sunday, the sixteenth after Trinity. At
11 a. m., in Trinity Church, Guthrie, Oklahoma Territory, I
said Morning Service, *preached and celebrated the Holy Eucharist.* At 7:30, I said Evening Prayer and *preached.*

September 22: Monday, at 7:30 p. m., in Trinity Church,
Guthrie, assisted by the Rev. Mr. Howard, of the Diocese of
Kansas, I *baptized* two children and one adult, *preached* and
confirmed twelve persons (four males and eight females) and
addressed the class.

September 23: Tuesday, in Trinity Church, Guthrie, at
7:30, I *baptized* a child, *preached* and *confirmed* one person
(male).

September 24: Wednesday, at Guthrie, I *baptized* one
adult and one child, and *confirmed* two persons (females). This
makes the whole number confirmed at Guthrie on this visitation fifteen, and two adults and four children have been baptized.

September 25: Thursday, in the Methodist Church, at
Oklahoma City, at 7:30 p. m., I said Evening Prayer and
preached. After the services I called a meeting of those interested in establishing church service at this point. About
twenty persons remained and took part in the meeting. I

appointed three gentlemen and three ladies as a committee to obtain subscriptions, and to secure a place for holding services, etc.

September 28: Sunday, the seventeenth after Trinity. In the Opera House, El Reno, Oklahoma Territory, I said Morning Service and *preached.* After visiting Darlington and Fort Reno I returned Monday evening and took the train for Wichita, Kansas, and thence homeward.

October 5: Sunday, the eighteenth after Trinity. At 11 a. m., in Trinity Cathedral, Little Rock, I said Morning Service, *preached* and *celebrated the Holy Eucharist.* At 4 p. m. I said Evening Prayer.

October 12: Sunday, the nineteenth after Trinity. In the Cathedral, Little Rock, I said Morning Service, *preached* and *celebrated the Holy Eucharist.* At 4 p. m., I said Evening Prayer.

October 19: Sunday, the twentieth after Easter. Having traveled incessantly since Tuesday last, and without taking a sleeping car, the day before being one of heavy rains, I rested in the neighborhood of Philadelphia, Penn.

October 21: Tuesday, attended the Missionary Council at Pittsburg, Penn.

October 22: Wednesday, at the Missionary Council in the morning, and attending the House of Bishops in the afternoon.

October 23: Thursday, attended the House of Bishops all day.

October 26: Sunday, the twenty-first after Trinity, at Little Rock, but forbidden by the physician to go to church.

October 29. Wednesday, I *administered the Holy Communion* to a sick person.

October 31: Friday, I officiated in Little Rock at the *funeral* of a communicant of Trinity Cathedral.

November 1: Saturday, All Saints' Day. In Trinity Cathedral, Little Rock I *lectured* on the day and *celebrated the Holy Eucharist.*

November 2 :   Sunday, the twenty-second after Trinity, I said Morning and Evening Services, *preached and celebrated the Holy Eucharist* in Trinity Cathedral.

November 4 : Tuesday, at 7 p. m., in St. Paul's Church, Batesville, Ark., I *baptized* an adult and *preached*, after which the Rev. William Jones presented, and I *confirmed*, six persons (females), and *addressed* the class.

November 5·: Wednesday, at 7:30 p. m., in St. Paul's Church, Newport, Ark., I said Evening Prayer, *preached* and made an *address* about calling a clergyman to fill the vacancy.

November 9 : Sunday, the twenty-third after Trinity, in Trinity Cathedral, Little Rock, I said Morning and Evening Services, *preached* and *celebrated the Holy Eucharist.*

November 16 : Sunday, the twenty-fourth after Trinity, in the Cathedral, Little Rock, I said Morning and Evening Services, *preached* and *celebrated the Holy Eucharist.*

November 20 : Thursday, assisted by Rev. Messrs. Vaulx and Galbraith, I examined Mr. Palin Saxby for the Diaconate.

November 23 : Sunday, the next before Advent, in the Cathedral, Little Rock, I said Morning Service, *preached* and *celebrated the Holy Eucharist.* At 2:30 p. m., I *baptized* two children. At 4 p. m., I assisted in saying Evening Prayer, and *baptized* a child. The baptisms are all registered at the Cathedral.

November 25 : Tuesday, in St. Luke's Church, Hot Springs, I *preached* and *confirmed* five persons, and *addressed* the class. During the afternoon I *confirmed* a sick man. Thus the whole number confirmed on this visitation is six, of whom two are males and four females.

November 27 : Thursday, Thanksgiving Day, at 9 a. m., in Trinity Cathedral, Little Rock, I *made a deacon*, Mr. Palin Saxby. The sermon was preached by the Rev. William Jones and the candidate presented by the Rev. John E. H. Galbraith. The Rev. Mr. Jones read the Epistle and I *celebrated the Holy Eucharist* and administered alone as usual. At 11 a. m. the service for Thanksgiving Day was duly said by the Rev. Mr. Jones and myself.

November 28 : Friday, at 7 p. m., in Trinity Church, Van Buren, Arkansas. I *preached, confirmed* three persons (three females) and *addressed* the class.

November 30: Sunday, the first in Advent. In the chapel of the State University, Fayetteville, Arkansas, I *preached* the Baccalaureate Sermon. At 4 p. m., I *preached* in St. Paul's Church, Fayetteville.

December 1 : Monday, at 8 p. m., I *preached* at Boonsboro, after Evening Prayer said by the Rev. J. J. Vaulx. The services were held in the Academy chapel.

December 2 : Tuesday in the chapel of the Academy, Boonsboro, at 11 a. m., I *preached*, and assisted by the Rev. Mr. Vaulx, *celebrated the Holy Eucharist.* At 7:30 p. m., I *preached* again and *confirmed* one person (one female). The congregations were large and very attentive. The Rev. Mr. Vaulx has been making occasional visits to this point, twenty miles from Fayetteville, and reached only by stage. In Dr. Blackburn and family (resident here) the church has intelligent and able representatives.

December 7 : Sunday, the second in Advent. In Trinity Cathedral, Little Rock, I said Morning Service, *preached and celebrated the Holy Eucharist.* At 4 p. m., I assisted in saying Evening Prayer.

December 14: Sunday, the third in Advent. In Trinity Cathedral, Little Rock, I said the Morning Service, *preached and celebrated the Holy Eucharist.* I assisted in saying Evening Prayer.

December 21 : Sunday, the fourth in Advent. Assisted by the Rev. C. A. Bruce, I said Morning Service and *celebrated the Holy Eucharist* in the Cathedral, Little Rock. Rev. Mr. Bruce preached. I assisted also in saying Evening Prayer.

December 25 : Thursday, Christmas Day. In the Cathedral, Little Rock, I said Morning Service, *preached and celebrated the Holy Eucharist.*

December 26 : Friday, St. Stephen's Day. I said the Communion Office, *lectured* on the day and *celebrated the Holy Eucharist* in the Cathedral.

December 27 : Saturday, St. John's Day. I *celebrated the Holy Eucharist* in the Cathedral.

December 28 : Sunday, the first after Christmas and Holy Innocents' Day. I said the Communion office and *preached* and *celebrated the Holy Eucharist* in Trinity Cathedral, Little Rock. I assisted in saying the Evening Prayer.

January 1 : Thursday, the Circumcision. In Trinity Cathedral I said the Communion Office, *lectured* and *celebrated the Holy Eucharist*, assisted by the Rev. Palin Saxby.

January 4 : Sunday, the second after Christmas. In Trinity Cathedral, Little Rock, at 11 a. m., the Rev. Mr. Saxby said the Litany and read the Epistle. I said the Communion Office, *preached* and *celebrated the Holy Eucharist*, assisted by the Rev. Mr. Saxby. I assisted, also, at Evening Prayer.

January 6 : Tuesday, the Epiphany. I *celebrated the Holy Eucharist* in Trinity Cathedral, assisted by the Rev. Mr. Saxby.

January 9 : Friday, I *gave my canonical consent* to the consecration of Rev. H. M. Jackson, D. D., to be Assistant Bishop of the Diocese of Alabama. I gave this day *Letters Dimissory* to the Rev. Ralph T. Jefferson to the Diocese of Pittsburg, Pa. Mr. Jefferson belonged formerly to the jurisdiction of the Indian Territory.

January 11 : Sunday, the first after Epiphany. In St. Andrew's Church, Marianna, assisted by the Rev. C. A. Bruce, Rector, I said the Communion Office, *preached* and *celebrated the Holy Eucharist.* At 3 p. m., after Evening Prayer, said by the Rev. Mr. Bruce, I *preached* again.

January 12: Monday, at the Rev. C. A. Bruce's request, I this day *licensed* as *lay reader* Mr. Clark.

January 16: Friday, in St. John's Church, Helena, Ark., at 4 p. m., after Evening Prayer, said by the Rector, the Rev. C. H. Lockwood, I *preached* and *confirmed* one person (male).

January 18: Sunday, the second after Epiphany. At 11 a. m., in St. John's Church, Helena, Ark., assisted by the Rector, I said the Communion Office, *preached*, *confirmed* twenty-one persons (8 males, 13 females), and *addressed* the class; after which I *celebrated the Holy Eucharist.* At 7 p. m., I *preached* again. The number of persons confirmed on this visitation is twenty-two.

January 25: Sunday, Septuagesima. At 11 a. m., in St. John's Church, Camden, Ark., the Rev. Homer J. Broadwell, Rector, said Morning Prayer and read the Epistle. I said the Communion Office, *preached* and *celebrated the Holy Eucharist* At 7 p. m. I *preached* and confirmed three persons (one male and two females), and *addressed* the class.

February 1: Sunday, Sexagesima. I attended Morning and Evening Service in the Church of the Nativity, in Philadelphia, Pa., and assisted in saying the Services. The Bishop of Easton preached in the morning, and delivered an address on " Woman's Work in the Church " in the evening.

February 3: Tuesday, in the Chapel of the See House, in the City of New York, I attended a meeting of the House of Bishops.

February 4: Wednesday. Attending the meeting of the House of Bishops all day. At 9:30 attended a celebration of the Holy Eucharist in Grace Church oratory, and received the sacrament. I this day received the Letters Dimissory of Rev. William Jones, from the Missionary Jurisdiction of Western Texas, and gave canonical notice of my acceptance of the same. I also gave notice to the Ecclesiastical Authority of the Diocese of Indiana of the acceptance of the Letters Di-

missory presented by the Rev. W. C. Tyler, Deacon, now officiating at Guthrie, Oklahoma Territory.

February 8: Sunday, Quinquagesima. In St. Peter's Church, Columbia, Tenn., I *preached* at Morning Service.

February 11: Wednesday (Ash Wednesday), I attended Evening Prayer in Trinity Cathedral, Little Rock. I reached home too late for Morning Service.

February 12: Thursday, at 9 a. m., I attended Lenten Service in Trinity Cathedral. The Very Rev. W. C. Rodgers, Dean of Little Rock, officiated.

February 13: Friday. Attended Lenten Service in the Cathedral.

February 15: Sunday, the first in Lent. In St. Andrew's Church, Mammoth Spring. Ark., assisted by the Rev. R. S. James, D. D., I said the Communion Office, *preached, confirmed* one person (one male), and *celebrated the Holy Eucharist.* At 3 p. m., I *confirmed*, in private, a sick man and his wife, making the number confirmed at Mammoth Spring, on this visitation, three (two males, one female.) At 7 p m. I *confirmed* at Thayer, Missouri, four persons (one male, three females), after Evening Prayer said by the Rev. Dr. James. On this occasion I *preached* and *addressed* the class. This confirmation was held at the request of the Bishop of Missouri, conveyed to me through Dr. James.

February 16: Monday, at Mammoth Spring, Ark., I *baptized* a child at the request of the Rector, Dr. James.

February 17: Tuesday. I *preached* at night in St. Andrew's Church, Mammoth Spring.

February 18: In St. Paul's Church, Newport, Ark., at 4 p. m., I said Evening Prayer and Litany and gave a *lecture.*

February 19: Thursday at 7:30 p. m., in St. Paul's Newport, I said Evening Prayer and *preached.*

February 20: Friday. The Rev. W. B. Guion, who is the newly called Rector of S. Paul's Church, Newport, Ark., arrived this morning and entered at once upon his duties. At 4 p. m., I attended Evening Service and he officiated.

February 21 : Saturday, at Batesville, Ark., at 4 p. m., I attended Evening Prayer in St. Paul's Church. At 7:30 I *confirmed* one person in private (one female).

February 22 : Sunday, the second in Lent. At 11 a. m., in St. Paul's Church, Batesville, Arkansas, the Rector, the Rev. William Jones, said Morning Prayer and read the Epistle. I said the Communion Office, *preached* and *celebrated the Holy Eucharist.* At 7:30 p. m., I *preached* and *confirmed* nine persons (five males and four females), and *addressed* the class. This makes sixteen confirmed in this Parish since the last Council.

February 23 : Monday, at 7:30 p. m., in St. Paul's Church, Newport, Arkansas, I *preached* and *confirmed* eight persons (five males and six females), and *addressed* the class. This Parish, though without a Pastor, has been having regular services during the vacancy by lay reading, and daily Lenten Services, and God has blessed them. This day the Rev. W. B. Guion's Letters Dimissory from the Diocese of Kansas were accepted.

February 25 : Wednesday, attended Lenten Services in the Cathedral, Little Rock, at 9 a. m. and 5 p. m.

February 26 : Thursday, attended Evening Prayer in the Cathedral.

March 1 : Sunday, the third in Lent. At 11 a. m., in St. John's Church, Fort Smith, Arkansas, assisted by the Rector, the Rev. George F. Degen, I said the Communion Office, *preached, confirmed* seventeen persons (four males and thirteen females), *addressed* the class and *celebrated the Holy Eucharist.* At night *preached* again.

March 2 : Monday, in St. Paul's Church, Fayetteville, I assisted in saying Evening Prayer.

March 3 : Tuesday, in St. Paul's Church, Fayetteville, I assisted in saying Evening Prayer and *preached.*

March 4 :   Wednesday, at 7:30 p. m., in St. James' Church, Eureka Springs, Ark., I *preached, confirmed* one person (female) and *joined in Holy Matrimony* Charles T. Arnett and Miss Dilla Blankenship.

March 5 :   Thursday, at 5 p. m., I attended Lenten Services, and at night *preached* in St. Paul's Church, Fayetteville.

March 6 :   Friday, I attended Lenten Services and *preached* at night in St. Paul's Church, Fayetteville.

March 7 :   Saturday, at Van Buren, I *confirmed* in private a sick person (female).

March 8 :   Sunday, the fourth in Lent.   In Trinity Church, Van Buren, Ark., at 10:30 a. m., I said the Communion Office, *preached, confirmed* one person (female), and *celebrated the Holy Eucharist,* assisted by the Rector, the Rev. L. F. Guerry. This makes the whole number confirmed for Trinity Church, Van Buren, since the last report, five.   In St. Agnes' Church, Morrilton, at 8 p. m., I *preached* and *confirmed* one person (male).

March 10 :   Tuesday, I attended Lenten Services in the Cathedral at 9 and 5 o'clock.

March 11 :   Wednesday, I attended Lenten Services in the Cathedral at 9 a. m. and 5 p. m.   At 10 a. m. I *confirmed* at the Cathedral one person (female).   The candidate was presented by the Rev. Mr. Galbraith and the confirmation is for Christ Church, Little Rock.

March 15 :   Sunday, the fifth in Lent.   At 11 a. m., in St. Luke's Church, Hot Springs, I said the Communion Office, *preached, confirmed* three persons (three females), and *addressed* the class.   This makes the whole number nine.   Assisted by the Rector, the Rev. Wm. J. Miller, I *celebrated the Holy Eucharist.*   At night I *preached* again in the same Church. *This day I accepted the Letters Dimissory* presented by Mr. Charles L. Mellard, a candidate for Deacon's and Priest's Orders from the Diocese of New York.

March 16: Monday, at 5 p. m., I attended Evening Prayer at the Cathedral, Little Rock.

March 17: Tuesday, I attended Evening Prayer in the Cathedral.

March 18: Wednesday, attended Morning and Evening Service in the Cathedral.

March 19: Thursday, attended Evening Prayer.

March 20: Friday, in St. Mark's Church, Hope, Ark., at 8 p. m., I *preached* and *confirmed* three persons (three females) and *addressed* the class. The whole number confirmed for St. Mark's, Hope, since the last Council, is now fourteen.

March 22: Sunday, the sixth in Lent. In St. Mark's Church, Hope, at 11 a. m., Rev. J. B. Whaling said Morning Prayer. I said the Communion Office, *preached* and *celebrated the Holy Eucharist*, assisted by the Rev. Mr. Whaling. At 8 p. m., in Grace Church, Washington, Ark., the Rev. Mr. Whaling baptized one adult. I *preached*, *confirmed* three persons (two males and one female) and *addressed* the class.

March 23: Monday in Holy Week. In the Church of the Redeemer, Nashville, Ark., at 8 p. m., after Evening Prayer said by the Rev. Mr. Whaling, I *preached*.

March 24: Tuesday in Holy Week. At 5 p. m., I attended Evening Prayer in the Cathedral, Little Rock.

March 25: Wednesday in Holy Week. Attended Evening Prayer in Trinity Cathedral.

March 26: Thursday in Holy Week. In St. John's Church, Fort Smith, the Rev. Mr. Degen baptized one adult. I *preached*, *confirmed* fourteen persons (fourteen females) and *addressed* the class. This makes the number confirmed for this Parish since the last Council, thirty-one.

March 27: Good Friday. In St. John's, Fort Smith, I assisted in saying Morning Service and *preached*.

March 29: Sunday, Easter Day. In Trinity Cathedral, Little Rock, at 11 a. m., I said the Communion Office, assisted by the Very Rev. W. C. Rodgers and the Rev. Palin Saxby.

D – 4.

Dean Rodgers preached. I *confirmed* four persons (one male, three females), *addressed* the class and *celebrated the Holy Eucharist.* At 3 p. m., in St. Philip's Church, Little Rock, I *preached, confirmed* four persons (two males, two females) and *addressed* the class. At 7:30 p. m., in Christ Church, Little Rock, I *preached, confirmed* twenty-two persons (nine males, 13 females) and *addressed* the class. This makes 23 confirmed for Christ Church since the last Council.

March 30: Monday in Easter Week. In the Cathedral, Little Rock, I attended Morning Prayer and *baptized* a child.

March 31: Tuesday, in Easter week, at 7 a. m., I received the Holy Communion in the Cathedral, Little Rock. At 7:30 p. m., in St. Paul's Church, Newport, Ark., I *preached, confirmed* four persons (two males, two females), and *addressed* the class. This makes the whole number confirmed for this Parish since the last Council, twelve.

April 3: Friday, at 5 p. m., I attended Evening Prayer in the Cathedral, Little Rock.

April 5: Sunday, the first after Easter, at 11 a. m., in Trinity Church, Pine Pluff, after the Litany, said by the Rector, I said the Communion Office, *preached* and *celebrated the Holy Eucharist*, assisted by the Rector, the Rev. I. O. Adams. At 4:30 p. m., I *preached, confirmed* eight persons (one male, seven females), and *addressed* the class. This makes the number confirmed in this Parish since the last Council, fifteen. At the close of the services I consecrated a beautiful processional cross, of solid brass, in memory of Samuel I. Jones, M. D., and made an address to the choir. The surpliced choir was introduced into this church for the first time on Christmas Day last. Their progress in this short time has been remarkable. This Parish has successfully solved the problem of uniting in the choir male and female voices. The arrangement of the seats for the female members, and the distinctive costume worn by them give evidence of the judgment and excellent taste of the Rector and his assistants.

To this abstract of my journal I append the customary

SUMMARY.

Sermons and addresses	118
Confirmed—For Arkansas, 168	
For the Indian Territory, 15	
For Diocese of Missouri, 4	187
Eucharists celebrated	58
Baptisms—In Arkansas, (adults) 2	
(infants) 5	7
Not in Arkansas, (adults) 2	
(infants) 4	6
Total Baptisms	13
Marriages	1
Funerals—In Arkansas, 1	
Not in Arkansas. 3	4
Ordinations (to the Diaconate)	1
Letters Dimissory accepted, Priests	4
Letters Dimissory accepted, candidates for Holy Orders	1
Admitted candidates for Holy Orders	1
Miles traveled	12,883

All of the baptisms administered by me for Arkansas, except four adults, are reported by the Parish wherever the services were performed. The same is true in regard to the marriages and the funerals.

It will be remembered that the conciliar year closing yesterday is a little less in length than a civil year. I always make my yearly report to cover all the time from the opening of one Council to the opening of the next, and I hope that in all parochial reports my example will be followed. It is not proper to extend them from Easter day to Easter day, since we wish to know what has been done during the past conclusive year, and it would be as correct in principle to end the report at Christmas as it is to end it at Easter.

Before closing this address, I wish to call your attention to my altered relations to the Indian Territory. At the meeting of the House of Bishops during the session of the Missionary Council, at Pittsburg, Penn., in October last, a committee was appointed to consider the question of creating a new missionary jurisdiction to embrace the two Territories, the Indian and Oklahoma. On the 4th of February, 1891, the Committee reported in favor of creating said new jurisdiction.

I had the satisfaction of moving that the recommendations be adopted. In doing so, I briefly stated my reasons for desiring this action to be taken. When some Bishops much younger than myself are striving to reduce the extent of their jurisdictions by making the least promising districts new Missionary Jurisdictions to be cared for by the General Board, it did not seem to me unreasonable to desire that my field, exceeding by about 3000 square miles the entire area of England, Wales, Scotland and Ireland, should be reduced to reasonable dimensions. After the Territories on our western border are cut off, there remains in Arkansas alone an extent numbering 6000 square miles more than the great State of New York, with its five Dioceses.

But this was not my main reason for desiring to be rid of the Indian Territory. I was physically able, and very willing to do all required of a Bishop in that field, but I could not bear to feel the responsibility of carrying on work there, and yet to know that I had not at hand, nor attainable by me, the means absolutely required even to fairly begin that work. I was aware that the Church expected me to do something; I knew that my hands were so tied that I could do nothing; I believed that a new man in that field would have a proper backing to enable him to carry out his plans. For the sake of the field itself, I was glad to see it pass into other hands.

In making this new arrangement, my own rights under the Canons were most scrupulously guarded. So far as its relation to the Board of Missions is concerned, Arkansas is still a Missionary Jurisdiction, and her Bishop entitled to draw his salary from the general missionary funds of the Church.

But this state of things lasts only till my death .terminates it, or till such time as I may feel myself justified in releasing the Board from its solemn contract, entered into with me in 1870.   Arkansas under this arrangement is receiving only what she is justly and legally entitled to under the Canon law of the Church, as I explained the matter to you when I became your Diocesan two years ago.   There have been some stupid utterances on this subject since then, but the utterers have merely made an exhibition of their profound ignorance of Canon law and the first principles of justice.

But though this Diocese is provided for as to the present, she must make provision for the future.   Yes; for a future by no means remote.   Therefore, more strenuous efforts ought to be put forth to increase the Episcopate Fund.   It is now at a point where it will grow faster than it has done of its own operation, as we may say.   But as soon as the stringency of the money market is loosened, I hope a course of more energetic action will be entered on.

Another matter to which I call your attention is the importance of doing more for Diocesan Missions.   The Rev. R. W. Anderson, Rector of St. James' Parish, Texarkana, in the Missionary Jurisdiction of Northern Texas, has most kindly held stated services at Rocky Comfort and Richmond, in Southwestern Arkansas.

I have promised him for these services, which have (as you will see from our last journal) already given rich results, $100 a year.   Last year I managed to pay him this sum by other means.   This year I was obliged to draw on our Diocesan Missions Fund.   When I did so, I found that the amount there was a little over $61.   Comparing this with the balance reported at last Council, it appears that not more than $20 have been contributed to this fund in the last twelve months.   I am sure this is not right.   Every cent appropriated by the General Board is now assigned. But we could open new places if I had a few hundred dollars more.   I hope, at least, that you will send in at once enough to enable me to redeem my pledge to the Rev. Mr. Anderson. I do not wish to be compelled to make extra visitations every year, so as to insure the receipt of more than $20 a year for Diocesan Missions. If I can do no better, I must begin to gradually reduce the missionary stipends at the points which have long been aided. I shall regret to be obliged to do this, as the time is hardly yet' ripe for such action.

Now, brethren, I wish you to consider whether the Canons of this Diocese do not call for some changes in order to make them more efficient.

I will ask you in the first place to review Section 2, of Canon I, Title I. This Canon provides for the assessment of the Parishes for the Episcopate Fund and the current expenses of the Diocese. I do not doubt that it was the intention of the framers to require any assessment once laid on a Parish to be paid in full, as a prerequisite to representation in the Diocesan Council, but it is so worded that no back dues can be legally demanded of a Parish that tenders payment of the dues to any Council at which its Delegates may present themselves, though several years may have elapsed since their previous appearance there.

I suggest that the Canon be so changed as to require the payment of all assessments when once laid upon a Parish, and that all assessments unpaid at the time they are due, shall be carried forward as a debt owed by said Parish, which must be paid in order to secure representation in the Council. This debt, however, may be remitted by the Council according to the proviso at the end of the section referred to. The Committee on Ways and Means should report to the Council a list of all delinquent Parishes and cause the same to be published in the Journal.

I would next call your attention to needed changes in Title V, Trial of Ministers. Section 1 is defective in that it omits from its list of offences for which a Clergyman shall be liable to presentment and trial, one which the Church in this country accounts as such. In Section 1, Canon II, Title II, of the Digest of the Canons of the General Convention, we find among the grounds of trial enumerated, this: "Any act which involves a breach of his ordination vows."

Now, while I deny the right of any Diocese to make an offence anything not considered such by the Church in this land, I hold that it has no right to omit from its list of offences anything that the General Canons have declared to be an offence. I presume that the omission referred to was not intentional, but a mere inadvertence.

A second fault found in this Canon is the long time necessarily occupied in proceedings under it. Ninety days and sixty days are not required in this age of postoffices and rapid transit. Not more than thirty days should be allowed to intervene between any two steps to be taken.

Another great defect is that the presentation of a Clergyman for any offence of whatever nature is left almost to chance or to the whims of individuals. While the provision that a charge may be made by two communicants of the Church, one of whom shall be a Priest, is a good one, and ought to be retained, the Canon ought to provide other ways also of reaching an offender. The Clerical members of the Standing Committee ought to be authorized to lay a charge before the Judiciary Committee, and as the Bishop is held responsible for the discipline of his Diocese, he ought to have some power to see that the laws of the Church are not violated with impunity.

I recommend, therefore, that Section 3 of said Canon may be amended by inserting at the close of the first sentence, a clause declaring that the Clerical members of the Standing Committee *may* make charges of their own motion, and that they *shall* make them when the Bishop so requests. This will enable the Bishop to have the case properly investigated when public rumor accuses a Clergyman of violating the

moral, canonical or ritual law of the Church. Now the
Bishop is blamed for not acting, though this Canon binds him
so that he cannot stir. For proof of this, see Section 16.

The fourth section also .requires amendment. The Church
has rights as well as the accused party. Both of these should
be regarded in constructing the Court Ecclesiastical, by whom
the trial is to be had. As the Canon now reads, the accused
has a very large right of challenge and the Church has none.
Let the seven names be drawn as the order now is. Then the
accused shall strike off, from the list of the seven drawn, one
name ; the Judge Advocate shall strike off a second name, then
the accused shall strike off a third name, and, lastly the Judge
Advocate shall strike off a fourth. Then, the Court will in all
cases consist of three members. Should the accused refuse
to exercise his right of striking off the names as proposed,
then the Standing Committee are to draw by lot from the
seven names first chosen, three to constitute the court. In
this way a fair and impartial court may be secured. It
should be furthermore provided that the accused, or someone
acting for him, may be present at the drawings, and in case no
such person appears, then the Chancellor of the Diocese shall
be present and preside at said drawing.

Assertions that have appeared in print within a few years
concerning the mode of rendering the verdict adopted by Ecclesiastical Courts, in some cases, suggests another amendment
of the Canon. It is said that in several cases, the Court, after
hearing the evidence, did not, while assembled, come to a verdict, but separated and went to their homes, and after a lapse
of several days or weeks even, agreed as to the verdict by
corresponding with each other. As to the truth or falsity of
these statements, I cannot say anything, but the wrong of
such a proceeding is so manifest, that I trust you will make
such a thing impossible in Arkansas. In such circumstances,
a Bishop's duty would be to treat the whole affair as a mis-
trial, and order a new Court to be formed. Whether this

Canon can be otherwise improved, I cannot now say. But with these changes, I think it will be the best disciplinary Canon in the American Church.

Before closing these protracted remarks, I have the sad duty of informing you of the affliction that has fallen upon one of the Clerical members of this body. A few weeks ago I met for the first time the beloved wife of the Rev. Dr. Potter, Rector of St. Agnes' Church, Morrilton. She was to start in a few days to visit a near relative in Missouri. I hoped to see her at this Council. A letter lately received informed me of her death, which took place while she was on her visit. A letter from Dr. Potter, dated April 3d, and written at Syracuse, informs me of her burial. The doctor sends kindly greetings to his brethren here assembled. He will make an effort to reach here in time to share in our deliberations, but he had some fears of not being able to do so, as he was then suffering from a severe cold. I know that you all share the sorrow of onr brother and extend to him the warmest sympathy in his great bereavement.

I conclude by asking you not to forget the Diocesan paper established by the authority of this Council in 1889, under the able management of its conservative editor. It is doing what no Church paper in this country can do for the Church in Arkansas. Do not rest till every family in your congregation receives it regularly, and send to the editor such items of news as will make its columns interesting to all readers.

But I have detained you too long, and I close with the prayer that the God of all peace will preside in this Council, and that the Holy Ghost will guide us in all our deliberations, and fill our souls with the grace of our Lord Jesus Christ.

H. N. PIERCE.

APPENDIX II.

REPORT OF THE STANDING COMMITTEE.

To the Ninteenth Annual Council of the Diocese of Arkansas :

The Standing Committee of the Diocese submits the following report :

April 18, 1890, the Committee met in Trinity Cathedral, and organized by electing the Rev. Innes O. Adams, President; and Mr. P. K. Roots, Secretary. The testimonials recommending Mr. Charles T. Arnett, of Mammoth Springs, as a candidate for the Order of Deacons, were read; and he was unanimously recommended to the Bishop as a candidate for the Diaconate.

October 20, 1890, the Committee met in the City of Little Rock on this date, and recommended Mr. Palin Saxby for ordination to the Order of Deacons.

On motion, the authority extended September 19, 1889, in regard to the McMurray property left the Episcopate Fund, was continued in full force and effect until September 30, 1891.

January 5, 1891, the Committee met and gave its consent to the consecration of the Rev. Henry Melville Jackson as Assistant Bishop of Alabama.

The consent of the Committee to the consecration of the Rev. John W. Chapman, as Missionary Bishop of Alaska, was withheld; but with no objection to him.

INNES O. ADAMS, *President.*

APPENDIX III.

REPORT OF THE TREASURER OF THE DIOCESE.

DIOCESAN FUND.

RECEIPTS.

April 19, 1890, balance on hand	$ 646	85
Error in voucher, April 17, 1890		04
April 1, 1891, St. Philip's, Little Rock	10	00
" 9, St. John's, Helena	100	00
" Trinity, Pine Bluff	60	00 ˙
" St. Paul's, Newport	11	50
" St. Paul's, Fayetteville	40	00
" Trinity, Little Rock	125	00
" St. Andrew's, Marianna	15	00
" St. John's, Fort Smith	125	00
April 10, St. Luke's, Hot Springs	50	00
" St. Mark's, Hope	10	00
" St. Paul's, Batesville	20	00
" Trinity, Van Buren	20	00
Total	$1,233	39

DISBURSEMENTS.

May 5, 1890, allowance of Council for Janitor	$ 10	00
May 28, binding five volumes Journal Annual Council	6	25
June 13, printing and distributing reports Investigating Committee	40	60
July 23, W. J. Miller, stationery, postage, etc.	20	73

September 23, printing Journals of the
Eighteenth Council..... ...   145 75
October 20, W. J. Miller. expenses of
Standing Committee ...:.....   4 00
Innes O. Adams, expenses of
Standing Committee 4 00
November 8, P. K. Roots, Trustee
Episcopate Fund...........   315 00
February 2, 1891, W. J. Miller, order
Standing Committee........   7 90   554 23

Balance on hand $679 16

FUND FOR DISABLED CLERGY, ETC.

April 19, 1890, balance on hand $172 38
November 29, Trinity Parish, Pine Bluff...........   9 50
December 1, St. Luke's, Hot Springs 7 10
    "   4, St. John's, Helena 6 75
    "   8, St. John's, Camden...................   5 20
    ..   St. Andrew's, Marianna 5 80
January 22, 1891, Trinity Church, Van Buren........   4 05

Total $210 78

DISBURSEMENTS.

April 29, 1890, expended in purchase, $500,
Building Association Stock, Series No. 7 $ 82 75
Since then, monthly dues for eleven months,
at $5......................... .... 55 00 $137 75

Balance on hand .... $ 73 03

DIOCESAN MISSIONS.

RECEIPTS.

April 19 1890, balance on hand .... $ 41 48
June 13, St. Luke's, Hot Springs 8 05
August 7, Trinity Parish, Van Buren.............. 3 05
February 16, 1891, St. Luke's, Hot Springs 8 40
"   25, Trinity Church, Pine Bluff............ 4 65
March 18, St. John's, Camden 4 60

Total.............................:.........$ 70 23

DISBURSEMENT.

March 25, 1891, Rt. Rev. H. N. Pierce.............$ 61 83

Balance on hand.......................$ 8 40

Respectfully and fraternally submitted,

LOGAN H. ROOTS,

Treasurer.

APPENDIX IV.

REPORT OF EPISCOPATE FUND.

1890   RECEIPTS.

April	21, Cash balance on hand............	$ 58 61
May	16, Loan from P. K. R	216 39
"	21, Int. on lots 10, 11 and 12, block 200..	100 00
July	1, Ladies' Building Association, series No. 4, forty shares, matured......	1000 00
Nov.	8, From Logan H. Roots, Treasurer Diocesan Fund................	315 00
1891		
Feb.	2, St. Luke's, Hot Springs...........	17 15
"	2, Trinity, Pine Bluff..............	7 60
March	2, P. K. Roots.	10 00
"	3, Logan H. Roots.............	15 00
"	31, L. R. Building Association, No. 3, eighty shares, matured.........	2000 00
April	1, St. John's, Camden	5 00
"	11, St. John's, Helena............	15 00
"	11, Interest	28 50
		$3788 25

DISBURSEMENTS.

Building Associations.

May	23, Purchased 20 shares L. R., series No. 7, at "face," 18×$5............	$ 90 00
Nov.	7, Paid in exchange of 40 shares, series No. 7, for 40 shares, series No. 5 .	290 50
		$380 50

Paid monthly dues as follows:

L. R., series No. 3, $20×11 ....$220 00
"   "   No. 5, $10× 6 .... 60 00
"   "   No. 7, $25× 1 . $ 25 00
"   "   No. 7, $30× 5 . 150 00
"   " .   No. 7, $20× 6 . 120 00

$295 00   295 00

L'dies', "   No. 4, $10×3, matured
                July 1................ 30 00
".   "   No. 6, $5×13, and exp. $2 . 67 00

Total paid monthly dues $672 00   672 00
P. K. R. loan returned................   216 39
Cash balance on hand...........   2519 36

$3788 25

PRESENT VALUE OF ASSETS.

Cash 2519 36
40 shares L. R. Building Associatian, No.
    5, paid in $10x52, worth now ......$ 600 00
80 shares L. R. Building Association, No.
    7, paid in $20x28, worth now...... 600 00
20 shares, Ladies' Building Association
    No. 6, paid in $5x52, worth now.... 350 00

Total value building ass'n stock..   1550 00
Bal. due on lots 10, 11 and 12, block 200.$1000 00
    and interest.................... 50 00   1050 00

Invested in McMurray bequest $865 60
Additional worth McMurray bequest es-
    timated by Rev. Mr. Adams..... . 3000 00   3865 60

Total present value of assets $8984 96
Value of funds last report......   7786 68

Increase of funds during year.... $1198 28

I was first chosen custodian of this fund in 1878, when there was none of it. The first asset secured was with money advanced to regain some lots. The money therefor was not all refunded at the time of my report in 1879, and during every year since, I have advanced more or less to make new loans before the old ones matured, in order to make the fund accumulate more rapidly, and I have never made any charge on these advances.

While the duties of the position have, during the entire period, been a labor of love, I now feel impelled to request that some other well wisher of the fund be chosen Trustee.

Respectfully submitted,

P. K. ROOTS,

Trustee Episcopate Fund.

The following is a copy of Mr. N. B. Trulock's receipt for all of the Episcopate Fund, except the "McMurray Bequest," which $3000.00 is still in the hands of Rev. Innes O. Adams as administrator

$5984.96

Received, Little Rock, April 29, 1891, of P. K. Roots, funds and values belonging to the Episcopate Fund of the Diocese to the amount of fifty-nine hundred and eighty-four dollars and ninety-six ($5984.96) cents, as follows, to-wit:

L. R. Bldg. Assn., Series 5, paid in 52×$10, worth..$	600 00
" " " " 7, " 28×$20, worth..	600 00
Ladies Bldg. Assn., Series 6, paid in 52×$5, worth..	350 00
Bishop Pierce's notes on lots 10, 11 and 12, block 200, Little Rock............................	1000 00
Interest due May 5, 1891, on these two notes......	50 00
Notes for amount invested in McMurray bequest..	865 60
Cash..	2519 36
Total...........................	$5984 96

N. B. TRULOCK,

Trustee Episcopate Fund.

REPORT OF INNES O. ADAMS, EXECUTOR OF THE ESTATE OF JAMES McMURRAY, DECEASED.

To P. K. Roots, Trustee of the Episcopate Fund:

Easter Monday, 1890, to Easter Monday, 1891.

The value of the property, the receipts from rents, etc., are about the same as reported last year. The debts have been so much decreased, that there now remains very little to be paid over and above the bequests and the amount borrowed from the Episcopate Fund, with the interest thereon. As a final settlement will probably be made in July, I recommend that the property, when turned over to the Trustee of the Episcopate Fund, be not sold but rented, as the amount invested in the property could not be made to bring a better rate of interest than in this way.

All of which is respectfully submitted,

I. O. ADAMS,
Executor.

D. - 5.

APPENDIX V.

REPORT OF THE COMMITTEE ON STATE OF THE CHURCH.

To the Diocesan Council:

Your Committee on the State of the Church respectfully report as follows :

The year just past has been fraught with much good to the Church. The number of confirmations has not been as large as that of the preceding year. One cause, we deem the greatest, in this falling off in the number of confirmations, is owing to the removal of some of the Clergy from the Diocese, and also to the death of an efficient worker. There are some Parishes yet vacant that would yield a rich harvest of precious souls if they were supplied with a Rector. Some of these Parishes that are now vacant are ably filled as often as possible from the Cathedral Church, as will be seen from the Bishop's Journal.

The Diocese will, we think, be blessed in the addition of the several clergymen who have recently become laborers in this portion of our Lord's vineyard. We bid them welcome, in His name, to this field where the number is comparatively few who rightly teach "the faith once delivered to the saints.

The financial condition of most of the Parishes is, we are glad to report, in better shape than they have been for several years previous to the one just closed. The Episcopate Fund, and the contributions to the Diocesan Missions is, as yet, a mere pittance, and this fact should prick the conscience of every communicant or churchman and churchwoman within the Diocese, and urge us to a more united effort to swell these funds to a far greater magnitude. We believe a better concert of action on the part of the Clergy, and upon the part of the Laity, will produce this desired result.

We regret to report that several Parishes and Missions have failed to pay their legal assessments, and hence, are not represented in the deliberations of this Council. We earnestly hope that hereafter they will comply with the requirements of the Church in this Diocese. The Canons of the Diocese govern every Parish alike, and the failure to attend or take part in the proceedings of the Council does not relieve such Parish of any obligation.

We rejoice to know that the Church is growing stronger each year, and as we believe the Sunday-school to be the nursery of the Church, we most earnestly ask the parents of the children throughout the Diocese to put forth a greater effort to secure the attendance of their children at the Sunday-schools, and upon the services of the Church.

St. John's Hospital, at Fort Smith, is the direct result of indefatigable energy and indomitable preseverance on the part of the Rector of St. John's Church and his estimable wife. It has during the past year been incorporated under the laws of the State of Arkansas, and is now a Diocesan institution. The Bishop is *ex-officio* member of the Board of Trustees. The purchase of grounds, and the erection of more extensive buildings for the accommodation of those who are in distress, is contemplated, and the attention of churchmen and others charitably disposed, is kindly called to this fact, together with the urgent necessity of help in the way of contributions, in order to further this good work, which is now second to none in its character of any in the State.

We would respectfully suggest to the Clergy of the Diocese that they fill out their Parochial reports more completely, as a partial report is misleading, and so indefinite that such a report causes much extra work and discussion for the Committee.

The following report from an unorganized Mission is of so encouraging a character as showing what aid a Mission may give, and has given in a large Parish, to assist the Rector, and to increase the number of communicants in that Parish, that your Committee unanimously adopted it as a part of their report on the State of the Church, and order it set out *verbatim* in this report:

"In regard to a report for St. Paul's Mission, Little Rock, I desire to say that St. Paul's has as yet no regular organization, and is what might be called a chapel of ease to Christ Church. I have heretofore sent in the report of baptisms, marriages and funerals, etc., in the general report of Christ Church Parish. I may add, as to my official acts for the past year, that I have baptized fifteen infants and three adults, performed two marriages, and conducted ten funerals. I also baptized one infant at Newport, when the Parish had no Rector. Except, during the months of July and August, I have assisted every Sunday at Christ Church, and have held divine service at St. Paul's Chapel weekly, and have conducted two Mission Sunday-schools weekly. I held daily Lenten Services at Christ Church during the sickness of the Rector. I presented one candidate for confirmation, and five others instructed at the Mission were confirmed at Christ Church. I have administered the Holy Communion once in private, and also once (7 a. m. Easter morning) at St. Paul's Chapel. St. Paul's Sunday-school has contributed $30 to Indian and Foreign Missions. Donations of Church furniture, etc., to the value of $75 have been contributed by persons connected with the Mission.

"I am, yours respectfully,

"JOHN E. H. GALBRAITH."

(Signed)   C. H. LOCKWOOD, *Chairman*,
R. S. JAMES,
J. B. WHALING,
ROBERT J. MATHEWS,
GEORGE H. BRISCOE,
J. C. FITZHUGH.

Committee.

APPENDIX VI.

PAROCHIAL ASSESSMENTS.

REPORT OF COMMITTEE ON WAYS AND MEANS.

Your Committee very sensibly feel the importance of the Bishop's recommendation that more strenuous efforts be put forth to increase the Episcopate Fund, and earnestly trust that every congregation and individual will be inspired with public spirit and loyalty enough to satisfy this expectation. It is encouraging to find that some Churches, not satisfied with raising the sums assessed by the Council, have, in addition, made liberal voluntary contributions.

The following assessments, made last year, have not been paid:

St. Agnes, Morrilton .... $ 15
St. Andrew's, Mammoth Springs...................... 10
St. Mary's, Pendleton...... 10
St. John's, Camden 15
St. James', Eureka Springs........................... 10
Grace Church, Washington........................... 10
Christ Church, Little Rock........................... 275
Witcherville Mission................................ 8

The following assessments have been made for the ensuing year:

St. Paul's, Batesville...... 25
St. John's, Camden 25
St. James', Eureka Springs........................... 5
St. Paul's, Fayetteville.............................. 50
St. John's, Helena................................. 100

St. Mark's, Hope ....

St. Luke, Hot Springs...............................   ¡

St. John's, Fort Smith................................   1.

Christ Church, Little Rock............................   2;

Trinity Cathedral, Little Rock........................   10

St. Philip's, Little Rock.............................   1(

St. Andrew's, Marianna..............................   15

St. Andrew's, Mammoth Springs......................   10

St. Agnes', Morrilton................................   10

Church of Redeemer, Nashville.......................   5

St. Paul's, Newport   15

St. Mary's, Pendleton.   5

Trinity, Pine Bluff..................................   75

Trinity, Van Buren   20

Grace Church, Washington   10

Mission at Witcherville..............................   5

     Total 960

Respectfully submitted,

            WM. JONES,

            LOGAN H. ROOTS,

            JOHN M. KEITH,

                  Committee.

APPENDIX VII.

PAROCHIAL REPORTS.

ST. MARK'S CHURCH, ARKADELPHIA.

No report.

UNORGANIZED MISSION, ARKANSAS CITY.

No report.

ST. PAUL'S CHURCH, BATESVILLE.

THE REV. WM. JONES, Rector.

E. M. DICKINSON, J. C. FITZHUGH, Wardens.

BAPTISMS: Infants, 3; adults, 3; total, 6. Confirmations, 16. Actual Communicants, 65. Number confirmed persons, 82. SUNDAY-SCHOOL: Teachers, 7; pupils, 80.

Estimated value Church and grounds..............$2600 00
Estimated value Rectory 400 00
Estimated value other Church property 500 00

Total.....................................$3500 00

ST. JOHN'S CHURCH, CAMDEN.

REV. H. J. BROADWELL, M. D., Rector.

C. H. STONE, J. A. REEVES, Wardens.

Number of families, 23. Whole number of souls, 75. Number baptized persons, 60. BAPTISMS: Adults, 1; total, 1.

Confirmations, 3. ACTUAL COMMUNICANTS: total added, 3; removed, 1; total lost, 1; present number, 39. Marriages, 1. Burials, 2. PUBLIC SERVICES: Sundays, 21; other days, 17; total, 38. HOLY COMMUNION: Public, 8. SUNDAY-SCHOOL: Teachers, 4; pupils, 41. Church Sittings, 250. Rectory? Yes.

OFFERINGS.

PAROCHIAL: Communion alms, $8.94; Rector's salary and Parish expenses, $259.55; miscellaneous, Ladies' Guild, from Easter, 1890, $160; total, $428.49.

DIOCESAN: Diocesan Missions, $4.60; aged and infirm clergy, $5.20; Episcopate Fund, $5; total, $14.80.

EXTRA DIOCESAN: University of the South, $5.40.

Total offerings, $448.69.

Estimated value Church and grounds.............$3000 00
Estimated value Rectory....................... 500 00

Total $3500 00
Amount of indebtedness on Church property 62 00

This has been made up almost by guess-work, the Parish register not having been kept up for the past two years. This report only dates from the time I came, the middle of November last (1890). The outlook for a good and healthy growth of the Parish is most encouraging.

ST. PAUL'S CHURCH, DARDANELLE.
No report.

ST. JAMES' CHURCH, EUREKA SPRINGS.
No report.

ST. PAUL'S CHURCH, FAYETTEVILLE.

THE REV. JAMES J. VAULX, Rector.

W. B. WELCH, M. D., AND COL. J. L. CRAVENS, Wardens.

Number of families, 52. BAPTISMS: Infants, 14; adults, 2; total, 16. Confirmations, 1. *Actual Communicants, 128. Marriages, 4. Burials, 5. PUBLIC SERVICES: Sundays, 144; other days, 168; total, 312. HOLY COMMUNION: Public, 85; private, 6; total, 91. SUNDAY-SCHOOL: Teachers, 6; pupils, 90. Church Sittings, 240. Rectory? Yes.

OFFERINGS.

PAROCHIAL: Communion alms, $103.75; Rector's salary and Parish expenses, $992.96; miscellaneous, $457.89. Total, $1554 60.

Diocesan assessment, $40.

EXTRA DIOCESAN: Society for Promulgating Christianity Among the Jews, $4.65.

Total offerings, $1599 25.

Estimated value of Church and grounds	$3500 00
Estimated value of Rectory	3000 00
Estimated value of other Church property	100 00
Total	$6600 00

It has been a matter of great gratification to the Rector that communion alms have so increased, thus enabling the Rector to do so much more, as the almoner of his people, for Christ's poor and afflicted.

ST. JOHN'S CHURCH, FORT SMITH.

THE REV. GEORGE F. DEGEN, Rector.

STEPHEN WHEELER, WM. M. MELLETTE, Wardens.

Number of families, 164. Whole number of souls, 589. Number of baptized persons, 496. BAPTISMS: Infants, 18;

*This includes those at Boonsboro, Bentonville and Huntsville.

adults, 9; total, 27. Confirmations, 31. ACTUAL COMMUNICANTS:
Admitted, 31; received, 31; total added, 62; removed, 21;
died, 3; total lost, 24. Present number of males, 76; females,
199: total, 275. Number of confirmed persons, 275. Marriages, 9. Burials, 26. PUBLIC SERVICES: Sundays, 159;
other days, 126; total, 285. HOLY COMMUNION: Public, 107;
private, 5; total, 112. SUNDAY-SCHOOL: Teachers, 7; pupils
120. Church sittings, 200. Rectory? Yes.

OFFERINGS.

PAROCHIAL: Communion alms, $115.65; Rector's salary
and Parish expenses, $1587.45; miscellaneous, $258; St. John's
Hospital, $1531.86; total, $3492.96.

DIOCESAN: Diocesan assessment, $125; Diocesan mis-
sions, $17; mission at Arkansas City, $4 45; total, $146.45.

EXTRA DIOCESAN: Domestic missions, $61.15; University
of the South, $10.45; American Church Building Fund, $10.3 5;
Jewish missions, $5.55; total, $87.50.

Total offerings, $3726 91.

Estimated value Church and grounds.............$10000   00
Estimated value Rectory.......................   1800   00
Estimated value other Church property..........   705   00

Total $12505   00

ST. JOHN'S CHURCH, HELENA.

THE REV. C. H. LOCKWOOD, Rector.

P. O. THWEATT, GREENFIELD QUARLES, Wardens.

Number of families, 91. Whole number of souls, 402. Number of baptized persons, 398. BAPTISMS: Infants, 15; adults,
6; total, 21. Confirmations, 22. ACTUAL COMMUNICANTS:
Admitted, 25; received, 3; total added, 28; removed, 15;
died, 2; total lost, 17; present number, male, 63; female,
138; total, 201. Number of confirmed persons, 222. Marriages, 2. Burials, 7. PUBLIC SERVICES: 'Sundays, 141;

other days, 150; total, 291.   HOLY COMMUNION: Public, 70;
private, 4; total, 74. SUNDAY-SCHOOL: Teachers, 18; pupils,
140.   Church Sittings, 400.   Rectory?   Yes.

PAROCHIAL: Communion alms, $24.40; Rector's salary
and Parish expenses, $2306.13; miscellaneous, $506.85; Lenten offering for Rectory, $366.90; King's Daughter's Christ-
mas Tree for poor children, $25; total, $3229.28.

DIOCESAN: Diocesan assessment, $100; aged and infirm
Clergy, $6.75; Episcopate fund, $15; for Cathedral, $14.50;
box to St. John's Hospital, $25; total, $161.25.

EXTRA DIOCESAN: Domestic missions, $30; University of
the South, $10; Church building fund, $11; Indian school,
from Woman's Auxiliary, $90; work among Jews, $11.28;
total, $152.28.

Total offerings, $3542.81.
Estimated value of Church and grounds.........$16,000 00
Estimated value of Rectory....................   6,000 00

Total $22,000 00
Amount of indebtedness on Church property.....$ 2,100 00

ST. MARK'S CHURCH, HOPE.

THE REV. J. B. WHALING, Rector.

Number of families, 16.   Whole number of souls, 58.   BAP-
TISMS: Infants, 6; adults, 2; total, 8.   Confirmations, 14.
ACTUAL COMMUNICANTS: Received, 1; removed, 1; total, 35.
Burials, 3. SUNDAY-SCHOOL: Teachers, 4; pupils, 20. Church
Sittings, 125.

PAROCHIAL :   Rector's salary, $300; miscellaneous, $83.20.
Total offerings, $383.20.
Estimated value of Church and grounds...........$1500 00

EMMANUEL CHURCH, LAKE VILLAGE.
No report.

ST. AGNES' CHURCH, MORRILTON.
No report.

ST. LUKE'S CHURCH, HOT SPRINGS.

THE REV. WM. JAMES MILLER, Rector.

JAMES P. MELLARD, GEORGE G. LATTA, Wardens.

Number of families, 82. BAPTISMS: Infants, 11; adults, 3; total, 14. Confirmations, 9. ACTUAL COMMUNICANTS: Admitted, 9; received, 9; total added, 18; removed, 4; died, 1; total lost, 5; present number, 110. Number of confirmed persons, 143. Marriages, 4. Burials, 9. PUBLIC SERVICES: Sundays, 111; other days, 73; total, 184. HOLY COMMUNION: Public, 60; private, 3; total, 63. SUNDAY-SCHOOL: Teachers, 9; pupils, 80. Church Sittings, 400.

OFFERINGS.

PAROCHIAL: Communion alms, $78.21; Rector's salary and Parish expenses, $1664.16; miscellaneous, $2224.50; miscellaneous, additional, $94; raised by "King's Daughters," $600. Total, $4660.87.

DIOCESAN: Diocesan assessment, $50; Diocesan missions, $8.40; aged and infirm Clergy, $7.10; Episcopate Fund, $17.15; Cathedral work, $42.25. Total, $124.90.

EXTRA DIOCESAN: Domestic missions, $8.05; foreign missions, $22.20; University of the South, $8.25. Total, $38.50.

Total offerings, $4830.27.

Estimated value of Church and grounds $25,000 00
Estimated value of other Church property 1,762 60

Total $26,762 60
Amount of indebtedness on Church property $5000

CHRIST CHURCH, LITTLE ROCK.

Rev. Wallace Carnahan, Rector.

Rev. J. E. H. Galbraith, Assistant Minister.

Major John D. Adams, Senior Warden ; Dr. William A. Cantrell, Junior Warden.

Number of families, 356. Souls (about), 1700. Communicants, 620. Sunday-School : Teachers, 36; pupils, (about) 400; total, 436. Baptisms: Adults, 6; infants, 32; total, 38. Confirmations, 23. Marriages, 10. Burials, 25.

OFFERINGS.

Parochial : Communion alms, $253.34 ; Parish expenses, $4299.68 ; city missions, $828.65 ; Church debt, $2443.06 ; Mission Chapel, $250. Total, $8074 73.

Diocesan : Cathedral work, $24.30.

Extra Diocesan : Domestic missions, $116; Jewish missions, $14.50; Indian missions, $23; Deaf-Mutes' missions, $21.60. Total, $195.10.

Total offerings, $8274.13.

VALUE OF CHURCH PROPERTY.

Church edifice and grounds..................$60,000 00
Rectory and grounds......................... 8,500 00
Mission Chapel and lot...................... 1,500 00

Total $70,000 00

TRINITY CATHEDRAL, LITTLE ROCK.

The Very Rev. William Cunningham Rodgers, Dean.

Messrs. G. W. Caruth, W. G. Whipple, Wardens.

Number of families, about 60. Baptisms, 16. Confirmations, 4. Actual Communicants, 100. Number of confirmed persons, about 200. Marriages, 3. Burials, 6. Public Services (Since February 8, 1891): Sundays, 27; other days, 80;

total, 107. Holy Communion (Since February 8, 1891), 19. SUNDAY-SCHOOL : Teachers, 6 ; pupils, 40.

OFFERINGS.

PAROCHIAL : Rector's salary and Parish expenses from February 1, 1891, to date, $350.

Estimated value of Church and grounds..........$18,000 00

Amount of indebtedness on Church property 1,500 00

This can only be a partial and approximate report, inasmuch as there has been no regular work for a large portion of the twelve months last past.

ST. PHILIP'S CHURCH, LITTLE ROCK.

THE REV. PALIN SAXBY, Minister.

OSCAR W. SHAW, CHARLES S. WALLACE, Wardens.

Report for December 1, 1890 to April 9, 1891.

*Number of families, 50. *Whole number of souls, 100. *Number baptized persons, 75. BAPTISMS : Infants, 11. Confirmations, 4. ACTUAL COMMUNICANTS : Admitted, 4 ; received, 1 ; total added, 5 ; removed, 6 ; died, 1 ; withdrawn, 1 ; total lost, 8 ; present number, male, 11 ; female, 18 ; total, 29. Number confirmed persons, 29. PUBLIC SERVICES : Sundays, 27 ; other days, 57 ; total, 84. Holy Communion, 2. SUNDAY-SCHOOL : Teachers, 4 ; pupils, 57. Church Sittings, 200.

OFFERINGS.

PAROCHIAL : Communion alms, 90 cents; Rector's salary and Parish expenses, $28 40; total, $29.30.

Diocesan assessment, $10.

Total offerings, $39.30.

Estimated value Church and grounds..............$1900 00

*Approximate.

PAROCHIAL REPORT OF ST. PHILIP'S CHURCH FROM APRIL 20, TO DECEMBER 1, 1890.

NUMBER OF SERVICES HELD: On Sundays, 62; on week days, 4; total, 66. Number of Communicants, 32. Marriages, 2. Total amount of offerings, $60.85. Number of Sunday-School scholars on roll, 50.

ST. ANDREW'S CHURCH, MAMMOTH SPRING.

THE REV. RICHARD S. JAMES, D. D., Rector.

Number of families, 12. Whole number of souls, 60. Number of baptized persons, 50. BAPTISMS: Infants, 7; adults, 3; total, 10. Confirmations, 4. ACTUAL COMMUNICANTS: Received, 4; total added, 7; removed, 3; died, 1; total lost, 4. Present number, males, 10; females, 15; total, 25. Burials, 2. PUBLIC SERVICES: Sundays, 64; other days, 16; total, 80. HOLY COMMUNION: Public, 14; private, 4; total, 18. SUNDAY-SCHOOL: Teachers, 5; pupils, 45. Church Sittings, 150. Rectory? Yes.

OFFERINGS.

· PAROCHIAL: Communion alms, $15; Rector's salary and Parish expenses, $325; total, $340.

DIOCESAN: Miscellaneous, $20.

Total offerings, $360.

Estimated value Church and grounds............ ....$1250 00
Estimated value Rectory........,................. 1000 00

Total ....,..........$2250 00
Amount of indebtedness on Church property...... 240 00

ST. ANDREW'S CHURCH, MARIANNA.

THE REV. C. A. BRUCE, Rector.

JAMES P. DUNHAM, F. H. GOVAN, Wardens.

Number of families, 22. Whole number of souls, 87. number baptized persons, 80. BAPTISMS: Infants, 2; adults,

1; total, 3. ACTUAL COMMUNICANTS: Received, 7; total added, 7; removed, 1; suspended, 1; total lost, 2; present number, male, 13; female, 29; total, 42. Number confirmed persons, 44. Marriages, 2. PUBLIC SERVICES: Sundays, 120; other days, 10; total, 130. HOLY COMMUNION: Public, 45: total, 45. SUNDAY-SCHOOL: Teachers, 6; pupils, 35. Church sittings, 115.

OFFERINGS.

PAROCHIAL: Communion alms, Rector's salary and Parish expenses, $345 35.

DIOCESAN: Diocesan assessment, $15.

EXTRA DIOCESAN: Domestic missions, $5; St. John's, Louisville, $4.40; total, $9.40.

Total offerings, $369.75.

Estimated value Church and grounds................$3000

CHURCH OF THE REDEEMER, NASHVILLE.

THE REV. J. B. WHALING, Rector.

Number of families, 4. Whole number of souls, 13. BAPTISMS: Adults, 1. Number confirmed persons, 8. Burials, 1.

ST. PAUL'S CHURCH, NEWPORT.

REV. W. B. GUION, M. A., PH. D., Rector.

COL. L. MINOR, G. JONES, Wardens.

BAPTISMS: Infants, 2; adults, 7; total, 9. Confirmations, 12. Number confirmed persons, 136. Burials, 1. PUBLIC SERVICES: Sundays, 22; other days, 35; total, 57. HOLY COMMUNION: Public, 3. Sunday-school, teachers and pupils, 88. Total offerings, $406.43.

This report is imperfect, as the Rector has been in charge about two months only, and previous to this length of time no records of the work for the year can be had.

GRACE CHURCH, PHILLIPS COUNTY.

No report.

TRINITY CHURCH, PINE BLUFF.

THE REV. INNES O. ADAMS, Rector.

M. L. BELL AND N. B. TRULOCK, Wardens.

Number of families, 107; whole number of souls, 371. Number baptized persons, 23. BAPTISMS: Infants, 10; adults, 1; Total, 11. Confirmations, 15. ACTUAL COMMUNICANTS: Admitted, 15; received, 24; total added, 39; removed, 2; died, 1; total lost, 3; present number, male, 51; female, 155; total, 206. Number confirmed persons, 222. Marriages, 5. Burials, 8. PUBLIC SERVICES: Sundays, 165; other days, 50; total, 215. HOLY COMMUNION: Public, 25; private, 2; total, 27. SUNDAY-SCHOOL: Teachers, 8 pupils, 100. Church Sittings, 450. Rectory? Yes.

OFFERINGS.

PAROCHIAL: Communion alms, $31 70; Rector's salary and Parish expenses, $1181.00; miscellaneous, $708.15; total, $1920.85.

DIOCESAN: Diocesan assessment, $60; Diocesan missions, $4.65; aged and infirm Clergy, $9.50; Episcopate fund, $7.60; total, $81.75.

EXTRA DIOCESAN: Prayer-book Society, $7; Domestic missions, $4; University of the South, $4; Church Society for promoting Christianity among the Jews, $3.55; Church building fund, $5; total, $19.55.

Total offerings, $2022.15.

Estimated value of Church and grounds.......... $12,000 00
Estimated value of Rectory 3,500 00
Estimated value of other Church property........ 1,000 00

Total $16,500 00
Amount of indebtedness on Church property ..... None

D—6.

ST. JAMES' CHURCH, PRESCOTT.
No report.

GRACE CHURCH, WASHINGTON.
Rev. J. B. Whaling, Rector.

Number of families, 11. Whole number of souls, 43. Number of baptized persons, 16. Baptisms: Infants, 4; adults, 3; total, 7. Confirmations, 4. Actual Communicants: Died, 1; present number, 27. Burials, 2.

OFFERINGS.

Parochial: Communion alms, $23.30; Rector's salary and Parish expenses, $225; miscellaneous, $15; total, $263.30.

Diocesan: Aged and infirm Clergy, $1.50; Good Friday offerings, $3.10; total, $4.60.

Total offerings, $277.90.

Estimated value Church and grounds............$900 00

ST. MARY'S CHURCH, PENDLETON.
No report.

TRINITY CHURCH, VAN BUREN.
Rev. L. F. Guerry, Rector.
S. A. Pernot, John Fritz, Wardens.

Number of families, 26. Whole number of souls, 136. Number of baptized persons, 142. Baptisms: Infants, 3; adults, 2; total, 5. Confirmations, 5. Actual Communicants: Admitted, 5; total added, 5; removed, 1; total lost, 1; present number males, 7; females, 49; total, 56. Number confirmed persons, 74. Marriages, 2. Burials, 3. Public Services: Sundays, 95; other days, 75; total, 170. Holy Com-

MUNION : Public, 18 ; private, 1 ; total, 19. SUNDAY-SCHOOL : Teachers, 6 ; pupils, 50. Church Sittings, 250. Rectory ? Yes.

OFFERINGS.

PAROCHIAL : Communion alms, $40.05 ; Rector's salary and Parish expenses, $690.37 ; miscellaneous, $107.33 ; Parish Guild, $246.95 ; total, $1094.70.

DIOCESAN : Diocesan assessment, $20 ; Diocesan Missions, $3.05 ; aged and infirm Clergy, $4.10 ; Church building fund, $3.35 ; total, $30.50.

EXTRA DIOCESAN : Domestic missions, $6.77 ; foreign missions, $2.60 ; University of the South, $3.65 ; missions to Jews, $1.25 ; total, $14.27.

Total offerings, $1139.47.

Estimated value Church and grounds.............$3000 00
Estimated value Rectory........................ 1000 00

Total $4000 00
Amount of indebtedness on Church property (Rectory) $500 00

Of the services above reported, several were held at Winslow, and in regard to this point it gives me pleasure to state that an interesting Sunday-school is being regularly taught there by a few zealous Church people. A good congregation is always in attendance upon the services, while steps have already been taken to erect a chapel by the opening of another season for summer visitors. A class for confirmation will also soon be ready for the Bishop. May God continue to bless this work.

TABLE OF PAROCHIAL STATISTICS.

Parishes and Missions.	No. of Families.	Baptisms — Infants	Baptisms — Adults	Baptisms — Total	Confirmations.	Communicants.	Marriages.	Burials.	Sunday Schools — Teachers.	Sunday Schools — Pupils.	Offering — Parochial.	Offering — Diocesan.	Offering — Extra Diocesan.	Offering — Total.	Value of Church Property.
Arkadelphia, St. Marks	23	3	8	6	16	8									600 00
Arkansas City, Mission						9			7	80					250 00
Batesville, St. Paul's				1	8	65		2							3,000 00
Bay, Mission						12			4	41	428 49	14 80	5 40	448 69	
Camden, St. John's			1		37	1									3,500 00
Conway, Mission					8										
Dardanelle, St. Paul's					24										2,825 00
Eureka Springs, St. James'	52	14	2	16		20			6	90	1,654 60	40 00	4 65	1,699 25	500 00
Fayetteville, St. Paul's	164	18	9	27	31	128	4	5	7	120	3,492 96	146 45	87 50	3,726 91	6,600 00
Fort Smith, St. John's	91	15	6	21	22	275	9	7	18	140	3,229 23	161 23	152 81	3,542 81	12,505 00
Helena, St. John's	16	6	2	14	14	35	2	9	4	20	388 20			383 20	22,000 00
Hope, St. Mark's	82	11	1	8	9	110	4	8	9	50	4,660 87	124 90	88 50	4,830 27	1,000 00
Hot Springs, St. Luke's															1,000 00
Lake Village, Emmanuel	60			16	4	100	3		6	40	850 00			250 00	26,762 60
Little Rock, Trinity Cathedral	356	82	6	38	23	620	10	6	38	400	8,074 78	24 80	195 10	8,274 13	1,000 00
Little Rock, Christ Church	60	11		11	4	29	2	4	4	67	90 15	10 00		100 15	15,000 00
Little Rock, St. Phillip's	12	7	3	10		25		5	5	45	840 00	20 00	9 40	360 00	70,000 00
Mammoth Spring, St. Andrew's	22	2	1	8	1	42	1	6	6	35	345 35	15 00		360 75	1,000 00
Marianna, St. Andrew's						80									2,250 00
Morrilton, St. Agnes						8	2								8,000 00
Nashville, Church of the Redeemer	4	2	1	1		45	1	1							2,776 00
Newport, St. Paul's			7	9	12	10									700 00
Pendleton, St. Mary's															2,500 00
Phillips County,											406 43	81 76	19 55	406 43	1,800 00
Pine Bluff, Trinity	107	10	1	11	15	206	8	8	8	100	1,920 85			2,022 15	150 00
Hot St. James						8									16,600 00
Richmond, Mission						10									600 00
Rocky Comfort, Mission						20	3								300 00
Van Buren, City	26	3	2	5	5	56	8		6	50	1,091 70	30 50	14 27	1,139 47	100 00
Washington, Grace	11	4	3	7	4	27	2				278 80	4 60		277 90	4,000 00
Ritchieville, Mission						10									900 00
Total		145	56	201	168	2173	12	99	184	1878	26,288 46	671 95	527 18	27,487 61	215,450 40

NOTE.— The reports of the number of families are so very imperfect, so few Parishes reporting, the Secretary has thought it best to omit this item in the total of statistics.

APPENDIX VII.

CONSTITUTION AND CANONS.

CONSTITUTION,

As Proposed at the Fifteenth Annual Council at Little Rock, April 20, 1857, and finally Adopted by the Sixteenth Annual Council.

PREAMBLE.

This Church conforms to the Constitution and Canons of the Protestant Episcopal Church in the United States of America, as set forth by the General Convention of the same; to which Constitution and Canons this Church hereby accedes and subordinates herself, according to the rules of ecclesiastical law.

ARTICLE I.

Of the Clergy and Laity.

There are three orders of the Clergy :*

First—The Bishop, who exercises all the functions of the Ministry, presides over the Church by Apostolic Authority, and has the sole right to ordain, to confirm, and to pronounce judicial sentence on offenders; and governs the Church in his Diocese according to the Holy Scriptures and the Canons of this Church.

Second—The Priests or Presbyters, who preach the Word, administer the Sacraments of the Church, and have the over-

---

*Amended by the Sixteenth Annual Council to read as here given. Confirmed by action of the Seventeenth Annual Council.

sight and pastoral care of the Laity in their several Congregations. They also have the right to advise their Bishop and to share in the government of the Church, according to the Canons.

Third—The Deacons, who having received limited office in the general Ministry, serve in the same where they may be appointed by the Bishop. They are subject to the orders of the Bishop, cannot take the Rectorship of a Church, and must be under the care and supervision of some priest, who shall direct them in their work.

The Laity are divided and organized, according to local convenience, into Parishes or Congregations. They commit the general management of their parochial business to a portion of their own number, annually elected, and called Wardens and Vestrymen. To these belong the administration of all the secular concerns of their particular Parish; but they have no part in the spiritual government of the Church, which belongs to the Clergy alone.

ARTICLE II.

Of the Council.

There shall be a Council of the Diocese annually, at such time and place as the Council may, from time to time, determine; and, in case of its failure to do so, the Bishop shall appoint the time and place. In the Council the Bishop shall preside by virtue of his office. The Clergy shall sit by right of their order, and the Laity shall be represented by Delegates chosen for that purpose by the Vestry of each Congregation.

The Chancellor, Secretary and Treasurer of the Diocese shall be entitled to seats in the Council, with privilege of debate, but shall have no vote by reason of their offices.

Special Councils may be called by the Bishop, or, in case of a vacancy in the Episcopate, by the Standing Committee,

n some urgent necessity may require the action of the
le Church.

Without the concurrence of the Clergy and the Laity, no rule or law of the Church can be adopted, changed or done away.

ARTICLE III.

Of the Organization of Congregations.

All Congregations and Parishes represented in the Primary Convention, shall be deemed duly organized; and thereafter, the organization of all Parishes shall be in the form provided by the Canon, and subject to the will of the Council. And no Parish shall have an organic existence, or corporate life in this Church, unless acknowledged by the Council and approved by the Bishop.

ARTICLE IV.

Of the Support and Advancement of the Church.

All Christian men are bound to bear their just share of the burdens which duty imposes.

The Council, by Canon and resolution, may establish special funds :

First—For the support of the Episcopate.

Second—For the support of Missionaries.

Third--For the support of aged and infirm Clergymen.

Fourth—For Church building.

Fifth—For education of men for the Ministry ; and take all other measures necessary for the advancement of Christ's Kingdom: *Provided,* That this article does not imply any power to make any assessment except for the necessary expenses of the Diocese, *"which shall include all current expenses and proper provision for the Episcopate Fund."

ARTICLE V.

Of the Administration of Justice.

The Clergy, Priests and Deacons, may be tried by an Ecclesiastical Court, composed of Presbyters chosen for that

*Amended by the Sixteenth Annual Council by adding the words in quotation marks. Confirmed by action of the Seventeenth Annual Council.

purpose   But there shall be no such trial except on due presentment, and according to the Canon for the trial of Clergymen set forth in this Diocese, and the rules of Ecclesiastical
law.

ARTICLE VI.

Of the Tenure of Church Property.

The Rector, Wardens, and Vestry, or other persons in
whose names the property of any Church or Parish may be
vested, shall not, by deed or any other means, without the
consent of the Bishop and Standing Committee, under their
hands given, grant, alienate or otherwise dispose of any lands,
messuages, or hereditaments in them vested for the use and
benefit of said Church, nor charge, nor encumber the same to
any person whatever.

ARTICLE VII.

Of Amending the Constitution.

A proposal to amend this Constitution must be laid before
the Council in writing, and, if approved, shall lie over until the
next annual Council, and in the meantime, shall be notified to
the Parishes; and then, if it be approved by the Bishop, and
by two-thirds of the Clergy, and by two-thirds of the Laity
present, voting by orders, the proposed amendment shall
become a part of the Constitution.

THE CANONS.

Enacted by the First Annual Council, A. D., 1872—Revised by
the Fifteenth Annual Council, A. D., 1887, also by the
Nineteenth Annual Council, A. D., 1891.

TITLE I.

OF THE COUNCIL OF THE DIOCESE.

CANON I.

OF THE COUNCIL.

SECTION 1. The Members of the Council shall consist of
the Clergy and Laity of the Diocese having the following
qualifications: Every Clergyman having been admitted canonically by the Ecclesiastical Authority shall be a member of
the Council; but no Clergyman shall be qualified to vote at
the election of a Bishop unless he shall have been canonically
and actually a resident of the Diocese for six months. Every
Parish regularly organized as required by the Constitution
shall be entitled to send three Delegates to the Council, and
every duly organized Mission Station shall be entitled to send
one delegate; *Provided always*, That such Delegates shall be
communicants of the Protestant Episcopal Church, and that
no person under ecclesiastical censure or process, whether
Clergyman or Layman, shall be allowed a seat in the Council.

SEC. 2. The first standing committee appointed by the
Bishop, after the Council has been duly organized, and the
last to make a report, shall be a Committee on Ways and
Means, consisting of one Priest and two Laymen, whose duty
it shall be to consider the condition of each Parish and Mission, and to make an equitable assessment upon them, to be

applied to the expenses of the Diocese, which shall include all current expenses and proper provision for the Episcopate Fund.* The Lay Delegates from each Parish to the Diocesan Council shall, as a necessary part of their credentials, present to the Council the receipt of the Treasurer of the Diocese, or other satisfactory evidence, showing the payment of this assessment and that their Parish is not in arrears on any prior assessment.† *Provided*, That the Council when formally organized may, for good and sufficient reasons, excuse any delinquent Parish or Mission from the payment of any portion or all of this assessment.

SEC. 3.   The Council shall, ordinarily, deliberate and vote without any distinction of orders; but any member may call for a division upon any question, and if this call is sustained by two other members, then the question shall be put first to the Clergy and next to the Laity, who shall vote by Parishes; and in such a case a majority of both orders shall be necessary to constitute an affirmative vote of the Council.

SEC. 4.   The Bishop presides in Council, by virtue of his office, and has the right to express his opinion upon every subject that may come before the Council.   In the absence of the Bishop, the Council shall elect a Chairman from the Clergy present.   At each Council a Secretary and Treasurer shall be elected by a joint ballot of the whole body.

SEC. 5.   When a Bishop is to be elected, the Council shall always vote by orders, in this wise :   The Clergy shall make a nomination by ballot, and a majority of Lay Delegates, voting by Parishes, shall concur by ballot, in order to constitute an election.

SEC. 6.   When any great necessity shall arise, the Bishop, or if there be no Bishop, the President of the Standing Com-

---

*Amended by the Sixteenth Annual Council by omitting the words "Episcopate Fund and the current," and in lieu thereof inserting the word "necessary." By the action of the Seventeenth Annual Council amended to read as now printed.

†Amended by the Nineteenth Annual Council by inserting the words, "and that their Parish is not in arrears on any prior assessment."

mittee, may call a special Council. In such case, four weeks' notice shall be given to every Clergyman and to one of the Wardens in every Parish in the Diocese, stating the time, place and objects of the special Council; and no other matters shall be proposed or acted upon than those specified in the call of said special Council.

CANON II.

OF THE SECRETARY AND TREASURER.

SECTION 1. The Secretary of the Council shall keep in a fit book, full and exact records of all its acts, and shall preserve all papers, documents, memorials, etc., belonging to the same, duly indorsed and filed in such way that they may be easily consulted whenever recourse to them may be necessary. He shall also prepare, under the direction of the Bishop, at least one week before the meeting of the Council, a list of all the Ministers canonically resident in the Diocese, annexing their respective stations, distinguishing Priests from Deacons, but not inserting the name of any Clergyman who is suspended from the Ministry. The list thus prepared shall be laid before the Council immediately after it shall be called to order, and the names of the clerical members shall be called therefrom. Nevertheless, the Council has power immediately to order the correction of any errors or omissions.

SEC. 2. The Treasurer shall have charge of the General Fund of the Diocese, and all other funds the Council may commit to his care, and shall keep a strict account of the same in a fit book, with a distinct place therein for all proper entries. He shall keep a regular account with all funds and with all persons and Parishes concerned, and shall annually exhibit a balance sheet to the Auditing Committee. He shall indorse and file away all warrants, orders or other papers belonging to his department, and shall have his accounts audited at each Council by the Finance Committee.

Sec. 3. When a vacancy occurs in the office of Secretary or Treasurer, or Trustee of any fund,* the Ecclesiastical Authority shall appoint a fit person to fill the vacancy, who shall receive all records, funds and papers from the hands of the former officer or his legal representatives, and such appointee shall continue in office and perform all the duties thereof until the ensuing Council shall have elected some one to fill the same.

CANON III.

OF THE REGISTRAR.

Section 1. A Registrar shall be elected by the Council, into whose keeping shall be committed all documents pertaining to the history of the Church in the Diocese of Arkansas, that are now, or may hereafter become the property of the Council. It shall be the duty of said Registrar to preserve all documents herein referred to, in some suitable place of deposit, and to hold them subject to such regulations as the Council may, from time to time, prescribe.

Sec. 2. Said Registrar shall hold his office for one year and until another shall be chosen in his place.

CANON IV.

OF REGULAR ATTENDANCE AT COUNCIL.

Section 1. Every Clergyman in the Diocese shall attend the Annual Council, unless he has a satisfactory excuse; and it is the duty of every Parish to send Lay Delegates, and it shall be the duty of the Vestry to make provision for their representation. A satisfactory excuse will be required for every failure.

Sec. 2. No member of the Council shall leave the same during the session without having obtained leave of absence from the Council.

---

*Amended by the Nineteenth Annual Council by inserting the words, "or Trustee of any fund."

CANON V.

OF THE NUMBER NECESSARY TO CONSTITUTE A QUORUM.

SECTION 1. A quorum for ordinary business at the Annual Council shall consist of such Clergy and Delegates from the Parishes as may be present; but, if the Bishop be not present, such quorum shall have power only to receive reports of committees and Parishes, and to refer the same; to elect the ordinary officers and committees, and to fix the time and place for the next Council. In the election of a Bishop, two-thirds of the Clergy and a majority of all the Parishes shall be present before the Council proceed to elect. At any *called* Council, other than as provided for in Article II of the Constitution, a quorum shall consist of a majority of all the Clergy entitled to seats, and Lay Delegates from four or more Parishes.

CANON VI.

OF THE OPENING OF THE COUNCIL.

SECTION 1. At the opening of every Council there shall be a celebration of the Holy Communion, and a sermon by a Priest appointed by the Bishop when the Bishop himself does not deliver at that time a sermon or charge. And this *may* be preceded by Morning Prayer.

CANON VII.

OF THE STANDING COMMITTEE OF THE DIOCESE.

SECTION 1. At every Annual Council there shall be elected three Priests and two Laymen, by ballot, as a Standing Committee for the ensuing year. They shall elect, from their own body, a President and Secretary. They shall meet on the summons of the President. To constitute a quorum two Priests must be present, and when required they shall vote by orders.

SEC. 2. It shall be the duty of the Secretary to keep a regular record of their proceedings, in a book which shall belong to the Diocese, and which, together with all papers in the possession of the Committee, shall be open to the inspection of the Committee, or the Council, when required.

Sec. 3. The Standing Committee shall be summoned on the requisition of the Bishop, whenever he shall wish their advice; and they may meet, of their own accord and agreeably to their own rules, when they may be disposed to advise the Bishop. And the President shall call a meeting at any time, on the request in writing of any two members, or when he may deem it necessary.

Sec. 4. When the Diocese is vacant, through any cause, it shall be the duty of the Standing Committee to call a meeting forthwith, and, after consultation as to the time and place, to summon a special Council of the Diocese, to elect a successor, with all convenient speed. *Provided*, That if such vacancy occur within less than six months before the Annual Council, there shall be no special Council, but the election of a Bishop shall be deferred until the Annual Council; and during the vacancy, the Standing Committee shall exercise all the powers of the Ecclesiastical Authority consistent with their character as the administrators of the Diocese under Council.

CANON VIII.

OF THE APPOINTMENT OF STANDING COMMITTEES.

Section 1. At every Council the Presiding Officer shall appoint standing committees on—

1. Credentials of Lay Delegates.
2. Ways and Means.
3. Admission of New Parishes.
4. State of the Church.
5. Auditing and Finance.
6. Unfinished Business.
7. Constitution and Canons.

And on such other subjects as he may deem requisite to put the Council in possession of properly proposed information for their action.

Sec. 2. He shall also appoint a committee to be known as the Committee on Judiciary, to be composed of three Laymen, the Chancellor to be one and to be Chairman, who shall remain as members of such committee until their successors are appointed.

CANON IX.

OF THE ELECTION OF TRUSTEES.

Section 1. Every Council shall elect Trustees for all funds that may be created.

Sec. 2. A Trustee shall be annually appointed by the Council, who shall be known as the Trustee of the Episcopate Endowment Fund, and who shall be specially charged with the responsibility for the accumulation and investment of said fund. As often as the amounts received by him shall aggregate the sum of $50 he shall invest the same, under the supervision of the Bishop and Standing Committee of the Diocese. It shall be the duty of the said Trustee to make annual reports to the Council of the condition of said fund and the investment thereof. The said Trustee shall execute a bond with the State of Arkansas, for the use of the Diocese of the State, in such sum as may be required by the Council each year, to be approved by the said Standing Committee, and filed there for the faithful discharge of the duties of his office.*

CANON X.

OF DEPUTIES TO THE GENERAL CONVENTION.

Section 1. Deputies to the General Convention shall be chosen at each Annual Council, and shall continue in office until others are chosen.

Sec. 2. The Deputies to the General Convention shall be elected by ballot, the Clergy and Laity separately electing the Deputies and Substitutes of their respective orders.

---

*Amended by the Nineteenth Annual Council by adding the sentence, "The said Trustee shall execute a bond," etc.

SEC. 3. Substitutes for Deputies shall be elected one at a time; and, in the event of the resignation or inability of any Deputy, Clerical or Lay, such vacancy shall be filled by the Substitutes in the order of election, and the Journal must show the order of election of substitutes, Clerical and Lay.

CANON XI.

OF PUBLISHING THE JOURNAL.

SECTION I. The proceedings of the Council shall be published by the Secretary, under the supervision of the Bishop, and duly distributed, unless the Council shall otherwise order.

CANON XII.

OF FAILURE TO ELECT OFFICERS.

SECTION I. In all cases of failure to elect officers, whether in the Council or in a Parish, the persons last elected shall continue to serve with full power until their successors are elected.

CANON XIII.

OF THE CHANCELLOR OF THE DIOCESE.

SECTION I. There shall be elected by the Council an officer learned in the law, under the title of Chancellor of the Diocese, whose duty it shall be to act as the legal counselor of the Bishop and of the Standing Committee, in matters affecting the interests of the Church, as his professional counsel may be asked or required. The Chancellor of the Diocese shall hold his office for the term of three years, and, in the event of a vacancy, the Annual Council next ensuing shall elect a successor for the full term of three years.

ORDER OF BUSINESS.

1. Calling the Roll.
2. Presentation of the Certificates of Lay Delegates.
3. Appointment of Committee on Credentials.
4. Report of Committee on Credentials.
5. Election of Secretary.
6. Appointment of Standing Committees.
7. Annual Address of the Bishop.
8. Report of the Standing Committee.
9. Report of Special Committees.
10. Report of Trustees of the several Funds.
11. Report of the Auditing Committee.
12. Election of Treasurer.
13. Election of the Standing Committee.
14. Report of the State of the Church.
15. Election of Deputies to the General Convention.
16. Election of Trustees of the several Funds.
17. *Election of Trustees of the University of the South and other Trustees not specified.
18. Election of Registrar.
19. Election of Chancellor.
20. Report of Committee on Unfinished Business.
21. Miscellaneous Business.
22. Report of Committee on Ways and Means.

TITLE II.

OF PARISHES AND PARISH MINISTERS.

CANON I.

SECTION 1. All vacant Parishes shall be under the pastoral care of the Bishop. He shall provide for public worship, as

*Amended by Sixteenth Annual Council by inserting order 17.
D - 7.

far as he can, by occasional services of the Clergy, and by first persons appointed as Lay readers.

CANON II.

SECTION I. When any Parish shall have elected a Rector, and he shall have accepted the call, it shall be the duty of the Vestry to file with the Bishop a minute of their proceedings, including the particular agreement on their part and the acceptance of the elected Minister, showing that he accepts on the terms and agreements stipulated by the Vestry. The Bishop shall make record thereof, and the same shall be binding on the parties concerned, and held as a firm contract.

CANON III.

SECTION I. The Rector shall preside at all Vestry meetings, if present, and open the same with prayer, and may advise, but not vote, on any question.

SEC. 2. To the Rector belongs the control of the keys of the Church, and the right to open the Church for public prayer, sermons, catechetical instruction, marriages, funerals, baptisms, and all rights and ceremonies authorized by the Protestant Episcopal Church in America, at all times when he may deem proper.

SEC. 3. The Church building shall never be used for any secular or profane purpose.

CANON IV.

SECTION I. Every Parish Minister shall keep a Parish Register, which shall be a well-bound book, and, as far as may be, uniform throughout the Diocese.

SEC. 2. In it shall be entered the names of all persons baptized, confirmed, married and buried in the Parish. It shall contain a list of all the communicants, of all families, and of individuals not thus included, belonging to the Parish, or regularly attending its services. It shall also contain a record of all collections made in the Church.

Sec. 3. From this Register shall the annual parochial reports be made to the Council, under all the heads that may be required by the Council or Canons.

CANON V.

Section 1. It shall be the duty of the Vestry to report, annually, to the Council, by their Delegates, a full statement of their financial condition, according to general order of the Council. This statement shall contain the amount and value of their property and the net income of their Parish.

CANON VI.

Section 1. It shall be the duty of the Vestry to make a full exhibit to the Bishop at the time of his annual visitation, if he shall so require, of all their affairs, and receive from him counsel and advice for the conduct of the affairs of the Parish.

CANON VII.

Section 1. The organization of a new Parish shall be forthwith notified to the Bishop, and, if approved by him, the Parish may elect a Rector, and send Delegates and apply for admission to the Council.

Sec. 2. But if the new Parish proposed to be organized be within the territorial bounds of any existing Parish, the Bishop shall notify the Rector and Wardens thereof, and, if objections be made thereto, notice shall be given to both parties, and the Bishop, within thirty days thereafter, shall hear the same before the Standing Committee, and the decision of the Standing Committee, approved by the Bishop, shall determine the case. *Provided*, That no Parish within any city shall be divided for the purpose of forming a new and independent Parish, within its boundaries, except by express order of the Council.

CANON VIII.

Section 1. Congregations, Parishes, and the members thereof, shall never recognize any suspended clergyman, otherwise than as declared by the Ecclesiastical Authority.

Sec. 2.   If any Parish, or the members thereof, shall take part with a contumacious Clergyman, they shall forfeit their rights in the Council.

Sec. 3.   All parochial property is held by a tenure subject to this rule.

Sec. 4.   In case any Congregation should be so far forgetful of the honor of God's Church as to transgress in this matter, it shall be the duty of the Treasurer of the Diocese, or of the Trustees of the General Fund, to proceed at once to recover all the Church's property in such contumacious Parish, and to reduce it to the control of the Diocese.

Sec. 5.   The organization of every Parish shall recognize this rule, and, if it be not expressed in the Articles of Association, their admission into union with the Council shall bind them to this law.

TITLE III.

OF CONVOCATIONS, DIOCESAN MISSIONS AND CHURCH EXTENSION.

CANON I.

Section 1.   The Bishop may divide the Diocese into Districts, naming the town in each District which shall be the center of a Missionary work; and every Clergyman in the Diocese of every Parish and Missionary Station, shall be assigned to one or the other of the Missionary centers.

Sec. 2.   The Clergy and Laity of each District, when organized, shall constitute a Convocation, and have charge of the Missionary work in the field assigned by the Bishop.

Sec. 3.   The Bishop shall appoint one of the Clergy in each District as Dean of Convocation.   The Convocation shall elect a Secretary, who shall be a Clergyman, and a Treasurer, who shall be a Layman.

Sec. 4. The Convocation shall be governed by such rules as they shall adopt, with the Bishop's approval, and each shall report, through its Dean, to the Bishop annually.

Sec. 5. The Deans of Convocation shall constitute the Missionary Committee of the Diocese. Until such time as the Bishop shall divide the Diocese into Districts, the Bishop and the Clerical members of the Standing Committee shall constitute said Missionary Committee.

Sec. 6. Every Parish shall, by its Vestry, appoint one Delegate to Convocation.

Sec. 7. In Missionary Stations, the Missionary in charge or Dean of Convocation shall appoint the Lay Delegate.

CANON II.

Section 1. All organized Mission Stations shall be under the control of the Bishop and Missionary Committee.

Sec. 2. All Missionaries shall be appointed by the Bishop.

Sec. 3. Missionary Stations duly organized shall report to the Annual Council the same as Parishes, and shall be entitled to send one Delegate, who shall have the right to debate but not to vote.

CANON III.

In any community where there are twelve baptized adults, one of whom shall be a male communicant, desirous of organizing a Missionary Station, they shall assemble themselves— their own Missionary being present, or, if they have no Missionary, any Clergyman of the Diocese being present and consenting—and adopt the following form of organization, affixing their signatures thereto, and sending a copy of the same to the Bishop of the Diocese for his approval:

" We, whose names are hereunto subscribed, desirous of enjoying the privileges of religious worship and instruction of the Holy Catholic and Apostolic Church, according to the forms and doctrines of the Protestant Episcopal Church in the United States of America, have, this —— day of ——, A. D.

———, at ———, in the State of Arkansas, formed ourselves
into a Congregation, and adopted the following Articles of
Association:

"Article I.   This Association or Congregation shall be
known by the name of the ——— Mission.

"Article II.   This Association acknowledges, accedes to,
and will be governed by the Constitution, Canons, doctrine,
discipline and worship of the Protestant Episcopal Church in
the United States, and the Constitution and Canons of the
Protestant Episcopal Church in the Diocese of Arkansas.

"Article III.   When any person uniting with this Association shall disclaim or refuse conformity to the authorities mentioned in the preceding Article, he shall cease to be a member
of this Association, and shall no longer enjoy the privilege of
voting in the election of officers, of being elected an officer, or
of exercising any function concerning or connected with the
said Association; *but this exclusion shall not affect the spiritual
standing of the excluded.*

"Article IV.   In this Mission, regular attendants at the
services of the Church shall be entitled to vote for officers and
on all matters brought before the Easter meeting.

"Article V.   The officers of this Association shall be:
The Minister in Charge as President *ex officio;* a Warden, who
must be a male communicant, and appointed by the Minister;
a Secretary and a Treasurer, elected by ballot annually the
Monday in Easter week, or as soon thereafter as possible, due
notice having been given of time and place of election.

"Article VI.   The duties of these officers shall be the same
as those of like officers in organized Parishes.

"Article VII.   All lands, tenements, or other property,
real or personal, of this Association, shall vest in the Bishop
of the Diocese, or under whose supervision it may for the
time be, and his canonical successors, to be by him and them
held in trust for the benefit of the Mission.

"Article VIII. We promise to pay the sum of $——— per annum for the support of the Missionary whom the Bishop or Missionary Committee may send to us." •

CANON IV.*

SECTION I. The Bishop of the Diocese shall be *ex officio* President of the Missionary Committee. The Committee shall report, through its Secretary, to the Annual Council. The Treasurer shall receive, hold, and pay out funds, subject to the order of the Committee. His accounts shall be audited by the Council as a separate and distinct fund.

TITLE IV.

OF VESTRIES AND WARDENS AND THEIR DUTIES, ETC.

CANON I.

SECTION I. Annually, at a meeting on Easter Monday, or as soon thereafter as may be, the members of the Parish entitled to vote shall elect not less than three nor more than eleven Vestrymen, of whom the Rector or Minister shall appoint one as Senior Warden and the Vestry shall elect another as Junior Warden. *Provided,* That the congregation worshiping in the Cathedral Church may, on the Monday in Easter week, or as early thereafter as practicable, elect three communicants to represent them, subject to the laws and regulations governing parochial representation.

SEC. 2. Notice of the election shall be given on Easter Day, or at the service last preceding the election, after Morning Prayer, and the Congregation duly warned of the importance of the election.

*By action of the Sixteenth Annual Council, Canon IV, as originally proposed, was repealed and Canon V ordered to be numbered IV.

Sec. 3.   The Vestry elect shall meet within ten days thereafter, and organize by the election of the Junior Warden, Treasurer and Secretary.   As soon as the offices are filled the Secretary and Treasurer, if not re-elected, shall pass over to their successors the books, papers, accounts and moneys in their hands.   The Vestry shall then proceed to elect Delegates to represent the Parish in the next Council of the Diocese, and the Secretary of the Vestry, or the Rector, shall give the Delegates-elect certificates to that effect.

Sec. 4.   It is, in general, the duty of the Wardens and Vestrymen to consider and determine upon the election of a Minister when the Parish is vacant ; to see that the Minister is well and properly supported, sufficiently and punctually paid ; to make and execute all contracts for the erection of Church edifices, rectories, and other Church buildings ; to provide for their furnishing and repair and due preservation ; to have and to hold all Church property as trustees of the Parish, and as such generally to transact all temporal and financial business of the Parish.

Sec. 5.   It is the special duty of the Wardens to see that the Church edifice be kept from unhallowed use ; that it be kept clean and in good repair, duly lighted and warmed ; to provide a sufficient supply of books and ecclesiastical vestments to be used in the public ministrations by the Minister, and to provide proper elements for the celebration of the Holy Communion and preserve due order during service.

Sec. 6.   In the absence of the Rector the Wardens preside at Parish and Vestry meetings.

Sec. 7.   In the absence of the Wardens their duties devolve on the Vestrymen.

Sec. 8.   It is the duty of the Secretary to attend all the meetings of the Vestry, and perform the proper functions of his office.

Sec. 9.   It shall be the duty of the Treasurer to receive all moneys collected under authority of the Vestry ; to collect all moneys due the Vestry or Congregation, and to pay them out on the order of the Vestry in the manner they shall provide. Two weeks before Easter, every year, the Treasurer shall present to the Vestry a full statement of his accounts, and the Vestry shall audit the same, and, if found correct, order the annual balance to be made up in accordance therewith.

SEC. 10. The Minister may call meetings of the Vestry whenever he shall desire, and shall call a meeting when requested by any two members of the Vestry, of which he shall give due notice ; but meetings may be held at regular periods by regulation of the Vestry. At every meeting the minutes in the former meeting shall be read and approved, or corrected and approved.

SEC. 11. It shall be the special duty of the Vestry, at the time of public service, or other meeting in the Church, to see that the Congregation is properly seated, and in the performance of this duty they shall give special attention to strangers.

CANON II.

NEW PARISHES—FORM FOR ORGANIZATION OF NEW PARISHES.

Hereafter all new Parishes shall be organized by the adoption of the following form of organization :

" We, whose names are hereunto subscribed, desirous of enjoying the privileges of religious worship and instruction of the Holy, Catholic and Apostolic Church, according to the forms and doctrines of the Protestant Episcopal Church in the United States of America, have, this —— day of ———, A. D. ——, at ———, in the State of Arkansas, formed ourselves into a Parish, and adopted the following Articles of Association :

" Article 1. This association shall be known by the name of ' The Rector, Wardens and Vestry of ——— Church.'

" Article 2. This Association acknowledges, accedes to, and will be governed by the Constitution, Canons, doctrine, discipline and worship of the Protestant Episcopal Church in

the United States, and the Constitution and Canons of the Protestant Episcopal Church in the Diocese of Arkansas.

"Article 3. When any person, uniting with this Association, shall disclaim or refuse conformity to the authorities mentioned in the preceding Article, he shall cease to be a member of the Association, and shall no longer enjoy the privilege of voting in the election of Vestrymen, of being elected a Vestryman, or of exercising any function concerning or connected with the said Association; *but this exclusion shall not affect the spiritual standing of the excluded.*

"Article 4. In this Parish all baptized members of the Church, who are duly registered as members of this Congregation, shall be entitled to vote for Vestrymen, and on all matters brought before the Easter meeting.

"Article 5. The Vestrymen of ———— Church shall be elected annually, on the Monday in Easter week, or as soon thereafter as may be, by a majority of the voters assembled for that purpose, notice to that effect having been given publicly to the Congregation on the preceding Sunday. The Vestrymen so elected shall continue in office one year or until their successors are chosen.

"Article 6. The Rector of ————— Church shall be elected by the Wardens and Vestrymen in open meeting, which shall be duly convened for that purpose, they having due regard in all such elections to the previously ascertained wishes of the Congregation, and *especially* of the *communicants* of the Church.

"Article 7. No person shall be chosen Rector or Minister, or Associate Rector or Assistant Minister, of ————— Church, or be allowed to exercise any of the functions of the Sacred Ministry in the same, unless he be recognized by the Bishop having charge of this Diocese, or, if there be no Bishop, by the Standing Committee of the same, as an ordained Minister of the Protestant Episcopal Church, in good standing. *Provided,* That nothing in this Article shall prevent the Wardens and

Vestry from inviting any Clergymen of the Protestant Episcopal Church, in good standing, to officiate occasionally in the Church, or interfere with the performance of the usual services by the Lay Readers, duly appointed to so officiate in the absence of the Rector or Minister.

" Article 8. The annual rents, contributions and other revenues raised by this Congregation, shall be applied by the Wardens and Vestry to the maintenance and support of the Rector or Minister, and to such other objects as are connected with the well-being of the Church. and to no other purpose whatever.

" Article 9. This Association, or the Rector, Wardens and Vestry, or other persons in whose name the property of —————— Church may be vested, shall not, by deed or any other means, without the consent of the Bishop of the Diocese, under his hand given, grant, alienate, or otherwise dispose of, any lands, messuages or hereditaments, in them vested for the use and benefit of said Church, nor charge, nor encumber the same to any person whatever.

" Article 10. In case of the dissolution or extinction of this Association for any cause whatever, the lands, tenements and other estate, real or personal, if such there be, shall vest in the Bishop of the Protestant Episcopal Church in this Diocese, or under whose supervision it may for the time be, and his canonical successors, to be by him and them held in trust for the benefit of a future Congregation of the Protestant Episcopal Church which may be formed in the same place or vicinity, and upon the same principles as the present Church and Association."

CANON III.

SECTION 1. Clergymen and Laymen shall exercise due care in signing the papers of candidates for the Ministry, and shall not sign, except on personal knowledge or reasonable evidence. And if any fraud or concealment may have been used to obtain certificates, the signers, on evidence of the facts, may revoke

their recommendation.   And if they shall rashly or unadvisedly, without due care and caution, or through favor, or
with corrupt purpose, sign the recommendation of candidates,
whereby unworthy or unfit persons may be admitted to the
Ministry, whether they be Clergymen or Laymen, they shall be
subject to ecclesiastical censure.

TITLE V.*

TRIAL OF MINISTERS.

SECTION I.   Every Clergyman in this Diocese shall be
liable to presentment and trial for the following offences, to-
wit :

First—Crime and immorality.

Second—Holding and teaching, publicly or privately and
advisedly any doctrine contrary to that expressly and generally
set forth in the standards of the Protestant Episcopal Church
in the United States.

Third—Violation of the Constitution and Canons of the
General Convention, or of the Constitution and Canons of the
Diocese of Arkansas.

Fourth—Any act that involves a breach of his ordination
vows.

SEC. 2.   If a Minister of this Church shall be found guilty
of any of the offences enumerated in the foregoing section, he
shall be admonished, suspended or degraded.

SEC. 3.   In order to bring a Clergyman to trial a charge or
charges with specifications shall be made to the Judiciary
Committee, signed by at least two male communicants of the
Church, affirming that the same is true and that the accusers
will make the charge or charges good.   Should the Bishop
have reason to believe that a Clergyman is guilty of any or all
of the above named offences, he shall notify the Standing Com-

*As amended by the Nineteenth Annual Council.

mittee of the fact, and the Clerical members of the Standing Committee shall at once proceed to an investigation of the case, and should they be convinced of the guilt of the Clergyman, they shall make the charges to the Judiciary Committee, affirming as above. Thereupon, it shall be the duty of the Secretary of the Committee to furnish the accused a copy of the charge, and require an answer to be filed thereto within thirty days from the date of the receipt of said copy. On the coming in of the answer, a copy of the same shall be furnished the parties making the charge, accompanied by a notice that all proof on the issue, of both parties, must be taken and filed with the Secretary within thirty days from the date of the notice. All proof must be by deposition, taken before an officer authorized to administer oaths, and must be upon reasonable notice. Both parties have the right to be present at the taking of the depositions and to be represented by counsel.

At the end of the thirty days the hearing shall close, and thereupon the said Committee shall consider the charges, and if two members of the same shall deem the charges clearly within the scope of the Canons, and sustained by the proof, it shall be so declared in writing, and they shall file all the papers in the case with the Standing Committee of the Diocese.

In case the accused is a member of the Standing Committee, the two remaining Clerical members shall choose a Priest of the Diocese to supply his place, and for the purposes of this trial the Priest so chosen shall be considered a member of the Standing Committee.

SEC. 4. On the receipt of the presentation and papers it shall be the duty of the Clerical members of the Standing Committee to consider of the charge, and if in the opinion of at least two of said Clerical members, the charge be clearly within the scope of the Canons and sustained by the proof adduced, they shall cite the accused to appear before them, either in person or by representative, together with the Chancellor of the Diocese, and in their presence they shall select by lot seven

Presbyters of the Diocese, to meet on a certain day after thirty days, at a certain place, within which the accused may reside. Immediately upon their selection, the accused shall strike off one name from the list of seven drawn; the Judge Advocate shall then strike off a second name; the accused shall strike off a third name; and lastly, the Judge Advocate shall strike off a fourth, and the three remaining shall constitute the court. Should the accused refuse to exercise his right of striking off the names as proposed, then the members of the Standing Committee present shall draw by lot from the seven names first chosen, three to constitute the Court. In case the accused, or his representative, should not appear, then the drawings shall proceed without him. The Court shall be judges both of law and fact.

SEC. 5. The Standing Committee shall be prosecutors in the case, and shall appoint a Judge Advocate, who shall be a Priest of this Diocese. The Standing Committee shall give the accused thirty days' notice of the time and place of trial, and shall, also, deliver to him at the same time a copy of the charges preferred against him; and he shall nct be required to answer to anything not contained in the presentment.

SEC. 6. At the time fixed for the trial, the members of the court shall assemble at the place designated, and choose a President and Clerk from their own number; and they shall, before they proceed, adopt and declare the rules by which the trial shall be conducted, if rules of ecclesiastical trial have not already been set forth by authority. *Provided, however*, That all the evidence heard at the trial shall be reduced to writing at the time it is given, and signed by the witness before he leaves the room.

SEC. 7. The accused shall be allowed counsel, whom he may choose from among the Priests of the Church, and he may also advise with a Lay communicant learned in the law. If the accused decline to choose counsel, the court shall appoint counsel for him from the Priests of the Diocese.

SEC. 8. If the accused shall not appear for trial, without assigning sufficient cause, the court shall proceed against him for contempt, and he shall be suspended by the Bishop from the exercise of all Clerical functions for the space of three months. And if, in the three months, he shall not apply for trial, at any time afterwards, with the consent and advice of the Standing Committee, the Bishop may proceed to pronounce upon the recusant the sentence of deposition from the Ministry.

SEC. 9. But if, in the three months above named, the accused shall appear for trial, the Court may proceed on the presentment originally made, and shall adjudge him guilty or not guilty, according to the evidence. The Court shall render their verdict before separation; and if it shall be guilty, they shall designate the penalty or degree of censure which, in their judgment, ought to be pronounced against him; which the Bishop may not exceed, though he may modify it.

Immediately upon rendering the verdict, it shall be the duty of the Clerk of the Court to notify the Bishop of the action of the Court, delivering to him all the pleadings and evidence in the case; and he shall, at the end of ten days, pronounce sentence, unless the condemned has appealed to him from the verdict of the Court. In case of appeal, the Bishop shall give notice to both the Judge Advocate and the accused, that on a day fixed he will hear the case on appeal. At such hearing the accused shall have the right to be represented by a Lay communicant learned in the law, and the Bishop may call two of the neighboring Diocesans, who shall sit with him at the hearing, to assist him in arriving at a correct determination.

SEC. 10. The Clerk of such Ecclesiastial Court shall keep a record of all the proceedings, which shall contain a copy of the presentment, the specifications under particular charges, the notice to the accused, his answer, his plea or pleas, a clear statement of the evidence for and against, both oral and writ-

ten, and the judgment of the Court. An attested copy of this record shall be forthwith delivered to the Bishop.

Sec. 11.   On hearing the case on appeal, the Bishop, or the Bishop and his Assessors, shall confirm the decision of the Court, and at once pronounce sentence; or, order a new trial stating in order the reason and grounds of such decision, in which case a new Court shall be formed, after the same manner as before ; or, reverse the decision of the Court, according to the finding in the case, and shall declare him innocent accordingly.   When the sentence of the Court is less than deposition, the Bishop may, for reasons satisfactory to him, reprieve or wholly pardon the condemned.

Sec. 12.   Every summons, notice or citation, mentioned in the proceedings, shall be deemed to be duly served by the delivery of a written notice to the person to be summoned, notified or cited, or by leaving it or a certified copy at his residence or last known residence, by a person duly appointed in writing by the Standing Committee or Court, as the case may require.   Depositions must be taken according to the rules of law.

Sec. 13.   The Court may adjourn from day to day, or to a day certain, for the purpose of allowing parties to obtain evidence that they may affirm to be necessary to the maintenance of their cause ; but to obtain a postponement of trial for more than three days, the party making the motion shall solemnly affirm that such postponement is sought, not for delay, but that justice may be done, and that he expects thereby to obtain evidence which is material to his cause, and which he cannot now produce.

Sec. 14.   Suspensions from the exercise of the functions of the Ministry shall, *ipso facto*, sever the connection between a Clergyman and his Parish.

Sec. 15.   If any Clergyman shall be contumacious when suspended, and attempt to perform any of the functions of the Sacred Ministry, the Bishop shall at once cite him before the

Standing Committee; and, if the alleged facts be admitted or proven by sufficient evidence, on having been duly cited, such suspended Clergyman shall not appear or give reasons for not appearing, the Bishop, with the consent of the Standing Committee, may proceed at once to pronounce upon said recusant the grave sentence of deposition from the Ministry.

Sec. 16. No Clergyman shall be suspended, or receive any public censure from the Ecclesiastical Authority of the Diocese, without having been adjudged thereto in the manner provided in this Canon.

Sec. 17. If an accused Clergyman shall, to avoid notice or citation, remove himself out of the Diocese, he may be duly served with all notices by publication in some newspaper published at the Capital of the State, or the Church-newspaper which the Bishop shall have adopted as the official organ of the Diocese.

Sec. 18. If there shall be a necessity for the trial of a Clergyman, at any time when the Episcopate of the Diocese is vacant, the Bishop of some neighboring Diocese may, at the request of the Standing Committee, perform all the acts assigned by this Canon to the Bishop of the Diocese.

Sec. 19. Any resort to a civil court on the part of the accused, for the purpose of impeding, delaying, or avoiding trial, shall be treated as contumacy, and shall be sufficient cause to suspend such Clergyman from the exercise of the Ministry for contumacy, until he shall appear and demand a trial.

Sec. 20. No Clergyman under trial, or suspension, or against whom charges have been presented by the Standing Committee, can be transferred to any other Diocese, or be received therefrom. And if charges are made against a Clergyman who has already obtained Letters Dimissory, said charges shall be sent to the Diocese to which the letters were taken, within six months after the date of said letters, and not later. And if such letters have not been presented and received

D.- 8

at the time, the party shall be remanded to his Diocese for trial, and his Letters Dimissory thereby revoked.

SEC. 21.   All rights, claims and privileges, which any Clergyman may enjoy, or have a right to enjoy or receive, in the Diocese, by virtue of her general law, or by particular Canon, are, by the sentence of suspension or deposition, *ipso facto*, forfeited and rendered void ; and every Clergyman shall hold his ecclesiastical rights subject to this tenure.

INDEX.

THE CONSTITUTION.

THE CANONS.

The Domestic and Foreign Missionary Society of the Protestant Episcopal Church in the United States of America.

The Society asks for stated offerings as follows, and on the dates given when possible:

Domestic Missions, the first Sunday in Advent.

Foreign Missions, the second Sunday after the Epiphany.

Missions to colored people, the third Sunday after the Epiphany.

Missions to Indians, the Fourth Sunday after Easter.

The Treasurer is now MR. GEORGE BLISS, to whom all remittances should be sent, at his office,

22 Bible House, New York City.

ANNOUNCEMENT.

The Twentieth Annual Council of the Diocese of Arkansas will be held (D. V.) in St. Luke's Church, Hot Springs, on the second Thursday after Easter, April 28th, 1892.

W. J. MILLER, Secretary.

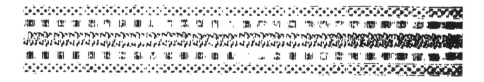

☆ THE SECRETARY
Diocese of Arkansas

JOURNAL

OF THE

Twentieth Annual Coun

* * 1892 * *

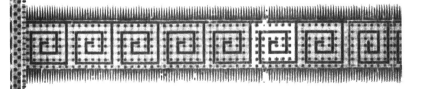

· Special · Offerings ·

Recommended by the Council, and the Dates on which They Shall be Made.

DIOCESAN MISSIONS, on the first Sunday in Lent, and on Trinity Sunday.

EPISCOPAL FUND, on Septuagesima Sunday, or on Easter Day.

AGED AND INFIRM CLERGY, and WIDOWS AND ORPHANS OF DECEASED CLERGY OF THE DIOCESE, on National Thanksgiving Day.

UNIVERSITY OF THE SOUTH, on the first Sunday in Advent.

JOURNAL

OF

THE PROCEEDINGS

OF THE

TWENTIETH ANNUAL COUNCIL

OF THE

Diocese of Arkansas.

Held in St. Luke's Church, Hot Springs, on the 28th, 29th and 30th
days of April and on the 1st day of May, 1892.

LITTLE ROCK, ARK.:
THE PRESS PRINTING COMPANY.
1892.

THE DIOCESE OF ARKANSAS.

ORGANIZED A. D. 1871.

DIOCESAN OFFICERS:

Bishop:

THE RT. REV. H. N. PIERCE, D. D., LL. D.

Standing Committee:

THE REV. INNES O. ADAMS, PRESIDENT.

REV. WM. J. MILLER.   MR. M. L. BELL.

REV. C. H. LOCKWOOD.   MR. P. K. ROOTS.

Secretary of the Council:

THE REV. WM. J. MILLER, Hot Springs.

Treasurer:

MR. LOGAN H. ROOTS, Little Rock.

Registrar:

MR. GEORGE H. VAN ETTEN, Little Rock.

Chancellor:

THE HON. M. L. BELL, Pine Bluff.

Trustee of the Episcopate Fund:

MR. S. S. FAULKNER, Helena.

Trustees of the University of the South:

REV. C. H. LOCKWOOD.

MR. GEO. G. LATTA.   MR. ROBT. J. MATTHEWS.

Trustee of the General Theological Seminary:

REV. WILLIAM JONES.

Deputies to the General Convention:

Clerical.	*Lay.*
REV. I. O. ADAMS.	DR. W. B. WELCH. ·
REV. W. J. MILLER.	MR. LOGAN H. ROOTS.
REV. J. J. VAULX.	MR. GEO. G. LATTA.
REV. C. H. LOCKWOOD.	MR. E. C. RATCLIFF.

Supplementary Delegates to the General Convention:

(In the order of their election.)

Clerical.	*Lay.*
1. REV. WM. JONES.	1. MR. GEO. W. CARUTH.
2. REV. DR. POTTER,	2. MR. R. B. BANCROFT.
3. REV. J. B. WHALING.	3. MR. W. M. MELLETTE.
4. REV. PALIN SAXBY.	4. MR. J. T. WEST.

Committee on Judiciary:

THE HON. M. L. BELL, PRESIDENT.

MR. W. M. MELLETTE.   MR. G. WHIPPLE, Sec'y.

Preacher of Council Sermon:

THE REV. R. S. JAMES, D. D., LL. D.

Alternate:

THE REV. D. S. C. M. POTTER, D. D., LL. D.

The Clergy of the Diocese.

BISHOP:

Rt. Rev. HENRY N. PIERCE, D. D., LL. D., Little Rock.

PRIESTS:

Rev. INNES O. ADAMS. Rector of Trinity, . . Pine Bluff.

Rev. C. A. BRUCE, serving at Marianna, Paragould
and Forrest City, ... P. O. Helena.

Rev. WALLACE CARNAHAN, Rector of Christ Church, Little Rock.

Rev. J. T. CHAMBERS, in charge of St. Paul's Church, Newport.

Rev. HERBERT EDWARDS, Missionary at St. James', Prescott.

Rev. R. S. JAMES, D. D., Rector of St. James', Eureka Springs.

Rev. WILLIAM JONES, Rector of St. Paul's, . . Batesville.

Rev. C. H. LOCKWOOD, Rector of St. John's, . . . Helena.

Rev. D. F. MacDONALD, D. D., . . . Diocese of Albany.

Rev. W. J. MILLER, Rector of St. Luke's, . . Hot Springs.

Rev. D. S. C. M. POTTER, D. D., Rector of St. Agnes', Morrilton.

Rev. PALIN SAXBY, Rector of Grace, Washington, St.
Mark's, Hope, and Church of the Redeemer,
Nashville, ... P. O. Washington.

Rev. D. L. TRIMBLE, ... Pine Bluff.

Rev. J. J. VAULX, Rector St. Paul's, ... Fayetteville.

Rev. J. B. WHALING, Canon in charge of Trinity
Cathedral, ... Little Rock.

LIST OF PARISHES AND MISSIONS,

WITH NAMES OF LAY DELEGATES.

ARKADELPHIA, St. Mark's.

ARKANSAS CITY, Mission.

BATESVILLE, St. Paul's—Messrs. J. C. Fitzhugh,* H. S. Coleman,* Jno. T. Warner.* *Alternates*—Dr. Wm. B. Lawrence,* Ed. M. Dickinson,* and Geo. W. Ball.*

CAMDEN, St. John's.

DARDANELLE, St. Paul's.

FORREST CITY, Mission of the Good Shepherd.

FORT SMITH, St. John's.

HELENA, St. John's—Messrs. P. O. Thweat,* S. S. Faulkner, E. C. Horner. *Alternates*—H. M. Grant,* G. Quarles,* J. B. Lambert.

HOPE, St. Mark's—Messrs. J. T. West, Edward Thomas,* M. H. Barlow.

HOT SPRINGS, St. Luke's—Messrs. Geo. G. Latta, Richard B. Bancroft, and J.ᐧP. Mellard.

LAKE VILLAGE, Emmanuel.

LITTLE ROCK, Trinity Cathedral—Messrs. Geo. W. Caruth,* P. K. Roots, R. J. Matthews. *Alternates*—W. G. Whipple,* F. H. H. Hewitt,* A. F. Adams.

LITTLE ROCK, Christ Church.

LITTLE ROCK, St. Philip's.

MAMMOTH SPRING, St. Andrew's.

MARIANNA, St. Andrew's.

MORRILTON, St. Agnes'.

NASHVILLE, Church of the Redeemer.

NEWPORT, St. Paul's—Messrs. L. Minor, E. L. Watson, Jr., H. A. Ridley.*

PARAGOULD, Mission Holy Communion.

PHILLIPS COUNTY, Grace.

PINE BLUFF, Trinity—Messrs. M. L. Bell, Geo. E. Valliant,* A. N. Smith.*

PRESCOTT, St. James—Mr. T. B. Blake.

VAN BUREN, Trinity.

WASHINGTON, Grace—Messrs. Wm. S. Eakin,* H. B. Holman, C. E. Ratcliff.

WITCHERVILLE, Mission.

Services are held with more or less regularity at the following places:

Altheimer,	Rocky Comfort,	Winslow,
Huntington,	Richmond,	Bentonville,
Huntsville,	Boonsboro,	Searcy.
Fulton,	Conway,	

* Not present at the Council.

PROCEEDINGS

OF THE

TWENTIETH ANNUAL COUNCIL.

.

The Twentieth Annual Council of the Diocese of Arkansas assembled in St. Luke's Church, Hot Springs, on the second Thursday after Easter, April 28, 1892.

The Holy Communion was celebrated by the Rt. Rev., the Bishop of the Diocese, assisted by the Rev. C. A. Bruce and the Rev. J. J. Vaulx.

Instead of a Council sermon the Bishop read a portion of his Annual Address. (See Appendix I.).

The Council was called to order immediately after the service by the Bishop.

On calling the roll of the Clergy canonically resident in the Diocese, the following answered to their names:

Bishop.

Rt. Rev. Henry N. Pierce, D.D. LL. D.

Priests:

Rev. C. A. Bruce,	Rev. J. J. Vaulx,
Rev. C. H. Lockwood,	Rev. J. T. Chambers,
Rev. Palin Saxby,	Rev. W. J. Miller,
Rev. D. S. C. M. Potter, D.D.,	Rev. H. Edwards.

The Rev. Mr. Chambers and the Rev. Palin Saxby were appointed a Committee on Credentials, who reported that the following Lay Delegates had been duly elected and were entitled to seats in this Council:

Trinity Cathedral —Messrs. Geo. W. Caruth, P. K. Roots, R. J. Matthews.   Alternates, Messrs. W. G. Whipple, F. H. H. Hewitt and A. F. Adams.

St. Paul's Church, Fayetteville—Dr. W. B. Welch, J. L. Cravens and R. V. McCracken.

Grace Church, Washington—Wm. S. Eakin, Henry Brown Holman and C. E. Ratcliff.

St. Mark's, Hope—Judson T. West, Edward Thomas and M. H. Barlow.

St. John's Church, Helena—P. O. Thweat, E. C. Horner, S. S. Faulkner.   Alternates, H. M. Grant, G. Quarles and J. B. Lambert.

St. Paul's, Newport—Lancelot Minor, Henry A. Ridley, Elbert L. Watson, Jr.   Alternates, John T. Flynn and Board B. Bond.

St. Luke's, Hot Springs—G. G. Latta, R. B. Bancroft and J. P. Mellard.

The Secretary calling the roll, the following answered to their names :

Mr. P. K. Roots,	Mr. E. L. Watson,
Mr. A. F. Adams,	Mr. E. C. Horner,
Mr. Geo. G. Latta,	Mr. S. S. Faulkner,
Mr. J. P. Mellard,	Mr. J. B. Lambert,
Mr. M. H. Barlow,	Dr. W. B. Welch.

There being a quorum, of both orders the Council proceeded to the election of a Secretary.

On motion of Mr. S. S. Faulkner, seconded by the Rev. J. J. Vaulx, the Rev. W. J. Miller was unanimously re-elected.

On motion, a recess was taken until 4 o clock p.m.

AFTERNOON SESSION.

THURSDAY, April 28.

The Council re-assembled at 4 p. m., the Bishop presiding.

On the calling of the roll, the following Clergy who were not present at the opening session, answered to their names : Rev. Wallace Carnahan, Rev. R. S. James, D. D., and Rev. J. B. Whaling.

The Committee on Credentials made the following additional report :

To the Diocesan Council :

Your Committee on Credentials beg leave to report that the credentials are received of Mr. Thomas B. Blake, Delegate from the Mission at Prescott, against which there is no assessment; and the assessment has been partially paid by Trinity Parish, Pine Bluff, $41.50 of the $75.00 assessed, having been received by the Diocesan Treasurer, and it is understood that the remainder will be paid within thirty days. It is hereby recommended that the Council admit the Delegate.

(Signed) J. TAYLOR CHAMBERS,
PALIN SAXBY.

On motion, the recommendation of the committee was adopted.

The roll of Lay Delegates being called, the following answered to their names, who were not present at the morning session :

Mr. R. J. Matthews, Trinity Cathedral.

Mr. H. B. Holman and C. E. Ratcliff, Grace Church, Washington.

Mr. J. T. West, St. Mark's, Hope.

Mr. T. B. Blake, Mission at Prescott.

Mr. M. L. Bell, Trinity, Pine Bluff.

Mr. R. B. Bancroft, St. Luke's, Hot Springs.

It not being possible to appoint the standing committees, the Council, on motion, adjourned to meet Friday morning at 9:30 o'clock.

SECOND DAY.

St. Luke's Church, Hot Springs, }
Friday, April 29, 1892. }

The Council re-assembled pursuant to adjournment at 9:30 a. m. Morning Prayer was read by Rev. J. B. Whaling and the Litany by the Rev. W. J. Miller. Immediately after the service the Council was called to order by the President. On the calling of the roll, the Rev. Wm. Jones and Col. L. Minor Lay Delegate from St. Paul's Church, Newport, answered their names, who were not present at the sessions of Thursday.

The minutes of the proceedings of the previous day were read and approved.

The Standing Committees were appointed as follows:

Ways and Means.

· Rev. Wallace Carnahan,

Mr. P. K. Roots,   Mr. J. T. West.

New Parishes.

Rev. J. Taylor Chambers,   Rev. D. L. Trimble,
Mr. T. B. Blake,   Rev. H. Edwards,
Mr. J. M. Lambert,   Mr. E. L. Watson, Jr.

State of the Church.

Rev. D. S. C. M. Potter, D.D. Rev. Wm. Jones,
Mr. E. C. Horner,   Rev. J. B. Whaling,
Mr. J. P. Mellard,   Mr. R. J. Matthews.

Auditing and Finance.

Mr. M. H. Barlow,

Mr. A. F. Adams,   Mr. H. B. Holman.

Unfinished Business.

Rev. W. J. Miller,   Mr. E. C. Ratcliff.

Constitution and Canons.

Rev. J. J. Vaulx,   Mr. M. L. Bell,
Rev. C. A. Bruce,   Mr. Geo. G. Latta,
Rev. C. H. Lockwood,   Mr. W. B. Welch,
Rev. R. S. James, D. D.,   Mr. S. S. Faulkner,
Rev. I. O. Adams,   Mr. L. Minor.

Credentials of Lay Delegates.

Rev. J. T. Chambers,   Rev. Palin Saxby.

The Rev. Mr. Vaulx offered the following resolution:

Resolved, That when this Council adjourns it adjourn to meet in St. Paul's. Church, Fayetteville, on the second Thursday after Easter, 1893.

The following communication was received:

HELENA, ARK., April 26, 1892.

At a meeting of the Vestry of St. John's Church on above date the following resolution was proposed and unanimously adopted:

Be it resolved, By the Vestry of St. John's Church, Helena, that our delegates to the Twentieth Annual Council, be, and they are hereby directed, to extend to the Council an invitation to hold the Twenty-first Annual Council at Helena, Ark.

S. S. FAULKNER,
Secretary.

The Rev. C. H. Lockwood moved that for St. Paul's Church,. Fayetteville, the words "St. John's Church, Helena," be substituted.

On motion the above resolution and substitute were made the order for the day at 4:30 p. m.

Dr. W. B. Welch offered the following resolution:

Resolved, That Title IV, Canon I, be amended by inserting after the word "Vestrymen," in the fourth line, the words "communicants of the Parish."

Which, on motion, was referred to the Committee on Constitution and Canons.

Mr. M. L. Bell read the report of Mr. N. B. Trulock, as Trustee of the Episcopate Fund, which on motion was referred to the Auditing and Finance Committee. (See Appendix IV.)

Rev. Mr. Saxby offered the following resolution:

Resolved, That Canon IV, Title I, of the Diocesan Canons be, and is hereby repealed.

Mr. Geo. G. Latta, offered as a substitute, that Canon IV, Title I, be referred to the Committee on Constitution and Canons for consideration, and that they be requested to report to this Council any amendments they may deem necessary. Adopted.

Mr. Latta also offered the following:

Resolved, That the explanation offered by the Chancellor of the Diocese of his action in the matters presented for his consideration during the year, are accepted as satisfactory by this Council.

Adopted.

On motion a recess was taken until 4 p. m.

AFTERNOON SESSION.

FRIDAY, April 29.

The Council re-assembled, the Bishop presiding.

The Rev. I. O. Adams appeared and took his seat.

The report of the Standing Committee of the Diocese was read by the Rev. Mr Adams. (See Appendix II.)

Mr. S. S. Faulkner read the following report of the Committee on Constitution and Canons:

To the Diocesan Council:

Your Committee on Constitution and Canons find upon examination of the proceedings of the last Council, that the resolution as offered this morning as follows: "*Resolved,* That Canon I, Title IV, be amended by inserting after the word 'Vestrymen' in the fourth line, the words 'communicants of the Parish,' was reported upon by the committee at the last Council, and said committee advised that action upon the same be deferred until the meeting of this Council, consequently the same thing will come before this Council as unfinished business. All of which is respectfully submitted.

J. J. VAULX, *Chairman.*

S. S. FAULKNER, *Secretary*

Mr. Faulkner also read the following report:

To the Diocesan Council:

Your Committee on Constitution and Canons, to whom was referred the following "*Resolved,* That Canon IV, Title I, be and is hereby repealed," recommend that the same be not adopted. In lieu thereof we recommend that said Canon be amended to read as follows:

CANON IV—TITLE I.

SECTION 1. Every Clergyman of the Diocese shall attend the Annual Council, unless he is excused by the Bishop.

SEC. 2. Every Parish shall send Lay Delegates to the Annual Council, and it shall be the duty of the Vestry to make provision for their representation, unless excused by the Council.

SEC. 3. Any Parish failing to comply with Section 2 of this Canon, for the period of two consecutive years, shall be no longer recognized as belonging to this Council, and shall forfeit all their rights and privileges. Upon said non-compliance the Bishop of the Diocese is hereby requested to refuse to give such Parish Episcopal recognition.

SEC. 4. No member of the Council shall leave the same during the sessions without having obtained leave of absence from the Council.

(Signed) J. J. VAULX, *Chairman.*

S. S. FAULKNER, *Secretary.*

On motion the report was received and the Council proceeded to consider the recommendation of the committee. After considerable discussion, the recommendation of the committee was adopted by the following vote: Ayes, 10; nays, 6.

The following communication was received from Christ's Church, Little Rock:

At a meeting of the Vestry of Christ's Church, Little Rock, Ark., held in the Parish office, Monday, April 25, 1892, it was resolved that the following address be presented to the Twentieth Annual Council of the Diocese of Arkansas:

To the Members of the Twentieth Annual Council of the Diocese of Arkansas:

DEAR BRETHREN: This Parish having had no Lay representation in the Diocesan Councils of 1890 and 1891, and sending none to the present Council, we deem it due our brethren of the Diocese to offer the following statement of our attitude, lest our non-representation should be construed as indifference to the welfare of the Diocese.

It is the object of this communication therefore to assure our brethren that we are desirous of participating in the counsels and legislation of the Diocese, and of bearing our due share of its burdens as soon as we can consistently do so.

We cannot do so at present for the same reasons that precluded our appearance in the last two Councils.

According to Article II of the Constitution of the Diocese of Arkansas, negro clergymen and negro Lay Delegates are entitled to admission to the Council; and there is no restriction on the organization and admission of negro Parishes to the Council.

We remind you, who know the negro character as we do, and who are familiar with the history of African participation in our civil affairs, that the negro is not qualified for the grave and difficult work of ecclesiastical legislation.

We remind you again that the direct tendency of such equality of responsibility is to bring about social equality, and its corollary—miscegenation; which can only result in the degradation of the white race, and social anarchy.

We remind you further of the notorious fact that every attempt to mix the two races in Church matters has proved unsatisfactory to the negro himself, and hindered his religious improvement. We believe that the participation of the negro in our Church government is unfavorable to his own spiritual welfare, and that subordination to the white race is essential to the religious progress of the negro.

We therefore solemnly protest against the continuance of the constitutional provision admitting negroes to Council; and we respectfully and earnestly suggest the following amendment to the Constitution of the Diocese:

WHEREAS, The full right of all men of every race to a participation in the privileges and blessings of the Gospel of our Lord Jesus Christ does not necessarily imply fitness or right to govern the Church; and,

WHEREAS, The black or African race is not yet far enough advanced in Christian civilization to be qualified for the great responsibility of legislating for the Church;

Be it Resolved, That Article II of the Constitution be amended by interpolating the word "*white*" before the word "Clergy," and before the word "Delegates," and before the word "congregation," as the same occur in said article, so that the first clause of said article shall, when so amended, read as follows:

"There shall be a Council of the Diocese annually, at such time and place as the Council may from time to time determine, and in case of its failure to do so, the Bishop shall appoint the time and place. In the Council the Bishop shall preside by virtue of his office. The Clergy shall sit by right of their order, and the Laity shall be represented by white Delegates chosen for that purpose by the Vestry of each white congregation."

If that amendment be adopted we pledge this Parish to a cordial participation in all Diocesan work and burdens.

Adopted by the Vestry.

JOHN D. ADAMS,
Chairman.

Attest: R. H. PARHAM,
          Secretary.

On motion, the above was referred to the Committee on Constitution and Canons.

The order for the day having arrived, viz., the determining of the place for the meeting of the next Annual Council, the Rev. Mr. Saxby offered the following substitute:

Resolved, That when this Council adjourns, it adjourns to meet in Trinity Cathedral, Little Rock, on the second Thursday after Easter, 1893.

Which was lost by the following vote: Ayes, 7; nays, 12.

^ motion being taken on the resolution substituting the name of "St. John's Church, Helena," for "St. Paul's Church, Fayetteville," it was adopted by the following vote: Ayes, 12; nays, 10.

On motion, the Council proceeded to consider the resolution offered at the last Council, which had been deferred to this Council for consideration, viz.:

Resolved, That Title IV, Canon I, Section 1, be amended by inserting after the words " eleven Vestrymen," the words " who shall be communicants."

The Rev. Dr. James moved that the word "baptized" be substituted for the word "communicants," which was lost by the following vote: Ayes, 10; nays, 12. The original resolution being put, it also was lost by the following vote: Ayes, 11; nays 12.

On motion, the Rev. Mr. Carnahan and Messrs. Welch, West and Ratcliffe were excused at their request from further attendance on the Council.

On motion, the Council adjourned to meet Saturday morning at 9:30.

THIRD DAY.

St. Luke's Church, Hot Springs, }
Saturday, April 30, 1892. }

Morning Prayer was said by the Rev. W. J. Miller. Immediately after the service, the Council was called to order by the President.

The roll was called, and all the members were found to be present.

The minutes of the proceedings of the previous day were read and approved.

The Rev. Mr. Saxby offered the following resolution :

Resolved, That the Canons of the Diocese be referred to the Judiciary Committee, with instructions to consider and report them with such additions and amendments as will make them effective.

D—2

A motion to lay the resolution on the table was lost by the following vote: Ayes, 7 ; nays, 11.   A vote being taken on the resolution as offered, it was adopted.

The Rev. Mr. Saxby offered the following resolution:

Resolved, That the Judiciary Committee examine into the condition of the Church in Arkansas, and report a scheme for the placing of the Church upon a firm legal basis to the next Council.

On motion the resolution was laid on the table by the following vote: Ayes, 11 ; nays, 10.

Mr. L. Minor read the following report of the Committee on Constitution and Canons:

To the Diocesan Council:

Your Committee on Constitution and Canons make the following report on the petition asking this Council to amend Article II of the Constitution as follows: "*Be it resolved*, That Article II of the Constitution be amended by interpolating the word " white " before the word " Clergy," and before the word " Delegates," and before the word " congregation." We recommend that the Article be not amended as proposed. The committee voting as follows: Ayes—I. O. Adams, J. J. Vaulx, R. S. James and W. B. Welch. Nays—M. L. Bell and L. Minor.

The following minority report of the committee was read :

To the Diocesan Council :

We, the undersigned minority of the Committee on Constitution and Canons, recommend that Article II of the Constitution be amended as proposed by the petition from Christ Church, Little Rock, except that the word "white" be omitted before the word " Clergy," in said petition, but retained as otherwise proposed.

(Signed)   L. MINOR,
M. L. BELL.

A motion having been made that the minority report be accepted, and a vote by orders being called for, it was not accepted by a non-concurrence of orders.

It being moved and seconded that the majority report be accepted and a vote by orders being called for, it also was not accepted by a non-concurrence of orders.

On motion, the Rev. J. Taylor Chambers was excused, at his request, from further attendance on the Council.

On motion, a recess was taken until 3 p. m.

ATERNOON SESSION.

SATURDAY, April 30, 1892.

The Council re-assembled and was called to order by the President.

Mr. P. K Roots read the reports of Mr. Logan .H. Roots, as Treasurer of the Diocese, which, on motion were referred to the Auditing and Finance Committee. (See Appendix III.)

On motion of Mr. E. C. Horner, it was resolved· that the Twenty-first Annual Council be held on the second Wednesday after Easter, 1893, instead of the second Thursday, as voted this morning.

The report of the Committee on the State of the Church was read by Mr. Robert J. Matthews. (See Appendix V.)

On motion, the Council proceeded to the election of the Standing Committee of the Diocese, which resulted as follows:

Standing Committee :

Rev. I. O. Adams,	Mr. M. L. Bell,
Rev. W. J. Miller,	Mr. P. K. Roots,
Rev. C. H. Lockwood.	

The Secretary was instructed to cast the ballot for the Council for the re-election of Mr. George H. Van Etten as Registrar.

A vote being taken for the election of a Trustee of the General Theological Seminary, the Rev. William Jones was elected.

On motion, the Council proceeded to the election of Deputies and Supplementary Deputies to the General Convention. A ballot being taken, the following were elected :

Deputies to General Convention.

Clerical.	Lay.
Rev. I. O. Adams,	Dr. W. B. Welch,
Rev. W. J Miller,	Mr. G. G. Latta,
Rev. J. J. Vaulx,	Mr. L. H. Roots,
Rev. C. H. Lockwood,	Mr. E. C. Ratcliff.

Supplementary Deputies.

(In the order of their election.)

Clerical.   *Lay.*

1. Rev. William Jones,   Mr. G. W. Caruth,
2. Rev. Dr. Potter,   Mr. R. B. Bancroft,
3. Rev. J. B. Whaling,   Mr. W. M. Mellette,
4. Rev. Palin Saxby,   Mr. J. T. West.

On motion of the Rev. Dr. James, it was ordered that the result of the balloting alone be printed in the Journal.

The Rev Mr. Bruce moved that the Secretary be instructed to have printed 500 copies of the Journal of the Proceedings of the Council. Carried.

Mr. A. F. Adams read the report of the Auditing and Finance Committee, as follows :

To the Diocesan Council :

Your Committee on Auditing and Finance respectfully report that they have examined the reports of Mr. Logan H. Roots, as Treasurer of the Diocesan Fund, and of Mr. N. B. Trulock, Trustee of the Episcopate Fund, as submitted by Mr. P. K. Roots and Mr. M. L. Bell, and find them correct.

We are glad to state that the reports show that the Fund for Disabled Clergymen has grown, and there is invested about $200 in Building Association stock, the value of which must be more than the amount paid in. We also find an uninvested balance in the hands of the Treasurer amounting to $82.30

We find that some Parishes have again failed to respond to the different fnnds, and would respectfully recommend that their attention be called to the necessity of doing so.   (Signed)   M. H. BARLOW,
                                                   A. F. ADAMS,
                                                   H. B. HOLMAN.

On motion, the report was received and the recommendation of the committee adopted.

On motion, the Secretary was directed to cast the ballot for the Council for the re-election of Mr. Logan H. Roots as Diocesan Treasurer.

Nominations for Trustee of the Episcopate Fund being in order, Mr. P. K. Roots nominated Mr. N. B. Trulock for re-election.

The Rev. Mr. Saxby nominated Mr. S. S. Faulkner.

Mr. L. Minor nominated Mr. George G. Latta.

The ballot being cast it was found that there was no election.

A second ballot being taken, Mr. S. S. Faulkner was elected.

On motion, the Secretary was directed to cast the ballot for the Council for the election of the Rev. C. H. Lockwood, as Clerical Trustee, and for the election of Messrs. George G. Latta and Robert J. Matthews as Lay Trustees of the University of the South.

The Committee on Unfinished Business made the following report:

To the Diocesan Council:

In addition to the business left over from the last Annual Council, already acted on by this Council, your committee find on the thirtieth page of the last Journal the following:

"*Resolved*, That any communicant who shall neglect for twelve months successively to receive the Holy Communion, having opportunity, may at the discretion of the Rector, be stricken from the list of communicants, unless satisfactory reasons for such neglect be assigned to the Rector."

On motion, the consideration of the above was postponed to the Twentieth Annual Council.   (Signed)   W. J. MILLER.

E. C. RATCLIFFE.

On motion, the consideration of the resolution was postponed until the next Annual Council.

The report of the Committee on Ways and Means was read by the Secretary, which, after certain changes was, on motion, adopted.   (See Appendix VI.)

The Rev. Mr. Adams offered the following resolution, seconded by the Rev. C. H. Lockwood:

Resolved, That the thanks of this Council be tendered the Rector, Vestry and parishioners of St. Luke's Church for their very kind and courteous hospitality.

Adopted.

The Rev. Mr. Adams also offered the following resolution, seconded by the Rev. C. H. Lockwood:

Resolved, That the sum of $10 be paid the Sexton for services rendered during the sessions of this Council.

Adopted.

The Rev. C. H. Lockwood offered the following :

Resolved by this Council, That the sum of one hundred dollars ($100), be voted to the Rev. W. J. Miller in recognition of his services as Secretary of the Diocese.

Adopted.

On motion, the Council adjourned to meet on Sunday immediately after the evening service.

FOURTH DAY.

St. Luke's Church, Hot Springs, }
Second Sunday after Easter, May 1, 1892. }

At 7 a. m., the Holy Eucharist was celebrated, the Rev. H. Edwards being celebrant.

At 11 o'clock, there was a second clebration, the Bishop being celebrant, and the Rev. C. A. Bruce, the Senior Presbyter of the Diocese, preaching the sermon.

At 8 p. m., Evensong was sung by the Rev. W. J. Miller, the Lessons being read by the Rev. I. O. Adams.   Missionary addresses were made by the Rev. Messrs. Adams, Lockwood, Vaulx, Bruce and the Rev. Dr. James.

Immediately after the service, the Council was called to order by the Bishop.

The Secretary being asked if there was any further business before the Council, reported that the Council Preacher for the next Annual Council had not been elected.

On motion of the Rev. Mr. Lockwood, the Rev. R. S. James, D. D., was elected, and the Rev. Dr. Potter as Alternate.

On motion of the Rev. W. J. Miller, the thanks of the Council were returned to the Memphis & Little Rock Railroad, the Missouri Pacific Railroad, and the Hot Springs Railroad for courtesies extended to the members of the Council.

The Rev. Mr. Vaulx moved that the minutes which had not

been submitted to the Council be submitted to the Bishop for his examination and approval. Carried.

After a few earnest words of encouragement by the Bishop and the bestowal of his blessing, the Council, on motion, adjourned *sine die*.

H. N. PIERCE,
Bishop of Arkansas.

W. J. MILLER, ·
Secretary.

APPENDIX I.

THE BISHOP'S ADDRESS TO THE TWENTIETH ANNUAL COUNCIL.

Brethren of the Clergy and Laity:

The Primary Convention of the Church in the State of Arkansas assembled at Little Rock on the 24th day of August, 1871. So far as depended on its own action, the Church in Arkansas then became a Diocese. It was recognized as such by the whole American Church a few months later, and admitted into union with the General Convention in October, 1871. In the Primary Convention, it was

"*Ordered*, That the term 'Council' be substituted for the word 'Convention' wherever it occurs in the Proceedings, when it pertains to the Diocese."

On the 9th day of May, 1872, the First Annual Council met in Christ Church, Little Rock. Twenty years have passed. We have now reached, as a Diocese, that age at which the civil law ascribes manhood to the individual, and I welcome you to your seats in this Twentieth Annual Council. The Diocese is yet far from strong. But it has grown and is still growing. The foundation has been well laid and the structure erected thereon will at last convince the world that we have not labored in vain. Few can realize how much patient toil, how much anxious care, how much earnest thought, how much self-sacrifice it has cost to attain the point already reached. And none can know as well as I do how many blasted hopes and bitter disappointments have burdened the heart, as we steadily advanced toward our sole end—the glory of God, the extension of His kingdom on earth, and the welfare of mankind. With all my imperfections and defects as a man, I can call God to witness that, as your Bishop, I have never known one selfish wish, nor thought of using my high office to attain one selfish end. My heart's strongest desire and my steady aim has been to be as one who serves for Christ's sake.

I need not now review the whole past of my more than twenty-two years in the Episcopate. If God grants me to reach the year 1895, with faculties unimpaired, such a review will then be most appropriate. If still in this mortal life, I hope then to see the Cathedral of the Diocese, now virtually completed, freed of its comparatively small debt and ready for consecration. It will be an exceeding joy to me if, on my jubilee, I can see the great work, planned so many years ago, fully accomplished. The grand work which the Cathedral is destined to accomplish lies in the future. I feel assured that one American Cathedral, humble indeed when compared with the noble structures that bear the name in older Dioceses, will ere long be doing what was done by the Bishop's See in the early Church. It was intended to benefit the whole Diocese— if it fail to do that, it will be a failure indeed.

But what have we to say of the Diocese during the past year?

First, clerical changes. The names of no less than seven Clergy have disappeared from our list during the past year. The Rev. B. W. Timothy had already personally left the Diocese at the time of our last Council. A few weeks after its close the Rev. W. B. Guion received Letters Dimissory to South Dakota. Then the Rev. J. E. H. Galbraith was transferred to Kentucky. On the 1st of December last, the Rev. L. F. Guerry, much to the regret of his parishioners, as well as to that of myself and the Clergy generally, returned to his native South Carolina. In November last the Rev. W. C. Rodgers resigned his Deanship of Trinity Cathedral, and is now in the Diocese of Iowa. Very recently the Rev. Homer J. Broadwell resigned his charge of St. John's Church, Camden, and removed to the Diocese of Southern Ohio. And only one week ago the Rev. George F. Degen, the energetic, able and much-loved Rector of St. John's, Fort Smith, started for his new field of labor in Charleston, South Carolina.

The vacancy at Newport caused by the removal of the Rev. W. B. Guion, has been admirably filled by the Rev. J. Taylor Chambers, received on Letters Dimissory from the Diocese of Western Missouri.

To fill the vacancy at Van Buren, the Vestry have called the Rev. D. L. Trimble, and I trust he will accept the call.

I am daily expecting to be informed that the vacancy at Camden is filled by a clergyman of fine ability and large exerience. The Rev. J. B. Whaling is now Canon of Trinity Cathedral and has pastoral charge of the Cathedral Parish.

I am assured that the strong and well organized Parish at Fort Smith will not be long without pastoral care.

The Rev. R. S. James, D. D., has resigned his charge of St. Andrew's Church, Mammoth Spring, and is now working most acceptably and successfully as Rector of St. James' Church, Eureka Springs. The parish there has never had so flourishing a present and so promising a future as now. St. Andrew's, Mammoth Spring, is at present supplied with stated services by the Rev. James B. Lytton, resident at West Plains, Mo. These Parishes have been worked in connection most of the time since St. Andrew's was built.

The Rev. Palin Saxby, who, as Deacon, was in charge of St. Philip's, Little Rock, has been priested and is in charge of the field vacated by the Rev. Mr. Whaling, Hope, Washington and Nashville. I am taking steps looking to filling the vacancy in St. Philip's, caused by Mr. Saxby's change.

Some months ago the Rev. Herbert Edwards, canonically resident in the Diocese of Missouri, on the invitation of the Rev. Wm. Jones, Rector of St. Paul's, Batesville, came to Arkansas, and has been acting as a General Missionary within the bounds of the Central Convocation, and at the request of the Convocation of Little Rock. His reports have created no little interest, and I trust he may accomplish much good. [Since reading this address, the Rev. Mr. Edwards has pre-

past twelve months is largely due to his attention to those not rich in the goods of this world.

I could spend an hour in giving details to show that we have much to encourage us in our future labors. But for many of the evidences of growth and increasing vigor I must refer you to the Parcohial reports.

To give you a glimpse of my labors, as Bishop, since the last Council, I here subjoin

AN ABSTRACT OF MY JOURNAL.

My last annual report closed with April 8, 1891.

April 9: Thursday, the Nineteenth Annual Council of the Diocese in Arkansas met in Trinity Cathedral, Little Rock, at 11 a. m., I said the Communion Office, the Rev. I. O. Adams reading the Epistle and the Rev. J. J. Vaulx reading the Gospel. The Rev. C. H. Lockwood *preached* the sermon and I *celebrated the Holy Eucharist*, assisted by the Rev. J. J. Vaulx. After the service, I called the Council to order. Afternoon, I read my annual *address*.

April 10: Friday, I attended Morning Prayer and presided in the Council all day.

April 11: Saturday, I presided in the Council till it adjourned *sine die* at 6 p. m.

April 12: Sunday, the second after Easter, at 11 a. m., I said the Communion Office, in Trinity Cathedral, Little Rock, the Very Rev. W. C. Rodgers reading the Epistle and the Rev. G. F. Degen reading the Gospel. Rev. Mr. Degen *preached* and I *celebrated the Holy Eucharist*, assisted by the Rev. Messrs. Degen and Rodgers. At 4:30, the Rev. J. B. Whaling *preached* and I closed.

April 15: Wednesday, I attended Morning Service in the Cathedral.

April 19: Sunday, the third after Easter, in the Cathedral, Little Rock, I assisted in saying Morning and Evening Service.

April 20: Attended Evening Prayer.

April 21: Attended Evening Prayer.

April 22 :   Attended Morning and Evening Prayer.

April 24 :   Friday, I attended Morning and Evening Service in the Cathedral.

April 26 :   Sunday, the fourth after Easter, at 11 a. m., in St. Philip's Church, Little Rock, I *preached* and *celebrated the Holy Eucharist.* At 4:30 p. m. I assisted in saying Evening Prayer in the Cathedral

April 28 :   Tuesday, in Trinity Cathedral, Little Rock, at 10:30, I joined in *holy matrimony* Edwin Witherell and Miss Fannie L Curtis.

April 29 :   Wednesday, I attended Evening Prayer.

April 30 :   In Pine Bluff I *confirmed*, in private, a sick man.

May 3 :   Sunday, the fifth after Easter, at 11 a. m., in the Cathedral, Little Rock, I *celebrated the Holy Eucharist*, assisted by the Dean.   At 4:30 p. m. I assisted in saying Evening Prayer.

May 5 :   Tuesday, I attended Evening Prayer in the Cathedral.

May 7 :   Thursday, Ascension Day, at 11 a. m., in the Cathedral, Little Rock, I *celebrated the Holy Eucharist*, assisted by the Dean.

May 10 :   Sunday, after Ascension, at 9:30 a. m., in the Cathedral, Little Rock, I *celebrated the Holy Eucharist*, assisted by the Dean.   At 11 a. m. I assisted in saying Morning Service, and at 4:30 in saying Evening Service.

May 15 :   Friday, I *confirmed* in private a sick person and her sister (two females).   The candidates were presented by the Rev. Mr. Galbraith.   They belong to Christ Church Parish.

May 17 :   Sunday, Whitsun day.   At 7:30 a. m. in Trinity Cathedral, I *celebrated* the Holy Eucharist.   At 11 a. m. I *preached*.   At 4:30 I assisted in saying Evening Prayer.

May 24 :   Sunday, Trinity Sunday.   At 11 a. m , in St Phillip's Church, Little Rock, I *preached and celebrated* the Holy Eucharist.   At 4:30 p. m. in the Cathedral, I *preached*.

May 26 :   Tuesday.   I this day, acting under the Canon of

the Diocese touching that matter, divided the Diocese of Arkansas into three Convocations, and appointed the Rev. C. H. Lockwood, the Rev. W. C. Rodgers and the Rev. G. F. Degen, Deans of the same.

May 31: Sunday, the first after Trinity, at 10:30 a. m., I assisted in saying Morning Service in Columbia, Tenn. At 8 p. m. I *preached* in the same church.

June 1: Monday, I delivered the medals to the pupils and made an *address*. I gave my *canonical consent* to the consecration of Rev. Davis Sessums as Assistant Bishop of Louisiana.

June 3: Wednesday, attended the commencement exercises of the Columbia Institute, delivered the diplomas and *addressed* the graduating class. Attended the meeting of the Board of Trustees.

June 7: Sunday, the second after Trinity. In St. Peter's Church, Columbia, at 10;30 a. m. I assisted in saying Morning Service, *preached* and *celebrated the Holy Eucharist.* At 8 p. m. I *preached* again.

June 14: Tuesday, the third after Trinity. At 9:30 a. m , in Trinity Cathedral, Little Rock, I *celebrated the Holy Eucharist.* At 11 a. m. and 8 p. m. I assisted in saying the services.

June 21: Sunday, the fourth after Trinity. At 10:30 a. m. in the Chapel at Fort Reno, Oklahoma Territory, I said Morning Service and *preached*. At night I said Evening Prayer and *preached* in the Arapahoe school house at Darlington, O. T.

June 23: Tuesday, at the residence of Col. Wade, Fort Reno, O. T., at 9 p. m., I *joined in holy matrimony* Lieut. John Murray Jenkins and Miss Clara Lyon Wade, daughter of Col. Wade.

June 24. Wednesday, nativity of St. John, Baptist. In the Chapel at Fort Reno, at 10:30 a m , I said the Communion Office, *preached* and *celebrated* the Holy Eucharist. I *baptized* a child also.

June 26: Friday, at 8 p. m. after Evening Prayer said by the Rev. G. F. Patterson, I *preached* at Oklahoma City, O. T.

June 28: Sunday, the fifth after Trinity. At 11 a. m., in Trinity Church, Guthrie, Oklahoma Territory, assisted by the Rev. C. W. Tyler, I said the Communion Office, *preached* and *celebrated the Holy Eucharist.* At night I *preached again.*

July 2: Thursday, at 11 a. m., in St. Paul's Church, Fayetteville, Ark., I *preached* and *ordered priest,* the Rev. Charles Whitecombe Tyler, Deacon. The Rev. L. F. Guerry read the Epistle; the Rev. J. J. Vaulx, the Gospel, and both united in imposition of heads. I *celebrated the Holy Eucharist,* and administered alone, as usual.

July 5: Sunday, the sixth after Trinity, at 11 a. m., at St. Paul's Church, Fayetteville, Ark. Rev. J. J. Vaulx said the Office and celebrated the Holy Eucharist. I *preached.* At 5 p. m. I *preached* again.

July 7: Gave canonical notice to the Ecclesiastical Authority of the Diocese of Milwaukee of my acceptance of the Letters Dimissory presented by the Rev. J. F. Patterson, Deacon, transferring him to the Missionary Jurisdiction of Oklahoma and Indian Territories.

July 12: Sunday, the seventh after Trinity, at 9:30 a. m., in the Cathedral, Little Rock, I *celebrated the Holy Eucharist.* At 11 o'clock I *preached.* At 8 p m., I assisted in saying Evening Service.

July 16: Thursday, at 8 p. m., in Grace Church, Washington, Ark., I *preached, confirmed* two persons (two females) and *addressed* the class.

July 19: Sunday, the eighth after Trinity, at 11 a. m., in the Cathedral, Little Rock, I *celebrated the Holy Eucharist.* At 8 p. m. assisted at Evening Service.

July 24: Friday, I attended Evening Prayer in the Cathedral.

July 25: Saturday, St. James' day. I received the Holy Communion in the Cathedral.

D—3

July 26: Sunday, the ninth.after Trinity. I *preached* at 11 a. m. in the Cathedral.

July 30: Thursday. I *preached* and received the Holy Communion in St. Augustine's Chapel, Sewanee, Tenn., at 9 a. m.

July 31: Attending the meeting of the Board of Trustees of the University of the South.

August 2: Sunday, the tenth after Trinity, at 7 a. m., in St. Augustine's Chapel, Sewanee, I received the Holy Eucharist. At 11 a. m. I attended the same Church. At 8 p. m. I *preached* in the Otey Memorial, Sewanee.

August 3: Attending the Board of Trustees.

August 4: As yesterday.

August 5: As yesterday.

August 6: Thursday. Commencement day at the University of the South.

August 9: Sunday, the eleventh after Trinity, in St. Peter's Church, Columbia, Tenn., at 10:30, I said Morning Service, *preached* and *celebrated the Holy Eucharist.*

August 16: Sunday, the twelfth after Trinity, in the Cathedral, Little Rock, at 11 a. m., I *preached* and *celebrated the Holy Eucharist.*

August 23: Sunday, the thirteenth after Trinity. I assisted in saying Morning and Evening Service in Trinity Cathedral, Little Rock.

August 24: I *gave my canonical* consent to the consecration of the Rev. I. L. Nicholson, D. D., to be Bishop of Milwaukee.

August 30: Sunday, the fourteenth after Trinity, at Paragould, Ark., at 11 a. m., assisted by the Rev. I. O. Adams, I *preached* and *celebrated the Holy Eucharist.* At 4 p. m. I *preachep* again. At 8 p. m., I *preached, confirmed* three persons (1 male, 2 females), and *addressed* the class.

September 6: Sunday, the fifteenth after Trinity, in the Cathedral, Little Rock, at 11 a. m., I *celebrated the Holy Eucharist.* At 8 p. m., I *preached.*

September 13: Sunday, the sixteenth after Trinity, in St. Paul's Church, Fayetteville, Ark., I *preached* at 11 a. m. At 4:30 p. m., I *preached* again.

September 16: Attended Litany Service in St. Paul's.

September 20: Sunday, the seventeenth after Trinity, in St. Paul's, Fayetteville, at 7 a. m., I received the Holy Communion. At 11 a. m., I *preached* and at 4.30 p. m., I *preached* again.

September 21: Monday, St. Matthew's day, in St. Paul's, Fayetteville, at 7 a. m., I *celebrated the Holy Eucharist.*

September 27: Sunday, the eighteenth after Trinity, in St. Philip's Church, Little Rock, at 11 a. m., I *preached,* made an *address,* and *celebrated the Holy Eucharist.* At 8 p. m, I *preached* in Trinity Cathedral.

September 29: Tuesday, the Festival of St. Michael and All Angels, I attended Evening Service in St. Paul's Church, Newport, Ark.

September 30: Wednesday, at 10 a. m., I *consecrated* to the service and worship of Almighty God, St. Paul's Church, Newport, Ark. The Rev. W. C. Rodges read the sentence of consecration and preached. Morning Prayer was said by the Rev. William J. Miller. I *celebrated the Holy Eucharist.* At 7 p. m. I assisted at Evening Prayer.

October 2: Friday, at 7:30 p. m., in St. Paul's Church, Batesville, I *preached* and *confirmed* six persons (6 females) and *addressed* the class.

October 4: Sunday, the nineteenth after Trinity, at 11 a. m., in St. Paul's Church, Newport, I said Morning Service and *preached* at 4 p. m. I said Evening Prayer, *baptized* a child and *lectured* on infant baptism. At 7:30 I said the Litany and *preached* again.

October 7: Wednesday, I this day gave Letters Dismissory to the Rev. William B. Guion transferring him to the missionary jurisdiction of South Dakota.

October 11: Sunday, the twentieth after Trinity, at 11 a. m., in St. Philip's church, Little Rock, I *celebrated the Holy*

Eucharist, Rev. P. Saxby read the Epistle and preached. At 7:30 I attended Evening Prayer in the Cathedral.

October 14: Wednesday, at 9 p. m., in Christ Church, Little Rock, I *joined in holy matrimony* George Hastings Lee and Miss Anna Viola Cohen.

October 18: Sunday, the twenty-first after Trinity. At 11 a.m., in St. Philip's Church, Little Rock, I said full Morning Service and *preached*. At 7:30 p.m., I *preached* in the Cathedral.

October 25: Sunday, the twenty-second after Trinity. At 11 a.m., in the Cathedral, Little Rock, I *preached* and *celebrated the Holy Eucharist*.

November 1: Sunday, the twenty-third after Trinity. At 11 a.m., in the Cathedral, Little Rock, I said Morning Service, *preached* and *celebrated the Holy Eucharist*.

November 8: Sunday, the twenty-fourth after Trinity. At 11 a.m., in Trinity Cathedral, Little Rock, I said Morning Service, *preached* and *celebrated the Holy Eucharist*.

November 10: Tuesday, at 3 p.m., in Calvary Church, Memphis, Tennessee, I *joined in holy matrimony* James Arthur Sample and Miss Ida Myrtle Gregory.

November 15: Sunday, the twenty fifth after Trinity. At 11 a.m., in Trinity Cathedral, Little Rock, I said Morning Service, *preached* and *celebrated the Holy Eucharist*.

November 22: Sunday, the next before Advent. At 11 a.m., in Trinity Cathedral, I said Morning Service, *preached* and *celebrated the Holy Eucharist*. At 4 p.m , I said Evening Prayer.

November 26: Thursday, Thanksgiving Day. At 11 a.m., in Trinity Cathedral, Little Rock, I said Morning Prayer and the Ante-Communion, and *preached*.

November 29: Sunday, the first in Advent. At 9 a.m., in St. Philip's Church, I *lectured* and *celebrated the Holy Eucharist*. At 11 a.m., in Trinity Cathedral, I said Morning Service, *preached* and *celebrated the Holy Eucharist*. At 4 p.m., I said Evening Prayer and *lectured*.

December 6: Sunday, the second in Advent At 9 a.m.,

in St. Philip's Church, Little Rock, I *celebrated the Holy Eucharist*. At 11 a.m., in the Cathedral, I said the Litany, *preached* and *celebrated the Holy Eucharist*. At 4 p.m., I said Evening Prayer and *lectured*.

December 8: Tuesday, at 9 p.m., in Christ Church, Little Rock, I *joined in holy matrimony* Lewis M. Cherry and Miss Lina V. Denison.

December 12: Saturday. I *officiated at a funeral* in Little Rock.

December 13: Sunday, the third in Advent. At 11 a.m., in Trinity Cathedral, I said Morning Service, *preached* and *celebrated the Holy Eucharist*. At 4 p.m., I said Evening Prayer and *lectured*.

December 20: Sunday, the fourth in Advent, at 11 a. m. in Trinity Cathedral, Little Rock, I said the Litany, *preached* and *celebrated the Holy Eucharist*. At 4 p. m. I said the Evening Prayer and *lectured*.

December 22: Tuesday, at 5 p. m. at Forrest City, I *confirmed*, in private, a lady aged and infirm. At 7:30 p. m. I *preached* and *confirmed* two persons (1 male and 1 female), and *addressed* the class.

December 25: Friday, Christmas day, at 11 a. m., in the Cathedral, Little Rock, I said Morning Service, *preached* and *celebrated the Holy Eucharist*.

December 26: Saturday, St. Stephen's day, at 11 a. m. in Trinity Cathedral, assisted by the Rev. Palin Saxby, I *lectured* and *celebrated the Holy Eucharist*.

December 27: Sunday, the first after Christmas and St. John's day, in St. Luke's Church, Hot Springs, I said the Communion Office, the Rev. Wm. J. Miller, the Rector, reading the Gospel and the Rev. I. O. Adams the Epistle. The Rev. I. O. Adams preached and I *celebrated the Holy Eucharist*. At 7:30 p. m. I *preached* and *confirmed* seven persons (one male and six females) and *addressed* the class.

December 28: Monday, Holy Innocents' Day, in St. Luke's Church, Hot Springs, at 3 p. m., I *joined in holy matrimony*, the Rev. William J. Miller and Mrs. Marietta Allen. I was assisted by the Rev. I. O. Adams.

December 30: Wednesday, I *officiated* (at 3 p. m.) *at a funeral* in Little Rock.

January 1, 1892: Friday, the Circumcision, at 11 a.m., in the Cathedral, Little Rock, being assisted by the Rev. Palin Saxby, I *celebrated the Holy Eucharist.* This day I gave *Letters Dimissory* to the Rev. L. F. Guerry, transferring him to the Diocese of South Carolina.

January 3: Sunday, the second after Christmas, at 11 a. m., in the Cathedral, Little Rock, I said Morning Service, *preached* and *consecrated Holy Eucharist.* At 4 p. m., I said Evening Prayer and *lectured.*

January 6: Wednesday, the Epiphany, the work going on in the Cathedral prevented the holding of services today as it has on several of the recent holy days.

January 10: Sunday, the first after Epiphany, at 11 a. m., in St. Paul's Church, Newport, I said Morning Service and *preached.* At 7 p. m. I said Evening Prayer and *preached* again.

January 17: Sunday, the second after Epiphany, at 11 a. m., in Trinity Cathedral, Little Rock, the Rev. Herbert Edwards said the Litany and assisted me. I *preached* and *celebrated the Holy Eucharist.* At 4 p. m. I said Evening Prayer and Mr. Edwards preached.

January 18: Monday, *this day I gave my canonical* consent to the consecration of Rev. Dr. Nelson to be Bishop of Georgia.

January 24: Sunday, the third after Epiphany, at 11 a. m. in Trinity Cathedral, I said Morning Service, *preached* and *celebrated the Holy Eucharist.* At 4 p. m. I said Evening Prayer and *lectured.*

January 28: Thursday, at 8 p. m., in Trinity Church, Pine Bluff, I *preached, confirmed* four persons (1 male, 3 female) and *addressed* the class.

January 31: Sunday, the fourth after Epiphany, at 11 a. m.,

I *consecrated* to the service and worship of Almighty God, St. John's Church, Camden, Arkansas. Mr. C. H. Stone, Senior Warden, read the instrument of donation, the Rev. Homer J. Broadwell, Rector, read the sentence of consecration, the Rev. I. O. Adams preached, I *celebrated the Holy Eucharist*, assisted by the Rector. At 7 p. m., I *preached, confirmed* four persons (1 male, 3 female), and *addressed* the class.

February 7: Sunday, the fifth after Epiphany, at 11 a. m., in St. John's Church, Fort Smith, I said the Communion Office, *preached* and *celebrated the Holy Eucharist*. At 7:30 p. m., I *preached, confirmed* two persons (females) and *addressed* the class. The Rector, the Rev. Geo. F. Degen was confined to his bed by very serious illness.

February 14: Sunday, Septuagesima, at 11 a. m., in St. Paul's church, Fayetteville, Rev. J. J. Vaulx said the Litany and read the Epistle, I said the Communion Office, *preached* and *celebrated the Holy Eucharist*. At 4 p. m. I *preached* again.

February 18: Thursday, at 3 p. m., in Christ Church, Little Rock, I officiated at the funeral of Mr. William B. Wait one one of the oldest and best known communicants of the Church in Arkansas, and I believe one of the founders of that, the oldest Parish in the Diocese. He was a man upright and influential.

February 21: Sunday, Sexagesima, at 11 a. m., in Trinity Cathedral, Little Rock, assisted by the Rev. Palin Saxby, I said Morning Service, *preached* and *celebrated the Holy Eucharist*. In the evening I made an *address* on the building of Trinity Cathedral and on its present encouraging financial condition.

February 27: Saturday, at 7:30 p. m., in St. Paul's Church, Batesville, I *preached, confirmed* twelve persons (8 males, 4 females), and *addressed* the class, alter service *confirmed*, in private, a sick person (1 female.)

February 28: Sunday, Quinquagesima, at 9 a. m., Rev. Mr. Jones, the Rector, and I drove a mile and a half out of town, where I *confirmed* a sick person (1 female), making the whole number confirmed on this visitation, 14. At 11 a. m., in St. Paul's Church, Batesville, I *preached* and *celebrated the Holy Eucharist.* At 7 p. m. in St. Paul's Church, Newport, I *preached* and *confirmed* one person (1 female).

March 2: Wednesday. Ash Wednesday, at 11 a. m., I assisted in saying Morning Service, in Trinity Cathedral, Little Rock, and *preached.* At 5 p. m. I assisted in saying Evening Prayer.

March 3: Thursday, I assisted at Evening Prayer at 5 p. m., and *lectured.*

March 5: Friday, in Trinity Cathedral, at 10 a. m., I attended Morning Service. At 5 p. m., I said Evening Prayer.

March 6: Sunday, the first in Lent, at 11 a. m., Trinity Cathedral, I *preached* and *celebrated the Holy Eucharist.* At 4 p. m. I made an *address* on Diocesan Missions.

March 7: Monday, at 5 p. m., I *lectured* in Trinity Cathedral.

March 8: Tuesday, at 5 p. m., I *lectured.*

March 9: Wednesday, at 11 a. m., I attended Morning Service. At 5 p. m., assisted in saying Evening Prayer.

March 10: Thursday, I assisted in saying Evening Prayer.

March 11: Friday. Said Morning Prayer and Litany at 11 a. m. Said Evening Prayer and *lectured* at 5 p. m.

March 13: Sunday, the second in Lent, at 11 a. m., in St. Mark's Church, Hope, Rev. J. B. Whaling said the Litany, read the Epistle and assisted me. I *preached* and *celebrated the Holy Eucharist.* At 7:30 p. m., I *preached, confirmed* three persons (3 females) and *addressed* the class.

March 14: Monday, in Grace Church, Washington, at 7:30, I *preached, confirmed* two persons (1 male, 1 female) and *addressed* the class.

March 15: Tuesday, at 7:30 p. m., in the Church of the Redeemer, Nashville, after Evening Prayer, said by the Rev. H. Edwards, I *preached.*

March 18: Friday, at 5 p. m., I attended Evening Service in Trinity Cathedral, Little Rock.

March 20: Sunday, the third in Lent, at 11 a. m., in Trinity Cathedral, Little Rock, the Rev. J. B. Whaling preached and I *celebrated the Holy Eucharist.* At 5 p. m., I *preached.*

March 21: Monday, in Trinity Cathedral, Little Rock, at 11 a. m. (Morning Prayer having been said at an earlier hour), I *ordered Priest*, the Rev. Palin Saxby, Deacon. The Rev. J. B. Whaling preached the sermon, the Rev. Innes O. Adams presented the candidate and Rev. Messrs. Adams and Whaling united in the imposition of hands, I *celebrated the Holy Eucharist* and administered alone as usual.

March 22: Tuesday, at 5 p. m., I assisted in saying Evening Prayer.

March 23: Wednesday, I assisted in saying Morning Service in the Cathedral.

March 24: Thursday, at 5 p. m., I attended Evening Prayer:

March 25: Friday, the Annunciation, at 11 a. m., in Trinity Cathedral, assisted by Canon Whaling, I *lectured* and *celebrated the Holy Eucharist.*

March 26: Saturday, in St. John's Church, Helena, at 5 p. m., after Evening Prayer said by the Rector, the Rev. C. H. Lockwood, I *preached.* The congregation, an ordinary Lenten, I was told, would not have been considered in many places a poor one on Sunday.

March 27: Sunday, the fourth in Lent, at 11 a. m., St. John's Church, Helena, the Rev. C. H. Lockwood, assisted by the Rev. D. B. Ramsey said the Ante-Communion, I *preached*, *confirmed* seventeen persons (8 males, 9 females), *addressed* the class and *celebrated the Holy Eucharist.* The more than crowded congregation, for many could not be seated, shows how full of life is this Parish under its devoted, energetic and much loved pastor. It is a great gratification to see a Parish so united and so co-operating with its pastor. At 7:30 p. m., in St. Andrew's Church, Marianna, the Rev. Mr. Lockwood said Evening Prayer, I *preached*, the Rev. C. A. Bruce, Rector, presented and I *confirmed* six persons (6 females) and *addressed* the class.

March 28:   Monday, at 8 p. m., in the Presbyterian Church, Forrest City, I *preached*, the Rev. Mr. Bruce presented and I *confirmed* two persons (2 females) and *addressed* the class. This makes five persons confirmed at this point since our last Council.

March 30:   Wednesday at 11 a. m., in the Cumberland Presbyterian Church, Paragould, I said Morning Prayer, the Rev. C. A. Bruce said the Litany and I *preached*. At 7:30 p. m., I *preached*, confirmed five persons (3 males, 2 females) and *addressed* the class. This makes the number confirmed at Paragould since the last Council eight.

March 31:   Thursday, at 5 p. m., I said Evening Prayer in the Cathedral, Little Rock.

April 3:   Sunday, the fifth in Lent, at 11 a. m., in Trinity Church, Pine Bluff, I assisted in saying Morning Service, *preached* and *celebrated the Holy Eucharist.* At 8 p. m., I *preached* again.

April 4:   Monday, at 11 a. m., I *confirmed* at Pine Bluff a sick man in private. This makes the whole number confirmed at Pine Bluff since the last Council six.

April 6:   Wednesday, at 8 p. m., in Trinity Church, Van Buren, I said Evening Prayer, *preached* and made an *address*.

April 7:   Thursday, at 7:45 a. m., I received the Holy Communion in St. Paul's Church, Fayetteville. At 3 p. m. I confirmed a person (1 female.) At 5 p. m. I assisted in saying Evening Prayer. At 8. p. m. I *preached* and *confirmed* ten persons (3 males, 7 females), and *addressed* the class.

April 8:   Friday, I *confirmed* a sick man in private at Fayetteville. This makes the whole number confirmed for St. Paul's Church, Fayetteville, since the last Council twelve.

April 10:   Sunday, next before Easter, at 11 a. m, in St. James' Church, Eureka Springs, the Rev. R. S. James, D. D., LL. D., Rector, baptized an adult, read the Epistle and assisted me. I said the Communion Office, *preached, confirmed* seven persons (5 males, 2 females), and *addressed* the class. Afterwards I *celebrated the Holy Eucharist.* At 3:30 p. m. I *addressed* the Sunday-School. At 7:30 p. m. I *preached* again and made an *address* concerning the Easter Monday Parish meeting.

April 12: Tuesday, in Holy Week, 7:45 a. m., in St. Paul's Church, Fayetteville, I received the Holy Communion. At 5 p. m. I attended Evening Prayer. At 8 p. m. I *preached.*

April 13: Wednesday, in Holy Week, in Fort Smith, I *confirmed* two persons in private (2 females). At 3:40 p. m. I *confirmed* at St. John's Hospital four persons (2 males, 2 females). At 8 p. m. in St. John's Church, Fort Smith, I *preached* and *confirmed* eleven persons (6 males, 5 females), and *addressed* the class.

April 14: Thursday, Maunday-Thursday, in St. John's Church, Fort Smith, at 9:45 a. m., I *confirmed* one person (1 female). This makes the whole number confirmed at Fort Smith since the last Council twenty. At 10 a. m. I *preached* and received the Holy Communion. The Rector, the Rev. G. F. Degen, celebrated.

April 15: Friday, Good Friday, at 11 a. m., in St. Agnes' Church, Morrilton, the Rev. Dr. Potter said Morning Prayer and Litany and read the Epistle. I said the Ante-Communion and *preached.* At 8 p. m. I *preached, confirmed* five persons (4 males, 1 female) and *addressed* the class.

April 17: Sunday, Easter Day, at 11 a. m., in Trinity Cathedral, Little Rock, I *preached* and made an *address* and *celebrated the Holy Eucharist.* At 4:30 p. m. I made an *address.* At 7:30 p. m., in Christ Church, Little Rock, I *preached* and *confirmed* thirty persons (7 males, 23 females), and *addressed* the class. This makes the whole number confirmed for Christ Church, Little Rock, since the last Council, thirty-two.

April 18: Monday, in Easter week, at 7 p. m., in St. Paul's

·Church, Newport, I *preached, confirmed* three persons (1 male, 2 females) and *addressed* the class.

April 19: Tuesday, at 7:30, in St. Paul's Church, Batesville, I *preached, coufirmed* six persons (1 male and 5 females) and *addressed* the class. The whole number confirmed at Batesville since the last Council is twenty-six.

April 20: Wednesday, at 8:30 p. m., I *confirmed,* in private, one person (1 male). The whole number confirmed for St. Paul's, Newport, the past year is five.

April 24: Sunday, the first after Easter, in St. Luke's Church, Hot Springs, assisted by the Rector, I said the Communion Office, *preached, confirmed* six persons (2 males, 4 females) and *addressed* the class. Then *celebrated the Holy Eucharist.* At night I *preached* again. The whole number confirmed for St. Luke's during the conciliar year is thirteen.

To this abstract of my journal I append the customary

SUMMARY.

Sermons and addresses 146
Confirmed 173
Eucharists celebrated................... 59
Baptisms (infants)...................... 2
Marriages... 6
Funerals.. 3
Ordinations, priesthood—Arkansas..................... .
                  Oklahoma ....
Letters Dimissory received—Arkansas.................. .
         .   Oklahoma....... 1
Letters Dimissory given................... 7
Miles traveled...... 7909

The distance traveled is much less than last year, and most all of it has been made in Arkansas.

The work upon the interior of the Cathedral, carried on continuously for more than four months, required my constant oversight and compelled me to spend more time than usual at .home.

Whether any new legislation is required from this Council, is for you to decide. Changes unless necessary are to be avoided, for a changeable Code is apt to lose the respect of those subject to it.

I wish to call your attention to Section 2, Canon IV, Title I. This reads as follows: " No member of the Council shall leave the same during the session without having obtained leave of absence from the Council." This law is frequently violated. If it cannot be respected without a penalty being added, then it should be enforced by a proper penalty. Leaves of absence should be granted only for urgent reasons. It has been customary for all the Clergy to remain over the Sunday following the Council. If this custom is not to continue, then I suggest that we meet one day earlier, or two days earlier in the week, if it be practicable. If our old custom is to continue, then Thursday is the best day to assemble. As a law from its very nature must make itself respected, I suggest that inquiry be made whether any of our canons require the addition of penalty clauses, in order to secure their better enforcement. I have nothing further to recommend pertinent to this question and leave it to your wisdom.

As the next General Convention will take its last action in the revision of the Prayer-Book, it will be a very important one. I hope you will have Arkansas fully represented there.

There are many questions which might be profitably discussed here. But as these concern the Church and even the world at large, and have no special bearing on the affairs of the Church in Arkansas, we leave their consideration to what we deem a more fitting time and place, and leave you to enter upon the work before you. May the Holy Ghost guide your hearts and understandings in all your deliberations.

H. N. PIERCE,
Bishop of Arkansas.

APPENDIX II.

· REPORT OF THE STANDING COMMITTEE.

To the Twentieth Annual Council:

The Standing Committee of the Diocese met in Trinity Cathedral, Little Rock, Saturday, April 11th, 1891, and organized by electing Rev. Innes O. Adams President, and Mr. P. K. Roots, Secretary.

The committee met in Little Rock, Wednesday, April 29th; approved the bond of N. B. Trulock, Trustee of the Episcopate Fund, and gave its consent to the consecration of the Rev. Davis Sessums as Assistant Bishop of Louisiana.

Met at Pine Bluff June 9th, 1891, and on the question of consent to the consecration of the Rev. Phillips Brooks, the committee stood divided. The Rev. Charles Whitcomb Tyler, Deacon, of Guthrie, was recommended to the Bishop for ordination to the Sacred Order of Priests.

Met at Pine Bluff November 24th, 1891, and recommended the Rev. George F. Patterson, Deacon, stationed in Oklahoma for ordination to the Sacred Order of Priests.

Met at Pine Bluff January 28th, 1892, and recommended the Rev. Palin Saxby, Deacon, to the Bishop for ordination to the Sacred Order of Priests.

Also gave its consent to the election of an Assistant Bishop, by the Diocese of Springfield, by reason of extent of territory.

Respectfully submitted,

INNES O. ADAMS,
President.

APPENDIX III.

REPORTS OF THE TREASURER OF THE DIOCESE.

DIOCESAN FUND.

RECEIPTS.

April 10, 1891, balance on hand....................	$ 679	16
" 26, 1892, St. Paul's, Newport...............	15	00
" 27, Trinity Cathedral, Little Rock...........	100	00
" 30, St. Mark's, Hope.....................	10	00
Grace Church, Washington..............	10	00
St. Paul's, Batesville....................	25	00
St. Paul's, Fayetteville,................	50	00
St. Luke's, Hot Springs................	50	00
St. John's, Helena.....................	100	00
" Trinity, Pine Bluff (part).	41	50
Total to be accounted for..............	$1080	66

DISBURSEMENTS.

April 14, 1891, Honorarium to W. J. Miller, Secretary, 1891...............	$ 50	00
Allowance of Council for Janitor..	10	10
" 29, Innes O. Adams, expenses Standing Committee	2	50
W. J. Miller, expenses Standing Committee	6	00
J. J. Vaulx, expenses Standing Committee	14	85
Honorarium to W. J. Miller, Secretary, 1890...............	25	00
May 28, Printing Journals Nineteenth Council	150	65

June 1, postage, distributing Journals......   15 07
"   9, J. J. Vaulx, expense, order Standing
          Committee.................   8 00
"   17, N. B. Trulock, Trustee Episcopate
          Fund..................... 220 09
"   W. J. Miller, expense, order Standing
          Committe............... ...   6 00
Dec. 2, W. J. Miller, expens,e order Standing
          Committee.................   7 80
Feb. 2, 1892, W. J. Miller, expense, order
          Standing Committee..........   6 00
                          ———   521 96
April 30, 1892, balance on hand........... $ 558 70

FUND FOR DISABLED CLERGY.

RECEIPTS.

Jan'. 22, 1891, balance on hand...................$ 73 03
April 11, Grace Church, Washington...............   4 60
Nov. 28, St. Paul's, Batesville....................   14 00
"   St. John's, Camden....................   5 15
Dec. 2, St. Paul's, Newport....................   3 45
"   Grace Parish, Washington...............   5 00
"   10, St. John's, Helena.....................   12 17
"   14, St. Luke's, Hot Springs.................   4 00
"   16, St. Paul's, Fayetteville.................   5 00
"   18, St. James', Eureka Springs...............   5 00
Jan. 6, 1892, Trinity Parish, Pine Bluff.............   2 50
"   St. John's, Helena.....................   8 00
Mar. 9, Trinity Cathedral, Little Rock.............   5 40
                                ———
April 30, total to be accounted for..................$147 30

DISBURSEMENTS.

April 30, 1892, monthly dues to Building Association
   since last report, 13 months, at $5..............   65 00
                                      ———
         Balance on hand......................$ 82 30

DIOCESAN MISSIONS.

RECEIPTS.

April 25, 1891, balance on hand.................$	8 40
May 26, St. Paul's Batesville.....................	9 60
" St. Paul's, Newport......................	6 61
St. Paul's, Fayetteville..................	5 00
" 27, St. John's, Camden.....................	2 50
Trinity Parish, Van Buren..............	3 45
" St. Luke's, Hot Springs.................	15 85
June 6, Trinity Cathedral, Little Rock...........	7 80
" St. Phlip's, Little Rock................	1 35
Mar. 10, 1892, St. Mark's, Hope.................	4 20
" St. John's, Fort Smith....................	10 60
Trinity Parish, Pine Bluff................	8 40
" 16, St. Luke's, Hot Springs................	36 82
St. Paul's, Newport......................	4 20
" Trinity Cathedarl, Little Rock.............	4 73
April 30, St. John's, Helena......................	10 00

Total to be accounted for........................$139 51

DISBURSEMENTS.

Sept. 4, 1891, Rt. Rev. H. N. Pierce..........$38 17	
Mar. 8, Rt. Rev. H. N. Pierce.............. 25 00	
" 23, 1892, Rt. Rev. H. N. Pierce........ 36 82	99 99

April 30, 1892, balance on hand............... .....$ 39 52

All of which reports are respectfully and fraternally submitted,

LOGAN H. ROOTS,

Treasurer.

D—4

APPENDIX IV.

REPORT OF EPISCOPATE FUND.

CASH ACCOUNT.

1891.   RECEIPTS.

April 29, Rec'd from P. K. Roots, former Trustee..$2519	36
June 19, From Logan H. Roots, Diocesan Treas'r. 220	09
July 22, Bishop Pierce note and interest......... 530	96
Dec. 24, Bishop Pierce note and interest......... 25	00
Dec. 30, Bishop Pierce note and interest........ 26	00
1892.	
March 11, Bishop Pierce note and interest 7	15
March 10, P. K. Roots' donation 10	00
Feb. 26, St. Paul's, Newport.................... 5	65
April 8, Ladies' Building Association 444	58
April 13, Rev. Innes O. Adams refunding part of amount advanced on McMurray Bequest notes 114	30
April 16, Bishop Pierce, part payment note........ 100	00
April 24, L. E. Cheek, interest 100	00
April 26, Trinity Church, Pine Bluff 4	55
April 29, St. John's, Helena.................... 10	50

Total cash receipts........................$4118   14

DISBURSEMENTS.

To Ladies' Bldg. Assn., 11x$5, monthly dues $55; expense assessment $2. .$	57	00
To L. R. Bldg. Assn., Series 5, 12x$10, monthly dues......................	120	00
To L. R. Bldg. Assn., Series 7, 12x$20, monthly dues.	240	00

1891.

April 30, L. E. Cheek loan.......... 1000 00

May 8, M. L. Bell loan........... 1000 00

1892.

April 8, A. B. Grace loan.......... 1000 00

April 26, Transfer Bldg. Assn. stock.. 1 00

April 26, Two trips to Little Rock... 6 50

Total disbursements.................. ....$3424 50

Balance cash on hand 693 64

$4118 14

1892.   PRESENT STATEMENT OF ASSETS.

April 29, Cash on hand........................ .....$ 693 64

L. R. Bldg, Assn., Series 5, 64x$10, worth. 800 00

L. R Bldg. Assn., Series 7, 40x$20, worth. 860 00

L. E. Cheek's note, secured by mortgage. 1000 00

M. L. Bell's note, secured by mortgage... 1000 00

M. L. Bell's note, interest due May 1 .... 100 00

A. B. Grace's note, secured by mortgage.. 1000 00

A. B. Grace's note, interest up to date.... 3 00

Bishop Pierce's note, secured by mortgage. 400 00

Interest and recording fees still due from
Bishop Pierce 10 00

Interest on Bishop Pierce's note up to date. 7 43

Cash originally invested in McMurray
Bequest notes .... $ 865 60

Additional worth McMurray Bequest.. 3000 00

Rent notes in hand ($11.50, $10.25)... 21 75

Amount McMurray Bequests and notes at this date.. 3887 35

Total present value of fund $9761 42

Value of fund at last report 8984 96

Increase of fund during year ....$ 776 46

N. B. TRULOCK,

Trustee.

PINE BLUFF, May 20, 1892.

Received of N. B. Trulock funds and values belonging to the Episcopate Fund of the Diocese, to the amount of $9761.42, as follows, to-wit:

Little Rock Bldg. Assn., Series 5, 64x$10, worth....	$ 800	00
Little Rock Bldg. Assn., Series 7, 40x$20, worth....	860	00
L. E. Cheek's note, secured by mortgage..........	1000	00
M. L. Bell's note, secured by mortgage............	1000	00
A. B. Grace's note, secured by mortgage..........	1000	00
H. N. Pierce's note, secured by deed of trust..... .	400	00
Interest and recorder's fees due from H. N. Pierce ..	10	00
Interest on H. N. Pierce's note up to April 29th	7	43
Interest on A. B. Grace's note up to April 29th	3	00
M. L. Bell's note for interest due....	100	00
Amt. of rents recd. from McMurray's Bequest, $114.30		
Invested in McMurray's Bequest....$ 865 60		
Additional worth McMurray's Bequest 3000 00......	3865	60
Rent notes in hand ($11.50, $10.25)................	21	75
Cash on hand	693	64
Total........ ....$9761	42

[Signed]   S. S. FAULKNER,

Trustee.

APPENDIX V.

REPORT OF THE COMMITTEE ON THE STATE OF THE CHURCH.

To the Diocesan Council :

We, the Committee on the State of the Church, respectfully submit the following report :

Another year has passed, and with it opportunities that ought to have been grasped and turned to good account for the betterment of the state of the Church in this Diocese. We rejoice to know that there has been some improvement, yet we are constrained to say that the efforts in all respects have not been as fruitful as we might have made them. We have an abiding hope that more good will have been accomplished ere the close of this year than the one just ended.

With unfeigned regret we have to report again to this Council that several Parishes and Missions have failed to pay their legal assessments, and to a great degree have by such action retarded the progress of the Church.

The Parochial reports from most of the Parishes are more complete than heretofore, which is a cause of congratulation, but some of these are yet indefinite.

The missionary work in the Diocese has in most sections been faithfully performed, and the results very beneficial. This part of the work for the advancement of the Holy Catholic Church in Arkansas should, in our humble opinion, be of greater moment than that with which it has been seemingly regarded. "The harvest is ripe, but the laborers are few."

We note with great satisfaction the improvement and advancement of the Church buildings throughout the Diocese, and we feel assured that with proper efforts and united action that in a few years more there would be a neat and comfortable building in each town where there is none which we can now call our own.

The number of confirmations during the year is encouraging.

The several convocations that have been held in the different parts of the Diocese have been successful and of great value to the people at large, and especially to Churchmen in those sections. We urgently ask the Clergy and Laity not to let this good work cease, and to use renewed zeal in this direction.

Chapters of the Brotherhood of St. Andrew have been organized by some of the Rectors in the Diocese, and wherever there has been an organization of a Chapter it has been prolific of good works in these Parishes. We recommend that a Chapter of such Brotherhood be organized in the different Parishes that are without this valuable aid.

The Episcopate fund has had little or no increase during the year. With deep regret this committee is compelled to urge again that Churchmen and Churchwomen have not realized the great need of this fund, and that of necessity it must be increased. There have been many gifts from generous Church people for the benefit of Parishes, but the contributions to this fund to sustain the Episcopate have been too small for consideration.

With great pleasure we report that two Church buildings have been consecrated since our last Council. We also feel encouraged when we call to mind the fact that nearly all of the Parishes are in a better financial condition than formerly, and we trust that with God's help to see in a few years every Church building within the Diocese free of debt and consecrated to Him who died to establish His Church.

With joy and thankfulness we report that there are evidences of spiritual growth throughout the Diocese. The Clergy and Laity are more united in their efforts to hold the faith in the bond of peace; more careful to avoid error; more charitable; more faithful.

. The vacant Parishes and Missions should not remain so, and we earnestly request every person who desires the advancement of God's kingdom in our Diocese to aid the Bishop with the means which God has given them to supply the vacancies with Priests and Missionaries. The urgent necessity of such aid is apparent to all.

We deplore the absence of Lay Delegates who are elected as representatives to the Councils. The Church will be benefited by their presence, their counsel and their labor in its up-building. We sincerely trust that the Laity throughout this Diocese will recognize that to them is committed a work as well as to the Clergy. We suggest that the Rectors of the various Parishes continue their good efforts towards the completion of the Cathedral work as requested by the Bishop in his annual address.

> D. S. C. M. POTTER, D. D., *Chairman,*
> J. B. WHALING,
> E. C. HORNOR,
> R. J. MATHEWS,
> J. P. MELLARD.

APPENDIX VI.

PAROCHIAL ASSESSMENTS.

REPORT OF COMMITTEE ON WAYS AND MEANS.

Your committee have no suggestions to make touching the ways and means of the Diocese, except to submit a list of assessments uupaid for the past year, and new assessments for the year now beginning, as follows:

The following assessments, made last year, have not been paid:

St. John's, Camden	$ 25 00
St. James', Eureka Springs	5 00
St. John's, Fort Smith	140 00
Christ Church, Little Rock	275 00
St. Philip's, Little Rock	10 00
St. Andrew's Marianna	15 00
St. Andrew's, Mammoth Springs	10 00
St. Agnes', Morrilton	10 00
Church of Redeemer, Nashville	5 00
St. Mary's, Pendleton	5 00
Trinity, Van Buren	20 00
Mission, at Witcherville	5 00
Total	$525 00

The following assessments have been made for the ensuing year:

St. Paul's, Batesville	$ 25 00
St. John's, Camden	10 00
St. James', Eureka Springs	5 00
St. Paul's, Fayetteville	50 00
St. John's, Helena	100 00

St. Mark's, Hope	10	00
St. Luke's, Hot Springs	50	00
St. John's, Fort Smith	100	00
Christ Church, Little Rock	275	00
Trinity Cathedral, Little Rock	100	00
St. Andrew's, Marianna	5	00
St. Andrew's, Mammoth Springs	5	00
St. Agnes, Morrilton	5	00
Church of Redeemer, Nashville	5	00
St. Paul's, Newport	15	00
Trinity, Pine Bluff	75	00
Trinity, Van Buren	20	00
Grace Church, Washington	10	00
Total	$875	00

Respectfully submitted,

WALLACE CARNAHAN,
P. K. ROOTS,
J. T. WEST,
Committee.

APPENDIX VII.

PAROCHIAL REPORTS.

ST. MARK'S CHURCH, ARKADELPHIA.
No report.

UNORGANIZED MISSION, ARKANSAS CITY.
No report.

ST. PAUL'S CHURCH, BATESVILLE.
THE REV. WM. JONES, Rector.

E. M. DICKINSON, I. C. FITZHUGH, Wardens.

BAPTISMS: Infants, 16; adults, 15; total, 31. Confirmations, 26. ACTUAL COMMUNICANTS: Total, 89. Number confirmed persons, 108. Marriages, 2. Burials, 10. PUBLIC SERVICES: 2 every Sunday, 2 weekly and Saints' days. Holy Communion, twice a month. SUNDAY SCHOOL: Teachers, 7; pupils, 105. Rectory? Yes.

OFFERINGS.

PAROCHIAL: Communion alms, $54.85 : Rector's salary and Parish expenses, $1046; total, $1100 85.

DIOCESAN: Diocesan assessment, $25; Diocesan missions, $9; aged and infirm Clergy, $14; miscellaneous, $30; the Cathedral, $14; total, $92.00.

EXTRA DIOCESAN: Domestic missions, $10.75; miscellaneous (Sunday School Lenten offering), $31; total, $41.75.

Total offerings, $1234.50.

Estimated value of Church and grounds $2700 00

Estimated value Rectory.................... .... 300 00

Estimated value of other Church property......... 500 00

Total................... ....$3500 00

Amount indebtedness on Church property......... 300 00

ST. JOHN'S, CAMDEN.

No report.

ST. PAUL'S, DARDANELLE.

No report.

ST. JAMES' CHURCH, EUREKA SPRINGS.

THE REV. RICHARD S. JAMES, D. D., Rector.

J. C. CUNNINGHAM, W. G. WEAR, Wardens.

Number of families, 18. Whole number of souls, 58. Number baptized persons, 45. BAPTISMS: Infants, 1; adults, 2; total, 3. Confirmations, 7. ACTUAL COMMUNICANTS: Total added, 9; died, 2; present number male, 9; female, 23; total, 32. Number of confirmed persons, 32. Marriages, 2. Burials, 5. PUBLIC SERVICES: Sundays, 66; other days, 14; total, 80. HOLY COMMUNION: Public, 11; private, 1; total, 12. SUNDAY SCHOOL: Teachers, 3; pupils, 33.

OFFERINGS.

PAROCHIAL: Communion alms, $18.50; Rector's salary and Parish expenses, $560; miscellaneous, Industrial school, $33; music, $27; rectory fund, $40; total, $678.50.

DIOCESAN: Aged and infirm Clergy, $5; for the Cathedral, $6 80; total. $11.80.

EXTRA DIOCESAN: Domestic missions, $4: foreign missions, $4; miscellaneous, $2; total, $10.

Total offerings, $700.30.

Estimated value of Church and grounds............$800 00
Estimated value of other Church property........... 150 00

Total...$950 00

ST. PAUL'S CHURCH, FAYETTEVILLE.

THE REV. JAS. J. VAULX, Rector.

W. B. WELCH, J. L. CRAVENS, Wardens.

Number of families, 60. BAPTISMS : Infants, 9; adults, 3 .
total, 12. Confirmations, 12. ACTUAL COMMUNICANTS : Total,
130.* Marriages, 5. Burials, 9. PUBLIC SERVICES : Each
Sunday, 3; other days, every holy day twice, daily during
Lent. HOLY COMMUNION : Public, every Sunday and holy
day; private, 12. SUNDAY SCHOOL : Teachers, 7; pupils,
(about) 80. Church sittings, (about) 250. Rectory? Yes.

OFFERINGS.

PAROCHIAL : Communion alms, $108.45 ; Rector's salary
and Parish expenses, $1154.05 ; miscellaneous, St. Paul's
Guild, $120.09 ; Miss Dickson's Memorial, $95 ; McIlroy's
Memorial, $25 ; Sunday school, $20 ; total, $1512.59.

DIOCESAN : Diocesan assessment, $50 ; Diocesan missions, $5 ;
aged and infirm Clergy, $5 ; Cathedral, $35.50 ; total, $95.50.

EXTRA DIOCESAN : Domestic missions, $10 ; Society for the
Promotion of Christianity among the Jews, $5 ; total, $15.

Total offerings, $1623.09.

Estimated value of Church and grounds............$3600 00
Estimated value rectory........................ 3000 00

Total...$6600 00

Amount of indebtedness on Church property...... None.

We hope soon to build a Guild hall to the memory of a former Senior Warden.

The Rector holds monthly services at two stations in the
country.

---

*This includes those at Springdale, Boonsboro, Rogers and Huntsville.

GOOD SHEPHERD CHURCH, FORREST CITY.

THE REV. C. A. BRUCE, Minister.

W. GORMAN, Warden.

Number of families, 7. Whole number of souls, 25. Number baptized persons, 25. BAPTISMS: Infants, 4; adults, 5; total, 9. Confirmations, 5. ACTUAL COMMUNICANTS: Admitted, 4; received, 2; total added, 6; removed, 3; total lost, 3; present number male, 3; female, 8; total, 11. Number of confirmed persons, 11. PUBLIC SERVICES: Two each month; Sundays, 12; other days, 6; total, 18. HOLY COMMUNION: Public, 6; total, 6.

OFFERINGS.

PAROCHIAL: Communion alms, $15; Parish expenses, $32; miscellaneous, Easter, $18.55; collected from various sources for Church building, $669.75; total, $735.30.

DIOCESAN: Miscellaneous, to the Bishop, $2.20; total, $2.20. Total offerings, 737.50.

Estimated value Church grounds and foundation of
Church........ ....·..................·..........$650 00

ST. JOHN'S CHURCH, FORT SMITH.

THE REV. GEORGE FREDERIC DEGEN, Rector.

STEPHEN WHEELER, WILLIAM M. MELLETTE, Wardens.

Number of families, 164. Whole number of souls, 589 Number baptized persons, 496. BAPTISMS: Infants, 32; adults, 7; total, 39. Confirmations, 20. ACTUAL COMMUNICANTS: Admitted, 20; received, 23; total added, 43; removed, 36; died, 6; withdrawn, 3; total lost, 45; present number males, 82; females, 191; total, 273. Number of confirmed persons, 273. Marriages, 3. Burials, 16. PUBLIC SERVICES: Sundays, 181; other days, 109; total, 290 HOLY COMMUNION: Public, 107; private, 5; total, 112. SUNDAY SCHOOL: Teachers, 8; pupils, 120. Church sittings, 200. Rectory? Yes.

OFFERINGS.

PAROCHIAL: Communion alms, $43.30; Rector's salary and Parish expenses, $2132.75; miscellaneous, $686.20; church building fund, $30; total, $2892.25.

DIOCESAN: Diocesan assessment, $125; Diocesan missions (including Cathedral), $34; miscellaneous, mission at Winslow, $11.90, St. John's Hospital, $1537.60; total, $1708.50.

EXTRA DIOCESAN: Domestic missions, $69 10; foreign missions, $14.85; University of the South, $8.40; miscellaneous, American Church Building Fund Committee, $8.30, Jewish missions, $1.60; total, $102.25.

Total offerings, $4703.

Estimated value Church and grounds............$10,000 00
Estimated value rectory 1,800 00
Estimated value other Church property........... 705 00

Total ....,......... ....$12,505 00
Amount of indebtedness on Church property...... None.

TRINITY CHURCH, GUTHRIE, OKLAHOMA.

REPORT OF TREASURER FOR YEAR ENDING MARCH 31. 1892.

RECEIPTS

Balance April 1 1891   ....$ 77 25
General offerings 124 84
Special offerings 4 56
Subscribers 173 62

Total   .... $351 --

ASSESSMENTS

Given to missions   ... . $ 7 25
Given to National 5 53
Given to Mr. Tyler   42 00
Paid Mr. Tyler   25 00
Offering given to Mr. Tyler   5 00

Building and Loan Association dues................ 66 25
Building and Loan Association interest............. 36 66
Mrs. Wells, organist................................ 32 00
Wire doors and screens...... .... 18 00
Insurance on building 8 50
Parish register, for Mr. Tyler..................... 6 00
Printing and postage.............................. 3 85
Miscellaneous expenses, which includes janitor, light,
    fuel, sundry help, etc......................... ... 93 45

    Total..$350 90
This leaves balance in this fund of 30 87

There was received from various sources $562.81 for real estate purchases, which amount included $45 borrowed from the bank and $20 advanced by Mr. Tyler, which amount is to be refunded. The lots purchased, adjoining on the east the Church lot, cost $515. The bank was paid $45 borrowed from it. The recording of the deed was $1, making the total amount paid out on this account $561, which leaves a balance of $1.81. During the year the Ladies' Guild paid $75 to the Building and Loan Association on account of the Church loan. So that the total amount now due the Building and Loan Association is less than $170, which amount is being reduced each week.

RECAPITULATION.

Balance in expense fund ....'................. ....$30 87
Balance in real estate fund 1 81
Old balance in building fund...................... 13

    Total cash on hand April 1, 1892 ....$32 81
        Respectfully submitted,
        FRANK R. PHISTER, *Treasurer.*

ST. JOHN'S CHURCH, HELENA.

The Rev. C. H. Lockwood, Rector.

P. O. Thweatt, Greenfield Quarles, Wardens.

Number of families, 93. Whole number of souls, 420. Number baptized persons, 416. BAPTISMS: Infants, 10; adults, 10; total, 20. Confirmations, 17. ACTUAL COMMUNICANTS: Admitted, 18; received, 14; total added, 32; removed, 11; died, 3; total lost, 14; present number of males, 71; females, 148; total, 219. Number of confirmed persons, 240. Marriages, 2. Burials, 11. PUBLIC SERVICES: Sundays, 143; other days, 146; total, 289. HOLY COMMUNION; Public, 70; private, 2; total, 72. SUNDAY SCHOOL: Teachers, 18; pupils, 137. Rectory? Yes.

OFFERINGS.

PAROCHIAL: Communion alms, $35.36: Rector's salary and Parish expenses, $2495.34; miscellaneous, $537.18; Ladies' Aid Society, $847.35; King's Daughters, $200; total, $4115.23.

DIOCESAN. Diocesan assessment, $100; Diocesan missions, $10; aged and infirm Clergy, $20.17; Episcopate fund, $10.50; miscellaneous, Cathedral, $23.60: Church of the Good Shepherd, Forrest City, $85; total, $249.27.

EXTRA DIOCESAN: Domestic missions, $27.50; miscellaneous, educational, $7. conversion of the Jews, $2.95; total, $37.45.

Total offerings, $4401.95.

Estimated value Church and grounds $16,000 00

Estimated value rectory 6,00 00

Total $22,000 00

Amount of indebtedness on Church property $1350 00

ST. MARK'S CHURCH, HOPE.

THE REV. PALIN SAXBY, RECTOR.

J. T. WEST, E. THOMAS, Wardens.

Number of families, 26. Whole number of souls, 78. Number baptized persons, 70. BAPTISMS: Infants, 4; adults, 1; total, 5. Confirmations, 3. ACTUAL COMMUNICANTS: Admitted, 3; received, 8; total added, 11; present number male, 17; female, 29; total, 46. Number confirmed persons, 46. Burials, 1. PUBLIC SERVICES: Sundays, 84; other days, 25; total, 109. HOLY COMMUNION: Public, 18; total, 18. SUNDAY SCHOOL: Teachers, 6; pupils, 30. Church sittings, 125. Rectory? No.

OFFERINGS.

PAROCHIAL: Communion alms, $2.70; Rector's salary and Parish expenses, $641.10; total, $643.80.

DIOCESAN: Diocesan assessment, $10; Diocesan missions, $4.50; Episcopate fund, $16.35; Convocation missionary, $8 Trinity Cathedral, $12; total, $50.85.

EXTRA DIOCESAN: Society for Promulgating Christianity Among the Jews, $1.30; American Church Building Fund, $2.50; total, $3.80.

Total offerings, $698.45.

Estimated value Church and grounds..............$1500 00

ST. LUKE'S CHURCH, HOT SPRINGS.

REV. WM. JAMES MILLER, Rector.

GEO. G. LATTA, R. B. BANCROFT, Wardens.

Number of families, 89. BAPTISMS: Infants, 11; adults, 4; total, 15. Confirmations, 14. ACTUAL COMMUNICANTS: Admitted, 14; received, 14; total added, 28; removed, 11; died, 2; total lost, 13; present number, 125. Marriages, 9. Burials, 10. PUBLIC SERVICES: Sundays, 128; other days, 75; total,

203. HOLY COMMUNION: Public, 64; private, 1; total, 65. SUNDAY SCHOOL: Teachers, 7; pupils, 80. Church sittings, 400.

OFFERINGS.

PAROCHIAL: Communion alms, $81.91; Rector's salary and Parish expenses, $1872.15; miscellaneous, $1414 65; offerings in Sunday School, $52.97; from King's Daughters, $943.15; total, $4364.84

DIOCESAN: Diocesan assessment, $50; Diocesan missions, $52.67; aged and infirm Clergy, $4; Bishop's Cathedral work, $25.37; total, $132.04.

EXTRA DIOCESAN: Domestic missions, $27 15; foreign missions, $10.25; University of the South, 16.25; total, $53.65.

Total offerings, $4550.52.

Estimated value of Church grounds $30,000 00
Amount of indebtedness on Church property......$ 5,000 00

In addition to the above, the Parish has been the recipient of many valuable gifts during the year. The beautiful, new brass Altar cross was the gift of Miss Gaines at Christmas. The handsome choir railing was Mrs. Sithen's Easter gift to the church. The Chancel Ten have also added much to the furnishing of the chancel, viz.: The Altar hangings for Advent and Trinity, and the very rich and elegant hangings which now grace the Altar was their Easter gift. The large, beautiful and costly window which adorns our sanctuary was the gift of Mr. and Mrs. Stitt, Mr. and Mrs. A. B. Gaines, and Miss Gaines, in loving memory of their mother, who for so many years was identified with the Parish, and who did so much for its welfare and prosperity. This window is truly a noble gift. It is next to the largest window that has been made in this country and its reception places St. Luke's Church among the notable churches in the United States.

EMMANUEL CHURCH, LAKE VILLAGE.
No report.

CHRIST CHURCH, LITTLE ROCK.
THE REV. WALLACE CARNAHAN, Rector.

MAJOR JOHN D. ADAMS, Senior Warden; DR. WILLIAM A. CANTRELL, Junior Warden.

Number of families, 360. Whole number of souls (about), 1700. Number of communicants, 631. Number of Sunday school teachers, 25; pupils (about), 300; total, 325. Number of baptisms, adults, 4; infants, 16; total, 20. Number of confirmations, 32. Marriages, 10. Burials, 20.

OFFERINGS.

PAROCHIAL: Communion alms, $247.49; Rector's salary, $2420; other current expenses, $1982.82; debt and interest, $2792.88; improvements, $129.65; total, $7572.84.

DIOCESAN: Missionary, $20.15; Church building, $24.80; total, $44.95.

EXTRA DIOCESAN: Domestic missions, $167.17; foreign missions, $111.18; deaf mute missions, $19.30; Jewish missions, $14.40; widows and orphans of Clergymen, $72.11; miscellaneous, $25; total, $409.16; aggregate, $8026.95.

Church edifice and grounds....................$60,000 00
Rectory and grounds 8,500 00
Mission chapel and lot........................ 1,500 00

Total $70,000 00

TRINITY CATHEDRAL, LITTLE ROCK.
THE REV. J. B. WHALING, Canon in Charge.

GEO. W. CARUTH, WM. G. WHIPPLE, Wardens.

Number of families, about 60. BAPTISMS: Infants, 6. ACTUAL COMMUNICANTS: Total, 87. Marriages, 1. Burials,

4. PUBLIC SERVICES: Sundays, 120; other days, 50; total, 170. HOLY COMMUNION: Public, 79. Rectory? Yes.

OFFERINGS.

PAROCHIAL: Offerings for choir fund, $33.70 ; Communion alms, $70.49; Rector's salary and Parish expenses, $1034.53 ; miscellaneous, $119.50; towards completing the Cathedral, $1200.00; by the Ladies' Guild, $502.05 ; total, $2960.27.

DIOCESAN: Diocesan assessment, $100; Diocesan missions, $7.80; disabled Clergy fund, 5.40 ; total, $113.20.

Total offerings, $3073.47.

Estimated value of Church and grounds............ $20,000

Estimated value of rectory........................ 1,350

Total...... .... $21,350

Amount of indebtedness on Church property........ $ 2,400

No record having been left—that is, record in full—therefore the data by which to get the results for report is missing, and it is impossible to make a full report.—J. B. WHALING.

ST. PHILIP'S CHURCH, LITTLE ROCK.

S. SPIGHT, C. S. WALLACE, Wardens.

Number of families, 49. Whole number of souls, 91. Number qaptized persons, 82. BAPTISMS: Infants, 3 : total, 3. ACTUAL COMMUNICANTS: Present number, male, 10; female, 17; total, 27. Number of confirmed persons, 27. Burials, 1. PUBLIC SERVICES: Sundays, 95 ; other days, 110; totals, 205. HOLY COMMUNION: Public, 16; total, 16. SUNDAY SCHOOL: Teachers, 3; pupils, 67. Church sittings, 200. Rectory? No.

OFFERINGS.

PAROCHIAL: Communion alms, $1.35 ; Rector's salary and Parish expenses, $118.52; miscellaneous, church debt (property), $100; total, $219.87.

DIOCESAN: Diocesan missions, $1.35 ; aged and infirm Clergy, .30; total, $1.65.

EXTRA DIOCESAN: Domestic missions, .20; miscellaneous, missions to Indians, $1.15 ; total. $1.35.

Total offerings, $222.87.

Estimated value Church and grounds............$2300 00
Estimated value rectory........................ 200 00

Total $2500 00
Amount of indebtedness on church property....... 400 00

ST. ANDREW'S CHURCH, MAMMOTH SPRINGS.

THE REV. I. P. LYTTON, Minister.

P. P. B. HYNSON, Junior Warden, acting Senior Warden.

Number of families, 16. Whole number of souls, 66. Number baptized persons, 64. BAPTISMS: Infants, 3. ACTUAL COMMUNICANTS: Present number, male, 12; female, 15; total, 27. PUBLIC SERVICES: Sundays, 29; other days, 6; total, 35. HOLY COMMUNION: Public, 5 ; total, 5. SUNDAY SCHOOL: Teachers, 6 ; pupils, 30.

OFFERINGS.

PAROCHIAL: Communion alms, estimated, $4 ; Rector's salary and Parish expenses, estimated, $180; miscellaneous, estimated, $12 ; total, $196.

Estimated value Church and grounds............$1500 00
Estimated value rectory.................. .... 1000 00

Total..$2500 00
Amount of indebtedness on Church property...... 260 00

ST. ANDREW'S CHURCH, MARIANNA.

THE REV. C. A. BRUCE, Rector.

J. P. DUNHAM, Warden.

Number of families, 23. Whole number of souls, 82. Number baptized persons, 76. BAPTISMS: Infants, 1 ; total, 1.

Confirmations, 6. Actual Communicants : Admitted, 4 ; received, 6 ; total added, 10 ; removed, 5 ; died, 2 ; total lost, 7 ; present number male, 12 ; female, 33 ; total, 45. Number of confirmed persons, 47. Marriages, 1. Burials, 5. Public Services : Sundays, 80 ; others days, 1 ; total, 81. Holy Communion : Public, 40 ; total, 40. Sunday School : Teachers, 4 ; pupils, 25. Church sittings, 115. Rectory ? No.

OFFERINGS.

Parochial : Rector's salary and Parish expenses, $190.65 ; total, $190.65.

Diocesan : Diocesan assessment, $15 ; Bishop, $5 ; total $20.

Extra Diocesan : Domestic missions, $5 ; total, $5.

Total offerings, $215.65.

Estimated value Church and grounds $3000 00

ST. AGNES CHURCH, MORRILTON.

The Rev. D. S. C. M. Potter, Rector.

W. M. Scarborough, T. P. Stout, Wardens.

Number of families, 10. Whole number of souls, 43. Number baptized persons, 57. Baptisms : Infants, 5. Confirmations, 6. Actual Communicants : Admitted, 3 ; removed, 5 ; died, 1 ; total lost, 6 ; present number male, 16 ; female, 22; total, 38. Burials, 1. Public Services : Sundays, 34 ; other days, 12 ; total, 46. Holy Communion : Public, 9. Sunday School : Teachers, 5 ; pupils, 26. Church sittings, 150. Rectory ? Yes.

OFFERINGS.

Parochial : Communion alms, $59.40 ; Rector's salary and Parish expenses, $294.33 ; total, $353.73.

Diocesan : Miscellaneous (collection Good Friday, paid to Bishop Pierce for the Cathedral), $2.05.

Total off rings, $355.78.

Estimated value Church and grounds..............$2300 00
Estimated value rectory 400 00

Total................................... .$2700 00
Amount of indebtedness on Church property....... 44 52

CHURCH OF THE REDEEMER, NASHVILLE.
No report.

ST. PAUL'S CHURCH, NEWPORT.
The Rev. J. Taylor Chambers, Priest in charge.

Launcelot Minor, Gustave Jones, Wardens.

Number of families, 33. Whole number of souls, 120. Baptisms: Infants, 5; adults, 1; total, 6. Confirmations, 5. Actual Communicants: Admitted, 11; died, 1; present number, male, 10; female, 43; total, 53. Number of confirmed persons, 71. Marriages, 2. Burials, 4. *Public Services: Sundays, 58; other days, 77; total, 135. Holy Communion: Public, 13; total, 13. Sunday School: Teachers, 5; pupils, 41. Church sittings, 175. Rectory? Yes.

OFFERINGS.

Parochial: Communion alms, $15.40; Rector's Salary and Parish expenses, $764.49; miscellaneous, $408.97; total, $1188.86.

Diocesan: Diocesan assessment, $15; Diocesan missions, $4.20; aged and infirm Clergy, $3.45; Episcopate fund, $5.65; Cathedral, $7.50; total, $35.80.

Extra Diocesan: Domestic missions, $15 90; foreign missions, $2.10; total, $18.

†Total offerings, $1742.66.

*The statistics of services are for the past six months.
†The financial statement covers the Council year.

Estimated value Church and grounds $2.500 00

Estimated value rectory . . . . , ...   400 00

Total $2,900 00

Amount of indebtedness on church property . . . . None

HOLY COMMUNION CHURCH, PARAGOULD.

THE REV. C. A. BRUCE, Minister.

Number of families, 4. BAPTISMS: Adults, 2. Confirmations, 8. ACTUAL COMMUNICANTS: Admitted, 15; removed, 1; total lost, 1; present number male, 6; females, 9; total, 15. Number of confirmned persons, 16. HOLY COMMUNION: Public, 6. SUNDAY SCHOOL: Teachers and pupils, 16

OFFERINGS.

PAROCHIAL: Communion alms, $8.90; Rector's salary and Parish expenses, $98.30; miscellaneous, on hand for Church lot, $300.

ST. MARY'S CHURCH, PENDLETON.

No report.

GRACE CHURCH, PHILLIPS COUNTY.

No report.

TRINITY CHURCH, PINE BLUFF.

THE REV. INNES O. ADAMS, Rector.

M. L. BELL, W. W. SCULL, Wardens.

Number of families, 107. Whole number of souls, 365. Number baptized persons, 268. BAPTISMS: Infants, 10; adults, 3; total, 13. Confirmations, 6. ACTUAL COMMUNICANTS: Admitted, 6; received, 3; total added, 9; removed, 7; died, 4; total lost, 11; present number male, 51; female,

133; total, 204. Number of confirmed persons, 220. Marriages, 7. Burials, 7. PUBLIC SERVICES: Sundays, 165; other days, 60; total, 225. HOLY COMMUNION: Public, 25; private, 2; total, 27. SUNDAY SCHOOL: Teachers, 8; pupils, 100. Church sittings, 450. Rectory? Yes.

OFFERINGS.

PAROCHIAL: Communion alms, $44.17; Rector's salary and Parish Expenses, $964.25; miscellaneous, $443.68; total, $1452.10.

DIOCESAN: Diocesan assessment, $41.50; Diocesan missions, $12.90; aged and infirm Clergy, $2.50; Episcopate fund, $4.55; miscellaneous, Cathedral, $8.90; total, $70.45.

EXTRA DIOCESAN·: Domestic missions, $6; miscellaneous, Sunday school for domestic missions, $6.70; Church building fund, $3.80; total, $16.50

Total offerings, $1539.10.

Estimated value Church and grounds $12,000 00

Estimated value rectory 3,500 00

Estimated value other Church property 1,000 00

Total..................................... $16,500 00

ST. JAMES CHURCH, PRESCOTT.
No report.

TRINITY CHURCH, VAN BUREN.
S. A. PERNOT, SR., JOHN FRITZ, JR., Wardens.

Number of families, about 29. BAPTISMS: Infants, 10; total, 10. ACTUAL COMMUNICANTS: Present number, male, 5; female, 50; total, 55. Marriages, 1. Burials, 1. PUBLIC SERVICES: Sundays, 50; other days, 24; total, 74. SUNDAY SCHOOL: Teachers, 4; pupils, 30. Rectory? Yes.

OFFERINGS.

PAROCHIAL. Rector's salary and Parish expenses, $553.28.

DIOCESAN: Diocesan missions, $3.40.

EXTRA DIOCESAN: Domestic missions, $8.20.

Total offerings, $564.88.

Estimated value Church and grounds $2000 00

Estimated value rectory 1000 00

Total $3,000 00

Amount of indebtedness on Church property .... $ 500 00

The Rector (Rev. L. F. Guerry) left in November, 1891.

GRACE CHURCH, WASHINGTON.

THE REV. PALIN SAXBY, Rector.

WILLIAM S. EAKIN, C. E. RATCLIFF, Wardens.

Number of families, 30. Whole number of souls, 84. Number baptized persons, 82. BAPTISMS: Infants, 12; adults, 5; total, 17. Confirmations, 2. ACTUAL COMMUNICANTS: Admitted, 3; received, 4; total added, 7; died, 1; total lost, 1; present number male, 8; female, 27; total, 35. Number confirmed persons, 35. Burials, 3. PUBLIC SERVICES: Sundays, 35; other days, 75; total, 110. HOLY COMMUNION: Public, 12; total, 12. SUNDAY SCHOOL: Teachers, 6; pupils, 44. Church sittings, 154. Rectory? No.

OFFERINGS.

PAROCHIAL: Communion alms, $1.40. Rector's salary and Parish expenses, $236.70; total, $238.10.

DIOCESAN: Diocesan assessment, $10; Diocesan missions, $8; aged and infirm Clergy, $2.50; Episcopate fund, $19.65; total, $40.15.

EXTRA DIOCESAN: Miscellaneous, S. P. C. among the Jews, $1.25; total, $1.25.

Total offerings, $279.50.

Estimated value Church and grounds..............$ 900 00
Estimated value other Church property..... ...... 300 00

Total.....................................$1200 00
Amount of indebtedness on Church property.......... None

REPORT OF THE REV. H. EDWARDS.

PRESCOTT, ARK., April 26, 1892.

During the time I have been in the Diocese of Arkansas I have had the pleasure of visiting and holding services in the Towns of Batesville, Cushman, Sulphur Rock, Jamestown (2), Searcy (2), Paragould, Dry Forks, Melbourne (2), Oxford, Salem, Mammoth Springs, Viola, Mountain Home, Newburgh, • Beebe, Judsonia, Stephen's Creek, Fairview, Little Rock, Hope (3), Washington, Capt. Holman's plantation, Nashville (4), Centre Point (4), Fulton (3), Arkadelphia, Gurdon, Prescott (3), Hot Springs, Camden (Good Friday and Easter). I baptized two children, one at Mountain Home and the other at Centre Point, and have promise of several more. Since Hope convocation I have have been quite ill with grippe, and therefore have confined my efforts as near headquarters at Prescott as possible.

I have lived at the hotel during the whole of my stay, and the Sunday offerings have been about sufficient to pay expenses.

I went to Nashville when the Bishop made his visitation. There was a fair congregation although the weather was unfavorable, and collections of 35 cents. I accompanied the Bishop as far as Prescott with directions from him to work up the Parish if possible, and I trust we have reason to believe that a good Church can be built up there in the near future, as soon as the Church building is removed to a more favorable location and $100 raised to place it in repair. A lady has promised to make the furnishing of the new altar her special care.

Hoping that my work will be blessed by God and approved by the Executive of the Diocese, I am,

Very obediently,

HERBERT EDWARDS,
Mission Priest.

TABLE OF PAROCHIAL STATISTICS.

PARISHES AND MISSIONS.	No. of Families	Baptisms Infants	Baptisms Adults	Baptisms Total	Confirmations	Communicants	Marriages	Burials	S.S. Teachers	S.S. Pupils	OFFERINGS Parochial	OFFERINGS Diocesan	OFFERINGS Extra Diocesan	OFFERINGS Total	Value of Church Property.
Arkadelphia, St. Mark's						8									$ 600 00
Arkansas City, Mission						9									250 00
Batesville, St. Paul's		16	15	31	26	108	2	10	7	105	1,100 85	92 00	41 75	1 234 50	3,500 00
Brinkley, Mission						12									
Camden, St. John's						37									3,500 00
Conway, Mn.						8									
Dardanelle, St. Paul's	18	1	2	3	7	24	2	5	3	83	678 50	11 80	10 00	740 30	2,875 00
Eureka Springs, St. James'	60	9	3	12	12	32		9	6	80	1,512 59	95 50	15 00	1,623 09	950 00
Fayetteville, St. Paul's	7	32	7	39	5	130	8	16	7	129	735 30	2 20		737 50	6,000 00
Forrest City, The Good Shepherd	164	4	16	20	20	11	2	1	18	187	2,892 25	249 27	102 25	4,708 50	12,665 00
Fort Smith, St. John's	91	1	10	9	17	273	9	1	16	6	4,115 25	50 85	37 45	4,401 95	22,000 00
Helena, St. Mk's	26	11	4	15	14	219		10	7	90	648 80	132 04	3 80	698 45	1,000 00
	99					46					4,364 83		53 65	4,550 52	30,000 00
Hot Springs, St. Luke's						125									260 00
Lake Village, Emmanuel	6	6		6		10	1	4	5	300	2,950 27	104 73	409 16	3,065 00	21,350 00
Little Rock, Trinity Cathedral	346	16		8	32	87	10	29	25	67	7,672 84	44 95	1 35	8,026 95	70,000 00
Little Rock, Christ Church	44	3		3		631		1	3		219 87	1 65		222 87	2,500 00
Little Rock, St. Philip's	16	1		1		27			6	80	196 65		5 00		3,000 00
Mammoth Spring, St. Andrew's	25	5		5	6	45	1	5	4	25	190 65	20 00		215 65	3,000 00
Marianna, St. Andrew's	10					38		1	6	26	353 78	2 05		355 78	2,700 00
Morrilton, St. Agnes'						8									700 00
Nashville, Church of the Redeemer	35	5	1	6	6	53	2	4	5	41	1,188 86	35 80	18 00	1,242 66	2,900 00
Newport, St. Paul's	4	2	1	3	8	15			2	16	407 20			407 20	
Paragould, Holy Communion						10									
Pendleton, St. Mary's															
Phillips County, Grace	107	10	3	13	6	204	7	7	8	100	1,452 10	70 45	16 50	1,539 10	150 00
Pine Bluff, Trinity						8									16,500 00
Prescott, St. James'					2	10	1								500 00
Richmond, Mission						20									800 00
Rocky Comfort, Mission	29	10	10	10		55	1	1	4	30	553 28	3 40	8 20	564 88	100 00
Van Buren, Trinity	30	12	5	17		35	2	8	6	44	238 10	40 15	1 25	279 50	8,000 00
Washington, Grace						10									1,200 00
Witcherville, Mission															4,000 00
Totals	1188	152	62	214	169	2200	45	108	123	1264	$31,884 25	$2,575 34	$728 36	$34,663 9	$216,690 00

INDEX.

117894

The Domestic and Foreign Missionary Society of The Protestant Episcopal Church in the United States of America.

The Society asks for stated offerings as follows, and on the dates given when possible :

Domestic Missions, the first Sunday in Advent.

Foreign Missions, the second Sunday after the Epiphany.

Missions to colord people, the third Sunday after the Epiphany.

Missions to Indians, the fourth Sunday after Easter.

The Treasurer is MR. GEORGE BLISS, to whom all remittances should be sent, at his office,

22 Bible House, New York City.

ANNOUNCEMENT.

The Twenty First Annual Council of the Diocese of Arkansas will be held (D. V.) in St John's Church, Helena, on the second Wednesday after Easter, April 12th, 1893.

W. J. MILLER, Secretary.

Lightning Source UK Ltd.
Milton Keynes UK
UKHW010321120219
337137UK00004B/380/P

9 780260 453488